Communications in Computer and Information Science 3175

Series Editors

Gang Li, *School of Information Technology, Deakin University, Burwood, VIC, Australia*
Joaquim Filipe, *Polytechnic Institute of Setúbal, Setúbal, Portugal*
Zhiwei Xu, *Chinese Academy of Sciences, Beijing, China*

AF892418

Rationale

The CCIS series is devoted to the publication of proceedings of computer science conferences. Its aim is to efficiently disseminate original research results in informatics in printed and electronic form. While the focus is on publication of peer-reviewed full papers presenting mature work, inclusion of reviewed short papers reporting on work in progress is welcome, too. Besides globally relevant meetings with internationally representative program committees guaranteeing a strict peer-reviewing and paper selection process, conferences run by societies or of high regional or national relevance are also considered for publication.

Topics

The topical scope of CCIS spans the entire spectrum of informatics ranging from foundational topics in the theory of computing to information and communications science and technology and a broad variety of interdisciplinary application fields.

Information for Volume Editors and Authors

Publication in CCIS is free of charge. No royalties are paid, however, we offer registered conference participants temporary free access to the online version of the conference proceedings on SpringerLink (http://link.springer.com) by means of an http referrer from the conference website and/or a number of complimentary printed copies, as specified in the official acceptance email of the event.

CCIS proceedings can be published in time for distribution at conferences or as post-proceedings, and delivered in the form of printed books and/or electronically as USBs and/or e-content licenses for accessing proceedings at SpringerLink. Furthermore, CCIS proceedings are included in the CCIS electronic book series hosted in the SpringerLink digital library at http://link.springer.com/bookseries/7899. Conferences publishing in CCIS are allowed to use our online conference service (Meteor) for managing the whole proceedings lifecycle (from submission and reviewing to preparing for publication) free of charge.

Publication process

The language of publication is exclusively English. Authors publishing in CCIS have to sign the Springer CCIS copyright transfer form, however, they are free to use their material published in CCIS for substantially changed, more elaborate subsequent publications elsewhere. For the preparation of the camera-ready papers/files, authors have to strictly adhere to the Springer CCIS Authors' Instructions and are strongly encouraged to use the CCIS LaTeX style files or templates.

Abstracting/Indexing

CCIS is abstracted/indexed in DBLP, Google Scholar, EI-Compendex, Mathematical Reviews, SCImago, Scopus. CCIS volumes are also submitted for the inclusion in ISI Proceedings.

How to start

To start the evaluation of your proposal for inclusion in the CCIS series, please send an e-mail to ccis@springer.com

Genoveva Vargas Solar · Kostas Stefanidis ·
Themis Palpanas · Patrick Marcel ·
Mirian Halfeld-Ferrari · Panos Vassiliadis ·
Tatjana Welzer · Enrico Gallinucci ·
Veronika Peralta
Editors

New Trends in Database and Information Systems

ADBIS 2026 Short Papers, Workshops and Doctoral Consortium,
Orléans, France, September 28 – October 1, 2026
Proceedings

Springer

Editors
Genoveva Vargas Solar
CNRS
Villeurbanne Cedex, France

Themis Palpanas
Université Paris Cité
Paris, France

Mirian Halfeld-Ferrari
Université d'Orléans
Orleans, France

Tatjana Welzer
University of Maribor
Maribor, Slovenia

Veronika Peralta
University of Tours
Tours, France

Kostas Stefanidis
Tampere University
Tampere, Finland

Patrick Marcel
Université d'Orléans
Orleans, France

Panos Vassiliadis
University of Ioannina
Ioannina, Greece

Enrico Gallinucci
Università di Bologna
Bologna, Italy

ISSN 1865-0929 ISSN 1865-0937 (electronic)
Communications in Computer and Information Science
ISBN 978-3-032-39822-2 ISBN 978-3-032-39823-9 (eBook)
https://doi.org/10.1007/978-3-032-39823-9

© The Editor(s) (if applicable) and The Author(s), under exclusive license
to Springer Nature Switzerland AG 2027

This work is subject to copyright. All rights are solely and exclusively licensed by the Publisher, whether the whole or part of the material is concerned, specifically the rights of translation, reprinting, reuse of illustrations, recitation, broadcasting, reproduction on microfilms or in any other physical way, and transmission or information storage and retrieval, electronic adaptation, computer software, or by similar or dissimilar methodology now known or hereafter developed. Unless otherwise expressly agreed by the Publisher in writing, the Publisher does not authorize use or reproduction of all or any part of this work in any manner for the purpose of training, fine-tuning, evaluating, or developing artificial intelligence models, technologies, or systems. In accordance with Article 4(3) of the EU Directive 2019/790 on copyright and related rights in the Digital Single Market, the Publisher expressly reserves all rights with respect to this work under the text and data mining exception of the directive.
The use of general descriptive names, registered names, trademarks, service marks, etc. in this publication does not imply, even in the absence of a specific statement, that such names are exempt from the relevant protective laws and regulations and therefore free for general use.
The publisher, the authors and the editors are safe to assume that the advice and information in this book are believed to be true and accurate at the date of publication. Neither the publisher nor the authors or the editors give a warranty, expressed or implied, with respect to the material contained herein or for any errors or omissions that may have been made. The publisher remains neutral with regard to jurisdictional claims in published maps and institutional affiliations.

This Springer imprint is published by the registered company Springer Nature Switzerland AG
The registered company address is: Gewerbestrasse 11, 6330 Cham, Switzerland

If disposing of this product, please recycle the paper.

Preface

This CCIS volume includes research and demonstration papers presented at the 30th European Conference on Advances in Databases and Information Systems (ADBIS 2026), research papers from the workshops accompanying ADBIS, and papers from the Doctoral Consortium School. The 30th ADBIS conference was held in Orléans, France, from September 28 to October 1, 2026, as a full on-site event.

The first ADBIS conference was held in Saint Petersburg, Russia, in 1997. Since then, ADBIS has been organized annually across Europe, most recently in Tampere, Finland (2025); Bayonne, France (2024); Barcelona, Spain (2023); Turin, Italy (2022); Tartu, Estonia (2021); Lyon, France (2020); and Bled, Slovenia (2019). Earlier editions took place in Budapest, Hungary (2018); Nicosia, Cyprus (2017); Prague, Czech Republic (2016); Poitiers, France (2015); Ohrid, North Macedonia (2014); Genoa, Italy (2013); Poznań, Poland (2012); Vienna, Austria (2011); Novi Sad, Serbia (2010); Riga, Latvia (2009); Pori, Finland (2008); Varna, Bulgaria (2007); Thessaloniki, Greece (2006); Tallinn, Estonia (2005); Budapest, Hungary (2004); Dresden, Germany (2003); Bratislava, Slovakia (2002); Vilnius, Lithuania (2001); Prague, Czech Republic (2000); Maribor, Slovenia (1999); and Poznań, Poland (1998). The official ADBIS portal, http://adbis.eu, provides information on the conference series, its publications, and the wider community.

The proceedings of ADBIS 2026 are the outcome of a rigorous review and selection process. The conference received 80 research submissions, of which 22 were accepted as full papers for presentation and publication in the Springer LNCS main proceedings volume, corresponding to an acceptance rate of 27.5%. Each submission was carefully evaluated by members of the Program Committee and additional reviewers, with at least three single-blind reviews informing the discussion and final decision. The broader technical program also included 18 short papers and 5 demonstration papers, published in this companion volume in Springer's Communications in Computer and Information Science (CCIS) series.

The selected papers span a broad spectrum of topics in data management and information systems. To provide a coherent presentation, they were organized into eight thematic sessions: (1) Core database systems and serialization; (2) Similarity, topic modeling, and knowledge graphs; (3) Knowledge graphs, text-to-SQL, and metadata extraction; (4) Data cleaning, semantic discovery, and AutoML; (5) Sustainability, privacy workflows, and clinical analytics; (6) Similarity search, truth discovery, and anomaly detection; (7) Text analysis, graph neural networks, privacy, and Ethereum analytics; and (8) Integration, auditing, diversification, and embeddings. Together, these sessions illustrate both the depth of foundational database research and the growing reach of data-management methods across scientific, industrial, and societal domains.

Following a successful ADBIS tradition, the authors of the best research papers presented at ADBIS 2026 will be invited to submit substantially extended and revised versions to a special issue of Elsevier's Information Systems. Invitations will be issued to top-ranked conference contributions, whose authors will be expected to add new results, deeper evaluations, and significant new material. All invited manuscripts will undergo an independent journal peer-review cycle, and the final set of accepted articles will be determined through that subsequent review process. The Program Committee Chairs gratefully acknowledge the Editors-in-Chief of Information Systems for endorsing and approving this initiative.

Beyond the peer-reviewed contributions, ADBIS 2026 offered an engaging program of keynote talks, tutorials, demonstrations, workshops, and a doctoral consortium school. Four keynote speakers addressed timely scientific and societal directions for the data-management community:

Zoi Kaoudi (IT University of Copenhagen, Denmark) delivered the keynote "Query Optimization in the Wild: From Cross-Platform Data Systems to Multi-Agent Systems." Her talk examined the evolving role of query optimization, from cost-based optimization in cross-platform data systems to emerging generate-and-explore approaches and the challenges of multi-agent systems.

Wolfgang Lehner (TU Dresden, Germany) delivered the keynote "Reproducible Query Optimization Research for Data Systems." His talk explored the challenges of evaluating and comparing query optimization techniques and outlined perspectives for reproducible optimizer research.

Maria-Esther Vidal (Leibniz University Hannover and TIB – Leibniz Information Centre for Science and Technology, Germany) delivered the keynote "From Normal Forms to Knowledge Graph Ecosystems: Foundations for Trustworthy AI." Her talk connected systematic data and knowledge modeling with trustworthy AI, emphasizing knowledge-graph ecosystems, data quality, and biomedical and clinical applications.

Tiziana Catarci (Institute of Cognitive Sciences and Technologies, National Research Council, Italy) delivered the keynote "Gender Gap in ICT: From Missing Women to Missing Data." This DEI keynote addressed gender gaps and stereotypes in ICT, bias in AI systems, and the need to make inclusion technically visible through data modeling, quality, integration, provenance, privacy, fairness, analytics, and information-systems design.

Five tutorials offered in-depth engagement with emerging methods, tools, and application domains:

- "***Deep Learning for Time Series Classification and Regression with aeon***", presented by Ali Ismail-Fawaz and Maxime Devanne (Université de Haute-Alsace, France), Antoine Guillaume (Novahé, France), Anthony Bagnall (University of Southampton, UK), and Germain Forestier (Université de Haute-Alsace, France, and Monash University, Australia).
- "***Navigating the Vector Search Landscape: ANN Indexes for Modern AI Systems***", presented by Ilias Azizi and Themis Palpanas (Université Paris Cité, France) and Vassilis Christophides (ETIS, CNRS, ENSEA, France).
- "***Towards Optimized Big Satellite Data Management in Agricultural Monitoring through Causal-Based xAI: A Tutorial from the EDEM***", presented by Michele Linardi (CYU, ENSEA, CNRS, Cergy, France) and Claudia Paris (University of Twente, The Netherlands).

- "***Digital Tourism - From Tripadvisor Circulation Graphs to Behavior Extraction and Characterization***", presented by Nicolas Travers (De Vinci Research Center, France).
- "***A Survey on Multisided Fairness in Recommender Systems***", presented by Reza Shafiloo, Maria Stratigi, and Kostas Stefanidis (Tampere University, Finland).

The conference participated in the Database Diversity, Equity and Inclusion initiative, encouraging authors and participants to adopt DEI-aware communication practices in papers and presentations. In addition to the dedicated keynote by Tiziana Catarci, the DEI4Teach workshop was organized as an interactive World Café. The workshop fostered collaborative reflection and the exchange of experiences on integrating diversity, equity, and inclusion into the teaching of advanced database and information systems topics. A dedicated plenary session later presented the principal insights, shared vision, and recommendations emerging from the workshop discussions. These activities reaffirmed the conference's commitment to a more inclusive, equitable, and representative research community.

This CCIS volume includes 18 short papers and 5 demonstration papers from the main ADBIS 2026 conference, 4 papers (1 from an invited talk and 3 regular papers) from the Doctoral Consortium School, 1 paper from the DEI4Teach workshop, and the papers accepted by the three remaining workshops co-located with ADBIS 2026. Each workshop established its own international Program Committee, whose members reviewed the corresponding submissions. Overall, MADEISD, ERGA, and FEHDA received 23 submissions, of which 12 were selected for presentation and publication. The acceptance rate for each workshop did not exceed 50%. DEI4Teach contributed one paper summarizing the main topics discussed in the workshop.

The following Doctoral Consortium School (DCS) was co-located at the ADBIS 2026 conference:

DCS 2026: Second Doctoral Consortium School, chaired by Enrico Gallinucci and Verónika Peralta.

Supported by the ACM Europe Council, the four-day ADBIS 2026 Doctoral Consortium School (DCS) offered doctoral students an inclusive and collaborative environment for developing their research, receiving expert feedback, and building academic connections. The scientific program featured the following courses:

- "NebulaStream—Data Stream Processing for the Edge-Cloud-Continuum", by Volker Markl (TU Berlin, Germany).
- "Challenges and Methods in Trajectory Analytics: Data Preparation, Management, and Mining", by Karine Zeitouni (UVSQ–Université Paris-Saclay, France).
- "Ethical & Equitable Data Science: Bridging Social Justice and Technical Innovation", by Genoveva Vargas-Solar (CNRS and LIRIS, France).
- "When Generative AI Meets the Data Lifecycle: New Capabilities, New Responsibilities", by Oscar Romero (Universitat Politècnica de Catalunya, Spain).
- "Data for the (Press) People: Using AI to Help Journalists Make Sense of Interesting Data", by Ioana Manolescu (Inria and École Polytechnique, France).

DCS participants also attended ADBIS keynote talks delivered by Zoi Kaoudi, Wolfgang Lehner, María-Esther Vidal, and Tiziana Catarci.

The program further included mentoring, networking activities, and a Research Innovation Sprint coordinated by Veronika Peralta and Enrico Gallinucci. Working in interdisciplinary teams and supported by experienced mentors, participants developed original research ideas and presented them in a concluding pitch session. Selected participants may subsequently be invited to expand the most promising proposals into a collaborative paper for a special issue associated with ADBIS 2026.

The following workshops were co-located at the ADBIS 2026 conference.

DEI4Teach: Diversity, Equity and Inclusion for Teaching Advanced Databases and Information Systems, chaired by Cécile Favre and Barbara Catania.

Diversity, Equity and Inclusion (DEI) are longstanding themes within the ADBIS community. In 2026, the ADBIS DEI Chairs launched DEI4Teach, a highly interactive workshop dedicated to DEI in the teaching of Advanced Databases and Information Systems. The topic will also be reflected in the broader DEI initiatives of ADBIS 2026 and the DEI keynote of this year's conference. While ADBIS traditionally focuses on scientific advances, DEI4Teach shifts the attention to how we teach them and to whom. It offers an opportunity to reflect on teaching practices from a DEI perspective in a concrete and practice-oriented way. In this context, DEI is understood broadly to include gender equity, cultural and linguistic diversity, accessibility, socio-economic background, and inclusion across national and institutional contexts.

MADEISD 2026: 8th Workshop on Modern Approaches in Data Engineering and Information System Design, chaired by Sonja Ristić, Ivan Luković, and Slavica Kordić.

For decades, in many particularly complex organization systems, there has been an open issue of how to support information management processes to produce useful knowledge and tangible business values from data being collected. Database and information systems still play a central role in addressing the issue. In recent years, we have witnessed great movements in business information management. Such movements are of both a technological and methodological nature. Today, we have a huge selection of technologies, tools, and methods in data engineering, a discipline that supports the whole data life cycle in organizational systems, as well as information system design, which supports the software process in data engineering. Despite that, one of the hot issues in practice is still how to effectively transform large amounts of daily collected operational data into useful knowledge from the perspective of declared company goals, and how to set up the information design process aimed at the production of effective software services in companies. It seems that nowadays we have great theoretical potential for the application of new and more effective approaches in data engineering and information system design. However, it is likely that real deployment of such approaches in industry practice is far behind their theoretical potential. The main goal of this workshop was to address open questions and real potentials for various applications of modern approaches and technologies in data engineering and information system design to develop and implement effective software services in support of information management in various organization systems. We addressed the interdisciplinary nature of theories, methodologies, processes, architectures, and technologies across disciplines such as Data Engineering, Information System Design, Big Data, NoSQL Systems, Data Streams, Internet of Things, Cloud Systems, and Model-Driven Approaches in the development of effective software services. We invited researchers from all over the world to present their contributions, interdisciplinary approaches, or case studies related to modern approaches in Data Engineering and Information System Design. We were interested in gathering scientists and practitioners who are interested in applying these disciplines in the industry, public, and government sectors, such as healthcare, education, public administration, or security services. Experts from all sectors and application domains were welcome.

FEHDA 2026: 2nd International Workshop on Fairness Exploration in Heterogeneous Data and Algorithms, chaired by Beatrice Amico, Anna Dalla Vecchia, and Maria Stratigi.

Fairness is a complex and multifaceted concept that has garnered increasing attention across many areas of computer science research. Defining and measuring fairness is often context-dependent, as different applications may require tailored approaches to address specific ethical concerns. Understanding the relationships between involved groups can be facilitated by defining an ontology or identifying key properties. However, achieving fairness demands ongoing evaluations, transparent decision-making, and adaptability to evolving contexts. In this effort, another crucial challenge is managing and analyzing heterogeneous data types - data from diverse sources, formats, and structures. To achieve fairness, there are several possible approaches: (i) Establishing standardized definitions for similar data fields to promote consistency; (ii) Identifying potential biases and designing mechanisms to reduce them; (iii) Handling missing data with appropriate imputation techniques and augmenting data to guarantee representation of different groups; (iv) Promoting diverse representation to support an equal decision-making system. Ultimately, guaranteeing fairness in computational systems depends not only on data management but also on the careful design and evaluation of algorithms at various stages, including pre-processing, modeling, and post-processing. Incorporating fairness into these stages is critical for mitigating biases and fostering equity in data-driven systems. This workshop aimed to serve as a small step forward in a field as vast as it is significant to the scientific community. We welcomed articles with a particular focus on descriptive ontologies, fairness metrics and properties, frameworks for managing data heterogeneity to ensure fairness, and fairness-aware algorithms. We were also open to discussing other fairness-related topics that are not explicitly mentioned.

ERGA 2026: 2nd International Workshop on Entity Resolution and Graph Alignment, chaired by Georgia Koloniari and Alexandros Karakasidis.

In the era of a connected world and abundant data, entity resolution and graph alignment have come to play an increasingly important role for ensuring data consistency, accuracy, and quality. Entity resolution identifies and links records referring to the same real-world entities (e.g., people, organizations) despite inconsistencies and has been a cornerstone of data integration, with applications in finance, healthcare, and various other domains. Graph alignment maps nodes and edges across different graphs, considering relationships and structures among entities, with applications in social network analysis, bioinformatics, and knowledge graphs. The tasks share common challenges, particularly in handling large-scale data, requiring efficient solutions and the deployment of techniques from a wide range of research areas, such as database management, big data and parallel processing, machine learning and AI-based techniques, and others. Recognizing the common ground between entity resolution and graph alignment, the goal of this workshop was to bring together researchers, practitioners, and experts in both fields to introduce new methods and techniques, discuss open challenges, and explore future research directions. The workshop aimed to facilitate the exchange of new ideas in each of the two fields, while also highlighting their shared goals and providing new opportunities for collaborations.

Acknowledgements. We would like to wholeheartedly thank all participants, authors, PC members, workshop organizers, session chairs, demonstration chairs, doctoral consortium chairs, workshop chairs, volunteers, and co-organizers for their contributions to making ADBIS 2026 a great success. We would also like to thank the ADBIS Steering Committee and all sponsors.

September 2026

Genoveva Vargas Solar
Kostas Stefanidis
Themis Palpanas
Patrick Marcel
Mirian Halfeld-Ferrari
Panos Vassiliadis
Tatjana Welzer
Enrico Gallinucci
Veronika Peralta

Organization

General Chairs

Patrick Marcel	Université d'Orléans, France
Mirian Halfeld-Ferrari	Université d'Orléans, France

Program Chairs

Genoveva Vargas-Solar	CNRS, France
Kostas Stefanidis	Tampere University, Finland
Themis Palpanas	Université Paris Cité, France

Workshop Chairs

Panos Vassiliadis	University of Ioannina, Greece
Tatjana Welzer	University of Maribor, Slovenia

Doctoral School Chairs

Enrico Gallinucci	University of Bologna, Italy
Verónika Peralta	Université de Tours, France

Tutorial Chairs

Matteo Francia	Università di Bologna, Italy
Nicolas Labroche	Université de Tours, France

Proceedings Chairs

Silvia Chiusano	Politecnico di Torino, Italy
Cristina Dutra de Aguiar	Universidade de São Paulo, Brazil

Test of Time Award Chairs

Yannis Manolopoulos	University of York, Europe Campus, Greece
Mirjana Ivanovic	University of Novi Sad, Serbia

Diversity and Inclusion Chairs

Barbara Catania	University of Genoa, Italy
Cécile Favre	Lumière University Lyon 2, France

Special Issues Chairs

Oscar Romero	Universitat Politècnica de Catalunya, Spain
Julien Aligon	Université Toulouse Capitole, France

Demonstration Chairs

Alexandre Chanson	Université de Tours, France
Madhulika Mohanty	Inria Saclay, France

Sponsorship Chairs

Francesca Bugiotti	CentraleSupélec, France
Johann Gamper	University of Bozen-Bolzano, Italy

Community Chair

Nicolas Travers	École Supérieure d'Ingénieurs Léonard de Vinci, France

Publicity Chairs

Lorena Etcheverry	Universidad de la República, Uruguay
Robert Wrembel	Poznań University of Technology, Poland
Carlos Ordonez	University of Houston, USA
Ladjel Bellatreche	National Engineering School for Mechanics and Aerotechnics, France

Website Chairs

Nicolas Hiot	Université d'Orléans, France
Lingchen Wang	Université d'Orléans, France
Yousif Elias	Université d'Orléans, France

Research Track Program Committee

Alberto Abelló	Universitat Politècnica de Catalunya, Spain
Maribel Acosta	Technische Universität München, Germany
Cristina D. Aguiar	Universidade de São Paulo, Brazil
Rocio A Aldeco-Pérez	Universidad Nacional Autónoma de México, Mexico
Bernd Amann	Sorbonne University, CNRS, France
Witold Andrzejewski	Poznań University of Technology, Poland
Sylvio Barbon Junior	University of Trieste, Italy
Nelly Barret	INSA Lyon & LIRIS, France
Andreas Behrend	Technical University of Cologne, Germany
Ladjel Bellatreche	ISAE-ENSMA, France
Nadia Bennani	INSA Lyon, France
Fadila Bentayeb	Université Lumière Lyon 2, France
Sandro Bimonte	INRAE, France
Paweł Boiński	Poznań University of Technology, Poland
Drazen R. Brdjanin	University of Banja Luka, Bosnia and Herzegovina
Francesca Bugiotti	CentraleSupélec, France
Barbara Catania	University of Genoa, Italy
Mónica Caniupán	Universidad del Bío-Bío, Chile
Silvia Chiusano	Politecnico di Torino, Italy
Antonio Corral	University of Almería, Spain
Jerome Darmont	Université Lumière Lyon 2, France
Christos Doulkeridis	University of Pireaus, Greece
Stefania Dumbrava	ENSIIE INRIA IRIF, France
Johann Eder	Universität Klagenfurt, Austria
Markus Endres	Technische Universität München, Germany
Javier A. Espinosa-Oviedo	University of Lyon 1 Claude Bernard, France
Lorena Etcheverry	Universidad de la República, Uruguay
Georgios Evangelidis	University of Macedonia, Greece
Johann Gamper	Free University of Bozen-Bolzano, Italy
Mirian Halfeld-Ferrari	Université d'Orléans, France
Herodotos Herodotou	Cyprus University of Technology, Cyprus

Mirjana Ivanovic	University of Novi Sad, Serbia
Alexandros Karakasidis	University of Macedonia, Greece
Eleftheria Katsiri	Democritus University of Thrace, Greece
Zoubida Kedad	University of Versailles Saint-Quentin-en-Yvelines, France
Georgia Koloniari	University of Macedonia, Greece
Yannis Manolopoulos	University of York, Europe Campus, Greece
Maude Manouvrier	Université Paris Dauphine-PSL, France
Patrick Marcel	Université d'Orléans, France
Jose-Norberto Mazon	Universidad de Alicante, Spain
Maria Medina	Universidad Politécnica de Puebla, Mexico
Sara Migliorini	University of Verona, Italy
Alex Mircoli	Università Politecnica delle Marche, Italy
Simona Nisticò	University of Calabria, Italy
Boris Novikov	Unaffiliated, Finland
George Pallis	University of Cyprus, Cyprus
George Papastefanatos	Athena Research Center, Greece
Veronika Peralta	University of Tours, France
Edelmira Pasarella	Universitat Politècnica de Catalunya, Spain
Giuseppe Polese	University of Salerno, Italy
Anna Queralt	Universitat Politècnica de Catalunya, Spain
Elisa Quintarelli	Università degli Studi di Verona, Italy
Franck Ravat	Institut de Recherche en Informatique de Toulouse, France
Sonja Ristić	University of Novi Sad, Serbia
Gunter Saake	University of Magdeburg, Germany
Ingo Schmitt	Brandenburg University of Technology, Germany
Sana Sellami	Université d'Aix-Marseille, France
Sergey A. Stupnikov	Russian Academy of Sciences, Russia
Panos Vassiliadis	University of Ioannina, Greece
Yannis Velegrakis	Utrecht University, Netherlands
Goran Velinov	Ss. Cyril and Methodius University in Skopje, North Macedonia
Maria-Esther Vidal	Leibniz University of Hannover and TIB-Leibniz Information Centre for Science and Technology, Germany
Szymon Wilk	Poznań University of Technology, Poland
Robert Wrembel	Poznań University of Technology, Poland
Tetiana Yemelianenko	Université Lumière Lyon 2 CNRS LIRIS, France
Demetrios Zeinalipour-Yazti	University of Cyprus, Cyprus
Zheying Zhang	Tampere University, Finland
Ester Zumpano	University of Calabria, Italy

Demonstration Track Program Committee

Alberto Abelló	Universitat Politècnica de Catalunya, Spain
Julien Aligon	Université Toulouse Capitole, France
Nelly Barret	INSA Lyon & LIRIS, France
Drazen R. Brdjanin	University of Banja Luka, Bosnia and Herzegovina
Javier A. Espinosa-Oviedo	University of Lyon 1 Claude Bernard, France
Johann Gamper	Free University of Bozen-Bolzano, Italy
Moncef Garouani	Université Toulouse Capitole, France
Tomáš Horváth	Edinburgh Napier University, UK
Alexandros Karakasidis	University of Macedonia, Greece
Zoubida Kedad	University of Versailles, France
Maude Manouvrier	Université Paris Dauphine-PSL, France
Sara Migliorini	University of Verona, Italy
Boris Novikov	Unaffiliated, Finland
Sergey A. Stupnikov	Russian Academy of Sciences, Russia
Robert Wrembel	Poznań University of Technology, Poland

Steering Committee Chair

Yannis Manolopoulos	University of York, Europe Campus, Greece

Steering Committee

Andreas Behrend	TH Köln, Germany
Ladjel Bellatreche	ENSMA Poitiers, France
Maria Bielikova	Kempelen Institute of Intelligent Technologies, Slovakia
Barbara Catania	University of Genoa, Italy
Tania Cerquitelli	Politecnico di Torino, Italy
Richard Chbeir	IUT de Bayonne et du Pays Basque, France
Silvia Chiusano	Politecnico di Torino, Italy
Jérôme Darmont	University of Lyon 2, France
Johann Eder	Alpen Adria Universität Klagenfurt, Austria
Johann Gamper	Free University of Bozen-Bolzano, Italy
Tomáš Horváth	Pavol Jozef Šafárik University, Slovakia
Mirjana Ivanović	University of Novi Sad, Serbia
Manuk Manukyan	Yerevan State University, Armenia

Kjetil Nørvåg	Norwegian University of Science and Technology, Norway
Boris Novikov	Unaffiliated, Finland
George Papadopoulos	University of Cyprus, Cyprus
Jaroslav Pokorny	Charles University in Prague, Czech Republic
Oscar Romero	Universitat Politècnica de Catalunya - BarcelonaTech, Catalunya
Kostas Stefanidis	Tampere University, Finland
Sergey Stupnikov	Russian Academy of Sciences, Russia
Bernhard Thalheim	Christian Albrechts University, Kiel, Germany
Goce Trajcevski	Iowa State University, USA
Valentino Vranić	Pan-European University, Slovakia
Tatjana Welzer	University of Maribor, Slovenia
Genoveva Vargas-Solar	CNRS, France
Robert Wrembel	Poznań University of Technology, Poland
Ester Zumpano	University of Calabria, Italy

Contents

Sustainability, Privacy Workflows and Clinical Analytics

Similarity Search, Truth Discovery and Anomaly Detection

Demos

Doctoral Consortium School

DEI4Teach: Diversity, Equity and Inclusion for Teaching Advanced Databases and Information Systems

MADEISD 2026: 8th Workshop on Modern Approaches in Data Engineering and Information System Design

Similarity, Topic Modeling and Knowledge Graphs

A Bimodal Gaussian Convolutional Jaro–Winkler Similarity for Token-Aware Entity Matching

Ondřej Rozinek(✉)

Faculty of Information Technology, Czech Technical University in Prague, Prague, Czech Republic
ondrej.rozinek@gmail.com

Abstract. Approximate string comparators are a core primitive of database systems, underpinning deduplication, record linkage and fuzzy joins. Convolutional Jaro–Winkler (ConvJW) [1] sharpens the classical comparator with a Gaussian-weighted matching window, but inherits its narrow positional reach. When two records contain the *same words in a different order*, such as *Mrs. Yvonne Abbott* and *Abbott, Yvonne*, the matching characters fall outside the window and the pair looks like noise: every ConvJW configuration scores below 5 % F1 on the Cohen2003 `ucd-people` set. We propose MGSA-JW (Multimodal Gaussian Shifted-Alignment Jaro–Winkler), which gives every character a *second* Gaussian peak placed where a token-level alignment predicts its word has moved, switched on by a single scalar Q^p measuring how strongly the two strings share words. A one-to-one greedy assignment keeps the score bounded and symmetric, and the ConvJW aggregation and Winkler prefix are reused unchanged, so MGSA-JW is a drop-in replacement for any Jaro–Winkler-class comparator. On the eleven Cohen2003 datasets it raises pooled max-F1 from 86.32 % to 88.32 % (+2.0 p.p.) and is the strongest of 24 comparators, with gains concentrated on reordered-token datasets (up to +95 p.p. on `ucd-people`) and within 0.7 p.p. of ConvJW on ordered data.

Keywords: Approximate string matching · Jaro–Winkler · Convolutional similarity · Entity resolution · Record linkage · Token alignment

1 Introduction

Approximate string matching is a building block of entity resolution, deduplication, record linkage and data cleaning. These are database operations with no clean equality predicate, such as joining customer records across heterogeneous CRM and ERP systems or merging product catalogues. The input is a stream of short, semi-structured strings (names, organisations, addresses) that may be re-tokenised, abbreviated or mistyped, and the comparator must run

© The Author(s), under exclusive license to Springer Nature Switzerland AG 2027
G. Vargas Solar et al. (Eds.): ADBIS 2026, CCIS 3175, pp. 3–12, 2027.
https://doi.org/10.1007/978-3-032-39823-9_1

inside block-then-compare pipelines yet let one global threshold separate true links from noise.

The Convolutional Jaro and Jaro–Winkler measures of Rozinek and Mareš [1], ConvJ and ConvJW, recently sharpened this regime by replacing Jaro's hard matching window with a smooth Gaussian-weighted one, obtaining higher F1 and lower running time than every classical competitor on the Cohen2003 benchmark.

The Blind Spot: Reordered Words. Write X and Y for the two strings being compared, and $X[i]$ for the character at position i of X. ConvJW looks for a partner for $X[i]$ only among characters $Y[j]$ whose position j is close to i. It weights a candidate match by a Gaussian of the offset $|j - i|$ with bandwidth σ, and that weight is essentially zero once the offset exceeds a radius $w \approx 3.29\sigma$. This is exactly right for typos, which sit a few positions from where they should be, but fatal when two records share whole tokens in a different order: a word moved to the other end of the string lands far outside the window, so none of its characters can find their partners. Three real pairs from Cohen2003 `ucd-people`, all the same person:

```
Mrs. Yvonne Abbott          Abbott, Yvonne
Dr. Cornelius P. Ahern      Ahern, Cornelius P.
Mr. Brad Anderson           Anderson, Brad
```

The surname and given name swap, so matching characters are offset by about one token length. At $\sigma = 2$ the window only reaches $w = 7$ and the matches vanish: all six ConvJ/ConvJW configurations score 0–5 % F1 here, while even plain Jaro recovers 50 %. Token reordering is a *structural* blind spot, not something a better σ can fix.

Our Idea, Informally. The fix is to let each character look in *two* places at once. Besides its usual neighbourhood (the standard peak, which still catches typos), $X[i]$ gets a *second* Gaussian peak centred where the character would land *if its whole word had moved.* To find where it moved, we match the strings at word level, scoring every word of X against every word of Y and greedily locking in the best pairs, and then aim the second peak at the matching position inside the partner word. This peak fires only when the strings genuinely share words. A single number $Q \in [0, 1]$, the average quality of the matched words, gates it through Q^p, which is near 1 only when nearly every word of the shorter string has a strong partner. When no words are shared $Q^p \to 0$ and MGSA-JW behaves exactly like ConvJW, so the method slides continuously from the character to the token regime with no discrete switch. For the clean swap *Yvonne Abbott / Abbott Yvonne*, where ConvJW scores about 0.36, MGSA-JW scores 1.0 (Example 1).

Contributions. We make four contributions. First, an *algorithm* (Sect. 4): a bimodal convolutional similarity that adds one token-aware Gaussian peak per character and resolves candidate pairs by a single one-to-one greedy assignment. Second, *theory* (Sect. 5): bounded matched mass, exact symmetry, and provable reduction to ConvJW absent token evidence. Third, *experiments* (Sect. 6): a reproduction-grade benchmark against 23 comparators on Cohen2003, where MGSA-JW leads pooled F1 by ≥ 2.0 p.p. Fourth, *negative findings*: an acronym peak and four metric-inspired aggregations that do not help.

2 Background: Convolutional Jaro–Winkler

We restate ConvJW here, explaining each quantity before its formula so the paper is self-contained. Jaro similarity [6] counts characters two strings share *at roughly the same position*, discounts transposed pairs, and averages three ratios. Jaro–Winkler [7] adds a shared-prefix bonus. ConvJW [1] keeps this skeleton but softens the window: a candidate match at offset $d = |j - i|$ is weighted by a Gaussian

$$G(d) = \exp\Big(-\tfrac{d^2}{2\sigma^2}\Big) \in (0, 1], \qquad w = \lceil 3.29\sigma \rceil,$$

where the bandwidth σ sets positional tolerance and w is the radius at which G has decayed to near zero. A perfectly aligned match ($d = 0$) gets full weight 1, and a match one position off gets a little less.

Let $n = |X|$, $m = |Y|$, and $J(i) = \{j : |j - i| \leq w\} \cap [0, m)$ the window around i. For each $X[i]$, ConvJW keeps its best in-window partner of the same character and accumulates the *matched mass* M_w (total Gaussian weight of those matches) and the *misalignment mass* A_w (the part contributed by matches that are not exactly aligned, a soft transposition penalty):

$$M_w = \sum_{i=0}^{n-1} \max_{j \in J(i)} G(|j - i|)\, \delta_{X[i],Y[j]}, \quad A_w = \sum_{i:\, j^\star(i) \neq i} G(|j^\star(i) - i|)\, \delta_{X[i],Y[j^\star(i)]}, \tag{1}$$

where $\delta_{a,b} = 1$ iff $a = b$ and $j^\star(i)$ attains the maximum. The scores combine these as Jaro and Jaro–Winkler do, with $\ell \in \{0, \dots, 4\}$ the common-prefix length and $p_{\mathrm{W}} = 0.1$:

$$s_{\mathrm{ConvJ}} = \tfrac{1}{3}\Big(\tfrac{M_w}{n} + \tfrac{M_w}{m} + \tfrac{M_w - A_w}{M_w}\Big), \qquad s_{\mathrm{ConvJW}} = s_{\mathrm{ConvJ}} + \ell\, p_{\mathrm{W}}\,(1 - s_{\mathrm{ConvJ}}),$$

the three terms being "how much of X matched", "how much of Y matched", and "how aligned". One loose end matters later. Equation (1) lets each $X[i]$ pick its $Y[j]$ *independently*, so several characters may claim the same $Y[j]$, and M_w can exceed m (for example, $X = \mathsf{aaa}$, $Y = \mathsf{a}$ gives $M_w = 3$). MGSA-JW closes this with a one-to-one assignment (Sect. 4.4).

3 Related Work

Jaro [6] and Jaro–Winkler [7] are character-level comparators with a hard window. Levenshtein [11], Damerau–Levenshtein [10], Needleman–Wunsch [13] and Smith–Waterman [12] are edit-distance or alignment methods. Monge–Elkan [9], SoftTFIDF [8] and the token-sort/token-set family lift a character similarity to bags of tokens, gaining order-invariance but discarding position. ConvJ/ConvJW [1] replace Jaro's hard window with a Gaussian convolution, and MGSA-JW adds a token-aware mode. The closest comparators in spirit are transposition-tolerant ones. N-gram similarity and distance [3] generalise edit distance to n-grams and tolerate local reordering, and Al-Hagree et al. [4] adapt this to names. Bag-of-n-gram cosine, our `Q-gram cosine` baseline, is the extreme case. It ignores order entirely, handling arbitrary transpositions but also matching unrelated strings sharing n-grams. MGSA-JW instead *keeps* positional information, adding a second alignment-predicted position. Learned and coarser-granularity matchers such as ChatGPT-as-matcher [5] are orthogonal, matching at the record level rather than the inner character comparison.

4 The MGSA-JW Algorithm

The algorithm has four stages. *Tokenisation* (Sect. 4.1) splits the strings into words. *Token alignment* (Sect. 4.2) matches words and yields the global quality Q. *Expected positions* (Sect. 4.3) predict where each character's word moved. Finally, the *bimodal kernel* (Sect. 4.4) scores candidate pairs with two peaks, resolves them one-to-one, and feeds the result into the unchanged ConvJW aggregation.

4.1 Tokenisation

We normalise both strings (Unicode NFKD, case-folding, diacritics stripped) and split on *any maximal run of separator characters* – whitespace and punctuation. Concretely we map punctuation to spaces and split on whitespace, so the exact delimiter set does not matter (adding separators such as \r leaves every Cohen2003 score unchanged). The rule is permissive, because the gate Q^p below tolerates spurious short tokens. We write the token sequences $(x_1, \dots, x_{n_t})$, $(y_1, \dots, y_{m_t})$ with start positions $b_X[t] \in [0, n]$, $b_Y[t] \in [0, m]$, and let $t(i) \in \{1, \dots, n_t\}$ be the index of the token containing character i.

4.2 Token Alignment and the Global Quality Q

We decide which word of X corresponds to which of Y. Every word pair is scored with the same comparator used for characters, $S_{ij} = s_{\mathrm{ConvJW}}(x_i, y_j; \sigma) \in [0, 1]$, and a partial one-to-one matching π is built greedily: sort word pairs from most to least similar and commit each pair whose two words are still free. Greedy (not globally optimal) matching is deliberate: it locks in the few strong, informative word pairs first and leaves stop-words and titles unmatched, instead of being forced to pair them (Sect. 7). To keep the comparator symmetric the sort uses the swap-invariant key $\kappa_{\mathrm{tok}}(a, b) = (-S_{ab}, \min(a, b), \max(a, b))$. The *global pair quality* is the average similarity of matched words, normalised by the larger token count,

$$Q = \frac{1}{\max(n_t, m_t)} \sum_{i:\,\pi(i)\neq\perp} S_{i,\pi(i)} \in [0,1], \tag{2}$$

answering "do these strings really consist of the same words?" Here $Q = 1$ when every word of the shorter side has an identical partner, and $Q \approx 0$ when no two words are similar.

4.3 Expected Positions and the Q^p Gate

If the word containing $X[i]$ is matched, we can predict where $X[i]$ should appear in Y: at the start of the partner word plus the same in-word offset $r = i - b_X[t(i)]$. This prediction and its confidence are

$$\begin{aligned} e_{\mathrm{tok}}(i) &= \begin{cases} b_Y[\pi(t(i))] + r & \text{if } \pi(t(i)) \neq \perp, \\ i & \text{otherwise;} \end{cases} \\ \mathrm{conf}_{\mathrm{tok}}(i) &= \begin{cases} S_{t(i),\pi(t(i))} \cdot Q^p & \text{if } \pi(t(i)) \neq \perp, \\ 0 & \text{otherwise.} \end{cases} \end{aligned} \tag{3}$$

with symmetric counterparts $e^*_{\mathrm{tok}}(j), \mathrm{conf}^*_{\mathrm{tok}}(j)$ for characters of Y. The confidence multiplies how good *this* word match is by Q^p, how good the *overall* alignment is. We stress that Q^p is a *gate*, not a smoother: all smoothing is done by the positional Gaussian G, whereas Q^p is deliberately switch-like so a moved word is rewarded only when the rest of the words line up too. At $p = 1$ the peak fires on incidental shared letters, whereas at our default $p = 15$ it stays essentially off until the alignment is near-complete ($Q = 0.9 \Rightarrow Q^{15} \approx 0.2$, $Q = 0.8 \Rightarrow 0.04$). This near-binary behaviour is intended, as it suppresses the false positives that sink the naive token baselines below. Any $p \in [8, 20]$ gives F1 within 0.1 p.p. of the reported numbers (Sect. 6.4).

4.4 The Bimodal Kernel and One-to-One Assignment

A pair (i, j) with $X[i] = Y[j]$ is a *candidate* if it lies inside the standard or either token-shifted window ($|j - i| \leq w$, $|j - e_{\mathrm{tok}}(i)| \leq w$, or $|i - e^*_{\mathrm{tok}}(j)| \leq w$). Its weight is the *strongest* available peak,

$$\begin{aligned} W(i,j) = \max\{\&G(|j-i|), \\ &\mathrm{conf}_{\mathrm{tok}}(i)\, G(|j - e_{\mathrm{tok}}(i)|), \\ &\mathrm{conf}^*_{\mathrm{tok}}(j)\, G(|i - e^*_{\mathrm{tok}}(j)|)\,\}. \end{aligned} \tag{4}$$

Taking the maximum (not the sum) stops two peaks aimed at the same character from double-counting and bounds W by $G(0) = 1$. The displacement $d(i, j) \in \{0, \ldots, w\}$ is the offset of the *winning* peak from its own centre, so a cleanly moved word incurs no penalty while a typo inside it still does. *If two peaks tie*, we take the one with the smaller displacement (ties broken toward the standard peak), so $d(i,j)$ is uniquely defined, and this rule is itself swap-invariant. Retaining the standard peak guarantees that pure typographical noise is scored exactly as in ConvJW.

A single $Y[j]$ may still be the best partner for several $X[i]$, so we resolve candidates one-to-one: we sort them by the swap-invariant key

$$\kappa(i,j) = \big(-W(i,j),\, d(i,j),\, \min(i,j),\, \max(i,j)\big),$$

and accept each whose i and j are both free. Over the accepted set $\mathcal{M}$,

$$M_w = \sum_{(i,j)\in\mathcal{M}} W(i,j), \qquad A_w = \sum_{(i,j)\in\mathcal{M}:\, d>0} W(i,j). \tag{5}$$

The score is $s_{\text{MGSA-JW}} = 0$ if $M_w = 0$, and otherwise $s + \ell p_{\text{W}}(1-s)$, where $s = \frac{1}{3}\left(\frac{M_w}{n} + \frac{M_w}{m} + \frac{M_w - A_w}{M_w}\right)$ and ℓ is the common-prefix length up to 4. This reuses the ConvJW aggregation and Winkler prefix unchanged. When the alignment is uninformative ($Q \to 0$), the last two peaks vanish, $W(i,j) = G(|j-i|)$, and MGSA-JW reduces to a one-to-one ConvJW (Theorem 3). Full pseudocode is in the extended version [2].

Example 1 (Clean reordering). For $X =$ `YVONNE ABBOTT`, $Y =$ `ABBOTT YVONNE` (length 13), token alignment pairs the two `YVONNE`s and `ABBOTT`s at $S = 1$, so $Q = 1$, $Q^p = 1$. Every character of `YVONNE` (positions 0–5) has shifted centre $e_{\text{tok}} = 7, \ldots, 12$, exactly its image in Y, contributing $1 \cdot G(0) = 1$ at $d = 0$, and likewise for `ABBOTT` and the space. All 13 pairs are accepted, $M_w = 13$, $A_w = 0$, so $s = 1$. The same pair scores $s_{\text{ConvJW}} \approx 0.36$ at $\sigma = 2$. With stop-word noise (`MRS YVONNE ABBOTT` / *Abbott Yvonne*), `MRS` is left unmatched, $Q \approx 0.667$ and $Q^{15} \approx 2 \cdot 10^{-3}$, giving a small $s \approx 0.09$ that is still *strictly above* any non-match, whose $Q \approx 0$ silences the peak. Ranking, which is what pooled F1 measures, is preserved.

5 Theoretical Properties

Three properties make MGSA-JW a safe drop-in. All follow from the one-to-one assignment and the swap-invariant ordering of Sect. 4.4, and are proved in the extended version [2].

Theorem 1 (Boundedness). *For all X, Y with $|X| = n, |Y| = m$: $M_w \le \min(n,m)$, $A_w \in [0, M_w]$, and $s_{\text{MGSA-JW}} \in [0,1]$.*

Theorem 2 (Symmetry). *With the swap-invariant keys and the displacement tie-break of Sect. 4.4, $s_{\text{MGSA-JW}}(X,Y) = s_{\text{MGSA-JW}}(Y,X)$.*

Theorem 3 (ConvJW reduction). *If each string is a single token, or every $S_{ij} = 0$, then $s_{\text{MGSA-JW}} = s^{1\text{-}1}_{\text{ConvJW}}$, the ConvJW score with a one-to-one character constraint.*

The one-to-one assignment bounds the matched mass (without it, X=aaa, Y=a would give $M_w = 3 > m$) and, with the swap-invariant key and displacement tie-break, makes the kernel symmetric. When no token evidence is present, the two shifted peaks vanish and the standard peak alone recovers ConvJW. In practice, $s^{1\text{-}1}_{\text{ConvJW}}$ and s_{ConvJW} differ only on pathologically repeated characters.

6 Experiments

We cover datasets and baselines (Sect. 6.1), accuracy and *where* gains arise (Sect. 6.2), running time (Sect. 6.3), parameter sensitivity (Sect. 6.4) and limitations (Sect. 6.5).

6.1 Setup

We use the eleven Cohen2003 entity-resolution datasets [8] exactly as the original ConvJW paper [1]. They are short, structured strings: animal and bird species names (1–4 words), business, park and restaurant names (multi-word), and person and census names. What matters for a positional comparator is how matching records vary. Most differ mainly by *typos* or spelling while keeping word order (the bird, park, business and census sets). A few are *reordered or re-tokenised*, chiefly `ucd-people` (*Given Surname* vs. *Surname, Given*), `animal` and `demo`. This is exactly where positional comparators fail and MGSA-JW is designed to help.[1]

We benchmark three baseline families. *Classical*: Jaro, Jaro–Winkler, Levenshtein, Damerau–Levenshtein, Needleman–Wunsch, Smith–Waterman (SimMetrics.NET implementations). *Convolutional*: ConvJ/ConvJW at $\sigma \in \{0.5, 1, 2\}$ [1]. *Token-level*: symmetric Monge–Elkan with JW or ConvJW inner [9], Token-Sort (both inners), Token-Set-Ratio, Hungarian token alignment, q-gram cosine (q=3, a bag-of-n-gram comparator [3,4]) and a corpus-free SoftTFIDF. Following [1] we report *pooled* max-F1 (all datasets in one ranked list, one global threshold) and *per-dataset* max-F1 means (per-domain thresholds), which probe the two deployment regimes. Timings: .NET 8.0 release, single thread, Windows 11, after a JIT/cache warm-up. MGSA-JW adds one parameter to ConvJW, the gate exponent $p = 15$ (Sect. 6.4).

6.2 Accuracy and Where the Gains Come From

Table 1 ranks all 24 comparators by pooled F1 with their running time. MGSA-JW occupies ranks 1–3 at 86.56–88.32 % (per-dataset mean F1 92.2 %), ahead of every other method by $\geq$ 2.0 p.p. The strongest token baseline, Monge–Elkan-ConvJW, trails by 2.20 p.p. The gains come precisely from reordering datasets.

[1] We trim trailing whitespace in the `bird3` ground-truth keys. The original source leaves it on some URL keys, so literal-equality ground truth returns 0 % F1 for every method until trimmed.

Against the best ConvJW per cell (max over σ), MGSA-JW(σ=2) records five wins (the reordering-heavy datasets above: +95.0 p.p. on `ucd-people`, +75.6 on `bird3`, +31.7 on `animal`), two ties at the ceiling, and four losses ≤ 0.7 p.p. on ordered data, for a mean cell-wise gain of +18.4 p.p. In short, MGSA-JW helps when records share words in a different order, and essentially never otherwise. The larger +22.1 p.p. figure sometimes quoted compares against a *single* ConvJW configuration and is optimistic, so we headline the defensible +2.0 p.p. pooled and +18.4 p.p. cell-wise. Our reproduction of every flat-character baseline matches the published numbers within 0.6 p.p. pooled.

Table 1. Pooled max-F1 and total CPU time on the eleven Cohen2003 datasets. **Bold** = MGSA-JW. The overhead is discussed in Sect. 6.3.

#	Method	F1 %	t (s)	#	Method	F1 %	t (s)
1	**MGSA-JW(σ2)**	**88.32**	29.1	13	Monge–Elkan-JW	82.24	15.4
2	**MGSA-JW(σ1)**	**87.35**	23.9	14	Jaro–Winkler	81.02	7.1
3	**MGSA-JW(σ.5)**	**86.56**	19.6	15	Q-gram cosine	79.73	16.6
4	ConvJW(σ2)	86.32	3.7	16	Hungarian-ConvJW	76.78	18.2
5	ConvJW(σ1)	86.12	2.7	17	Damerau–Lev.	76.55	24.9
6	Monge–Elkan-ConvJW	86.12	12.5	18	Levenshtein	76.52	15.7
7	ConvJW(σ.5)	85.49	2.0	19	Needleman–Wunsch	76.13	35.0
8	ConvJ(σ1)	84.99	2.4	20	Smith–Waterman	75.53	34.2
9	ConvJ(σ2)	84.72	3.6	21	Token-Sort-JW	75.36	10.1
10	ConvJ(σ.5)	84.54	1.9	22	Jaro	74.89	7.4
11	SoftTFIDF-JW	84.31	14.0	23	Token-Sort-ConvJW	74.78	5.1
12	Token-Set-Ratio-JW	83.98	21.7	24	Hungarian-JW	71.16	20.4

6.3 Running Time

The time column of Table 1 shows the cost, which we do not hide. MGSA-JW is the slowest convolutional variant: at $\sigma = 2$ it takes 29.1 s against ConvJW's 3.7 s, a 7–8$\times$ overhead from building the token matrix S, the symmetric kernel and the $\mathcal{O}(nw \log nw)$ greedy sort. This is a constant factor, not a change of class (MGSA-JW runs in $\mathcal{O}(n_t m_t \bar{c} w) + \mathcal{O}(nw \log nw)$, $\bar{c}$ the mean token length). It stays faster than Smith–Waterman (34.2 s) and Needleman–Wunsch (35.0 s) and comparable to Damerau–Levenshtein (24.9 s), the workhorses it would replace. At scale it runs *inside* a blocking stage, scoring only surviving pairs, so the cost is a per-deployment decision, with a SIMD kernel and cached token matrix the obvious remedies.

6.4 Sensitivity to the New Parameters

Gate Exponent p. Sweeping p at $\sigma = 2$, pooled F1 is monotone, crosses the ConvJW baseline at $p \approx 3$ and saturates near 88 % for $p \geq 6$. Per-dataset F1 is non-monotone (highest at $p = 1$, dipping at $p \in [2, 4]$, recovering as noise is suppressed). Any $p \in [8, 20]$ lands within 0.1 p.p., so we fix $p = 15$. *Bandwidth σ.* The best σ here is 2, whereas ConvJW preferred 0.5. This is expected, because in ConvJW a wide window lets distant non-matching characters leak in, while in MGSA-JW the token peak already handles long-range structure, so a wider standard peak can absorb within-token jitter safely. Sensitivity is mild (all three σ rank 1–3 pooled), but σ remains a tunable. *Two negative results*, for honesty: an acronym-aware third peak changes F1 by < 0.01 p.p. here (Cohen2003 has no acronym pairs), and four metric-inspired aggregations (Jaccard, Dice, Cosine, Overlap) lose 1.5–3 p.p. pooled. Both are detailed in the extended version [2].

6.5 Limitations

Two caveats bound the claims. First, $p = 15$ was tuned on these same eleven datasets, so the accuracy is an in-distribution best (sensitivity is mild, ± 0.1 p.p. over $p \in [8, 20]$, but out-of-distribution performance may differ, and leave-one-dataset-out selection is the proper next step). Second, and most important for deployment, both protocols pick the F1-maximising threshold *using ground truth*, which is unavailable in production, so absolute F1 is optimistic. What transfers label-free is the *ranking* of pairs, exactly what the pooled protocol stresses and where MGSA-JW's +2.0 p.p. lead is measured.

7 Discussion

Why MGSA-JW Beats the Token Baselines. Hungarian token alignment is the mathematically "correct" one-to-one scheme, yet it is the *worst* token baseline on pooled F1: short names are a few informative tokens surrounded by stop-words, and a globally optimal assignment is forced to pair the noise too, inflating scores for non-matches. MGSA-JW's greedy alignment instead commits the strong pairs first and leaves the residue unmatched, exactly what Q^p rewards, so it keeps ConvJW's character robustness and the token peak's structural advantage while suppressing the failures of both pure token and pure character methods.

When to Choose What. We can key the choice to the dataset characteristics of Sect. 6.1. *Use MGSA-JW* for short, structured records that may be reordered or re-tokenised (people, organisations, addresses merged across sources), where its +95 p.p. swings appear. Because it never costs more than 0.7 p.p. on ordered data, it is a safe default whenever order cannot be guaranteed. *Use plain* ConvJ/ConvJW on already-canonicalised data when latency dominates (4–8× faster). *Prefer a bag-of-n-gram comparator* [3,4] only when order is *completely* unreliable. MGSA-JW beats q-gram cosine by +8.6 p.p. pooled precisely because it keeps positional information.

8 Conclusion

MGSA-JW adds one token-aware Gaussian peak per character, gated by a scalar Q^p, on top of ConvJW. A one-to-one assignment keeps the score provably bounded and exactly symmetric, making it a true drop-in replacement that slides continuously between the character and token regimes, recovering reordered matches while leaving ordered data untouched. On the eleven Cohen2003 datasets it raises pooled max-F1 from 86.32 to 88.32 % and is the strongest of 24 comparators, with gains on reordering datasets (+95 p.p. on `ucd-people`) and losses never above 0.7 p.p., at a 7–8× cost and one extra parameter. Open problems remain: an unsupervised threshold to replace the current ground-truth one, out-of-distribution selection of p and σ, and closing the runtime gap. Calibrating the absolute score, so that reordered matches score near 1 rather than just above the noise floor, is the most valuable next step toward label-free deployment.

References

1. Rozinek, O., Mareš, J.: Fast and precise Convolutional Jaro and Jaro-Winkler similarity. In: Proceedings of FRUCT (2024)
2. Rozinek, O.: A bimodal Gaussian convolutional Jaro–Winkler similarity (extended version with full proofs) (2025)
3. Kondrak, G.: N-gram similarity and distance. In: Consens, M., Navarro, G. (eds.) SPIRE 2005. LNCS, vol. 3772, pp. 115–126. Springer, Heidelberg (2005). https://doi.org/10.1007/11575832_13
4. Al-Hagree, S., Al-Sanabani, M., Hadwan, M., Al-Hagery, M.A.: An improved N-gram distance for names matching. In: Proceedings of ICOICE, Hadhramout, Yemen, pp. 1–7 (2019). https://doi.org/10.1109/ICOICE48418.2019.9035154.
5. Peeters, R., Bizer, C.: Using ChatGPT for entity matching. In: Proceedings of ADBIS Short Papers, LNCS, vol. 14186, pp. 221–230 (2023). https://doi.org/10.1007/978-3-031-42941-5_20
6. Jaro, M.A.: Advances in record-linkage methodology as applied to matching the 1985 census of Tampa, Florida. J. Amer. Stat. Assoc. **84**(406), 414–420 (1989)
7. Winkler, W.E.: String comparator metrics and enhanced decision rules in the Fellegi–Sunter model of record linkage. Technical report, U.S. Bureau of the Census (1990)
8. Cohen, W.W., Ravikumar, P., Fienberg, S.E.: A comparison of string distance metrics for name-matching tasks. In: Proceedings OF IJCAI Workshop on Information Integration on the Web, pp. 73–78 (2003)
9. Monge, A.E., Elkan, C.P.: The field matching problem: algorithms and applications. In: Proceedings of ACM SIGKDD, pp. 267–270 (1996)
10. Damerau, F.J.: A technique for computer detection and correction of spelling errors. Comm. ACM **7**(3), 171–176 (1964)
11. Levenshtein, V.I.: Binary codes capable of correcting deletions, insertions, and reversals. Soviet Phys. Doklady **10**(8), 707–710 (1966)
12. Smith, T.F., Waterman, M.S.: Identification of common molecular subsequences. J. Molec. Biol. **147**(1), 195–197 (1981)
13. Needleman, S.B., Wunsch, C.D.: A general method applicable to the search for similarities in the amino acid sequence of two proteins. J. Molec. Biol. **48**(3), 443–453 (1970)

Evaluating Accuracy and Probabilistic Reliability of Zero-Shot Time Series Foundation Models

Panagiotis Michael[1], Moysis Symeonides[2], and Demetris Trihinas[1](✉)

[1] Department of Computer Science, University of Nicosia, Nicosia, Cyprus
michael.p15@live.unic.ac.cy, trihinas.d@unic.ac.cy
[2] Department of Computer Science, University of Cyprus, Nicosia, Cyprus
msymeo03@ucy.ac.cy

Abstract. Time Series Foundation Models (TSFMs) promise a paradigm shift toward zero-shot forecasting by eliminating task-specific training. However, existing works often overlook trade-offs between predictive accuracy and probabilistic calibration. This paper presents a benchmark study of six TSFMs evaluated on energy, traffic, and financial datasets. We contrast their performance against statistical baselines and a supervised DL model. The study reveals that while TSFMs outperform statistical methods and supervised models, they are subject to a fundamental trade-off between point accuracy and probabilistic reliability. Specifically, xLSTM architectures provide robust probabilistic calibration across horizons. In contrast, patch-based transformers offer competitive accuracy but face calibration issues at long horizons, while transformer-based models exhibit context saturation points for optimal zero-shot reasoning. These findings offer evidence-based guidance for balancing generalization and uncertainty quantification in real-world deployments.

Keywords: Time Series · Foundation Models · Zero-Shot Learning

1 Introduction

Time series forecasting is important for decision-making in critical domains, including energy grid management, supply chain logistics, and traffic planning. Although statistical models are common, the focus has shifted toward task-specific DL models setting new benchmarks for supervised forecasting [9]. However, these models require extensive historical data, considerable compute for optimization, and frequent retraining under new distributions or domains [13].

The success of large language models (LLMs) has inspired a new wave of forecasting research known as Time Series Foundation Models (TSFMs). TSFMs are neural networks pre-trained on thousands of time series to enable zero-shot forecasting [4]. This approach bypasses task-specific training, enabling direct deployment on unseen data through mechanisms such as token patching [6], numerical

© The Author(s), under exclusive license to Springer Nature Switzerland AG 2027
G. Vargas Solar et al. (Eds.): ADBIS 2026, CCIS 3175, pp. 13–23, 2027.
https://doi.org/10.1007/978-3-032-39823-9_2

quantization [1], and generative flow matching [7]. Consequently, TSFMs offer a practical alternative for cold-start scenarios, such as forecasting demand for new retail products or power generation for newly installed renewable microgrids where historical data is limited [5]. From a data engineering perspective, TSFMs enable a model-as-a-service paradigm, integrating directly into data pipelines and reducing the complexity of maintaining localized ML/AI workflows.

However, current TSFM evaluations are sparse and fragmented. Recent benchmarks show that while TSFMs are competitive, they do not exceed finely tuned task-specific baselines [8] and under-perform statistical methods for irregular time series [12]. Moreover, with TSFMs trained on public data, their performance can be artificially inflated on standard benchmarks. Another critical gap in the literature is the emphasis on point accuracy, neglecting probabilistic calibration. Our work bridges the gap between point accuracy and probabilistic reliability by benchmarking trade-offs among recurrent, generative, and transformer TSFMs, and evaluating them on unseen data to verify their generalization.

The contributions of this work are summarized as follows:

- A comprehensive, reproducible, and open-source[1] benchmark study on zero-shot time series forecasting, where we evaluate 6 TSFMs (Chronos-2, TiRex, Moirai-2.0, Sundial, TimesFM, and Toto) against statistical baselines and a state-of-the-art supervised DL architecture (PatchTST).
- We contrast model performance across diverse data representations and utilize newly collected datasets to ensure zero-shot forecasting on data unseen by TSFMs during their training to assess model robustness.
- The evaluation extends beyond point-error metrics, by using Interval Coverage Error (ICE) and Interval Mean Absolute Error (IMAE) to quantify the reliability of the uncertainty estimates from the TSFMs.

The rest of this paper is organized as follows: Sect. 2 reviews related work, Sect. 3 describes datasets and experimental setup, Sect. 4 presents the experiments and key takeaways, and Sect. 5 concludes and outlines future work.

2 Related Work

Prior to foundation models, the state-of-the-art was dominated by task-specific DL architectures trained on target datasets. The Transformer advanced this generation through self-attention, enabling models to capture long-range dependencies, with early adaptations such as Informer reducing the quadratic complexity of attention to handle longer contexts [13]. The paradigm matured with PatchTST [9], which segments time steps into discrete patches and processes variables independently, reducing memory overhead and setting a new supervised benchmark. Despite high accuracy, these models are constrained by large volumes of domain-specific data and significant optimization overhead, limiting their utility in zero-shot or cold-start scenarios [5].

[1] https://github.com/unic-ailab/TSFM-Eval.

TSFMs overcome the limitations of task-specific training by pre-training on large, diverse datasets and using zero-shot inference to generalize across unseen distributions and domains. A key challenge is translating continuous numerical data into a format compatible with architectures designed for natural language. Chronos-2 [1] applies strict quantization, mapping continuous values into a discrete token vocabulary and treating forecasting as language modeling. Moirai-2.0 [6] and TimesFM [4] instead adopt patch-based, decoder-only autoregressive architectures, where Moirai-2.0 predicts multiple future patches simultaneously via multi-token prediction, and TimesFM lets the output patch length exceed the input patch length for long-horizon generation. Toto [3], a transformer-based TSFM embeds a Student-T mixture output head to capture heavy-tailed distributions common in time series observability data.

While attention transformers dominate, recent work proposes generative and state-tracking architectures to better model predictive uncertainty and temporal continuity. Sundial [7] approaches forecasting through generative modeling, using continuous tokenization and a flow-matching objective to sample multiple future trajectories and construct probabilistic bounds without a fixed parametric distribution, making it adaptable to volatile data. In contrast, TiRex [2] abandons attention in favor of an extended LSTM (xLSTM) architecture, where its recurrent backbone explicitly tracks hidden states over time, maintaining continuous internal memory for consistent long-range predictions.

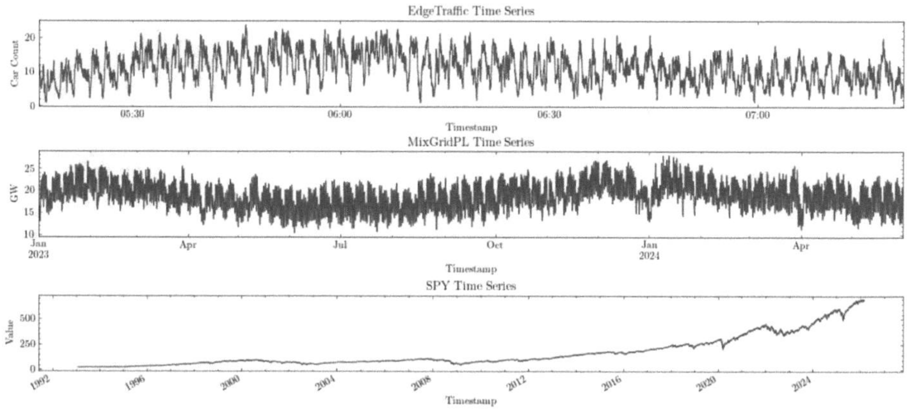

Fig. 1. High-Level Overview of the Datasets Embraced for the Benchmarking Study

3 Experimental Methodology

3.1 Datasets

We evaluate zero-shot generalization across three modalities (Fig. 1): discrete traffic counts (EdgeTraffic), continuous energy load (MixGridPL), and stochastic financial indices (SPY). These span a wide range of characteristics, including high versus low volatility, periodic versus stationary behavior, and temporal granularity. EdgeTraffic and MixGridPL are recently curated data outside known training corpora, isolating true zero-shot reasoning from data leakage.

The **EdgeTraffic** dataset [10] provides high-frequency vehicle counts from a road intersection in Iasi, Romania (7478 observations at 1 s resolution over 2h window). The data (Fig. 1a) exhibits high volatility, periodic patterns, and a discrete modality that is challenging for continuous-value foundation models.

The **MixGridPL** dataset [11] tracks aggregate electricity for Poland's national power grid (12407 observations at 1h resolution) over 17 months in 2024–25 (Fig. 1b). A continuous, highly seasonal series whose recent collection ensures its temporal patterns were unavailable during TSFM development.

The Yahoo! **SPY** dataset consists of 8324 daily closing prices for SPDR S&P 500 ETF from 1993 to 2025 (Fig. 1c). SPY is non-stationary with a long-term positive trend but significant short-term volatility, and percentage shifts are evaluated to gauge model responsiveness to economic trends.

Table 1. Experimental configurations for varied context (C) and horizon (H)

Dataset	Scenario	Fixed Value	Varying Range
EdgeTraffic	FixedC	$C = 900$	$H \in \{10, 60, 300, 600, 900, 1,200, 1,800\}$
	FixedH	$H = 60$	$C \in \{120, 300, 600, 900, 1,200, 1,800, 2,400\}$
MixGridPL	FixedC	$C = 240$	$H \in \{12, 24, 72, 144, 288, 576, 672\}$
	FixedH	$H = 24$	$C \in \{96, 120, 168, 240, 336, 480, 600\}$
SPY	FixedC	$C = 60$	$H \in \{1, 5, 21, 42, 63, 126, 252\}$
	FixedH	$H = 5$	$C \in \{20, 40, 60, 126, 252, 378, 504\}$

3.2 Problem Description

We define a univariate time series as an ordered sequence of observations $\mathcal{X} = \{x_1, x_2, \ldots, x_N\}$. For any given reference time T, which represents the current moment in the series, the goal of zero-shot forecasting is to predict a future sequence of observations $\hat{\mathcal{X}}_{fut} = \{\hat{x}_{T+1}, \ldots, \hat{x}_{T+H}\}$ for a defined horizon H by utilizing a historical context of length C $(x_{T-C+1}, \ldots, x_T)$ without performing any gradient updates or fine-tuning on the target dataset.

To evaluate this goal across our experimental scenarios, we employ a non-overlapping rolling window evaluation scheme where each instance is constructed from a segment of length $L = C + 2H$. Each segment is divided into three parts: a context window of length C and two consecutive horizon windows of length H. The first horizon window provides ground-truth data to fairly train the supervised DL baseline (PatchTST, Sect. 3.4), while for the zero-shot models it is merged with the context to form an extended input of $C+H$. The second horizon window remains the consistent inference target across all models, ensuring all models are evaluated on the exact same unseen data. Subsequent segments are produced by sliding the start index forward by H, continuing while a full segment of length $C + 2H$ fits within the series.

3.3 Experiment Scenarios

To evaluate model performance, two parameters are varied for experimentation: the historical context C and prediction length H, as shown in Table 1.

- **Scenario 1 - Fixed Context (FixedC).** For each dataset, we fix a representative context C while varying the forecast horizon H from short to long-range. This assesses how accuracy scales as the prediction distance increases.
- **Scenario 2 - Fixed Horizon (FixedH).** We keep the horizon H constant and vary the context length C. This identifies the point of "context saturation", beyond which additional history no longer improves zero-shot reasoning.

3.4 Benchmark Baselines and TSFMs

We evaluate three statistical baselines: (i) a fixed-order **ARIMA** model with local autocorrelation and non-stationarity; (ii) a **Running Average (RA)** adopting the context mean over the prediction horizon; and (iii) a **Random Walk with Drift (RWD)**, setting each future value to the previous plus a drift estimated from historical variance. These are configured in their best settings across the datasets. We also use a supervised DL baseline, **PatchTST**, configured for architectural and computational parity with the TSFMs (single encoder layer and attention head, hidden dimension of 32, and 0% dropout), to achieve inference latency comparable to benchmarked TSFMs. It also uses robust scaling to manage outliers, and is optimized with Multi-Quantile Loss (MQLoss) to estimate 10th, 50th, and 90th percentiles for direct probabilistic comparison.

We evaluate six state-of-the-art TSFMs that span diverse architectures and scales (detailed in Sect. 2), enabling a comparative analysis of how internal structure influences forecasting accuracy across the evaluated modalities. All adopt optimal pre-trained configurations to ensure standardized zero-shot evaluation and only adjust each model to emit the quantile forecasts required by the calibration metrics in Sect. 3.5. The benchmarked models and their parameter counts are: **Moirai-2** (11.4M), **TiREX** (35M), **Chronos-2** (120M), **Sundial** (128M), **Toto** (151M), and **TimesFM** (200M).

3.5 Testbed and Evaluation Metrics

Experiments are run in a virtual realm with an Nvidia T4 GPU (15GB VRAM) and 12GB of system RAM. Implementation is based on PyTorch, with all TSFMs

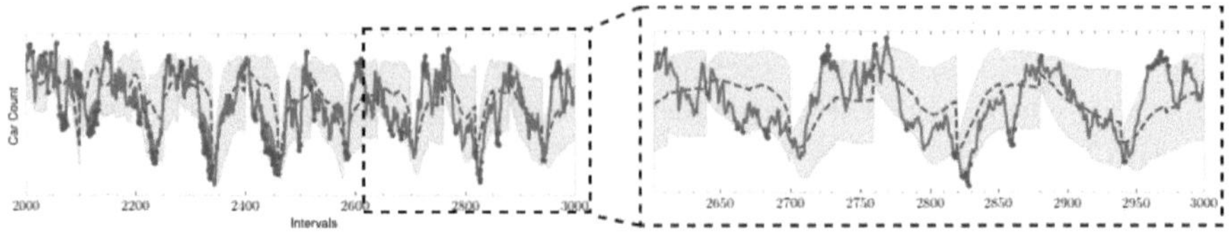

Fig. 2. Example TSFM with EdgeTraffic dataset depicting ground truth (blue line), forecast (purple line), confidence interval (shaded area), and interval violations (pink points). Zoomed-in highlight of last 500 datapoints provides a detailed overview. (Color figure online)

originating from Hugging Face in their default settings. Inference is performed without task-specific fine-tuning to evaluate zero-shot forecasting.

We employ three metrics for predictive accuracy and calibration. For point accuracy, the Symmetric Mean Absolute Percentage Error (sMAPE, Eq. 1) provides a percentage error measure robust to scale variations normalizing the absolute error by the mean magnitude of the observed and predicted values. For probabilistic reliability, we use Interval Coverage Error (ICE) and Interval Mean Absolute Error (IMAE) to evaluate prediction intervals. We use an 80% prediction interval with quantiles $\alpha = 0.1$ and $\beta = 0.9$. Figure 2 depicts this setting, with the ground truth, point predictions, and shaded intervals between the quantile bounds. ICE in Eq. (2) measures calibration error by comparing the observed miscoverage, the fraction of points outside the shaded band, with the nominal miscoverage of 0.20. A value of zero indicates perfect calibration. IMAE in Eq. (3) complements ICE by measuring the magnitude of these violations, the vertical distance between each out-of-interval point and the nearest interval bound in Fig. 2. Thus, ICE captures how often the interval fails, while IMAE captures how severe these failures are. A model may therefore achieve low ICE but high IMAE if only a few observations fall outside the interval, but by a large margin.

$$\text{sMAPE} = \frac{100}{H}\sum_{h=1}^{H}\begin{cases}0, & \text{if } |x_{T+h}| + |\hat{x}_{T+h}| = 0\\ \dfrac{2\,|x_{T+h} - \hat{x}_{T+h}|}{|x_{T+h}| + |\hat{x}_{T+h}|}, & \text{otherwise}\end{cases} \tag{1}$$

$$\text{ICE}_{\alpha,\beta} = \left|\frac{1}{H}\sum_{h=1}^{H}(\mathbb{1}_{\{x_{T+h} < \hat{x}^{\alpha}_{T+h} \vee x_{T+h} > \hat{x}^{\beta}_{T+h}\}}) - (1 - (\beta - \alpha))\right| \tag{2}$$

$$\text{IMAE}_{\alpha,\beta} = \frac{1}{H}\sum_{h=1}^{H}\left[\max(0, \hat{x}^{\alpha}_{T+h} - x_{T+h}) + \max(0, x_{T+h} - \hat{x}^{\beta}_{T+h})\right] \tag{3}$$

Here, $\hat{x}^{\alpha}_{T+h}$ and $\hat{x}^{\beta}_{T+h}$ represent the predicted α- and β-quantiles at horizon step h, respectively. In turn, T denotes the reference time, while $h = 1, \ldots, H$ indexes the forecast horizon of length H. The variable x_{T+h} represents the ground-truth, and $\hat{x}_{T+h}$ denotes the corresponding median point prediction.

4 Evaluation

This section examines the benchmark results for predictive accuracy and probabilistic calibration, visualized per dataset in Figs. 3, 4 and 5. For brevity, findings are presented as plots. Full tabular data and reproduction instructions are openly available in the benchmark repository.

4.1 Predictive Accuracy Evaluation of Forecasting Models

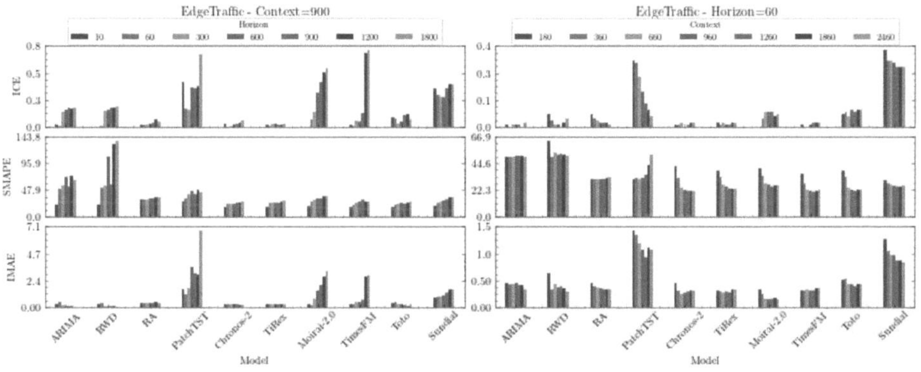

Fig. 3. Overview of Benchmark Results for the EdgeTraffic Dataset

The accuracy results show that TSFMs perform strongly across diverse settings, though their advantage depends on the structure of the underlying series. In volatile realms they remain more robust than traditional statistical methods, particularly as the forecast horizon extends.

For the discrete EdgeTraffic dataset and FixedC scenario, TimesFM and Chronos-2 achieve the best short-horizon sMAPE (17%) at $H = 10$, surpassing ARIMA (22%) and RA (32%). The gap widens at long horizons: at $H = 1800$ Chronos-2 remains the most stable (28%), while ARIMA, RA, and RWD exceed 65%, 35%, and 136%. Under FixedH, TSFMs show non-monotonic sensitivity to context. TimesFM improves from 36% at $C = 180$ to 21% at $C = 1260$, then marginally degrades at $C = 2460$ (22.5%), indicating that excessive history can introduce noise rather than improve accuracy. In contrast, supervised PatchTST collapses as context grows, rising from 31.5% at $C = 180$ to 52% at $C = 2460$. This exposes a key limitation of task-specific architectures, where they lack the "context reasoning" of TSFMs and overfit as input dimensionality grows.

Gains are more pronounced in the MixGridPL dataset, where TSFMs substantially outperform statistical baselines for all scenarios. For FixedC, Chronos-2, TiRex, and Sundial reach 3.92% to 3.95% at $H = 12$, versus 14% for ARIMA and 13% for RA; at $H = 672$, Chronos-2 and Moirai-2.0 stay at 6.4% and

6.6% while ARIMA reaches 19%. The FixedH scenario confirms that TSFMs exploit longer contexts for seasonal data, with Chronos-2 improving from 6.70% at $C = 120$ to 4.4% at $C = 624$ and Moirai-2.0 following a similar trend.

For SPY, short-horizon results are nearly identical across methods (at $H = 1$, RWD 0.79%, TiRex 0.80%, Chronos-2 0.82%), but TSFMs become competitive at long horizons, where TiRex (8.34%) and Chronos-2 (8.64%) at $H = 252$ improve over ARIMA (9.68%) and RWD (9.74%). Under FixedH ($H = 5$), most TSFMs remain stable as context grows (TiRex from 1.40% at $C = 25$ to 1.26% at $C = 509$), whereas the RA worsens from 2.50% to 14.83%, confirming that a constant-mean approach is unsuitable for trending financial data.

Key Takeaway: *TSFMs consistently match or exceed traditional baselines, with the largest gains in seasonal and structurally rich series where long-context reasoning provides a clear zero-shot advantage.*

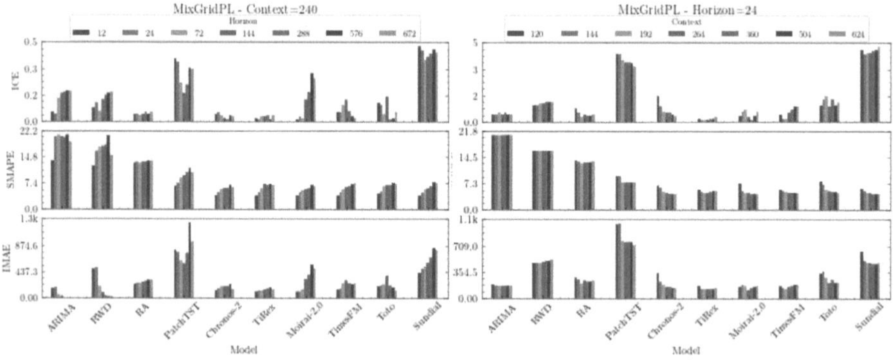

Fig. 4. Overview of Benchmark Results for the MixGridPL Dataset

4.2 Probabilistic Reliability and Interval Calibration

Several of the TSFMs maintain low sMAPE at extended horizons, but their uncertainty estimates deteriorate, leading to significant miscalibration, as shown by their ICE and IMAE scores.

For EdgeTraffic (FixedC), several transformer models suffer a *calibration collapse* as the horizon extends. TimesFM and Moirai rise from near-perfect calibration at $H = 10$ to ICE values of 0.73 and 0.56 at $H = 1800$, indicating severe over-confidence and a failure to capture observed traffic peaks where their IMAE also scales poorly (reaching 2.8 and 3.2). This denotes that missed values are missed by a wide margin. Toto is the exception among transformers, holding an ICE of 0.07 at $H = 1800$, which suggests its Student-T mixture head captures heavy-tailed distributions more robustly than the standard density heads of other patch-based models. The best performers are Chronos-2 and TiRex, both keeping ICE below 0.06 across all horizons and their slightly higher IMAE (averaging ~0.28) reflects a conservative profile that is preferable when missing a traffic burst is costlier than overestimating variance. PatchTST performs worst, with an ICE of 0.7 and IMAE of 6.8 at $H = 1800$, showing that task-specific training fails to generalize uncertainty to long-range and out-of-distribution shifts.

For MixGridPL, high seasonality yields more stable behavior, although differences persist. TiRex has an ICE between 0.01 and 0.04 across all scenarios. Under FixedH, Chronos-2 improves its calibration as context grows, with ICE dropping from 0.17 ($C = 120$) to 0.04 ($C = 624$). In contrast, Sundial and PatchTST are over-confident regardless of context (ICE ~0.45). Moirai achieves good short-horizon calibration (ICE 0.01 at $H = 12$), but long-range reliability degrades sharply, with IMAE rising from 109 to 479, indicating patch-based transformers struggle to propagate uncertainty through long autoregressive chains.

For SPY, the stochastic signal exposes narrow interval risk. Sundial and PatchTST exceed a 0.50 ICE, missing half of the price movements they target, while TimesFM and Moirai-2.0 show similar decay as the horizon extends. TiRex and Chronos-2 are the most robust. Under FixedH, as context grows to $C = 509$, TiRex reaches a near-perfect ICE of 0.01 with a low IMAE (0.34), confirming its intervals are safe without being excessively loose. This balance makes recurrent (TiRex) and quantized-encoder (Chronos-2) architectures more suitable for risk-sensitive financial applications than purely generative or patch-based ones.

Key Takeaway: *Point accuracy does not guarantee probabilistic. TimesFM and Moirai often lead in sMAPE yet become over-confident at long horizons, whereas Chronos and TiRex provide calibrated uncertainty across modalities.*

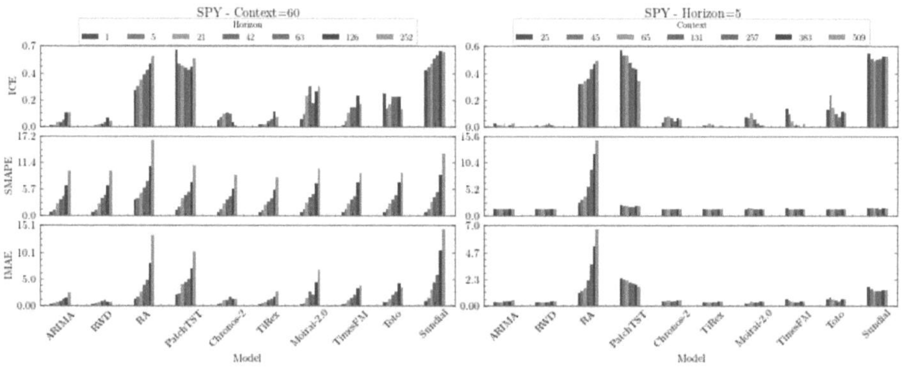

Fig. 5. Overview of Benchmark Results for the SPY Dataset

5 Conclusion and Future Directions

This paper presented a benchmark of zero-shot TSFMs across different data modalities. TSFMs emerge as a strong alternative to statistical and lightweight supervised baselines, especially in seasonal settings where longer context windows improve performance. However, point accuracy alone is insufficient to assess real-world deployment where forecasting quality depends on a trade-off between predictive accuracy and uncertainty calibration. TSFM architecture drives this trade-off. The xLSTM-based TiRex gives the most consistent, conservative calibration across modalities, staying stable as the horizon extends, whereas patch-based transformers such as Moirai-2.0 and TimesFM often lead on accuracy yet suffer a calibration collapse, becoming over-confident at long horizons. Chronos-2 is the most balanced, pairing competitive accuracy with well-calibrated intervals. Success is also signal-dependent, where seasonal data (MixGridPL) is most favorable, discrete high-frequency traces (EdgeTraffic) challenge calibration, and stochastic financial series (SPY) with short-term volatility remain hardest. TSFM selection should thus weigh forecast horizon, signal volatility, and the cost of under-estimating uncertainty, not sMAPE alone.

Future work includes extending the benchmark to multivariate forecasting and to robustness under missing data, irregular sampling, and concept drift. A dedicated study of computational efficiency is left to forthcoming work, alongside calibration-aware forecasting and adaptive model-selection strategies.

References

1. Ansari, A.F., et al.: Chronos-2: from univariate to universal forecasting (2025). https://arxiv.org/abs/2510.15821
2. Auer, A., Podest, P., Klotz, D., Böck, S., Klambauer, G., Hochreiter, S.: Tirex: zero-shot forecasting across long and short horizons with enhanced in-context learning. In: The Thirty-Ninth Annual Conference on Neural Information Processing Systems (2025)
3. Cohen, B., et al.: This time is different: an observability perspective on time series foundation models. In: The Thirty-Ninth Annual Conference on Neural Information Processing Systems (2026)
4. Das, A., Kong, W., Sen, R., Zhou, Y.: A decoder-only foundation model for time-series forecasting. In: Proceedings of the 41st International Conference on Machine Learning, ICML'24. JMLR.org (2024)
5. Jin, M., et al.: Time-LLM: time series forecasting by reprogramming large language models. In: The Twelfth International Conference on Learning Representations (2024)
6. Liu, C., et al.: Moirai 2.0: when less is more for time series forecasting (2026). https://arxiv.org/abs/2511.11698
7. Liu, Y., et al.: Sundial: a family of highly capable time series foundation models. In: Forty-Second International Conference on Machine Learning (2025)
8. Meyer, M., Gonzalez, D.Z., Kaltenpoth, S., Müller, O.: Benchmarking time series foundation models for short-term household electricity load forecasting. IEEE Access **13**, 218141–218153 (2025)

9. Nie, Y., Nguyen, N.H., Sinthong, P., Kalagnanam, J.: A time series is worth 64 words: long-term forecasting with transformers. In: The Eleventh International Conference on Learning Representations (2023)
10. Symeonides, M., Trihinas, D., Cleju, N.: Edgetraffic: an edgeai dataset integrating road traffic dynamics with system telemetry. In: Proceedings of the 4th International Workshop on Testing Distributed Internet of Things Systems, TDIS '26, pp. 13–18. Association for Computing Machinery, New York (2026)
11. Symeonides, M., Tsiopani, N., Maouris, G., Trihinas, D., Pallis, G., Dikaiakos, M.D.: Carbonoracle: automating energy mix & renewable energy source forecast modeling for carbon-aware micro data centers. In: 2024 IEEE/ACM 17th International Conference on Utility and Cloud Computing (UCC), pp. 246–255 (2024)
12. Toner, W., Lee, T.L., Joosen, A., Singh, R., Asenov, M.: Performance of zero-shot time series foundation models on cloud data. arXiv preprint arXiv:2502.12944 (2025)
13. Zhou, H., et al.: Informer: beyond efficient transformer for long sequence time-series forecasting. In: Proceedings of the AAAI Conference on Artificial Intelligence, vol. 35 (2021)

Enhancing Topic Modeling Through Adaptive Similarity Thresholding: The Case of Large-Scale Citizen Contributions

Sami Guembour[1(✉)], Catherine Domingues[1], and Sabine Ploux[2,3]

[1] Univ Gustave Eiffel, Géodata Paris, IGN, LASTIG, 77420 Champs-sur-Marne, France
{sami.guembour,catherine.domingues}@ign.fr

[2] Centre d'Analyse et de Mathématique Sociales CNRS-UMR 8557, Paris, France
sabine.ploux@ehess.fr

[3] Ecole des Hautes Etudes en Sciences Sociales, Paris, France

Abstract. In this paper, we propose a topic modeling method aimed at identifying the most salient themes in a large-scale collection of citizen contributions. Our method explicitly distinguishes between different proposals expressed within the same theme by assigning them to separate clusters, rather than grouping all occurrences into a single cluster. We leverage multiple language models to compute sentence embeddings which are organized into similarity graphs using model-specific similarity thresholds. Community detection algorithms are then applied to these graphs to identify semantically coherent clusters. We conduct experiments to determine the optimal threshold for each model and to evaluate different combinations of embedding models and community detection algorithms in order to identify the most effective configuration. The proposed configurations are evaluated on two large-scale corpora of citizen contributions and compared with state-of-the-art baselines using a comprehensive set of evaluation metrics, including topic modeling measures (topic diversity, NPMI) and clustering validity indices (Davies-Bouldin, intra- and inter-cluster distances). The results show that the selected configuration improves cluster quality, outperforms state-of-the-art baselines, and more accurately captures the diversity of proposals within each theme, providing an effective framework for large-scale thematic analysis.

Keywords: Topic Modeling · Semantic Clustering · Community Detection · Sentence Embeddings · Similarity Thresholding · Clustering Evaluation · Large-Scale Text Analysis

1 Introduction

In January 2019, the French government launched the *Grand Débat National* [Large National Debate] (GDN), which enabled citizens to contribute through a digital platform and physical supports known as *Cahiers Citoyens* [Citizens'

© The Author(s), under exclusive license to Springer Nature Switzerland AG 2027
G. Vargas Solar et al. (Eds.): ADBIS 2026, CCIS 3175, pp. 24–34, 2027.
https://doi.org/10.1007/978-3-032-39823-9_3

Notebooks] (CC). The latter were placed in various public locations and allowed citizens to freely express their views on themes of their choice. By March 2019, CC had collected 225 224 contributions from 17 014 municipalities.

Due to the volume and heterogeneity of the data, a key challenge is to automatically identify the main themes emerging from the CC while capturing the diversity of proposals expressed within each theme (salaries, voting, etc.). For example, regarding salaries, some contributors suggest increasing the minimum wage and low salaries, while others advocate lowering the highest salaries. Similarly, the theme of voting includes proposals such as recognizing blank votes, making voting mandatory, or introducing proportional representation. The objective is therefore to group sentences addressing the same theme with the same proposal into coherent clusters, while separating sentences that either address different themes or express different proposals within the same theme. Referring to the voting example, three distinct groups are expected. In previous work, we applied a clustering method to a subset of 50 000 sentences extracted from the CC [1], enabling an initial exploration of semantic structures. This method relied on a language model (LM) to compute sentence embeddings and on community detection algorithms for clustering. A more detailed review of this approach, the topic modeling and community detection methods on which it builds, and existing analyses of the CC are provided in the preprint version of this paper[1] [2].

In this work, we extend this approach by systematically investigating the impact of three key parameters: the LM, the similarity threshold, and the community detection algorithm. Their combination defines a configuration of the method. We enhance the approach by proposing a procedure that adapts the similarity threshold to each LM and conduct experiments to identify the configuration that maximizes sentence coverage while preserving semantic coherence. The selected configuration is then applied to the full *Cahiers Citoyens* corpus (*CC-Corpus*) to assess its scalability and robustness, and to a second GDN corpus collected through the digital platform (*Platform-Corpus*) to examine its generalizability across different forms of citizen contributions.

The main contributions of this paper are threefold: (i) a clustering framework designed to distinguish between proposals within the same theme, (ii) an adaptive similarity thresholding strategy tailored to different language models, and (iii) a comprehensive evaluation combining clustering and topic modeling metrics on large-scale corpora.

2 Corpora Description

The objective of this study is to identify the themes developed in the *CC-Corpus*. This corpus is therefore presented in Sect. 2.1, while the *Platform-Corpus*, used for method evaluation, is described in Sect. 2.2. The same preprocessing was applied to both corpora, following the procedure used for the sample of 50 000 sentences in our previous work [1] and detailed further in the preprint [2].

---

[1] https://doi.org/10.13140/RG.2.2.34184.17927.

2.1 CC-Corpus

The *CC-Corpus* contains 225 224 contributions collected through the *Cahiers Citoyens*. A comprehensive textometric and spatial analysis of this corpus is presented in [3]. Since individual contributions may address several themes [4], sentences were used as the basic unit of analysis. The contributions were segmented using a SpaCy transformer-based model [5]. After preprocessing, the resulting version of the corpus used in this study contains 2 789 465 sentences.

2.2 Platform-Corpus

The *Platform-Corpus* contains contributions collected through the GDN digital platform. The platform included both closed-ended questions, mainly requiring *yes/no* answers, and open-ended questions. Only responses to open-ended questions were retained, resulting in 4 905 322 contributions. These contributions were segmented into sentences using SpaCy [5]. After preprocessing, the version of the corpus used in this study contains 4 304 513 sentences.

3 Proposed Method

The proposed methodology for clustering sentences into thematic groups, relies on sentence embeddings, graph-based representations which depend on the similarity threshold, and community detection algorithms. A key component of the method is the definition of model-specific similarity thresholds, designed to ensure that sentences expressing the same theme and proposal are grouped together, while sentences referring to different themes or expressing different proposals are assigned to distinct clusters.

3.1 Combination of Language Models and Community Detection Algorithms

Three French transformer-based language models (LMs) were selected: CamemBERT-large [6], DistilCamemBERT [7], and Solon-large[2], based on their performance in semantic tasks [8]. Each sentence is represented by an embedding produced by the selected LM [9], and sentence similarity is computed using cosine similarity.

For clustering, two community detection algorithms were selected for their accuracy and computational efficiency on large datasets: Louvain [10] and the Label Propagation Algorithm (LPA) [11]. To apply these algorithms, for each model m, an unweighted similarity graph $G(m)$ is constructed by creating an edge between two sentences when their similarity exceeds a model-specific threshold $T(m)$. Louvain and LPA are then applied to $G(m)$ to obtain semantically coherent clusters. Isolated nodes, whose similarity does not exceed the threshold with any other node, are grouped into a dedicated cluster of unassigned sentences.

[2] https://huggingface.co/OrdalieTech/Solon-embeddings-large-0.1.

3.2 Threshold Definition Rules

To determine suitable thresholds, an experiment was conducted on 100 manually selected sentence pairs[3] representing the semantic configurations defined by rules R1–R4 below. Each sentence is described through an *object*, corresponding to its theme, and a *predicate*, corresponding to the proposal expressed about that theme. The threshold must be lower than the similarity values associated with R1 and R2, and higher than those associated with R3 and R4.

- **R1 (Acronym equivalence):** Sentences differing only by an acronym and its expanded form should be assigned to the same cluster. Example: P1 = *Rétablir l'ISF* [Reinstate the ISF] and P2 = *Rétablir l'Impôt de Solidarité sur la Fortune* [Reinstate the Solidarity Wealth Tax].
- **R2 (Synonymy):** Sentences expressing the same predicate using synonymous terms should be assigned to the same cluster. Example: P3 = *Il faut augmenter les salaires* [Salaries should be increased] and P4 = *Il faut revaloriser les salaires* [Salaries should be raised].
- **R3 (Different objects):** Sentences sharing the same predicate but referring to different objects should be assigned to different clusters. Example: P5 = *Stop à l'immigration* [Stop immigration] and P6 = *Stop à la hausse des prix de l'électricité et du gaz* [Stop the rise in electricity and gas prices].
- **R4 (Different predicates):** Sentences referring to the same object but expressing different or opposite predicates should be assigned to different clusters. Example: P7 = *Il faut conserver les taxes* [Taxes should be retained] and P8 = *Il faut supprimer les taxes* [Taxes should be abolished].

These rules reflect the objective defined in Sect. 1: grouping sentences expressing the same theme and predicate, while separating those that differ in either component. Table 1 reports the similarity values observed across the 100 sentence pairs for rules R1–R4. When "Same Cluster" is 1, the reported value is the minimum similarity observed for the corresponding rule and model; when it is 0, it is the maximum observed similarity.

Table 1. Similarity ranges and selected thresholds for rules R1–R4.

Rule	CamemBERT-large	Distil-CamemBERT	Solon large	Same Cluster
R1	0.74	0.75	0.49	1
R2	0.84	0.72	0.79	1
R3	0.48	0.51	0.67	0
R4	0.70	0.57	0.67	0
Valid Range	[0.70; 0.74]	[0.57; 0.72]	No valid range	–
Selected T(m)	**0.74**	**0.72**	**0.79**	–

[3] Sentence pairs available at: https://github.com/SamiGuembour/CC-Topic-Clusters.

3.3 Model-Specific Threshold Selection

The similarity values computed for the 100 sentence pairs were used to determine, for each LM, a valid threshold range satisfying rules R1–R4. These ranges are summarized in Table 1. The threshold must be lower than or equal to the minimum similarity observed for pairs that should be grouped together (R1 and R2), and strictly higher than the maximum similarity observed for pairs that should belong to different clusters (R3 and R4). The resulting valid range is therefore defined by these two values. For each model, $T(m)$ is set to the upper bound of the valid range. This choice satisfies the four rules while limiting the creation of edges between semantically distinct sentences. The "Same Cluster" column indicates whether the sentence pairs associated with each rule should belong to the same cluster (1) or to different clusters (0).

For CamemBERT-large, the minimum similarity for R1 and R2 is 0.74, while the maximum similarity for R3 and R4 is 0.70. The valid range is therefore $]0.70; 0.74]$, and the selected threshold is **0.74**. For Distil-CamemBERT, these values are respectively 0.72 and 0.57, resulting in the valid range $[0.57; 0.72]$ and a selected threshold of **0.72**. For Solon-large, however, the minimum similarity for R1 and R2 is 0.49, whereas the maximum similarity for R3 and R4 is 0.67. Since a threshold cannot be both greater than 0.67 and lower than or equal to 0.49, no value can simultaneously satisfy all four rules. The observations made on the sentence pairs suggest that Solon-large representations give more importance to object-related information than to predicate distinctions. In particular, the model does not correctly associate some acronyms with their expanded forms, preventing rule R1 from being satisfied. A threshold satisfying only rules R2–R4 was therefore selected, namely **0.79**.

4 Experiments and Evaluation

The experiments combine three LMs, CamemBERT-large, Distil-CamemBERT and Solon-large, with their adapted similarity thresholds, and two community detection algorithms: Louvain and LPA. These algorithms were selected because the number of clusters is not known in advance and because they can be directly applied to similarity graphs. In total, six combinations were evaluated. The combinations were first applied to the *CC-Corpus*, which is the main target corpus of this study, in order to identify the best configuration. However, no ground truth is available regarding either the number of themes or the content of the clusters. The government-commissioned [12] cannot be used as a baseline, since its "expressed ideas" were identified through the GDN platform's closed questions. The evaluation therefore relies on unsupervised clustering and topic modeling metrics, described in Sect. 4.1 The same experiments are also conducted on the *Platform-Corpus* (Sect. 4.2) to examine whether corpus quality[4] affects the metric values. Finally, the evaluation is extended to two topic modeling baselines (Sect. 4.3).

[4] The *CC-Corpus* contains a large number of misspellings [3].

4.1 Evaluation Metrics

The evaluation aims to assess semantic coherence and diversity, cluster structure, and corpus coverage. Semantic coherence is measured using Normalized Pointwise Mutual Information (NPMI) and Topic Diversity (TD). NPMI evaluates the internal coherence of clusters from the co-occurrence of their most representative words, while TD measures the proportion of unique keywords among the K most frequent terms in each cluster. In our experiments, we set $K = 10$, following standard practice in topic modeling to capture the most salient terms per cluster [13]. Higher NPMI and TD indicate more coherent and diverse clusters.

Cluster structure is evaluated using the Davies–Bouldin Index (DBI) and the inter/intra-cluster variance ratio (R). DBI measures the average similarity between each cluster and its closest neighboring cluster, while R compares inter-cluster and intra-cluster variance. Better clustering corresponds to a higher R and a lower DBI.

Corpus coverage is measured by the proportion of classified sentences (P_c), where higher values indicate that more sentences are assigned to clusters. To enable fair comparison, all metrics are normalized in the range $[0, 1]$, using an inverse normalization for metrics to be minimized. The overall score S is defined as the arithmetic mean of the five normalized metrics. All metrics are equally weighted to avoid favoring one criterion over another, and the combination with the highest score is considered the most effective.

4.2 Comparative Evaluation of Model-Algorithm Combinations

Table 2 summarizes the metric values obtained for each combination and corpus. The combination of Distil-CamemBERT for sentence embeddings and Louvain for community detection achieved the highest overall score on both the *CC-Corpus* (**0.989**) and the *Platform-Corpus* (**0.804**). It was therefore selected as the optimal configuration, hereafter referred to as *DC+Lo*, for identifying themes in the *CC-Corpus*. This combination also provided the widest coverage, with 69.9% of sentences classified in the *CC-Corpus* and 76.0% in the *Platform-Corpus*. This suggests that Distil-CamemBERT connects a larger proportion of sentences in the similarity graph, reducing the number of isolated sentences. In terms of structural quality, Solon-large with Louvain obtained the lowest DBI, closely followed by Distil-CamemBERT with Louvain. However, *DC+Lo* achieved the best inter/intra-cluster variance ratio on both corpora, indicating compact and well-separated clusters. It also obtained the highest NPMI scores, showing strong semantic coherence; these high values are likely supported by the large corpus sizes, which stabilize word co-occurrence statistics. For topic diversity, *DC+Lo* achieved the best value on the *CC-Corpus*, tied with Distil-CamemBERT with LPA.

4.3 Comparison with Topic Modeling Baseline Methods

To further strengthen the evaluation, *DC+Lo* is compared with two topic modeling baselines: BERTopic [14] and Top2Vec [15]. The results are reported in

Table 2. Evaluation of LM and community detection combinations on both corpora. CamemBERT, Distil-CamemBERT, and Solon refer to CamemBERT-large, Distil-CamemBERT, and Solon-large, respectively.

	Metric	CamemBERT + Louvain	CamemBERT + LPA	Distil + Louvain	Distil + LPA	Solon + Louvain	Solon + LPA
CC-Corpus	% Classified Sentences	65.5	65.5	**69.9**	**69.9**	67.7	67.7
	Ratio (R)	5.129	4.622	**5.919**	5.169	0.961	0.468
	DBI	4.788	5.741	4.691	6.133	**4.610**	5.570
	NPMI	0.122	0.124	**0.130**	0.118	0.129	0.125
	TD	0.262	0.254	**0.276**	**0.276**	0.268	0.273
	Overall ($S1$)	0.487	0.303	**0.989**	0.572	0.628	0.463
Platform-Corpus	% Classified Sentences	72.7	72.7	**76.0**	**76.0**	71.4	71.4
	Ratio (R)	5.422	4.208	**6.248**	4.798	0.563	0.449
	DBI	5.355	7.808	5.412	8.148	**4.870**	7.338
	NPMI	0.956	0.950	**0.961**	0.953	0.960	0.941
	TD	0.051	0.072	0.058	0.083	0.059	**0.088**
	Overall ($S1$)	0.548	0.410	**0.804**	0.642	0.437	0.249

Table 3. The overall scores in Table 2 (*S1*) and Table 3 (*S2*) differ because the metrics are normalized separately within each comparison set, using the minimum and maximum values observed in the corresponding table.

DC+Lo outperforms both baselines, reaching an overall score of **0.677** on the *CC-Corpus* and **0.713** on the *Platform-Corpus*. Although Top2Vec assigns all sentences to clusters and therefore achieves full coverage, *DC+Lo* deliberately groups only sentences that are sufficiently semantically related. Despite this more selective clustering, it obtains higher inter/intra-cluster variance ratios, NPMI, and Topic Diversity on both corpora, producing clusters that are more structurally consistent and thematically richer.

Table 3. Comparison of DC+Lo with topic-modeling baselines.

Corpus	Method	P_c	R	DBI	NPMI	TD	$S2$
CC	DC+Lo	69.9	**5.919**	4.691	**0.130**	**0.276**	**0.677**
	BERTopic	50.9	0.319	**2.609**	0.106	0.216	0.256
	Top2Vec	**100.0**	0.010	3.010	0.107	0.198	0.369
Platform	DC+Lo	76.0	**6.248**	5.412	**0.961**	**0.058**	**0.713**
	BERTopic	44.3	0.351	**2.758**	0.950	0.033	0.263
	Top2Vec	**100.0**	0.008	3.172	0.951	0.024	0.386

5 Results and Discussions

Using the model-specific thresholds defined from rules R1–R4 in Sect. 3.2, we first analyze the thematic structure and interpretability of the resulting clusters

(Sect. 5.1). We then assess whether the clusters satisfy the intended semantic constraints through a validation of rules R1–R4 (Sect. 5.2).

5.1 Cluster Analysis

The clustering was performed using the selected configuration, *DC+Lo*, and produced 127 279 clusters. The complete list of clusters is available as a CSV file on GitHub[5]. Cluster numbers reported below correspond to cluster identifiers in this file, not to their rank by size. Each cluster is characterized by its five most frequent lemmas and its central sentence, obtained with closeness centrality [16].

The analysis of the largest clusters shows that citizen contributions mainly address major societal and economic issues, including public services, taxation, purchasing power, institutional reforms, and ecological transition. A comparison with the government-commissioned report [12] highlights the fine-grained nature of the proposed approach. While the report identifies broad themes such as "purchasing power", our method distinguishes several specific proposals within this theme, including the indexation of pensions to inflation (cluster 1), increasing salaries and the minimum wage (cluster 2), and increasing purchasing power more generally (cluster 38). A similar pattern appears for the report's broad theme "organization of the state and public services". The proposed method separates proposals related to the preservation of public services (cluster 66), the reduction of the number of deputies and the abolition of the Senate (cluster 28), the removal of privileges for former presidents and ministers (cluster 22), and the strengthening of local elected officials' powers (cluster 12). The same granularity is observed for "ecological transition", with distinct clusters on stopping nuclear energy (cluster 151), banning glyphosate and pesticides (cluster 76), and other more specific environmental proposals.

These comparisons show that, unlike the broad thematic categorization of the report, the proposed method captures a finer level of granularity by distinguishing different proposals expressed within the same theme.

5.2 Assessment of Clustering Rules

The clusters available in the CSV file on GitHub were examined to assess whether the clustering results satisfy rules R1–R4. Regarding R1, cluster 18, which focuses on the reinstatement of the ISF, contains sentences using both the acronym *ISF* and its expanded form *Impôt sur la Fortune*, such as *Rétablir l'impôt sur la fortune* [Reinstate the wealth tax] and *Il faut rétablir l'Impôt sur la fortune* [The wealth tax should be reinstated]. This confirms that acronym expansion is correctly handled.

R2 is also satisfied in the same cluster, where synonymous predicates express the same proposal, as in *Remettre l'ISF* [Reintroduce the ISF] and *Restaurer l'ISF* [Restore the ISF]. Cluster 27 provides another example with *Réduction de la TVA* [Reduction of VAT] and *Baisse de la TVA* [Decrease of VAT].

[5] https://github.com/SamiGuembour/CC-Topic-Clusters.

Clusters 66 and 108 illustrate R3: the first concerns *arrêter la suppression des services publics* [Stop the removal of public services], while the second addresses *arrêter l'immigration* [Stop immigration]. Although both share the predicate *arrêter* [stop], they are correctly separated because they concern different objects.

Finally, R4 is illustrated by clusters 216 and 80, which both relate to voting but express different predicates: *rendre le vote obligatoire* [make voting mandatory] and *le vote blanc soit compté* [count blank votes]. Similarly, clusters 2 and 35 address salaries from different perspectives: *augmentation des salaires* [increase salaries] and *égalité salariale entre les hommes et les femmes* [equal salaries for men and women]. These examples show that the method separates semantically distinct proposals referring to the same object.

A complementary intra-cluster evaluation, currently under review, was also conducted to assess internal semantic coherence. Each cluster was represented by a theme–predicate pair, and an LLM was used as a semantic judge to assess whether each sentence was consistent with this pair. This evaluation confirms the quantitative results: Distil-CamemBERT + Louvain achieved the best F-score (**0.825**), followed by Distil-CamemBERT + LPA (**0.812**). Overall, these results indicate that the proposed method produces clusters that are coherent both structurally and in terms of theme–predicate consistency.

6 Conclusion and Perspectives

In this study, we proposed a topic modeling approach to group into distinct clusters the different proposals expressed within the same theme in French citizens' contributions. The method combines transformer-based language models with community detection algorithms and introduces a procedure for defining model-specific similarity thresholds used to construct the similarity graphs.

Among the evaluated configurations, Distil-CamemBERT combined with Louvain proved to be the most effective. It achieved the best performance on both citizen consultation corpora, the *CC-Corpus* and the *Platform-Corpus*, producing coherent and well-structured clusters in a fully unsupervised setting, without requiring prior knowledge of the number of clusters. This confirms that topic modeling can also be formulated as a combination of language models, similarity thresholds, and community detection techniques (instead of clustering algorithms) which better correspond to corpora segmented into sentences.

This work contributes to the *Cahiers Citoyens* project, whose aim is to identify and structure the themes emerging from large-scale citizen consultations. Future work will explore additional community detection algorithms and other types of corpora, such as literary or domain-specific texts, to further assess the robustness and generalizability of the method. Another perspective is to develop an automatic evaluation framework for checking the impact – through the rules R1–R4 which involve acronym expansion, synonymy, and semantic opposition – of lexical and morpho-syntactic transformations on clusters.

Finally, 69% of the sentences in the *CC-Corpus* were assigned to clusters. Many remaining sentences contain noisy or corrupted tokens, probably due to

OCR errors during digitization. Improving corpus quality through automatic or manual correction and re-evaluating the method could therefore help determine whether clustering coverage and performance can be further enhanced.

Acknowledgments. This project was provided with computing AI and storage resources by GENCI at IDRIS thanks to the grant 2025-AD011015849 on the supercomputer Jean Zay's A100 partition.

References

1. Guembour, S., Dominguès, C., Ploux, S.: Semantic analysis experiments for French citizens' contribution: combinations of language models and community detection algorithms. In: Proceedings of the 16th International Conference on Computational Semantics, pp. 231–241. Association for Computational Linguistics, Düsseldorf (2025)
2. Guembour, S., Dominguès, C., Ploux, S.: Enhancing Topic Modeling Through Adaptive Similarity Thresholding: The Case of Large-Scale Citizen Contributions (2026)
3. Dominguès, C., Jolivet, L.: Analyse textométrique et spatialisée des Cahiers citoyens. In: Dister, A., Longrée, D. (eds.) JADT 2024, pp. 309–318. Presses universitaires de Louvain, Bruxelles (2024)
4. Guembour, S.: Analyse sémantique du corpus des Cahiers citoyens. In: 26ème Rencontre des Étudiants Chercheurs en Informatique pour le TAL, pp. 17–27. ATALA, AFPC, Toulouse (2024)
5. Honnibal, M., Montani, I., Van Landeghem, S., Boyd, A.: spaCy: industrial-strength natural language processing in Python. J. Open Source Softw. (2020)
6. Martin, L., et al.: CamemBERT: a tasty French language model. In: Proceedings of the 58th Annual Meeting of the Association for Computational Linguistics, pp. 7203–7219. Association for Computational Linguistics, Online (2020)
7. Delestre, C., Amar, A.: DistilCamemBERT: une distillation du modèle français CamemBERT. In: Conférence sur l'Apprentissage automatique,, Vannes (2022)
8. Guembour, S., Dong, C., Dominguès, C.: Characterization of the city of the future from a science fiction corpus. In: Métais, E., Meziane, F., Sugumaran, V., Manning, W., Reiff-Marganiec, S. (eds.) Natural Language Processing and Information Systems, pp. 313–325. Springer, Cham (2023). https://doi.org/10.1007/978-3-031-35320-8_22
9. Reimers, N., Gurevych, I.: Sentence-BERT: sentence embeddings using Siamese BERT-networks. CoRR arxiv:1908.10084 (2019)
10. Blondel, V.D., Guillaume, J.-L., Lambiotte, R., Lefebvre, E.: Fast unfolding of communities in large networks. J. Stat. Mech: Theory Exp. **2008**(10), P10008 (2008)
11. Zhu, X., Ghahramani, Z.: Learning from labeled and unlabeled data with label propagation, Carnegie Mellon University. Technical report (2003)
12. Berger, R., Bluenove, C.: Analyse des contributions libres: Cahiers citoyens, courriers et emails, comptes-rendus des réunions d'initiative locale (2019)
13. Abilasha, S., Boutalbi, R., Delliaux, S.: Multi-view topic modeling using multi-text representations. In: Companion Proceedings of the ACM Web Conference 2025, pp. 1278–1282. ACM, New York (2025)

14. Grootendorst, M.: BERTopic: neural topic modeling with a class-based TF-IDF procedure. arXiv preprint arXiv:2203.05794 (2022)
15. Angelov, D., Inkpen, D.: Topic modeling: contextual token embeddings are all you need. In: Findings of the Association for Computational Linguistics: EMNLP 2024, pp. 13528–13539. Association for Computational Linguistics, Miami (2024)
16. Bavelas, A.: Communication patterns in task-oriented groups. J. Acoust. Soc. Am. **22**(6), 725–730 (1950)

Efficient Knowledge Graph Evolution Through Learning-Guided Exploration

Bochra Kader(✉), Maude Manouvrier, and Khalid Belhajjame

Université Paris-Dauphine, PSL Research University CNRS UMR [7243] LAMSADE, Paris, France
{bochra.kader,maude.manouvrier,khalid.belhajjame}@dauphine.fr

Abstract. Knowledge graphs (KGs) structure domain knowledge and increasingly support reliable AI. As ontologies evolve, new concepts and properties must be integrated via mappings from heterogeneous data sources–a complex, expert-dependent bottleneck, especially when multiple interrelated concepts are added together. We propose the joint generation of mappings for multiple concepts using a pivot-based schema graph to shrink the search space and a joint Steiner Tree formulation to capture inter-concept dependencies; integrated with a Reinforcement Learning framework, this reduces computation and required user feedback, as shown in our evaluation on the benchmark Burr.

Keywords: Ontology Evolution · Knowledge Graph · Schema Mapping · Reinforcement Learning · Steiner Tree

1 Introduction

Knowledge Graphs (KGs) are a key method for structuring knowledge across domains, enabling semantic interoperability and advanced data analytics [11,21,28], and they increasingly ground generative AI to improve factual consistency and reduce hallucinations [1,18].

A central challenge is defining mappings from heterogeneous data sources to the target ontology, which transform data instances into RDF triples for the KG. As ontologies evolve and introduce new concepts and properties [8,22,25], corresponding mappings must be generated or updated. A substantial body of work has addressed the problem of mapping specification in Ontology-Based Data Access (OBDA) and data integration settings (see, e.g., [12,29]). Early approaches rely heavily on manual or semi-automatic mapping design, which is both time-consuming and error-prone [10,23].

Recent approaches automate mapping generation using schema matching, query discovery, and search-based techniques [7–9,27], but they still struggle with large search spaces and typically generate mappings for each target concept in isolation, ignoring dependencies among concepts introduced together.

In prior work [14], we introduced Hologram, which automatically derives mappings for individual concepts using a graph-based abstraction of data sources

© The Author(s), under exclusive license to Springer Nature Switzerland AG 2027
G. Vargas Solar et al. (Eds.): ADBIS 2026, CCIS 3175, pp. 35–45, 2027.
https://doi.org/10.1007/978-3-032-39823-9_4

and framing mapping discovery as an RL-guided search. However, it handles only one new concept at a time, missing inter-concept interactions and causing redundant computation when multiple concepts or relations are added simultaneously. Additionally, as attribute counts grow the data-source graph becomes highly connected, expanding the search space, lengthening learning, and increasing user feedback demands.

We address these limitations by proposing a joint mapping-generation approach for ontology evolution. First, we introduce a pivot-based compact representation of the source schema to reduce structural redundancy and focus the search on relevant graph regions. Second, we replace independent concept-level mapping with a joint formulation that constructs mappings for a set of newly introduced concepts and their relations simultaneously, capturing inter-concept dependencies and avoiding redundant exploration.

We focus on adding new concepts to an existing KG, a common scenario as ontologies evolve incrementally. Concept removal can be handled by deactivating associated mappings, and updates to existing concepts can be modeled as a combination of removal and addition. We frame mapping discovery as a Reinforcement Learning problem guided by feedback on candidate mappings. Using a pivot-based schema graph together with a joint search strategy reduces the candidate space and, consequently, required user feedback. Experiments show improved scalability while preserving mapping quality, particularly when multiple concepts are added simultaneously.

Specifically, the contributions of this paper are as follows: (1) a formalization of the problem of joint mapping generation for multiple newly introduced concepts in evolving KGs; (2) a pivot-based schema graph representing the structure of the underlying data sources, which reduces graph density and limits the size of the search space; (3) a joint Steiner-tree approach that generates mappings covering multiple concepts and their associated properties simultaneously; and (4) experimental results showing that the proposed method improves search efficiency and scalability while preserving the quality of the generated mappings.

The remainder of this paper is organized as follows. Sections 2–6 present, respectively, the foundations and problem statement, proposed approach, experimental evaluation, related work, and conclusion.

2 Foundations and Problem Statement

We consider RDF KGs populated from relational or tabular data via mapping rules: given an ontology $\mathcal{O}$ that defines the KG vocabulary and constraints, mappings specify how source data are extracted and transformed into assertions compatible with $\mathcal{O}$.

Definition 1 (KG, Ontology, and Assertions). *A KG is represented as a pair $(\mathcal{O}, \mathcal{A})$, where $\mathcal{O}$ denotes the ontology, or TBox, and $\mathcal{A}$ denotes the assertions, or ABox. We consider the RDFS formalism, so $\mathcal{O}$ contains triples defining subclass, sub-property, property domain, and property range. Assertions are* *triples of the form* s τ C*, stating that* s *is an instance of class* C*, and* (s p o)*, stating that* s *is connected to* o *via property* p*, where* o *may be a resource or a literal.*

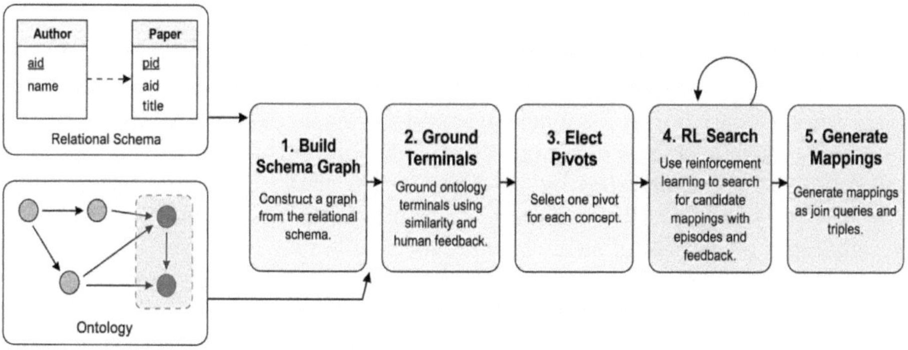

Fig. 1. Overview of the proposed approach. (Color figure online)

Definition 2 (Data Source Schema and Instance). *A data source schema* $\mathcal{S}$ *consists of a set of relational schemas* $\{R_1, \ldots, R_n\}$ *and integrity constraints* Γ*. Each relation is denoted* $R_i(A_{i,1}, \ldots, A_{i,m_i})$ *and defines typed attributes. An instance* $\mathcal{I}$ *of* $\mathcal{S}$ *is a set of relational instances* $\{r_1, \ldots, r_n\}$*, where each* r_i *is an instance of* R_i*. The constraints* Γ *include primary keys and foreign keys. A primary key* $PK_i \subseteq \{A_{i,1}, \ldots, A_{i,m_i}\}$ *uniquely identifies tuples in* R_i*. A foreign key* FK_i *in* R_i *references a primary key* PK_j *of* R_j *when, for each tuple* $t \in r_i$*, there exists* $t' \in r_j$ *such that* $t[FK_i] = t'[PK_j]$*.*

Definition 3 (Mapping Rules). *The KG* $(\mathcal{O}, \mathcal{A})$ *is populated from an instance* $\mathcal{I}$ *of* $\mathcal{S}$ *using mapping rules* $\mathcal{M}$*. A mapping rule* $m \in \mathcal{M}$ *is a pair* $m = (q_m, \theta_m)$*, where* q_m *is a conjunctive query over* $\mathcal{I}$*, possibly involving joins and existentially quantified variables, and* θ_m *is a template that transforms the values returned by* q_m *into KG assertions. The template generates class assertions* (s τ C) *and/or property assertions* (s p o)*. Applying* $\mathcal{M}$ *to* $\mathcal{I}$ *produces the ABox* $\mathcal{A}$*.*

Problem Statement. Given a KG $(\mathcal{O}, \mathcal{A})$ and a set of mapping rules $\mathcal{M}$ used to populate it from data sources described by a schema $\mathcal{S}$, we suppose that new user requirements require the introduction of a set $\mathcal{C}$ of new concepts, each new concept $C_{\text{new}} \in \mathcal{C}$ being associated with properties $p_1, \ldots, p_k$, where C_{new} serves as the domain and/or range of these properties. The problem is to automatically generate a minimal set of new mapping rules $\mathcal{M}_{\text{new}}$ that extends $\mathcal{M}$ to populate the new concepts and their properties, minimizing human intervention; we focus on addition of concepts (removal is straightforward to automate).

3 Our Approach

Figure 1 embodies our solution; the relational schema $\mathcal{S}$ and its associated ontology $\mathcal{O}$, updated with new concepts $\mathcal{C}$ (in blue in the figure), serve as input. Steps 1 and 2 are preparatory: Step 1 builds the *Schema Graph* $\mathcal{G}$ from $\mathcal{S}$, a unified representation that brings the relational schema and the ontology fragment into a single structure, enabling graph-theoretic mapping discovery. Step 2 grounds each property of each concepts of $\mathcal{C}$ as a terminal node by combining lexical similarity with user feedback on sampled values, yielding $\mathcal{G}^+$. Step 3 elects one *pivot* terminal per new concept, selecting the property with the highest feedback score. This is motivated by the fact that by first finding the Steiner Tree that correctly connects all new concepts through their pivots, and then resolving the remaining properties of each concept, the search requires fewer RL iterations and less user feedback. Step 4 searches for the optimal Steiner tree in $\mathcal{G}^+$, which is NP-hard [15], so an RL agent is used, guided by user feedback on sampled query results. Step 5 is a deterministic translation of the resulting tree into a join query and an RDF triple template, yielding $\mathcal{M}_{\text{new}}$.

3.1 Schema Graph, Terminal Nodes and Steiner Tree

We represent the data sources using a compact structure called the *Schema Graph*. The key motivation for this representation is twofold: it provides a unified graph that brings together both the relational schema structure and the new ontology fragment within a single formalism, and it enables the use of Steiner Trees as a graph-theoretic mechanism for deriving the source queries of the mapping rules. In our previous formulation [14], every pair of attributes within a relation was connected by an intra-relation edge, producing a dense graph that enlarges the search space, increases the number of RL episodes needed to converge to correct mappings, and raises the amount of user feedback required. In the definition below, intra-relation edges are restricted to connections between the *primary key* attributes and each non-key attribute of the same relation, yielding a substantially sparser graph.

Definition 4 (Schema graph). *A* schema graph $\mathcal{G}$ *associated with a source schema* $\mathcal{S} = \{R_1, \ldots, R_n\}$ *is a weighted, connected graph* (V, E, W)*. The node set* $V = \bigcup_{i=1}^{n}\{A_{i,1}, \ldots, A_{i,m_i}\}$ *contains one node for each attribute of the relational schema* $\mathcal{S}$*, where* m_i *is the arity of relation* R_i*. We assume attribute names to be unique and use the terms* attribute *and* node *interchangeably. The edge set* $E \subseteq V \times V$ *is undirected and partitioned into* E_{intra} *and* E_{inter}*. The set* E_{intra} *connects primary-key attributes to non-key attributes of the same relation:* $E_{\text{intra}} = \{\{A_{i,j}, A_{i,k}\} \mid A_{i,j} \in PK_i,\ A_{i,k} \in (R_i \setminus PK_i)\}$*. The set* E_{inter} *encodes foreign-key relationships: for each foreign key* $FK_i \subseteq R_i$ *referencing a primary key* $PK_j \subseteq R_j$*, we include edges* $\{A_{i,k}, A_{j,\ell}\}$ *between corresponding key attributes. Finally,* W *assigns each edge* $e \in E$ *a weight* $w_e \in [0, 1]$*; initially, intra-relation edges receive weight 0 and inter-relation edges receive weight 1.*

Definition 5 (Terminal Nodes and Augmented Schema Graph). *Given a set $\mathcal{C}$ of new concepts, each $\mathcal{C}_i \in \mathcal{C}$ is characterized by properties $\{p_{i1}, \ldots, p_{ik}\}$, the schema graph $\mathcal{G}$ is augmented with a set of terminal nodes T, one per property p_{ij} whose values are literals. Each terminal is linked to the most similar attribute nodes in $\mathcal{G}$ based on name and type. The resulting Augmented Schema Graph is denoted $\mathcal{G}^+ = (V^+, E^+, W^+)$, where $V^+ = V \cup T$, $E^+ = E \cup E_T$, and each edge in E_T carries weight $1 -$ **Similarity** between the terminal and its matched attribute node.*

$\mathcal{G}^+$ allows us to frame the derivation of mapping rules as the problem of finding a *Steiner Tree* spanning T in $\mathcal{G}^+$, whose inter-relation edges encode the join conditions of the source query. The similarity between terminal nodes and schema attributes is detailed in Sect. 3.2.

Definition 6 (Steiner Tree). *A Steiner Tree $\mathcal{T} = (V_\mathcal{T}, E_\mathcal{T}, W_\mathcal{T})$ of $\mathcal{G}^+$ is a connected sub-graph spanning all terminals $T \subset V^+$, possibly including Steiner vertices from $V^+ \setminus T$, that minimizes $\sum_{e \in E_\mathcal{T}} w_e$ (see [5]).*

3.2 Construction of $\mathcal{G}^+$ and Pivot Selection

For each property p_{ij} of each new concept $\mathcal{C}_i \in \mathcal{C}$, a similarity score with every type-compatible attribute $a \in V$, $\text{sim}(p_{ij}, a)$, is computed as a weighted average of three measures: Levenshtein distance [19], Jaccard similarity [13], and Token Sort Ratio [6]; type-incompatible attributes receive a score of zero. The k most similar candidates $\text{Cand}_k(p_{ij}) = \text{TopK}_{a \in V}\ \text{sim}(p_{ij}, a)$ are then selected.

Lexical similarity alone may be insufficient, since two attributes may share similar names but contain incompatible data, so the top-k candidates are validated by showing the user a small sample of actual values, whose feedback both selects the best match and encodes grounding confidence into the edge weight of $\mathcal{G}^+$. Formally, let $n_{p_{ij},a}$ denote the number of values marked as correct out of the sample $S_{p_{ij},a}$; the feedback score is $F(p_{ij}, a) = \frac{n_{p_{ij},a}}{|S_{p_{ij},a}|}$, and terminal t is linked to $a^\star(p_{ij}) = \arg\max_{a \in \text{Cand}_k(p_{ij})} F(p_{ij}, a)$ with edge weight $1 - F(p_{ij}, a^\star(p_{ij}))$.

Definition 7 (Pivot node). *The pivot node τ_i of concept $\mathcal{C}_i \in \mathcal{C}$ is the terminal with the highest feedback score: $\tau_i = \arg\max_{p_{ij} \in \{p_{i1}, \ldots, p_{ik}\}} F\big(p_{ij}, a^\star(p_{ij})\big)$.*

The pivot configuration $\tau = \{\tau_1, \ldots, \tau_{|\mathcal{C}|}\}$ drives a two-phase search. In **Phase 1**, RL constructs a single Steiner Tree spanning only the pivot terminals, keeping the terminal set small (size $|\mathcal{C}|$) and the search tractable. In **Phase 2**, the remaining terminals of each concept are connected to the pivot tree individually. This joint design, contrasting with our prior work [14] where a separate tree was built per concept, captures inter-concept dependencies and significantly reduces both RL episodes and user feedback required to converge. The resulting tree encodes the conjunctive query of the mapping rule via its inter-relation edges E_{inter}.

3.3 Reinforcement Learning-Based Optimization

We formulate the Steiner Tree search as a Markov Decision Process (MDP) [24] $(\mathsf{S}, \mathsf{A}, \mathsf{K}, \mathsf{r})$, where S is the state space, A the action space, K the transition function, and r the immediate reward. The MDP is instantiated twice: once for Phase 1 over pivot terminals τ, and once for Phase 2 over the remaining terminals of each concept.

State. A state $s_i^j = (\mathcal{G}^+, \tau, T_i^j, \mathcal{T}_i^j)$ captures the augmented graph, the pivot configuration, the set of terminals covered so far, and the partial Steiner Tree at iteration i of episode j. The initial state is $s_0^j = (\mathcal{G}^+, \tau, \emptyset, \perp)$ and the terminal state is $s_f^j = (\mathcal{G}^+, \tau, T, \mathcal{T}_j)$, where $\mathcal{T}_j$ spans all terminals in T.

Table 1. Evaluation scenario groups.

Ontology	Scenarios	#C	#P	Link to github
Burr micro	B1–B5	1–3	3–8	`burr-micro`
ISWC	I1–I5	8–10	24–25	`iswc`
Mondial	M1–M4	25–26	61–63	`mondial`
NPD	N1–N4	82–83	331–332	`npd`

Action. At each iteration, an action consists of selecting a path in $\mathcal{G}^+$ that extends the current partial tree to at least one uncovered terminal. The admissible action set $\mathsf{A}(s_i^j)$ is the set of simple paths from $\mathcal{T}_i^j$ to an uncovered terminal.

Reward. The reward r is derived from the quality of the query induced by the current Steiner Tree. The tree at episode j is converted into a conjunctive query q_j, executed over the source data to produce tuples U_j. The user assesses a small sample, judgments accumulate in H^+ (correct) and H^- (incorrect), giving: $TP_j = |U_j \cap H^+|$, $FP_j = |U_j \cap H^-|$, and $FN_j = |H^+ \setminus U_j|$. Precision and recall are computed over labeled tuples only, and the episode reward is their harmonic mean F_1.

Weight Adjustment. After each episode, each edge of the selected tree is updated by a weight-adjustment coefficient ρ, as $w_e \leftarrow \rho\, w_e + (1-\rho)(1-F_1)$, steering future episodes toward better-scoring join paths.

4 Experimental Evaluation

Our solution[1], implemented in Python, is evaluated on whether it produces correct mappings for new ontology fragments and how much feedback it requires.

[1] available at https://github.com/bouchrakdr/Feedback-guided-KG-evolution.

The evaluation addresses four research questions: RQ1 whether correct mappings are generated across controlled and real-world scenarios; RQ2 how fast the search converges; RQ3 how feedback behaves across different schema organizations and output sizes; and RQ4 how the approach compares with Similarity-only, Greedy-ST, and Hologram [14].

We use Burr [17] for controlled relational-to-ontology mapping scenarios with reference mappings: five micro-benchmarks and thirteen real-world tasks from ISWC, Mondial, and NPD FactPages. Table 1 summarizes the evaluation: #C and #P are the concepts and properties present before extension; the last column links to a GitHub repository containing the tested scenarios.

We compare four methods under identical inputs. **Similarity-only** maps each ontology property independently to the most similar source attribute and then uses the shortest available join path. **Greedy-ST** greedily builds a Steiner-like tree from the initial edge weights without feedback-based revision. **Hologram** is our previous RL-based method; it handles concepts independently and does not use pivot nodes or F_1-based edge updates. **Ours** is the proposed joint pivot-based method.

The tabular Q-learning hyperparameters used are: $\alpha = 0.45$, $\gamma = 0.9$, $\epsilon_0 = 0.6$ (decayed by a factor of 0.95 after each episode down to a minimum of 0.05), and $\rho = 0.3$; $\rho \in \{0.3, 0.5, 0.6\}$ yielded the same final F_1, with 0.3 converging fastest.

Table 2 reports the detailed results. *Episodes* denotes the number of learning episodes to converge. Feedback rows are tuples sampled from candidate-query results and inspected by the user; they accumulate across episodes.

On the micro-benchmarks, our approach reaches perfect F_1 on all five tasks, converging in 2–4 episodes and requiring 36 feedback rows over 2,266 query rows. B2 needs more feedback than B1 because its normalized schema spreads evidence across more tables. B3 is harder than B4 because the new concept must satisfy multiple relational constraints simultaneously, not due to output size.

On real-world scenarios, the approach reaches perfect F_1 on 11/13 tasks (for M2 : $F_1 = 0.93$, for M3: $F_1 = 0.95$), average $F_1 = 0.991$. Convergence ranges from 1 to 6 episodes, with 126 feedback rows over 14,289 query rows. High I4/I5 percentage%s reflect tiny outputs, and M2/M3 drop from multiple plausible relational realizations of the same ontology fragment.

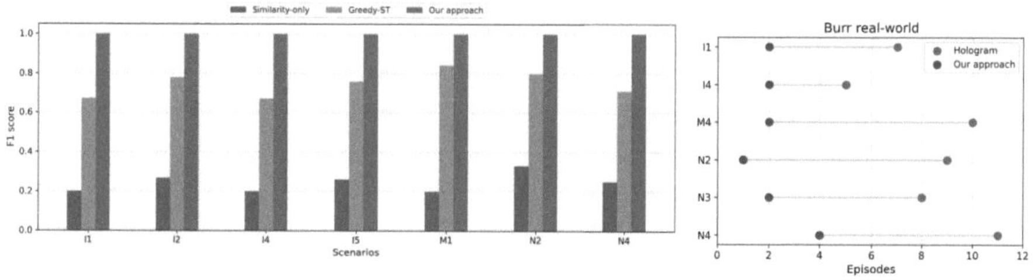

Fig. 2. Left: F_1 comparison on real-world scenarios. Right: Convergence speed of Hologram [14] vs. our approach.

Table 2. Results on Burr scenarios.

ID	F_1	Episodes	# Query rows	# Feedback rows	Feedback (%)
Micro-benchmark					
B1	1.00	3	981	9	0.92
B2	1.00	3	422	9	2.13
B3	1.00	4	230	8	3.48
B4	1.00	2	171	4	2.34
B5	1.00	3	462	6	1.30
Real-world					
I1	1.00	2	6	4	66.67†
I2	1.00	1	9	2	22.22
I3	1.00	1	21	2	9.52
I4	1.00	2	3	3	100†
I5	1.00	1	2	2	100†
M1	1.00	3	27	6	22.22
M2	0.93	4	125	8	6.40
M3	0.95	6	105	12	11.43
M4	1.00	2	12300	69	0.56
N1	1.00	1	48	2	4.17
N2	1.00	1	120	2	1.67
N3	1.00	2	58	4	6.90
N4	1.00	4	1465	10	0.68

† High percentage due to very small output size; absolute feedback remains 2–4 rows.

The left panel of Fig. 2 shows our approach consistently outperforming Similarity-only and Greedy-ST. Similarity-only is sensitive to ambiguous names and cannot optimize joins. Greedy-ST uses structure but cannot revise poor initial weights. Our RL-based updates use feedback to escape suboptimal joins. The right panel of Fig. 2 compares our method with Hologram: on real-world tasks, average episodes drop from 8.33 to 2.17, showing that pivot-guided joint search reduces redundant exploration while preserving mapping quality.

Results show the proposed feedback-guided approach effectively supports ontology evolution. On micro-benchmarks it recovers intended fragments with perfect structural accuracy, confirming that terminal grounding, Steiner-tree search, and reinforcement learning work across schema variations. Real-world experiments confirm effectiveness beyond controlled settings: strong results on ISWC, Mondial, and NPD show good transfer to realistic schemas and fragments. Comparison with Hologram [14] corroborates the benefit of pivot-based exploration and feedback-driven edge updates.

Results support framing ontology evolution as interactive structural search, where user feedback validates mappings and guides the search. Future work will test more real-world datasets and explore full mapping synthesis, including explicit URI construction for new concepts.

5 Related Work

KGs have become long-term strategic infrastructures by providing a backbone for encoding, interlinking, and reasoning over data [11]. A particular class of KGs relevant to our work consists of those constructed over tabular data sources via Ontology-Based Data Access (OBDA). In OBDA frameworks, such as Ontop [4], an ontology provides a conceptual layer over heterogeneous sources, and declarative mappings specify how source data are exposed as ontology instances.

Two distinct categories of approaches have been identified in the context of mapping between data sources and ontologies: *bottom-up* approaches [3,16], which extract an ontology from the sources, and *top-down* approaches [10,20], which map a data source to an already existing ontology.

Maintenance tasks are commonly categorized according to where changes originate [22]. *Instance-level* approaches address changes that arise from the underlying data at the *ontology level* (ABox), when data already integrated into the KG are modified [27], as well as *source-level* updates, when new input sources are integrated [23], or both [9]. The problem then becomes how to update the ontology and mappings to reflect schema or content evolution at the data level. Conversely, among *Schema-level* approaches, the authors of [8] start from changes at the ontology (TBox) level, such as the introduction of new concepts or the modification of existing ones, and aim to determine how mappings (and potentially data sources) must be adapted accordingly.

Among recent work on instance-level evolution, Wandji et al. [27] propose a framework where users add assertions directly at the KG instance level, and the system automatically determines the tuples that must be inserted into the underlying data sources to make these assertions valid with respect to the ontology-mapping specification. While their focus is on propagating changes from the KG to the data, our contribution addresses the complementary problem of extending the ontology itself and deriving the corresponding mappings in a controlled and incremental manner.

Our work belongs to the category of schema-level approaches. As far as we know, only two approaches [7,8] are close to our work. The authors of [8] automate the impact of ontology changes on mappings. OntoRipple [7] propagates ontology changes to RML mappings and SHACL shapes. Unlike our approach, these works do not use source instances to generate mapping updates; in our case, instances linked to the ontology update are explicitly considered when updating the mappings. Finally, there are proposals that use Steiner Trees to find optimal join paths [2,26]. As far as we know, no approach except ours combines RL, ST and User Feedback for ontology update mapping.

6 Conclusion

This paper addressed mapping generation in an ontology-evolution setting, where new concepts and relations must be integrated into an existing knowledge graph from relational sources. We proposed a method that combines an Augmented Schema Graph, pivot selection, Steiner-Tree search, and Reinforcement Learning to guide the generation of mapping rules. The experiments on Burr [17] show that the method remains highly accurate while requiring limited feedback and only a few episodes. The results also indicate that the proposed formulation improves over *Hologram* [14] in both mapping quality and convergence speed, while requiring limited feedback across Burr scenarios with different output sizes. Future work will investigate simultaneous ontology and relational-schema evolution, where mappings must be adapted to changes on both sides.

References

1. Agrawal, G., Kumarage, T., Alghamdi, Z.: Can knowledge graphs reduce hallucinations in llms?: a survey. In: NAACL Conference, pp. 3947–3960 (2024)
2. Baik, C., Jagadish, H.V., Li, Y.: Bridging the semantic gap with sql query logs in natural language interfaces to databases. In: ICDE Conference, pp. 374–385 (2019)
3. Ben Mahria, B., Chaker, I., Zahi, A.: A novel approach for learning ontology from relational database: from the construction to the evaluation. J. Big Data **8**(1), 1–22 (2021). https://doi.org/10.1186/s40537-021-00412-2
4. Calvanese, D., Cogrel, B., Komla-Ebri, S., et al.: Ontop: answering sparql queries over relational databases. Semantic Web **8**(3), 471–487 (2016)
5. Chlebík, M., Chlebíková, J.: The steiner tree problem on graphs: inapproximability results. Theor. Comput. Sci. **406**(3), 207–214 (2008)
6. Cohen, S.: Fuzzy string matching in python (2011). https://github.com/seatgeek/fuzzywuzzy
7. Conde-Herreros, D., Corcho, O., Chaves-Fraga, D.: Ontoripple: making waves in the knowledge graph lifecycle. SoftwareX **33**, 102542 (2026)
8. Conde-Herreros, D., Stork, L., Pernisch, R.: Propagating ontology changes to declarative mappings in construction of knowledge graphs. In: KGCW@ ESWC Workshop, vol. 3718 (2024)
9. De Giacomo, G., Lembo, D., Oriol, X.: Practical update management in ontology-based data access. In: ISWC Conference, pp. 225–242 (2017)
10. Futia, G., Vetrò, A., De Martin, J.C.: Semi: a semantic modeling machine to build knowledge graphs with graph neural networks. SoftwareX **12**, 100516 (2020)
11. Hogan, A., Blomqvist, E., Cochez, M., et al.: Knowledge graphs. ACM Comput. Surv. **54**(4), 1–37 (2021)
12. Hoseini, S., Theissen-Lipp, J., Quix, C.: A survey on semantic data management as intersection of ontology-based data access, semantic modeling and data lakes. JWS **81**, 100819 (2024)
13. Jaccard, P.: Étude comparative de la distribution florale dans une portion des alpes et des jura. Bull. Soc. Vaudoise Sci. Nat. **37**, 547–579 (1901)
14. Kader, B., Manouvrier, M., Belhajjame, K.: Human-guided reinforcement learning for knowledge graph maintenance. In: IoTBDS Conference (2026)

15. Karp, R.M.: Reducibility among combinatorial problems. In: Miller, R.E., Thatcher, J.W. (eds.) CCC Symposium. The IBM Research Symposia Series, pp. 85–103. Plenum Press, New York (1972)
16. Lakzaei, B., Shamsfard, M.: Ontology learning from relational databases. Inf. Sci. **577**, 280–297 (2021)
17. Laskowski, L., Hladik, M., Portisch, J., et al.: Burr: a benchmark for ontology learning from relational databases. In: ACM SIGMOD Conference, vol. 3, no. 6, pp. 1–27 (2025)
18. Lavrinovics, E., Biswas, R., Bjerva, J., et al.: Knowledge graphs, large language models, and hallucinations: an NLP perspective. JWS **85**, 100844 (2025)
19. Lcvenshtcin, V.: Binary coors capable or 'correcting deletions, insertions, and reversals. Soviet Phys.-Doklady **10**(8) (1966)
20. de Medeiros, L.F., Priyatna, F., Corcho, O.: Mirror: automatic r2rml mapping generation from relational databases. In: ICWE Conference, pp. 326–343 (2015)
21. Peng, C., Xia, F., Naseriparsa, M., et al.: Knowledge graphs: opportunities and challenges. Artif. Intell. Rev. **56**(11), 13071–13102 (2023)
22. Polleres, A., Pernisch, R., Bonifati, A., et al.: How does knowledge evolve in open knowledge graphs? Trans. Graph Data Knowl. **1**(1), 11–1 (2023)
23. Pomp, A., Lipp, J., Meisen, T.: You are missing a concept! enhancing ontology-based data access with evolving ontologies. In: ICSC Conference, pp. 98–105 (2019)
24. Puterman, M.L.: Markov Decision Processes: Discrete Stochastic Dynamic Programming. John Wiley & Sons, Hoboken (2014)
25. Shi, M., Janowicz, K., Liu, Z., et al.: The geography of evolving concepts: quantifying spatial, temporal, and semantic consequences of ontology changes. Int. J. Digital Earth **19**(1), 2605865 (2026)
26. Talukdar, P.P., Jacob, M., Mehmood, M.S., et al.: Learning to create data-integrating queries. VLDB Endow. **1**(1), 785–796 (2008)
27. Wandji, R.E., Calvanese, D.: Ontology-based update in virtual knowledge graphs via schema mapping recovery. In: RuleML+RR Conference, pp. 59–74 (2024)
28. Weikum, G.: Knowledge graphs: a data odyssey. VLDB Endow. **14**(12), 3233–3238 (2021)
29. Xiao, G., Calvanese, D., Kontchakov, R.: Ontology-based data access: a survey. In: IJCAI Conference (2018)

Knowledge Graphs, Text-to-SQL and Metadata Extraction

A Multi-layer Knowledge Graph for Motive Detection in Social Engineering Attacks

Alexandra Gialama(✉) and Georgia Koloniari

Department of Applied Informatics, University of Macedonia, Thessaloniki, Greece
aid23011@uom.edu.gr

Abstract. Understanding the reasoning behind social engineering attacks, which rely less on technical expertise and more on communication skills, has become essential. This paper introduces a labeling method designed to identify the attackers' motives in such attacks that use text and associate them semantically with their common linguistic patterns. To this end, we define a multi-layer knowledge graph, which incorporates basic language components and enables the application of graph analytics algorithms in order to visualize and gain insights into the complex text relationships. The effectiveness of the proposed methodology is evaluated against a widely used public dataset for studying phishing attacks. The results show that while similar language features may indicate shared motive, they are mostly influenced by the discussion topic. Also, through our evaluation, we identify two new attack motives, extending corresponding previously developed ontologies.

Keywords: Cybersecurity · Social Engineering · Phishing · Knowledge Graph · Natural Language Processing

1 Introduction

Social Engineering (SE) attacks, a type of attack that involves social interaction between the victim and the attacker(s) with the objective of exploiting their vulnerabilities [17], have highlighted the importance of alerting users to recognize suspicious behavior. Among the most common types of such attacks, *phishing* is defined as a fraudulent process of obtaining sensitive and personal information by posing as a trustworthy entity, most commonly conducted via email [7].

Many AI solutions using NLP, Machine and Deep Learning [15,16] have enhanced the mitigation of such attacks with high success rates, but often providing limited insight into their decision-making processes. Consequently, users may over-trust algorithmic outputs, even when they are incorrect, leading to lack of understanding of the source of the problem and remaining in danger in the next incident. Thus, it may be advisable to shift the focus to the reasoning behind these attacks. In [18], a comprehensive domain ontology of SE is provided that includes, among other aspects, some of the basic attack motives such as financial gain, revenge, personal interest, prank, and politics.

© The Author(s), under exclusive license to Springer Nature Switzerland AG 2027
G. Vargas Solar et al. (Eds.): ADBIS 2026, CCIS 3175, pp. 49–59, 2027.
https://doi.org/10.1007/978-3-032-39823-9_5

In text-based SE attacks, the use of language is the basic tool for manipulation containing indications of the attacker's motive. The key challenge lies in effectively managing these indicators and formulating conclusions about their meaning. Given the linguistic diversity, it is essential to consider how useful information can be found in whole sentences, expressions or even individual words. Knowledge graphs (KGs) facilitate the process of representing these verbal indicators and allow inference based on their relationships by handling different types of data and integrating diverse information. Our work aims to address the lack of explainability of AI methods, by providing the means of understanding the root causes of SE attacks. To this end, we introduce a *labeling* method that associates attack texts with their possible motive. The proposed approach relies on defining a *multi-layer KG* to capture the relationships between these texts and graph analytics algorithms, such as PageRank and degree centrality, along with NLP technologies to reveal hidden patterns. The effectiveness of our approach is evaluated on phishing attacks, which as evidenced by the Anti-Phishing Working Group [2] in the 2nd quarter of 2025 continue to be one of the most harmful attacks. Based on our results, there are language patterns associated with the attack motives indicating the intention for deception, but the choice of expressive means depends on the topic of the text. Lastly, our work contributes to the existing research of [18] with the detection and addition of two new attack motives, which achieve high semantic association with the analyzed data.

The paper is organized as follows. Section 2 reviews related work. The proposed framework is explained in Sect. 3. Our case study is presented in Sect. 4, while Sect. 5 concludes and suggests directions for future research.

2 Related Work

The advent of direct communication, a consequence of the growth of social networks, has significantly altered the security landscape [3]. The term *SE* represents attacks based on communication and psychological manipulation. This study relies on the definition in [17], which defines it as a form of attack where the attacker(s) exploits human vulnerabilities via social interaction to breach cybersecurity. A taxonomy in [6] discerns between human- and technical-based attacks presenting defensive strategies. Other works [7] divide the attacks based on the media used and the physical or non-physical presence of the attacker, while describing the methods of execution and the objectives behind the attacks, as well as the emotions that are typically exploited. In [9], the physical, technical, social, and socio-technical attack categories are identified, with the channel, operator, and attack type considered, and the attacker tactics outlined.

Besides taxonomies, ontologies have also been developed encompassing the involved entities and their relationships, providing examples of communication forms and definitions of SE concepts [12]. In [10], a universally applicable ontology based on established theories on safety and insights from psychology and sociology is proposed with axioms providing a clear distinction between attacks and description logic enabling the inference of attack classes. A more recent and complete ontology is defined in [18], including attack motives, and its usefulness is demonstrated by analyzing attacks and identifying threats. We use the motives in [18] in a complementary manner to associate them with their linguistic patterns through the newly proposed labeling method applied on our multi-layer KG, which comprises a representation framework for text data, enabling graph analysis to generate actionable insights.

Social science insights are essential to understand human behavior; in this context, in [14], Twitter data is used to identify instances of user-generated content that can be interpreted as attacks based on the users relationship graph and the textual semantics of tweets. This method combines graph and text analysis for cyberattack detection, whereas our KG preserves textual information for attack motive association. KGs have been used for vulnerability assessment in [8] defining a multi-layered graph model for the representation of SE attack scenarios in various states. The KG built in [13] analyzes human behavior in phishing attacks, assessing their susceptibility and potential risks of their reactions. Another application is presented in [11], where unstructured cyber threat intelligence reports are converted to structured attack technique graphs and combined into a unified technique KG. To the best of our knowledge, there is no such application regarding the attack motives that we analyze in this work.

3 Methodology

The proposed methodological framework has two key objectives: to represent the text data derived from SE attacks by capturing their relationships through the definition of a *multi-layer KG* and by applying a novel labeling method based on graph analysis to attribute attack motives to these texts.

Fig. 1. Multi-layer knowledge graph structure

3.1 Multi-layer Knowledge Graph Definition

The key component of our approach is a newly defined *multi-layer KG*, whose multiple layers allow the efficient representation of different aspects of relationships between texts. The graph follows a hierarchical structure, from the most general to the most specific, facilitating the flow of information. As shown in Fig. 1, it comprises a total of 5 layers with nodes representing fundamental linguistic elements.

The lower (most specific) layer, called *Texts Layer*, includes *Text* and *Duplicate* nodes, with the first representing the text content and the second the repeated words within the text body, as the latter is considered an important feature for discerning illegitimate texts. This is the only layer that contains two different node labels. The *COMMON_WORDS* relationship connects *Text* nodes that share common words, while maintaining as a property the number of words they share, and the *HAS_DUPLICATE* relationship connects *Text* to *Duplicate* nodes to represent words that appear multiple times within a text, with a property indicating how many times each duplicate word occurs.

The *Trigrams Layer* goes one step further and analyzes the trigrams of each text. The 1st and 2nd layers have a text-to-trigram relation and are connected with the *HAS_TRIGRAM* relationship. The bigrams that occur in the trigrams constitute the *Bigrams Layer*, enabling analysis of the different pairs of words, and the *HAS_BIGRAM* relationship represents the trigram-to-bigram relation. The 4th layer, named *Keywords Layer*, consists of nodes representing the most significant keywords, as identified by NLP during the preprocessing stage. The *HAS_KEYWORD* relationship connects the *Bigrams Layer* with the *Keywords Layer* denoting that a given keyword belongs to a bigram.

Lastly, the *Topics Layer*, which is the highest (most general) graph layer. Each *Topic* node can be interpreted as a combination of words which encapsulate the text subjects. Therefore, the keyword-to-topic relation, *BELONGS_TO*, connecting the fourth and fifth layers, establishes a connection between the keywords and the topics, indicating their relevance.

3.2 Multi-layer Knowledge Graph Construction

The proposed *multi-layer KG* is developed using the Neo4j[1] graph database, which enables efficient management of scientific-domain graphs and exploration of complex networks through its native Cypher language.

To construct the graph, data from SE attacks is preprocessed using NLP to extract the linguistic elements that populate its different layers. To determine text features that differentiate legitimate from fraudulent texts, both are statistically analyzed and, in accordance with related research [1], we rely on: (i) existence of URLs; (ii) text length; (iii) special characters such as repeated punctuation marks or marks that do not normally occur together; (iv) percentage of words written in capital letters; (v) presence of large words; (vi) references to

[1] https://neo4j.com.

entities such as person names, organizations and locations collected using Named Entity Recognition (NER); and finally, (vii) numbers within the context of their surrounding words. Figure 2 presents the overall preprocessing workflow.

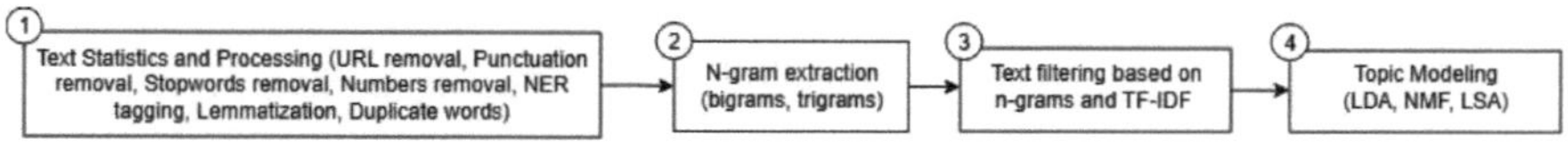

Fig. 2. Data preprocessing workflow scheme.

In Step 1, common NLP techniques (stopword removal, lowercase conversion, lemmatization, etc.) are applied to clean attack messages and extract their textual features, including repeated words within each. The output of this step provides the data for the *Texts Layer*. The *Duplicate* nodes have as a single property the frequently occurring terms, while the *Text* nodes maintain the cleaned text and all other attributes we have mentioned above.

In Step 2, N-gram extraction (trigram and bigram) is performed to provide a richer understanding of each text's content and populate the *Trigrams Layer* and *Bigrams Layer*, respectively. Filtering may be applied to bigrams using Term Frequency-Inverse Document Frequency (TF-IDF) to preserve the most informative terms as described in Step 3 of the workflow. Only bigrams associated with at least two trigrams and their corresponding trigrams are retained.

In Step 4, topic modeling is applied to the preprocessed texts. Latent Dirichlet Allocation (LDA), Non-Negative Matrix Factorization (NMF) and Latent Semantic Analysis (LSA) are utilized for the detection of the number of topics to determine the most suitable model, since dataset size and text length significantly influence performance. Based on their coherence, which measures the semantic consistency of words within a topic, the approach with the highest score is selected. While the topics detected form the *Topics Layer*, the words describing each topic form the *Keywords Layer*.

3.3 Labeling Method

The labeling method's goal is to associate *Text* nodes with attack motives. Using graph analysis, *Trigram* and *Bigram* nodes along with their corresponding relationships propagate motives to *Text* nodes.

Initially, each *Text* node is assigned its most relevant topic by traversing the KG from the given node to all its connected *Keyword* nodes and summarizing the edge weights that connect the latter to the various *Topic* nodes. The topic with the highest score is identified as the most relevant. A subset of trigrams is randomly selected, as they are more informative than bigrams, being more specific. Their embeddings are generated using sentence transformers (SBERT) and particularly the 'all-MiniLM-L6-v2' pre-trained model. The cosine similarity of trigram-motive is calculated and the motive with the highest similarity is then incorporated as a new property into these *Trigram* nodes. The propagation

Algorithm 1 Labeling Algorithm

```
Input: List of trigrams partially labeled
Output: List of labeled texts
1: for all t1 ∈ Trigrams do
2:     if t1.label = ∅ then
3:         LabelPR ← ∅
4:         for all t2 ∈ Neighbors(t1, HAS_BIGRAM) do
5:             if t2.label ≠ ∅ then
6:                 add (t2.label, t2.pagerank) to LabelPR
7:         if LabelPR ≠ ∅ then
8:             sort LabelPR by PageRank descending
9:             t1.label ← LabelPR[0].label
10: for all t1 ∈ Trigrams do
11:     t1.inDegreeCent ← InDegreeCentrality(t1)
12: for all txt ∈ Texts do
13:     LabelDC ← ∅
14:     for all t1 ∈ Neighbors(txt, HAS_TRIGRAM) do
15:         if t1.label ≠ ∅ then
16:             add (t1.label, t1.inDegreeCent) to LabelDC
17:     if LabelDC ≠ ∅ then
18:         sort LabelDC by inDegreeCent descending
19:         txt.label ← LabelDC[0].label
20: return Texts
```

of motives to the rest of the *Trigram* nodes and finally to the *Text* nodes is detailed in Algorithm. 1, and is split into two phases using different measures of node importance. Influential trigrams are determined by their Pagerank as evaluated based on their connections to *Text* nodes, as in large-scale sparse graphs, Pagerank effectively captures the flow of information and influence. In particular, a PageRank property is added to each *Trigram* node evaluated based on the PageRank values of all connected *Text* nodes, divided by their out-degree.

For Phase A (lines 1–9), trigrams without a motive label that have common bigrams with already labeled trigrams are matched based on the *HAS_BIGRAM* relationship. The labeled trigrams are sorted in descending order of PageRank value and the one with the highest score shares its label with the given unlabeled trigram. In Phase B (lines 10–20), label propagation proceeds to *Text* nodes. Since the focus is on direct connections between texts and trigrams rather than broader influences (e.g. bigrams), trigram degree centrality is preferred over PageRank as it captures local influence, is computationally simpler and directly reflects a node's immediate prominence. Since the graph is directed, the trigrams in-degree is considered to identify those that appear in most *Text* nodes and a similar process as in Phase A is followed to propagate the motives to the texts.

4 Evaluation – Case Study

The curated CEAS 2008 Challenge Lab Evaluation Corpus [4,5] aligns with our goals, enabling us to extract features and patterns of phishing and legitimate emails. Our code is publicly available[2]. From the original dataset, only the phishing emails were used to construct the multi-layer KG. Along with the presence of URLs, the subject line was incorporated into the email body instead of being analyzed separately. After the exploration of both legitimate and non-legitimate messages, following our preprocessing procedure, we determined the important features detailed in Sect. 3.2. Table 1 illustrates some of the basic statistics of the extracted features. The results suggest that named entities and URL(s) are of great significance in phishing emails, whilst the use of special characters and words written in uppercase letters are comparatively less prevalent.

Table 1. Distribution of texts by presence of properties after preprocessing

Text Properties	Description of Values	Presence (%)
length	Number of words	100
ner	Contain named entities	90.8
special_chars	Include special characters	31.9
uppercase_percentage	Positive uppercase percentage	40.9
url_exists	URL(s) exist(s)	65.2

Following preprocessing, LDA, NMF and LSA were applied for topic modeling. Based on the coherence score and their graphical representation, NMF was selected for this dataset deriving 7 topics, and only the 5,000 most important keywords per topic were retained for subsequent analysis. Table 2 shows for each topic, the keywords that most accurately represent it, alongside the number of emails ultimately associated with it.

4.1 Evaluation Results

A significant result of the application of our methodology and the construction of the multi-layer KG is the definition of two new attack motives. As mentioned earlier, the 19 attack motives in [18], such as financial gain, personal interest, etc., formed the basis for our study. Based on the emails' context and keywords identified using topic modeling, we detected texts that did not adequately fit any of these motives. Thus, the original list is expanded with two additional attack motives: *misinformation* and *data theft*. Misinformation refers to the deliberate sharing of false or inaccurate information as fact such as fake news and health scams. Data theft may also occur without a specific immediate purpose, with data often gathered in excess under the assumption of future usefulness.

[2] https://github.com/alexandragial/graph-construction-python-cql.

Table 2. Most representative keywords per topic

Topic	#Emails	Keywords
0	3206	life, health, time, work, site, summer
1	490	american, news, explosion, terrorist, world, special
2	1543	increase, month, size, inch, notice, benefit
3	2597	replica, watch, rolex, quality, visit, price
4	1326	customer, fast, price, offer, device, click
5	2144	guarantee, herbal, product, breakthrough, increase, read
6	461	prince, emperor, time, germany, political, wish

The distribution of emails per topic and motive (Fig. 3) reveals that every topic includes emails from all motives, with approximately 1 to 3 always standing out. To assess whether attackers adopt the same language for the same motive, linguistic features are compared across texts using Neo4j queries. For example, personal interest is mainly observed in Topics 0 and 4. Topic 0 is characterized by short messages, with 94.3% containing fewer than 80 words and 91.1% not including URLs. In contrast, 60% of Topic 4 texts exceed 80 words and 84.8% contain external links. Financial gain is prevalent in Topics 2 and 5, which share short text length, absence of special characters and frequent inclusion of external links. The main difference lies in Topic 5, which exhibits a higher repetition rate, with 68.9% of texts containing duplicate terms associated with financial gain.

For the two new motives, attackers motivated by data theft rarely use URLs; instead they rely on short messages with repeated words and references to credible organizations and platforms. Misinformation emails contain one or more external links and remain under 80 words. Although repeated word roots are absent, they include multiple recognized entities such as organizations, well-known people, events, and geopolitical entities. Capitalized text is also a notable feature of this motive category, appearing in 85.8% of cases.

Summarizing our results, we conclude that attack motives grouped within the same topic tend to share similar linguistic features. However, expression styles vary across topics even when the attack motives remain unchanged, indicating stronger correlation between language and topic rather than motive. This may indicate that learning methods based solely on linguistic features are not appropriate for motive association. Finally, the newly introduced motives are associated with a substantial number of emails (292 with misinformation and 549 with data theft), demonstrating the practical value of the expansion and its potential for further investigation.

Labeling Method Performance. To facilitate evaluation in the absence of inherent ground truth, a subset of the dataset (45 texts) was manually annotated and used as a proxy ground truth. While these annotations inevitably introduce a degree of subjectivity, consistent annotation provides a reasonable level of valid-

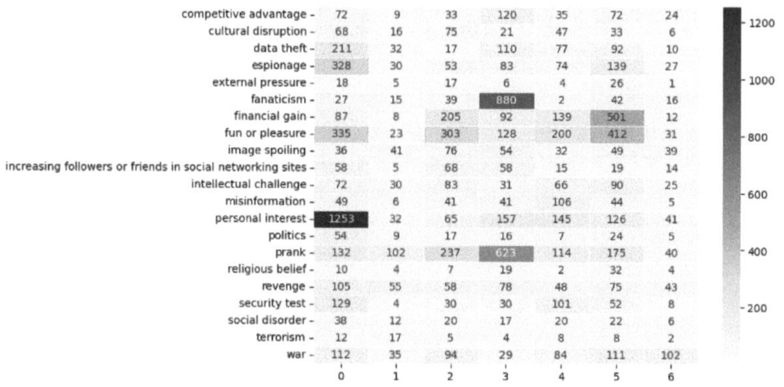

Fig. 3. Heatmap showing the distribution of emails across attack motives and topics.

ity and a practical basis for assessing the effectiveness of the proposed method. On 10 out of 21 motives (Table 3), the method achieves an overall accuracy of 0.69 and F1-Score of 0.70. Cohen's Kappa, a measure of inter-rater agreement for categorical data ranging from -1 to 1, is 0.654, indicating substantial agreement between predicted and manual labels. Specifically, data theft, image spoiling and intellectual challenge achieve the strongest performance, followed by financial gain with a solid F1-score. In contrast, fun or pleasure, personal interest and prank show moderate results, whereas war remains the most challenging category. Despite the differences across classes, the evaluation metrics show considerable alignment with human annotation, validating the approach as a scalable method for annotating unlabeled data.

Table 3. Classification performance per motive and evaluation metrics

Category	Precision	Recall	F1-Score	Support
competitive advantage	1.00	0.50	0.67	6
data theft	1.00	0.80	0.89	5
financial gain	1.00	0.60	0.75	5
fun or pleasure	0.50	0.75	0.60	4
image spoiling	0.80	1.00	0.89	4
intellectual challenge	0.75	1.00	0.86	3
personal interest	0.50	0.75	0.60	4
politics	1.00	0.50	0.67	4
prank	0.60	0.60	0.60	5
war	0.43	0.60	0.50	5

5 Conclusion and Future Work

The main purpose of this study is the association of text data derived from SE attacks with their attack motives. We introduced a graph-based labeling method relying on a newly defined *multi-layer KG*, structured based on fundamental concepts of NLP. The development of the model incorporates the application of (i) NLP methods as part of text analysis and (ii) graph analysis algorithms, which efficiently navigate relationships between entities and reveal hidden patterns. The results of our evaluation on the CEAS 2008 dataset provide a solid foundation for understanding the proposed methods capabilities and indicate that the labeling method performs reasonably well in identifying underlying attack motives. Finally, we managed to contribute to the existing ontology of [18], which presented 19 common attack motives by expanding it with two new additions: misinformation and data theft. Future research will extend the evaluation first through a direct comparison against a non-KG baseline by using SBERT and second through a broader analysis investigating additional SE attacks.

Acknowledgement. This paper is a result of research conducted within the "MSc in Artificial Intelligence and Data Analytics" of the Department of Applied Informatics of University of Macedonia. The presentation of the paper is funded by the University of Macedonia Research Committee.

Disclosure of Interests. The authors have no competing interests to declare that are relevant to the content of this article.

References

1. Al-Yozbaky, R.S., Alanezi, M.: Detection and analyzing phishing emails using NLP techniques. In: 2023 5th International Congress on Human-Computer Interaction, Optimization and Robotic Applications (HORA), pp. 1–6 (2023)
2. Anti-Phishing Working Group (APWG): Phishing activity trends report: 2nd quarter 2025. Report, Anti-Phishing Working Group (2025)
3. Carley, K.: Social cybersecurity: an emerging science. Comput. Math. Organ. Theory **26**, 365–381 (2020)
4. Champa, A.I., Rabbi, F., Zibran, M.F.: Why phishing emails escape detection: a closer look at the failure points. In: 2024 12th International Symposium on Digital Forensics and Security (ISDFS), pp. 1–6 (2024)
5. Champa, A.I., Rabbi, M.F., Zibran, M.F.: Curated datasets and feature analysis for phishing email detection with machine learning. In: 2024 IEEE 3rd International Conference on Computing and Machine Intelligence (ICMI), pp. 1–7 (2024)
6. Foozy, C.F.M., Ahmad, R., Abdollah, M.F., Yusof, R., Mas'ud, M.Z.: Generic taxonomy of social engineering attack and defence mechanism for handheld computer study. In: Malaysian Technical Universities International Conference on Engineering & Technology, pp. 1–7 (2011)
7. Ivaturi, K., Janczewski, L.: A taxonomy for social engineering attacks. In: International Conference on Information Resources Management, pp. 1–12 (2011)

8. Jaafor, O., Birregah, B.: Multi-layered graph-based model for social engineering vulnerability assessment. In: 2015 IEEE/ACM International Conference on Advances in Social Networks Analysis and Mining (ASONAM), pp. 1480–1488 (2015)
9. Krombholz, K., Hobel, H., Huber, M., Weippl, E.: Advanced social engineering attacks. J. Inf. Secur. Appl. **22**(C), 113–122 (2015)
10. Li, T., Ni, Y.: Paving ontological foundation for social engineering analysis. In: Advanced Information Systems Engineering, pp. 246–260. Springer Cham (2019)
11. Li, Z., Zeng, J., Chen, Y., Liang, Z.: Attackg: constructing technique knowledge graph fromnbsp;cyber threat intelligence reports. In: 27th European Symposium on Research in Computer Security, 2022, Proceedings, Part I, pp. 589–609 (2022)
12. Mouton, F., Leenen, L., Malan, M.M., Venter, H.S.: Towards an ontological model defining the social engineering domain. In: ICT and Society, pp. 266–279 (2014)
13. Omowumi, A., McDermott, C.D., Munasinghe, L.: Leveraging knowledge graphs for analysing human vulnerabilities in phishing attacks. In: 2025 International Conference on Software, Knowledge, Information Management Applications (SKIMA), pp. 1–6 (2025)
14. Park, J.H., Kwon, H.Y.: Cyberattack detection model using community detection and text analysis on social media. ICT Express **8**(4), 499–506 (2022)
15. Tsinganos, N., Fouliras, P., Mavridis, I., Gritzalis, D.: CSE-ARS: deep learning-based late fusion of multimodal information for chat-based social engineering attack recognition. IEEE Access **12**, 16072–16088 (2024)
16. Wang, Z., Ren, Y., Zhu, H., Sun, L.: Threat detection for general social engineering attack using machine learning techniques (2022). arXiv:2203.07933
17. Wang, Z., Sun, L., Zhu, H.: Defining social engineering in cybersecurity. IEEE Access **8**, 85094–85115 (2020)
18. Wang, Z., Zhu, H., Liu, P., Sun, L.: Social engineering in cybersecurity: a domain ontology and knowledge graph application examples. Cybersecurity **4**, 31 (2021)

Calibrated Multi-agent Consensus for Knowledge Graph Validation Using Open-Source LLM

Hadsaw Kakazai(✉) and Jyrki Nummenmaa

Tampere University, Tampere, Finland
hadsaw.kakazai@tuni.fi , jyrki.nummenmaa@tuni.fi

Abstract. Knowledge graphs are being used with Large Language Model applications such as question answering, recommendation, and factual grounding, but real graphs contain errors that propagate into downstream tasks. Manually finding and resolving these errors takes time and can lead to human errors. Automated validation of knowledge graph triples is, therefore, a long-standing problem. Recent works used commercial Large Language Models for the validation of Knowledge Graphs, and showed strong results, but have struggled with open-source alternatives. The confidence values that open-source models report are systematically unreliable, for example, a model that predicts a triple is true with 90% confidence is correct on those predictions far less often than 90% of the time.

This paper investigates whether post-hoc calibration combined with dual-perspective evidence fusion can produce reliable triple validation using a single open-source language model. The proposed framework has a plug-and-play architecture containing two agents, an External Agent that retrieves factual evidence from an external source and an Internal Agent that extracts subgraphs from the knowledge graph's own training data, both running on Meta-Llama-3-8B-Instruct. Each agent's raw logits are passed through a calibration layer that evaluates post-hoc methods (temperature, Platt, isotonic) and a consensus engine that combines the calibrated probabilities through fusion strategies. The framework is evaluated on FB13, a knowledge graph derived from Freebase.

The results indicate that the framework is effective: isotonic calibration reduces Expected Calibration Error from 0.144–0.191 to 0.005–0.010, and the calibrated dual-agent consensus reaches 87.51% accuracy versus 82.48% for the best single agent, showing that calibrated confidence estimates can contribute to more reliable and accurate knowledge graph validation.

Keywords: knowledge graph validation · calibration · multi-agent systems · open-source language models · probability fusion

© The Author(s), under exclusive license to Springer Nature Switzerland AG 2027
G. Vargas Solar et al. (Eds.): ADBIS 2026, CCIS 3175, pp. 60–71, 2027.
https://doi.org/10.1007/978-3-032-39823-9_6

1 Introduction

A knowledge graph (KG) represents factual information as a collection of triples of the form (head, relation, tail), providing real-world knowledge in a structured representation that enables machines to reason and query the information. The structured semantics form a foundation for a wide range of downstream applications: web search engines use them to answer entity-centric queries, recommender systems utilize the KG's relational structure to improve personalization, and, more recently, retrieval-augmented generation (RAG) pipelines integrate KGs to mitigate hallucination in large language models [9,13].

However, to use a knowledge graph in any domain, the correctness of the triples must be ensured. Even a small error rate propagates into downstream tasks and can produce misleading answers, biased recommendations, or factually incorrect results. Manual audit work on major KGs repeatedly shows non-trivial issues, encouraging research into automatic knowledge graph validation. Errors enter knowledge graphs during construction, editing, or integration [10]. Resolving them is framed as binary triple classification: a validation system predicts whether a triple (h,r,t) holds in the real world, the formulation established when the FB13 and WN11 benchmarks were introduced [14].

Two broad families of methods address automated KG validation. Embedding models learn vector representations of entities and relations and score a triple by how well a geometric relationship holds; this captures structural error patterns well but lacks an external reference point for purely factual errors. The second family uses LLMs to bring external knowledge to bear, framing validation as a natural-language inference task rather than a geometric one. KGValidator [2] showed GPT-4 with Wikidata context reaches strong accuracy, but open-source models failed almost completely. FactCheck [13] showed that aggregating predictions across multiple models through majority voting does not consistently improve over the best single model—miscalibration, single-perspective evidence, and naive aggregation are the likely causes.

A model is calibrated when its predicted confidence matches its actual accuracy. Modern neural networks are systematically overconfident [5], and open-source LLMs in particular generate high-certainty epistemic markers even on incorrect responses—meaning stated confidence reflects training distribution rather than actual correctness. KGValidator [2] found Llama-2 predicted nearly every triple as true regardless of evidence, producing near-random accuracy. Post-hoc calibration methods (temperature scaling, Platt scaling, isotonic regression) operate on raw logits—pre-softmax, unnormalized class scores—to correct this [5]. Commercial LLM APIs do not expose raw logits, motivating the use of open-source models here, which additionally support reproducibility, accessibility, and external oversight.

Calibration alone is insufficient, because LLMs are limited to knowledge available at training time, so KG validation also requires supporting evidence supplied as context—retrievable from sources such as Wikidata or the web [2]. The KG's own structure is itself a useful evidence source: which relations co-occur, which entity pairs appear together, which triples are consistent with the graph's local neighbourhood [6]. Relying on a single evidence source risks a systematic blind spot that scaling the model or improving prompts alone does not close [10].

This paper frames each evidence source as an agent: a specialized inference pipeline that retrieves context, structures a prompt, and produces a probability estimate over the true/false label—not an autonomous system with planning or tool-calling capability. The External Agent retrieves evidence from Wikidata/web; the Internal Agent extracts bidirectional subgraphs from the KG, following the decomposition strategy of Li et al. [6]. The architecture is modular: new agents register through a configuration layer, so any evidence source or model can be swapped without changing the calibration or consensus engine.

This work proposes a calibrated dual-agent consensus framework addressing these gaps in a single pipeline. Both agents produce raw logit outputs rather than binary verdicts, preserving confidence information that majority-voting systems discard. These outputs pass through a calibration layer supporting several post-hoc methods, and calibrated probabilities feed into a consensus engine implementing both static and adaptive fusion strategies, enabling a systematic ablation of which combination is most effective. The framework is evaluated on FB13 [14], an encyclopedic knowledge graph derived from Freebase. No existing work has combined these components in this way. The closest prior work, Shami, Marchesin, and Silvello [13], addresses multi-model consensus but without calibration. Li et al. [6] addresses internal graph structure but without external evidence or confidence calibration. Lin and Hooi [7] addresses calibrated multi-agent consensus, but in general NLP, not the KG validation domain. Lu et al. [8] apply dual calibration to a KG-augmented reasoning pipeline but use a single agent and do not address multi-perspective fusion. Each of these works resolves one part of the problem while leaving the other parts open. This paper addresses their intersection directly, evaluated on FB13.

2 Previous Work

Boylan et al. [2] (KGValidator) prompt an LLM to judge a triple's validity given context retrieved from Wikidata, the web, or a user-provided document corpus; with GPT-4 and external context, accuracy reaches 95% on WN18RR and 90% on CoDEx-S. Open-source models tell a different story: Llama-2-70B predicted nearly every triple as true regardless of the evidence retrieved, producing near-random accuracy across every setting tested, and the framework returns only binary verdicts with no confidence estimation. The most comprehensive evaluation to date, Shami, Marchesin, and Silvello's FactCheck [13], benchmarks four open-source LLMs alongside GPT-4o-mini on 13,530 facts and finds that combining predictions across models through naive majority voting does not consistently outperform the best individual model.

Li et al. [6] (MAKGED) propose four trainable agents, each specialized to one direction of a triple's bidirectional local subgraph, encoded via a graph convolutional network and combined with a Llama-2 model fine-tuned via LoRA; after multi-round discussion (avg. 1.8 rounds) and majority voting, the framework reaches 77.48% on FB15K and 82.83% on WN18RR. Their design cost is high—four agents each requiring task-specific fine-tuning—and the voting mechanism is binary. This paper adopts MAKGED's four-direction decomposition for the Internal Agent but without per-graph fine-tuning: the same frozen LLM reasons directly over formatted subgraph context. Wu et al. [15] instead fuse seven non-LLM structural and embedding features through a multilayer perceptron, reaching 0.963 accuracy on WN18RR error detection; their ablation finds path-frequency evidence the single strongest feature, supporting the case that structural signal alone carries substantial predictive power.

Lin and Hooi [7] (ConfMAD) show that in LLM debate, groups of models frequently fail to converge on a correct answer even when one member already holds it, because models are overconfident; eliciting and calibrating per-turn confidence—Platt scaling performing most stably across GPT-4o-mini, LLaMA, and Phi—restores the correlation between an agent's debate win rate and its standalone accuracy. Their framework targets question answering rather than KG validation. Guo et al. [5] establish temperature scaling, Platt scaling [11], and isotonic regression [16] (via the Pool-Adjacent-Violators algorithm [1]) as the standard post-hoc calibration toolkit, with isotonic typically achieving the lowest error given sufficient validation data but at risk of overfitting otherwise. Lu et al. [8] calibrate a RAG pipeline at both the evidence-scoring and reasoning stages, showing that removing evidence-stage calibration alone spikes ECE from roughly 4% to over 20% while accuracy barely changes—evidence that calibration and prediction correctness are separable concerns, a premise this paper shares.

Across this literature, three gaps recur: each work treats either external or internal evidence, not both; few examine whether the underlying LLM's confidence is itself trustworthy before aggregating it; and where multi-agent or multi-model aggregation is attempted [13], it discards confidence entirely rather than calibrating and fusing it. This paper addresses all three within a single pipeline.

3 Our Methodology

3.1 Research Design Overview

Three design principles run through the architecture. Shared model isolation: both agents use the same underlying LLM, so any behavioral difference is attributable to the evidence pipeline, not the model. Preserved confidence: neither agent collapses its output to a binary verdict before calibration—raw logits are carried forward so the calibration step operates on the model's actual confidence rather than a thresholded approximation. Modularity: agents, calibrators, and fusion strategies are connected through fixed data interfaces, so any one stage can be replaced without touching the others (Fig. 1).

3.2 Problem Formulation

A knowledge graph $G = (E, R, T)$ consists of entities E, relations R, and triples $T \subseteq E \times R \times E$. Given a triple $x = (h, r, t)$, the goal is to learn $f : E \times R \times E \rightarrow$

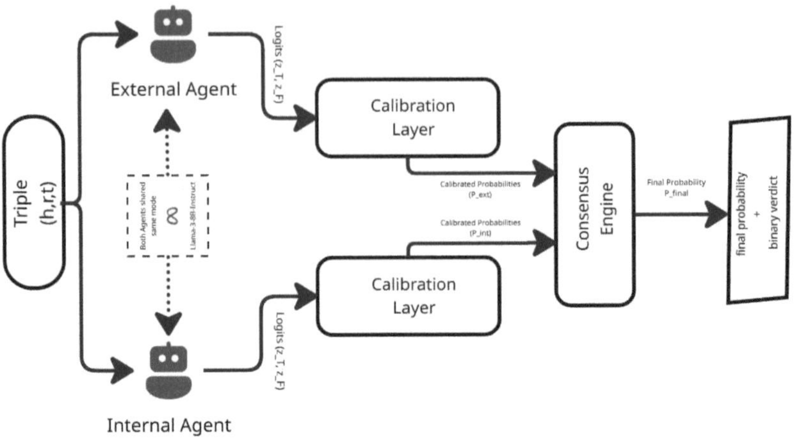

Fig. 1. Architecture of the calibrated dual-agent consensus framework

$\{0, 1\}$, induced from a predicted probability $\hat{p}(x) \in [0, 1]$ thresholded at 0.5.
An **agent** here is a specialized inference pipeline that retrieves context for a triple, constructs a prompt from a fixed template, queries an LLM exactly once, and returns a logit pair (z_T, z_F) over the True/False output tokens. Agents are stateless and deterministic given fixed retrieval results, with no planning, tool invocation, or feedback loop – a narrower scope than the autonomous-agent definition common in the broader AI literature.
Expected Calibration Error (ECE), used throughout Sect. 5, bins predictions into $M = 10$ equal-width confidence bins:

$$\mathrm{ECE} = \sum_{m=1}^{M} \frac{|B_m|}{N} \left|\mathrm{acc}(B_m) - \mathrm{conf}(B_m)\right| \tag{1}$$

where $\mathrm{acc}(B_m)$ and $\mathrm{conf}(B_m)$ are bin m's accuracy and mean predicted confidence.

3.3 Dual-Agent Pipelines

The **External Agent** retrieves Wikidata evidence. The cleaned triple's head and tail entities are looked up in a static, offline-built Wikidata subset – avoiding live-API rate limits and temporal drift – and each retrieved (entity, property, value) fact is formatted as a natural-language sentence. The triple and all candidate sentences are embedded with `all-MiniLM-L6-v2` [12], and the top-k ($k = 3$) sentences by cosine similarity are selected as evidence ($k = 3$ balances evidence diversity against the risk that more chunks add noise that degrades the LLM's judgment). The retrieved evidence and triple are inserted into a fixed prompt template, and a single forward pass through Meta-Llama-3-8B-Instruct [4] yields

$$(z_T, z_F) = (l_{\mathrm{True}}, l_{\mathrm{False}}) \tag{2}$$

the logits at the final position restricted to the True/False vocabulary entries.

The **Internal Agent** extracts bidirectional subgraphs. After verifying both entities exist in the training graph (otherwise returning a fallback of verdict = 0, confidence = 0), it extracts four directional subgraphs around the candidate triple following Li et al.'s decomposition [6] – head-forward, head-backward, tail-forward, tail-backward – each capped at five triples to bound prompt length. The candidate triple itself is explicitly removed from all four subgraphs even when present in the training set: this **data-leakage guard** is critical because calibration is fit on a subset of the same test triples, and any leakage would both inflate accuracy and corrupt the calibration fit. The leak-free subgraphs are rendered as a labeled context block and passed through the same prompt-template-and-LLM procedure as the External Agent.

3.4 Calibration Layer

Raw logits are converted to probabilities via softmax, which is severely miscalibrated for both agents (Sect. 5.1). Four post-hoc calibrators are evaluated, each fit on a 60% train split and **selected by lowest ECE on a held-out** 20% **validation split** – selection is performed entirely on validation, never on the test split, which is touched only for final reporting. **Temperature scaling** [5] rescales both logits by a single learned scalar T:

$$p_{\text{temp}}(x;T) = \frac{\exp(z_T/T)}{\exp(z_T/T) + \exp(z_F/T)} \tag{3}$$

Being rank-preserving, it is accuracy-preserving by construction – a confidence-only correction that cannot fix a systematic class bias. **Platt scaling** [11] fits a logistic regression on the logit difference $\Delta z = z_T - z_F$:

$$p_{\text{platt}}(x;A,B) = \sigma(A \cdot \Delta z + B) = \frac{1}{1 + \exp(-(A \cdot \Delta z + B))} \tag{4}$$

The intercept B gives Platt scaling a second degree of freedom that temperature scaling lacks, letting it correct systematic over-prediction of one class. **Isotonic regression** [16], fit via the Pool-Adjacent-Violators algorithm [1], is a non-parametric monotonic step function with no fixed functional form – more flexible than the parametric methods, at the cost of needing sufficient validation data to avoid overfitting. **Chained temperature-then-Platt** fits T first, then (A, B) on the temperature-scaled logits:

$$p_{\text{chain}}(x;T,A,B) = \sigma\left(A \cdot \frac{\Delta z}{T} + B\right) \tag{5}$$

This is algebraically identical to plain Platt scaling with a re-parameterized slope:

$$\sigma\left(A \cdot \frac{\Delta z}{T} + B\right) = \sigma(A' \cdot \Delta z + B), \quad \text{where } A' = \frac{A}{T} \tag{6}$$

proven both algebraically here and empirically in Sect. 5, where the chained calibrator reproduces Platt's ECE and accuracy exactly, confirming it is not an independent fifth method.

3.5 Consensus Engine

Let $P_{\text{ext}}(x), P_{\text{int}}(x) \in [0,1]$ be the agents' calibrated True-class probabilities. A fusion strategy

$$\Phi : [0,1] \times [0,1] \to [0,1] \tag{7}$$

maps these to a final probability, thresholded at 0.5.

Static fusion [3]? applies a fixed linear-opinion-pool weight to every triple:

$$\Phi_{\text{static}}(P_{\text{ext}}, P_{\text{int}}; w) = w \cdot P_{\text{ext}} + (1-w) \cdot P_{\text{int}} \tag{8}$$

evaluated at $w = 0.5$, 0.7 (external-favored), and 0.3 (internal-favored). **Adaptive fusion** weights agents per-triple by confidence,

$$c_a(x) = |P_a(x) - 0.5|, \quad a \in \{\text{ext}, \text{int}\} \tag{9}$$

the distance from the decision boundary. The three strategies differ in how they use this signal:

- *Max-Confidence* is a hard, discontinuous rule:

$$\Phi_{\text{max-conf}} = \begin{cases} 0.5 \cdot P_{\text{ext}} + 0.5 \cdot P_{\text{int}} & \text{if } |c_{\text{ext}} - c_{\text{int}}| < \tau, \\ P_{\text{ext}} & \text{if } c_{\text{ext}} \geq c_{\text{int}} \text{ and gap} \geq \tau, \\ P_{\text{int}} & \text{otherwise.} \end{cases} \tag{10}$$

  It selects the more confident agent outright when the confidence gap exceeds $\tau = 0.05$, and falls back to an equal 50/50 blend below that threshold.
- *Decisiveness* is continuous:

$$\Phi_{\text{decisive}} = \frac{c_{\text{ext}}}{c_{\text{ext}} + c_{\text{int}}} \cdot P_{\text{ext}} + \frac{c_{\text{int}}}{c_{\text{ext}} + c_{\text{int}}} \cdot P_{\text{int}} \tag{11}$$

  There is no cutoff – it reduces exactly to 50/50 when both agents are equally confident, and shifts smoothly toward the more confident agent otherwise, never fully discarding either.
- *ECE-weighted decisiveness* further scales each agent's decisiveness weight by a validation-split trust term

$$q_a = \frac{1}{1 + \text{ECE}_a} \tag{12}$$

  discounting an agent that has proven less calibrated overall, even on triples where it is locally confident:

$$\Phi_{\text{ece-dec}} = \frac{q_{\text{ext}} \cdot c_{\text{ext}}}{q_{\text{ext}} \cdot c_{\text{ext}} + q_{\text{int}} \cdot c_{\text{int}}} \cdot P_{\text{ext}} + \frac{q_{\text{int}} \cdot c_{\text{int}}}{q_{\text{ext}} \cdot c_{\text{ext}} + q_{\text{int}} \cdot c_{\text{int}}} \cdot P_{\text{int}} \tag{13}$$

Because Max-Confidence and Decisiveness both collapse to the 50/50 blend whenever the confidence gap is small, the two can produce identical predictions to Static 50/50 on triples where neither agent strongly dominates (Sect. 5.3).

4 Results

4.1 Calibration Reduces Miscalibration (RQ1)

Both agents are severely miscalibrated before correction. The External Agent reports a mean confidence of 0.9652 while achieving only 82.21% accuracy; the Internal Agent reports 0.9187 mean confidence against 72.78% accuracy (Table 1).

Table 1. Test-split ECE and accuracy per calibration method, FB13. Bold marks the best value per column. The chained calibrator is numerically identical to Platt in every cell, confirming the equivalence proven in Sect. 3.4.

Method	Ext. ECE	Ext. Acc.	Int. ECE	Int. Acc.
Uncalibrated	0.1445	0.8221	0.1909	0.7278
Temperature	0.0454	0.8221	0.0499	0.7278
Platt	0.0570	**0.8248**	0.0210	0.7968
Isotonic	**0.0046**	0.8221	**0.0102**	**0.7978**
Chained (T→P)	0.0570	0.8248	0.0210	0.7968

Isotonic regression achieves the lowest ECE for both agents – 0.0046 for the External Agent and 0.0102 for the Internal Agent, roughly an order of magnitude below the uncalibrated baseline (0.1445 and 0.1909, respectively). Temperature scaling reduces ECE substantially (to 0.0454 and 0.0499) while leaving accuracy exactly unchanged, confirming it is a confidence-only transformation. Platt and isotonic both shift accuracy upward for the Internal Agent specifically, from 0.7278 to 0.7968 (Platt) and 0.7978 (isotonic), because their fitted functions are not constrained to be rank-preserving and can move the effective decision threshold. The External Agent's fallback rate (no usable Wikidata evidence) is 0.30%, and the Internal Agent's is 0.00%; coverage does not materially limit either agent's evaluated accuracy on FB13.

4.2 Dual-Agent Consensus vs. Single-Agent Baselines (RQ2)

The best calibrated single agent on FB13 is the External Agent at 0.8248 (Platt scaling); the Internal Agent's best is 0.7978 (isotonic), a margin of 0.0270 in the External Agent's favor. The best configuration across the full calibration $\times$ fusion grid reaches **0.8751 accuracy** (isotonic calibration, under any of the three symmetric fusion strategies), a gain of **+0.0503** over the best single agent. Statistical significance is evaluated with McNemar's test on paired binary predictions, with continuity correction:

$$\chi^2 = \frac{(|b - c| - 1)^2}{b + c} \tag{14}$$

Table 2. Best single agent vs. best consensus and McNemar's test, FB13 ($n = 6{,}364$).

Accuracy comparison	
Best single agent (External, Platt)	0.8248
Best consensus (isotonic, symmetric fusion)	0.8751
Δ	+0.0503
McNemar's test	
b	577
c	257
χ^2	122.02
p-value	2.3×10^{-28}
Significant at $\alpha = 0.05$	**Yes**

where b is the number of triples the consensus predicts correctly and the single agent predicts incorrectly, and c is the reverse (Table 2).

The improvement is overwhelmingly significant. $b \gg c$ (577 vs. 257) indicates the gain is not an artifact of a handful of discordant predictions but a broad-based correction across hundreds of triples the single best agent got wrong (Table 3).

4.3 Fusion Strategy Comparison (RQ3)

Table 3. Consensus accuracy across the six fusion strategies at fixed isotonic calibration, FB13.

Fusion strategy	Accuracy
Static 50/50	**0.8751**
Static 70/30 (external-heavy)	0.8668
Static 30/70 (internal-heavy)	0.8371
Max-Confidence	**0.8751**
Decisiveness	**0.8751**
ECE-weighted decisiveness	0.8686

Static 50/50, Max-Confidence, and Decisiveness tie exactly at 0.8751. This is not coincidental: both adaptive strategies reduce to the 50/50 blend whenever the per-sample confidence gap between agents falls below the $\tau = 0.05$ threshold (Sect. 3.5), and on FB13 this condition holds for a large share of test triples, so all three select identical predictions. The asymmetric static splits underperform: weighting the weaker Internal Agent more heavily (30/70) costs 0.0380 relative to the symmetric strategies – the largest spread observed across the six strategies – while over-weighting the stronger External Agent (70/30) costs a smaller 0.0083.

5 Conclusion and Future Work

This paper investigated whether post-hoc calibration combined with dual-perspective evidence fusion produces reliable knowledge graph triple validation using a single open-source LLM, evaluated on FB13. Three findings follow the three research questions.

First, post-hoc calibration substantially reduces miscalibration (RQ1): isotonic regression cuts ECE by roughly an order of magnitude for both agents ($0.1445 \rightarrow 0.0046$ External; $0.1909 \rightarrow 0.0102$ Internal), with calibration-method selection performed strictly on a held-out validation split rather than the test split. Llama-3-8B-Instruct's miscalibration profile is not well approximated by the parametric families that temperature and Platt scaling represent, which is why the non-parametric isotonic calibrator wins on both agents. Notably, the Internal Agent's accuracy itself improves under calibration ($0.7278 \rightarrow 0.7978$) – not a coincidence, since temperature scaling, which is accuracy-preserving by construction, leaves it unchanged, while Platt and isotonic, which are free to shift the decision threshold, both move it in the same direction. This indicates the uncalibrated Internal Agent systematically over-predicts the True class, and calibration corrects a genuine class bias rather than introducing noise.

Second, dual-agent consensus significantly outperforms the best calibrated single agent (RQ2): 0.8751 vs. 0.8248, a highly significant gain (McNemar's test, $p = 2.3 \times 10^{-28}$) driven by $b = 577$ triples the single agent got wrong and consensus corrected, against only $c = 257$ in the opposite direction.

Third, fusion strategy matters moderately on FB13 (RQ3): the symmetric strategies (Static 50/50, Max-Confidence, Decisiveness) tie at the top (0.8751), while internal-heavy weighting (Static 30/70) costs 0.0380 relative to them – consistent with the External Agent being the stronger of the two on this dataset.

Limitations. This evaluation covers a single encyclopedic KG (FB13) and a single LLM backbone; whether the same calibration and fusion patterns hold on structurally different KGs or other open-source LLM families remains an open question. We do not re-implement MAKGED [6], TCM [15], KGValidator [2], or FactCheck [13] as live baselines under identical splits: MAKGED requires per-graph LoRA fine-tuning of four separate agents, FactCheck's strongest configuration requires live web search access, and none of the four report ECE or calibrated probabilities, making a like-for-like calibration comparison without re-implementing each from scratch not meaningful within this paper's scope. The External Agent's $k = 3$ retrieval depth and the Internal Agent's five-triple-per-direction subgraph cap were chosen on prompt-length grounds rather than via a hyperparameter sweep.

Future Work includes: (1) extending evaluation to structurally distinct KG types (lexical-semantic, sparse RDF-derived) to test whether the patterns observed here generalize, which a single-dataset study cannot establish; (2) replicating the experiments with other open-source LLM backbones; (3) an ablation over the External Agent's retrieval depth and the Internal Agent's subgraph cap; and (4) extending beyond binary verdicts to multi-class or ordinal validation (outdated facts, partial truths), which would require generalizing both the calibration layer and the fusion strategies to richer probability distributions.

Disclosure of Interests. The authors have no competing interests to declare that are relevant to the content of this article.

References

1. Ayer, M., Brunk, H.D., Ewing, G.M., Reid, W.T., Silverman, E.: An empirical distribution function for sampling with incomplete information. Ann. Math. Stat. **26**(4), 641–647 (1955)
2. Boylan, J., Mangla, S., Thorn, D., Ghalandari, D.G., Ghaffari, P., Hokamp, C.: KGValidator: a framework for automatic validation of knowledge graph construction. arXiv preprint arXiv:2404.15923 (2024). https://arxiv.org/abs/2404.15923
3. Genest, C., McConway, K.J.: Allocating the weights in the linear opinion pool. J. Forecast. **9**(1), 53–73 (1990)
4. Grattafiori, A., et al.: The llama 3 herd of models. arXiv preprint arXiv:2407.21783 (2024). https://doi.org/10.48550/arXiv.2407.21783. https://arxiv.org/abs/2407.21783
5. Guo, C., Pleiss, G., Sun, Y., Weinberger, K.Q.: On calibration of modern neural networks. In: International Conference on Machine Learning (ICML), pp. 1321–1330. PMLR (2017)
6. Li, Y., et al.: Harnessing diverse perspectives: a multi-agent framework for enhanced error detection in knowledge graphs. In: International Conference on Database Systems for Advanced Applications (DASFAA), pp. 446–458. Springer Nature Singapore, Singapore (2025)
7. Lin, Z., Hooi, B.: Enhancing multi-agent debate system performance via confidence expression. In: Findings of the Association for Computational Linguistics: EMNLP 2025, pp. 6453–6471. Association for Computational Linguistics, Suzhou, China (2025)
8. Lu, Y., Liang, Z., Rao, Y., Fan, W., Wang, F.L., Li, Q.: Double-calibration: Towards trustworthy LLMs via calibrating knowledge and reasoning confidence. arXiv preprint arXiv:2601.11956 (2026). https://arxiv.org/abs/2601.11956
9. Pan, S., Luo, L., Wang, Y., Chen, C., Wang, J., Wu, X.: Unifying large language models and knowledge graphs: a roadmap. IEEE Trans. Knowl. Data Eng. **36**(7), 3580–3599 (2024)
10. Paulheim, H.: Knowledge graph refinement: a survey of approaches and evaluation methods. Semantic Web **8**(3), 489–508 (2017)
11. Platt, J.C.: Probabilistic outputs for support vector machines and comparisons to regularized likelihood methods. In: Smola, A.J., Bartlett, P.L., Schölkopf, B., Schuurmans, D. (eds.) Advances in Large Margin Classifiers, pp. 61–74. MIT Press (1999)
12. Reimers, N., Gurevych, I.: Sentence-BERT: sentence embeddings using siamese BERT-networks. In: Proceedings of the 2019 Conference on Empirical Methods in Natural Language Processing and the 9th International Joint Conference on Natural Language Processing (EMNLP-IJCNLP), pp. 3982–3992. Association for Computational Linguistics, Hong Kong, China (2019). https://doi.org/10.18653/v1/D19-1410, https://aclanthology.org/D19-1410

13. Shami, F., Marchesin, S., Silvello, G.: Benchmarking large language models for knowledge graph validation. arXiv preprint arXiv:2602.10748 (2026). https://arxiv.org/abs/2602.10748
14. Socher, R., Chen, D., Manning, C.D., Ng, A.: Reasoning with neural tensor networks for knowledge base completion. In: Advances in Neural Information Processing Systems (NIPS), vol. 26. Curran Associates, Inc. (2013). https://proceedings.neurips.cc/paper/2013/hash/b3377a10425a350029349c6565bc9c6d-Abstract.html
15. Wu, T., et al.: Triple confidence measurement in knowledge graph with multiple heterogeneous evidences. World Wide Web **27**(6), 70 (2024)
16. Zadrozny, B., Elkan, C.: Transforming classifier scores into accurate multiclass probability estimates. In: Proceedings of the 8th ACM SIGKDD International Conference on Knowledge Discovery and Data Mining (KDD), pp. 694–699. ACM Press (2002)

Towards Natural Language Reasoning and Hybrid Querying over Virtual Knowledge Graphs

Indeewari Balasooriya(✉), Anna Dalla Vecchia, and Elisa Quintarelli

Department of Computer Science, University of Verona, Verona, Italy
{indeewari.balasooriya,anna.dallavecchia,elisa.quintarelli}@univr.it

Abstract. Virtual Knowledge Graphs (VKGs) provide a semantic layer for unified access to heterogeneous, distributed data sources, but still require expertise in formal query languages such as SPARQL. In this work, we present a framework that combines VKGs with Large Language Models (LLMs) to support natural language querying and reasoning. The approach leverages LLMs for both mapping generation, linking data sources to the VKG, and natural language-to-SPARQL translation.

Our preliminary findings indicate that not all user queries can be expressed as declarative queries. While factual questions can be answered through SPARQL, analytical requests, such as preference inference, require data-driven reasoning. To address this limitation, we propose a hybrid architecture that combines symbolic querying with model-based inference modules. This work highlights the opportunities and challenges of integrating declarative and statistical approaches, paving the way for more expressive natural language interfaces in complex data environments.

Keywords: Natural Language Interface · Virtual Knowledge Graphs · NL2SPARQL

1 Introduction

The widespread use of heterogeneous and distributed data sources has made unified, user-friendly data access both a challenge and an opportunity. Traditional data integration approaches, such as Local-as-View and Global-as-View [7], often rely on costly data warehousing or manual schema alignment, limiting scalability and flexibility. Knowledge graphs have emerged as a powerful paradigm for representing and querying structured data through a semantic layer, but building and maintaining centralized knowledge graphs remains resource-intensive, particularly in dynamic or decentralized environments.

Virtual Knowledge Graphs (VKGs) offer a lightweight alternative by enabling unified access to distributed data without physical integration. Through semantic mappings that connect data sources to a shared ontology, VKGs allow heterogeneous data to be queried as a single knowledge graph. However, they still

© The Author(s), under exclusive license to Springer Nature Switzerland AG 2027
G. Vargas Solar et al. (Eds.): ADBIS 2026, CCIS 3175, pp. 72–81, 2027.
https://doi.org/10.1007/978-3-032-39823-9_7

require expertise in formal query languages such as SPARQL, creating a barrier for non-expert users.

Recent advances in Large Language Models (LLMs) offer new opportunities to address this limitation. LLMs can support both the automatic generation of semantic mappings and the translation of natural language queries into formal query languages. To achieve this goal, we present a framework that integrates LLM-driven generation and natural language-to-SPARQL (NL2SPARQL) translation within a VKG setting.

However, our preliminary findings suggest that not all natural language queries can be effectively mapped to SPARQL. While factual and relational questions, such as "Which museums are open in Verona in winter?" or "Which hotels are located near the Arena?" can be directly translated into declarative queries, more analytical questions, such as "What are the preferences of tourists in Verona during winter?", require a different form of reasoning. These queries involve aggregating across multiple behavioral observations, interpreting latent concepts (e.g., "preferences"), and potentially performing predictive or clustering analyses of user behavior. Such information is typically not explicitly represented in the underlying data sources or in the VKG itself, and therefore cannot be directly retrieved through SPARQL. Instead, it must be inferred using statistical or machine learning techniques. This observation highlights the need for hybrid approaches that combine symbolic querying (e.g., SPARQL) with data-driven inference. At the same time, this direction introduces several challenges, including determining when to trigger an appropriate analytical workflow, integrating symbolic and statistical reasoning, and designing unified interfaces that remain interpretable to end users. These findings point to a promising yet complex research direction toward more expressive and flexible natural language querying systems.

Contribution. In this paper, we propose a preliminary framework shown in Fig. 1 that leverages a VKG to provide a unified semantic abstraction across multiple, possibly heterogeneous, data sources. In particular, we exploit OnTop [4], an open-source OBDA system that exposes relational databases as virtual RDF graphs by linking ontology terms, namely classes and properties, to underlying data sources through mappings. The resulting VKG can be uniformly queried using SPARQL, which Ontop transparently translates into SQL queries executed over the relational databases. Unlike a purely NL2SPARQL pipeline, our approach introduces a reasoning step that analyzes the user input before query generation. This step determines whether the natural language request corresponds to a query over the integrated data sources or to an analytical inference task. In the former case, the input is translated into SPARQL and executed over the VKG through OnTop. In the latter case, the request is routed to an inference component, where relevant data retrieved from the underlying sources are processed by a machine learning or deep learning model according to the specific inference needs, such as preference inference. Building on this hybrid architecture, we introduce a natural language interface that supports both declarative querying and model-based reasoning over heterogeneous data. Declarative queries are handled by translating natural language requests into SPARQL, while analytical or preference-oriented requests are addressed by a dedicated model inference component. The pipeline integrates schema-aware mapping, controlled query generation, and intent-aware reasoning, ensuring that user requests are aligned with the most suitable execution mechanism and the underlying data schema. This design bridges the semantic gap between non-expert users and formal query languages while extending the expressiveness of VKG-based access beyond factual retrieval, enabling both precise querying and inference-oriented analysis across distributed data sources.

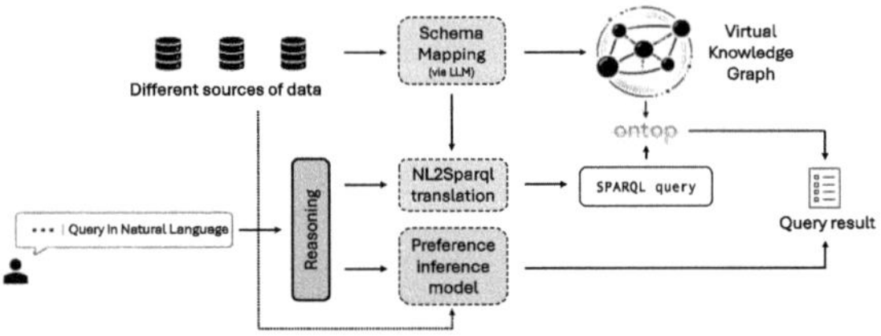

Fig. 1. Hybrid NL pipeline over a VKG integrating multiple data sources.

Running Example. We consider a tourism scenario in the city of Verona, integrating heterogeneous data sources related to points of interest (PoIs): (i) a relational database containing information on cultural attractions and tourist access through the Verona Card, and (ii) an image repository containing visual content associated with PoIs. These sources differ in structure and semantics, making them a suitable case study for evaluating a VKG-based approach.

The proposed pipeline virtually integrates these sources into a unified semantic layer. Through semantic mappings, the relational data is exposed as a VKG linking each PoI to its attributes, access rules, and multimedia resources. Users can then issue natural language queries such as "Which museums can I visit with the Verona Card?" or "Show me images of monuments included in the Verona Card circuit." The system translates these requests into SPARQL queries over the VKG, enabling user-friendly access to distributed tourism data without requiring knowledge of the underlying schemata or query language.

However, not all requests correspond to declarative retrieval tasks. For example, answering "What are the preferences of adult tourists visiting Verona during winter?" requires aggregating user behavior and inferring preferences from historical data. Such queries go beyond SPARQL-based retrieval and require integrating statistical or machine learning techniques.

Structure of the Paper. The remainder of the paper is organized as follows. In Sect. 2, the related work is discussed, while Sect. 3 introduces the framework and the case study. Finally, Sect. 4 summarizes the findings and outlines the future directions.

2 Related Work

Ontology-Based Data Access (OBDA) and, more recently, Virtual Knowledge Graphs (VKGs) provide a well-established paradigm for integrating heterogeneous data sources through a semantic layer without requiring data materialization [14]. In this setting, OnTop is one of the most widely adopted systems for exposing relational data as a virtual RDF graph and answering SPARQL queries by rewriting them into SQL over the original sources [4].

In VKG construction, there is the problem of mappings between source schemata and the target ontology. For instance, the authors in [10] introduced a benchmark specifically designed to evaluate automatic mapping generation in relational-to-ontology integration scenarios. Recent work has systematized recurrent solutions into a catalog of conceptually grounded mapping patterns for VKGs, highlighting that mapping design, validation, and maintenance remain key practical challenges [5]. Likewise, LLM4VKG [15] has been proposed to leverage large language models for automating VKG construction.

A complementary line of research investigates natural-language access to knowledge graphs and the translation of user questions into executable graph queries. Some preliminary studies rely on template-based approaches that map natural-language questions to SPARQL query structures [13]. With the widespread use of large language models, this problem has been revisited, showing that LLMs can generate competitive SPARQL queries from natural language, even with in-context learning and without task-specific fine-tuning [6]. At the same time, recent work has shown that LLM-based semantic parsing is still affected by faithfulness and hallucination issues, especially when generating entities, relations, or URIs that must match the target graph exactly [11,16]. The task of identifying the correct path for managing a user's natural language query aligns with recent work on intent detection and query routing, where LLMs are used to infer user intent and dispatch queries to the most suitable processing pipeline. For example, in [2], the authors demonstrate how LLMs can effectively classify intents, enabling the distinction between declarative queries and analytical tasks such as recommendation or preference inference.

Compared with these works, our framework combines all the above-mentioned aspects: LLM-assisted intent detection, the construction of a VKG across multiple heterogeneous data sources, and the translation of natural-language questions into executable SPARQL queries over that virtual semantic layer.

3 Framework

In this section, we present the proposed framework and describe its components in detail. As illustrated in Fig. 1, we consider a setting in which data is distributed across heterogeneous sources, potentially adopting different storage technologies and schemas, while remaining in their original sources and without requiring data replication or centralization. The goal is to enable users to query such data through natural language, without requiring knowledge of the underlying data structures, query languages, or inference models.

The Virtual Knowledge Graph and the Mappings with Data Sources. The first step aims to define a unified, abstract representation of the data. In our approach, we adopt a Virtual Knowledge Graph (VKG) that provides a semantic abstraction layer over heterogeneous data sources without requiring materialization. The mapping between the original data sources and the VKG is automatically generated using a prompt-based approach built on GPT-4.1 mini [9]. The model is leveraged to infer semantic correspondences between source schemas and the VKG ontology. These mappings are formulated following the Ontology-Based Data Access (OBDA) paradigm [4]. Each mapping rule specifies (i) a source query, expressed in SQL, that retrieves a set of tuples from the underlying relational database, and (ii) a target template, expressed in the RDF mapping language, that instantiates the ontology terms (e.g., classes, object properties, and datatype properties) from the retrieved tuples.

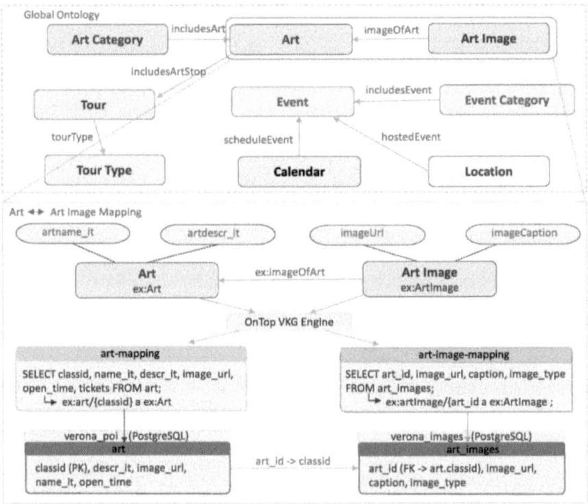

Fig. 2. OBDA mapping architecture for the Verona PoIs Virtual Knowledge Graph, illustrated for the Art-ArtImage sub-schema.

Figure 2 provides a two-level view of the resulting Virtual Knowledge Graph. The upper layer shows the global ontology structure, comprising the classes `Art`, `ArtImage`, `ArtCategory`, `Tour`, `TourType`, `Event`, `EventCategory`, `Calendar`, and `Location`, together with the object properties that relate them. The lower layer focuses on the `Art`–`ArtImage` sub-graph, showing the two OBDA mapping rules, the corresponding SQL source queries, and the relational tables from which the virtual triples are generated. This diagram illustrates how OnTop exposes data from two physically separate PostgreSQL databases as a coherent, queryable RDF graph without requiring data replication.

Multi-source Integration. A key feature of the present setting is that the data sources span multiple, physically separate databases. In our Verona tourism case study, the main relational database (`verona_poi`) stores descriptive and operational data about PoIs, while a second database (`verona_images`) stores images associated with those PoIs. Cross-database references are resolved at the mapping level: the `art-image-mapping` rule joins the `art_images` table on the foreign key `art_id`, which corresponds to `art.classid` in the primary database, and instantiates the `ex:ArtImage` class with an `ex:imageOfArt` object property linking each image to its associated `ex:Art` instance. At runtime, OnTop translates the incoming SPARQL query into federated SQL that spans both databases, exploiting PostgreSQL Foreign Data Wrappers (FDW) to materialize the cross-database join transparently.

Natural Language Query Reasoning. Our framework analyzes the user's natural language request to determine whether it corresponds to a factual query over the integrated data sources or to an analytical inference task. In the first case, the expected output can be obtained by querying the data sources through the VKG, without requiring additional processing beyond query translation and execution. These requests are therefore routed to an NL2SPARQL component, which generates a SPARQL query to be executed over the VKG. In the second case, the request cannot be satisfied by simply retrieving explicitly represented data. Instead, it requires a more complex analytical process to derive implicit information from the available data. These requests are routed to a model-based inference component, where the relevant data are processed using a machine learning or deep learning model according to the specific task.

From Text to SPARQL. To translate natural language queries into SPARQL, we integrated SPARQL-LLM [12], a competitor in the Text2SPARQL challenge, into our pipeline. It is an open-source, triplestore-agnostic framework for translating natural language queries into SPARQL. The approach leverages standardized metadata automatically extracted from SPARQL endpoints. Two main categories of metadata are required:

1. pairs of SPARQL query examples and their natural language descriptions, encoded as RDF graphs and annotated with SHACL-based vocabularies.
2. a data-aware schema that captures the structural characteristics of the underlying dataset, potentially enriched with frequency indicators. To obtain this information, SPARQL-LLM retrieves VoID [1] descriptions from each endpoint.

The overall data flow of SPARQL-LLM consists of a multi-stage pipeline. The process begins with question decomposition, in which the input natural language query is analyzed to extract potential sub-questions and identify relevant schema classes. Subsequently, embeddings are computed for both the extracted sub-questions and the identified classes. These embeddings are then used to perform similarity-based retrieval of relevant contextual information, including related query examples and schema elements.

Once the SPARQL query is generated, it is executed over the Virtual Knowledge Graph through OnTop [4]. OnTop is an Ontology-Based Data Access (OBDA) system that enables querying relational data as if it were exposed as an RDF graph, without requiring data materialization. It achieves this by rewriting SPARQL queries into equivalent SQL queries based on predefined mappings between the ontology and the underlying data sources.

In our framework, the generated SPARQL query is then provided as input to OnTop, which handles the translation and execution over the original data sources. The results are then returned to the user in a structured format consistent with the semantics of the VKG.

Model-Based Inference. Analytical and preference-oriented questions often require inferring latent information that is not explicitly encoded in the underlying data sources or the semantic layer.

In these cases, the framework orchestrates a dedicated inference workflow that combines data retrieval with machine learning or deep learning models. The retrieved data are processed to infer behavioral patterns, preferences, or predictive insights, and the resulting output is returned to the user as the answer to the original query.

As an initial step, we consider a lightweight preference inference module to derive aggregate tourist preferences from interaction and contextual data, currently limited to temporal data. Given a natural language request such as "What are the preferences of tourists visiting Verona during winter?", the framework first identifies the relevant temporal context, such as the season. It then retrieves corresponding data from the underlying sources, including visits through Verona cards. In addition to these data, a simple analytical model, such as frequency-based ranking, is applied to identify recurrent patterns in tourist behavior. For example, the module may infer that winter visitors tend to prefer museums included in the Verona Card circuit or monuments located near the city center [3]. The output is therefore not a direct fact retrieved from the VKG, but an inferred preference profile derived from observed behavioral patterns.

3.1 Case Study

We evaluate the proposed framework on a real-world case study in the tourism domain, focusing on Points of Interest (PoIs) in Verona, Italy.

The dataset, introduced in [8], includes heterogeneous information for each PoI, including descriptive metadata, events, tourist affluence data spanning 2014 to 2022, and daily weather conditions. Furthermore, geospatial information, such as the location of PoIs and tourist routes, is stored, enabling the representation and querying of spatial data. In addition to this information, a separate CSV file collects links to images associated with each PoI. This setting provides a representative example of heterogeneous data sources with different schemas and modalities, making it particularly suitable for evaluating the effectiveness of our approach for integrating and querying data via natural language.

To better illustrate the behavior of the proposed system, we developed a web application that allows users to observe the execution of natural language queries on the VKG. More specifically, Fig. 3a shows the query formulation phase, in which a user-provided natural-language question is processed through the entire translation and execution pipeline. Figure 3b presents the corresponding query results retrieved from the heterogeneous data sources integrated within the VKG.

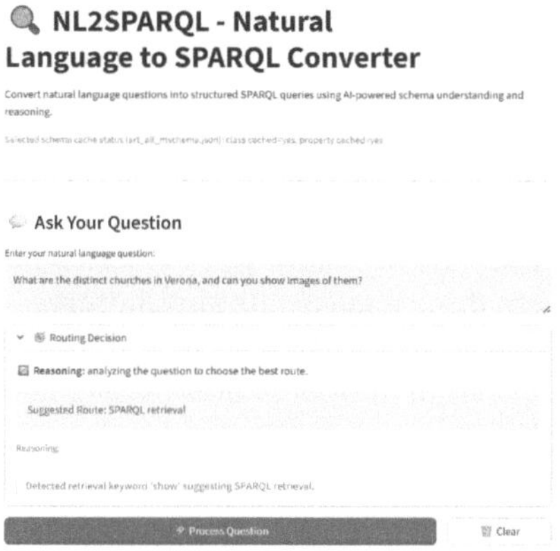

(a) User interface for natural language query processing.

(b) Query results returned from the VKG. The output integrates structured data with associated multimedia content.

Fig. 3. Overview of the NL query interface and the generated VKG results.

Preliminary Evaluation. To assess the feasibility of the proposed framework, we conducted a preliminary qualitative evaluation using a set of 50 natural language questions over the Verona tourism dataset. The question set comprises 40 factual questions expected to be answered via SPARQL over the VKG, and 10 analytical questions requiring model-based inference. The evaluation focuses on two aspects: (i) the correctness of the routing decision, i.e., whether the framework correctly identifies whether a question should be directed to the NL2SPARQL component or to the inference module; and (ii) the quality of the generated SPARQL queries for the factual subset. Table 1 summarizes the evaluation results across the two execution paths.

Routing Accuracy. The reasoning component, implemented as a prompt-based classifier using GPT-4.1 mini, correctly routed all 50 questions to the appropriate execution path. All 40 factual questions were correctly assigned to the NL2SPARQL component, and all 10 analytical questions were correctly directed to the model-based inference module. While the dataset is small and the evaluation is qualitative, this result indicates that the prompt-based intent classifier

Table 1. Preliminary qualitative evaluation of the framework.

Path	Component	Questions	Correct	Accuracy
Factual	Routing (NL2SPARQL)	40	40	100%
	SPARQL correctness	40	28	70%
Analytical	Routing (Inference)	10	10	100%
Total	Routing (All Questions)	**50**	**50**	**100%**

is effective at distinguishing between declarative and analytical user requests in the tourism domain.

SPARQL Generation Quality. For the 40 factual questions routed to the NL2SPARQL component, we evaluated the correctness of the generated SPARQL queries by executing them over the VKG using SPARQL-LLM. Of the 40 queries, 28 (70%) returned correct results. The remaining 12 queries produced either incorrect results, empty result sets due to entity-linking failures, or syntactically invalid SPARQL queries.

This simple evaluation highlights how the system supports non-expert users by exposing both the intermediate reasoning steps and the final integrated results.

4 Conclusion and Future Work

This work presents a preliminary framework that combines VKGs with LLMs to enable natural language querying across heterogeneous and distributed data sources. The proposed approach includes an intent-aware reasoning step that distinguishes between factual queries, which can be answered through SPARQL over the VKG, and analytical requests, which require model-based inference.

The Verona tourism case study highlights the potential of the proposed hybrid architecture. By combining a VKG with a natural language interface, the system enables non-expert users to query heterogeneous data sources. Preliminary results show effective handling of both factual and analytical queries, as well as promising performance on NL2SPARQL.

These findings highlight the potential of combining symbolic querying with data-driven inference to move beyond factual retrieval in VKGs. Future work will investigate intent detection and support for advanced analytical tasks, such as recommendations.

Acknowledgements. This work has been partially supported by DataGEMS, funded by the European Union's Horizon Europe Research and Innovation programme, under grant agreement No 101188416.

Declaration of use of Generative AI. During the preparation of this work, the authors used Grammarly to improve the grammar and readability of the manuscript. The authors take full responsibility for the final content of the manuscript and the associated software artifacts.

References

1. Describing linked datasets with the void vocabulary. https://www.w3.org/TR/void/
2. G. Arora, S. Jain, and S. Merugu. Intent detection in the age of LLMs. In: Proceedings of the 2024 Conference on Empirical Methods in Natural Language Processing: Industry Track, pp. 1559–1570 (2024)
3. Belussi, A., Cinelli, A., Vecchia, A.D., Migliorini, S., Quaresmini, M., Quintarelli, E.: Forecasting poi occupation with contextual machine learning. In: European Conference on Advances in Databases and Information Systems, pp. 361–376. Springer (2022)
4. Calvanese, D., et al.: Ontop: answering sparql queries over relational databases. Semantic Web **8**(3), 471–487 (2016)
5. Calvanese, D., Gal, A., Lanti, D., Montali, M., Mosca, A., Shraga, R.: Conceptually-grounded mapping patterns for virtual knowledge graphs. Data Knowledge Eng. **145**, 102157 (2023)
6. D'Abramo, J., Zugarini, A., Torroni, P.: Investigating large language models for text-to-sparql generation. In: Proceedings of the 4th International Workshop on Knowledge-Augmented Methods for Natural Language Processing, pp. 66–80 (2025)
7. Lenzerini, M.: Data integration: a theoretical perspective. In: Proceedings of the twenty-first ACM SIGMOD-SIGACT-SIGART symposium on Principles of database systems, pp. 233–246 (2002)
8. Migliorini, S., Vecchia, A.D., Belussi, A., Quintarelli, E.: ARTEMIS: a context-aware recommendation system with crowding forecaster for the touristic domain. Inf. Syst. Front. 1–27 (2024)
9. OpenAIs. Gpt-4 Technical report (2024)
10. Pinkel, C., et al.: Rodi: a benchmark for automatic mapping generation in relational-to-ontology data integration. In: European Semantic Web Conference, pp. 21–37. Springer (2015)
11. Sharma, A., Pal, C., Zouaq, A.: Reducing hallucinations in language model-based SPARQL query generation using post-generation memory retrieval. In: Findings of the Association for Computational Linguistics: EACL, vol. 2026, pp. 4657–4668 (2026)
12. Smeros, P., Emonet, V., Wang, R., Sima, A.-C., de Farias, T.M.: Sparql-llm: real-time sparql query generation from natural language questions. arXiv preprint arXiv:2512.14277 (2025)
13. Unger, C., Bühmann, L., Lehmann, J., Ngonga Ngomo, A.-C., Gerber, D., Cimiano, P.: Template-based question answering over RDF data. In: Proceedings of the 21st International Conference on World Wide Web, pp. 639–648 (2012)
14. Xiao, G., et al.: Ontology-based data access: a survey. In: Proceedings of the 27th International Joint Conference on Artificial Intelligence IJCAI-18, pp. 5511–5519 (2018)
15. Xiao, G., Ren, L., Qi, G., Xue, H., Di Panfilo, M., Lanti, D.: Llm4vkg: leveraging large language models for virtual knowledge graph construction. In: Proceedings of the Thirty-Fourth International Joint Conference on Artificial Intelligence, IJCAI-25, pp. 4715–4723 (2025)
16. Zhao, R., Zhao, F., Zhang, H.: Correcting on graph: Faithful semantic parsing over knowledge graphs with large language models. In: Findings of the Association for Computational Linguistics: ACL, vol. 2025, pp. 5364–5376 (2025)

Content Learning for Metadata Extraction and Enrichment of Historical Hand-Drawn Illustrations

Rajae El-Idrissi(✉), Juba Agoun, Jérôme Darmont, and Sabine Loudcher

UR ERIC, Université Lumière Lyon 2, Lyon, France
{rajae.el-idrissi,juba.agoun1,jerome.darmont,sabine.loudcher}@univ-lyon2.fr

Abstract. The digitisation of cultural heritage collections requires automated metadata generation to improve resource discovery and reuse. This paper presents the Content Learning for Metadata Extraction and Enrichment (CLEAD), a multimodal approach for generating metadata from illustrations in digitised archaeological diaries. CLEAD combines illustration detection and segmentation with vision-language and large language models to generate and enrich illustration descriptions using page-level textual context. Experiments on the DataLAC and IlluHisDoc datasets show that integrating visual and textual information improves the semantic quality and relevance of the generated metadata. These results demonstrate that CLEAD effectively supports the indexing and retrieval of visual heritage resources in digital archives and data lakes.

Keywords: Data Lakes · Metadata · Artificial Intelligence · Vision-Language Models · Historical Documents · Document Analysis

1 Introduction

Data lakes are widely used to store large, heterogeneous digitised collections, but storing data alone is insufficient. Without metadata, a data lake becomes a so-called data swamp that cannot be found or reused [7,20]. This issue appears across diverse domains where collection growth outpaces metadata creation [7].

The description of each data entity within a data lake is often created manually and is therefore time-consuming. Several research studies have proposed machine learning approaches to support metadata generation [1,2]. In this paper, we address the problem of metadata generation for image entities within a data lake, with the aim of automatically producing image descriptions. In this work, we focus on a specific type of image, namely hand-drawn illustrations. To the best of our knowledge, no existing approach is capable of automatically generating descriptions for hand-drawn illustrations. We selected this particular type of image because it reflects a real-world challenge encountered in the DataLAC

© The Author(s), under exclusive license to Springer Nature Switzerland AG 2027
G. Vargas Solar et al. (Eds.): ADBIS 2026, CCIS 3175, pp. 82–91, 2027.
https://doi.org/10.1007/978-3-032-39823-9_8

project, which aims to develop a data lake for organizing, querying, and analyzing the archaeological archives of a site in Spain [6].

In the DataLAC project we handle excavation diaries, which mix handwritten text, drawings and sketches called illustrations. Though Handwritten Text Recognition (HTR) can transcribe texts [16,18], illustrations remain undescribed. A vision-language model can caption an illustration, but it doesn't take into account the archaeological context (e.g., excavation sector, related artefact) recorded in the surrounding text (Fig. 1).

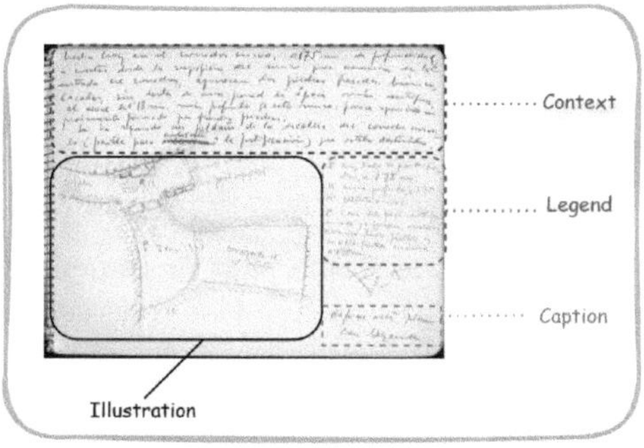

Fig. 1. Example excavation diary page

Combining visual content with page-level textual information transforms generic captions into meaningful metadata that supports retrieval and analysis. This work addresses two questions: how can vision-language models accurately describe illustrations, and how can these descriptions be enriched with textual context? To address these questions, we propose the Content Learning for Metadata Extraction and Enrichment (CLEAD), an approach that detects, segments, describes and enriches illustrations through multimodal analysis.

The remainder of this paper is structured as follows. Section 2 reviews related works. Section 3 presents the CLEAD approach. Section 4 describes two corpus and an evaluation protocol. Section 5 reports experimental results. Finally, Sect. 6 concludes and discusses future research.

2 Related Work

Automatically generating metadata has become a key research direction for managing large, heterogeneous digital collections. Early approaches relied on supervised learning, clustering, and topic modeling [3], while more recent work has shifted toward deep learning and large language models to produce richer, semantically grounded metadata with less human effort.

In multimodal settings, Boukhers and Bouabdallah [2] combined Bi-LSTM and Maks R-CNN to extract metadata from mixed- content documents, and He and Wang [8] used Bi-LSTM networks to standardise metadata across heterogeneous sources. LLM-based frameworks such as AutoDDG [25] and LEDD [1] further demonstrated that models like GPT and LLaMa can generate structured metadata directly from raw documents, substantially reducing annotation costs. For semantic enrichment, Mihindukulasooriya et al. [13] paired large language models with knowledge graphs to align metadata with domain ontologies, while Lobo et al. [12] used fondation models to produce human-readable semantic descriptions. Despite this progress, most existing work targets textual or tabular content. Automatic description of visual embedded in historical handwritten documents remains underexplored. ClEAD addresses this gap by combining vision-language models with page-level transcription context to generate enriched metadata for illustrations in digitised archaeological diaries.

3 CLEAD Approach

CLEAD consists of three sequential stages that incrementally enrich illustration metadata: identification and segmentation of visual regions within heterogeneous page layouts, followed by automated generation of context-sensitive descriptions linking visual and semantic data to each illustration (Fig. 2).

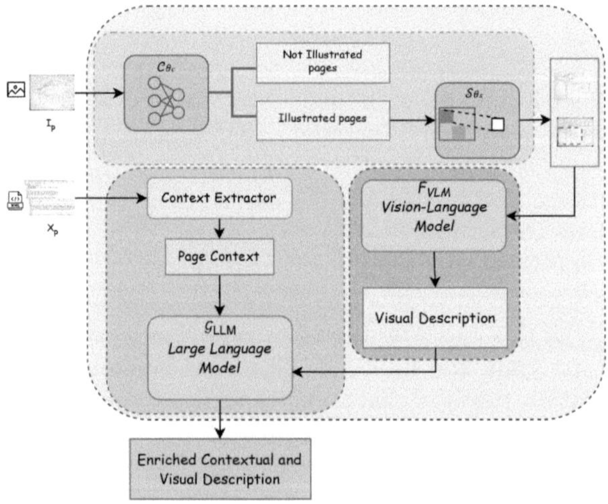

Fig. 2. CLEAD approach: from illustration detection to enriched metadata

3.1 Formalization

The CLEAD approach generates enriched illustration metadata for each page in a digital collection of archaeological diaries through three sequential steps.

For any given page, e.g., page number p, the page image is denoted as I_p and its XML/ALTO transcription as $\mathcal{X}_p$. The progressive development of the final illustration metadata M_p within CLEAD is formalised by Eq. 1.

$$M_p = \mathcal{G}_{\text{LLM}}\left(\mathcal{F}_{\text{VLM}}\left(\mathcal{S}_{\theta_s}(\mathcal{C}_{\theta_c}(I_p))\right), \mathcal{X}_p\right) \tag{1}$$

In Eq. 1, each element below corresponds to a distinct stage of the approach.

1. **Illustration Classification** $\mathcal{C}_{\theta_c}$. This initial stage automatically determines whether a page image I_p contains any illustrations, using a specific classifier with parameters θ_c.
2. **Illustration Segmentation** $\mathcal{S}_{\theta_s}$. For pages identified as containing illustrations, this stage further isolates and outlines the corresponding illustration regions by employing a segmentation model with parameters θ_s.
3. **Visual Description and Enrichment** $\mathcal{F}_{\text{VLM}}, \mathcal{G}_{\text{LLM}}$. This stage first utilises a vision-language model $\mathcal{F}_{\text{VLM}}$ to generate initial visual captions. Subsequently, a large language model $\mathcal{G}_{\text{LLM}}$ refines these descriptions by incorporating contextual information from the page transcription $\mathcal{X}_p$ to ensure relevance and accuracy.

This formalism captures the full CLEAD approach, from visual detection to context-aware semantic enrichment of archaeological diary illustrations.

3.2 Illustration Identification and Segmentation

The first stage of CLEAD identifies and localises illustrations on digitised diary pages using a supervised ResNet classifier [22], which effectively distinguishes illustrated pages from text-only pages despite challenges such as handwriting variability and image degradation. Where pages contain illustrations, a U-Net [19] segmentation model then isolates the precise contours of each illustration, generating distinct regions that serve as the foundation for subsequent metadata enrichment, as formalised by $\left(\mathcal{S}_{\theta_s}(\mathcal{C}_{\theta_c}(I_p))\right)$.

3.3 Visual-Based Illustration Description

CLEAD's second step creates descriptive metadata for each identified illustration, focusing on visual content. This stage uses the function $\mathcal{F}_{\text{VLM}}$, where advanced vision-language models, such as BLIP-2 [10], CLIP [17], GIT [23], ViT-GPT2 [14] and large-scale multimodal systems like LLaVA-1.5 [11], Gemini 2.5 [5] and GPT-4o [9], automatically generate natural language descriptions that accurately capture the salient visual characteristics of each illustration. Such models train on large-scale image and text corpora, which enables CLEAD to produce context-free captions as the initial layer of metadata. This visually grounded metadata is critical for effective indexing, retrieval and organisation of illustrations within extensive digital diary collections.

3.4 Contextual Enrichment with Page Transcriptions

In the third stage, formalised as G_{LLM}, initial visual descriptions are enriched with contextual information extracted from page-level transcriptions, including captions, labels, and XML/ALTO metadata. Gemini 2.5 [5], GPT-4o, GPT-4-turbo [9], and GPT-3.5-turbo [24] combine visual descriptions with textual context to generate more precise and interpretable metadata for indexing and retrieval. By generating visual captions first and enriching them with transcription data in a second step, CLEAD preserves visual grounding, limits transcription noise, and ensures compatibility with models that do not support contextual inputs, while enabling independent evaluation of each stage.

4 Experimental Protocol

4.1 Datasets

To evaluate the effectiveness of the CLEAD approach, experiments are conducted on two datasets: the DataLAC corpus and the IlluHisDoc benchmark [15].

DataLAC (Archaeological Excavation Diaries). The DataLAC dataset [6] originates from the digitisation of archaeological archives from the Puig de Sant Andreu (Ullastret) excavation site[1,2], comprising thirteen excavation diaries written between 1947 and 1977 by Miquel Oliva i Prat and collaborators. These documents mix handwritten notes, sketches, plans, photographs, and technical observations related to archaeological fieldwork. The digitised collection includes 2,558 scanned pages, of which 563 contain illustrations such as drawings, excavation plans, stratigraphic profiles, artefact representations, and maps. Illustrations were manually extracted by domain experts, and the dataset provides partial XML/ALTO transcriptions describing page content and layout.

IlluHisDoc (Historical Document Benchmark). The IlluHisDoc, introduced by Monnier and Aubry [15], is a public benchmark designed for illustration segmentation in historical documents. The dataset contains 400 annotated pages from various manuscript and printed sources, including scientific diagrams, illuminations, and mixed-layout documents. Pixel-level annotations enable accurate evaluation of segmentation methods across diverse document layouts and illustration styles.

4.2 Preprocessing and Training

Stratified splits address class imbalance, and data augmentation is applied through rotations, scaling, brightness adjustments, and horizontal flips. Polygonal annotations are converted into binary masks for segmentation training.

[1] http://datalac.huma-num.fr/.
[2] http://www.macullastret.cat/.

XML/ALTO files are parsed to extract captions and surrounding text, with relevant sentences selected based on spatial proximity to illustration regions. Non-English segments are translated using Helsinki-NLP MarianMT models [21]. ResNet is fine-tuned from pretrained weights using cross-entropy loss and Adam $lr = 10^{-4}$ over 3 epochs, while the U-Net architecture is trained with the same loss and Adam $lr = 10^{-3}$ for 100 epochs. All experiments ran on a single NVIDIA RTX A6000 GPU (48 GB VRAM), and the implementation is publicly available[3].

4.3 Prompting Procedure

State-of-the-art vision–language models are evaluated using a prompt-based approach without additional fine-tuning. Prompts were designed in collaboration with archaeologists to produce detailed, factual, and domain-relevant descriptions (Table 1), and are available in the project repository [3]. The evaluated models – GIT, ViT-GPT2, BLIP-2, CLIP, Gemini 2.5, GPT-4o, and LLaVA-1.5 – are tested under zero-shot and few-shot settings, with BLIP-2 and CLIP combined with FlanT5 [4] to improve output quality. For contextual enrichment, visual descriptions and XML/ALTO metadata are provided to Gemini 2.5, GPT-4o, GPT-4-turbo, and GPT-3.5-turbo through dedicated prompts.

Table 1. Prompting Protocol in Visual Description

Model	Zero-shot	Few-shot	Prompt
Git	✓	✓	Prompt 1 and 2 and 4
ViT-GPT2	✓	✓	Prompt 1 and 2 and 4
BLIP-2	✓	✓	Prompt 1 and 2 and 4
CLIP	✓	✓	Prompt 1 and 2 and 4
Gemini 2.5	✓	×	Prompt 1 and 2
GPT-4o	✓	×	Prompt 1 and 2
LLaVA-1.5	✓	✓	Prompt 1 and 3

4.4 Evaluation Metrics

To evaluate the performance of CLEAD, we use a combination of quantitative metrics and qualitative expert assessment, reflecting the different tasks involved in the approach.

For illustration classification, we report *precision*, *recall*, and *F1-score*. For segmentation, we use the *Dice coefficient*, *mean Intersection over Union (mIoU)*, and *pixel accuracy*. As the CLEAD approach includes generative description and

[3] https://git.msh-lse.fr/rajaeel-idrissi/clead-approach.

contextual enrichment stages, metadata quality is assessed through expert evaluation. Archaeological specialists evaluated the outputs according to visual accuracy, archaeological relevance, contextual consistency, and usefulness for indexing and retrieval. The protocol, designed in collaboration with domain experts, was applied to 34 illustrations for visual description and 14 illustrations for contextual enrichment. Experts examined both the illustrations and their associated transcriptions before selecting the most relevant model output based on overall quality, accuracy, and interpretability.

5 Results and Discussion

5.1 Visual Description

Both model architecture and prompting strategy significantly influence the quality of generated visual descriptions. On DataLAC, smaller models such as GIT and ViT-GPT2 fail to produce accurate archaeological descriptions even with few-shot prompting, indicating limited generalisation to this domain. BLIP-2 and CLIP combined with FlanT5 generate more relevant and context-specific descriptions, particularly when expert examples are included in the prompts. Among large multimodal models, Gemini 2.5 and GPT-4o consistently produce the richest descriptions when using structured prompts, effectively capturing the salient visual characteristics of each illustration such as drawing type, layout, visible annotations, and possible archaeological context. LLaVA with few-shot Prompt 3 also produces results comparable to archaeologist-written descriptions. Expert evaluation confirms these findings, with Expert 1 unanimously selecting Gemini 2.5 and Expert 2 unanimously selecting GPT-4o as the most coherent, informative, and contextually appropriate model across all 34 evaluated illustrations. Results on IlluHisDoc further confirm that prompt engineering and model selection are critical factors, with GPT-4o combined with a structured descriptive prompt producing the most accurate and informative descriptions by effectively distinguishing illustrations from surrounding textual content.

Prompt 1: Expert Prompt for Visual Description
You are an archaeological archivist. Describe this illustration in detail: 1. What objects or scenes are shown?
2. Drawing style and technique
3. Any visible text or labels
4. Likely archaeological context
5. Purpose of the drawing. Be factual and detailed.

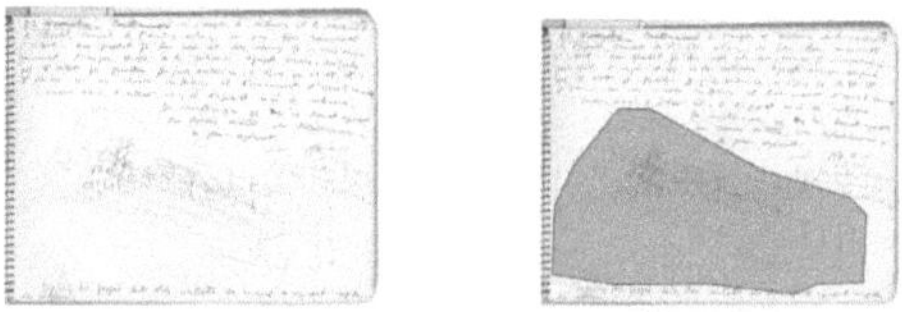

(a) Original page image *(b) Segmented illustration*

(c) Initial visual description.
Sketch of the profile of both sides of the corner walls of the cabin on the eastern slope.

(d) Contextually enriched description.
The image appears to be a detailed sketch depicting the profile of both sides of the corner walls of a cabin situated on the eastern slope. The drawing likely illustrates the structural design and architectural elements of the cabin's corner, focusing on how the walls intersect and form the angle. Despite the caption being absent, the sketch serves to provide visual insight into the construction and layout of this specific part of the cabin. Positioned at coordinates (94, 746) with dimensions measuring 2694 × 1439, the illustration may be intended for architectural planning.

Fig. 3. Example of the CLEAD Approach: from illustration detection to enriched description. Starting from a digitised historical document *(a)*, the U-Net segmentation model isolates the illustration region *(b)*. A vision–language model then produces an initial visual description *(c)*, subsequently enriched with archival context *(d)*.

Prompt 1: Expert Prompt for Enriching with Context
Input contains English + Spanish/Catalan. Output English only.
Description (English): ***Visual Description***
Metadata (Catalan/Spanish): ***Paper context***
Enrich description with metadata. Output English only.

5.2 Contextual Enrichment

The contextual enrichment experiments demonstrate that combining page transcriptions with visual descriptions significantly improves the semantic quality of the generated metadata. Across all evaluated models – Gemini 2.5, GPT-4o, GPT-4-turbo, and GPT-3.5-turbo – both enrichment prompts produce high-quality outputs, though with notable differences. While Prompt 2 generates more elaborate interpretations incorporating broader archaeological context, Prompt 1 provides clearer and more concise descriptions better aligned with expert archaeological documentation practices. GPT-4o achieves the best overall performance, selected by the expert in 13 out of 14 cases (92.9%), confirming its superior ability to integrate visual and textual cues into coherent and contextually relevant metadata. Gemini 2.5 and GPT-4-turbo produce no satisfactory outputs, while GPT-3.5-turbo is selected in only one case, highlighting the importance of model capability for this task. As illustrated in Fig. 3, the enrichment stage refines the initial visual description by incorporating contextual information from the page transcription. GPT-4o again produces the most coherent enriched descriptions on IlluHisDoc, though some limitations remain in generating numerical measurements and spatial dimensions.

6 Conclusion and Future Work

This paper presents CLEAD, an approach for the automatic generation of enriched metadata. By combining vision-language models with page transcription context, CLEAD produces more informative and semantically meaningful metadata than visual analysis alone. Experiments on the DataLAC and IlluHisDoc datasets show the effectiveness of integrating visual and textual information for improving metadata quality and supporting the indexing and retrieval of visual heritage resources. Future work will focus on incorporating domain knowledge and expert validation mechanisms to further enhance metadata accuracy and reliability.

References

1. An, Q., Ying, C., Zhu, Y., Xu, Y., Zhang, M., Wang, J.: Ledd: large language model-empowered data discovery in data lakes. arXiv preprint arXiv:2502.15182 (2025)
2. Boukhers, Z., Bouabdallah, A.: Vision and natural language for metadata extraction from scientific pdf documents: a multimodal approach. In: Proceedings of the 22nd ACM/IEEE Joint Conference on Digital Libraries, pp. 1–5 (2022)
3. Cherradi, M., El Haddadi, A.: Enhancing data lake management systems with LDA approach. J. Data Sci. Intell. Syst. **3**(1), 58–66 (2025)
4. Chung, H.W., et al.: Scaling instruction-finetuned language models (2022). https://arxiv.org/abs/2210.11416
5. Comanici, G., et al.: Gemini 2.5: pushing the frontier with advanced reasoning, multimodality, long context, and next generation agentic capabilities (2025). https://doi.org/10.48550/arXiv.2507.06261
6. El-Idrissi, R., Makhlouf, E., Sahrane, M.R., Elohounkpon, D.R., Cristancho, J.A.S., Reig, J.S., Romero, L., Agoun, J., Girard, J.P., de Prado, G., Darmont, J., Loudcher, S.: Datalac: intelligence artificielle dans un lac de données pour valoriser les archives archéologiques. Revue des Nouvelles Technologies de l'Information Extraction et Gestion des Connaissances, RNTI-E-42, 545–552 (2026)
7. Hai, R., Koutras, C., Quix, C., Jarke, M.: Data lakes: a survey of functions and systems. IEEE Trans. Knowl. Data Eng. **35**(12), 12571–12590 (2023)
8. He, F., Wang, D.: Cloze: a building metadata model generation system based on information extraction. In: Proceedings of the 9th ACM International Conference on Systems for Energy-Efficient Buildings, Cities, and Transportation, pp. 109–118 (2022)
9. Islam, R., Moushi, O.M.: Gpt-4o: The cutting-edge advancement in multimodal LLM (2024). https://doi.org/10.36227/techrxiv.171986596.65533294/v1
10. Li, J., Li, D., Savarese, S., Hoi, S.: Blip-2: bootstrapping language-image pretraining with frozen image encoders and large language models. In: International Conference on Machine Learning, pp. 19730–19742. PMLR (2023)

11. Liu, H., Li, C., Wu, Q., Lee, Y.J.: Visual instruction tuning (2023). https://arxiv.org/abs/2304.08485
12. Lobo, E., Hassanzadeh, O., Pham, N., Mihindukulasooriya, N., Subramanian, D., Samulowitz, H.: Matching table metadata with business glossaries using large language models. arXiv preprint arXiv:2309.11506 (2023)
13. Mihindukulasooriya, N., et al.: Unleashing the potential of data lakes with semantic enrichment using foundation models. In: ISWC (Posters/Demos/Industry) (2023)
14. Mishra, S., et al.: Image caption generation using vision transformer and GPT architecture. In: 2024 2nd International Conference on Advancement in Computation & Computer Technologies (InCACCT), pp. 1–6. IEEE (2024)
15. Monnier, T., Aubry, M.: docextractor: an off-the-shelf historical document element extraction. In: 2020 17th International Conference on Frontiers in Handwriting Recognition (ICFHR), pp. 91–96. IEEE (2020). https://doi.org/10.1109/icfhr2020.2020.00027
16. Nockels, J., Gooding, P., Ames, S., Terras, M.M.: Understanding the application of handwritten text recognition technology in heritage contexts: a systematic review of transkribus in published research. Archival Sci. **22**, 367 – 392 (2022). https://doi.org/10.1007/s10502-022-09397-0
17. Radford, A., et al.: Learning transferable visual models from natural language supervision. In: International Conference on Machine Learning, pp. 8748–8763. PmLR (2021)
18. Rakesh, S., Reddy, P.K., Prashanth, V., Reddy, K.S.: Handwritten text recognition using deep learning techniques: a survey. MATEC Web Conferences (2024). https://doi.org/10.1051/matecconf/202439201126
19. Ronneberger, O., Fischer, P., Brox, T.: U-Net: Convolutional Networks for Biomedical Image Segmentation (2015)
20. Sawadogo, P., Darmont, J.: On data lake architectures and metadata management. J. Intell. Inf. Syst. **56**(1), 97–120 (2021)
21. Tiedemann, J., et al.: Democratizing neural machine translation with opus-mt (2023). https://arxiv.org/abs/2212.01936
22. Tomandl, A., Fuchs, K.P., Federrath, H.: Rest-net: A dynamic rule-based ids for vanets. In: 2014 7th IFIP Wireless and Mobile Networking Conference (WMNC), pp. 1–8 (2014). https://doi.org/10.1109/WMNC.2014.6878854
23. Wang, J., et al.: Git: a generative image-to-text transformer for vision and language (2022). https://arxiv.org/abs/2205.14100
24. Ye, J., et al.: A comprehensive capability analysis of GPT-3 and GPT-3.5 series models (2023). https://arxiv.org/abs/2303.10420
25. Zhang, H., Liu, Y., Santos, A., Hung, W.L., Freire, J.: Autoddg: automated dataset description generation using large language models. Proc. ACM Manag. Data **4**(1 (SIGMOD), 1–27 (2026)

Sustainability, Privacy Workflows and Clinical Analytics

RL-Based Carbon-Aware Profit-Oriented Data Replication Strategy in Cloud Systems

Amir Najjar(✉), Riad Mokadem, and Jean-Marc Pierson

Université de Toulouse, CNRS, IRIT, Toulouse, France
{amir.najjar,riad.mokadem,jean-marc.pierson}@irit.fr
https://www.irit.fr/

Abstract. Data replication is an essential technique to ensure fault tolerance, improve performance and provide higher availability in scalable distributed systems such as the cloud. It is often triggered using ad-hoc thresholds. The responsibility of adjusting them falls on administrators and requires prior knowledge of the workload and the architecture. Reinforcement learning is a promising framework that has been proposed to dynamically adapt to environment changes and to avoid human intervention. In this paper, we propose a data replication strategy based on Deep Q-Networks that optimizes a trade-off between cloud provider profit and carbon footprint, a combined objective generally missing in the literature. The proposed strategy dynamically learns the system characteristics and adapts to workload changes. Results show satisfactory quality of service in terms of response time while improving provider profit and carbon footprint compared to other strategies.

Keywords: Cloud Systems · Data Replication · Reinforcement Learning · Quality of Service · Provider Profit · Carbon Footprint

1 Introduction

The increased popularity of social media, video streaming and online gaming has resulted in the generation of very large data volumes in distributed systems. As such, distributed systems needed to evolve to ensure satisfactory Quality of Service (QoS), which can be measured via response time (RT), throughput, availability and fault tolerance. Data replication has emerged as a technique to satisfy such requirements; it provides improved RT, fault tolerance and availability [17].

Data replication strategies proposed in the literature often utilize thresholds that require human intervention as well as prior knowledge of the system. The thresholds are set by administrators based on the nature of the workload and the underlying system architecture. As a solution to manual adjustment, statistical methods have been used to predict thresholds automatically, such as the use of controls charts in [15].

© The Author(s), under exclusive license to Springer Nature Switzerland AG 2027
G. Vargas Solar et al. (Eds.): ADBIS 2026, CCIS 3175, pp. 95–104, 2027.
https://doi.org/10.1007/978-3-032-39823-9_9

Consequently, it seems promising to explore Machine Learning (ML) to design a data replication strategy that automatically learns the characteristics of the system and the workload. The strategy can use workload traces or a simulated environment to predict the necessary thresholds for replication. In fact, ML has seen increased use in data replication through supervised learning [13], unsupervised learning [14], and reinforcement learning (RL) [19]. Among these methods, RL appears to be the most suitable as it can learn directly from a simulated or a real environment. In contrast, supervised learning relies on labeled datasets, and unsupervised learning requires underlying clusters within the environment [9].

Current strategies, particularly those incorporating ML [13,14,19] often focus on ensuring QoS without considering economic profitability, an essential aspect in commercial contexts such as the cloud [8]. In addition, they fail to tackle the environmental impact and the carbon footprint of distributed systems [16].

In this paper, we introduce an RL-based data replication strategy for cloud systems that optimizes the trade-off between cloud provider profit and carbon footprint, in terms of both emissions and machine procurement. The proposed strategy consists of a static and a dynamic component. The static component aims to ensure availability and fault tolerance and utilizes VM consolidation to minimize the purchase of additional machines. The dynamic component is based on Deep Q-Networks (DQN) and ensures satisfactory RT while optimizing a trade-off between cloud provider profit and carbon footprint. From our preliminary design in [10], we have improved the system model to be more representative of a real environment. In addition, we have introduced query batching as well as improved the modeling of the reward signal.

The rest of the paper is organized as follows: Sect. 2 analyzes the data replication strategies in the literature that utilize RL. Section 3 provides an overview of the considered architecture and its specifications. Section 4 describes the proposed RL-based strategy. Section 5 describes the experiment setup, validates the RL model and presents the obtained results. Section 6 concludes and presents future plans.

2 Existing Work

RL can be used to train agents in an environment modeled on the underlying distributed cloud system, allowing them to learn replication strategies or adjust the thresholds that trigger the replication mechanism. An overview of RL based data replication strategies for the cloud is presented in [9].

Morffi et al. [12] to allocate replicated fragments in a distributed database. Ferreira et al. [2] employ Deep Q-Networks (DQN) to dynamically tune the parameters of a replication middleware to increase throughput. Lu et al. [7] also utilize them to improve read latency in distributed storage systems. Double Deep Q-Networks (DDQN), an extension of DQN, have also seen use in data replication. Zheng et al. [20] utilize them to improve RT and provide load balancing, while Lee and Song [5] employ them to optimize a trade-off between video quality and storage demands in Content Delivery Networks (CDNs).

Lee [6] uses Proximal Policy Optimization (PPO) to determine replication factors and aims to provide load balancing.

Previously proposed strategies do not address two key concerns in cloud systems: profitability and environmental impact. In this paper, we propose a strategy that optimizes a trade-off between the two aforementioned objectives.

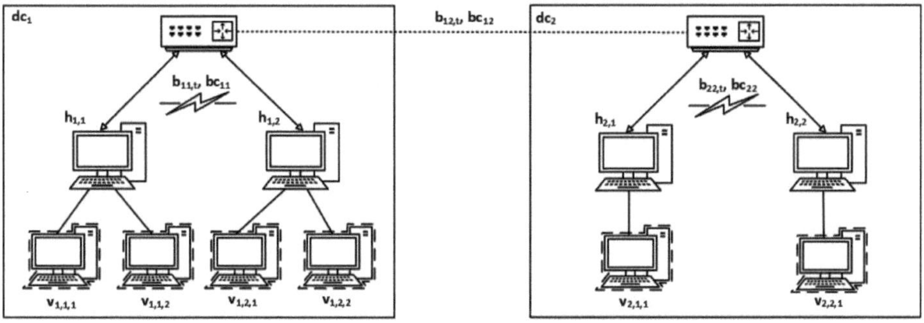

Fig. 1. Example of a simplified CDN with two data centers.

3 Architecture

3.1 Overview

For our strategy, we consider three modules defined as follows:

- Replica Management Module (RMM): Serves as an intermediary between the LDM and CMM. Replication actions are relayed from the LDM. They are checked for validity and sent as replication decisions to the CMM. System state is sent from the CMM and is then processed and transformed to fit the Deep Q-Network for the LDM.
- Learning Decision Module (LDM): Using updates in the system state, a DQN model takes a replication decision and relays it to the RMM.
- Cloud Management Module (CMM): measures static and dynamic information about the system and relays it to the RMM. Static information includes data center specifications and economic costs (for example, in USD). Dynamic information includes current network and resource utilization, as well as performance metrics such as RT.

3.2 Specification

The cloud system consists of a set of N data centers $DC = \{dc_1, ..., dc_N\}$. Each data center $dc_i, (1 \leq dc_i \leq N)$ is characterized by a carbon intensity factor $CI = [ci_i]$. O data files are available on the cloud $D = \{d_1, ..., d_O\}$ with sizes

$SZ = \{sz_1, ..., sz_O\}$. The system services a set of L clients $U = \{u_1, ..., u_L\}$. Each client $u_l, (1 \leq l \leq L)$ has a certain latency to each of the data centers $\text{LAT}_l = \{\text{lat}_{l1}, ...\text{lat}_{lN}\}$. Each data center has a set of M_i homogeneous hosts $H_i = \{h_{ij}\}, 1 \leq j \leq M_i$. In the case of a data center having heterogeneous hosts, it can be modeled as multiple homogeneous data centers sharing a common backbone. Hosts of dc_i are characterized by a CPU with $C = \left[c_i\right]$ cores, a core frequency of $F = \left[f_i\right]$, an economic cost per execution cycle of $CC = \left[cc_i\right]$, a storage capacity $S = \left[s_i\right]$ bytes and a storage cost of $SC = \left[sc_i\right]$ per byte.

Several VMs can be deployed on a host depending on the core count and the required resources. A VM on h_{ij} is denoted by v_{ijk}. A VM v_{ijk} can occupy one or more cores of the host h_{ij}. The number of cores occupied by v_{ijk} is referred to by nco_{ijk}.

Network links are established between all pairs of data centers: for dc_i and $dc_{i'}$ and at time t, the bandwidth available is denoted by $b_{ii'}$ and the bandwidth cost per byte is denoted by $bc_{ii'}$. Network information can therefore be represented as matrices $B_t = \left[b_{ii'}\right]$ and $BC = \left[bc_{ii'}\right]$. Figure 1 presents an example of a simplified CDN with two data centers. dc_1 has two hosts, each with two VMs. dc_2 has two hosts with one VM each.

A Service Level Agreement (SLA) is established between the provider and a client u_l to access datum d_{ud_l}, with $1 \leq ud_l \leq O$ the index of the datum. The client pays a fixed rate per query $RATE_l$. Multiple Service Level Objectives (SLOs) are defined: (i) Availability objective AVO_l: minimum replication factor to respect at all times and (ii) Response time objective RTO_l: maximum allowed response time before incurring a penalty RT_PEN_l.

The client requests their datum at time t by executing query Q_t. Query arrival rates follow a Poisson process and are divided into different categories depending on complexity. With DB systems as an example, the queries complexity scales with the amount of joins. The complexity factor of the query is defined as CF_{Q_t}. Therefore, the amount of execution cycles $EC_{Q_t} = CF_{Q_t} \cdot sz_{ud_l}$. We also calculate the average utilization percentage of hosts containing d_{ud_l} per data center $UTIL_{l,t} = \left[util_{l1,t}, ..., util_{lN,t}\right]$ and track the amount of replicas for each client's data $R_{l,t} = \left[r_{l1,t}, ..., r_{lN,t}\right]$ with $r_{li,t} \geq 0$.

In addition, we keep track of the current load on all pairs of links between each data center as well as all backbones and model it as a matrix $BU_t = \left[bu_{ii',t}\right]$ with $bu_{ii',t}$ being the bandwidth utilization between dc_i and $dc_{i'}$ at time t.

4 Proposed Strategy

Our strategy consists of a static component and a dynamic component. First, static replication is performed when the SLA is established to ensure satisfactory QoS and availability. Then, dynamic replication is performed as queries arrive to maintain satisfactory QoS and to adapt to workload changes. VM consolidation is adopted to reduce the carbon footprint associated with hardware provisioning.

4.1 Static Replication

To satisfy the availability objective for each client u_l, AVO_l replicas need to be created. The RMM places the initial copies in different data centers to ensure fault tolerance. The initial datum is placed in the data center with the lowest latency to the client to ensure fast response time.

Afterwards, the datum is replicated until the minimum availability AVO_l is satisfied. The copies are placed in the data centers with the lowest carbon intensity factor ci_i. Hosts that are already on are prioritized following the principle of VM consolidation. Response time is less critical for the remaining replicas, as they serve as backups in case of a failure of the VM hosting the primary copy.

It is worthy to note that multiple clients can access the same datum. Replicas therefore can be reused to satisfy other clients' SLO requirements.

4.2 Dynamic Replication

The LDM uses a Deep Q-Network with experience replay and target network to take actions based on a state, which is encoded in the input layer and provides an accurate representation of the environment. The value of actions is encoded in the output layer. For each datum, the associated queries are batched and then processed by the LDM. Therefore, some of the variables in the state space are averaged over the batch. The state space consists of:

- Data center information: core frequencies F, core counts C, costs per execution cycle CC, storage costs SC, carbon intensity factor CI;
- Network information: bandwidth available at time t B_t, bandwidth costs BC, link loads at time t BU_t;
- Client information: latencies $avg(\mathrm{LAT}_l)$, average utilization $UTIL_{l,t}$, complexity factor $avg(CF_{Q_t})$, RT objective $avg(RTO_l)$.

The action space consists of either replicating in a data center dc_i (N candidates) or not performing any replication, for a total of $N+1$ possible actions. Action masking is applied for invalid actions (e.g. insufficient storage, availability).

The reward for a batch is the sum of the rewards for each query and the penalty incurred while replicating. With $QS_{o,k}$ as the k-th batch of queries associated to datum d_o, the reward can be expressed as follows:

$$Batch\_Reward_{o,k} = \Big(\sum_{Q_t \in QS_{o,k}} Reward_{Q_t}\Big) - REPL_{o,k} \tag{1}$$

The reward for each query is constructed from economic profit and a penalty for carbon emissions.

$$Reward_{Q_t} = \alpha \cdot Economic - (1-\alpha) \cdot Carbon \tag{2}$$

where $0 \leq \alpha \leq 1$ is a parameter set by the provider to control the trade-off between profit and carbon footprint. A higher value gives more emphasis on profit rather than carbon footprint reduction. Economic and carbon terms are rescaled to the unit interval [0, 1] via min-max normalization.

The economic component is defined as the difference between the query rate and the total cost incurred in processing and replicating data. The latter includes CPU, storage, and bandwidth costs, as well as a penalty cost incurred when the response time constraint is violated.

$$Economic = RATE_l - (CPU + STOR + PEN) \tag{3}$$

The CPU cost can be calculated using the execution cycles EC_{Q_t}, the core count nco_{ijk} and the cost per execution cycle cc_i. For simplicity, we assume that task performance scales linearly with core count:

$$CPU = \frac{EC_{Q_t}}{\cancel{nco_{ijk}}} \cdot cc_i \cdot \cancel{nco_{ijk}} = EC_{Q_t} \cdot cc_i \tag{4}$$

The storage cost is the size of the datum sz_l multiplied by the sum of storage costs incurred for each data center dc_i, which can be calculated using the product of the replication factor $r_{li,t}$ and the storage cost sc_i:

$$STOR = sz_o \cdot \sum_{i=1}^{N} sc_i \cdot r_{li,t} \tag{5}$$

The final part of is the penalty RT_PEN_l incurred if RTO_l is not respected:

$$PEN = \mathbb{1}_{RT(Q_t) > RTO_l} \cdot RT\_PEN_l \tag{6}$$

Given $E(Q_t)$ energy consumed in Joules in energy by data center dc_i with ci_i, the carbon emissions in gCO_2/kWh 2 is defined as follows:

$$Carbon = \frac{E(Q_t)}{3.6 \times 10^6} \cdot ci_i \tag{7}$$

The penalty for replication (if replication occurs) in Eq. 1 consists of the bandwidth cost and the carbon footprint for replication:

$$REPL_{o,k} = \alpha \cdot BW_{o,k} + (1 - \alpha) \cdot Carbon_{REPL_{o,k}} \tag{8}$$

Replication can occur either between two hosts in the same data center ($h_{ij} \rightarrow h_{ij'}, j \neq j'$) or between two hosts in different data centers ($h_{ij} \rightarrow h_{i'j'}, i \neq i'$), the bandwidth cost associated is calculated accordingly:

$$BW_{i,j} = \begin{cases} sz_o \cdot bc_{ii} & \text{in same DC} \\ sz_o \cdot bc_{ii'} & \text{in different DCs} \\ 0 & \text{no replication} \end{cases} \tag{9}$$

Table 1. Data center specifications

Location	Host Count	CPU	Disk	Carbon Intensity [11]
Frankfurt	64	Intel Xeon Gold 5320	1.92 TB	0.179 gCO_2/kWh
Northern Virginia	124	Intel Xeon Gold 5220	1.44 TB	0.185 gCO_2/kWh
Sao Paulo	64	AMD Epyc 7301	480 GB	0.123 gCO_2/kWh
Tokyo	32	Intel Xeon E5-2660	480 GB	0.201 gCO_2/kWh
Mumbai	32	Intel Xeon E5-2630 v3	200 GB	0.282 gCO_2/kWh

Table 2. Network latency

	Frankfurt	Northern Virginia	Sao Paulo	Tokyo	Mumbai
Frankfurt	55 μs	87 ms	213 ms	230 ms	371 ms
Northern Virginia	87 ms	55 μs	127 ms	150 ms	278 ms
Sao Paulo	213 ms	127 ms	55 μs	258 ms	371 ms
Tokyo	230 ms	150 ms	258 ms	55 μs	98 ms
Mumbai	371 ms	278 ms	371 ms	98 ms	55 μs

5 Evaluation

5.1 Experiment Setup

To validate the proposed strategy, we use SimGrid [1] version 4.1 to simulate a platform consisting of 5 data centers located in Frankfurt, Northern Virginia, Sao Paulo, Tokyo and Mumbai. The specifications of the platform are described in Table 1. Intra and inter-DC latencies are detailed in Table 2. The energy consumption is modeled as a linear function of CPU utilization [4]. Inter-DC bandwidth is 7 Gbps and intra-DC bandwidth is 100 Gbps. The network parameters are taken from the specifications of the Google Cloud Platform (GCP) [3]. The platform services 1,000 clients with varying data sizes and 3 different query types. The probability for simple, intermediate and advanced queries are 40%, 30% and 30% respectively. In order to establish the response time objective RTO_l in the SLA, we consider, for each query type that a client may issue, the maximum RT observed across all data centers when the query is executed in isolation. This value is then multiplied by a tolerance factor of 1.5 [18].

The neural network consists of an input layer of 82 neurons, representing the state space of the cloud system. The hidden layer consists of 128 neurons. Finally, the output layer consists of 6 neurons, representing the action space. We use the ϵ-greedy policy to explore the action space with a decaying ϵ from 1.0 to 0.0. As queries are batched, short term rewards should be prioritized. Therefore, we use a discount factor γ of 0.3. We compare the following strategies:

- Hadoop strategy: statically replicates in random locations until AVO_l is satisfied

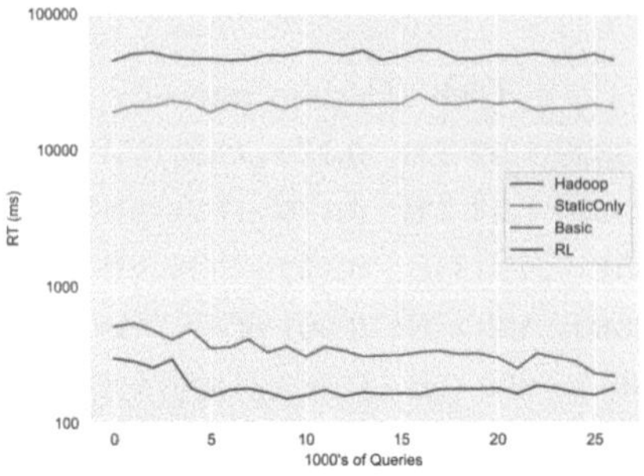

Fig. 2. Evolution of RT over time.

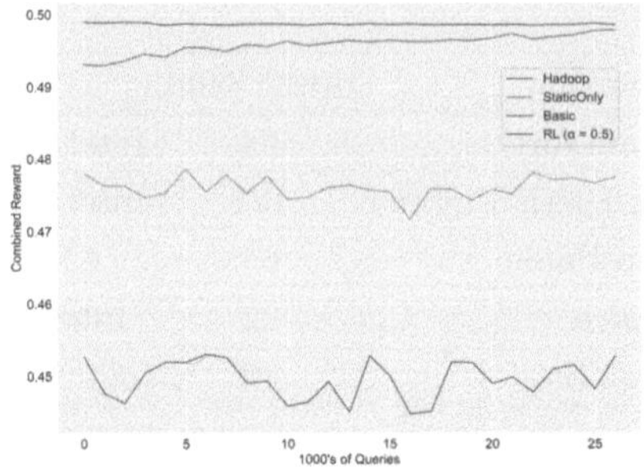

Fig. 3. Evolution of reward over time.

- Static strategy: the static strategy described in Sect. 4.1
- Basic strategy: the static strategy combined with dynamic replication only when penalties are incurred. Location is chosen based on client proximity.
- RL strategy: static strategy combined with the RL-based dynamic strategy

5.2 Results

First, we compare RT over time for all strategies on the balanced reward ($\alpha = 0.5$). The results are presented in Fig. 2 on a log-scale. Hadoop and Static strategies fail to provide satisfactory QoS due to the limited replication, with an average RT of 49,110 ms and 21,514 ms respectively. Basic and RL strategies scale dynamically to meet demands, with an average RT of 350 ms and 186 ms respectively. As the Hadoop and Static strategies do not dynamically replicate, there is no perceived change over time. On the other hand, Basic strategy scales up as more penalties are incurred while RL's proactiveness reduces RT over time.

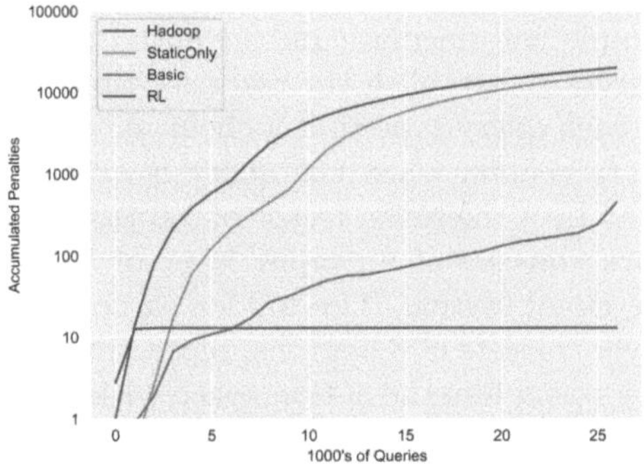

Fig. 4. Penalty accumulation over time.

We then compare the combined reward over time for all strategies as shown in Fig. 3. As profit is considered in the reward, we see a significant drop in performance between the static strategies and dynamic strategies. The Hadoop and Static strategies achieve average rewards of 0.4496 and 0.4760 respectively. The Basic strategy's performance improves over time (from 0.4930 to 0.4979) as penalties are incurred and load is reduced, resulting in a reduction in both penalties and carbon emissions. The RL strategy outperforms all other strategies with an average of 0.4986 and remains relatively stable.

To better distinguish the difference between the Basic and RL strategies, we visualize the evolution of penalties incurred over time in Fig. 4 on a log-scale. The Hadoop and Static strategies incur 20,852 and 17,352 penalties respectively. Overall, the Basic strategy incurs significantly more penalties than the RL strategy, with 744 penalties compared with only 12 for the RL strategy.

6 Conclusion and Future Work

In this paper, we have proposed an RL-based data replication strategy to optimize the trade-off between provider profit and carbon footprint while providing a satisfactory QoS. The proposed strategy consists of (i) a static component that provides availability and minimizes carbon footprint and (ii) a dynamic component that aims to adapt to workload changes using RL. Results show significant improvements in RT, profitability and carbon footprint compared to other strategies while ensuring satisfactory QoS by incurring fewer penalties.

As the strategy requires learning to adapt to the architecture and the workload, it could be first deployed on a simulated environment and trained on past traces. Once the learning is complete, the agent is deployed in inference mode.

In the future, we plan to consider the carbon footprint of the Learning Decision Module and the cost of its usage. We also plan to compare our strategy against other state of the art strategies, notably ML-based strategies.

References

1. Casanova, H., Giersch, A., Legrand, A., Quinson, M., Suter, F.: Lowering entry barriers to developing custom simulators of distributed applications and platforms with SimGrid. Parallel Comput. **123**, 103–125 (2025). https://doi.org/10.1016/j.parco.2025.103125
2. Ferreira, L., Coelho, F., Pereira, J.: Self-tunable DBMS replication with reinforcement learning. In: Remke, A., Schiavoni, V. (eds.) DAIS 2020. LNCS, vol. 12135, pp. 131–147. Springer, Cham (2020). https://doi.org/10.1007/978-3-030-50323-9_9
3. Google: Google cloud platform. https://cloud.google.com/. Accessed 15 Jan 2026
4. Heinrich, F.C., et al.: Predicting the energy consumption of MPI applications at scale using a single node. In: Cluster 2017. IEEE, Hawaii (2017). https://inria.hal.science/hal-01523608
5. Lee, D., Song, M.: Optimizing video quality in distributed storage systems via deep reinforcement learning (DRL)-based adaptive replication. IEEE Trans. Circuits Syst. Video Technol. (2025). https://doi.org/10.1109/TCSVT.2025.3538916

6. Lee, H.: Intelligent Replication Management for HDFS Using Reinforcement Learning (2020). https://arxiv.org/abs/2008.08665
7. Lu, K., Zhao, N., Wan, J., Fei, C., Zhao, W., Deng, T.: RLRP: high-efficient data placement with reinforcement learning for modern distributed storage systems. In: IEEE International Parallel and Distributed Processing Symposium (IPDPS), pp. 595–605 (2022). https://doi.org/10.1109/IPDPS53621.2022.00064
8. Mokadem, R., Hameurlain, A.: A data replication strategy with tenant performance and provider economic profit guarantees in Cloud data centers. J. Syst. Softw. **159**, 110447 (2020). https://doi.org/10.1016/j.jss.2019.110447
9. Najjar, A., Mokadem, R., Pierson, J.M.: A review of data placement and replication strategies based on machine learning. In: IEEE 30th International Conference on Parallel and Distributed Systems (ICPADS), pp. 278–285. IEEE (2024)
10. Najjar, A., Mokadem, R., Pierson, J.M.: Towards designing an energy aware data replication strategy for cloud systems using reinforcement learning. In: Conférence francophone d'informatique en Parallélisme, Architecture et Système (COMPAS) (2025). https://hal.science/hal-05118691
11. Ritchie, H., Rosado, P., Roser, M.: CO2 and Greenhouse Gas Emissions. Our World in Data (2023). https://ourworldindata.org/co2-and-greenhouse-gas-emissions
12. Rodriguez Morffi, A., Paz, D., Mainegra Hing, M., González, L.: A Reinforcement learning solution for allocating replicated fragments in a distributed database. Computacion y Sistemas **11**, 117–128 (2007)
13. Shwe, T., Aritsugi, M.: Proactive re-replication strategy in HDFS based cloud data center. In: Proceedings of The 10th International Conference on Utility and Cloud Computing, UCC '17, pp. 121–130. Association for Computing Machinery (2017). https://doi.org/10.1145/3147213.3147221
14. Symvoulidis, C., et al.: A user mobility-based data placement strategy in a hybrid cloud/edge environment using a causal-aware deep learning network. IEEE Trans. Comput. **72**(12), 3603–3616 (2023). https://doi.org/10.1109/TC.2023.3311921
15. Séguéla, M., Mokadem, R., Pierson, J.M.: Dynamic energy and expenditure aware data replication strategy. In: 2022 IEEE 15th International Conference on Cloud Computing (CLOUD), pp. 97–102 (2022). https://doi.org/10.1109/CLOUD55607.2022.00027
16. Thakur, S., Chaurasia, A.: Towards green cloud computing: impact of carbon footprint on environment. In: 6th International Conference - Cloud System and Big Data Engineering, pp. 209–213 (2016). https://doi.org/10.1109/CONFLUENCE.2016.7508115
17. Tos, U., Mokadem, R., Hameurlain, A., Ayav, T., Bora, S.: A performance and profit oriented data replication strategy for cloud systems. In: Int. IEEE Conferences on UIC/ATC/ScalCom/CBDCom/IoP/SmartWorld, pp. 780–787 (2016)
18. Yin, S., Morvan, F., Martinez-Gil, J., Hameurlain, A.: MTD-DS: an SLA-aware decision support benchmark for multi-tenant parallel DBMSs. IEEE Trans. Knowl. Data Eng. **37**(5), 2743–2755 (2025). https://doi.org/10.1109/TKDE.2025.3543727
19. Zhang, T., Gupta, A., Rodríguez, M.A.F., Spjuth, O., Hellander, A., Toor, S.: Data management of scientific applications in a reinforcement learning-based hierarchical storage system. Expert Syst. Appl. **237**, 121443 (2024). https://doi.org/10.1016/j.eswa.2023.121443
20. Zheng, M., Du, X., Lu, Z., Duan, Q.: A balanced and reliable data replica placement scheme based on reinforcement learning in edge–cloud environments. Futur. Gener. Comput. Syst. **155**, 132–145 (2024). https://doi.org/10.1016/j.future.2024.02.004

From BPMN to TLAQ: A Privacy-Preserving Framework for Executable Clinical Pathway Analytics in Federated Big Data Healthcare Systems

Alfredo Cuzzocrea[1,2](✉) and Abderraouf Hafsaoui[1]

[1] iDEA Lab, University of Calabria, Rende, Italy
{alfredo.cuzzocrea,abderraouf.hafsaoui}@unical.it
[2] Department of Computer Science LIPADE, University of Paris City, Paris, France

Abstract. This paper introduces *BPMN-to-TLAQ wrapping methodology* that enables the transformation of formal *Business Process Model and Notation* (BPMN) clinical pathway models into executable *Tree-Like Analytical Queries* (TLAQ) within the *QFLS Federated Analytics Framework*. Our approach leverages the innovative *Lazy Aggregation paradigm* of TLAQ, where parent-child query nodes do not adhere to strict containment relations, thereby supporting *granular, step-wise medical investigation processes*. This methodology bridges declarative process modelling with *privacy-preserving distributed data analytics*, which allows healthcare institutions to quantitatively evaluate guideline-based clinical workflows across fragmented, sensitive datasets without raw data centralization. We demonstrate the practical utility and scalability of the approach through a comprehensive case study based on a *real-life clinical scenario* within the context of the *EU H2020 QUALITOP Research Project*.

Keywords: Big Healthcare Data · Big Healthcare Data Analytics · Multidimensional Big Healthcare Data Analytics

1 Introduction

Modern healthcare delivery is increasingly guided by standardized *Clinical Pathways*, structured multidisciplinary care plans that translate evidence-based guidelines into actionable workflows. These pathways aim to improve patient outcomes, reduce variability in care, and enhance clinical efficiency. However, their real-life implementation and impact are often difficult to measure quantitatively due to the fragmented, heterogeneous, and *privacy-sensitive nature of healthcare data*. With the proliferation of *Electronic Health Records* (EHR), *Genomic Data Streams*, and *Internet of Medical Things* (IoMT) devices (e.g., [1–3]), healthcare institutions are now generating data with unprecedented *volume*, *velocity*, and *variety*, characteristics that define the *Big Data Paradigm in Medicine*. This explosion of data presents a dual challenge and opportunity: while it holds the potential to unlock deeper insights into *disease progression*, *treatment efficacy*, and population health, its effective analysis is hindered by significant technical, regulatory, and methodological barriers.

© The Author(s), under exclusive license to Springer Nature Switzerland AG 2027
G. Vargas Solar et al. (Eds.): ADBIS 2026, CCIS 3175, pp. 105–116, 2027.
https://doi.org/10.1007/978-3-032-39823-9_10

Big data analytics paradigm in healthcare (e.g., [4, 5]) promises to transform raw, multi-source data into actionable clinical intelligence through advanced computational techniques, such as *Machine Learning* (ML), *predictive modelling*, and *Process Mining* (e.g., [6]). Yet, key obstacles remain, particularly concerning *data privacy*, *interoperability* across disparate systems, and the semantic gap between high-level clinical guidelines and *low-level, Distributed Data Traces* (e.g., [7]). Traditional centralized analytics models often require data consolidation, which conflicts with stringent regulations like *GDPR* (e.g., [8]) and *institutional data sovereignty policies* (e.g., [9]). Consequently, there is a pressing need for novel methodological frameworks that can perform sophisticated, guideline-aware analytics directly over federated data landscapes without necessitating raw data movement or compromising patient confidentiality.

Following these considerations, this paper introduces a *BPMN-to-TLAQ wrapping methodology* as a novel approach for bridging formal clinical process modelling with executable, data-driven analytics within *federated data environments* (e.g., [10]). This innovative methodology is developed within the *EU H2020 QUALITOP Research Project* [11] and its core technological framework, *QUALITOP Federated Big Data Analytics Learning System* (QFLS) [12]. Our approach enables the automated transformation of *Business Process Model and Notation* (BPMN) clinical pathway models into hierarchical *Tree-Like Analytical Queries* (TLAQ) [13], thereby allowing healthcare institutions to operationalize guideline-based processes into privacy-preserving, distributed analytical investigations.

The proposed methodology aims to address key challenges in modern healthcare informatics, notably the gap between documented clinical workflows and their quantitative evaluation across fragmented, sensitive datasets. By systematically mapping BPMN *decision points*, *tasks*, and *gateways* into a TLAQ query structure, our wrapping technique supports granular, temporal analysis that mirrors clinical reasoning while adhering to stringent data privacy regulations. This linkage of declarative process modelling with lazy aggregation-based querying enables refined tracking of patient cohorts through complex, branching care pathways without the need for raw data centralization.

The *BPMN-to-TLAQ transformation* is implemented within the QFLS framework, a Cloud-based federated system designed for secure, large-scale healthcare analytics. QFLS employs a *privacy-by-design architecture* (e.g., [14]), where data remains at its source institution, and analytics are performed via distributed query orchestration using *Apache Spark* and *Apache Hadoop* components, according to state-of-the-art paradigms (e.g., [15]). The methodology is realized through dedicated system modules to support data anonymization and ingestion, and query formulation and visualization, which ensures an end-to-end, user-accessible analytical workflow. Through this integration of process modelling, temporal logic querying, and federated analytics, our work provides a scalable foundation for enhancing clinical audit, compliance monitoring, and outcomes research. It enables healthcare researchers and decision-makers to move beyond static guideline documentation toward dynamic, data-informed evaluation of care processes in real-life multi-institutional settings.

2 QFLS System Overview

In this Section, we provide a concise overview of the QFLS system by detailing its structural components and core functionalities.

QFLS System [12] is a *Cloud-based federated framework* specifically engineered to address the critical challenges of *big healthcare data management and analytics*. Being developed as the core technological pillar of the *EU H2020 QUALITOP research project* [11], QFLS is designed.

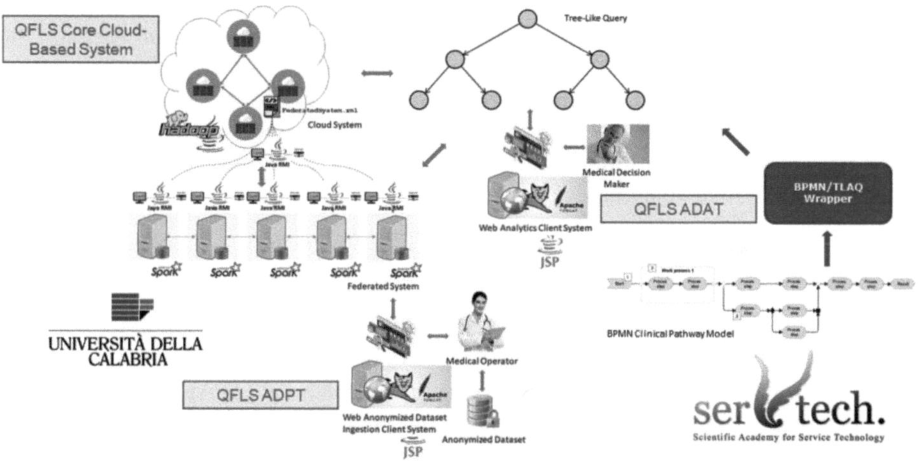

Fig. 1. QFLS Core Cloud-Based System Architecture

to support precision medicine and *Quality-of-Life* (QoL) research for cancer patients undergoing immunotherapy. Its primary innovation is the seamless integration of a privacy-preserving federated architecture with the powerful TLAQ model [13], which enables advanced analytics on distributed, sensitive medical datasets without the need for raw data centralization. It should be noted that QFLS architecture bridges the gap between distributed data sources and end-user clinical decision-making. Its design is governed by several core principles, such as *data security* (e.g., [16]), *privacy-by-design* (e.g., [14]), *federated processing* (e.g., [10]), and clinical workflow. The system's end-to-end workflow is shown in Fig. 1.

As shown in Fig. 1, QFLS operates on a *Federated Learning* (FL) and analytics paradigm. Unlike centralized data lakes, it does not pool raw patient data into a single repository. Instead, it connects a federation of autonomous data provider nodes (e.g., hospitals, medical centers across Europe) to a central Cloud-based analytics core. The core principle is that data remains local at its source institution. Analytics are performed via distributed querying, where only aggregated results, never individual patient records, are exchanged. This architecture directly addresses the paramount concerns of medical *Data Privacy*, *GDPR compliance* (e.g., [8]), and institutional willingness to participate in collaborative research.

Specifically, the QFLS framework is structurally organized into the following three main software pillars, each serving a distinct phase in the data analytics lifecycle.

2.1 QFLS Core – the Distributed Analytics Engine

QFLS Core is the Cloud-based brain of the system. It is not a data repository but a coordinator and processor of federated computations. Its operations are powered by *Apache Hadoop* for distributed storage and *Apache Spark* for in-memory, high-velocity data processing. As the federated orchestrator, the Core maintains a configuration file that registers all participant nodes, their network locations (i.e., IPs, logical names), and the metadata of their available anonymized datasets. All coordination between the Core and the remote data nodes is facilitated through *Java Remote Method Invocation* (RMI). The Core uses RMI to dispatch query fragments and collect aggregated results. Its primary function is to receive analytical requests (TLAQ queries) from the front-end, decompose them, dispatch sub-queries to relevant nodes, aggregate the returned results, and structure the final analytical output.

2.2 QFLS-ADPT (Anonymized Dataset Population Tool)

The QFLS-ADPT is a web-based client application deployed at each federated data provider node (e.g., a hospital in France). Its sole purpose is the secure ingestion and preparation of local data for the federation. Specifically, QFLS-ADPT is used by a medical operator at the node to realize the following operation: (*i*) select and upload a local healthcare dataset (e.g., in CSV format); (*ii*) anonymize the data by applying strict *k-Anonymity* (e.g., [17]) and other sanitization techniques to generate an anonymized version D' of the original dataset D, where sensitive identifiers and *Quasi-Identifier* (QID) attributes are generalized; (*iii*) store and register the anonymized dataset D' locally within Hive table. Simultaneously, QFLS-ADPT updates the local configuration and notifies the QFLS Core about the new dataset metadata, making it discoverable for analytics. Finally, access to QFLS-ADPT is controlled through *Role-Based Access Control* (RBAC), permitting only authenticated medical operators to use it.

2.3 QFLS-ADAT (Anonymized Dataset Analytics Tool)

The QFLS-ADAT is the primary interface for end-users, *data scientists,* and *medical decision-makers.* Specifically, QFLS-ADAT is a *web-based analytical workbench* that provides tools to explore federated data, build complex analyses, and visualize insights. Also, secured with RBAC authentication, QFLS-ADAT differentiates between *data analysts* with full access and medical operators who have restricted access. Its key functional modules include the following ones: (*i*) *Data Federation Discoverer* (DFD), which allows users to browse and discover available anonymized datasets across all registered federated nodes; (*ii*) *Anonymized Dataset Analysis* (ADA), providing a diagnostic view of any selected dataset, and showing anonymization percentages per attribute, data types, and basic statistical informations; (*iii*) *Anonymized Analytics Environment* (AAE), the core module which features TLAQ Graphical Editor, where users can visually see

TLAQ queries along with defined nodes, attributes, constraints, and aggregations; (*iv*) *SQL Query Environment* (SQE), allowing execution of standard SQL queries on a single target dataset for users more comfortable with traditional querying; (*v*) *Predictive Analytics Environment* (PAE), a dashboard that generate advanced predictive metrics such as *2D Clustering*, *Icicle Plots*, *Confusion Matrices*, *Pearson/Spearman Correlation*, and *Outlier Detection*, with results exportable as *PDF*.

3 BPMN-to-TLAQ Wrapping Methodology

In this Section, we present a formal methodology for the automated transformation of *BPMN clinical pathways* into executable TLAQ. The methodology, termed *BPMN-to-TLAQ Wrapping*, enables the QFLS framework to bridge declarative process modelling with quantitative, data-driven analysis.

It should be noted that the imperative to transform clinical process models into analytical query structures arises from a fundamental observation about the nature of medical investigation, *clinical protocols*, *epidemiological studies*, and *patient management pathways*, which are inherently procedural. They prescribe sequences of actions, decision points conditional on patient characteristics or laboratory findings, parallel investigations of correlated physiological systems, and termination criteria defined by clinical endpoints. When these protocols are to be executed against large-scale, federated healthcare datasets, the procedural logic must be mapped onto an analytical query paradigm (i.e., *TLAQ query*) that can express hierarchical refinement, conditional branching, and multi-dimensional aggregation while respecting the stringent privacy constraints that govern access to sensitive medical data.

The *BPMN-to-TLAQ wrapping methodology* addresses this mapping challenge through a novel approach grounded in the *theory of semantic model transformation*. Unlike conventional query generation systems that produce *flat, monolithic SQL statements*, our methodology preserves the full structural and semantic richness of the original process model within the resulting analytical artifact. TLAQ query is not merely a translation of BPMN model into a different notation; it is a homomorphic image that retains the decision topology, condition dependencies, and aggregation intent of the source process while adapting its execution semantics to the *lazy aggregation paradigm* (e.g., [18]) that distinguishes the TLAQ model from traditional hierarchical query systems. Formally, given a dataset D, a TLAQ model defined over D is an *n-ary tree* T, where each node is a tuple $\langle A, AP, \langle Cond \rangle \rangle$, where A is the *selected attribute* in D; AP represents a *user-defined aggregation predicate* on A; $Cond$ is a *filtering operation* applied to D.

This preservation of structural semantics is particularly critical in the healthcare domain, where investigational protocols must be auditable, reproducible, and traceable. Regulatory frameworks governing clinical research require that analytical results be linked to the precise methodological steps that produced them. Furthermore, our proposed *BPMN-to-TLAQ* wrapping methodology does not operate in isolation but rather constitutes a critical intermediary layer within a sophisticated multi-component architecture that spans the *MILA DSL* [11], *QFLS system* [12], and the federated healthcare data nodes. Understanding this architectural embedding is essential for appreciating both the operational context of the wrapping transformation and the design decisions that have shaped its implementation. The *Query Language component* of *MILA DSL* allows investigators to retrieve and analyze patterns across the repository of stored blueprints, identifying common pathway structures, treatment variations, and outcome correlations that inform the design of new protocols. This query capability operates at the metadata level, analyzing the structural properties of BPMN models rather than the patient data that those models are designed to investigate. The Composition language, meanwhile, enables the assembly of complex, composite blueprints from simpler constituent elements, supporting hierarchical model construction and the reuse of validated pathway fragments across multiple contexts.

With this ontological foundation established, we define a set of correspondence rules that map each BPMN construct type to its TLAQ node. These rules are formalized as inference rules in a deduction system, enabling both deterministic transformation and the detection of modelling inconsistencies.

For *BPMN Start Events*, the correspondence rule establishes that the unique start event of a BPMN process model maps to the root node of the TLAQ tree. The root node filtering condition is derived from any cohort definition annotations attached to the start event; in the absence of such annotations, the root condition defaults to the universally true predicate, indicating analysis of the entire federated dataset.

For *BPMN Task*, the correspondence rule distinguishes three task subtypes based on their semantic annotation. Data filtering tasks, identified by labels containing selection predicates, map to TLAQ nodes that introduce a new conjunct in the accumulated path condition. Data aggregation tasks, identified by labels containing statistical function keywords, map to TLAQ nodes that specify an aggregation operator and target attribute. Hybrid tasks that both filter and aggregate, such as "*number of female patients with complete response*", are mapped to TLAQ nodes that both extend the path condition and specify an aggregation, with the filtering condition applied.

For *BPMN Exclusive Gateways*, the correspondence rule establishes that each outgoing sequence flow becomes a distinct child node of the TLAQ node corresponding to the gateway incoming context. The condition annotating each flow becomes the local filtering condition for its corresponding child node, specialized through conjunction with the parent accumulated condition. This rule embodies the lazy aggregation principle in its purest form.

For *BPMN Parallel Gateways*, the correspondence rule diverges from conventional interpretations of parallel execution in process models. Rather than attempting to model true concurrency in the analytical domain, a semantic impossibility given the sequential nature of query execution, the rule establishes that each outgoing flow from *Parallel Gateway* becomes a child node that inherits its parent's accumulated condition without specialization. The analytical intent of parallel investigation is preserved, but the implementation semantics are adapted to the query processing paradigm.

Finally, for *BPMN End Events*, the correspondence rule establishes that TLAQ nodes corresponding to BPMN end events are designated as *leaf nodes* in TLAQ tree. Leaf nodes represent terminal analytical states at which no further refinement occurs; the aggregate value computed at a leaf node constitutes the final result for that analytical pathway.

Specifically, Fig. 2 shows Algorithm `BPMN-to-TLAQ Model`, which summarizes TLAQ model construction from BPMN model.

As shown in Fig. 2, Algorithm `BPMN-to-TLAQ Model` takes as input: the set of BPMN nodes $\mathcal{V}$, the set of sequence flows E, and the starting point s, and returns as output the TLAQ query $\mathcal{T}$. Specifically, the algorithm constructs a TLAQ query $\mathcal{T}$ from the BPMN model by traversing the process graph in a *Breadth-First Search* (BFS) [19] and converting each BPMN element into corresponding TLAQ nodes. The algorithm begins by initializing a work queue Q with the starting node s and a null parent. Then, while Q is not empty, it pops a node v along with its parent p and determines the type t of v. The algorithm processes each node type differently to build the hierarchical TLAQ structure depending on the following cases. **(1)** If t corresponds to a *BPMN Task*, the method `extractSemantics` is invoked to extract the attribute *Att*, constraint σ_A, and aggregation predicate *Pred* from the BPMN task annotation. Subsequently, a new TLAQ node n is created and added to $\mathcal{T}$. The parent of n is set to p, and if p is not null, n is appended to p children list. To continue the traversal, for each outgoing edge (v, u) in E, the algorithm pushes (v, u) for further processing. **(2)** If t is a *BPMN ExclusiveGateway*, the algorithm does not create a TLAQ node but instead handles the branching logic. For each outgoing edge (v, u) in E, the method getCondition retrieves the condition *cond* labeling that branch and then pushes $(u, p, cond)$. This ensures that the condition is propagated to subsequent nodes in that branch. **(3)** If t is a *BPMN ParallelGateway*, the algorithm similarly does not create a TLAQ node. For each outgoing edge (v, u) in E, it pushes $(u, p, null)$, thereby allowing all parallel branches to share the same parent p while processing concurrently. **(4)** If t is a *BPMN EndEvent* and p is not null, the algorithm invokes `extractSemantics` to obtain the terminal semantics $(Att, \sigma_A, Pred)$, creates a new TLAQ node n adds n to $\mathcal{T}$, sets its parent to p, and adds n as a child of p. This step finalizes the branch in the TLAQ tree. Once all nodes have been processed, algorithm returns a fully constructed TLAQ query $\mathcal{T}$.

Algorithm 1 `BPMN-to-TLAQ Model`

Input: Set of BPMN Node $\mathcal{V}$, Set of Sequence Flows E, Starting Point s
Output: TLAQ Query $\mathcal{T}$

```
Begin
  Q.push(s, null));
  while (Q ≠ ∅) do
    (v, p) ← Q.pop();
    t ← v.type();
    if (t = Task) then
      (Att, σ_A, Pred) ← v.extractSemantics();
      n ← newNode(A, Σ_A, P);
      T.add(n);
      n.parent ← p;
      if p ≠ null then
        p.children.add(n);
      end if
      for (v, u) ∈ E do
        Q.push(u, n);
      end for
    else if (t = ExclusiveGateway) then
      for all (v, u) ∈ E do
        cond ← getCondition((v, u));
        Q.push((u, p, cond));
      end for
    else if (t = ParallelGateway) then
      for all (v, u) ∈ E do
        Q.push((u, p, null));
      end for
    else if (t = EndEvent) then
      if p ≠ null then
        (Att, σ_A, Pred) ← v.extractSemantics();
        n ← newNode(Att, Σ_A, Pred)
        T.add(n);
        n.parent ← p;
        p.children.add(n);
      end if
    end if
  end while
  return T;
End
```

Fig. 2. Algorithm `BPMN-to-TLAQ Model`

4 From BPMN-To-TLAQ Model in Practice: A Case Study

In this Section, we present a practical case study that demonstrates the transformation and execution of BPMN clinical pathway models into TLAQ queries within the QFLS system.

This case study demonstrates the practical application of *BPMN-to-TLAQ transformation methodology* within the QFLS framework, using a real-life clinical scenario: the management of *Grade 3 Cytokine Release Syndrome* (CRS) [20] in *pediatric* patients (see Fig. 3). As described in Sect. 3, the transformation from a formal BPMN model into an executable TLAQ query follows a rigorous, hierarchical wrapping methodology, which systematically translates each clinical decision point, task, and gateway in the BPMN model into a corresponding TLAQ node.

Figure 4 shows the complete TLAQ query for this case study, which enables a powerful top-down analytical drill-down. Executing this query across the federated QFLS environment provides, at each node, the count of patients whose clinical journey satisfied all conditions from the root down to that specific node.

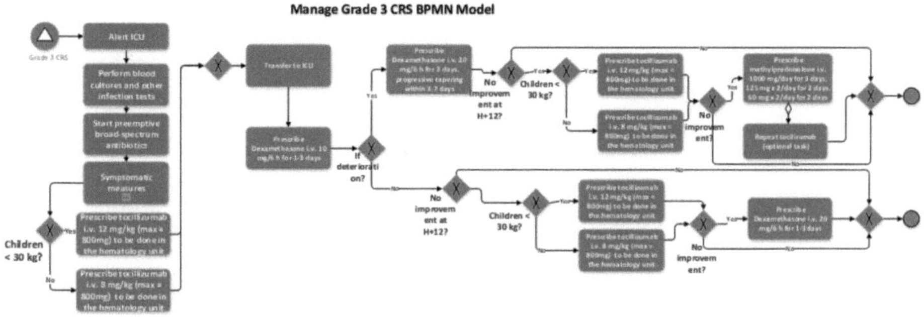

Fig. 3. BPMN Clinical Pathway Modelling of Grade 3 CRS Case Study

For example, the value at a leaf node like (Dose, "20", COUNT) under the branch: (Weight, " < 30") - > (Treatment, "Tocilizumab") - > (Dose, "8") - > (ICU, "Yes") - > (Treatment, "Dexamethasone") - > (Dose, "10") would represent: "*The number of sub-30kg patients treated with Tocilizumab 8mg/kg, who were transferred to the ICU, and started on Dexamethasone 10mg/6h and whose condition deteriorated requiring escalation to 20mg/6h*".

Moreover, it is worth noting that this transformed TLAQ, shown in Fig. 4, is not a static artifact. It is deployed within the QFLS system via the QFLS-ADAT. The QFLS Core orchestrates the distributed processing: each node query (e.g., (ICU, "Yes", COUNT)) is executed locally at participating hospitals via *Spark SQL* on their anonymized data, with only aggregated results returned and assembled into the final result tree.

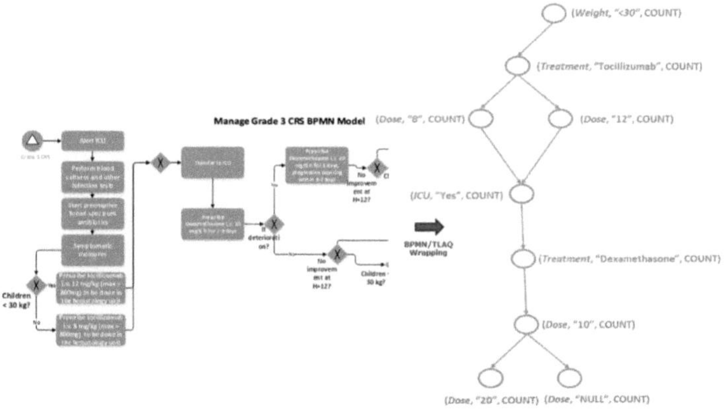

Fig. 4. Final TLAQ Branching for Deterioration Response and Dose Adjustment

5 Experimental Assessment

In this Section, we experimentally evaluate the proposed BPMN-to-TLAQ wrapping methodology within the QFLS federated healthcare analytics framework. The experimental assessment is conducted using anonymized healthcare datasets related to the CRC dataset [20] within the QFLS federated analytics environment. Upon this dataset, we construct multiple datasets of increasing.

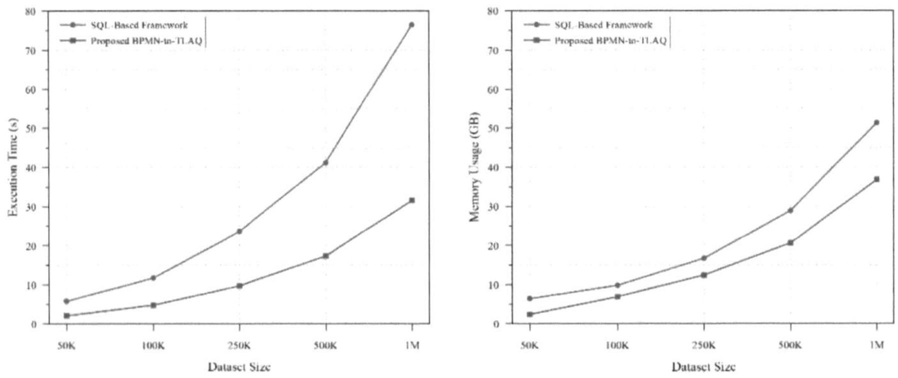

(*a*) (*b*)

Fig. 5. Performance Evaluation Between Traditional SQL-Based Analytical Framework and our Proposed BPMN-To-TLAQ Methodology: (*a*) Query Execution time; (*b*) Memory Usage.

size through a *controlled sampling-based data generation process* (e.g., [21]). For each dataset, we compare two analytical approaches: (*i*) a *traditional federated SQL-based analytical framework* executed over distributed healthcare nodes; (*ii*) the proposed BPMN-to-TLAQ wrapping methodology within the QFLS framework in terms of two critical aspects of distributed healthcare analytics: (*i*) *query execution efficiency*; (*ii*) *memory utilization scalability*.

Figure 5 presents the comparative performance evaluation in terms of execution time and memory usage over healthcare datasets of increasing size.

As shown in Fig. 5, the proposed BPMN-to-TLAQ framework consistently achieves lower query execution times and memory consumption compared to the conventional SQL-based analytical approach. As the dataset size increases, the performance gap becomes progressively more significant.

6 Conclusions and Future Work

In this paper, we introduce a BPMN-to-TLAQ wrapping methodology that enables the transformation of formal clinical pathway models into executable *Tree-Like Analytical Queries* within the QFLS federated analytics framework. By systematically mapping *BPMN decision points*, *tasks*, and *gateways* into TLAQ hierarchical query structure, our approach bridges process modelling with privacy-preserving data analytics. The practical case study demonstrates the model's effectiveness in supporting detailed, temporal investigations across distributed healthcare datasets without compromising data privacy. Future work is mainly oriented toward exploring the applicability of the BPMN-to-TLAQ model across different healthcare domains, as well as investigating enhanced *privacy* and *security* aspects of data (e.g., [22, 23]).

References

1. Secco, C.A., Sina, L.B., Nazemi, K.: Medical visual analytics - an interactive approach for analyzing electronic health records. In: IEEE IV 2024, pp. 143–149 (2024)
2. Gururaj, T., Siddesh, G.M.: Hybrid approach for enhancing performance of genomic data for stream matching. Int. J. Cogn. Inf. Nat. Intell. **15**(4), 1–18 (2021)
3. Tang, Y., Mishra, S., Alduaiji, N., Shukla, P.K., Yahya, M.A., Pang, T.: An advanced data analytics approach to a cognitive cyber-physical system for the identification and mitigation of cyber threats in the medical internet of things (MIOT). J. Supercomput. **81**(4), 623 (2025)
4. Leung, C.K., Chen, Y., Hoi, C.S.H. Shang, S., Cuzzocrea, A.: Machine learning and OLAP on big COVID-19 data. In: IEEE BigData 2020, pp. 5118–5127 (2020)
5. Cuzzocrea, A.: BigMDHealth: Supporting multidimensional big data management and analytics over big healthcare data via effective and efficient multidimensional aggregate queries over key-value stores. In: DaSET 2022, pp. 187–194 (2022)
6. Aversano, L., Iammarino, M., Madau, A., Pirlo, G., Semeraro, G.: Process mining applications in healthcare: a systematic literature review. PeerJ Comput. Sci. **11**, e2613 (2025)
7. Chatzimilioudis, G., Cuzzocrea, A., Gunopulos, D., Mamoulis, N.: A novel distributed framework for optimizing query routing trees in wireless sensor networks via optimal operator placement. J. Comput. Syst. Sci. **79**(3), 349–368 (2013)
8. Machado, P., Vilela, J., Peixoto, M., Silva, C.: A systematic study on the impact of gdpr compliance on organizations. In: ACM SBSI 2023, pp. 435–442 (2013)
9. Martin, A.: Why sovereignty matters for humanitarian data. Big Data Soc. **12**(3), 1–13 (2025)
10. Chen, Y., Pang, X., Li, X., Wang, H., Niu, B., Hu, S.: U-DPAP: utility-aware efficient range counting on privacy-preserving spatial data federation. Proc. ACM Manag. Data **3**(1), 1–25 (2025)
11. EU Committee, The EU H2020 QUALITOP Project. https://h2020qualitop.liris.cnrs.fr/wordpress/index.php/project/
12. Cuzzocrea, A., Soufargi, S.: Supporting Big healthcare data management and analytics: the cloud-based QFLS framework. In: DaWaK 2023, pp. 372–379 (2023)
13. Cuzzocrea, A., Belmerabet, I., Hafsaoui, A.: TLAQ: enhanced big healthcare data analytics via lazy aggregations. In: BigData 2025, pp. 88–103 (2025)
14. Spiekermann, S.: The challenges of privacy by design. Commun. ACM **55**(7), 38–40 (2012)
15. Cuzzocrea, A., Fortino, G., Rana, O.F.: Managing data and processes in cloud-enabled large-scale sensor networks: state-of-the-art and future research directions. In: IEEE CCGRID 2013, pp. 583–588 (2013)
16. Verma, P., Tripathi, V., Pant, B.: Secure hashgraph for healthcare: strengthening privacy and data security in patient records. IEEE Trans. Cons. Electron. **70**(1), 1205–1213 (2024)
17. Sweeney, L.: k-Anonymity: a model for protecting privacy. Int. J. Uncertain. Fuzziness Knowl. Based Syst. **10**(5), pp. 557–570 (2002)
18. Yan, W.P., Larson, P.A.: Eager aggregation and lazy aggregation. In: VLDB 1995, pp. 345–357 (1995)
19. Tan, W., Xie, N., Zhao, L., Xu, L., Sun, Y.: A New Method for business process retrieval using breadth-first traversal. Enterp. Inf. Syst. **14**(1), 83–109 (2020)

20. Lee, D.W., Santomasso, B.D., Locke, F.L., Ghobadi, A., Turtle, C.J., Brudno, J.N., et al.: ASTCT consensus grading for cytokine release syndrome and neurologic toxicity associated with immune effector cells. Biol. Blood Marrow Transplant. **25**(4), 625–638 (2019)
21. Liu, C.L., Hsieh, P.Y.: Model-Based Synthetic Sampling for Imbalanced Data. IEEE Trans. Knowl. Data Eng. **32**(8), 1543–1556 (2019)
22. Coronato, A., Cuzzocrea, A.: An innovative risk assessment methodology for medical information systems. IEEE Trans. Knowl. Data Eng. **34**(7), 3095–3110 (2022)
23. Mehmood, S., Amin, R., Costanzo, A., Alshehri, A.H., Alsubaei, F.S.: GEN-SECHEALTH: an ai-powered generative architecture for self-scalable cybersecurity and flexible data privacy protection in intricate healthcare systems. J. Big Data **13**(1), 58 (2026)

Multimodal Survival Analysis on Hierarchical Representation of Clinical Trial Data

Jyotishka Das[1,2](✉), Aaron Mamann[1], Francesca Bugiotti[2], and Paul-Henry Cournède[1]

[1] Université Paris-Saclay, CentraleSupélec, Gustave Roussy, INSERM, IHU PRISM, Cancer Data Science Unit, MICS Laboratory, Paris, France
jyotishka.das@centralesupelec.fr

[2] Université Paris-Saclay, CentraleSupélec, LISN, Paris, France

Abstract. Modern clinical trials generate heterogeneous biomedical data spanning multiple physiological scales, from molecular measurements to patient-level clinical variables. While considerable effort has been devoted to improving survival analysis through statistical or deep learning modeling, the structural organization of the input data is usually assumed to be a fixed prior. We demonstrate that partitioning the input data into hierarchical levels through informed heuristics can improve survival predictions. Experiments conducted using a Neural Cox model on the phase III IMpower150 clinical trial dataset demonstrate that a well-chosen hierarchical representation achieves a higher concordance index (C-index) and reduced overfitting than other candidate representations, signifying the importance of data organization as a key modeling and system design consideration.

Keywords: Hierarchical Survival Model · Multimodal Prediction · Deep Learning · Document Database · Heterogeneous Data · Learning Representation

1 Introduction

Deep learning models built on integrated multi-modal clinical trial data offer the potential to improve survival prediction substantially over single-modality models [10, 13]. However existing approaches address this primarily through model optimization, while assuming the organization of the input data to be a fixed prior [14]. In this work, we formalize this prior as a learning problem and then demonstrate that introducing hierarchies in the input *data representation* can improve predictive performance in survival modeling.

Section 2 discusses recent work related to the concepts and technologies that this study draws upon. In Sect. 3, we formulate the problem and present relevant theoretical results. The experimental setup is described in detail in Sect. 4. In Sect. 5, we evaluate the results. Finally, in Sect. 6, we present our conclusions and discuss potential directions for future work.

© The Author(s), under exclusive license to Springer Nature Switzerland AG 2027
G. Vargas Solar et al. (Eds.): ADBIS 2026, CCIS 3175, pp. 117–126, 2027.
https://doi.org/10.1007/978-3-032-39823-9_11

2 Related Work

Survival analysis is a cornerstone of clinical trial methodology, concerned with modelling time-to-event outcomes such as death, relapse, or disease progression. The Cox proportional hazards model [4] remains the most widely adopted framework, expressing the hazard function as $h(t \mid X) = h_0(t)\exp(\beta^\top X)$, where $h_0(t)$ is an unspecified baseline hazard and the linear predictor $\beta^\top X$ gives a patient-specific *risk score*. Regularized extensions address high-dimensional covariate settings by penalizing regression coefficients in order to reduce overfitting [12]. DeepSurv introduced a neural extension by relaxing the linearity assumption while retaining the Cox partial likelihood as the training objective [7].
Structural organisation of a human body into nested levels is recognised as a foundational principle of anatomy. Modern physiology usually shows this progression into a multi-scale hierarchy, as illustrated in Fig. 1 (a), and has directly informed multiscale modeling in clinical applications [3]. Although clinical trials have evolved from predominantly clinical feature sets [6] toward high-dimensional molecular and imaging-derived representations, to our knowledge, no prior work has systematically exploited an induced hierarchical input representation to inform downstream tasks such as survival analysis.
Document databases have emerged as a compelling alternative to relational database management systems (RDBMS) for integrating heterogeneous and longitudinal clinical data [8]. While relational systems offer strong consistency guarantees, document databases (for example, MongoDB) support a flexible schema that can be advantageous for storing hierarchical data [5].
Curriculum learning is conceived as a machine learning paradigm demonstrating that structured presentation of training examples from easiest to hardest improves convergence and generalization over random sampling [2,11]. The paradigm has already been applied across natural language processing, computer vision, and medical imaging [15].

3 Problem Formulation

We first review key preliminary concepts. Then, we analyze our proposed method theoretically to motivate the experimental design and empirical evaluation.

Neural Cox Framework. For n patients, each patient i has a survival outcome (T_i, δ_i) with observed time T_i and event indicator $\delta_i \in \{0,1\}$ ("death"). Under the Neural Cox framework of [7] and proportional hazards assumption, the *risk score* r_i can be modeled by a neural network with learnable parameters θ, patient features X_i, and continuous time t:

$$r_i = f_\theta(X_i), \quad \text{where} \quad h(t \mid X_i) = h_0(t)\exp(r_i) \tag{1}$$

It can be trained by minimizing the negative Cox partial log-likelihood with ℓ_2 regularization [12] where $\mathcal{R}(T_i) = \{j \mid T_j \geq T_i\}$ is the risk set at time T_i.

$$L(\theta) = -\sum_{i=1}^{n} \delta_i \left[r_i - \log \sum_{j \in \mathcal{R}(T_i)} \exp(r_j) \right] + \lambda \|\theta\|_2^2 \tag{2}$$

Concordance Index. The concordance index (C-index) measures the probability that, for a randomly selected comparable pair of individuals, the patient with the shorter observed survival time is assigned a higher predicted risk. The C-index ranges from 0.5 (random chance) to 1.0 (perfect discrimination). It is defined as:

$$\mathcal{C} = \frac{1}{|\mathcal{P}|} \sum_{(i,j) \in \mathcal{P}} \mathbf{1}(r_i > r_j), \qquad \mathcal{P} = \{(i,j) \mid T_i < T_j,\ \delta_i = 1\} \tag{3}$$

Mutual Information. Let R and T be random variables denoting the patient risk score and survival time. The mutual information between them is:

$$I(R;T) \;=\; H(T) - H(T \mid R) \;\geq\; 0, \tag{4}$$

where $H(T)$ measures marginal uncertainty in T and $H(T \mid R)$ the residual uncertainty after observing R. Since $H(T)$ is fixed by the data distribution, maximizing $I(R;T)$ is equivalent to minimizing $H(T \mid R)$ [11]. Therefore, if new informative external features can be introduced through a strategy that maximizes $I(R;T)$, the predictive performance of a model can be improved.

3.1 Proposed Method Hierarchical Data Representations

We run a Neural Cox model over a set $\mathcal{L}$ of m ordered partitions:

$$\mathcal{L} = (l_1, \ldots, l_m \mid l_i \prec l_j,\ \forall i < j) \tag{5}$$

$\mathcal{L}$ may follow physiological abstraction levels (Fig. 1 (a)) or a data-driven metric. For patient i and level k, let $X_i^{(k)} \in \mathbb{R}^{p_k}$ be the feature vector at L_k and $\oplus$ denote concatenation. We compare two representations for the input X_i to f_θ.

Naïve Representation. Discarding the structure of $\mathcal{L}$ concatenates all features into one vector [1], giving the risk score (from (1)):

$$r_i^{\text{naïve}} = f_\theta\left(\bigoplus_{k=1}^{m} X_i^{(k)} \right), \qquad \bigoplus_{k=1}^{m} X_i^{(k)} \in \mathbb{R}^p,\ p = \sum_{k=1}^{m} p_k. \tag{6}$$

Hierarchical Representation. Our approach organizes the same features along $\mathcal{L}$ via *recursive stacking* ($r_i^{(0)} = 0$):

$$r_i^{(k)} = f_{\theta_k}\left(X_i^{(k)} \oplus r_i^{(k-1)} \right) \in \mathbb{R}, \qquad k = 1, \ldots, m \tag{7}$$

Algorithm 1. Hierarchical Survival Analysis via Risk Score Propagation

Require: Feature sets $\{X^{(k)}\}_{k=1}^{m}$, outcomes (T_i, δ_i), regularization λ
Ensure: Final risk scores $r^{(m)}$

$r_i^{(0)} \leftarrow 0$
for $k = 1$ to m **do**
  Fit θ_k via penalized Cox loss (λ) on $(X^{(k)} \oplus r^{(k-1)}, T, \delta)$
  $r_i^{(k)} \leftarrow f_{\theta_k}(X_i^{(k)} \oplus r_i^{(k-1)})$
end for
return $r_i^{(m)}$

Unrolling (7) yields the following nested composition through Algorithm 1.

$$r_i^{\text{hier}} = f_{\theta_m}\Big(X_i^{(m)} \oplus \cdots \oplus f_{\theta_1}\Big(X_i^{(1)} \oplus r_i^{(0)}\Big)\Big) \tag{8}$$

As shown in Fig. 1(b), both (6) and (8) use the same features $\{X_i^{(k)}\}_{k=1}^{m}$ and model family f_θ. The difference in predictive performance can therefore be attributed to the structure of the data representation used.

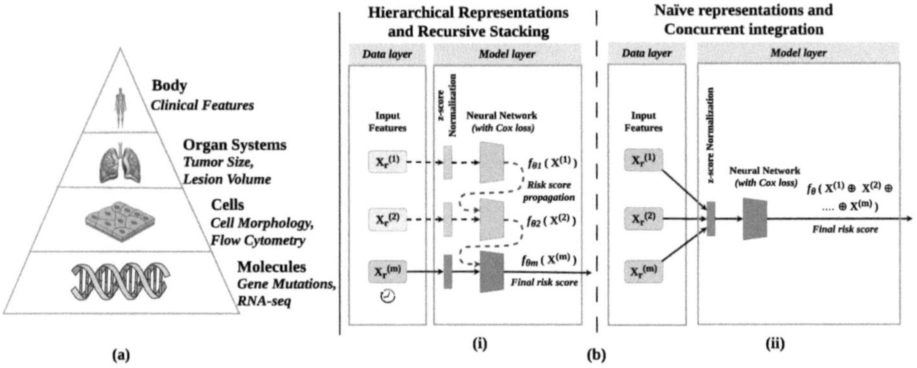

Fig. 1. (a) Hierarchical physiological abstraction of the human body. (b) Running a Neural Cox model on a (i) hierarchical, and a (ii) naïve representation.

Theoretical Results

Proposition 1 (Mutual Information as a Heuristic for Stacking Strategy). *Let $R^{(1)}, \ldots, R^{(m)}$ be risk scores from successive levels of a recursive stacking procedure over $\mathcal{L}$. If the representations are* information monotone, *i.e., $I(R^{(1)}; T) \leq \cdots \leq I(R^{(m)}; T)$, then the conditional uncertainty $H(T \mid R^{(k)})$ decreases across levels, suggesting that higher-level representations capture progressively more survival-relevant information and may improve ranking performance as measured by the concordance index in practice.*

Proof. For a consecutive pair $(R^{(k-1)}, R^{(k)})$, since $H(T)$ is fixed, the *information monotone* condition implies $H(T \mid R^{(k)}) \leq H(T \mid R^{(k-1)})$. For a comparable pair $(i,j) \in \mathcal{P}$, lower $H(T \mid R)$ suggests more consistent pairwise ordering. Therefore, $P(R_i^{(k)} > R_j^{(k)} \mid T_i < T_j) \gtrsim P(R_i^{(k-1)} > R_j^{(k-1)} \mid T_i < T_j)$. Since the concordance index (3) estimates this quantity over $\mathcal{P}$, this provides a heuristic justification that $\mathcal{C}(R^{(k)}) \gtrsim \mathcal{C}(R^{(k-1)})$ in practice.

Comments. Overfitting is acute when all modalities are trained jointly in the $p \gg n$ regime [12]. A hierarchical physiological ordering of $\mathcal{L}$ reflects the biological reality that macroscopic signals emerge from interactions of microscopic processes. Since low-dimensional clinical features arise from complex gene-gene interactions, they are more discriminative than individual genes alone [9]. Since a neural network exploits hidden structure in high-dimensional data well, it can be opted as a default model for progressively integrating weaker (molecular) into stronger (clinical) predictors. This recursive stacking is thus inspired by *curriculum learning*, introducing modalities by decreasing dimensionality $p_1 \geq p_2 \geq \cdots \geq p_m$. When information monotonicity does not hold empirically, or a broader search space is desired due to longitudinal dynamics, alternative orderings should be explored, motivating the data-driven approach of Sect. 5.

4 Experimental Setup

The dataset was integrated into MongoDB to ease the evaluation of input representations for survival modeling. Two versioned collections were created, one per dataset: *Static*, and *Dynamic*. The pipeline is shown in Fig. 2.

4.1 Dataset

The dataset is derived from the randomized phase III IMpower150 clinical trial (NCT02366143), corresponding to 466 patients from a non-blinded study to evaluate the efficacy of anti-PD-L1 atezolizumab in combination with carboplatin and paclitaxel with or without bevacizumab, in comparison to treatment with bevacizumab along with a combination of carboplatin and paclitaxel in chemotherapy-naïve participants with Stage IV nonsquamous non-small-cell lung cancer [1]. It comprises three relational tables. The *clinical table* holds 9 patient-level features (age, sex, smoking history, number of metastatic sites, ECOG, SLD, PD-L1 high/low, ctDNA positive/negative, treatment arm) plus survival outcomes for 466 patients, re-baselined across treatment cycles: Baseline (BL), C2D1 (C2), C3D1 (C3), C4D1 (C4), and C8D1 (C8). The *aggregated table* contains 331 ctDNA biomarkers; we retain four non-redundant ones: cfDNA concentration (cfDNA_conc), variant allele frequency (VAF), tumor molecules per mL of plasma (TMPMP), and mutation count (n). The *gene table* covers 393 ctDNA-positive patients with longitudinal per-gene VAF. Since later cycles improve prediction but reduce cohort size due to mortality and follow-up loss, potentially introducing survival bias [1], we constructed two datasets. A *Static*

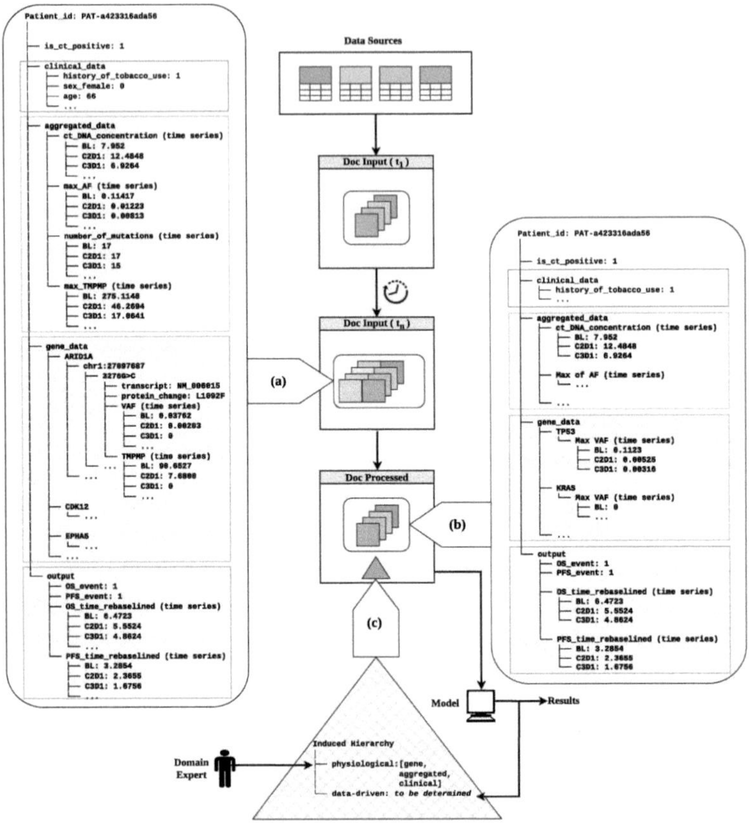

Fig. 2. Data integration pipeline in MongoDB for the *Dynamic* collection, with snippets showing the hierarchical structure for (a) raw data, (b) processed data, and (c) the induced hierarchy.

Dataset was constructed to support analysis at a single timepoint, BL, for all 466 patients. A *Dynamic Dataset* was constructed to support analysis for the 398 patients who survived till C3, with the survival outcome re-baselined. We included static clinical measurements along with longitudinal *gene* and *aggregated* metrics from BL to C3 during the early treatment phase.

4.2 Data Cleaning and Processing

The following processing steps were carried out. Firstly, since retaining all genes introduces sparsity, we restricted the *gene* feature space to the top 10 genes with the highest number of patients carrying at least one detected mutation at any chromosomal position within that gene. For each retained gene, the VAF was aggregated across all chromosomal positions and mutation sites by taking the element-wise maximum at each cycle. This gave a single longitudinal profile per gene per patient. Secondly, it was observed that in the *Dynamic* collection, some patients have missing *aggregated* and *gene* measurements at cycles C2 or C3 because they were not tested at those cycles. To ensure consistent longitudinal feature vectors, we apply a simple imputation heuristic: a missing value is propagated from the preceding observation (BL for C2, C2 for C3) under a conservative assumption that no improvement in tumor-related biomarkers occurs between consecutive cycles. Figure 2 (b) shows the collection after the application of these two processing steps.

4.3 Data Hierarchy

We organize the integrated patient data into hierarchical representations for downstream modeling. The *intrinsic hierarchy* follows directly from the document-oriented schema. For example, Fig. 2 (a, b)) shows the nested hierarchies for each of the feature groups (*clinical*, *aggregated*, and *gene*). The *induced hierarchy*, our main focus, is instead constructed during the experimental setup to order features by task-relevant heuristics. For flexibility, induced hierarchies are stored separately from the patient documents as a hash table in an auxiliary `Induced Hierarchy` document (Fig. 2 (c)), so that multiple alternatives can be defined and evaluated easily. We further investigate two forms of induced hierarchies. Firstly, a *physiological* hierarchy, derived from the biological organization of the body, progressing from molecular measurements (e.g., *gene* mutations) to *aggregated* biomarker values and finally patient-level *clinical* outcomes, yielding increasingly compact levels. Next, a *data-driven* hierarchy, constructed algorithmically by a surrogate model by arranging the data into partitions of increasing perceived "difficulty".

5 Results

To obtain reliable performance estimates, all experiments were repeated $K = 50$ times with different randomized data splits. Survival outcomes used the overall survival event indicator (`OS_event`) and time-to-event variable (`OS_month`). In each run, the dataset was partitioned into 70%/30% training/test subsets using `scikit-learn`, with `random_state` incremented from 1 to K to obtain distinct partitions per iteration. Performance was evaluated using the C-index, for which we report the mean and standard deviation (SD) across the $K = 50$ runs on both training and test sets. To isolate the effect of the data representations, the same Neural Cox model and hyperparameters were used across all experiments. After Z-score normalization, inputs pass through a fully connected hidden layer with 128 units, ReLU activation, batch normalization, and dropout ($p = 0.4$). A linear output layer produces a scalar *risk score*, trained using the Cox partial-likelihood loss with L_2 regularization ($\lambda = 0.5$). Optimization uses Adam (learning rate 10^{-3}). All experiments were run with a batch size of 64 for 200 epochs.

Table 1. C-index from physiological hierarchy-based survival modeling reported as mean ± SD. Green arrows indicate improvement across hierarchical stages.

Approach	Feature Representation	Static Collection (Time: BL)		Dynamic Collection (Time: BL, C2, C3)	
		Train	Test	Train	Test
Hierarchical	Gene	0.632 ± 0.008	0.594 ± 0.034	0.698 ± 0.011	0.611 ± 0.039
	Gene → Agg.	$0.691 \pm 0.009 \nearrow$	$0.648 \pm 0.034 \nearrow$	$0.751 \pm 0.009 \nearrow$	$0.653 \pm 0.037 \nearrow$
	Gene → Agg. → Clin.	$0.738 \pm 0.007 \nearrow$	$\mathbf{0.665 \pm 0.027} \nearrow$	$0.798 \pm 0.007 \nearrow$	$\mathbf{0.679 \pm 0.034} \nearrow$
Naïve	Gene ⊕ Agg. ⊕ Clin.	0.752 ± 0.006	0.643 ± 0.028	0.827 ± 0.008	0.657 ± 0.039

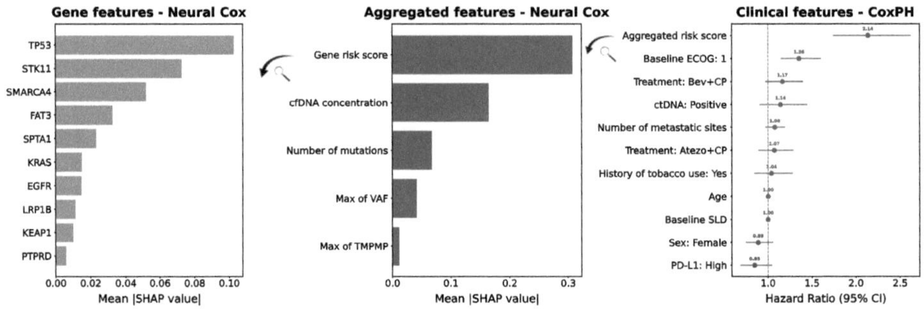

Fig. 3. Feature importance through SHAP and Hazard Ratios on the *Static* collection.

Physiological Hierarchy-Based Modeling. We evaluate survival modeling on the physiological ordering (*gene* $[X_i^{(g)}]$ → *aggregated* $[X_i^{(a)}]$ → *clinical*$[X_i^{(c)}]$), separately on *Static* and *Dynamic* collections with flattened longitudinal features. The final risk score is:

$$r_i^{\text{hier-physiological}} = f_{\theta_c}\left(X_i^{(c)} \oplus f_{\theta_a}\left(X_i^{(a)} \oplus f_{\theta_g}\left(X_i^{(g)}\right)\right)\right) \tag{9}$$

Scores are evaluated with the C-index (Table 1). Although the hierarchical approach yields a lower training C-index than the naïve approach at the final stage, it achieves a higher test C-index, indicating better generalization and more accurate survival predictions. This demonstrates the benefit of incorporating the physiological hierarchy in improving survival predictions. The framework also stays interpretable. At the final stage, the Neural Cox layer can be replaced with a standard CoxPH regression, yielding interpretable hazard ratios for the *clinical* variables. For the *gene* and *aggregated* levels, SHAP is used to quantify how these features drive their respective intermediate risk scores (Fig. 3).

Data-Driven Hierarchy-Based Modeling. Since the physiological ordering need not be optimal, we enumerate all feature-group permutations and select the hierarchy maximizing the mean test C-index, storing it in the `Induced Hierarchy` document for reuse (Fig. 4). For the *Static* collection, the best hierarchy (C-index: 0.665) matches the physiological ordering (*gene* → *aggregated* → *clinical*). For the *Dynamic* collection, the best hierarchy (C-index: 0.685) differs (*aggregated* → *clinical* → *gene*). This demonstrates that longitudinal *gene* mutation profiles strongly signal tumor progression and survival, and therefore reserving them for the final stage leads to better predictions.

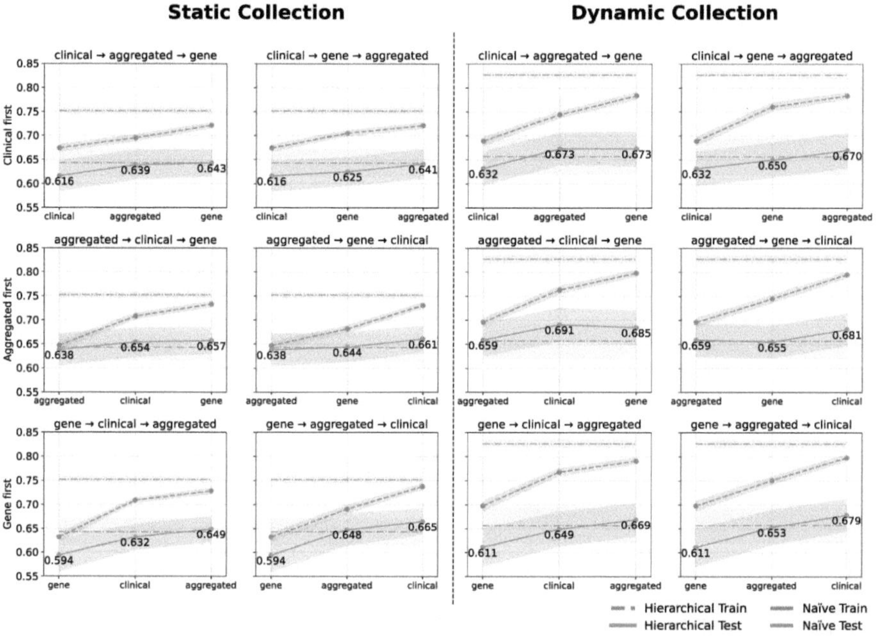

Fig. 4. C-index from data-driven hierarchy-based survival modeling. Lighter shades show SD from the mean. In the *Dynamic* collection, after the final stage, the hierarchical test (yellow) C-indices consistently exceed the naïve test (green) reference C-indices. (Color figure online)

6 Conclusion

This study underscores the importance of data organization strategies for managing heterogeneous clinical trial data within a survival analysis framework. We introduced an information-theoretic evaluation methodology that enables a systematic comparison of alternative organizational schemes. The ordering of feature groups meaningfully affects generalization: introducing weaker predictors early encourages broader pattern learning before stronger predictors refine later stages, whereas the converse promotes overfitting. This reveals the complementary roles of domain knowledge and data-driven optimization. In a *Static* collection, the physiologically motivated hierarchy already reflects a favorable ordering and achieves the best performance; in a *Dynamic* collection, algorithmic search instead places the most informative group last, improving the overall C-index. As future work, this framework opens avenues for adaptive database systems that dynamically learn and refine hierarchical organization strategies from downstream predictive performance, with extensions to other multimodal clinical data to further enhance scalability and generalization.

References

1. Assaf, Z.J.F., et al.: A longitudinal circulating tumor dna-based model associated with survival in metastatic non-small-cell lung cancer. Nat. Med. **29**(4), 859–868 (2023)
2. Bengio, Y., Louradour, J., Collobert, R., Weston, J.: Curriculum learning. In: Proceedings of the 26th International Conference on Machine Learning (ICML), pp. 41–48. ACM (2009)
3. Clancy, C.E., et al.: Multiscale modeling in the clinic: drug design and development. Ann. Biomed. Eng. **44**(9), 2591–2610 (2016)
4. Cox, D.R.: Regression models and life-tables. J. Roy. Stat. Soc.: Ser. B (Methodol.) **34**(2), 187–202 (1972)
5. Dhanagari, M.R.: Mongodb and data consistency: bridging the gap between performance and reliability. J. Comput. Sci. Technol. Stud. **6**(2), 183–198 (2024)
6. Huang, Y., Li, J., Li, M., Aparasu, R.R.: Application of machine learning in predicting survival outcomes involving real-world data: a scoping review. BMC Med. Res. Methodol. **23**(1), 268 (2023)
7. Katzman, J.L., Shaham, U., Cloninger, A., Bates, J., Jiang, T., Kluger, Y.: Deepsurv: personalized treatment recommender system using a cox proportional hazards deep neural network. BMC Med. Res. Methodol. **18**(1), 24 (2018)
8. Marshall, I.J., et al.: Trialstreamer: a living, automatically updated database of clinical trial reports. J. Am. Med. Inf. Assoc. **27**(12), 1903–1912 (2020)
9. Millar-Wilson, A., Ward, O., Duffy, E., Hardiman, G.: Multiscale modeling in the framework of biological systems and its potential for spaceflight biology studies. iScience **25**(11), 105421 (2022). https://doi.org/10.1016/j.isci.2022.105421
10. Namiot, E.D., Smirnovová, D., Sokolov, A.V., Chubarev, V.N., Tarasov, V.V., Schiöth, H.B.: The international clinical trials registry platform (ictrp): data integrity and the trends in clinical trials, diseases, and drugs. Front. Pharmacol. **14**, 1228148 (2023)
11. Semeraro, O., Bucci, M.A., Hosseinkhan-Boucher, R., Chibbaro, S., Allauzen, A., Mathelin, L.: On the use of entropy-based metrics for data-driven modeling and reinforcement learning control. In: Joint Event Euromech Colloquium on Data-Driven Fluid Dynamics/2nd ERCOFTAC Workshop on Machine Learning for Fluid Dynamics, Londres, United Kingdom (2025). https://hal.science/hal-05379611
12. Simon, N., Friedman, J.H., Hastie, T., Tibshirani, R.: Regularization paths for cox's proportional hazards model via coordinate descent. J. Stat. Softw. **39**, 1–13 (2011)
13. Wiegrebe, S., Kopper, P., Sonabend, R., Bischl, B., Bender, A.: Deep learning for survival analysis: a review. Artif. Intell. Rev. **57**(3), 65 (2024)
14. Zhou, F., Chen, H.: Cross-modal translation and alignment for survival analysis. In: Proceedings of the IEEE/CVF International Conference on Computer Vision, pp. 21485–21494 (2023)
15. Zhu, J., et al.: Curriculum trustworthy multi-modal learning. Expert Syst. Appl. 131541 (2026)

Efficient Pruning of Range Queries Under Fréchet Distance

Paul Walther(✉), Carla Rieger, and Martin Werner

Department of Aerospace and Geodesy, TUM School of Engineering and Design, Technical University of Munich, Munich, Germany
{paul.walther,carla.rieger,martin.werner}@tum.de

Abstract. Processing geospatial objects, such as trajectories, requires efficient indexing, which often relies on similarity measures, like the Hausdorff and Fréchet distances. While such distances allow for a detailed comparison of spatial objects, their computational complexity is high. Therefore, various methods for upper and lower bounds for these distance measures were proposed, which mostly rely on bounding-box approaches or start- and endpoint-based indexing to prune out-of-range elements. Though, for circular objects or objects with similar start and end points, these state-of-the-art approaches do not work. To address this issue, we propose a randomized representation of complex geometric objects using Bloom filters (BFs) as an index data structure, allowing efficient pruning of up to 95% of the comparisons of similarity-based range queries in our analysis and thus vastly reducing the number of distance measures to be calculated for the exact query. We evaluate our method on three distinct datasets (hand-written Characters, artificially generated Freespace, and the real-world Roma Taxi dataset). Our method demonstrates a 10 to 100% higher pruning ratio than a standard R-Tree and improves processing times by more than 30% for recurring queries.

Keywords: Range queries · similarity measure · Fréchet distance · Bloom filter · GloBiMaps

1 Introduction

Recently, large collections of vector-like geospatial data have been generated and collected, e.g., trajectories, ordered sequences of locations with timestamps. For this data a fast retrieval based on specific query predicates is a core task of every database management system, with similarity queries being a core functionality. In this case, similarity is usually described by complex distance metrics, e.g., the Hausdorff and Fréchet distances, which compare the query object element-wise with all other objects in the database. Building efficient indices for distance-based queries is non-trivial and was also the basis of the 2017 GISCUP [29]. The proposed solutions mainly addressed the problem by pruning the search space based on locality-sensitive hashing [4,11,13].

© The Author(s), under exclusive license to Springer Nature Switzerland AG 2027
G. Vargas Solar et al. (Eds.): ADBIS 2026, CCIS 3175, pp. 127–137, 2027.
https://doi.org/10.1007/978-3-032-39823-9_12

In this work, we present an approach based on the small-data representation *GloBiMaps* [27] and the BACR approach [26], whose basic idea got patented in [28]. Our approach allows for more efficient indexing of geometric objects and pruning the search space for range queries. We combine the following aspects:

- introducing a lower bound for complex geometric object similarity based on a query object being buffered with a given value of the distance, and
- efficiently pruning the search space for distance range queries by simple bit comparisons of pre-computed buffered discrete GloBiMaps representations.

Compared to previous approaches, our contribution provides a lower bound on the distance measures of complex geometric objects, effectively pruning the search space in range queries without any false negatives.

2 Theoretical Background

A *spatial geometric object* $o \in G$, G being the set of all objects, is modelled as a sequence of points $\mathbf{p}_i$ connected by line segments $l_{i,(i+1)}$, with each point $\mathbf{p}_i := (\mathbf{x}_i, t_i)$ having a spatial position $\mathbf{x}_i \in \mathbb{R}^{n-1}$ and an ordering attribute $t_i \in \mathbb{R}$.

Throughout this work, we focus on *non-time-sensitive similarity measures*, namely the Hausdorff and Fréchet distance. The *Hausdorff distance* δ_H is the largest minimal distance between two point sets and ignores ordering [20].

In contrast, the *Fréchet distance* δ_F intuitively is the maximum needed leash length of a man on a geometric object U walking his dog on the object V when both are not allowed to backtrack and, thus, only walk forward [8,16]. This takes ordering into account and therefore refines δ_H.

In practice, its discrete counterpart δ_{dF} [14] is used, defined for discrete spatial geometric objects U and V by

$$\delta_{dF}(U, V) := \min_{L}\{\max_{i=1,\ldots,m} d(\tilde{u}_{a_i}, \tilde{v}_{b_i})\}. \tag{1}$$

Here, $L = ((\tilde{u}_{a_1}, \tilde{v}_{b_1}), \ldots, (\tilde{u}_{a_m}, \tilde{v}_{b_m}))$ ranges over all monotone couplings between the vertex sequences $\sigma(U) := (\tilde{u}_1, \ldots, \tilde{u}_u)$ and $\sigma(V) := (\tilde{v}_1, \ldots, \tilde{v}_v)$ with u, v being the lengths of objects U, V, respectively, and m being the amount of distinct pairs. Algorithms for computing δ_F require a point-to-point distance evaluation with almost never subquadratic time complexity [8], with the baseline resulting in $\mathcal{O}(uv)$ [14]. Other distance measures, e.g., Dynamic Time Warping [32], also require point-wise comparisons.

Bloom filters (BFs) [6] are probabilistic data structures introduced in the 1970s and are commonly used to efficiently store sets with no false negatives. *GloBiMaps* are based on BFs and provide a method for efficiently storing and managing rasterized geometric objects [27]. The spatial object is represented by the set of all raster cells it intersects, stored in a BF, resulting in a small representation of the initial geometric object with a low false positive rate.

3 Related Work

To *improve efficiency* of calculating geometric distance functions non-exact approximations can be computed [9,12,25] using easy-to-be-calculated lower and upper bounds of the distance function, or algorithm can be improved [1,2,10]. Alternatively, *building indexes* of complex geometric objects can reduce the number of explicit calculations [24]. The main approaches of those indexes are differentiated into four groups: *Model-based indexes* resemble complex geometric objects in a parametrized way, which leaves a reduced memory footprint. This offers possibilities for searching and comparing the indexed objects based on the model parameters. Examples are the B-spline [15] and curve fitting [31] indexed with structures like KD-trees [5]. Other indexes are built based on *geometric summaries* of the objects. This includes circular approximations, e.g., the Ball-tree method [23], minimum bounding rectangles (MBRs) used in the R-tree-based approaches [18] and GloBiMaps [26]. A third group of indexes is based on *locality-sensitive hashing* (LSH) [17] and approaches the indexing by overlapping the hash values of similar objects. LSH approaches do not necessarily provide the optimal result but, a valid solution. For distance range queries, this was used by applying LSH on the start and end point of a trajectory [11] or the corner of an MBR [13]. Alternatively, with distance based hashes are used [19]. The most advanced approach is the representation of trajectory summaries in LSH arrays based on the Geohash [26]. The newest approaches include *learned index structures*, which fit a probabilistic model to both the data and the queries, e.g., LISA, which promises to outperform standard R-trees [21].

4 Methodology and Mathematical Description

The main idea for the proposed efficiency gain for distance based range queries is a precomputed representation of the geometric objects, which allows for low-cost retrieval of lower bound distances (Fig. 1).

Definition 1. *Given the metric space* $(\mathbb{R}^n, d)$ *a geometric R-Buffer for a complex geometric object* $o \in G$ *is the set of all points* $\mathbf{p}$ *with a distance to* o *smaller than* R *[22]:*

$$BUFFER(o, R) := \left\{ \mathbf{p} : \inf_{\mathbf{x} \in o} d(\mathbf{x}, \mathbf{p}) \leq R \right\}. \tag{2}$$

The buffer can also be calculated in an approximate way to reduce computational effort. Based on this, we define a *range query* for geometric objects as follows:

Definition 2. *A range query for complex geometric objects retrieves all complex geometric objects* $o \in G$ *given the metric space* $(\mathbb{R}^n, d)$*, which are within a distance bounded by* R *between the query object* $q \in G$ *and* o*. Hence,* $\forall o \in G$ *and*

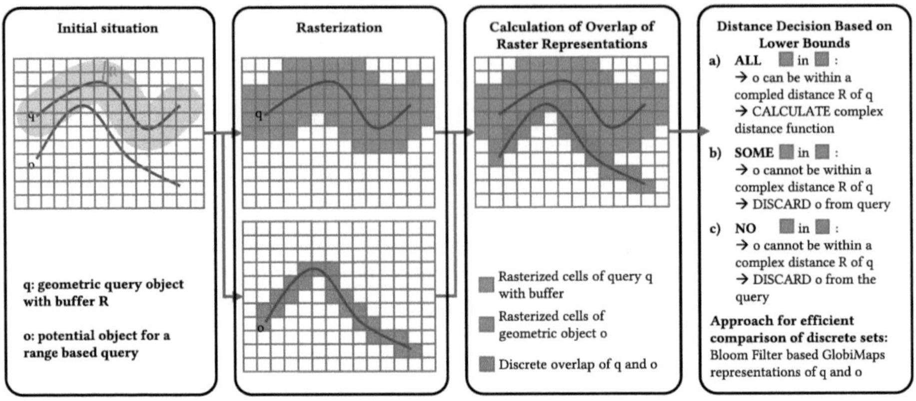

Fig. 1. Overview of the general methodological approach to efficiently prune range queries on complex geometric objects.

$\forall \mathbf{p} \in o$ it holds that $\inf_{\mathbf{g} \in q} d(\mathbf{g}, \mathbf{p}) \leq R$. Therefore, this range query returns the following set:

$$BUFFER_{GO} := \bigcup_{o \in G} \{o \mid \inf_{g \in q} d(g, p) \leq R \, \forall p \in o\} . \tag{3}$$

Thereby, all geometric objects that do completely lie in the R-Buffer are returned in the set BUFFER_{GO}. The previously described distance functions play a crucial role in our further argumentation. As known, the Hausdorff distance forms a lower bound to the Fréchet distance as shown in [3].

Lemma 1. *The maximum of a simple element-wise distance metric δ_{simple} between two polygonal curves is smaller or equal to a distance metric with applied ordering constraint $\delta_{simple} \leq \delta_{complex}$. Therefore, the Hausdorff distance δ_H forms a lower bound for the Fréchet distance $\delta_H \leq \delta_F$.*

The proof is given in [3] and follows from imposing additional constraints for computing the distance measure. For the Hausdorff distance, we can further formulate a lower bound based on a buffer of size R.

Lemma 2. *For a geometric buffer of size R around object $q \in G$, another object $o \in G$ has a Hausdorff distance larger than R if one of the object elements $o_i \in o$ for some i is not an element of the respective R-buffer. This is formalized as follows:*

$$\exists \, o_i \in o \setminus BUFFER(q, R) \Rightarrow \delta_H > R . \tag{4}$$

Proof. If an element $o_i \in o$ lies outside $\text{BUFFER}(q, R)$, the distance to every point of q exceeds R, i.e., $\inf_{g \in q} d(g, o_i) > R$, leading to $\sup_{p \in o} \inf_{g \in q} d(g, p) > R$, and hence $\delta_H > R$.

Consequently, with efficient buffer calculation we can formulate a lower bound to the Hausdorff distance and therefore set a lower bound for complex distances

$\delta_{complex}$ such as Fréchet. To profit from this, we propose using GloBiMaps representations for objects $o \in G$: They pose a *sketch* s of each o by fixing a global raster, transforming the geometries o into raster pixels, and subsuming those with a GloBiMaps into a BF representation of size m; the sketch s. For querying all o with respect to a query element $q \in G$ and $d(q, o) \leq R$, we compute the buffered query BUFFER$(q, R+\tau)$, where $\tau > 0$ accounts for inaccuracies due to rounding, discretization and generation errors. Selecting this τ not smaller than the maximal displacement occurring to a point during rasterization ensures no point within range is pruned. Its GloBiMaps sketch is computed with similar configurations as during the initial sketch generation of $o \in G$. The sketch of q and all database objects $o \in G$ can then be cheaply compared.

Theorem 1. *We can exclude geometric objects $o \in G$ from geometric range queries with query predicate $d(q, o) \leq R$, if there is a 1 in position i in the sketch of o and a 0 in the same position i of the sketch of the buffered query.*

Proof. Having a *1* in the database object while having a *0* in the query object means that there is some cell c in the raster that is occupied by the database object but not the query object. Based on the observations in Lemma 2, subsequent discussions, and the definition of a *sketch*, we can conclude that the distance between the query object and the respective object in the database cannot be $\leq R$.

This has significant implications as in large datasets, pruning potential objects outside the queried Fréchet distances reduces the computational effort as the number of candidates for the complex exact calculation of the Fréchet distance (with time complexity of $\mathcal{O}(n^2)$) is reduced.

5 Evaluation of Correctness and Efficiency

As described before, we account for potential *discretization and rounding errors* when generating the buffered query objects by adding $\tau > 0$ to R. An inherent property of GloBiMaps representations is that they allow only for false positives. A GloBiMaps sketch represents at least all raster cells initially occupied by the geometric object, but, the limited size of the used BF data structure can result in overlapping hashes of different raster cells. Consequently, the bit representations in the sketch may also embed additional cells accidentally. The effectiveness of our approach is inverse to the risk of a false positive p_{FP} depending on the chosen number of hash functions k, in the optimal case $k^* = \frac{m}{n} \log 2$, and the BF length m [26]:

$$p_{FP} \approx \left(1 - \exp\left(-k\frac{n}{m}\right)\right)^k . \tag{5}$$

As an *efficiency* baseline, range queries require pairwise distance computations between the query and all database objects, leading to linear complexity. Our approach adds a one-time cost for generating sketches and computing a buffered sketch for each query, which depends only on the query size. Querying involves cheap comparisons of compressed sketches, reducing memory use and computation time, while exact distance calculations are performed only on the remaining candidates. Pruning *effectiveness* depends on detecting zero bits in sketches and on parameters such as grid size, hash functions, and memory, which can be tuned per application. The method also supports efficient summaries via lossless sketch unions using bitwise OR, and its bitwise independence enables parallel, hardware-accelerated, and distributed implementations.

6 Experiments

We conduct experiments on three datasets to evaluate our approach (Fig. 2). The *Chars* dataset includes spatially-overlapping hand-written character traces forming three-dimensional trajectories [30]. We only use two dimensions. The *Freespace* dataset is a self-created dataset of 2061 trajectories with similar start and endpoints in a constrained free space. It was generated using three obstacles and a penalty algorithm. This dataset was chosen because it holds very similar trajectories, which are not separable by traditional methods such as MBR pruning. The *Roma* dataset contains trajectories of $\approx$ 320 taxis in Rome over 30 days [7] and was chosen because of its unsteady sampling frequencies resulting in gaps influencing similarity calculation. For evaluation, we cut the trajectories into parts of around 100 points and remove outliers.

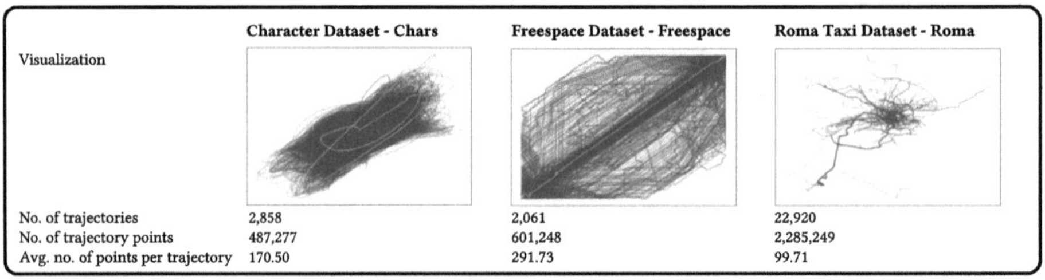

Fig. 2. Visualization and key properties of the three distinct selected datasets *Chars*, *Freespace*, *Roma* with one highlighted sample trajectory in orange for each dataset.

Evaluation of Algorithmic Steps. The code base is written in C++ based on open-source libraries, the proposed method, and the patent [28] and is executed single-threaded on a device with 16GB RAM and a 4-core, 2.6GHz CPU. It is designed for arbitrary dimensions, while only 2D is examined here, and requires the input data to be normalized to $[0, 1]$. For comparability, we fix the rasterization grid to 100×100 for all datasets and use two BF hash functions.

First, we measure the time to *create the GloBiMaps index* (Fig. 3, Step 1)) done once before querying by rasterizing the trajectories and inserting their representation. Wall clock times for various BF sizes show that runtime mainly depends on the number of trajectories and covered grid cells per trajectory, not

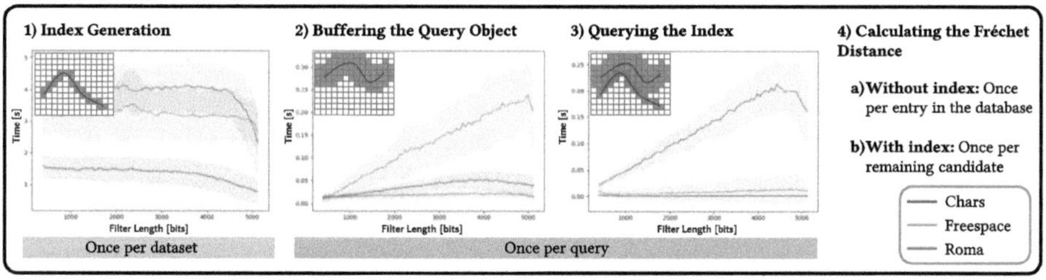

Fig. 3. Algorithmic steps of our pruning approach with average wall clock times [s] (with standard deviations) depending on the filter length [bits] for the three datasets *Chars*, *Freespace* and *Roma* ($n_{\text{queries}} = 200$ per index size).

filter length. Slight decreases for longer filters are observed and are likely due to sparser filters. Overall index creations takes only seconds in all cases. For the *preparation of the query object* the processing times are given in Fig. 3, Step 2), being in the range of ms. Finally, the times for *index query* are given in Fig. 3, Step 3. The results mainly depend on the dataset and the filter size, as those correlate with the number of bits to be checked.

For the *pruning ratio* $\text{PR} = \frac{\text{omitted elements}}{\text{total elements}}$ we achieve $\geq 95\%$ (Chars), $\geq 85\%$ (Freespace), and $\geq 53\%$ (Roma), with BF lengths of <512 bits only and marginal gains from larger BFs. Differences are dataset inherent, e.g., Freespace contains many elements with a low Fréchet range, limiting pruning. For Roma the fixed grid size and large area result in coarse resolution and lower PR.

Computing the Fréchet Distance. As a reference for the measured wall clock times, we investigate the time to calculate the Fréchet distance between randomly chosen trajectories in the dataset using three different standard implementations of fast, sparse, and linear discrete Fréchet distance[1]. The results are given in Table 1. Additionally, the computation time for a query in the set without any index structure, assuming that all distances between the query object and all objects have to be calculated, is presented. These queries are relatively long and, hence, are unsuitable for fast retrieval of trajectories from a database with many entries. It is obvious that our approach with pruning capabilities of more than 50% cuts the standard times without pruning by a huge factor.

Comparison to R-Tree Based Pruning of the Search Space. To show the pruning advantage of our approach, we compare it with a standard R-Tree-based pruning based on MBRs of the trajectories. For the evaluation we fix the BF size to 1024 bits. To evaluate the *pruning power*, we queried the database with 10 different trajectories under a fixed maximum Fréchet distance. For the R-Tree-based index, we compute each trajectories' MBR, insert them as a tuple `(id, MBR)` in the index, and query with the MBR of the R-buffered search trajectory, yielding candidate matches. Alternatively, we apply our pruning algorithm. The

[1] https://github.com/joaofig/discrete-frechet, last accessed Jun 06, 2024.

Table 1. Wall clock times for a) calculating the Fréchet distances between randomly chosen trajectories and b) a whole range query. Assumption: for full queries, the Fréchet distance between a query item and all items in the dataset is calculated.

	Calculation Method	Chars	Freespace	Roma
a) time for a distance calculation*	fast	2.5 ± 5.3 ms	1.7 ± 2.9 ms	0.9 ± 2.2 ms
	sparse	12.5 ± 7.0 ms	9.1 ± 28.7 ms	4.4 ± 2.3 ms
	linear	3.2 ± 1.6 ms	8.3 ± 3.6 ms	1.1 ± 0.7 ms
b) time for a full query**	fast	142.3 ± 3.6 s	52.2 ± 29.9 s	325.8 ± 6.2 s
	sparse	715.9 ± 19.9 s	282.7 ± 166.8 s	1509.1 ± 28.9 s
	linear	181.2 ± 3.8 s	255.2 ± 40.1 s	366.8 ± 4.8 s

*Average and standard deviation of the pairs of 15 query objects with all dataset objects each (Fig. 2).
**Average and standard deviation of 15 random queries. This means n-1 distance calculations each.

results (Table 2) report the mean and standard deviation over 10 random queries, each conducted 20 times (200 queries per dataset).

Table 2. Average Pruning Ratio, Creation Time, Index Query Time, and calculated Overall Query Time of the R-Tree in comparison to our index with 1024 bits length (average and standard deviation for $n_{\text{queries}} = 200$ per case).

Dataset	Chars		Freespace		Roma	
	R-Tree	Our Index	R-Tree	Our Index	R-Tree	Our Index
Pruning Ratio	81.9 ± 21.4%	97.6 ± 1.9%	0.0 ± 0.0%	88.7 ± 25.4%	41.6 ± 20.7%	53.0 ± 7.2%
Index Creation Time	604 ± 98 ms	1718 ± 323 ms	391 ± 22 ms	2959 ± 1012 ms	4558 ± 172 ms	4017 ± 788 ms
Index Query Time	0.14 ± 0.04 ms	24.3 ± 7.7 ms	0.20 ± 0.03 ms	44.5 ± 22.8 ms	0.94 ± 0.29 ms	65.4 ± 13.9 ms
Overall Time, 1 Query, calc.	1.90 s	1.91 s	3.99 s	3.39 s	16.61 s	13.78 s
Avg. Overall Time per Query, 1000 Queries	1.29 s	0.20 s	3.50 s	0.44 s	12.05 s	9.76 s

Our approach is especially effective for pruning Freespace, as all trajectories share the same MBR, which fails with the traditional approach of R-Tree-based MBR pruning. More general, it excels if many trajectories have identical or similar MBRs but differ significantly within these MBRs, as in spread-out trajectories or complex trajectories in constrained spaces.

For the *runtime analysis*, we compare index creation and query time (Table 2). Querying includes both preparing the query object and executing it. R-Tree-based pruning is faster for both creation and querying. However, our higher pruning power results in overall outperformance, as element-wise Fréchet Ranges computations are costly (*Overall Time*). Especially for repeated queries with one-time index creation, our approach reduces query time by at least 30%.

7 Conclusion

In this work, we propose and evaluate an approach for efficient pruning of the search space for range queries based on a pointwise distance measure, like the

Fréchet distance. Our approach relies on the compressed data representation GloBiMaps based on BFs. It allows for computing lower bounds for distance measures by simple bitwise comparisons of these representations of complex geometric objects. This leads to a low additional one-time cost of preparing the newly defined index structure but allows for efficient processing. Especially for widespread spatial objects with similar bounding boxes, we achieve higher pruning ratios than traditional MBR and R-tree-based pruning. We evaluated our approach on three datasets where it outperforms the pruning ratio of traditional methods, especially in resource-constrained settings. In the future, the solution can be extended to hierarchical GloBiMap structures for more efficiency.

Acknowledgments. This work is funded by the Deutsche Forschungsgemeinschaft (DFG, German Research Foundation) – 507196470. CR is sponsored by the Wolfgang Gentner Programme of the German Federal Ministry of Education and Research – 13E18CHA and the CERN Quantum Technology Initiative.

References

1. Agarwal, P.K., Avraham, R.B., Kaplan, H., Sharir, M.: Computing the discrete Fréchet distance in subquadratic time. SIAM J. Comput. **43**(2), 429–449 (2014). https://doi.org/10.1137/130920526
2. Alt, H., Godau, M.: Computing the Fréchet distance between two polygonal curves. Int. J. Comput. Geom. Appl. **05**(01n02), 75–91 (1995). https://doi.org/10.1142/S0218195995000064
3. Alt, H., Knauer, C., Wenk, C.: Comparison of distance measures for planar curves. Algorithmica **38**(1), 45–58 (2004). https://doi.org/10.1007/s00453-003-1042-5
4. Baldus, J., Bringmann, K.: A fast implementation of near neighbors queries for Fréchet distance (GIS Cup). In: Proceedings of the 25th ACM SIGSPATIAL International Conference on Advances in Geographic Information Systems, ACM, New York, NY, USA (2017). https://doi.org/10.1145/3139958.3140062
5. Bentley, J.L.: Multidimensional binary search trees used for associative searching. Commun. ACM **18**(9), 509–517 (1975). https://doi.org/10.1145/361002.361007
6. Bloom, B.H.: Space/time trade-offs in hash coding with allowable errors. Commun. ACM **13**(7), 422–426 (1970). https://doi.org/10.1145/362686.362692
7. Bracciale, L., Bonola, M., Loreti, P., Bianchi, G., Amici, R., Rabuffi, A.: CRAWDAD dataset roma/taxi (v. 2014-07-17) (2022). https://doi.org/10.15783/C7QC7M
8. Bringmann, K.: Why walking the dog takes time: frechet distance has no strongly subquadratic algorithms Unless SETH Fails. In: Proceedings of the 2014 IEEE 55th Annual Symposium on Foundations of Computer Science, pp. 661–670. IEEE Computer Society, USA (2014). https://doi.org/10.1109/FOCS.2014.76
9. Bringmann, K., Mulzer, W.: Approximability of the discrete Fréchet distance. J. Comput. Geom. **7**(2), 46–76 (2015). https://doi.org/10.20382/jocg.v7i2a4
10. Buchin, K., Buchin, M., Meulemans, W., Mulzer, W.: Four soviets walk the dog—with an application to alt's conjecture. In: Chekuri, C. (ed.) Proceedings of the Twenty-Fifth Annual ACM-SIAM Symposium on Discrete Algorithms, pp. 1399–1413. PR, ACM and SIAM (2014). https://doi.org/10.1137/1.9781611973402.103

11. Buchin, K., Diez, Y., van Diggelen, T., Meulemans, W.: Efficient trajectory queries under the Fréchet distance (GIS Cup). In: Proceedings of the 25th ACM SIGSPATIAL International Conference on Advances in Geographic Information Systems, pp. 1–4. ACM, New York, NY, USA (2017). https://doi.org/10.1145/3139958.3140064
12. Colombe, C., Fox, K.: Approximating the (Continuous) Fréchet Distance: Schloss Dagstuhl – Leibniz-Zentrum für Informatik. LIPIcs, Volume 189, SoCG 2021 **189** (2021). https://doi.org/10.4230/LIPICS.SOCG.2021.26
13. Dütsch, F., Vahrenhold, J.: A filter-and-refinement-algorithm for range queries based on the Fréchet Distance (GIS Cup). In: Proceedings of the 25th ACM SIGSPATIAL International Conference on Advances in Geographic Information Systems, pp. 1–4. ACM, New York, NY, USA (2017). https://doi.org/10.1145/3139958.3140063
14. Eiter, T., Mannila, H.: Computing discrete Fréchet distance. CD-TR **94**(64) (1994)
15. Farin, G.: B-Splines. In: Farin, G. (ed.) Kurven und Flächen im Computer Aided Geometric Design, pp. 122–145. Vieweg+Teubner Verlag, Wiesbaden (1994). https://doi.org/10.1007/978-3-663-10602-9_10
16. Fréchet, M.M.: Sur quelques points du calcul fonctionnel. Rendiconti del Circolo Matematico di Palermo **22**(1), 1–72 (1906). https://doi.org/10.1007/BF03018603
17. Gionis, A., Indyk, P., Motwani, R.: Similarity search in high dimensions via hashing. In: Proceedings of the 25th International Conference on Very Large Data Bases. VLDB 1999, pp. 518–529. Morgan Kaufmann Publishers Inc, San Francisco, CA, USA (1999)
18. Guttman, A.: R-Trees: a dynamic index structure for spatial searching. In: Proceedings of the 1984 ACM SIGMOD International Conference on Management of Data. pp. 47–57. SIGMOD 1984, ACM, New York, NY, USA (1984). https://doi.org/10.1145/602259.602266
19. Haase, J., Brefeld, U.: Finding similar movements in positional data streams. In: Davis, J., van Haaren, J., Zimmermann, A. (eds.) Proceedings of the 2nd Workshop on Machine Learning and Data Mining for Sports Analytics co-located with 2013 ECML PKDD 2013, Prague, Czech Republic, September 27th, 2013, vol. 1969, pp. 49–57. CEUR-WS.org (2013). https://ceur-ws.org/Vol-1969/paper-07.pdf
20. Hausdorff, F.: Grundzüge der Mengenlehre, vol. 7. von Veit (1914)
21. Li, P., Lu, H., Zheng, Q., Yang, L., Pan, G.: LISA: a learned index structure for spatial data. In: Maier, D. (ed.) Proceedings of the 2020 ACM SIGMOD International Conference on Management of Data, pp. 2119–2133. ACM, New York, NY, United States (2020). https://doi.org/10.1145/3318464.3389703
22. Maekawa, T.: Overview of offset curves and surfaces. CAD Comput. Aided Des. **31**(3), 165–173 (1999). https://doi.org/10.1016/S0010-4485(99)00013-5
23. Omohundro, S.: Five Balltree Construction Algorithms. California, Berkeley (1989)
24. Su, H., Liu, S., Zheng, B., Zhou, X., Zheng, K.: A survey of trajectory distance measures and performance evaluation. VLDB J. **29**(1), 3–32 (2020). https://doi.org/10.1007/s00778-019-00574-9
25. Vlachos, M., Kollios, G., Gunopulos, D.: Discovering similar multidimensional trajectories. In: Agrawal, R. (ed.) Proceedings / 18th International Conference on Data Engineering, pp. 673–684. IEEE Computer Society Press, Los Alamitos, Calif (2002). https://doi.org/10.1109/ICDE.2002.994784
26. Werner, M.: BACR: set similarities with lower bounds and application to spatial trajectories. In: Proceedings of the 23rd SIGSPATIAL International Conference on Advances in Geographic Information Systems, pp. 1–10. ACM (2015). https://doi.org/10.1145/2820783.2820802

27. Werner, M.: GloBiMaps - a probabilistic data structure for in-memory processing of global raster datasets. In: Proceedings of the 27th ACM SIGSPATIAL International Conference on Advances in Geographic Information Systems, pp. 3–12. ACM, New York, NY, USA (2019). https://doi.org/10.1145/3347146.3359086
28. Werner, M.: A Method and System for Range Query Processing of Complex Geometric Data - EP 4 336 377 A1 (2024)
29. Werner, M., Oliver, D.: ACM SIGSPATIAL GIS Cup 2017. SIGSPATIAL Special **10**(1), 24–27 (2018). https://doi.org/10.1145/3231541.3231549
30. Williams, B.: Character Trajectories (2008). https://doi.org/10.24432/C58G7V
31. Woodford, C., Phillips, C.: Curve fitting. In: Woodford, C., Phillips, C. (eds.) Numerical Methods with Worked Examples: Matlab Edition, pp. 71–96. Springer, Dordrecht (2012). https://doi.org/10.1007/978-94-007-1366-6_4
32. Yi, B.K., Jagadish, H.V., Faloutsos, C.: Efficient retrieval of similar time sequences under time warping. In: Proceedings 14th International Conference on Data Engineering, pp. 201–208. IEEE, Los Alamitos, Calif (1998). https://doi.org/10.1109/ICDE.1998.655778

SmartIVF: A Z-Order Inverted File for Filtered Approximate Nearest-Neighbor Search

Henrique G. Zanin(✉), André M. S. Magalhães, Elaine P. M. de Sousa, and Cristina D. Aguiar

University of São Paulo (USP), São Carlos, SP, Brazil
{henrique.zanin,andre.moreira.souza}@usp.br, {parros,cdac}@icmc.usp.br

Abstract. Hybrid vector search, the problem of approximate nearest neighbor retrieval under scalar range predicates, is a core issue in modern vector databases. Existing graph-based indexes for this problem fall into two families, each with limitations: (i) *predicate-coupled* designs, which embed the scalar structure directly into the graph topology and therefore support only one or two filtering dimensions; and (ii) *predicate-agnostic* designs, which build a single shared graph and apply the predicate as a filter at query time, but whose memory usage scales with dataset size and tuning parameters. We present `SmartIVF`, which extends the inverted file by using a Z-order space-filling curve to encode all scalar dimensions into a single key. This design enables budget-controlled range decomposition at query time without structural limits on dimensionality, thus overcoming the limitations of existing approaches. Experiments on the SIFT-1M, AudioSet, and LAION-1M datasets, with up to five scalar dimensions, show that `SmartIVF` consistently achieves recall above 0.9 across all configurations, in contrast to graph-based competitors, which fail to reach 0.9 recall on the high-dimensional LAION-1M dataset. On SIFT-1M, `SmartIVF` builds 130× faster than iRangeGraph, and across the three datasets uses 3–6× less search memory than iRangeGraph and 4–30× less than ACORN. These results demonstrate that `SmartIVF` is well-suited to memory-constrained settings and frequent index rebuilding.

Keywords: Approximate nearest neighbor search · Hybrid query processing · Multidimensional indexing · Space-filling curves · Inverted file

1 Introduction

Modern transformer encoders and diffusion models represent documents, images, and audio segments as high-dimensional embeddings, and many applications, such as Retrieval-Augmented Generation (RAG), recommendation, and multimedia search, depend on efficient Approximate Nearest Neighbor (ANN)

© The Author(s), under exclusive license to Springer Nature Switzerland AG 2027
G. Vargas Solar et al. (Eds.): ADBIS 2026, CCIS 3175, pp. 138–147, 2027.
https://doi.org/10.1007/978-3-032-39823-9_13

retrieval [9]. Queries in these settings are rarely similarity-only. For instance, a product search may retrieve the ten most similar items to a query image, with a price between $40 and $120 and a given rating level. Real workloads combine a vector query with one or more scalar range predicates [6].

Existing approaches (Sect. 2) build on graph-based ANN indexes and fall into two families: *predicate-coupled* designs bake the scalar structure into the graph topology, while *predicate-agnostic* designs filter a single shared graph at query time. Neither supports filtering over multiple independent scalar attributes without incurring structural or memory overhead.

These limitations raise a practical question: can an inverted-file design, augmented with a Space-Filling Curve (SFC) to encode all scalar dimensions into a single key, achieve high recall across varying selectivities and dimensionalities while preserving memory efficiency and low construction cost?

We answer this question by introducing the following contributions:

- `SmartIVF`, a hybrid strategy that maps scalar attributes to Z-order keys and organizes the dataset into an equi-depth inverted file (IVF) over the scalar domain. At query time, the scalar predicate is decomposed into a budget-controlled set of SFC intervals via breadth-first search (BFS), probing only matching partitions in vector-proximity order. The design imposes no limit on the number of scalar dimensions and requires no auxiliary graph structure.
- **Safe-adaptive probing**, a stopping rule that counts only non-empty SFC-filtered clusters toward the probe budget, allowing probe depth to scale with predicate selectivity without additional tuning parameters.

We evaluated `SmartIVF` on the SIFT-1M, AudioSet, and LAION-1M datasets with up to five scalar dimensions at 1% selectivity. Results show that `SmartIVF` consistently maintains Recall@10 above 0.9 across all evaluated configurations while achieving the highest query throughput. Moreover, `SmartIVF` is the only algorithm that meets the prescribed quality threshold on LAION-1M, and it further achieves up to 130× lower index construction time, 3–6× less search memory than iRangeGraph, and 4–30× less than ACORN.

The remainder of this paper is organized as follows. Section 2 reviews related work, Sect. 3 presents the construction and search procedures of `SmartIVF`, Sect. 4 details the empirical evaluation, and Sect. 5 concludes the paper.

2 Related Work

Graph-based methods such as HNSW [5] dominate ANN search over high-dimensional vectors but do not address the scalar-range predicates that are our focus.

Methods that target scalar-range predicates build on graph-based ANN and split into two families that differ in how scalar structure is incorporated. *Predicate-coupled* designs embed the scalar structure directly into the graph topology. SeRF [11] creates a dedicated graph for each scalar interval and compresses these graphs to reduce memory usage. UNIFY [4] combines pre-, hybrid-, and post-filtering within a unified graph, selecting among them at query time using a cardinality heuristic; it also supports incremental insertion but targets only single-attribute scalar predicates. iRangeGraph [10] reduces the number of dedicated graphs to $O(\log n)$ by organizing objects in a segment tree over the scalar attribute and merging the relevant graphs on demand during query execution. It supports single-attribute predicates, but multi-attribute filtering requires secondary in- or post-filtering. Across this family, filtering is constrained to one or two scalar dimensions because the scalar structure is baked into the graph, and recall degrades under high-selectivity predicates when this limit is exceeded.

Predicate-agnostic designs, in contrast, build a single graph that ignores the scalar attributes at construction time and applies the predicate as a filter during search. ACORN [7] is the representative example: it constructs an overconnected HNSW graph, where neighborhood expansion is controlled by a tunable parameter γ, and predicates are applied as filters during query execution. Although this design avoids index reconstruction and supports arbitrary predicates, memory overhead and index construction time both grow with γ and the dataset size. Furthermore, ACORN has not been evaluated under high-selectivity queries.

These limitations motivate structuring the scalar attributes differently. Space-Filling Curves, notably the Z-order (Morton) curve, map a multidimensional domain to a one-dimensional key while approximately preserving locality [3], turning axis-aligned range queries into contiguous key intervals, yet classical SFC structures do not natively support ANN search under scalar filters. `SmartIVF` closes this gap: it organizes the dataset into an equi-depth inverted file over the Z-order key and probes only matching partitions in vector-proximity order, sustaining recall under high-selectivity queries while keeping construction time and memory low (Sect. 4).

3 The Proposed `SmartIVF`

`SmartIVF` is a hybrid strategy that unifies multidimensional scalar-range filtering with ANN search. Each object is assigned a Z-order key over its scalar attributes; the dataset is then organized into an equi-depth inverted file over the key domain, so that at query time only the partitions whose scalar ranges intersect the predicate are probed. Probing order within each partition follows vector proximity to the query, and a configurable probe budget controls the recall-throughput trade-off without modifying the index structure.

3.1 Index Layout and Query Processing

`SmartIVF` is built in two nested levels: scalar-domain partitioning via SFC keys (Level 1), followed by vector clustering within each partition (Level 2).

Level 1: SFC-Based Scalar Partitioning. We quantize each object's D scalar attributes to a fixed number of bits per dimension and bit-interleave them into a single Z-order (Morton) key, mapping the multidimensional scalar values to one dimension while preserving spatial locality. The dataset is then divided into equi-depth partitions of approximately equal size, each storing a bounding box that records, for each dimension, its scalar range and the extent of its Z-order key.

We use equi-depth rather than equi-width binning: under skewed distributions, equi-width partitioning creates highly imbalanced buckets that degrade search efficiency and recall uniformity, whereas equi-depth partitioning ensures balanced partition sizes regardless of the distribution of the scalar values.

We adopt the Z-order (Morton) curve because its bit-interleaved encoding maps cleanly to integer arithmetic and offers competitive locality with the Hilbert order for the dimensionalities considered here ($D \leq 5$); a Hilbert-curve variant is straightforward and left for future work.

We further note that the equi-depth balance guarantee is marginal: under strong correlation between scalar dimensions, equi-depth buckets can still exhibit elongated bounding boxes.

Level 2: Vector-based Partitioning. Within each partition, the vectors are organized adaptively: small partitions are kept as a flat list sorted by Z-order key, while larger ones are clustered with K-Means, using a centroid count that grows with the square root of the partition size, and each cluster's list is likewise sorted by key. Sorting each list by key enables binary search to extract only the contiguous segments that fall within the query's key intervals, avoiding a full scan.

Figure 1 shows the resulting structure: (a) the Voronoi cells in the embedding space, (b) the scalar bounding boxes for each partition, and (c) the sorted inverted lists for one partition, where each cell shows the quantized SFC key z (4-bit per dimension; repeated values reflect ties in the quantized grid).

Search. A filtered k-NN query supplies a query vector and a scalar range predicate over the D attributes, and is answered in two phases without scanning the full dataset. *Partition Selection* projects the scalar predicate onto the Z-order key line as a set of key intervals and uses them to prune partitions that cannot contain any in-range object, without touching their vectors. *Safe-Adaptive Probing* then visits each surviving partition, probing its clusters in order of proximity to the query and stopping once the candidate pool is large enough, or the probe budget is exhausted, so computation concentrates on partitions that intersect both the scalar range and the vector neighborhood.

Partition Selection. The scalar predicate is transformed into a set of key intervals using a breadth-first decomposition of the scalar domain. The process begins with the entire domain: regions disjoint from the query are discarded, regions fully contained within the query (or refined to a single cell) are emitted as intervals, and partially overlapping regions are split along their longest dimension. The traversal terminates early when a predefined budget on the number of intervals is reached. The emitted intervals over-approximate the predicate due to both the early termination and the well-known Z-order false positives, where the key range of a query box may include keys whose values lie outside the intended range. This over-approximation is acceptable because the exact

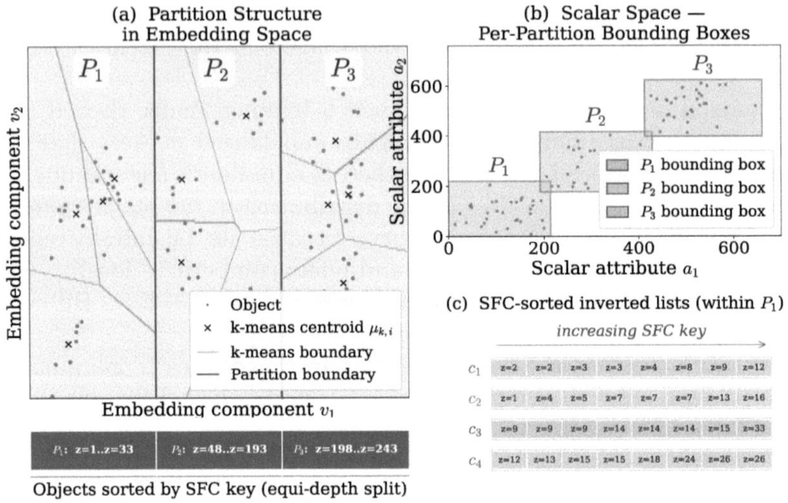

Fig. 1. Two-level structure of `SmartIVF`: (a) Voronoi cells in the embedding space; (b) scalar bounding boxes per partition; (c) SFC-sorted inverted lists inside P_1, each cell is a quantized SFC key z (4-bit per dimension; ties arise from grid quantization).

scalar predicate is re-evaluated for every candidate downstream. The intervals are then sorted, and contiguous intervals are fused. If the number of intervals still exceeds the budget, the closest pairs are merged until the budget is met. Each partition's stored key range is then tested against these intervals. Partitions that do not overlap any interval are discarded without further processing. The remaining partitions are further checked against their raw scalar bounding boxes to reject those whose key ranges overlap but whose per-dimension scalar bounds fall entirely outside the query. For instance, a query over two attributes on a 4×4 grid produces nine matching cells that are consolidated into four key intervals.

Safe-Adaptive Probing. The surviving partitions are then searched for the candidates that form the final k-NN pool. A flat partition is scanned directly: a binary search over each key interval extracts the matching contiguous slice, and every retrieved object is checked against the exact scalar predicate. An inverted-file partition is probed cluster by cluster, in order of distance to the query centroid, applying the same key-interval slicing and scalar check to each cluster's sorted list. A cluster counts toward the probe budget only when its key-filtered slice is non-empty, so empty clusters are skipped, and the effective probe depth adapts to predicate selectivity; probing stops at a maximum number of clusters, or earlier once a minimum has been probed, and the pool holds enough candidates. Finally, the exact distance to the query is computed for every pooled object, and the top k are returned.

Table 1. Dataset summary. †: derived or always-pass attribute that does not add independent filtering power. L2: Euclidean distance; Cosine: cosine similarity.

Dataset	# Embeddings	# Vector Dim.	# Scalar Dim.	Scalar Attributes	Metric
SIFT-1M	1M	128	1–5	Synthetic, uniform in $[0, 1000]$	L2
AudioSet [1]	2M	128	1–4	*start time*, *end time*† *num labels*, *duration*†	L2
LAION-1M [8]	1M	768	1–3	*cosine similarity*, *width*, *height*	Cosine

4 Performance Evaluation

4.1 Experimental Setup

Datasets. Table 1 summarizes the employed datasets: (i) SIFT-1M, containing synthetic uniform scalar attributes; (ii) AudioSet, including real temporal metadata; and (iii) LAION-1M, consisting of real CLIP (Contrastive Language-Image Pretraining) embeddings paired with image-level scalars. Regarding AudioSet, the number of derived attributes limits the filter's dimensionality to at most 2, regardless of the number of scalar columns included.

Query Workload. Each query combines a vector with D scalar range predicates calibrated to a target selectivity of 1%, and each configuration is evaluated with 10,000 queries. For SIFT-1M, the range widths are derived analytically assuming a uniform distribution, whereas for AudioSet and LAION-1M, they are calibrated by bisecting the empirical cumulative distribution function until the resulting window matches the target selectivity. Ground truth is the top-10 nearest neighbors among the predicate-passing vectors, computed with a brute-force FAISS [2] index, and Recall@10 measures the fraction of these neighbors retrieved.

Competitors and Setup. Among the related indexes (SeRF, iRangeGraph, UNIFY, and ACORN; Sect. 2), we evaluate iRangeGraph and ACORN as the most robust and recent competitors supporting multi-attribute scalar range filtering, using the official C/C++ implementation released by each author. Experiments ran on a Dell PowerEdge T430 with an Intel Xeon E5-2630 v3 CPU and 96 GiB RAM, under Debian GNU/Linux in CPU-only mode with all indices loaded into memory; `SmartIVF` is implemented in C/C++, and we report index construction cost, recall, memory usage, and query throughput (queries per second, QPS). Unless otherwise stated, `SmartIVF` uses q=256 equi-depth quantiles, b=8 bits per scalar dimension, an interval budget M=256, a flat/IVF threshold τ_{flat}=2000, probe bounds $p_{\min}$=1 and $p_{\max}$=200, and a candidate-pool target τ=1000. Source code, query workload generators, and ground-truth construction scripts for the three datasets are released alongside the camera-ready version of this paper.[1]

[1] https://github.com/henriquezanin/smartivf-index.

4.2 Index Construction

Construction time is a distinct advantage of `SmartIVF` (Fig. 2(a)). On SIFT-1M, it builds in 12 s, whereas iRangeGraph (which the original paper does not benchmark on SIFT-1M; we built it from the authors' open-source release on the same machine) requires 1,537 s, corresponding to a 130× reduction. ACORN ranges from 88 s to 980 s depending on γ, yielding a speedup for `SmartIVF` between 7.3× and 82× depending on the configuration. On AudioSet and LAION-1M, increasing the scalar structure does not materially affect `SmartIVF`'s construction time, and `SmartIVF` retains a large build-time margin over both competitors.

The differences stem from each index's structure: iRangeGraph performs a neighbor search for every data point at each level of the scalar segment tree, over progressively larger candidate pools; ACORN's build cost scales with γ, since denser multilayer graphs require more work. `SmartIVF` instead encodes the scalar structure once via Z-order keys, partitions the data by equi-depth binning, and runs a single K-means pass per partition on the embeddings, with no repeated neighbor searches.

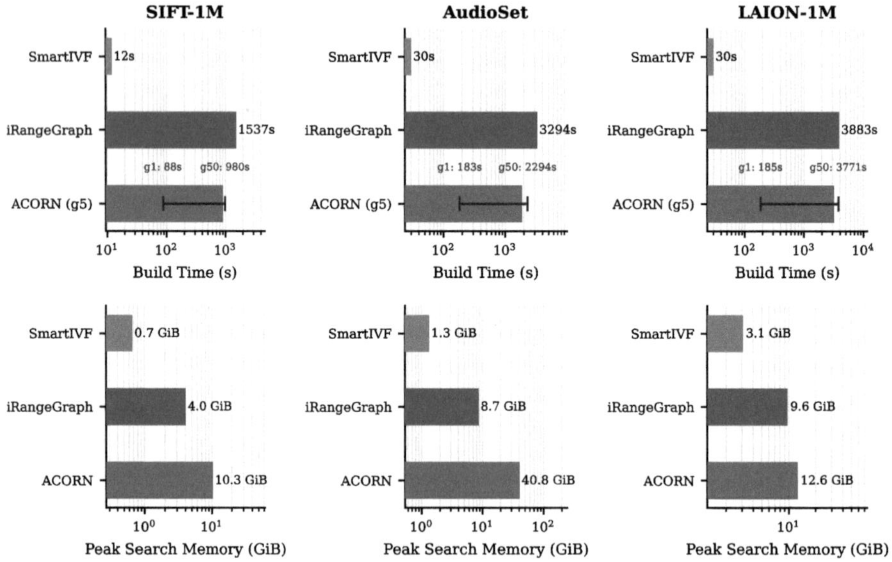

Fig. 2. (a) Index build time and (b) peak resident memory during search (both log scale). ACORN error bars / range span $\gamma \in \{1, 2, 5, 10, 50\}$; build-time bars are placed at γ=5.

4.3 Recall Consistency and Memory Usage

`SmartIVF` is the only index that consistently achieves high recall across all evaluated datasets and dimensionalities. Figure 3 shows the per-configuration

Recall@10 values, with the median marked for each method. SmartIVF maintains recall values near 1.0, indicating that its SFC-based partitioning reliably directs queries to the correct candidates. In contrast, iRangeGraph exhibits high variability. ACORN exhibits a broader recall distribution, driven by the choice of γ=5.

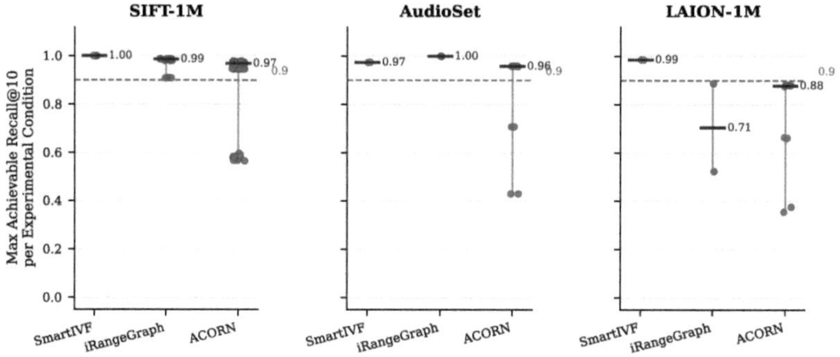

Fig. 3. Distribution of Recall@10 across all experimental configurations. The dashed line marks the 0.9 quality target common in ANN benchmarks. Recall is measured as best across all probe depths for each (dataset, dimensions) configuration.

Beyond maintaining consistent recall, SmartIVF also achieves the lowest memory usage during the search phase across all evaluated datasets. Figure 2(b) reports the peak resident memory observed at query time. On SIFT-1M, SmartIVF achieves a 6× speedup over iRangeGraph and a 15× speedup over ACORN with γ=5. The 2M-point AudioSet dataset amplifies graph-related overhead, yet SmartIVF maintains its construction-time advantages, achieving a 6.4× speedup over iRangeGraph and a 30× speedup over ACORN. On LAION-1M, SmartIVF continues to outperform both competitors, reducing memory usage by 3.3× relative to iRangeGraph and by 4.1× relative to ACORN.

4.4 Scalability Under Varying Scalar Dimensionality

Figure 4 presents three Recall–QPS Pareto plots, one per evaluated dataset. Each line corresponds to D=3 (the median scalar dimensionality), and the shaded band around it covers the full range of D tested on that dataset (D=1–5 on SIFT-1M, D=3–4 on AudioSet, D=1–2 on LAION-1M). The top boundary of the band corresponds to lower scalar dimensionalities (e.g., D=1), whereas the bottom boundary corresponds to higher dimensionalities (e.g., D=5). ACORN appears at γ=5, the median setting. Points further toward the top-right are better. The width of each shaded band reflects the QPS spread observed across the D range; ACORN's band is almost invisible because it shares a single graph index across all D configurations, so only scalar-filter overhead (not the graph structure) changes with D.

Figure 4 corroborates the findings from Fig. 3, also showing SmartIVF's robustness to increasing scalar dimensionality, as recall remains near perfect across all plots regardless of changes in D (staying above 0.9 beyond the dashed vertical line).

Above the 0.9 recall target that SmartIVF reaches consistently, ACORN performs poorly on every dataset, while SmartIVF achieves 1.9× higher QPS than iRangeGraph and 5.3× higher than ACORN on SIFT-1M, and 3.9× higher than iRangeGraph on AudioSet; on LAION-1M, neither competitor reaches the target. Below 0.9 recall, SmartIVF remains competitive in QPS.

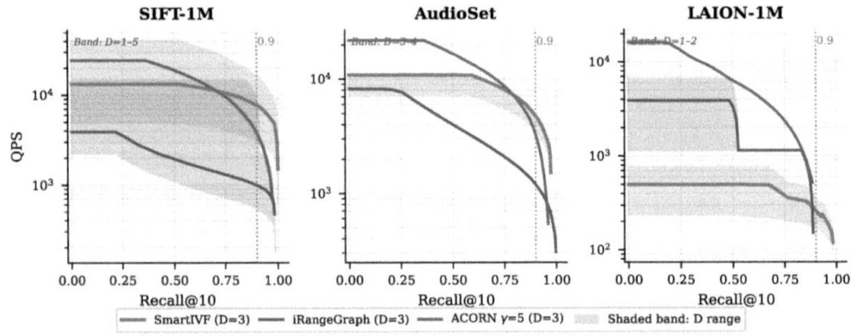

Fig. 4. Recall–QPS Pareto curves as scalar dimensionality D varies, for SIFT-1M (left), AudioSet (center), and LAION-1M (right), at 1% selectivity. For each curve, the shaded band spans the full D range tested on that dataset, and the central line corresponds to a representative D within that range (D=3 for SIFT-1M; the lowest tested D for AudioSet and LAION-1M). On AudioSet, only two of the four scalar attributes are effective independent filters (the other two are derived or always-pass), so the D=3 and D=4 curves should be read as upper bounds on filtering effectiveness. ACORN is shown at γ=5.

5 Conclusion

SmartIVF closes a structural gap in range-filtered ANN: encoding all scalar dimensions into a single Z-order key overcomes the dimensionality limits of graph-based designs without the memory cost of predicate-agnostic ones. Across SIFT-1M, AudioSet, and LAION-1M with up to five scalar dimensions at 1% selectivity, SmartIVF keeps Recall@10 above 0.9 in every configuration, builds up to 130× faster than iRangeGraph, uses 3–6× less memory than iRangeGraph and 4–30× less than ACORN, and is the only method clearing the threshold on LAION-1M, making it well-suited to memory-constrained settings and frequent index rebuilding.

As future work, we plan to investigate search-refinement heuristics that reduce distance computations and to extend the evaluation to georeferenced datasets with scalar timestamps, a workload that matches SmartIVF's multidimensional scalar handling and modest memory profile.

Acknowledgements. This work was supported by the São Paulo Research Foundation (FAPESP), the Brazilian Federal Research Agency (CNPq), and the Coordenação de Aperfeiçoamento de Pessoal de Nível Superior, Brasil (CAPES), Finance Code 001. The work is supported by the project "IntegraSanca: Conectando Dados, Transformando São Carlos" (Grant FAPESP Nr. 2025/07160-0).

Declaration of generative AI use. *Grammarly* was used for language polishing; authors take full responsibility for the content.

References

1. Gemmeke, J.F., et al.: Audio set: an ontology and human-labeled dataset for audio events. In: Proceedings of ICASSP, pp. 776–780 (2017)
2. Johnson, J., Douze, M., Jégou, H.: Billion-scale similarity search with gpus. IEEE Trans. Big Data **7**(3), 535–547 (2019)
3. Li, M., et al.: A survey of multi-dimensional indexes: past and future trends. IEEE Trans. Knowl. Data Eng. **36**(8), 3635–3655 (2024)
4. Liang, A., Zhang, P., Yao, B., Chen, Z., Song, Y., Cheng, G.: UNIFY: Unified index for range filtered approximate nearest neighbors search. Proc. VLDB Endowment **18**(4), 1118–1130 (2024)
5. Malkov, Y.A., Yashunin, D.A.: Efficient and robust approximate nearest neighbor search using hierarchical navigable small world graphs. IEEE Trans. Pattern Anal. Mach. Intell. **42**(4), 824–836 (2020)
6. Pan, J.J., Wang, J., Li, G.: Survey of vector database management systems. VLDB J. **33**(5), 1591–1615 (2024)
7. Patel, L., Kraft, P., Guestrin, C., Zaharia, M.: ACORN: performant and predicate-agnostic search over vector embeddings and structured data. Proc. ACM Manage. Data **2**(3), 1–27 (2024)
8. Schuhmann, C., et al.: LAION-5B: an open large-scale dataset for training next generation image-text models. In: Proceedings of NeurIPS, vol. 35, pp. 25278–25294 (2022)
9. Wang, M., Xu, X., Yue, Q., Wang, Y.: A comprehensive survey and experimental comparison of graph-based approximate nearest neighbor search. Proc. VLDB Endowment **14**(11), 1964–1978 (2021)
10. Xu, Y., Gao, J., Gou, Y., Long, C., Jensen, C.S.: iRangeGraph: improvising range-dedicated graphs for range-filtering nearest neighbor search. Proc. ACM Manage. Data **2**(6), 1–26 (2024)
11. Zuo, C., Qiao, M., Zhou, W., Li, F., Deng, D.: SeRF: segment graph for range-filtering approximate nearest neighbor search. Proc. ACM Manage. Data **2**(1), 1–26 (2024)

Similarity Search, Truth Discovery and Anomaly Detection

Schema-Free Truth Discovery via Wasserstein Barycenters

Xiufeng Liu[1(✉)], Ruyu Liu[1], Nadeem Iftikhar[3], and Yanyan Yang[2]

[1] Department of Technology, Management and Economics, Technical University of Denmark, 2800 Kgs. Lyngby, Denmark
{xiuli,ruyli}@dtu.dk

[2] School of Computing, University of Portsmouth, Portsmouth PO1 3HE, UK
Linda.Yang@port.ac.uk

[3] University College of Northern Denmark, Sofiendalsvej 60, Aalborg, Denmark
naif@ucn.dk

Abstract. Truth discovery recovers reliable values from multiple conflicting sources, but most methods assume that observations can be aligned through shared keys or regridded onto a common grid before fusion. This assumption breaks down in multi-granular settings, where sources report at different spatial or temporal resolutions and key matching is unavailable or lossy. We propose **GeoTD**, a schema-free truth discovery framework that models each source as a probability measure and estimates consensus as a reliability-weighted Wasserstein barycenter. Disagreement is measured by optimal transport, which captures both value differences and spatial displacement without prior alignment, while source reliabilities are learned jointly with the barycenter through an entropy-regularized objective solved with Sinkhorn iterations. On a synthetic misalignment benchmark and an open Mediterranean sea-surface-temperature bundle, transport-based fusion improves substantially over common-grid aggregation, and learned reliability weighting adds further gains when source quality differs across inputs.

Keywords: Data Fusion · Truth Discovery · Optimal Transport · Wasserstein Barycenters · Schema-Free Integration

1 Introduction

Organizations increasingly rely on multiple autonomous sources – satellite products, sensor networks, financial aggregators – to describe the same phenomenon. When they disagree, recovering the most reliable value is known as *truth discovery* [8,15]: one alternates between estimating each source's trustworthiness and a consensus value. This is central to data integration, since conflicting observations propagate errors downstream [3,9] and classical quality dimensions such as accuracy and completeness do not address structural misalignment across sources [3,13].

© The Author(s), under exclusive license to Springer Nature Switzerland AG 2027
G. Vargas Solar et al. (Eds.): ADBIS 2026, CCIS 3175, pp. 151–160, 2027.
https://doi.org/10.1007/978-3-032-39823-9_14

Most truth discovery methods first align observations on a *key* – a shared identifier, such as a grid coordinate or entity id, on which sources are joined – before fusion begins. TruthFinder [15], CRH [11], CATD [10], and probabilistic variants for numerical data [16,17] differ in how they score reliability but all rely on this assumption. In multi-granular settings a common key may not exist: a source on a 0.04° grid and another on a 0.05° grid cannot be matched without regridding, a preprocessing step that discards fine-scale structure and injects an arbitrary resolution choice that can change the fused result.

Recent work on discord measurement exposes this limitation but does not remove it. Eris [1] models disagreement through symbolic tables and convex optimization, more expressive than voting or weighted averaging yet still requiring a known key and a common representation; earlier LP-based reconciliation for multi-granular data shares the same dependence on a predefined alignment space [5]. Current approaches thus conflate two issues that should be separated: genuine disagreement among sources, and distortion from preprocessing.

We instead model each source as a discrete probability measure and reformulate truth discovery as a Wasserstein barycenter [2]. Here *optimal transport* – moving probability mass between measures at minimum cost [14] – compares sources through transport geometry, so correspondence is inferred from the data rather than imposed by a key. The barycenter is the consensus truth, transport costs provide a natural basis for reliability, and Sinkhorn iterations [4,6] make the optimization practical. The result is *schema-free*: no shared schema, key, or common grid is required. Our contributions are:

- A schema-free formulation of truth discovery that represents each source as a probability measure, eliminating key alignment and common-grid preprocessing.
- The GeoTD framework, which couples Wasserstein discordance, barycenter-based consensus, and reliability learning in a single entropy-regularized procedure with a closed-form reliability update.
- An empirical study on synthetic misalignment data and an open Mediterranean SST bundle, showing that GeoTD improves consensus quality over Eris and classical baselines while remaining computationally practical.

2 Related Work

Truth discovery infers reliable values by alternating between source-reliability and truth estimation. Early methods such as TruthFinder [15] targeted categorical data; later models extended to continuous values, heterogeneous attributes, and domain-aware reliability [8,10,11,16,17]. A parallel family applies fixed weighting rules after projecting sources to a common grid. Both share one assumption – observations must be aligned to known entities before fusion – which is restrictive when sources observe the same process at different resolutions with no stable key.

Data Quality and Discord. Quality frameworks emphasize agreement, consistency, and completeness, but are usually defined over schema-aligned relations [3,9,13]. The most relevant recent system, Eris [1], measures discord through symbolic tables and convex optimization and connects to uncertainty-aware query processing and multi-granular integration [5], yet still requires a known key and common representation. GeoTD instead defines both discord and consensus directly on the native supports of the sources.

Optimal Transport. The Wasserstein distance compares measures while respecting domain geometry [14]; entropic regularization and Sinkhorn iterations made it practical at scale [4,6], and barycenters give a natural notion of consensus [2,7,12]. Transport has been applied widely in vision and geometry but not to truth discovery under conflicting multi-granular observations; GeoTD uses transport costs both to define disagreement and to replace hand-crafted weighting with a truth-discovery objective on the transport geometry.

3 Preliminaries

We recall the optimal-transport concepts that underpin GeoTD and fix notation.

Definition 1 (Discrete Empirical Measure). *Given a source S_k over a bounded domain $\Omega \subset \mathbb{R}^d$ with grid points $\{x_i^{(k)}\}_{i=1}^{n_k}$ and observed values $\{v_i^{(k)}\}_{i=1}^{n_k}$, the discrete empirical probability measure of S_k is*

$$\mu_k = \sum_{i=1}^{n_k} w_i^{(k)} \delta_{(x_i^{(k)}, v_i^{(k)})}, \qquad w_i^{(k)} = v_i^{(k)} \Big/ \textstyle\sum_{j=1}^{n_k} v_j^{(k)}, \tag{1}$$

where δ_z is the Dirac measure at z. When only locations with values are given, the value is absorbed into the weight; when both matter, the point is bound in $\Omega \times \mathbb{R}$. Crucially, the grids $\{x_i^{(k)}\}$ need not coincide across sources – the multi-granular setting where key-based alignment fails.

Definition 2 (Wasserstein-2 Distance). *For probability measures μ, ν on $\mathbb{R}^d$,*

$$W_2(\mu, \nu) = \Big(\inf_{\pi \in \Pi(\mu,\nu)} \int_{\mathbb{R}^d \times \mathbb{R}^d} \|x - y\|^2 \, d\pi(x, y) \Big)^{1/2}, \tag{2}$$

where $\Pi(\mu, \nu)$ is the set of transport plans with marginals μ and ν [14].

W_2 respects the geometry of the domain: two measures differing by a small spatial shift incur a small distance, whereas mass placed at distant locations incurs a large one. Unlike pointwise divergences (KL, total variation), which require a shared reference or grid and are insensitive to the metric structure, W_2 operates directly on the native supports [12].

Definition 3 (Wasserstein Barycenter). *Given measures $\mu_1, \dots, \mu_K$ and non-negative weights $\lambda_1, \dots, \lambda_K$ summing to one, the Wasserstein barycenter [2] is*

$$\mu^* = \arg\min_{\mu} \sum_{k=1}^{K} \lambda_k W_2^2(\mu, \mu_k). \tag{3}$$

For discrete measures on a fixed grid the barycenter exists and is unique [2]. In GeoTD the μ_k are the source measures, the λ_k reliability weights, and μ^* the consensus truth: a more reliable source receives a larger weight, pulling μ^* toward its measure.

Example 1 (Why transport, not averaging). Two 1-D sources measure temperature on a line: S_1 at spacing 0.04, S_2 at 0.05. A sharp front places unit mass at $x = 0.50$ in S_1 but, on the coarser grid, at $x = 0.55$ in S_2. Key-based joining finds no matching coordinate and must regrid, smearing the front. Transport instead moves S_2's mass left at cost 0.05^2, recognizing one displaced feature rather than two unrelated values; the equal-weight barycenter (3) places the front at $x = 0.525$, preserving its sharpness. If S_2 is less reliable, its weight shrinks and μ^* moves toward $x = 0.50$.

Entropic Regularization. Computing W_2 exactly needs a linear program with $O(n^2)$ variables ($n = \max_k n_k$). Cuturi [6] replaces the marginal constraint with an entropy penalty,

$$W_{2,\varepsilon}(\mu, \nu)^2 = \inf_{\pi \in \Pi(\mu,\nu)} \int \|x - y\|^2 \, d\pi + \varepsilon \, H(\pi), \tag{4}$$

where $H(\pi) = \int \pi \log \pi$ and $\varepsilon > 0$. The solution is $\pi^* = \mathrm{diag}(u) \, K \, \mathrm{diag}(v)$ with Gibbs kernel $K_{ij} = \exp(-c_{ij}/\varepsilon)$, recovered by Sinkhorn's alternating projections [4,6] at $O(n^2)$ cost per iteration.

4 Methodology

GeoTD models sources as probability measures and computes consensus through a reliability-weighted Wasserstein barycenter.

4.1 Framework Overview

GeoTD follows one principle: when sources disagree because they observe the same phenomenon at different resolutions, correspondence should be inferred from geometry rather than imposed by a chosen grid. The pipeline (Fig. 1) has three stages: each source S_k becomes a discrete measure μ_k on its native support; pairwise discordance is measured by W_2, aligning mass through transport rather than key matching; and a reliability-weighted barycenter is computed as the consensus while source weights are updated from it through a Gibbs rule (below). In discrete form S_k is a support matrix $X^{(k)} \in \mathbb{R}^{n_k \times d}$ with weights $a_k \in \Delta^{n_k - 1}$, and the consensus is $X^* \in \mathbb{R}^{n^* \times d}$ with weights $b \in \Delta^{n^* - 1}$. Crucially, truth estimation and source weighting share one transport geometry, so reliability is coupled to the barycenter objective rather than a hand-crafted proxy.

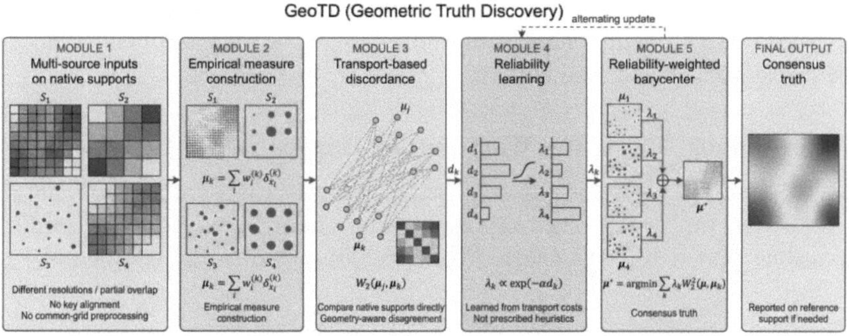

Fig. 1. Overview of GeoTD. Conflicting sources are represented on their native supports without key alignment or common-grid preprocessing. Each source becomes an empirical measure, discordance is computed through optimal transport, source reliabilities are updated from the resulting transport costs, and the consensus truth is obtained as a reliability-weighted Wasserstein barycenter.

Assumptions. GeoTD assumes (i) each source's observations are non-negative (so they normalize to a probability measure, Definition 1) or are mapped to one by a fixed monotone transform; (ii) all supports lie in a common metric domain Ω so transport cost is defined; and (iii) sources observe the same phenomenon, possibly at different resolutions, offsets, and noise levels. No shared key, schema, or common grid is assumed.

4.2 Source Modeling as Probability Measures

Consider K sources $S_1, \ldots, S_K$ over a domain Ω, where S_k has its own resolution producing n_k grid points $\{x_i^{(k)}\}$ with values $\{v_i^{(k)}\}$; the grids need not coincide. We convert each S_k to a measure μ_k via Definition 1. When the value field carries the information (sea surface temperature, air quality index), we set the support to the spatial grid and absorb values into weights, giving $\mu_k = \sum_i w_i^{(k)} \delta_{x_i^{(k)}}$; when location and value are independent we work on $\Omega \times \mathbb{R}$, with a cost combining spatial-displacement and value-discrepancy terms. Unlike the symbolic-table representation of Eris [1], which requires a known key, each source here contributes its own measure at its own resolution, and the transport plan between any two measures determines the correspondence between their grids.

4.3 Geometric Discordance via Wasserstein Distance

Agreement between S_j and S_k should reflect not only value differences but also *where* they occur, which W_2 (Definition 2) captures: for Gaussian measures W_2^2 splits into a mean-shift term and a covariance (shape) discrepancy, and for general discrete measures it penalizes mass displacement by squared Euclidean distance. A source that places mass at the wrong *location* is thus penalized more than one that errs only in value – a property absent from pointwise divergences (KL, RMSE, MAE), which need a shared reference or grid and hence regridding before comparing misaligned sources.

4.4 Consensus Truth via Wasserstein Barycenter

Reliability-Coupled Objective. A weighted barycenter (3) assumes the reliabilities λ_k are known, but truth discovery must infer them from the same conflicting observations that define the truth. We therefore optimize the coupled objective

$$\min_{b\in\Delta^{n^*-1},\,\lambda\in\Delta^{K-1}} \sum_{k=1}^{K} \lambda_k\, T_\varepsilon\big(b, a_k; C^{(k)}\big) + \frac{1}{\alpha}\sum_{k=1}^{K} \lambda_k \log \lambda_k, \tag{5}$$

where $C_{ij}^{(k)} = \|x_i^* - x_j^{(k)}\|^2$, $T_\varepsilon(b, a_k; C^{(k)})$ is the entropic OT cost between the barycenter and source k, and $\alpha > 0$ controls how sharply reliability concentrates on low-discordance sources. The first term says trustworthy sources lie close to the consensus in Wasserstein geometry; the second is an entropy barrier preventing the degenerate solution that assigns all mass to one source.

Closed-Form Reliability Update. For fixed b, let $d_k = T_\varepsilon(b, a_k; C^{(k)})$. Minimizing (5) over λ on the simplex is a strictly convex problem whose unique minimizer is the Gibbs distribution

$$\lambda_k = \frac{\exp(-\alpha\, d_k)}{\sum_{\ell=1}^{K} \exp(-\alpha\, d_\ell)}. \tag{6}$$

Equation (6) is not heuristic but the optimal solution of the entropy-regularized objective, so $d_i < d_j \Leftrightarrow \lambda_i > \lambda_j$: trust is rank-equivalent to transport agreement with the emerging consensus. The temperature α only controls separation sharpness: as $\alpha \to 0$ weights become uniform and (5) reduces to the equal-weight entropic barycenter, while as $\alpha \to \infty$ they concentrate on the lowest-discordance sources, so α interpolates between neutral fusion and reliability-aware truth discovery. Unlike picking a single "best" source, the barycenter pools partially overlapping supports – recovering structure no single source observes completely – while discounting rather than discarding weaker sources.

Barycenter Update. For fixed λ, the barycenter subproblem is solved by iterative Bregman projections [4,7]. With Gibbs kernels $K_{ij}^{(k)} = \exp(-C_{ij}^{(k)}/\varepsilon)$ and scaling form $P^{(k)} = \mathrm{diag}(u_k) K^{(k)} \mathrm{diag}(v_k)$, the update is the weighted geometric mean

$$b^{(t+1)} = \exp\Big(\sum_{k=1}^{K} \lambda_k \log\big(K^{(k)} v_k^{(t)}\big)\Big), \tag{7}$$

followed by normalization. The consensus is thus a multiplicative average of transport-adjusted marginals, not an arithmetic average of values. Alternating (6) and (7) (Algorithm 1) mirrors classical truth discovery but in transport geometry, so reliability is updated from geometric concordance and the truth estimate stays well defined even with no common key.

Algorithm 1:. GeoTD: Reliability-Weighted Wasserstein Barycenter

Input: Source supports $X^{(k)}$, weights a_k, barycenter support X^*, regularization ε, temperature α, tolerance τ
Output: Consensus weights b^* and reliabilities λ^*
for $k = 1, \ldots, K$ **do**
  Compute $C_{ij}^{(k)} = \|x_i^* - x_j^{(k)}\|^2$ and $K_{ij}^{(k)} = \exp(-C_{ij}^{(k)}/\varepsilon)$; initialize $u_k \leftarrow \mathbf{1}$, $v_k \leftarrow \mathbf{1}$;
Initialize $\lambda_k \leftarrow 1/K$ and $b \leftarrow \mathbf{1}/n^*$;
repeat
  for $k = 1, \ldots, K$ **do**
    Update (u_k, v_k) by Sinkhorn scaling so $P^{(k)} = \mathrm{diag}(u_k)K^{(k)}\mathrm{diag}(v_k)$ matches marginals $(b^{(t)}, a_k)$; set $d_k \leftarrow T_\varepsilon(b^{(t)}, a_k; C^{(k)})$;
  Update λ with (6); update $b^{(t+1)}$ with (7) and normalize;
until $\|b^{(t+1)} - b^{(t)}\|_1 \leq \tau$;
return (b^*, λ^*)

4.5 Complexity and Convergence

Each outer iteration of Algorithm 1 runs in $O(K\,n^*\,\bar{n}\,L)$ time and $O(K\,n^*\,\bar{n})$ space, with $\bar{n} = \frac{1}{K}\sum_k n_k$ and L the number of Sinkhorn iterations. This compares favorably with the LP/QP approach of Eris, whose variable count scales with the product of source sizes; each Sinkhorn step is matrix–vector products that benefit from GPU parallelism. The regularized barycenter converges to the exact one as $\varepsilon \to 0$ [4], and the alternation is block-coordinate descent on (5) (convex in b for fixed λ; closed-form (6) in λ for fixed b), giving a monotone decrease of the objective.

5 Experiments

We evaluate GeoTD on a synthetic benchmark that stresses multi-granular misalignment and on a real Mediterranean SST bundle from open NOAA products, asking whether reliability-weighted transport improves consensus quality under misalignment and whether it stays competitive on real data without ground truth.

5.1 Experimental Setup

Synthetic Benchmark. We generate a positive ground-truth field on a 24×24 grid over $[0,1]^2$ and create four sources at 12×12 to 28×28 resolution, each spatially shifted, corrupted with additive noise, rescaled by a source-specific bias, and restricted to a partial window – reflecting different resolutions, supports, and incomplete overlap. We run 16 trials with fixed seeds.

Real SST Data. The real benchmark uses an open NOAA CoastWatch/ERDDAP bundle over the western Mediterranean for three dates in February 2020, with four products: night-only, day–night, and diurnally corrected blended SST (all 0.05°) and ACSPO SST (0.02°). The blended products are aggregated to 0.5° and ACSPO to 0.25°, with the consensus on a 0.5° grid.

Baselines and Metrics. We compare against common-grid baselines (Simple, Weighted, and Inverse-MAD Weighted Average, Trimmed/Winsorized/Huber Mean, Geometric Mean, Pointwise Median) and transport baselines (Equal-weight and inverse-variance OT Barycenter), separating gains from stronger aggregation, OT geometry, and reliability weighting. The NumPy implementation uses the fixed-support Sinkhorn barycenter of Sect. 4; grid searches give $\varepsilon = 0.05$ (both datasets), $\alpha = 6$ (synthetic), $\alpha = 4$ (real). We report RMSE/MAE against ground truth (synthetic) and the mean regularized transport disagreement to the four sources plus runtime (real); lower is better throughout.

5.2 Results

Table 1 shows a clear ranking on synthetic data. Among common-grid methods weighted averaging is strongest, but all remain worse than transport-based fusion: the equal-weight OT barycenter improves on weighted averaging by 5.6% in RMSE. Weighting inside OT also matters – both the inverse-variance OT variant and GeoTD improve over it. The inverse-variance heuristic is strongest here, as expected because the generator injects source-level noise and bias that variance captures well; GeoTD is second best, improves on weighted averaging by 6.9% in RMSE, and learns reliabilities directly from transport agreement rather than a specified proxy. The mean learned reliabilities $(0.227, 0.266, 0.259, 0.248)$ consistently downweight the noisiest source, and increasing α improves GeoTD monotonically toward this regime (Fig. 2(a)).

On real SST (Table 1) the picture is similar: robust common-grid methods cluster around 3.44×10^{-2} disagreement, still worse than OT-based methods. The inverse-variance OT barycenter is best, improving on the equal-weight barycenter by 3.3% and on GeoTD by 3.4%, while GeoTD is essentially tied with the equal-weight barycenter (within 0.15%). This is consistent with a bundle dominated by closely related blended products, where a variance prior already captures most source-quality variation; even so, the learned reliabilities still flag the night-only product as least trusted (weight 0.188 versus ≈ 0.271 for the others). Figure 2(b) adds the ε sensitivity: very small regularization is less effective, while $\varepsilon \in [0.04, 0.08]$ is stable, so $\varepsilon = 0.05$ lies in a robust regime.

All OT variants remain computationally practical: GeoTD averages 0.40 s on synthetic trials and 6.6 s on the real bundle, versus 0.13 s and 1.9 s for the inverse-variance heuristic, which skips outer reliability updates.

Table 1. Results on the synthetic benchmark (16 trials) and the real Mediterranean SST bundle (3 dates). Lower is better; best per column in **bold**, second underlined. Disag. is the mean regularized transport cost to the sources.

Method	Synthetic			Real SST	
	RMSE	MAE	Time (s)	Disag.	Time (s)
Simple Average	0.000832	0.000674	0.00007	0.04150	0.00016
Weighted Average	0.000789	0.000649	0.00014	0.04218	0.00034
Inverse-MAD Wtd. Average	0.000853	0.000680	0.00113	0.04150	0.00543
Trimmed Mean	0.001065	0.000882	0.00009	0.03443	0.00030
Winsorized Mean	0.001065	0.000882	0.00008	0.03443	0.00032
Huber Mean	0.000984	0.000797	0.00151	0.03442	0.00334
Geometric Mean	0.002880	0.002415	0.00007	0.05576	0.00026
Pointwise Median	0.001065	0.000882	0.00011	0.03443	0.00044
Equal-weight OT Bary.	0.000745	0.000605	0.10156	0.03355	1.76162
OT Bary. + inverse-variance	**0.000717**	**0.000572**	0.12973	**0.03245**	1.91638
GeoTD	0.000734	0.000594	0.40410	0.03360	6.60703

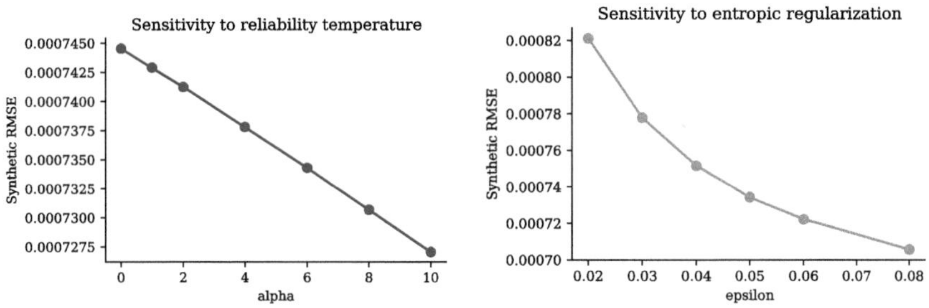

(a) Sensitivity to the reliability temperature α.

(b) Sensitivity to the entropic regularization ε.

Fig. 2. Sensitivity analysis of GeoTD on the synthetic benchmark (lower RMSE is better): (a) reliability temperature α; (b) entropic regularization ε.

6 Discussion and Conclusion

GeoTD estimates consensus as a reliability-weighted Wasserstein barycenter, removing key alignment and coupling source trust with geometric discordance. The experiments show that the dominant, most stable gain comes from replacing common-grid fusion with a Wasserstein barycenter; once OT is in place, learned weighting helps when source quality is not already summarized by global variance, while inverse variance is a strong competitor otherwise. GeoTD should thus be read not as a claim that learned weighting always wins, but as a principled formulation that learns reliabilities directly from transport disagreement.

Limitations. Three limitations remain: the fixed-support barycenter uses a prescribed reference grid rather than the full free-support formulation; the real benchmark is a reproducible proof of concept on an open NOAA bundle, not a strict replication; and GeoTD is slower than simple averaging, since Sinkhorn solves a richer problem, so it suits settings where alignment-free fusion quality outweighs minimal runtime. Future work includes free-support barycenters, richer source types, and larger benchmarks where source quality is less easily captured by variance.

Acknowledgments. The work was supported by the S3EM project funded by Marie Skłodowska-Curie Postdoctoral Individual Fellowship under Grant No. 101154277.

References

1. Abelló, A., Cheney, J.: Eris: efficiently measuring discord in multidimensional sources. VLDB J. **33**(2), 399–423 (2024)
2. Agueh, M., Carlier, G.: Barycenters in the Wasserstein space. SIAM J. Math. Anal. **43**(2), 904–924 (2011)
3. Batini, C., Scannapieco, M.: Data and Information Quality: Dimensions, Principles and Techniques. Springer, Heidelberg (2016)
4. Benamou, J.D., Carlier, G., Cuturi, M., Nenna, L., Peyré, G.: Iterative Bregman projections for regularized transportation problems. SIAM J. Sci. Comput. **37**(2), A1111–A1138 (2015)
5. Bimonte, S., Ren, L., Koueya, N.: A linear programming-based framework for handling missing data in multi-granular data warehouses. Data Knowl. Eng. **128**, 101832 (2020)
6. Cuturi, M.: Sinkhorn distances: lightspeed computation of optimal transport. In: Advances in Neural Information Processing Systems (NeurIPS), vol. 26 (2013)
7. Cuturi, M., Doucet, A.: Fast computation of Wasserstein barycenters. In: Proceedings of the 31st International Conference on Machine Learning (ICML) (2014)
8. Dong, X.L., Naumann, F.: Data fusion: resolving data conflicts for integration. Proc. VLDB Endowment **2**(2) (2009)
9. Ilyas, I., Chu, X.: Data Cleaning, ACM Books, vol. 28. ACM (2019)
10. Li, Q., Li, Y., Gao, J., Zhao, B., Fan, W., Han, J.: A confidence-aware approach for truth discovery on long-tail data. Proc. VLDB Endowment **8**(4), 425–436 (2014)
11. Li, Y., et al.: Conflicts to harmony: a framework for resolving conflicts in heterogeneous data by truth discovery. IEEE Trans. Knowl. Data Eng. **28**(8), 1986–1999 (2016)
12. Peyré, G., Cuturi, M.: Computational optimal transport with applications to data sciences. Found. Trends Mach. Learn. **11**(5–6), 355–607 (2019)
13. Pipino, L., Lee, Y., Wang, R.: Data quality assessment. Commun. ACM **45**(4), 211–218 (2002)
14. Villani, C.: Optimal transport: old and new. Grundlehren Math. Wiss. **338** (2009)
15. Yin, X., Han, J., Yu, P.S.: Truth discovery with multiple conflicting information providers on the web. IEEE Trans. Knowl. Data Eng. **20**(6), 796–808 (2008)
16. Zhao, B., Han, J.: A probabilistic model for estimating real-valued truth from conflicting sources. In: Proceedings of International Workshop on Quality in Databases (QDB), p. 1817 (2012)
17. Zhi, S., Yang, F., Zhu, Z., Li, Q., Wang, Z., Han, J.: Dynamic truth discovery on numerical data. In: IEEE International Conference on Data Mining (ICDM), pp. 817–826 (2018)

Using Distances and Pair Counting Correlations to Estimate Hierarchical Density-Based Clustering Parameters

Gabriel L. Melo(✉) and Caetano Traina Jr.

Institute of Mathematics and Computer Science, University of São Paulo (USP), São Carlos, Brazil

melogabriel@usp.br, caetano@icmc.usp.br

Abstract. Unsupervised clustering is essential for exploring large unlabeled datasets, yet hierarchical density-based methods often suffer from over-fragmentation in high-dimensional semantic spaces. This paper introduces **Core-HDBSCAN**, a deterministic approach for estimating spatial thresholds (ϵ^*) using fractal correlation analysis. By measuring distance correlations between data subsets, the method identifies macrostructural boundaries separating semantic manifolds and derives a geometrically grounded threshold for dendrogram pruning. Experimental results demonstrate improved clustering calibration, reducing parameter tuning while achieving F1-score gains of up to 37% over the baseline and better preserving the underlying domain structure.

Keywords: Hierarchical Density-Based Clustering · Fractal Correlation Analysis · Spatial Threshold Estimation

1 Introduction

As fully labeled datasets become increasingly difficult to obtain and process, unsupervised clustering has emerged as a key tool for exploring large unlabeled collections. HDBSCAN is particularly appealing because it can generate clusters using only a minimum cluster size parameter. However, meaningful results often still require iterative parameter tuning. This study addresses that limitation by deterministically estimating the hierarchical spatial threshold (ϵ^*), promoting well-structured partitions that capture broad semantic categories without excessive fragmentation into specialized subtopics. While previous methods, such as the hybrid approach of Malzer and Baum [10], attempts to identify an optimal cut-off value, their effectiveness tends to diminish in high-dimensional spaces.

To address this limitation, we introduce **Core-HDBSCAN**, a methodology that estimates the clustering threshold directly from high-dimensional semantic spaces using fractal correlation analysis. By exploiting the scaling behavior of pairwise spatial correlations, the fractal dimension reveals boundaries between distinct manifolds, providing a geometrically grounded threshold that mitigates

© The Author(s), under exclusive license to Springer Nature Switzerland AG 2027
G. Vargas Solar et al. (Eds.): ADBIS 2026, CCIS 3175, pp. 161–171, 2027.
https://doi.org/10.1007/978-3-032-39823-9_15

the dimensionality curse [8] affecting conventional density-based heuristics. The proposed technique can be applied to a wide range of datasets. For validation, we used the PIESP dataset, a collection of embeddings derived from investment-related news articles and organized into macroeconomic sectors and subsectors (Sect. 4). Extensively refined and used by a government institution to support public policy for several years, the dataset provides a reliable ground truth for evaluating the proposed approach.

The remainder of this paper is organized as follows. Section 2 reviews the related work and theoretical foundations. Section 3 presents the proposed fractal-correlation-based methodology. Section 4 describes the experimental setup, dataset, evaluation metrics, and results analysis. Finally, Sect. 5 concludes the paper and discusses future research directions.

2 Background and Related Work

Clustering is an unsupervised learning technique for discovering latent patterns and grouping similar instances in unlabeled data. K-Means is widely used for its simplicity and efficiency but requires a predefined number of clusters, assumes spherical cluster shapes, and is sensitive to noise [7]. For noisier datasets with arbitrary shapes, density-based approaches like DBSCAN are preferred. It identifies clusters as dense regions, detects arbitrary geometries, and filters out noise [4] using two parameters: the neighborhood radius ϵ and the minimum number of neighbors required (`MinPts`). To overcome DBSCAN's sensitivity to ϵ and its difficulty with varying densities, extensions have been proposed. OPTICS addresses density variations by ordering points to reveal multi-level cluster structures [1]. HDBSCAN further generalizes this by constructing a density hierarchy and extracting the most stable clusters [2] using three parameters: `min_cluster_size`, `min_samples` (for noise classification), and `cluster_selection_epsilon` (to limit over-fragmentation).

HDBSCAN incorporates the GLOSH outlier score to identify points deviating from dense regions, enabling unsupervised outlier detection. While refinements have improved its robustness and reduced parameter sensitivity [5], extracting meaningful clusters still depends on density-bounding parameters like `cluster_selection_epsilon`. To prevent HDBSCAN from over-fragmenting clusters in highly dense regions, Malzer and Baum [10] proposed a hierarchical threshold parameter ($\hat{\epsilon}$) within the FOSC framework. This threshold acts as a spatial floor that halts cluster divisions below a specified distance. However, selecting an appropriate value remains challenging in high-dimensional spaces where empirical heuristics fail, particularly in semantic embedding spaces where geometric distances often distort the underlying topological structure.

Other researchs characterize datasets by analyzing the relationship between pairwise distances and neighborhood growth within a given radius, a multiscale property formalized as the intrinsic dimensionality (D). While statistical [6] and fractal-based [9] methods have been proposed to estimate D, most provide only global or local estimates, failing to explicitly model multiple clusters.

The TriPlot technique addresses this limitation by analyzing two datasets embedded in a common space, possibly with distinct spatial distributions [11]. It examines how neighborhood counts grow with distance, capturing both intra- and inter-cluster structures across scales. To isolate inter-cluster behavior, TriPlot employs the cross-cloud function, which measures the cumulative number of cross-pairs as the radius increases. The resulting log–log cross-plot provides an estimate of the intrinsic dimensionality (D) through its average slope. Figure 1 illustrates a TriPlot for the PIESP dataset (Sect. 4.1). The dotted curves represent the neighborhood growth within the "Industries" and "Services" subsets, while the solid blue curve depicts their cross-group interaction. The average slope of each curve corresponds to D, with differences reflecting variations in the underlying spatial distributions.

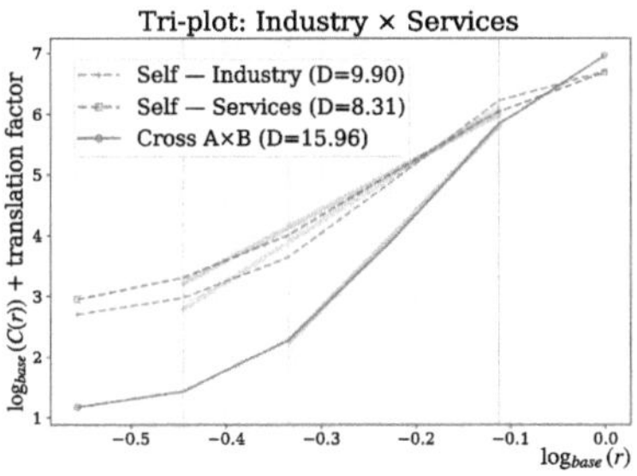

Fig. 1. Cross-plot of topological interaction between "Industry" and "Services news".

In this paper, we investigate how TriPlots-based analysis can be used to derive principled estimates for the ϵ parameter in HDBSCAN. Our objective is to replace heuristic or ad hoc parameter selection with a data-driven strategy, yielding a more reliable and stable configuration of the algorithm.

3 The Core-HDBSCAN Technique

When using HDBSCAN, practitioners typically tune `min_cluster_size` and `min_samples` parameters, while leaving `cluster_selection_epsilon` at its default value due to the difficulty of estimating it. This work introduces Core-HDBSCAN, a data-driven approach that leverages distance and pair-count correlations to estimate intrinsic dimensionality. By analyzing topological acceleration in the Cross-Cloud Plot, Core-HDBSCAN derives an informed spatial threshold (ϵ^*), enabling systematic calibration of `cluster_selection_epsilon` and reducing reliance on trial-and-error tuning in multiscale datasets.

Our heuristic models the interaction between high-dim textual embedding sets $\mathcal{A}$ and $\mathcal{B}$ across distinct semantic domains. The dissimilarity between elements $\mathbf{a} \in \mathcal{A}$ and $\mathbf{b} \in \mathcal{B}$ is defined as $r(\mathbf{a}, \mathbf{b}) = \|\mathbf{a} - \mathbf{b}\|_2$, with their structural relationship characterized by the cross-cloud correlation function $\text{Cross}_{\mathcal{A},\mathcal{B}}(r)$.

Core-HDBSCAN assumes a coherent macrostructure emerges at a characteristic scale, identified by the elbow (maximum acceleration) on a log–log Cross-plot.

Let $x = \log_{base}(r)$ denote the spatial scale (base 10 in our experiments). Since the slope of the log–log Cross-plot approximates the local correlation dimension, structural transitions are identified through the curvature of the cross-cloud curve, estimated via finite differences:

$$\frac{d^2}{dx^2} \log_{base}(\mathrm{Cross}_{\mathcal{A},\mathcal{B}}(base^x)) . \qquad (1)$$

The characteristic interaction distance is defined as the scale of maximum curvature within the informative region of the curve, excluding the final plateau.

Definition 1 (Optimal Fractal Threshold). *Let $X_{\mathrm{valid}} \subset X_{\mathrm{domain}}$ denote the range preceding the final plateau of the cross-cloud curve. The optimal spatial threshold is defined as $\epsilon^* = base^{x_{\mathrm{ref}}}$, where*

$$x_{\mathrm{ref}} = \arg\max_{x \in X_{\mathrm{valid}}} \left(\frac{d^2}{dx^2} \log_{base}(\mathrm{Cross}_{\mathcal{A},\mathcal{B}}(base^x)) \right) . \qquad (2)$$

Using ϵ^* as a scale-selective filter, Core-HDBSCAN prevents the clustering algorithm from prematurely isolating dense sub-clusters at microscales ($r < \epsilon^*$).

3.1 Deriving the Macro-structural Boundary Using Fractal Scaling

Analyzing the cross-correlation curve, we obtain the structural properties of the data distribution in the distance space induced by cross-domain interactions. By identifying internal subclusters and global macrostructure boundaries, the following properties and rule are derived:

Property 1 (Homogeneous Correlation). A straight cross-plot curve with a single constant slope and no intermediate plateaus indicates a homogeneous structural relationship, and the analyzed dataset pair contains no macroscopic subclusters.

Property 2 (Heterogeneity and Subclusters). Conversely, varying slopes and plateaus indicate a heterogeneous relationship with subclusters. A sharp increase in steepness marks the onset of exponential pair-counting growth, while the final top plateau reveals the maximum spatial distance between the datasets.

Rule 1 (Macro-structural Extraction): To identify the entire, cohesive dataset rather than isolated subclusters, locate the start of the steepest slope. If multiple slopes exist, the last steep slope before the final saturation plateau represents the complete macroscopic correlation between the sets.

3.2 Determining the Optimal Clustering Threshold

To illustrate the proposed method, we extract ϵ^* step-by-step using cross-plots from the PIESP dataset pairs (economic sectors). Figure 2 shows the cumulative cross-pair distribution against the expanding spatial radius r (in log scale). The evaluated bounds define the clustering limits. The lower bound is the minimum inter-dataset distance. Setting ϵ here causes severe micro-cluster fragmentation, treating most data as noise. The upper bound is the maximum distance before the final saturation plateau. Setting ϵ here merges distinct economic sectors into a single cluster, obscuring domain boundaries. As these curves lack a purely homogeneous distribution (as defined in Property 1), a detailed topological breakdown is required to find the optimal scale.

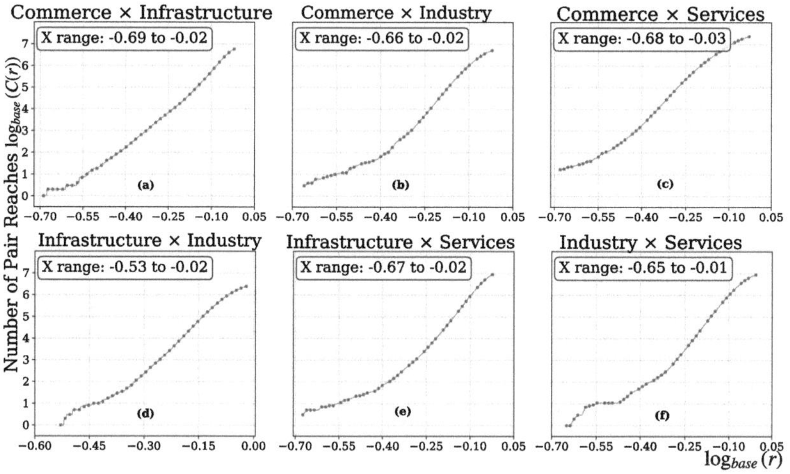

Fig. 2. Cross-correlation analysis (log–log scale) after initial and final plateau removal, spotting regions of linear growth in the cumulative inter-cluster pair distances.

Figure 3 details the cross-plot for the Industry × Services pair. This example exhibits a heterogeneous distribution (Property 2), where distinct slopes and plateaus, shown with vertical markers and piecewise dashed segments, reveal the formation of internal subclusters before the dominant macroscopic growth. The extraction of the optimal window follows Rule 1, which bypasses the early micro-cluster structures and defines the start of the useful region (red vertical line) at the onset of the final steep rise. This ensures that the measured spatial correlation reflects the interaction between the macroscopic sets. Finally, the linear fit within the selected region provides the fractal correlation dimension (D_2), estimated as the slope of the regression line:

$$D_2 = \frac{dy}{dx} \approx \frac{\Delta \log(\text{Cross}_{A,B}(r))}{\Delta \log(r)} \tag{3}$$

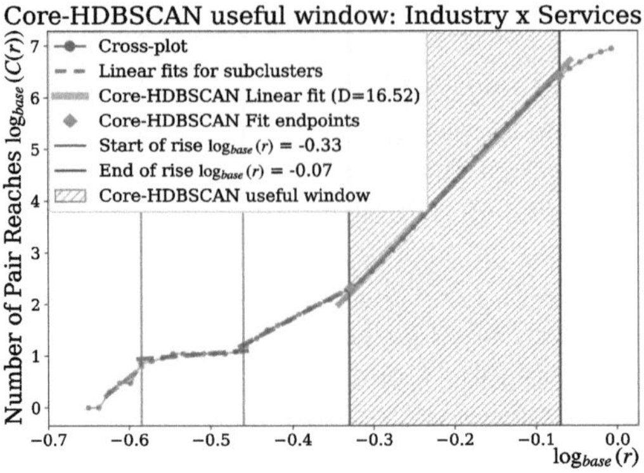

Fig. 3. Cross-plot for the Industry × Services pair, showing the Core-HDBSCAN useful window (hatched region) bounded by the rise onset and offset (red/green vertical lines), subcluster linear fits (dashed lines), and boundary markers (colored vertical lines). (Color figure online)

As described, the macroscopic correlation window begins at the point of maximum topological acceleration (x_{ref}), where $y''(x)$ reaches its peak.

In this example, the extracted range ($[-0.33, -0.07]$) spans the steepest growth region and yields an optimal spatial threshold for $\epsilon^* = 10^{-0.33} \approx 0.468$. Using this value as the `cluster_selection_epsilon` parameter provides HDBSCAN with a deterministic geometric boundary, reducing fragmentation and aligning the clustering with the macroscopic structure of the semantic data.

4 Experimental Results

4.1 Dataset and Domain Partitioning

The PIESP dataset: the Survey of Announced Investments in the State of São Paulo (*Pesquisa de Investimentos Anunciados no Estado de São Paulo*) was obtained from the SEADE website[1] It comprises approximately 14.5 thousand investment records in the State of São Paulo over 13 years (2012–2025). It tracks productive investments, including companies, localities, descriptions, economic sectors, and announcement dates. For our experiments, we used two attributes: the textual investment description and the sector description (excluding the minor Agribusiness category), which serves as the ground-truth label for clustering evaluation.

Dataset Distribution: The dataset encompasses investment records across five primary economic sectors: Services (6,792 records; logistics, delivery, multi-use

[1] https://repositorio.seade.gov.br/dataset/seade-investimentos/resource/3ee8eb9b-a3b5-4d53-925f-71e5dabb263c.

facilities), Commerce (4,134 records; retail, wholesale, distribution), Infrastructure (1,990 records; water, energy, sanitation), Industry (1,540 records; manufacturing, factories, tech development), and Agribusiness (134 records; agriculture, rural infrastructure).

The dataset exhibits a natural class imbalance across sectors. We preserved the original distribution without synthetic balancing (e.g., over/undersampling) to evaluate the robustness of the topological ϵ^* extraction under realistic conditions, leaving imbalance adjustments for future work. To embed the Portuguese corpus, raw texts were processed via the sentence-transformers library using the Bertimbau model(`neuralmind/ bert-base-portuguese-cased`)[2]. which generated 768-dimensional dense embeddings, providing the continuous spatial representation needed to compute Euclidean distances for our fractal-based cross-plot methodology.

4.2 Experimental Evaluation and Clustering Results

With the dataset embedded in a high-dimensional space and the optimal threshold (ϵ^*) extracted via cross-cloud, we evaluate our methodology by comparing baseline HDBSCAN (H_{def}, using default parameters with no active spatial constraint) against our proposed model (*Core*, incorporating ϵ^* as a deterministic cluster extraction boundary).

$$\text{H}_{\text{def}} = \text{HDBSCAN}(\text{min\_cluster\_size} = 5, \text{cluster\_selection\_epsilon} = 0.0) \tag{4}$$

$$\text{Core} = \text{HDBSCAN}(\text{min\_cluster\_size} = 5, \text{cluster\_selection\_epsilon} = \epsilon^*) \tag{5}$$

The specific ϵ^* values for each pair, derived from their fractal acceleration points (x_{ref}), are detailed in Table 1. We evaluate how this structural restriction affects the ratio of valid clustered points versus noise, factoring in the dataset's distribution. Table 2 summarizes the comparative performance across the analyzed economic domains.

Table 2 shows that Core-HDBSCAN consistently reduces both noise and cluster counts relative to the baseline. By controlling spatial strictness, ϵ^* mitigates premature noise assignment and over-fragmentation, promoting denser, more cohesive clusters. Their semantic quality was assessed using the purity metric.

As detailed in Table 3, the proposed method improved semantic purity in four of the six analyzed pairs. The exceptions were 'Commerce x Services' (decreasing from 97.83% to 96.90%) and 'Industry x Services' (from 99.40% to 97.34%). Consequently, the overall average purity dropped slightly by 0.46% (from 98.75%

[2] https://huggingface.co/neuralmind/bert-base-portuguese-cased.

Table 1. Spatial threshold (ϵ^*) calibration parameters, derived by converting the logarithmic rise onset (x_{ref}) back to the original distance scale.

Pair	x_{ref}	ϵ^*
Commerce × Infrastructure	−0.45	0.355
Commerce × Industry	−0.39	0.407
Commerce × Services	−0.50	0.316
Infrastructure × Industry	−0.35	0.447
Infrastructure × Services	−0.34	0.457
Industry × Services	−0.33	0.468

Table 2. Comparative clustering performance of HDBSCAN (H_{def}) × *Core* across sector pairs, detailing instance counts, formed clusters, and noise percentages.

Pair	**Total Points**	H_{def} **Clusters**	H_{def} **Noise (%)**	*Core* **Clusters**	*Core* **Noise (%)**
Commerce × Infrastructure	6124	98	72.24	**76**	**65.45**
Commerce × Industry	5674	80	76.84	**40**	**59.43**
Commerce × Services	10926	168	79.75	**144**	**77.24**
Infrastructure × Industry	3530	32	81.93	**28**	**81.16**
Infrastructure × Services	8782	118	82.60	**55**	**65.67**
Industry × Services	8332	103	86.02	**39**	**67.02**

to 98.29%). This trade-off is highly acceptable, as the topological ϵ^* maintains strong semantic cohesion while expanding cluster boundaries to capture thousands of instances previously discarded as noise.

To complement absolute purity and assess agreement between predicted partitions and ground-truth labels, we adopted pairwise counting metrics: precision, recall, and F1-score. These metrics evaluate clustering quality across all unordered instance pairs, treating noise points as misclassifications by verifying whether each pair is placed in the same cluster in both partitions.

Pairwise precision and recall measure the proportion of correctly co-clustered pairs relative to all predicted and true within-class pairs, respectively, balanced by the pairwise F1-score. To prevent macro-averaging from overemphasizing minority classes, we used weighted averaging to scale metric contributions by

Table 3. Clustering Purity Comparison

Pair	H_{def} **Purity %**	*Core* **Purity%**
Commerce × Infrastructure	99.59	**99.62**
Commerce × Industry	98.71	**98.78**
Commerce × Services	97.83	**96.90**
Infrastructure × Industry	98.28	**98.35**
Infrastructure × Services	98.69	**98.77**
Industry × Services	99.40	**97.34**

class frequencies. This accounts for sector-pair imbalances and ensures a representative performance evaluation (Table 4).

Table 4. Pairwise counting evaluation.

Pair	Precision	Recall	F1-Score
Commerce × Infrastructure	0.996 **0.996**	0.276 **0.344**	0.432 **0.508**
Commerce × Industry	0.982 **0.982**	0.229 **0.401**	0.359 **0.533**
Commerce × Services	0.981 **0.969**	0.198 **0.221**	0.325 **0.354**
Infrastructure × Industry	0.974 **0.975**	0.178 **0.185**	0.294 **0.303**
Infrastructure × Services	0.989 **0.987**	0.172 **0.339**	0.291 **0.504**
Industry × Services	0.992 **0.972**	0.139 **0.321**	0.243 **0.468**

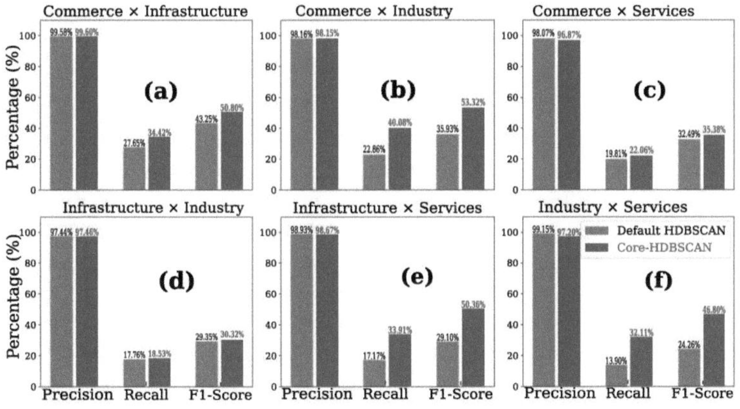

Fig. 4. Comparison of clustering metrics (Precision, Recall, F1-Score) between default HDBSCAN (gray) and Core-HDBSCAN (blue) across sector pairs. Subplots display percentages for each pair, highlighting differences in classification quality. (Color figure online)

Finally, to visually characterize topological boundaries and identify semantic overlap, we generated the confusion matrix for the calibrated extractions, mapping true classes (rows) against predicted classes (columns). Unclassified points are explicitly penalized as "noise." Because the ground truth covers the entire semantic space with no outliers, assigning a point as noise represents an error in mapping the topological manifold. This penalty ensures the evaluation reflects each technique's ability to capture structural completeness rather than just internal cluster homogeneity.

Complementing the global metrics in Fig. 4, the confusion matrices highlight that our method matches or outperforms the baseline along the main diagonal (true positives) in 5 of the 6 evaluated pairs. The exception occurs in the Industry vs. Services pair (f), where the calibrated threshold significantly increases correct classifications for Services but slightly reduces them for Industry. This behavior naturally reflects the dataset's asymmetric densities; under class imbalance, the larger manifold inherently assimilates boundary points. Rather than forcing a compressed fit like traditional dimensionality reduction, the fractal dimension threshold adapts to each domain's specific topology, driving the overall improvements observed in the weighted F1-Score.

5 Conclusions

This paper introduces a new approach for identifying an optimal spatial threshold from pairwise dataset correlations. By deriving the cut-off parameter ϵ^* through fractal correlation analysis, our method reveals the intrinsic dimensional structure of the semantic space and directly calibrates density-based algorithms, bypassing empirical tuning. Empirical results validate the structural consistency of this extracted threshold, yielding an average relative F1-Score improvement of **37.35%** over the baseline configuration.

Core-HDBSCAN is particularly effective for hierarchical algorithms, like HDBSCAN, where ϵ^* acts as a spatial constraint for dendrogram pruning that mitigates over-fragmentation while preserving domain structure. Future work will investigate the scalability of this topological mapping across different embedding architectures and textual corpora.

Acknowledgments. This research was supported by the São Paulo Research Foundation (FAPESP, grants No. 2025/15710-0, 2023/18026-8, 2024/13328-9), the Brazilian Federal Agency for Support of Graduate Education (CAPES), and the National Council for Scientific and Technological Development (CNPq).

Disclosure of Interests. The authors have no competing interests relevant to the content of this article. Generative AI tools were used only for linguistic revision and textual reorganization. The responsibility for the scientific content and final manuscript remains with the authors.

References

1. Ankerst, M., Breunig, M.M., Kriegel, H.P., Sander, J.: Optics: ordering points to identify the clustering structure. In: ACM SIGMOD International Conference on Information and Knowledge Management, vol. 28, pp. 49–60. ACM Press, Philadelphia, PA, United States (1999). https://doi.org/10.1145/304182.304187

2. Campello, R.J.G.B., Moulavi, D., Sander, J.: Density-based clustering based on hierarchical density estimates. In: Pei, J., Tseng, V.S., Cao, L., Motoda, H., Xu, G. (eds.) PAKDD 2013. LNCS (LNAI), vol. 7819, pp. 160–172. Springer, Heidelberg (2013). https://doi.org/10.1007/978-3-642-37456-2_14
3. Deng, D.: DBSCAN clustering algorithm based on density. In: 2020 7th International Forum on Electrical Engineering and Automation (IFEEA), 949–953 (2020). https://doi.org/10.1109/IFEEA51475.2020.00199
4. Ester, M., Kriegel, H.P., Sander, J., Xu, X.: A density-based algorithm for discovering clusters in large spatial databases with noise. In: ACM Interntional Conference on Knowledge Discovery and Data Mining, pp. 226–231. ACM Press (1996)
5. Ghosh, K., Naldi, M.C., Sander, J., Choo, E.: Unsupervised parameter-free outlier detection using hdbscan* outlier profiles. In: 2024 IEEE Interntional Conference on Big Data (BigData), pp. 7021–7030 (2024). https://doi.org/10.1109/BigData62323.2024.10825917
6. Houle, M.E.: Local intrinsic dimensionality i: an extreme-value-theoretic foundation for similarity applications. In: Beecks, C., Borutta, F., Kröger, P., Seidl, T. (eds.) Similarity Search and Applications, pp. 64–79. Springer, Cham (2017). https://doi.org/10.1007/978-3-319-68474-1_5
7. Jain, A.K.: Data clustering: 50 years beyond k-means. Pattern Recognit. Lett. **31**(8), 651–666 (2010). https://doi.org/10.1016/j.patrec.2009.09.011
8. Katayama, N., Satoh, S.: Distinctiveness-sensitive nearest-neighbor search for efficient similarity retrieval of multimedia information. In: Georgakopoulos, D., Buchmann, A. (eds.) IEEE International Conference on Data Engineering (ICDE), pp. 493–502. IEEE Computer Society, Heidelberg, Germany (2001). https://doi.org/10.1109/ICDE.2001.914863
9. Korn, F., Pagel, B.U., Faloutsos, C.: On the 'dimensionality curse' and the 'self-similarity blessing'. IEEE TKDE **13**(1), 96–111 (2001). https://doi.org/10.1109/69.908983
10. Malzer, C., Baum, M.: A hybrid approach to hierarchical density-based cluster selection. In: 2020 IEEE International Conference on Multisensor Fusion and Integration for Intelligent Systems (MFI), pp. 223–228 (2020). https://doi.org/10.1109/MFI49285.2020.9235263
11. Traina, A.J.M., Traina, Caetano, J., Papadimitriou, S., Faloutsos, C.: Tri-plots: scalable tools for multidimensional data mining. In: Provost, F., Ramakrishnan, S. (eds.) ACM SIGKDD International Conference on Knowledge Discovery and Data Mining, pp. 184–193. ACM Press, San Francisco, CA (2001). https://doi.org/10.1145/502512.502538

SparkADLS: Robust Semi-supervised Anomaly Detection in Log Series

Nayef Roqaya(✉) and Thorsten Papenbrock

Philipps University of Marburg, Marburg, Germany
roqaya@staff.uni-marburg.de, papenbrock@informatik.uni-marburg.de

Abstract. Large-scale computing systems generate massive amounts of log data, making accurate and timely anomaly detection critical for system reliability. Although previous work has achieved strong detection performance, most existing approaches rely on sequential processing pipelines, which inherently limit runtime efficiency and scalability – in particular for large-scale datasets in CPU-only environments. While GPU-based solutions can partially alleviate these limitations, such solutions introduce additional cost and deployment complexity, thereby reducing their practical applicability. In this paper, we present SparkADLS, a semi-supervised and scalable log anomaly detection system that translates the sequential pipeline of the known NovaADLS algorithm into a PySpark-based parallel execution environment. While preserving the high-level architectural principles of NovaADLS, SparkADLS redesigns all core components by introducing a probabilistic modeling of normal behavior, reconstruction-based anomaly scoring with a hybrid novelty decision mechanism, hybrid training layer with real and pseudo labels, principled pseudo-anomaly training layer, and a unified decision rule for multi-layer anomaly scoring. All components are tightly integrated and optimized for PySpark's distributed computing paradigm. SparkADLS reduces computational runtime, demonstrates effective scalability to large-scale datasets, and improves anomaly detection accuracy. More specifically, extensive experiments on real-world datasets, including BGL, HDFS, Thunderbird, and Spirit, show that SparkADLS achieves F1-scores of up to 0.999 and reduces training time on average by 57%.

Keywords: Anomaly Detection · Semi-Supervised Learning · PySpark · Efficiency · Scalability · Sequential · Parallel · Distributed

1 Introduction

Modern computing infrastructures generate system logs on an unprecedented scale, making accurate and efficient anomaly detection essential to maintain system reliability and to allow timely fault diagnosis [26]. Effective solutions must, therefore, achieve not only high detection accuracy but also efficient and scalable runtimes in large-scale environments [4,12,13]. Although anomaly detection has been widely studied [3,8,11,14,16,23], applying it to system logs remains

© The Author(s), under exclusive license to Springer Nature Switzerland AG 2027
G. Vargas Solar et al. (Eds.): ADBIS 2026, CCIS 3175, pp. 172–188, 2027.
https://doi.org/10.1007/978-3-032-39823-9_16

challenging due to their heterogeneous nature. However, existing methods still struggle to balance *detection accuracy*, *computational efficiency*, and *scalability*, limiting their practicality in large-scale systems.

1. **Parallel and distributed computation.** Anomaly detection in distributed environments requires consistency across distributed workers. These workers perform feature extraction, model training, and anomaly inference. Ensuring correctness and stability is critical so results remain reproducible and semantically equivalent.
2. **Scalable and efficient computation.** Modern IT systems generate massive amounts of log data, making sequential pipelines impractical. As the amount of data grows, training and inference costs increase and start causing resource bottlenecks. For this reason, anomaly detection methods need to support high-throughput, low-latency processing while using resources efficiently, highlighting the need for scalable solutions.

These challenges call for a unified, scalable, and correct distributed solution. Our contributions are as follows:

a. **Distributed anomaly detection pipeline.** We design a distributed anomaly detection approach that partitions log data across workers while enforcing consistent feature extraction, model training, and inference. This design offers high accuracy, stability, and resource scalability.
b. **Scalable and efficient execution.** We develop a scalable computation strategy that leverages distributed parallelism to enable high-throughput, low-latency anomaly detection and effectively mitigate computational bottlenecks in large-scale log analysis.

The remainder of this paper is organized as follows: Section 2 reviews related work, Section 3 introduces key concepts, Section 4 presents SparkADLS and compares SparkADLS with NovaADLS, Sect. 5 reports the experimental results, and Sect. 6 concludes the paper.

2 Related Work

This section reviews state-of-the-art methods for log-based anomaly detection.

Learning Paradigms in Anomaly Detection. Anomaly detection can be supervised, unsupervised, or semi-supervised. Since labeled anomalies are often unavailable and unsupervised methods may be less accurate, SparkADLS adopts a semi-supervised approach that uses a small set of normal data while maintaining high detection accuracy.

Supervised Learning. CNN [14] uses convolutional neural networks to log sequences, where log events are encoded using logkey2vec embeddings and processed through multiple convolutional layers to capture event patterns and dependencies. LogRobust [11] improves robustness to unstable log patterns by representing events with semantic embeddings and employing an attention-based

Bi-LSTM to capture contextual dependencies while highlighting informative events.

Unsupervised Learning. DeepLog [23] models logs as sequences and uses LSTM networks to learn normal event patterns. During detection, it continuously predicts the next event; if the observed event is not among the top candidates, the sequence is flagged as anomalous. LogAnomaly [8] improves DeepLog by using semantic event representations and frequency information to detect unusual event occurrences.

Semi-Supervised Learning. Semi-supervised learning has been widely used in log-based anomaly detection to reduce the dependency on large amounts of manually labeled anomalous data. PLELog [16] follows a semi-supervised strategy that, first, estimates probabilistic labels for unlabeled log sequences and, then, trains an attention-based GRU model to capture sequential dependencies among log events. On the one hand, PLELog improves anomaly detection when log patterns are unstable and reduces the need for manual labeling by combining probabilistic label estimation with sequence modeling. On the other hand, NovaADLS [3] uses a semi-supervised strategy that improves log-sequence representations and pseudo-label generation before supervised classification. It extracts multiple event-level features, aggregates them into fixed-size sequence representations, and applies OC-SVM-based novelty detection with LOF and Silhouette-guided tuning to infer pseudo-labels. Finally, It uses labeled and pseudo-labeled data to train a voting and stacking ensemble anomaly detector.

3 Key Concepts in Log Data Processing

This section introduces the key concepts of log data, single-node parallel processing and distributed processing.

Key Concepts of Log Data. A *log entry* is a textual record generated during the execution of a software system, application, or service. Each entry describes an event that occurred at a specific time. Because logs are typically written as unstructured text, transformation into structured data is required through *log parsing*, which is a process that extracts the characteristic components from the logs. In this work, a *log event* represents the fixed textual template defined by the developers, while a *log parameter* refers to the variable values embedded in the message (e.g., identifiers, numbers, or IP) [10].

Key Concepts of Distributed Processing. To efficiently process large log datasets, distributed computing frameworks, such as *Spark* or *Flink*, are commonly used. *PySpark* is the Python API for *Apache Spark* and enables scalable processing in cluster environments. A Spark cluster *node* refers to a physical or virtual machine. *Worker nodes* perform data processing tasks, while an *executor* is a process on a worker node that executes computations, manages resources, and stores intermediate results [4]. A *driver* program coordinates the executions by scheduling their tasks and communicating with the different executors.

Key Concepts of Parallel Processing. *PySpark* is used not only as a distributed cluster framework, but also as a local parallelization engine for scalable log processing. On every single machine, Spark decomposes datasets into partitions and schedules operations over these partitions using the available local CPU cores for parallelization [4].

4 Anomaly Detection with SparkADLS

In this section, we introduce **SparkADLS**[1], a semi-supervised and distributed system for batch-based **A**nomaly **D**etection in **L**og **S**eries. The system is designed for *efficient* and *scalable* anomaly detection in large-scale log datasets and requires only a small set of labeled normal log events. Similar to prior work [3,16], SparkADLS analyzes sequences of log events; however, it leverages distributed data processing to improve runtime efficiency while maintaining high detection accuracy. The overall architecture (see Fig. 1) consists of five phases: (1) log parsing and reading, (2) feature engineering, (3) feature aggregation, (4) novelty detection and label estimation, (5) and anomaly detection.

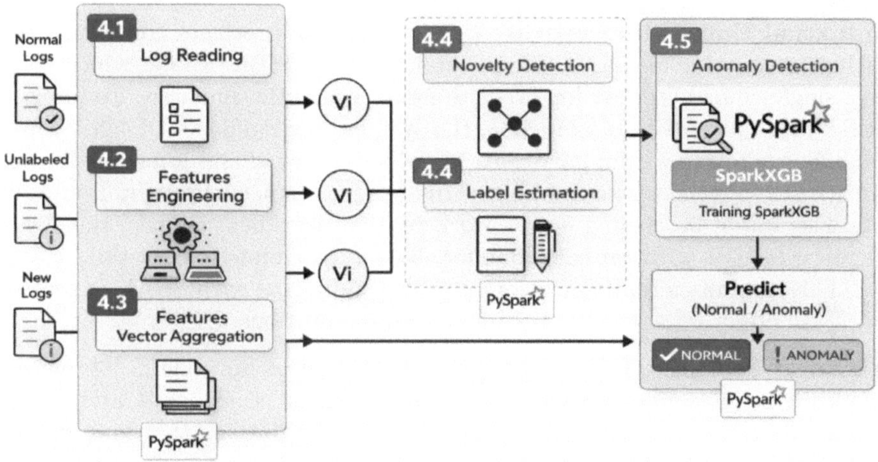

Fig. 1. Overview of SparkADLS.

4.1 Log Parsing and Reading

In the first phase, following prior work [3,16], we use the Drain log parser [18, 20,21] to transform raw log messages into structured event templates. Because Drain is implemented in Python and no native PySpark version exists, we treat log parsing as a traditional preprocessing step without using PySpark and store parsed logs as CSV files. SparkADLS then loads the data using

[1] SparkADLS: https://github.com/nayefroqaya/NovaAD_Plus.

spark.read.csv(), optionally with schema inference or predefined schemas, into PySpark DataFrames for subsequent processing, which enable parallel computation on a single node cluster and distributed parallel computation on multiple nodes of a cluster.

4.2 Feature Engineering

The second phase implements feature representations from parsed log templates using parallel transformations. We redesign the feature pipeline of *NovaADLS* [3] to enable its distributed execution while preserving semantic properties.

Topic-based Features. We apply Latent Dirichlet Allocation (LDA) from PySpark [7] to capture latent semantic patterns in log messages. In this context, we treat each log event as a short document and represent it by a topic distribution. From this, we derive two compact features: the dominant topic index and the entropy of the distribution. The dominant topic captures the primary semantic theme, while entropy quantifies uncertainty in the topic mixture. These features, together, summarize semantic structure and help identify anomalous patterns.

Contextual Embedding Features. Our approach processes contextual relationships among log messages using Sentence-BERT (SBERT) [5], which generates a single embedding per log event to model semantic similarity. To integrate SBERT into the distributed pipeline, the system uses Pandas UDFs in PySpark for batch processing within partitions to reduce overhead and improve efficiency compared to element-wise executions. This design enhances throughput and supports distributed processing across workers. For sentiment signals, the system uses SieBERT [19] with `mapInPandas` for efficient batch inference at the partition level. This minimizes redundant computation and aligns with Spark's execution model. We apply PCA to obtain compact representations.

Structural Features. Following the feature design of NovaADLS [3], our system extracts lightweight structural features, such as *word count* and *character count*, from log messages to capture structural variations that may indicate anomalous behavior. These features are implemented using PySpark transformations, including `length()` for character count and `size(split())` for word count computation. Transformations are applied using `withColumn()` to efficiently process large-scale log data in a distributed setting.

Temporal Features. Although timestamps are available, metadata features, such as the year component, provide limited discriminative value in datasets due to their short time spans (e.g., one or two values: 2005–2006 and 2008), resulting in near-zero variance. Such features introduce dataset-specific bias or spurious correlations. Hence, we focus on finer-grained temporal components. Temporal features are extracted from the `Timestamp` field using PySpark SQL functions (`month`, `dayofmonth`, `hour`, `minute`, `second`) via `withColumn` operations, producing numerical features in a distributed manner. These features capture fine-grained temporal patterns in log events.

4.3 Feature Vector Aggregation

Following the sequence-level representation strategy used in [3,16], SparkADLS maps variable-length log sequences to fixed-size feature vectors. Each log sequence consists of a set of event-level feature vectors, where the number of events may differ across sequences. To obtain a uniform representation, SparkADLS applies mean poolingin over the event dimension [3]. Given a sequence with n event vectors, the resulting sequence embedding is computed as the element-wise average of the corresponding feature dimensions across all n events. This operation yields one fixed-length vector per sequence, enabling downstream classification independent of sequence length. In the PySpark implementation, events are grouped by their sequence identifier using `groupBy()`, and the event-level feature vectors are collected and passed to a mean-pooling aggregation function. For vector-valued attributes, this function computes the element-wise mean of the collected vectors at the sequence level.

4.4 Novelty Detection and Label Estimation

The goal of the novelty detection and label estimation phase is to expand the training set by using the small set of labeled normal events to infer provisional labels for similar unlabeled events.

Stage 1: Data Preparation and Feature Transformation. We split the training set into a small labeled normal subset and a remaining unlabeled subset using PySpark. The labeled normal subset defines the reference distribution used for learning the normal-behavior model. We represent each sequence using the fixed-length feature vector that we generated during feature engineering and aggregation. Finally, we apply PCA to suppress noise, reduce dimensionality, and lower computational costs, while selecting components from a predefined candidate set according to an explained-variance threshold.

Stage 2: Probabilistic Modeling of Normal Behavior. To model the distribution of normal log sequences [1], SparkADLS trains a Gaussian Mixture Model (GMM) [22] on the PCA-transformed normal feature vectors. Let $z_i \in \mathbb{R}^d$ denote the PCA representation of sequence i, then the probability density of z_i under the mixture model is defined as ($p(z_i) = \sum_{k=1}^{K} \pi_k \mathcal{N}(z_i \mid \mu_k, \Sigma_k)$), where π_k denotes the mixture weight of component k, and $\mathcal{N}(z_i \mid \mu_k, \Sigma_k)$ represents a Gaussian distribution with mean μ_k and covariance matrix Σ_k. The optimal number of mixture components K is selected using the Bayesian Information Criterion (BIC) [25] over a predefined set of candidate values. For each sequence, we compute the negative log-likelihood [1] anomaly score which measures how unlikely the sequence is under the learned normal distribution.

$$S_{\mathrm{GMM}}(z_i) = -\log p(z_i) \tag{1}$$

Stage 3: Reconstruction-Based Anomaly Scoring. To capture structural deviations in the feature space, we compute an additional anomaly score based on the PCA reconstruction error [1,6]. Let x_i denote the input scaled feature vector and $\hat{x}_i$ its projection-based reconstruction from the PCA representation. The reconstruction error is defined as follows:

$$S_{\mathrm{PCA}}(x_i) = \|x_i - \hat{x}_i\|_2 \tag{2}$$

where $\|\cdot\|_2$ denotes the Euclidean norm. Sequences that deviate from the learned structure of normal data typically produce larger reconstruction errors.

Stage 4: Hybrid Novelty Decision. The final decision on novelty detection combines two anomaly indicators [1,22]. The thresholds τ_{GMM} and τ_{PCA} are determined from the score distributions of the normal train sequences using quantile-based estimation with a target upper-tail rate. An unlabeled sequence is assigned an anomalous label if ($S_{\mathrm{GMM}}(z_i) > \tau_{\mathrm{GMM}}$ or $S_{\mathrm{PCA}}(x_i) > \tau_{\mathrm{PCA}}$), otherwise, the sequence is labeled as normal. This hybrid decision strategy improves robustness by detecting both distributional deviations and structural anomalies. Because all stages are implemented using PySpark, the novelty detection pipeline can scale efficiently to large log datasets while maintaining accurate modeling of normal system behavior.

4.5 Anomaly Detection

After provisional labeling, SparkADLS expands the training data and reduces pseudo-label noise through performance-guided layer selection as the following:

4.5.1. Hybrid Training with Real and Pseudo Labels Layer. The first layer uses real and weighted pseudo-labels with validation-based thresholding.

Dataset Construction.
The train dataset combines (1) real labeled normal sequences and (2) all pseudo-labeled sequences from the novelty detection stage. Each sequence is represented by its aggregated feature vector.

Deterministic Split and Class Weighting. A hash-based partition of sequence identifiers divides the dataset into train (90%) and validation (10%) sets. This approach ensures stable and reproducible splits across runs. The method assigns lower weights to pseudo-labeled samples and higher weights to real labels to reduce impact of noise. It also applies class weighting to address the imbalance between normal and anomalous sequences, with an upper cap to avoid extreme values. The final sample weight is the product of class and source weights [2].

Model Training and Threshold Selection. *SparkXGB Classifier* [24] trains on the weighted dataset and outputs an anomaly probability $p_i \in [0, 1]$ for each sequence. The method selects a threshold τ on the validation set by searching over values in $[0.01, 0.999]$. It considers different target recall levels (e.g., 0.60, 0.80, 0.90, 0.95), and first identifies the target recall level that achieves the best validation F1-score among thresholds satisfying the corresponding recall constraint. Based on the selected target recall, the system chooses the final threshold that maximizes precision while maintaining recall above the selected target. If no threshold satisfies the constraint, it falls back to the threshold with the highest F1-score. If the selected threshold produces no anomalous predictions on the validation set, it uses the 90th percentile of validation probabilities.

4.5.2. Pseudo-Anomaly Training Layer. The second layer trains a classifier using real normal sequences and pseudo-labeled anomalous sequences.

Dataset Construction. Unlike layer 1, this layer excludes pseudo-labeled normal sequences and retains only pseudo-labeled anomalies. The training set is constructed by combining real normal with pseudo-labeled anomalous sequences.

Anomaly Oversampling. To reduce class imbalance, pseudo-labeled anomalies are repeated until their count approaches that of normal sequences, improving their representation during training [2].

Train-Validation Split. The method splits the resulting dataset into a train subset (90%) and a validation subset (10%). The validation set supports threshold selection before final inference.

Model Training and Threshold Selection. *SparkXGB Classifier* [24] trains on the resulting dataset and produces an anomaly probability $p_i \in [0, 1]$ for each sequence. The method selects the decision threshold on the validation set by testing thresholds in the range $[0.05, 0.95]$ with step size 0.01. It chooses the threshold that maximizes the weighted F1-score.

4.5.3. Unified Decision Rule for Multi-Layer Anomaly Scoring. Both layers use a classifier-only decision rule: $\hat{y}_i^{(\ell)} = \mathbb{I}\left(p_i^{(\ell)} \geq \tau_\ell\right)$, where $\ell \in \{1, 2\}$ denotes the layer, $p_i^{(\ell)}$ is the anomaly probability produced by the classifier in layer ℓ, and τ_ℓ is the validation-selected threshold for that layer [1,8,18,23]. Layer 1 uses τ_1, selected using the precision-at-recall criterion on the validation set. Layer 2 uses τ_2, selected by maximizing the weighted F1-score in the validation set.

Layer-wise Comparison. SparkADLS converts the parsed log sequences into aggregated feature vectors. Figure 2 shows that both layers share a common pipeline with training and inference phases. The features train a *SparkXGB Classifier* to produce anomaly probabilities p_i, while a validation set determines decision thresholds. The layers capture trade-offs between robustness to label noise and sensitivity to rare anomalies. The $layer_1$ hybrid layer combines real normal labels and all pseudo labels with sample weighting. It then applies a classifier-only threshold rule, where a sequence is predicted as anomalous if $p_i \geq \tau_1$. In contrast, $layer_2$ pseudo-anomaly layer combines real normal labels with pseudo-anomalies only and uses oversampling to increase anomaly sensitivity. It also applies a classifier-only threshold rule, where a sequence is predicted as anomalous if $p_i \geq \tau_2$. During inference, unseen sequences follow the same pipeline for prediction. When multiple layers are evaluated, the final step selects the model with the highest anomaly-class F1-score, with anomaly recall and precision used as secondary criteria.

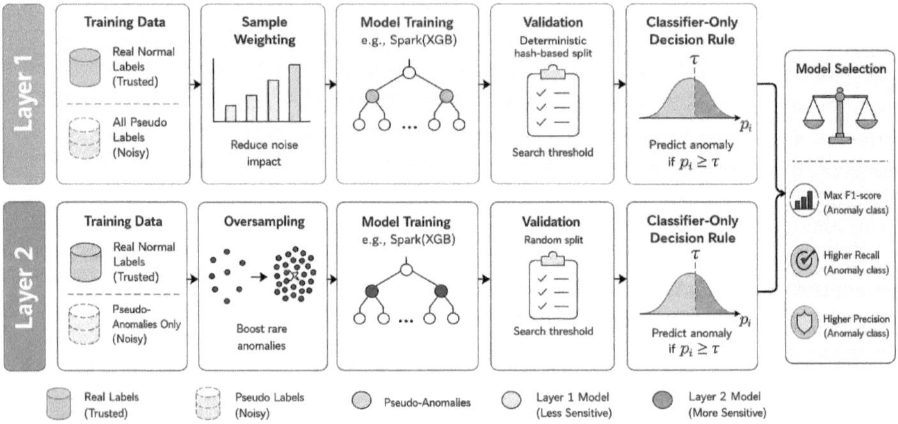

Fig. 2. Architecture Anomaly Detection Pipeline in SparkADLS.

Key Differences between NovaADLS and SparkADLS. NovaADLS [3] and SparkADLS follow the same high-level anomaly detection workflow, including feature extraction, sequence aggregation, novelty labeling, and final anomaly detection. However, SparkADLS advances this workflow by redesigning its internal components for distributed, large-scale, and more adaptive learning. While NovaADLS relies on sequential feature extraction and OC-SVM-based novelty detection with LOF/Silhouette tuning [3], SparkADLS implements feature extraction and aggregation in PySpark and introduces a hybrid GMM–PCA novelty estimator. This estimator combines GMM likelihood [22] with PCA reconstruction error, enabling more robust pseudo-label generation from unlabeled log sequences. In the final stage, SparkADLS further improves NovaADLS by replacing the voting/stacking ensemble with layered SparkXGB [24] training, weighted pseudo-labels, and validation-guided threshold tuning. Thus, SparkADLS is an advanced distributed extension of NovaADLS that provides scalable processing, as well as effective, robust and more efficient final anomaly detection.

5 Evaluation

In our evaluation, we focus on three research questions: How does the PySpark-based SparkADLS impact (RQ1) detection accuracy, (RQ2) runtime efficiency and scalability, and (RQ3) robustness compared to its competitors?

5.1 Experimental Setup

Implementations and Environments. All baselines [3,8,11,14,16,23] were re-implemented under a unified protocol using the same datasets and hardware for fair comparison. The proposed approach was evaluated offline over three runs.

Single-Node Configurations. Only one server evaluates anomaly detection accuracy and runtime efficiency on all datasets. Baselines and experiments run on a single-node AMD EPYC 7513 server with 32 CPU cores and ~251 GB RAM. The PySpark environment uses eight workers, each with four CPU cores. Each worker has 28 GB of memory (224 GB total for all executors). The remaining memory is reserved for the OS and Spark overhead. The driver is also assigned 28 GB for stable coordination. This setup provides balanced compute and memory resources for efficient parallel processing.

Multi-Node Configurations. The multi-node setup evaluates the anomaly detection accuracy, runtime efficiency, and scalability. All experiments are executed on a Google Cloud Dataproc cluster, with one master and (one to three) worker nodes. Each node uses an *n4-standard-8* machine (8 vCPUs, 32 GB RAM) with 30–50 GB boot disks, running Dataproc image (Debian 12). This configuration enables scalable distributed processing using Spark's resource management.

Datasets. We evaluate four widely used log datasets: BGL, Thunderbird, Spirit, and HDFS v1 [10]. For BGL, Thunderbird (TH), and Spirit (SP), sequences are generated using a sliding window of 120 events [3,16], while HDFS uses block IDs. Each dataset is chronologically split into train, validation, and test sets (60%, 10%, 30%) to prevent information leakage [16]. We ensure block ID groups do not overlap and verify that each block ID appears in only one split. Sequences involve abnormal behavior are labeled anomalous; otherwise, they are normal. In the semi-supervised setting, only 50% of normal train data is labeled [3,16], with the rest treated as unlabeled. Table 1 summarizes the datasets statistics.

Table 1. Datasets Statistics.

Dataset	Size	Logs	Anom. Ratio (%)	Blocks	Norm Seq.	Anom. Seq.
SP_a	150M	1,225,059	2.6%	7,590	6,266	1,324
BGL	708.7M	4,747,963	7.39%	84,926	49,247	36,251
HDFS	1.47G	11,175,629	2.5%	575,071	558,223	16,838
TH_a	1G	6,013,029	5.04%	52,333	44,732	7,601
TH_b	3G	18,170,704	4.3%	153,695	127,661	26,034
TH_c	9G	53,283,518	3.2%	446,442	402,705	43,73
TH_d	12G	73,055,215	2.4%	611,167	564.623	46.544

Evaluation Metrics. We evaluate the quality of anomaly detection using the standard metrics F_1-score, Precision, and Recall [6], which are defined as follows:

$$F_1 = \frac{2 \cdot \text{Precision} \cdot \text{Recall}}{\text{Precision} + \text{Recall}} \quad \text{Precision} = \frac{TP}{TP + FP} \quad \text{Recall} = \frac{TP}{TP + FN} \tag{3}$$

with true positives TP, false positives FP, and false negatives FN.

5.2 RQ1 - Detection Accuracy of SparkADLS

Table 2 reports the anomaly detection performance (Precision, Recall, F1-score) between datasets and learning paradigms in a single-node configuration, allowing comparison with reproduced baselines. On HDFS, unsupervised methods show high precision but low recall, indicating difficulties with rare anomalies, whereas semi-supervised methods improve recall. SparkADLS achieves a competitive result (F1-score = 0.969) on HDFS with a strong precision–recall balance. On BGL, most methods perform well due to the data being more balanced; deep models, such as CNNs, reach near-perfect scores, while SparkADLS remains competitive and stable. The table also evaluates TH_a and SP_a. On TH_a, SparkADLS achieves near-perfect performance (F1-score = 0.999), clearly outperforming the baselines, while on SP_a it obtains the highest F1-score (0.959), demonstrating robustness across datasets. In general, SparkADLS matches or exceeds state-of-the-art methods, particularly in the cases of imbalance or noisy labels. Experimentally, by running the system three times, SparkADLS shows low F1 variations ($\approx \pm 0.01$ on HDFS and BGL) while the performance of PLELog ($\approx \pm 0.27$) and LogAnomaly ($\approx \pm 0.15$) varies more strongly. SparkADLS's variations remain within ($\approx \pm 0.03$) on TH_a and ($\approx \pm 0.001$) on SP_a.

Table 2. Anomaly Detection Performance (Precision/Recall/F1).

C.	Method	HDFS	BGL	TH_a	SP_a
Sup.	LogRobust	.370/.236/.211	.900/.861/.879	.997/.954/.932	.982/.898/.938
	CNN	.471/.821/.602	.995/.993/.993	.999/.955/.977	.995/.920/.956
Uns.	LogAnomaly	.997/.255/.385	.987/.989/.987	.785/.049/.092	.900/1.0/.947
	DeepLog	.997/.233/.377	.977/.998/.987	.683/.050/.094	.847/1.0/.917
Sem.	PLELog	.262/.721/.443	.732/.966/.832	.299/.997/.455	.822/.863/.842
	NovaADLS	.982/.995/.988	.919/.983/.952	.998/.995/.996	.921/.928/.924
	SparkADLS	*.943/.998/.969*	*.987/.873/.926*	*1.0/.999/.999*	*.946/.971/.959*

5.3 RQ2 - Runtime Performance and Scalability of SparkADLS

To answer the second research question, we evaluate runtime and scalability.

Runtime Analysis. Table 3 reports training and inference times in minutes across four datasets in a single-node configuration. Overall, SparkADLS achieves the lowest runtime in both cases, i.e., training and inference. On large datasets, such as HDFS, supervised methods (e.g., LogRobust, CNN) require high training costs, which often exceed hundreds of minutes. LogAnomaly also shows notable overheads. We report training and inference runtime to provide a fairer comparison across methods. Full end-to-end runtimes are not comparable because the baselines and SparkADLS use different architectures and pipelines.

Table 3. Runtime (train/test ± mean std, minutes) on HDFS, BGL, TH_a, and SP_a.

Cat.	Method	HDFS	BGL	TH_a	SP_a
Sup.	LogRobust	298.9/1.15±2.0	17.15/.35±1.2	20.35/.47±.01	4.22/.12 ±.03
	CNN	371.1/.95±1.7	19.25/.15±1.44	22.6/.38±.04	4.4/.09 ±.01
Unsup.	LogAnomaly	126.1/.09±.001	10.05/.10±.10	282.8/1.1±.03	7.5/0.06±.01
	DeepLog	7.80/.07±.19	4.10/.04±.11	11.07/.05±.01	1.74/0.01 ±.01
Semi.	PLELog	67.10/.67±.44	29.1/.26±.01	24.08/.20±.01	4.85/.06±.01
	NovaADLS	21.40/.07±.53	3.12/.01±.001	1.98/.01±.01	.63/.01±.001
	SparkADLS	*.84/.001±.04*	*.33/.001±.001*	*.34/.001±.001*	*.24/.001±.001*

SparkADLS, in contrast, greatly reduces training times (0.84 min on HDFS) and keeps near-constant minimal latency (≈ 0.01 min). The mean standard deviation confirms runtime stability: SparkADLS shows negligible variation (0 to ≈ ±0.001), while baselines fluctuate more – especially LogRobust/CNN on HDFS (±2.0/±1.7) and BGL (±1.2/±1.44), and NovaADLS on HDFS (±0.53). Although DeepLog trains faster than other baselines, its detection performance is lower (cf. Table 2), showing an accuracy/efficiency trade-off. In general, SparkADLS remains the fastest, most stable, and effective solution for all datasets.

Scalability Analysis. This experiment evaluates the scalability of SparkADLS on large-scale Thunderbird and Spirit subsets using Google Cloud Dataproc. We used three separate cluster configurations, denoted as C1, C2, and C3, with the number of workers increasing from 2 to 4. This expands the cluster from 3 to 5 nodes and increases the available Spark executor cores from 12 to 24.

Table 4. Dataproc and Spark Configurations.

Cluster	Workers	Nodes	vCPUs/RAM	Exec	Cores/Exec	Mem./Exec
C1	2	3	24/96 GB	2	6	20 GB
C2	3	4	32/128 GB	3	6	20 GB
C3	4	5	40/160 GB	4	6	20 GB

As summarized in Table 4, each cluster assigns one Spark executor to each worker node, with 6 cores and 20 GB memory per executor. Dynamic allocation is disabled to keep the resource configuration fixed, allowing runtime changes to reflect the effect of increasing distributed resources. Table 5 shows that SparkADLS benefit from additional resources in Thunderbird. The training time decreases consistently from C1 to C3. For example, $TH_b/3G$ improves from 1.0 to 0.71 min, while $TH_d/12G$ decreases from 1.70 to 1.20 min, reaching the highest speedup of 1.42×. The scaling is sub-linear, which is expected due to scheduling, communication, and synchronization overhead. However, F1 remains stable across cluster sizes, showing that runtime efficiency improves without reducing detection quality.

Table 5. Scalability of SparkADLS on large-scale Thunderbird subsets.

Dataset	Cluster	(Train/Test) minutes	F1	Speedup
$TH_b/3G$	C1	1.0/0.0010	0.996	1.00
$TH_b/3G$	C2	0.79/0.0009	0.996	1.27
$TH_b/3G$	C3	0.71/0.0008	0.996	1.41
$TH_c/9G$	C1	1.40/0.0014	0.936	1.00
$TH_c/9G$	C2	1.23/0.0012	0.936	1.14
$TH_c/9G$	C3	1.08/0.0011	0.950	1.30
$TH_d/12G$	C1	1.70/0.0018	0.948	1.00
$TH_d/12G$	C2	1.60/0.0015	0.948	1.06
$TH_d/12G$	C3	1.20/0.0013	0.945	1.42

Table 6 reports the scalability results on the Spirit subsets, where SP_{X10}, SP_{X20}, and SP_{X50} denote Spirit datasets generated by duplicating the original subset (SP_a) 10, 20, and 50 times, respectively.

Table 6. Scalability of SparkADLS on large-scale Spirit subsets.

Dataset	Cluster	(Train/Test) minutes	F1	Speedup
$SP_{X10}/1.5G$	C1	0.36/0.0014	0.944	1.00
$SP_{X10}/1.5G$	C2	0.34/0.0012	0.951	1.06
$SP_{X10}/1.5G$	C3	0.33/0.0011	0.957	1.09
$SP_{X20}/3G$	C1	0.39/0.0019	0.962	1.00
$SP_{X20}/3G$	C2	0.36/0.0018	0.943	1.08
$SP_{X20}/3G$	C3	0.35/0.0017	0.945	1.11
$SP_{X50}/7.5G$	C1	0.41/0.0013	0.959	1.00
$SP_{X50}/7.5G$	C2	0.39/0.0012	0.936	1.05
$SP_{X50}/7.5G$	C3	0.38/0.0011	0.950	1.08

The training time decreases from C1 to C3 for all Spirit subsets, with speedups between 1.08× and 1.11×. These gains are lower than those on Thunderbird because the Spirit runs are already fast on C1, making the distributed overhead more visible. The F1-scores remain competitive, showing that scaling preserves detection performance. In general, SparkADLS improves runtime efficiency as resources increase, while inference time remains very low due to inference on log-sequence representations rather than single log events.

5.4 RQ3 - Robustness of SparkADLS

We evaluate robustness under varying conditions, showing stable performance across different dataset sizes and anomaly ratio.

Robustness Analysis. Table 7 demonstrates that SparkADLS maintains a consistently high performance across datasets with varying anomaly ratios and scales. Even in highly imbalanced scenarios (2.4%–2.6%), the method achieves F1-scores above 0.94, indicating a strong capability in detecting rare anomalies. Although recall slightly decreases for larger datasets with lower anomaly ratios, precision remains consistently close to 1.0, leading to stable overall performance measurements. This robustness stems from trainable layers that enhance the model's ability to distinguish subtle anomalous patterns. As a result, SparkADLS effectively generalizes across different data distributions, making it suitable for many real-world log analysis scenarios. In the same context, (cf. Table 2) compares precision, recall, and F1 across datasets with different anomaly ratios. The results show that several baselines are sensitive to anomaly prevalence: LogAnomaly and DeepLog perform well on BGL (7.39%) and SP_a (2.6%), but their recall and F1 drop on HDFS (2.5%) and TH_a (5.04%). PLELog also shows unstable precision. In contrast, NovaADLS remains consistently strong, while SparkADLS achieves the best or comparable F1 in most settings.

Table 7. Robustness of SparkADLS under varying anomaly ratios.

Dataset	Size	Anomaly (%)	Precision	Recall	F1
SP_a	150 MB	2.6%	0.946	0.971	0.959
BGL	708.7 MB	7.39%	0.987	0.873	0.926
HDFS	1.47 GB	2.5%	0.943	0.998	0.969
TH_a	1 GB	5.04%	1.0	0.999	0.999
TH_b	3 GB	4.3%	1.0	0.992	0.996
TH_c	9 GB	3.2%	0.946	0.918	0.932
TH_d	12 GB	2.4%	1.0	0.901	0.948

5.5 Ablation Study

We finally present the results of an ablation study that assesses the importance of the features and the contributions of Layer 1 and Layer 2 across datasets.

Layer-wise Analysis of the Anomaly Detection Pipeline. We conduct an ablation study to assess layer contributions in the detection pipeline. Figure 3 shows that Layer 1 (hybrid) consistently achieves high F1-scores by combining real and pseudo labels with a stricter decision rule, preserving a strong precision–recall balance. Layer 2 (pseudo-anomaly) performs best on HDFS but drops on BGL and TH_a, as its permissive rule improves recall while increasing false positives. On SP_a, both layers perform similarly, suggesting better alignment of pseudo-labels. In general, the hybrid layer is more robust, while the pseudo-anomaly layer is more sensitive to dataset-specific trade-offs.

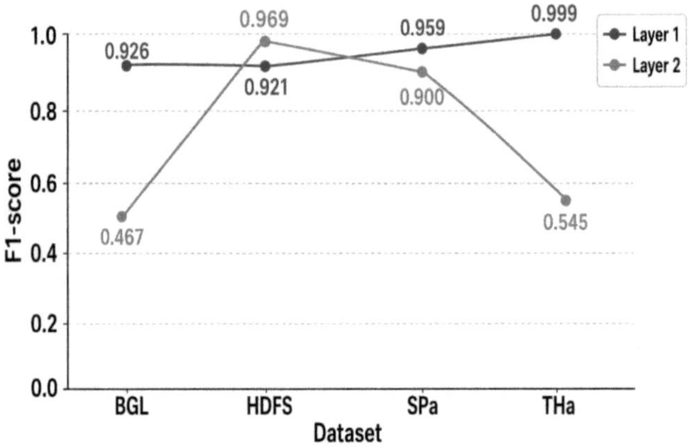

Fig. 3. F1-scores of Layer 1 and Layer 2 across datasets.

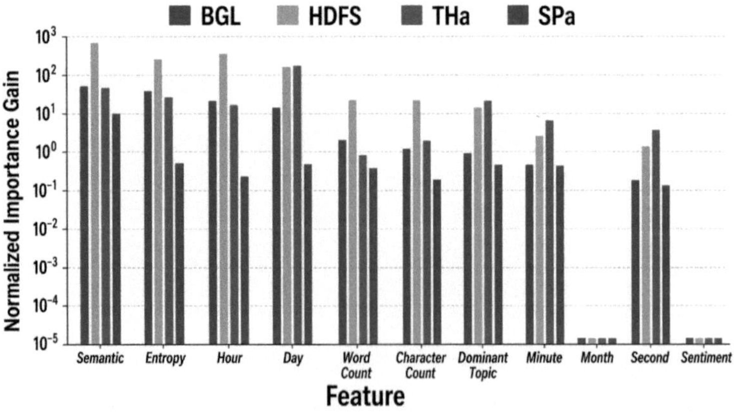

Fig. 4. Results of the ablation study analyzing feature importance.

Feature Importance Analysis. Figure 4 shows the normalized feature importance across BGL, HDFS, TH_a, and SP_a. Semantic features remain highly influential, especially in BGL, HDFS, and SP_a, indicating their strong discriminative power. Topic-related features (Dominant Topic) are also important, particularly in TH_a, reflecting dataset-specific structural patterns. The Entropy feature achieves a notably contribution across BGL, HDFS, TH_a datasets. Temporal features (`dayofmonth`, `hour`, `minute`) show notable contributions, with day being dominant in TH_a and hour being important in HDFS. Word and Character Count provide moderate but dataset-dependent importance. In contrast, Month and Sentiment are found to be negligible across the datasets. In general, these results highlight the most effective features for log-based learning.

6 Conclusion

In this paper, we presented SparkADLS, which is a scalable PySpark-based framework that redesigns NovaADLS for distributed log anomaly detection. SparkADLS combines probabilistic normal-behavior modeling, reconstruction-based anomaly scoring, hybrid novelty decisions, and training with real and pseudo labels. By parallelizing key components while preserving feature semantics, SparkADLS improves runtime efficiency and scalability. The experiments show competitive or superior accuracy, reduced training time, negligible inference cost, and robust performance across different datasets. Overall, SparkADLS demonstrates the effectiveness of combining semi-supervised learning with distributed processing for large-scale log analytics.

Future Work. As future work, we plan to improve the scalability and adaptability of SparkADLS through adaptive thresholding, dynamic pseudo-label weighting, and richer temporal, semantic, and sequence-aware features. We also aim to extend SparkADLS to streaming and online log analysis in real-world distributed environments.

Disclosure of Interests. The authors have no competing interests to declare.

References

1. Zong, B., et al.: Deep autoencoding Gaussian mixture model for unsupervised anomaly detection. In: International Conference on Learning Representations (2018)
2. He, H., Garcia, E.A.: Learning from imbalanced data. IEEE Trans. Knowl. Data Eng. **21**(9), 1263–1284 (2009). https://doi.org/10.1109/TKDE.2008.239
3. Roqaya, N., Papenbrock, T., Jabeen, H.: NovaADLS: semi-supervised anomaly detection in log series. In: Proceedings of Intelligent Systems Conference (IntelliSys) (2026)
4. Zaharia, M., Chowdhury, M., Franklin, M.J., Shenker, S., Stoica, I.: Spark: cluster computing with working sets. In: Proceedings of HotCloud, p. 10 (2010)
5. Reimers, N., Gurevych, I.: Sentence-BERT: sentence embeddings using siamese BERT-networks. In: Proceedings of EMNLP-IJCNLP, pp. 3982–3992 (2019)
6. Powers, D.M.W.: Evaluation: from precision, recall and F-Measure to ROC, informedness, markedness and correlation. J. Mach. Learn. Technol. **2**(1), 37–63 (2011)

7. Blei, D.M., Ng, A.Y., Jordan, M.I.: Latent dirichlet allocation. J. Mach. Learn. Res. **3**, 993–1022 (2003)
8. Meng, W., et al.: LogAnomaly: unsupervised detection of sequential and quantitative anomalies in unstructured logs. In: Proceedings of IJCAI, pp. 4739–4745 (2019). https://api.semanticscholar.org/CorpusID:199466044
9. Parekh, M., Shukla, M.: TEDA-powered anomaly detection on USPS images using PySpark streaming and MLAutoCloud framework: a comparative study. In: Rajagopal, S., Sajja, P., Thanki, R., Kumar, A. (eds.) Artificial Intelligence Based Smart and Secured Applications, pp. 311–338. Springer, Cham (2026)
10. He, S., Zhu, J., He, P., Lyu, M.R.: LogHub: a large collection of system log datasets towards automated log analytics. In: *Proceedings of ICSE Companion*, pp. 1–4 (2020). https://doi.org/10.1145/3377812.3381366
11. Zhang, X., et al.: Robust log-based anomaly detection on unstable log data. In: Proceedings of ESEC/FSE, pp. 807–817 (2019)
12. Lighari, S.N., Hussain, D.M.A.: Testing of algorithms for anomaly detection in big data using apache spark. In: Proceedings of CICN, pp. 97–100 (2017)
13. Garcia-Gil, D., et al.: Developing big data anomaly dynamic and static detection algorithms: AnomalyDSD spark package. Inf. Sci. **690**, 121587 (2025). https://doi.org/10.1016/j.ins.2024.121587
14. Lu, S., Wei, X., Li, Y., Wang, L.: Detecting anomaly in big data system logs using convolutional neural network. In: Proceedings of DASC/PiCom/DataCom/CyberSciTech, pp. 151–158 (2018)
15. Ali, S., Boufaied, C., Bianculli, D., Branco, P., Briand, L.: A comprehensive study of machine learning techniques for log-based anomaly detection. Empirical Softw. Eng., **30**(5) (2025). https://doi.org/10.1007/s10664-025-10669-3
16. Yang, L., et al.: PLELog: semi-supervised log-based anomaly detection via probabilistic label estimation. In: Proceedings of ICSE Companion, pp. 230–231 (2021)
17. He, S., Zhu, J., He, P., Lyu, M.R.: Experience report: system log analysis for anomaly detection. In: Proceedings of ISSRE, pp. 207–218 (2016). https://doi.org/10.1109/ISSRE.2016.21
18. He, P., Zhu, J., Zheng, Z., Lyu, M.R.: Drain: an online log parsing approach with fixed depth tree. In: Proceedings of ICWS, pp. 33–40 (2017)
19. Hartmann, J., Heitmann, M., Siebert, C., Schamp, C.: More than a Feeling: accuracy and application of sentiment analysis. Int. J. Res. Mark. **40**(1), 75–87 (2023)
20. Zhu, J., et al.: Tools and benchmarks for automated log parsing. In: Proceedings of ICSE-SEIP, pp. 121–130 (2019)
21. He, P., Zhu, J., He, S., Li, J., Lyu, M.R.: An evaluation study on log parsing and its use in log mining. In: Proceedings of DSN, pp. 654–661 (2016)
22. Reynolds, D.: Gaussian mixture models. In: Li, S.Z., Jain, A. (eds.) Encyclopedia of Biometrics, pp. 659–663. Springer, Boston (2009)
23. Du, M., Li, F., Zheng, G., Srikumar, V.: DeepLog: anomaly detection and diagnosis from system logs through deep learning. In: Proceedings of CCS, pp. 1285–1298 (2017). https://doi.org/10.1145/3133956.3134015
24. Quinto, B.: Next-Generation Machine Learning with Spark: Covers XGBoost, LightGBM, Spark NLP, Distributed Deep Learning with Keras, and More. Apress, Berkeley, CA (2020). https://doi.org/10.1007/978-1-4842-5783-4
25. Neath, A.A., Cavanaugh, J.E.: The Bayesian information criterion: background, derivation, and applications. Wiley Interdisc. Rev. Comput. Stat. **4**(2), 199–203 (2012)
26. Le, V.-H., Zhang, H.: Log-based anomaly detection with deep learning: how far are we? In: Proceedings of ICSE, pp. 1356–1367 (2022)

Description Generation of JSON Data for Fuzzy Joins Processing

Alan Petit[1], Matthew Damigos[2], Laurent d'Orazio[3](✉), and Eleftherios Kalogeros[2]

[1] Polytech Nantes, Nantes Université, Nantes, France
[2] Laboratory on Digital Libraries and Electronic Publishing, Department of Archives, Library Science and Museology, Ionian University, Corfu, Greece
{mgdamigos,kalogero}@ionio.gr
[3] Univ Rennes, CNRS, IRISA, Lannion, France
laurent.dorazio@univ-rennes.fr

Abstract. Fuzzy joins are important for integrating, cleaning, and matching heterogeneous data, but they remain difficult to apply to JSON collections. These methods often fail when JSON documents describe the same real-world entities using different keys, nesting schemes, or value organizations. This paper investigates a framework for semantic fuzzy joins over JSON collections. The proposed approach transforms each JSON document into a textual description that preserves both content and structural context, encodes this description as an embedding, and evaluates joins using vector similarity. In this context, we study deterministic rule-based textualization strategies, including an anchor-aware path method, as well as LLM-based prompt-driven descriptions. An experimental analysis compares rule-based and LLM-based transformations, showing their impact on join quality and accuracy.

Keywords: Fuzzy join · JSON similarity · semantic similarity · embeddings · structural comparison

1 Introduction

The rising volume and diverse formats of semi-structured data, notably JSON documents, pose major difficulties for data integration and analysis. Organizations increasingly need to integrate, deduplicate, and correlate JSON documents that describe the same real-world entities or events but originate from different sources and production pipelines. Such documents are rarely uniform: they may use different key names, value conventions, and nesting schemes. As a result, conventional equality joins fail to identify many relevant correspondences.

Fuzzy joins address this limitation by replacing strict equality with a similarity measure; i.e., returning pairs of documents whose similarity exceeds a predefined threshold [13]. While fuzzy-join techniques have been extensively studied for relational data and for text-centric matching (e.g., edit distance, Jaccard,

© The Author(s), under exclusive license to Springer Nature Switzerland AG 2027
G. Vargas Solar et al. (Eds.): ADBIS 2026, CCIS 3175, pp. 189–198, 2027.
https://doi.org/10.1007/978-3-032-39823-9_17

cosine over token sets) [1,13], to evaluate fuzzy joins over collections of semi-structured data is not straightforward since not only the text-values but also the hierarchical structure need to be taken into account. Since JSON data is self-descriptive, multiple structures of the same information might be found. To overcome this issue, computing structural similarity has been extensively investigated in the past for tree structures (e.g., [17,29,31]), XML documents (e.g., [7,24]), and graphs (e.g., [9,14]). In the last decade, structural similarity over JSON document has also attracted attention [2,5,11,19], where the main challenge is to support both ordered (i.e., arrays) and unordered (i.e., objects) set of values. These approaches [2,5,11,19] focus on variations of tree edit distance to measure structural similarity, and focus on single-machine computation. Taking into account both structure and content of JSON documents, however, is still an open problem.

In this work, we present a semantic fuzzy-join approach for JSON collections. The proposed framework converts JSON documents first into textual descriptions and then into document embeddings, aiming to preserve both content and structural context through natural-language representations. The main contributions are: (1) we formalize our preliminary work on semantic fuzzy joins over heterogeneous JSON collections, called FLESHJ-Join, a framework presented at DOLAP'26 [18]. (2) We study JSON-to-text transformations for preserving semantic content and structural context, including deterministic rule-based descriptions, anchor-aware path textualization, and LLM-based prompt-driven descriptions. (3) We provide an experimental analysis, comparing these strategies in terms of accuracy, precision, recall, and F1-score.

The remaining part of this paper is organized as follows. Section 2 analyzes the related work, and Sect. 3 presents the preliminary definitions and concepts used throughout this paper. Section 4 provides an overview of the proposed approach, while Sect. 5 presents the JSON-to-text transformation. Section 6 presents a preliminary experimental analysis. Finally, Sect. 7 concludes and discusses future work.

2 Related Work

Existing work on fuzzy joins has largely focused on structural or token-based similarity measures [12,16,23,26,32]. These approaches often combine similarity functions with filtering, indexing, or partition-based pruning in order to reduce the number of candidate comparisons. While effective for structure-oriented matching, they remain limited when documents are structurally different but semantically equivalent. In the specific context of semi-structured data, JSON-Vec [30] and ORIGAMI [21] are relevant because they encode JSON structure into vector representations. In contrast, our approach transforms JSON documents into semantic descriptions before embedding generation, thereby aiming to capture both content and structural context in a unified representation.

Recent work on semantic similarity, sentence embeddings, and LLM-based representations has shown that vector models can capture meaning beyond surface lexical overlap [20]. Related studies have also used semantic similarity for clustering files or JSON-like data [6,8,22,27]. Our work differs by focusing specifically on fuzzy joins between JSON collections and by comparing deterministic and LLM-based textualization strategies as alternative ways to construct embeddings for join evaluation.

3 Preliminary Definitions

A JSON document is either an object, i.e., an unordered set of key–value pairs enclosed in curly brackets, or an array, i.e., an ordered list of values enclosed in square brackets [4]. Values may be objects, arrays, or primitive values such as strings, numbers, booleans, or nulls. A JSON collection is a multiset of JSON documents, which do not necessarily share the same schema or structure.

Large Language Models (LLMs) [33], such as GPT and LLaMA-based models, are transformer-based neural architectures trained on large text corpora [25,28] to generate coherent natural language. Their use requires prompt engineering, namely the design of inputs that guide the model toward a desired output [15]. In this paper, LLMs are used only for JSON-to-text generation. The generated descriptions are then encoded into dense vector representations, or embeddings, so that semantic similarity can be estimated geometrically, for example through cosine similarity [3,20].

4 Fuzzy Join Based on Semantic Similarity

Unlike conventional equality joins, a fuzzy join matches records from two collections according to a similarity function rather than exact equality. Given a threshold $\tau \in [0,1]$, the fuzzy join between two collections C_1 and C_2 is defined as $C_1 \bowtie_{sim \geq \tau} C_2 = \{(J_1, J_2) \mid J_1 \in C_1, J_2 \in C_2, sim(J_1, J_2) \geq \tau\}$, where $sim(J_1, J_2)$ is a similarity measure applied to the compared elements.

For JSON collections, similarity cannot be reduced only to lexical overlap or structural distance. The documents in each collection may differ in nesting, key naming, field ordering, and value organization. Figure 1 illustrates this problem: J_1 and J_2 describe the same real-world entities using different structures and vocabularies, while J_3 has a similar structure to J_1 but different semantic content. Our approach, named **FLESHJ-Join** evaluates similarity through representations that combine content and structural context. FLESHJ-Join transforms each JSON document into a dense embedding that encodes its semantic content and structure. The embeddings are compared through cosine similarity[1], $sim_{cos}(\boldsymbol{V_1}, \boldsymbol{V_2}) = \frac{\boldsymbol{V_1} \cdot \boldsymbol{V_2}}{\|\boldsymbol{V_1}\| \cdot \|\boldsymbol{V_2}\|}$, where $\boldsymbol{V_1}$ and $\boldsymbol{V_2}$ are the vector representations of two JSON documents. Figure 2 summarizes the proposed pipeline.

The framework separates an offline phase from an online phase. In the offline phase, each document in the source collections $\mathcal{C}_1$ and $\mathcal{C}_2$ is transformed into a natural-language description, producing $\mathcal{T}_1$ and $\mathcal{T}_2$. These descriptions are

[1] Other vector-space similarity measures [10] could be used as alternatives to cosine similarity.

Fig. 1. Example - Semantically similar and dissimilar JSON documents

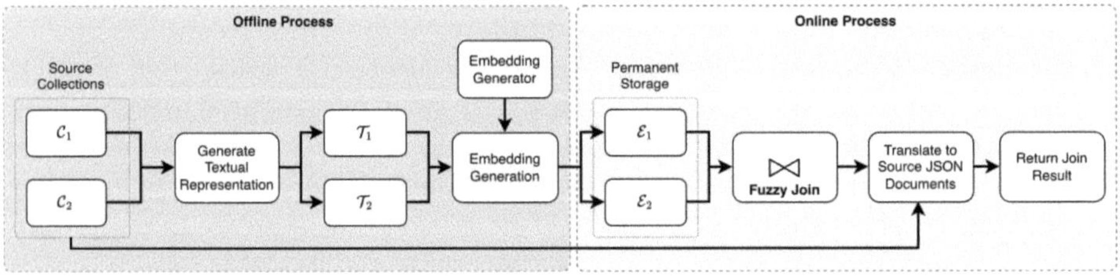

Fig. 2. Overall processing pipeline of FLESHJ-Join

then encoded by a sentence/document embedding model, producing embedding collections $\mathcal{E}_1$ and $\mathcal{E}_2$. The original documents, descriptions, and embeddings are stored together so that the embeddings can be reused during join execution. In the online phase, the precomputed embeddings are compared, pairs above the threshold are selected, and the corresponding source JSON documents are returned as the final join result.

Formally, let t_1 be the transformation from a JSON document to a textual description and t_2 the transformation from a description to an embedding. FLESHJ-Join is defined as $C_1 \bowtie_{\geq \tau} C_2 = \{(J_1, J_2) \mid J_1 \in C_1, J_2 \in C_2, sim_{cos}(t_2(t_1(J_1)), t_2(t_1(J_2))) \geq \tau\}$. Its quality is assessed through standard information-retrieval metrics, namely accuracy, precision, recall, and F1-score, computed against a gold-standard set of matching and non-matching pairs.

5 Transforming JSON Documents Into Text Representations and Embeddings

The primary challenge is to design effective methods for representing JSON documents through natural language. Each document $J \in C_1 \cup C_2$ is transformed into a text representation $t_1(J)$ that should preserve: (i) the semantic content of the document, namely what real-world entity, event, or concept it describes; and (ii) enough structural context to indicate how values are related. The descriptions must also remain compact and homogeneous, so that the embedding model captures semantic differences rather than arbitrary variation in style or length. To generate the representative descriptions, we consider two main families of transformations. The first follows deterministic text-generation rules over a tree representation of the JSON document. The second uses LLM prompts to generate concise descriptions. In both cases, the generated text is encoded by the same sentence/document embedding model, ensuring that all documents are compared in a common vector space.

Using Text-Generation Rules: To define rule-based descriptions, each JSON document J is first modeled as a labeled tree $T(J) = (V, E, r)$ rooted at a special *document* node. Keys and primitive values are represented as nodes, while object elements in arrays are represented as item nodes (e.g., "Item i", for an element in a JSON array at position i). Edges encode parent-child relations from objects or arrays to their components. Primitive values are leaves. To construct $T(J)$, we follow a top-down approach, starting from the document node. Note here that we encode the nested arrays of primitive values using their flattened form since we do not want to have an impact of the nested arrays on the similarity.; e.g., the array [["*a*", "*b*"],"*c*"] is similarly treated as the array ["*a*", "*b*", "*c*"]. For example, in Fig. 1, the tree representation of document J_1 is the tree $T(J_1)$.

The basic textualization strategy traverses $T(J)$ from the root and converts internal nodes and their children into declarative sentences. For each internal node n we generate *"[n] has fields* $k_1, \ldots, k_r$*"*, where $k_1, \ldots, k_r$ are the children of $n \in T(J)$; especially for the root, the sentence is *"document is described by* $k_1, \ldots, k_r$*"*. For each node $n \in T(J)$ having at least one leaf value, we generate a sentence of the form: *"[n] has values:* $x_1, \ldots, x_n$*"*. If n has a single leaf node "v″, then the sentence can be modified to *"The value of [n] is [v]"*. For example, we generate the following description from the $T(J_1)$ illustrated in Fig. 1: *"document is described by actors. actors has fields Item1, Item2. Item1 has fields name, role. The value of name is Matthew. The value of role is scientist. Item2 has fields name, role. The value of name is Julie. The value of role is artist"* This basic strategy is consistent with the JSON structure, but it may fail to distinguish identical local keys, such as `name` or `role`, appearing in different branches. It may also introduce an undesirable dependence on array positions through labels such as "Item 1" and "Item 2". To address this limitation, we introduce an *anchor-aware path textualization* strategy. The idea is to replace positional item labels with semantic anchors, whenever possible, using identifying keys such as `id`, `name`, `title`, `label`, or `code`. Thus, the path $\langle document, actors, Item\ 1, role\rangle$ can become $\langle document, actors, Matthew, role\rangle$.

Let n be a node of the $T(J)$ of a JSON document J, and $path(n)$ be the unique root-to-node path of n in $T(J)$, where the last node in $path(n)$ is n, and the first is *document*. For $v, m \in V$ so that v is a value and m is its parent in $T(J)$, we define the *context path* of v, denoted as $PVpath(v)$, which is given by the path $path(m)$. To reduce sensitivity to array ordering, we initially consider a list (an ordered set) of entity identifying keys K_{id} (e.g., K_{id} = [`id`, `ID`, `identifier`, `name`, `title`, `label`, `code`])) and define an anchor function $Anchor(o)$ from item nodes o (i.e., nodes of the form "Item i"). For each child node $k \in K_{id}$ of o having a leaf node v as a child (i.e., v is a value and k is a primitive field of the form $k : v$ in J), we have $Anchor(o) = x$; otherwise, $Anchor(o) = o$. If several identifying fields exist, the first according to the order in K_{id} is used; otherwise, the original item label is kept. The *anchor-enriched context path* $APath(v)$ of a value node v is obtained from $PVpath(v)$ by replacing each item node with its anchor whenever possible. For example, the path $PVpath(scientist) = \langle document, actors, Item\ 1, role \rangle$ in $T(J_1)$ illustrated in Fig. 1 becomes $APath(scientist) = \langle document, actors, Matthew, role \rangle$.

In anchor-aware path textualization strategy, we use the anchor-enriched context path to preserve the path of an item node in the description and focus on semantics rather than being dependent on arbitrary array positions. In addition, we apply further improvements to better capture the document's semantics. In particular the rules of the anchor-aware path textualization strategy are summarized as follows. **Root:** If the root *document* has a single dominant field k, we generate the sentence "*This document describes* k"; otherwise, for top-level fields $k_1, \ldots, k_m$, we generate: "*This document contains information about* $k_1, \ldots, k_m$". For example, in Fig. 1, the description of J_1 starts with the sentence "This document describes actors", while J_2 description starts with "This document contains information about scientist and artist". **Compact semantic grouping:** If an object contains primitive key-value pairs $(k_1, x_1), \ldots, (k_m, x_m)$, we generate: "*This object is characterized by* $k_1\ x_1, \ldots,\ k_m\ x_m$'. If the object o is an array item and an anchor exists, we generate: "*The entity* $Anchor(o)$ *is characterized by* $k_1\ x_1, \ldots, k_m\ x_m$". For arrays of primitive values $x_1, \ldots, x_m$, we generate: "*The field* k *has the values* $x_1, \ldots, x_m$". For example, in Fig. 1, the description of J_1 includes the sentence "The entity Matthew is characterized by role scientist" for the Item 1. **Anchor-enriched context path:** For each child $a_m \in K_{id}$ of an item node which has a leaf node v as a child, where $PVpath(v) = \langle a_0, a_1, \ldots, a_m \rangle$, we generate: "*In* $a_0\ a_1\ \ldots\ a_{m-1}$, *the value of* a_m *is* v". For example, in Fig. 1, the description of J_1 includes the sentence "In document actors Julie, the value of role is artist" for the Item 1.

Applying the anchor-aware path textualization strategy to $T(J_1)$ illustrated in Fig. 1, the following description is generated: "*This document describes actors. The field actors contains two entities. The entity Matthew is characterized by role scientist. The entity Julie is characterized by role artist. In document actors Matthew, the value of role is scientist. In document actors Julie, the value of role is artist.*". Notice that although the anchor-aware path textualization might produce duplication between grouped semantic sentences and path-aware sentences, this redundancy is intentional because it reinforces both the semantic interpretation of each value and its structural context in the original JSON document. The transformation is deterministic, faithful to the input JSON document, explicitly path-aware, and less sensitive to array ordering. Both the basic and anchor-aware strategies require a single traversal of $T(J)$, i.e., $O(|V|)$ node visits. If anchor-enriched paths are materialized, the additional cost is bounded by $O(p \cdot d)$, where p is the number of primitive values and d is the maximum depth of the tree.

Using LLMs: The second family of transformations uses LLMs. In this case, the text-generation function is defined by a prompt that instructs the model to convert a JSON document into a concise natural-language description that captures the true meaning of the document. We focus on zero-shot prompt design, using roles, constraints, and output instructions to encourage faithfulness to the input, avoid hallucinated attributes or values, and produce compact descriptions suitable for embedding generation.

The four prompts in Fig. 3 correspond to different points in the design space. Prompts 1 and 2 mainly capture hierarchical relationships and high-level semantic organization. Prompts 3 and 4 focus more explicitly on faithful, human-readable descriptions of the document's meaning. For example, Prompt 4 transforms J_1 into: *"This document describes two actors. One actor is Matthew, whose role is a scientist. The other actor is Julie, whose role is an artist. It identifies each actor by name and role."* In this case, both the content and the relevant structure of the JSON document are expressed in natural language.

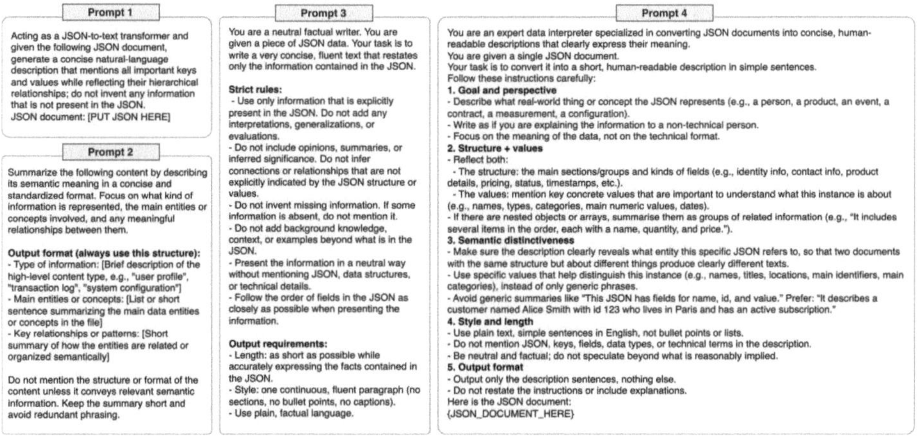

Fig. 3. Prompts transforming a JSON document to a text-representation.

6 Evaluation

This section presents a preliminary evaluation focused on the generation of text representations from JSON documents. We generated a dataset[2] of approximately 200K JSON documents using ChatGPT, with about 5% of the documents designed to be at least 80% similar in content, structure, or both. From this collection, we selected two samples: dataset A, containing 31 documents and 9 joining pairs with $sim_{cos} \geq 80\%$, and dataset B, containing 1000 documents, corresponding to approximately 1M candidate pairs, with 500 joining pairs having $sim_{cos} \geq 90\%$ and the remaining pairs having $sim_{cos} < 70\%$.

[2] The dataset is available at: https://github.com/DLIB-Ionian-University/fuzzyjoin-json-dataset.

To generate the descriptions of the documents, we applied the four LLM prompts (presented in Sect. 5) and the two rule-based approaches to both datasets. Dataset A was evaluated using Meta Llama 3.3–70b-instruct through the OpenRouter API, while dataset B was evaluated using GPT-OSS-20b with a 4-bit K-quants implementation through llama.cpp. The generated descriptions were encoded with the all-MiniLM-L6-v2 model, and embeddings were compared using cosine similarity. Join quality was evaluated against the gold-standard pairs using accuracy, precision, recall, and F1-score; precision, recall, and accuracy respectively quantify correct predicted matches, retrieved gold-standard matches, and correct match/non-match classifications over all candidate pairs.

The results in Fig. 4 show that Prompt 3 and the anchor-aware path textualization strategy, reported as "Improved", achieve the strongest overall performance. At the 80% threshold, Prompt 3 reaches high accuracy and F1-score in both datasets, while the improved rule-based strategy performs particularly well at stricter thresholds. Prompt 4 also remains competitive, especially because it combines semantic distinctiveness with controlled output style. Prompt 2 obtains high recall but low precision, suggesting that overly broad summaries may over-match semantically different documents. Overall, the evaluation indicates that faithful semantic descriptions are more effective than generic summaries for embedding-based fuzzy joins. Moreover, focusing on high-similarity document pairs, the analysis distinguishes the effectiveness of specific prompting and rule-based strategies in accurately capturing semantic and structural relationships for fuzzy joins.

Dataset/Model:	Dataset B / gpt-oss-20b-Q4_K_M												Dataset A / llama-3.3-70b-instruct			
Similarity Threshold:	70%				80%				90%				80%			
Textualization	Accuracy	Precision	Recall	F1	Accuracy	Precision	Recall	F1	Accuracy	Precision	Recall	F1	Accuracy	Precision	Recall	F1
Prompt 1	85.4%	1.3%	97.5%	2.6%	98.6%	11.2%	83.4%	19.8%	99.9%	93.8%	42.2%	58.2%	95.5%	47.1%	88.9%	61.5%
Prompt 2	40.7%	0.2%	70.6%	0.5%	66.4%	0.3%	46.2%	0.5%	80.7%	0.3%	26.2%	0.5%	73.6%	13.4%	100.0%	23.7%
Prompt 3	93.6%	3.1%	100.0%	5.9%	99.0%	16.3%	100.0%	28.0%	100.0%	86.8%	91.2%	88.9%	99.1%	81.8%	100.0%	90.0%
Prompt 4	95.0%	3.8%	99.8%	7.4%	98.6%	12.3%	99.8%	21.9%	99.7%	39.9%	99.5%	57.0%	97.7%	64.3%	100.0%	78.3%
Basic	29.1%	0.3%	100.0%	0.6%	92.3%	2.5%	100.0%	5.0%	100.0%	90.4%	94.6%	92.5%	94.5%	42.9%	100.0%	60.0%
Improved	76.2%	0.8%	100.0%	1.7%	97.7%	7.9%	100.0%	14.7%	100.0%	95.6%	98.8%	97.1%	97.7%	64.3%	100.0%	78.3%

Fig. 4. Performance of the Prompts - an overview

7 Conclusion and Future Work

This paper formalizes FLESHJ-Join, a semantic fuzzy-join framework for JSON collections. The approach textualizes each JSON document to preserve content, structure, and semantics, encodes the generated text as an embedding, and compares embeddings using vector similarity. We studied two families of JSON-to-text transformations: deterministic rule-based methods, including an anchor-aware path strategy, and LLM-based prompt-driven descriptions. The preliminary evaluation shows that faithful and semantically explicit descriptions, especially Prompt 3 and the improved rule-based strategy, provide the most effective basis for embedding-based fuzzy joins.

Future work will further investigate prompt design, embedding-generation options, and larger benchmark datasets. We also plan to study update-aware indexing, batching and caching of model calls, and extensions of JSONVec and ORIGAMI for semantic join scenarios.

References

1. Afrati, F.N., Sarma, A.D., Menestrina, D., Parameswaran, A., Ullman, J.D.: Fuzzy joins using MapReduce. In: ICDE, pp. 498–509 (2012)
2. Ben Hadj Yahia, E., Falleri, J.R., Réveillère, L.: Polly: a language-based approach for custom change detection of web service data. In: ICSOC, pp. 430–444. Springer (2017)
3. Bengio, Y., Ducharme, R., Vincent, P., Jauvin, C.: A neural probabilistic language model. J. Mach. Learn. Res. **3**, 1137–1155 (2003)
4. Bray, T.: The JavaScript object notation (JSON) data interchange format. RFC **7158**, 1–16 (2014)
5. Cao, H., Falleri, J.R., Blanc, X., Zhang, L.: JSON patch for turning a pull REST API into a push. In: ICSOC, pp. 435–449. Springer (2016)
6. Chandrasekaran, D., Mago, V.: Evolution of semantic similarity - a survey. ACM Comput. Surv. **54**(2), 1–37 (2022)
7. Cobena, G., Abiteboul, S., Marian, A.: Detecting changes in XML documents. In: ICDE, pp. 41–52. IEEE (2002)
8. Dharmaraj, U.P., Thilagam, P.S.: JSON document clustering based on schema embeddings. J. Inf. Sci. (2022)
9. Donnat, C., Holmes, S.: Tracking network dynamics: a survey of distances and similarity metrics. arXiv preprint: arXiv:1801.07351 (2018)
10. Gomaa, W.H., Fahmy, A.A., et al.: A survey of text similarity approaches. Int. J. Comput. Appl. **68**(13), 13–18 (2013)
11. Hütter, T., Augsten, N., Kirsch, C.M., Carey, M.J., Li, C.: JEDI: these aren't the JSON documents you're looking for? In: SIGMOD, pp, pp. 1584–1597 (2022)
12. Hütter, T., Augsten, N., Kirsch, C.M., Carey, M.J., Li, C.: JEDI: these aren't the JSON documents you're looking for... SIGMOD '22 (2022)
13. Jiang, Y., Li, G., Feng, J., Li, W.S.: String similarity joins: an experimental evaluation. Proc. VLDB Endow. **7**, 625–636 (2014)
14. Koutra, D., Parikh, A., Ramdas, A., Xiang, J.: Algorithms for graph similarity and subgraph matching. In: Proceedings of the Ecological Inference Conference, vol. 17. Citeseer (2011)
15. Liu, P., Yuan, W., Fu, J., Jiang, Z., Hayashi, H., Neubig, G.: Pre-train, prompt, and predict: a systematic survey of prompting methods in natural language processing. ACM Comput. Surv. **55**(9), 1–35 (2023)
16. Mizokami, T., Bou, S., Amagasa, T.: Subtree similarity search based on structure and text. In: Big Data Analytics and Knowledge Discovery (2024)
17. Pawlik, M., Augsten, N.: Tree edit distance: robust and memory-efficient. Inf. Syst. **56**, 157–173 (2016)
18. Petit, A., Damigos, M., d'Orazio, L., Kalogeros, E.: Computation of fuzzy joins over large collections of JSON data using semantic similarity. In: Proceedings of the 28th International Workshop on Design, Optimization, Languages and Analytical Processing of Big Data (DOLAP 2026) Co-located with the EDBT/ICDT 2026, pp. 107–115 (2026)

19. Priya, D.U., Thilagam, P.S.: JSON document clustering based on schema embeddings. J. Inf. Sci. **50**(5), 1112–1130 (2024)
20. Reimers, N., Gurevych, I.: Sentence-BERT: sentence embeddings using Siamese BERT-networks. arXiv preprint: arXiv:1908.10084 (2019)
21. Rückstieß, T., Huang, A., Vujanic, R.: ORIGAMI: a generative transformer architecture for predictions from semi-structured data. arXiv preprint: arXiv:2412.17348 (2024)
22. Santana, D.R., Lima, P.H.S., Ribeiro, L.A.: EM-Join: efficient entity matching using embedding-based similarity join. In: Proceedings of the International Conference on Enterprise Information Systems (2025)
23. Sevim, A., Eldawy, A., Carman, E.P., Carey, M.J., Tsotras, V.J.: FUDJ: flexible user-defined distributed joins. In: IEEE International Conference on Fuzzy Systems (2024)
24. Tekli, J., Chbeir, R., Yetongnon, K.: An overview on XML similarity: background, current trends and future directions. Comput. Sci. Rev. **3**(3), 151–173 (2009)
25. Touvron, H., et al.: LLaMA: open and efficient foundation language models. arXiv preprint: arXiv:2302.13971 (2023)
26. Uhartegaray, R., D'Orazio, L., Damigos, M., Kalogeros, E.: Scalable computation of fuzzy joins over large collections of JSON data. In: IEEE International Conference on Fuzzy Systems (FUZZ-IEEE) (2023)
27. Uma Priya, D., Santhi Thilagam, P.: JSON document clustering based on structural similarity and semantic fusion. In: International Conference on Computational Intelligence and Data Engineering, pp. 51–62. Springer (2022)
28. Vaswani, A., et al.: Attention is all you need. In: Advances in Neural Information Processing Systems, vol. 30 (2017)
29. Wang, L., Zhang, K.: Space efficient algorithms for ordered tree comparison. Algorithmica **51**, 283–297 (2008)
30. Woof, W., Chen, K.: A framework for end-to-end learning on semantic tree-structured data. arXiv preprint: arXiv:2002.05707 (2020)
31. Yang, R., Kalnis, P., Tung, A.K.: Similarity evaluation on tree-structured data. In: SIGMOD, pp. 754–765 (2005)
32. Yu, M., Li, G., Deng, D., Feng, J.: String similarity search and join: a survey. Front. Comput. Sci. (2015)
33. Zhao, W.X., et al.: A survey of large language models **1**(2). arXiv preprint: arXiv:2303.18223 (2023)

Towards Semantics-Aware Resilience in Composable Data Systems

Frédéric Loulergue(✉) and Jolan Philippe

Université d'Orléans, INSA Centre Val de Loire, LIFO UR 4022, Orléans, France
{frederic.loulergue,jolan.philippe1}@univ-orleans.fr
{frederic.loulergue,jolan.philippe1}@univ-orleans.fr

Abstract. Modern data management systems are increasingly assembled from specialized software components such as query optimizers, execution engines, and storage backends. They must also adapt to variations in available hardware resources, including accelerators, and to the availability of external analytical services. This composability is usually exploited for extensibility and performance. We argue that it should also be exploited for resilience. When resources become scarce, services disappear, or hardware capabilities change, a data system should be able to reconfigure itself and continue to deliver useful answers rather than fail abruptly. The difficulty is that reconfiguring a software component, changing an execution plan, or switching an execution backend may silently change the meaning of the computation. This paper presents a vision of semantics-aware resilience in composable data systems, in which a contract-guided resilience layer couples dynamic reconfiguration with semantic contracts. These contracts classify substitutions as exact, conditionally equivalent, or approximate with explicit bounds, and thereby turn resilience into controlled degradation rather than best-effort fallback. We discuss the main research challenges in contract design, multi-objective decision-making, benchmarking, and mechanically checkable substitution conditions.

Keywords: Composable data systems · dynamic reconfiguration · resilience · controlled degradation · formal semantics

1 Introduction

Digital infrastructures are increasingly exposed to disruptions that are not exceptional corner cases but recurring operational conditions: energy pressure, cooling limitations, partial hardware failures, network degradation, and service withdrawal. They must also cope with heterogeneous and sometimes ageing equipment. Resilience, understood as the ability to preserve useful service under adverse conditions, is therefore becoming a primary system's requirement rather than a secondary operational concern [25].

At the same time, the architecture of data management systems is changing. Instead of relying on monolithic database engines, modern platforms are

© The Author(s), under exclusive license to Springer Nature Switzerland AG 2027
G. Vargas Solar et al. (Eds.): ADBIS 2026, CCIS 3175, pp. 199–208, 2027.
https://doi.org/10.1007/978-3-032-39823-9_18

increasingly composed of specialized software components for storage management, query planning, and query execution [1,18]. They are also increasingly deployed on heterogeneous hardware, including accelerators. Systems and frameworks such as Apache Calcite [6], Velox [23], Apache Arrow DataFusion [19], BOSS [22], and CompoDB [14] show that composability has become a practical design principle in data management. This shift creates an opportunity: if multiple components or plans can realize the same analytical intent, then a system may reconfigure itself when its operating context changes [4,11].

However, resilience by reconfiguration is not just switching to a cheaper component. Replacing a GPU-accelerated operator with a CPU one, moving from full-data processing to sampling, or orchestrating several tools may affect semantics, precision, completeness, diversity, coverage, or cross-checking, not only latency and energy. Across several tools, orchestration choices may further affect the diversity and coverage of exploratory outputs, as well as the possibility of cross-checking them. In short, composability enables reconfiguration, but it also makes semantic drift easier. While prior work on component reconfiguration highlights the need for correctness arguments [10], and adaptive or robust query processing shows the value of runtime adaptation while preserving query semantics by construction [4,5,11,21], our concern is with explicit guarantees for degraded execution and cross-configuration substitution.

This paper presents a vision of *semantics-aware resilience* in composable data systems, where dynamic reconfiguration is guided by semantic contracts. These contracts allow a system to distinguish exact substitutions, substitutions valid only under explicit assumptions, and bounded quality degradation. Resilience then becomes controlled degradation rather than best-effort fallback. The novelty is not exact, conditional, and approximate substitutions taken separately, but their unification into a resilience-oriented contract layer for composable data systems.

The contributions of this vision paper are threefold. First, it frames resilience in composable data systems as a problem of semantic substitutability under changing resource and infrastructure constraints. Second, it proposes a contract-guided resilience layer for vertical reconfiguration in composable analytics stacks, discusses horizontal orchestration for exploratory analytics, and treats hybrid reconfiguration as the combination of these two dimensions. Third, it identifies the main research challenges raised by semantics-aware resilience, namely the design of semantic contracts, the design of resilient controllers, the construction of suitable benchmarks, and the mechanization of substitution reasoning.

The rest of the paper is organized as follows. Section 2 discusses the background and missing semantic layer. Section 3 introduces semantics-aware resilience and its reconfiguration scopes. Section 4 discusses the research agenda and a corresponding research path. We conclude in Sect. 5.

2 Background and Motivation

Composable Data Systems Change the Design Space. Composable data systems let engineers assemble platforms from reusable components rather than rebuild monolithic engines for each workload. Query planning can be delegated to Calcite [6], execution kernels can be reused through Velox [23], and modular analytics engines such as DataFusion [19] and BOSS [22] show that open, embeddable architectures can remain performant. The Cambridge Report on Database Research emphasizes research trends around modern hardware, sustainability, and heterogeneous application demands [1].

Yet the main benefits usually associated with composability remain performance, extensibility, and engineering reuse. The ability to *survive* degraded conditions is rarely treated as a first-class objective. When a service loses a GPU, exceeds an energy budget, experiences a cloud connector outage, or must run on older hardware, the common outcomes are performance collapse, emergency manual intervention, or outright service interruption. This is a poor match for many analytical settings where a slower, partial, or approximate answer may be far better than no answer at all.

From Failure Avoidance to Controlled Degradation. In constrained situations, continuity of service may matter as much as peak quality. For data analytics, this means preserving a useful service while adapting properties such as latency, update frequency, precision, or completeness. It may also require a temporary reduction in the set of available features. Such situations may be caused by climate-related events, supply-chain disruptions, geopolitical instability, or more routine operational incidents. Whatever the original cause, the data system eventually observes technical perturbations such as fewer nodes, a lower energy budget, missing accelerator resources, network instability, or the unavailability of an external software service.

This suggests a shift of perspective. We should not ask only whether the original configuration can still be executed. We should ask which alternative configuration can still satisfy the analytical intent under the new constraints, with the strongest guarantee that remains available. In this sense, resilience means controlled degradation rather than abrupt interruption. The system may have to move from exact processing to approximate processing, or from a full pipeline to a partial one. Such choices should be explicit, justified, and auditable.

The Missing Semantic Layer. Existing cost models, adaptive query processing [4, 11], robust query processing [5, 21], and resource schedulers can determine that one execution plan is cheaper than another, but they do not explain whether the substitute remains semantically valid. This limitation is particularly important in composable systems, where one may replace an operator implementation, change the data-consumption strategy, switch execution backends, or orchestrate several tools for the same analytical task. Such changes require more than performance comparisons:

- Some substitutions are *exact*: they preserve the intended result.
- Some are *conditionally equivalent*: they are correct only under explicit assumptions about the data, the workload, or the absence of nondeterminism.
- Some are *approximate*: they deliberately relax exactness but should provide explicit bounds or contracts on the deviation introduced.

What is missing, therefore, is a unified semantic layer to express and reason about these distinctions, which remain fragmented across the data stack. As a consequence, resilience choices remain ad hoc, hard to trust, and hard to compare.

3 A Vision of Semantics-Aware Resilience

3.1 A Contract-Guided Resilience Layer

Our vision is a data-system architecture in which runtime reconfiguration is governed not only by resource observations but also by semantic knowledge about candidate configurations. The starting point is an *analytical intent*: for example, compute an aggregate, execute a join-heavy pipeline, estimate a correlation, or carry out an interactive exploratory task. A configuration realizes this intent through a particular assembly of software components and a particular set of execution choices. These choices include parameter settings, data-access strategies, and hardware assignments.

We propose a *contract-guided resilience layer* between analytical intent and physical execution. It associates substitutable components, plans, and parameterization with semantic contracts. It observes perturbations such as memory pressure, missing accelerator resources, network instability, service unavailability, or explicit energy caps. It then selects and applies a substitute according to both resource constraints and semantic guarantees, and records the guarantee that is preserved. Under this view, adaptation is not merely a fallback mechanism. It is an explicit and traceable semantic choice. The proposed resilience layer could be realized within an autonomic management loop such as MAPE-K [17,26].

The primary target of this layer is *vertical reconfiguration*: changing components or parameters within one analytical stack while preserving the strongest guarantee available. A second dimension is *horizontal orchestration* across several tools or services for the same analytical task, especially in exploratory analytics. *Hybrid reconfiguration* combines these two dimensions. It covers cases where a system both reconfigures one analytical stack and orchestrates several tools or services within the same adaptive scenario.

3.2 Three Classes of Semantic Guarantees

The proposed contracts distinguish three classes of substitution. These classes describe the semantic relation between the original intent and the replacement configuration. A substitution may therefore replace one component by another component, one component by a composition of components, or one configuration by another configuration.

1. *Exact Substitutions.* These substitutions preserve the intended output. Typical examples include switching between two execution backends that implement the same operator semantics, or replacing one join algorithm with another under the same data model and query semantics. Exact substitutions support resilience without modifying user-visible meaning.

2. *Conditional Substitutions.* These substitutions preserve behaviour only under stated assumptions. For instance, two configurations may be equivalent only if the input satisfies a schema property, if duplicates are absent, or if ordering is irrelevant. Such substitutions are still valuable, but the assumptions must be represented rather than left implicit.
3. *Approximate Substitutions.* These substitutions intentionally trade quality for frugality or continuity. Examples include sampling, sketch-based aggregation, or reduced update frequency. Here the contract should provide a bounded notion of acceptable deviation: error on a numerical result, loss on a ranking metric, coverage reduction, or a more domain-specific measure of quality [15, 16].

A simple vertical case illustrates the idea. Consider a service that computes `SUM(sales)` by region every five minutes for operational monitoring. Following a climate-related infrastructure incident, the service is moved from a primary site to a secondary site with fewer machines and no GPU accelerators. The resilience layer may then consider an exact CPU-based configuration that preserves the intended result but no longer meets the original refresh objective, or an approximate configuration based on sampling or sketches that preserves the refresh frequency with a declared error bound. A semantic contract makes this choice explicit: it records whether the substitute is exact or approximate, under which assumptions it is valid, and what degradation is introduced when the service continues under tighter resource constraints.

This example illustrates how the classification supports controlled degradation. The resilience layer can record whether the chosen substitute is exact, equivalent only under explicit assumptions, or approximate with a declared bound while respecting the new resource constraints. More generally, the classification provides a language for explaining and comparing resilience decisions.

3.3 Primary and Secondary Reconfiguration Scopes

Vertical Reconfiguration. In vertical reconfiguration, the system changes the internal composition of one analytical stack. This may involve replacing an operator implementation, changing a parameter, reassigning a computation between CPU and GPU, or activating or deactivating a module within the same pipeline. The analytical task remains the same, but the way it is carried out changes. This is the simplest setting in which to study semantics-aware resilience, because it allows one to compare several configurations for the same task within one stack.

Horizontal Orchestration. Polystore systems such as BigDAWG [12] show the practical interest of orchestrating heterogeneous engines. Different engines may support different data models, execution strategies, or cost and quality trade-offs. Orchestration then makes it possible either to distribute parts of one analytical task across several engines or to compare several candidate results for the same task. In a resilience setting, the issue is then no longer only exact equivalence or bounded numerical error. It also concerns the diversity of the answers, the coverage of the explored search space, and the possibility of cross-checking one tool by another. If one service becomes unavailable, or if resource constraints force the system to reduce the number of active tools, the analytical service may continue with a reduced orchestration, but with reduced diversity, reduced coverage, or weaker cross-checking. In exploratory settings, one may also consider interestingness criteria such as novelty, relevance, surprise, or peculiarity [9]. This calls for contract notions different from those of vertical reconfiguration. Vertical contracts concern semantic preservation or bounded degradation of a task result, whereas horizontal contracts may concern evidence diversity, or source coverage.

Hybrid Reconfiguration. Hybrid reconfiguration combines vertical reconfiguration within one stack and horizontal orchestration across several tools or services. For example, an exploratory task may use multiple tools while one pipeline relies on sampling or approximate operators for a rapid first result. If confidence is too low or resources recover, selected parts of the analysis may then be refined through a more expensive configuration or through another tool. Hybrid reconfiguration is therefore relevant when resilience depends both on internal adaptation and on cross-tool coordination

4 Research Agenda

This vision raises four main research challenges.

4.1 Contracts for Analytical Intent and Substitutability

A first challenge is representational. What is the object that a contract talks about? One promising approach is to make the contract attach not merely to components in isolation but to well-defined parts of an analytical task: relational operators, distributed collection transformations, and pipeline fragments, with exploratory primitives treated as a later extension. The contract should state (i) the interface expected from the component or configuration; (ii) the assumptions under which the guarantee holds; (iii) the semantic guarantee provided; (iv) the resource envelope and observability requirements.

This raises a granularity trade-off. Contracts that are too coarse are easy to write but too weak for safe substitution. Contracts that are too fine become difficult to maintain and difficult for automated tooling to exploit. A central research question is therefore how rich a contract language must be to support useful resilience decisions without becoming unusable. In practice, such contracts may be introduced by different actors (e.g., system developers, library maintainers), with different versions. The resilience layer should treat these contracts as versioned artifacts, to avoid invalid substitution by introducing new semantics.

4.2 Decision-Making Under Multiple Objectives

A second challenge concerns decision-making under multiple objectives and semantic guarantees. Once several candidate substitutions are available, the controller must choose among them. The objective is not a single latency minimum but a compromise between resource consumption, analytical quality, and semantic status. Existing optimization techniques can help explore trade-offs between latency, energy, and quality. The difficulty here is that the controller must also account for whether a substitution is exact, valid only under explicit assumptions, or approximate with a declared bound. The precise optimization criteria may vary across scenarios: maintain exactness at all costs, preserve refresh frequency, or minimize energy under an acceptable error bound. In some settings, it may also be necessary to retain only a critical subset of analytical features.

This calls for a richer decision layer than a classical cost model. A resilient controller must reason over resource metrics, semantic guarantees, user-facing service policies, and the cost of reconfiguration itself. In other words, the decision problem is not *which plan is fastest?* but *which plan preserves the most valuable semantics under the current constraints?*

4.3 Benchmarks and Crisis Scenarios

A third challenge is empirical. A semantics-aware resilience benchmark must define perturbation scenarios, degradation policies, and metrics. Such metrics should include at least the preserved guarantee class, the observed quality loss and, when relevant, the error bound declared by the substitute, a service continuity measure such as latency or refresh frequency, and the cost of reconfiguration, for example the time needed to recover a stable service. Such a benchmark would be useful beyond this specific vision because it would make resilience properties measurable and comparable.

4.4 Mechanized Reasoning for Trustworthy Adaptation

A fourth challenge is formal. A large body of work exists on verification for component-based reconfiguration [10], and formal semantics have been mechanized for realistic fragments of SQL and Datalog [7,8]. However, the space of modern data-processing stacks remains too large to expect full mechanization in one step. Property-graph and modern query-language semantics illustrate the scale of the problem [2,13].

For this reason, we propose to start with Apache Spark as a practical platform for experimentation and as an initial target for formalization. Spark is expressive enough to cover both collection-style transformations and relational operations such as filtering, joins, grouping, and aggregation. It is also rich enough to express representative analytical pipelines while remaining more tractable than a full industrial query ecosystem. Previous work has already explored verified scalable parallel computing with Coq and Spark [20], as well as a Spark implementation based on a refined specification proved equivalent to an initial formal specification [24]. Spark also remains a practical reference platform in large-scale analytics deployments [3]. A realistic first result is therefore a formalized kernel of Spark transformations together with mechanically checkable lemmas for exact vertical substitutions. Horizontal orchestration, hybrid reconfiguration, and richer forms of contract management can then be treated as later extensions.

4.5 Representative Cases

To make the vision concrete, we propose to start from a small set of representative cases. A first family of cases consists of exact vertical substitutions over representative analytical tasks such as filtering, aggregation, joins, and descriptive statistics. Examples include replacing execution backends, switching from GPU to CPU, or choosing between exact operator implementations with different cost profiles while showing that the resulting answers are unchanged.

A second family of cases consists of horizontal orchestration cases for exploratory analytics. Such cases involve several tools or services capable of addressing the same task, with attention to diversity, coverage, and cross-checking under resource constraints.

A third family covers hybrid cases that combine both dimensions. For example, several tools may be orchestrated to produce an initial result, while one pipeline already relies on sampling or approximate operators. If confidence is insufficient or resources recover, selected parts can later be refined using a more expensive configuration or another tool.

Another important object of study is the resilience layer itself. A prototype does not need to be a full new DBMS. It should demonstrate that perturbations can be mapped to contract-aware substitutions, that the preserved guarantee can be recorded, and that reconfiguration decisions can be explained in terms of both resource constraints and semantic guarantees.

Finally, some representative substitution patterns should be backed by *mechanically checkable reasoning*. A mechanized Spark core can serve as a reference semantics for selected operations, enabling proofs of equivalence for exact substitutions and proof obligations for conditional or approximate contracts.

5 Conclusion

In this paper, we presented a vision of semantics-aware resilience in composable data systems, where dynamic reconfiguration is guided by semantic contracts. These contracts classify substitutions as exact, conditional, or approximate with bounded quality loss. In this view, resilience becomes controlled degradation rather than best-effort fallback.

The contribution of this paper is to identify semantics-aware resilience as a data-management research problem in its own right. It requires work on specification, decision, benchmarking, and mechanized reasoning. It also suggests that composable architectures should be studied not only for performance and reuse, but also for their ability to preserve a useful analytical service under degraded operating conditions.

As future work, we plan to design contract languages, define resilience benchmarks, develop representative prototypes, and mechanize representative substitution results. We will also study representative vertical cases, representative horizontal cases for exploratory analytics, and hybrid cases combining both dimensions, in order to assess the practical value and the semantic guarantees of the proposed approach. A natural first step is a Rocq formalization of core Spark transformations together with mechanically checkable lemmas for exact vertical substitutions. This would provide a first concrete basis on which to build.

Acknowledgements. Research on semantics-aware resilience in composable data systems is supported by the BQR programme of Université d'Orléans through the RADyD project, entitled "Resilience through dynamic adaptation for data processing".

References

1. Ailamaki, A., et al.: The Cambridge report on database research. CoRR abs/2504.11259 (2025). https://doi.org/10.48550/ARXIV.2504.11259
2. Angles, R., et al.: PG-schema: schemas for property graphs. Proc. ACM Manag. Data **1**(2) (2023). https://doi.org/10.1145/3589778
3. Armbrust, M., et al.: Scaling spark in the real world: performance and usability. PVLDB **8**(12) (2015). http://www.vldb.org/pvldb/vol8/p1840-armbrust.pdf
4. Avnur, R., Hellerstein, J.M.: Eddies: continuously adaptive query processing. In: International Conference on Management of Data (SIGMOD). ACM (2000). https://doi.org/10.1145/342009.335420
5. Babcock, B., Chaudhuri, S.: Towards a robust query optimizer: a principled and practical approach. In: International Conference on Management of Data (SIGMOD). ACM (2005). https://doi.org/10.1145/1066157.1066172
6. Begoli, E., Camacho-Rodríguez, J., Hyde, J., Mior, M.J., Lemire, D.: Apache calcite: a foundational framework for optimized query processing over heterogeneous data sources. In: International Conference on Management of Data (SIGMOD). ACM (2018). https://doi.org/10.1145/3183713.3190662
7. Benzaken, V., Contejean, E.: A Coq mechanised formal semantics for realistic SQL queries: formally reconciling SQL and bag relational algebra. In: Certified Programs and Proofs (CPP). ACM (2019). https://doi.org/10.1145/3293880.3294107
8. Benzaken, V., Contejean, E., Dumbrava, S.: Certifying standard and stratified Datalog inference engines in SSReflect. In: Interactive Theorem Proving (ITP). LNCS, vol. 10499. Springer (2017). https://doi.org/10.1007/978-3-319-66107-0_12
9. Chanson, A., Labroche, N., Marcel, P., Peralta, V., Vassiliadis, P.: Interestingness measures for exploratory data analysis: a survey. In: ADBIS (Short Papers). Springer (2024). https://doi.org/10.1007/978-3-031-70421-5_2
10. Coullon, H., Henrio, L., Loulergue, F., Robillard, S.: Component-based distributed software reconfiguration: a verification-oriented survey. ACM Comput. Surv. **56**(1) (2024). https://doi.org/10.1145/3595376
11. Deshpande, A., Ives, Z.G., Raman, V.: Adaptive query processing. Found. Trends Databases **1**(1) (2007). https://doi.org/10.1561/1900000001
12. Duggan, J., et al.: The BigDAWG polystore system. SIGMOD Rec. **44**(2) (2015). https://doi.org/10.1145/2814710.2814713

13. Francis, N., et al.: Cypher: an evolving query language for property graphs. In: International Conference on Management of Data (SIGMOD). ACM (2018). https://doi.org/10.1145/3183713.3190657
14. Gavriilidis, H., Behme, L., Munz, C., Pandey, V., Markl, V.: CompoDB: a demonstration of modular data systems in practice. In: Simitsis, A., Kemme, B., Queralt, A., Romero, O., Jovanovic, P. (eds.) International Conference on Extending Database Technology, (EDBT). OpenProceedings.org, (2025). https://doi.org/10.48786/EDBT.2025.97
15. Haas, P.J., Hellerstein, J.M.: Ripple joins for online aggregation. In: International Conference on Management of Data (SIGMOD). ACM Press (1999). https://doi.org/10.1145/304182.304208
16. Hellerstein, J.M., Haas, P.J., Wang, H.J.: Online aggregation. In: International Conference on Management of Data (SIGMOD). ACM (1997). https://doi.org/10.1145/253260.253291
17. Kephart, J.O., Chess, D.M.: The vision of autonomic computing. Computer **36**(1) (2003). https://doi.org/10.1109/MC.2003.1160055
18. Khurana, A., Le Dem, J.: The modern data architecture: the deconstructed database. Login Usenix Mag. **43**(4) (2018). https://www.usenix.org/publications/login/winter-2018-vol-43-no-4/khurana
19. Lamb, A., et al.: Apache arrow DataFusion: a fast, embeddable, modular analytic query engine. In: International Conference on Management of Data (SIGMOD). ACM (2024). https://doi.org/10.1145/3626246.3653368
20. Loulergue, F., Philippe, J.: Towards verified scalable parallel computing with Coq and spark. In: Formal Techniques for Java-like Programs (FTfJP). ACM (2023). https://doi.org/10.1145/3605156.3606450
21. Markl, V., Raman, V., Simmen, D.E., Lohman, G.M., Pirahesh, H.: Robust query processing through progressive optimization. In: International Conference on Management of Data (SIGMOD). ACM (2004). https://doi.org/10.1145/1007568.1007642
22. Mohr-Daurat, H., Sun, X., Pirk, H.: BOSS - an architecture for database kernel composition. SIGMOD Rec. **54**(1) (2025). https://doi.org/10.1145/3733620.3733629
23. Pedreira, P., et al.: Velox: Meta's unified execution engine. Proc. VLDB Endow. **15**(12) (2022). https://doi.org/10.14778/3554821.3554829
24. Philippe, J., Tisi, M., Coullon, H., Sunyé, G.: Executing certified model transformations on Apache spark. In: Software Language Engineering (SLE). ACM (2021). https://doi.org/10.1145/3486608.3486901
25. Welsh, T., Benkhelifa, E.: On resilience in cloud computing: a survey of techniques across the cloud domain. ACM Comput. Surv. **53**(3) (2020). https://doi.org/10.1145/3388922
26. White, S.R., Hanson, J.E., Whalley, I., Chess, D.M., Kephart, J.O.: An architectural approach to autonomic computing. In: International Conference on Autonomic Computing (ICAC). IEEE (2004). https://doi.org/10.1109/ICAC.2004.1301340

Demos

EFaST: An Explainable Framework for Fair Sequential Task Assignment

Anna Dalla Vecchia[1(✉)], Sara Migliorini[1], Elisa Quintarelli[1], and Kostas Stefanidis[2]

[1] Department of Computer Science, University of Verona, Verona, Italy
{anna.dallavecchia,sara.migliorini,elisa.quintarelli}@univr.it
[2] Data Science Research Centre, Tampere University, Tampere, Finland
konstantinos.stefanidis@tuni.fi

Abstract. In this demo, we present EFaST, an interactive framework for exploring and understanding fairness in multi-stakeholder sequential task assignment problems. EFaST allows users to iteratively define and modify stakeholder soft constraints, execute a fairness-aware optimization process, and observe how adjustments to these constraints influence fairness outcomes. Fairness is evaluated at two complementary levels: *local fairness* captures the satisfaction of individual stakeholders, while *global fairness* jointly measures overall satisfaction and balance across stakeholders. Users can inspect intermediate solutions, explore fairness trade-offs arising from conflicting constraints, and request natural-language explanations grounded in structured outputs. These explanations summarize constraint satisfaction, highlight critical violations, and provide guidance on potential constraint refinement, making fairness dynamics observable and controllable.

Keywords: Sequential tasks · Multi-stakeholder fairness · Explanations

1 Introduction

Incorporating fairness as a core ethical principle enhances productivity, positivity, long-term relationships, job satisfaction, and goal achievement within organizations and, more generally, in various social environments [4]. Fair task distribution ensures equal opportunities for individuals to showcase their skills, while also preventing bias in recommendation systems and promoting inclusivity [1,3]. However, fairness is a complex, context-dependent concept that varies across cultures and stakeholder perspectives [5]. This paper presents EFaST (Explainable FAir Sequential Task assignment), a framework for determining fair sequential task assignments among multiple stakeholders, a problem with competing interests and constraints that must be managed over time. The term *stakeholder* refers to any individual or group affected by or influencing task assignments. In the presence of multiple stakeholders, achieving fairness involves balancing the

© The Author(s), under exclusive license to Springer Nature Switzerland AG 2027
G. Vargas Solar et al. (Eds.): ADBIS 2026, CCIS 3175, pp. 211–219, 2027.
https://doi.org/10.1007/978-3-032-39823-9_19

needs of all of them and, thus, is a process that involves multiple points of view. We distinguish between local fairness, which measures satisfaction for a single stakeholder, and global fairness, which captures the overall balance across all stakeholders. Achieving optimal global fairness is a challenge, as a perfectly fair solution for all may not always exist.

Case Study. We consider the problem of timetable creation in the university domain, where professors and students share lessons, have constraints, and they also may have preferences. In this case, the goal is to automatically generate a fair timetable, with fairness evaluated from the perspectives of both stakeholder groups. EFaST addresses this by solving two sub-problems separately to ensure local fairness for students and each professor, then combines the found best local solutions to produce a globally fair timetable.

Contribution. EFaST tackles the challenge of assigning shared tasks in domains with multiple stakeholders, aiming to ensure fairness by respecting each party's preferences and constraints. It relies on the FaST-AMOSA optimization algorithm [2], a multi-objective simulated annealing approach tailored for fair sequential task assignment. This demonstration focuses on making the fairness computation explainable and fully interactive in practice, allowing stakeholders to inspect, modify, and iteratively refine fairness configurations in real time. The key contributions provided are: (i) an interactive constraint specification layer that allows non-technical stakeholders to directly manipulate time slot preferences without requiring them to disclose motivations; (ii) real-time monitoring of the task assignment process, allowing users to observe how local and global fairness evolve across iterations; and (iii) the integration of a natural language explanation layer that complements numerical fairness metrics, helping users understand the numerical values and the unsatisfied constraints.

Demonstration. EFaST is a web-based, interactive platform that enables users to define, modify, and experiment with stakeholders' constraints and preferences in a flexible manner. Users can specify availability and preference levels directly on a weekly timetable, actively monitor the assignment process, and observe how different choices influence fairness outcomes. Once constraints are defined, the system executes the FaST-AMOSA optimization process, allowing users to explore algorithm iterations and visualize, in real time, both local and global fairness scores at each step. This interactive exploration, coupled with natural language explanations, makes fairness trade-offs explicit, helping users understand how individual constraints and preferences contribute to the overall solution. By enabling direct user control and immediate feedback, the demo supports informed decision-making and highlights the practical relevance of EFaST for analyzing and refining fairness in complex, multi-stakeholder settings.

2 EFaST Overview

EFaST is an interactive system built on top of the FaST algorithm [2] to support the exploration of fair sequential task assignment problems involving multiple stakeholders with heterogeneous preferences and constraints. Here, sequential means that assignments are performed across time slots (e.g., hours and days). In this demo, we focus on the class scheduling problem in the university domain, where the stakeholders are represented by professors and students. As illustrated in Fig. 1, the shared resource is a calendar, in which classes are assigned to ordered time slots, yielding task sequences both within a day and across the week. Professors are modeled as individual stakeholders who can state their personal scheduling preferences. While students are represented at the cohort level, grouped by degree program and year of study, this reflects the standardized structure of university curricula.

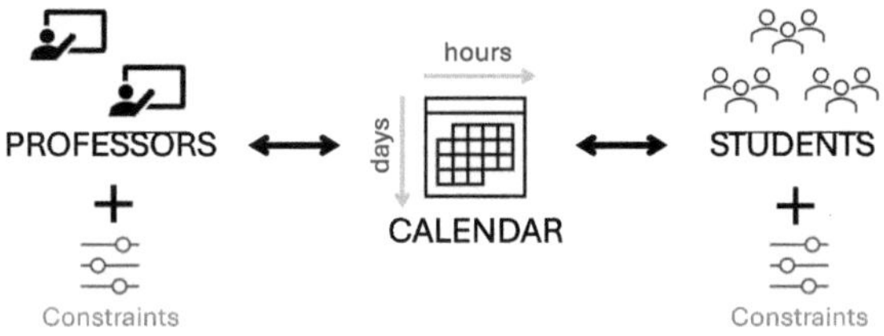

Fig. 1. Schematic representation of the considered sequential task assignment problem.

As in [2], we distinguish between two types of constraints. *Hard constraints* are mandatory requirements that are intrinsic to the problem definition and must be satisfied by any valid solution (e.g., a professor cannot be assigned to two classes at the same time), whereas *soft constraints* encode a set of preferences and may be violated at the cost expressed by the stakeholder, e.g., a user may prefer a task in a specific time slot. Tasks (i.e., classes) are assigned over a discrete temporal domain defined by two orthogonal granularities (e.g., days and hours). Each professor specifies their preferences through a calendar where each time slot is associated with a value $n \in [-1, 0]$, where values closer to -1 indicate more undesirable slots. In addition to the calendar-based preferences, further soft constraints can be modeled through objective functions, for instance, to guarantee a lunch break. The final goal is to produce valid schedules that satisfy all hard constraints while minimizing the number of unsatisfied soft constraints.

To compute fair solutions, EFaST relies on the FaST-AMOSA algorithm, a fairness-aware extension of Multi-Objective Simulated Annealing (MOSA) [6]. Unlike traditional simulated annealing, which randomly selects perturbations at each iteration, this algorithm uses soft constraints to guide the process, accelerating convergence toward fair solutions. In line with the FaST formulation, fairness is evaluated at two complementary levels. **Local fairness** measures how well a valid solution $\mathcal{A}$ satisfies the soft constraints of a stakeholder k and is denoted as $f(\mathcal{A}, k)$. **Global fairness** assesses how evenly satisfaction is balanced across all stakeholders involved and is represented as $g(\mathcal{A}) = \langle g_a(\mathcal{A}), g_s(\mathcal{A}) \rangle$, where g_a is the average local fairness across stakeholders and g_s is its standard deviation. This formulation captures both overall satisfaction and the balance among stakeholders, preventing solutions that favor some stakeholders at the expense of others. Beyond fairness computation, this demo emphasizes fairness understanding. EFaST integrates an explanation layer that helps users interpret fairness outcomes by highlighting how constraints are violated, which conflicts are most critical, and why certain still persist even in globally fair solutions. This enables users to inspect the underlying reasons for the final fairness score.

3 EFaST Architecture and User Interface

EFaST is implemented as a web-based interactive platform designed to support the exploration and understanding of fairness in sequential task assignment. The architecture follows a client–server model in which users interact with a web interface to define constraints and preferences, trigger the optimization process, and inspect both local and global fairness outcomes. The backend executes the FaST-AMOSA optimization algorithm and generates intermediate and final results in real time. The user interface is designed to make fairness trade-offs explicit and inspectable. Stakeholders interact with a weekly timetable view where each time slot is annotated with a preference value n, following the formalization introduced earlier. In particular, slots can be marked as available ($n = 0$), mildly undesirable ($n = -0.5$), or strongly undesirable ($n = -1$). Constraints are validated at insertion time according to administrator-defined limits to ensure feasibility. During execution, the interface visualizes the evolution of the solution by showing: (i) the student fairness across different cohorts, (ii) professor fairness, and (iii) the global fairness indicators.

The core of the web app is the explainability module, which supports the interpretation of fairness outcomes. For any solution, users can request a natural language explanation describing which constraints are violated, which stakeholders are most affected, and why specific unfair values persist. Explanations are generated through an external LLM service accessed via API. The demonstration supports interactive selection among different models, allowing the user to balance explanation quality, latency, and computational cost depending on the deployment context. LLMs have demonstrated the ability to translate structured representations into coherent natural language descriptions [7]. In EFaST, these models process fairness scores, violated constraints, and the current assignment solely to translate formal structured output into textual explanations. The prompt enforces a fixed three-part structure (fairness summary, structural conflicts, and preference adjustment) and does not introduce new numerical values or modify results. This approach enhances interpretability for non-expert users, which can be challenging in multi-stakeholder scenarios where explanations need to address multiple types of constraints and conflicting preferences.

EFaST supports incremental execution of the optimization algorithm. As the algorithm progresses, intermediate fairness results are displayed in the interface, allowing users to observe how local and global fairness evolve over time through a plot. Administrators can monitor convergence, inspect stakeholder conflicts, and request explanations at different stages of the optimization. This interactive loop enables users to explore how modifying constraints or preferences affects fairness trade-offs, transforming fairness optimization from a black-box process into an analyzable, controllable decision-support workflow.

4 Demonstration

In this section, we demonstrate how users can interact with the EFaST web application in a real-world university timetabling scenario. As illustrated in previous sections, we have two groups of stakeholders: students and professors. The latter are those that can express their own preferences in a calendar, while students are modeled as cohorts associated with degree programs. To showcase the potential of our proposal, we apply the EFaST system to data from the Department of Computer Science at the University of Verona, comprising three bachelor's degree programs in Computer Science, Bioinformatics, and Biotechnology. Participants can interact with the web application to (i) change constraints, (ii) inspect optimization results, and (iii) explore their explanations in real time. Overall, the demonstration is designed to show how fairness trade-offs emerge under different preference configurations and how stakeholders can interpret them. The following subsections illustrate the main interaction points offered by EFaST during the demonstration[1].

Constraint Specification. The demonstration starts with the specification of stakeholder constraints, in which each professor can specify their individual availability on a weekly calendar. For each time slot, the professor can select one of three options (Fig. 2): *Available* (blue), *Better not* (yellow), representing a soft constraint with $n = -0.5$, and *Impossible* (red), representing a stronger soft constraint ($n = -1$). To avoid unrealistic configurations in which only a few time slots remain effectively usable, the system allows the administrator to impose a limit on the number of constraints per professor. For instance, in Fig. 2, *prof8* expresses a preference to avoid classes scheduled between 1:30 and 3:30 p.m. on any day, while explicitly marking it as strongly unavailable on Wednesday.

Fair Solution Generation. Once preferences for each professor are collected by assessing the administrator dashboard, it is possible to inspect the submitted configurations. From the interface, the administrator can review and download detailed information for each professor and, if needed, adjust the professors' preferences thresholds. The optimization process is then triggered by selecting the maximum number of iterations for the FaST-AMOSA algorithm, which is set to 100 by default. Before the first iterations of the algorithm, EFaST estimates and displays the expected end time. As soon as the first solution is generated, the interface visualizes the current fairness status. Figure 3 shows an example of the monitoring interface displayed during the optimization process. The upper table provides a summary of the current fairness status, including the Global Fairness value $\langle g_a(A), g_s(A)\rangle = \langle -0.66, 0.31\rangle$, as well as the average and standard

[1] The source code and data have been made available at https://github.com/4nnina/EFaST.

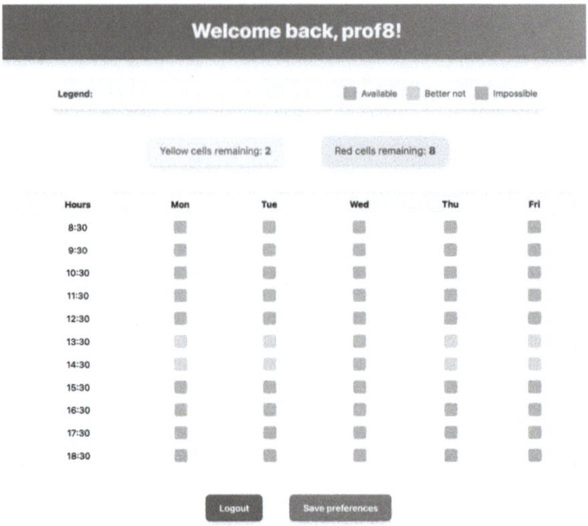

Fig. 2. User preferences webpage illustrating how professors express constraints for weekly classes. (Color figure online)

deviation of local fairness for professors and student cohorts. It also reports the number of professors whose preferences are not fully satisfied. In the shown configuration, all professor preferences are satisfied; consequently, the indicator corresponding to the percentage of satisfied constraints reaches 100%. The second table details student cohort fairness by degree program and academic year. Each value can be inspected interactively to visualize the corresponding timetable, highlighting in the assignment the professor constraints that are violated in that specific schedule. At the bottom of the page, a plot shows the evolution of fairness scores across iterations, allowing users to observe how global and local fairness improve over time.

This monitoring becomes particularly informative in configurations where stakeholder preferences conflict structurally. For example, if multiple professors mark Wednesday as strongly undesirable while student cohorts require compact weekly schedules, satisfying all professor constraints forces lectures to be redistributed across the remaining days, leading to fragmented timetables for students and a decrease in their local fairness score. In such cases, users can observe how prioritizing professor satisfaction increases the global fairness average $g_a(A)$, while simultaneously increasing its standard deviation $g_s(A)$, revealing a growing imbalance across stakeholders. While the interface makes these trade-offs quantitatively visible, the underlying reasons for persistent dissatisfaction are not immediately evident from numerical indicators alone. To clarify the causes behind these fairness dynamics, the violet pop-up on the right side of the interface provides direct access to the fairness explanation of the current assignment, supporting the interpretation of the reported scores and trade-offs.

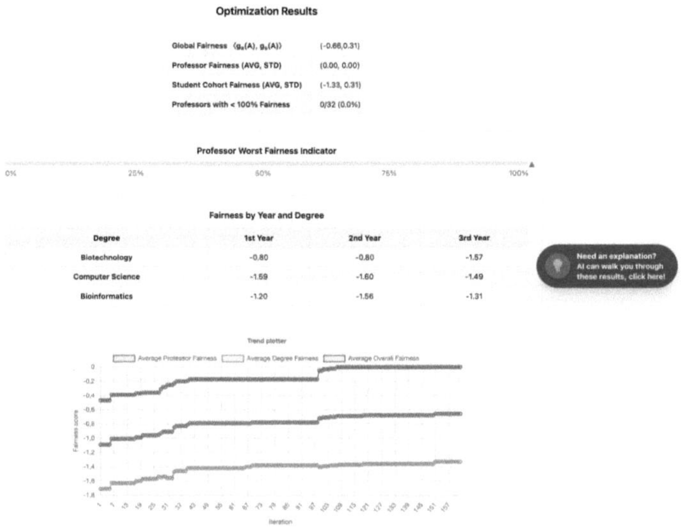

Fig. 3. Monitoring interface showing fairness indicators during the optimization process.

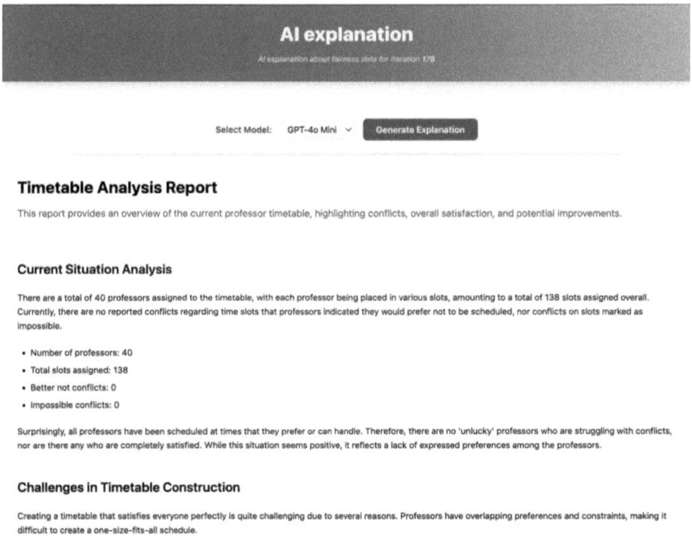

Fig. 4. Example of EFaST fairness explanation.

Fairness Explanation. In realistic scenarios, a perfectly fair solution satisfying all soft constraints is often unachievable, as schedules may violate some preferences due to structural conflicts among stakeholders. To support fairness, EFaST allows users to request an explanation of the current assignment at any stage of the optimization process. The system produces a structured explanation that summarizes the overall fairness score and highlights the constraint violation. Figure 4 shows an example of such an explanation. First, the current fairness is analyzed by qualitatively identifying which constraints remain unsatisfied and which stakeholders are most affected. Second, it articulates the structural conflicts underlying these violations, clarifying why certain constraints cannot be jointly satisfied. Finally, the explanation provides illustrative directions for improving fairness, including which preference adjustments could reduce imbalance, supporting the administrator in exploring alternative, potentially fairer configurations. The explanation relies on an LLM that translates structured outputs produced by the optimization process into natural language. This model can be iteratively configured by the user, and it does not perform any independent computations or optimizations, nor does it influence the algorithms' decision-making process. Any illustrative suggestions included in the explanation are interpretative and require an explicit human validation before any constraint edits.

5 Conclusion

This demo presented EFaST, an interactive framework for exploring fairness in sequential task assignment problems. EFaST enables users to monitor local and global fairness in real time, analyze trade-offs among stakeholders, and inspect why specific constraints remain unsatisfied. By combining optimization with natural language explanations grounded in structured outputs, the system transforms fairness-aware optimization from a black-box process into an inspectable and human-controllable decision-support workflow. Overall, EFaST illustrates how fairness-aware optimization can become transparent, interactive, and practically actionable in complex multi-stakeholder environments.

Disclosure of Interests. The authors have no competing interests to declare that are relevant to the content of this article.

References

1. Borges, R., Sahlgren, O., Koivunen, S., Stefanidis, K., Olsson, T., Laitinen, A.: Multi-objective fairness in team assembly. In: New Trends in Database and Information Systems - ADBIS 2023 Short Papers, Doctoral Consortium and Workshops Proceedings. CCIS, vol. 1850, pp. 106–116. Springer (2023)
2. Dalla Vecchia, A., Migliorini, S., Quintarelli, E., Stefanidis, K.: Multi-sided fairness in sequential task assignment. Inf. Syst.,102700 (2026)
3. Migliorini, S., Quintarelli, E., Gambini, M., Belussi, A., Carra, D.: Sequence recommendations for groups: a dynamic approach to balance preferences. Inf. Syst. **108**, 102023 (2022)
4. Pitoura, E., Stefanidis, K., Koutrika, G.: Fairness in rankings and recommendations: an overview. VLDB J. **31**(3), 431–458 (2022)

5. Shafiloo, R., Stratigi, M., Peltonen, J., Olsson, T., Stefanidis, K.: The many facets of fairness in recommender systems: consumers, providers and items. Inf. Syst. **137**, 102643 (2026)
6. Suman, B.: Study of simulated annealing based algorithms for multiobjective optimization of a constrained problem. Comput. Chem. Eng. **28**(9), 1849–1871 (2004)
7. Zhao, W.X., et al.: A survey of large language models (2025). https://arxiv.org/abs/2303.18223

HARPY: Human-AI Collaboration for Database Error Resolution via LLMs

Maximilian Plazotta(✉) and Meike Klettke

University of Regensburg, Bajuwarenstraße 4, 93053 Regensburg, Germany
{maximilian.plazotta,meike.klettke}@informatik.uni-regensburg.de
https://www.uni-regensburg.de/informatik-datascience/fakultaet/einrichtungen/data-engineering

Abstract. Maintaining database integrity is an essential task for researchers and practitioners alike due to inherent data errors that evade detection by conventional statistical or rule-based methods. While Large Language Models (LLMs) excel in finding anomalies in a scalable way, they are susceptible to hallucinations. To address this limitation, we introduce HARPY, an iterative LLM-powered pipeline for database error remediation with human-in-the-loop oversight. The system showcases a modular architecture compatible with any chosen LLM, incorporating TOON-encoding to reduce token consumption. HARPY provides an interactive front-end with a pre-scan cost estimator and an error review pane where the human expert can review each detected anomaly.

Keywords: Data Cleaning · LLMs · Human-in-the-Loop

1 Introduction

The coherence of database systems depends on reliable and accurate data. However, most real-world datasets lack data quality and cannot identify complex anomalies such as logical errors or context-dependent discrepancies. In recent research, the application of LLMs to data cleaning problems shows great potential, despite hallucination – the generation of plausible but incorrect output. Such behavior can lead to populating the dataset with even more errors if left unsupervised. Therefore, we present **HARPY**, an LLM-powered system for automated error detection and correction, featuring integrated human-in-the-loop oversight. HARPY combines the efficiency of LLM automation with expert validation by leveraging a modular architecture that allows for a seamless integration with any open- or closed-source LLM. To reduce token consumption, the system uses TOON-encoding; a cost estimator displays the expense for each scan in advance. Through the interactive user interface, the human expert can accept, modify, or drop suggested errors. To summarize, the key **contributions** of this paper are: a distinctive approach in prompt engineering, a human-in-the-loop for validating results, significant cost reduction through token minimization, and an ex-ante cost estimation engine. The subsequent sections highlight HARPY's operational workflow, its system architecture, and the demonstration scenarios.

© The Author(s), under exclusive license to Springer Nature Switzerland AG 2027
G. Vargas Solar et al. (Eds.): ADBIS 2026, CCIS 3175, pp. 220–227, 2027.
https://doi.org/10.1007/978-3-032-39823-9_20

2 Related Work

Traditionally, the discipline of data cleaning has relied on statistical or rule-based techniques to detect anomalies, which are accompanied by some well-researched limitations [1]. With the general accessibility of LLMs, researchers quickly adopted its offerings, yielding new data cleaning and correction systems such as `ZeroEC` [7] and `LLMClean` [2]. Such LLM-based systems generally provide convincing results but come along with the key problem of LLM inference: hallucination. To tackle hallucination, a human-in-the-loop approach has shown itself to be effective in checking inference output [5]. Another important aspect to such systems is the cost which occur through token-based consumption. Efficient data (pre-) processing, optimized query selection, and varying batching strategies have a significant impact on lowering token expenses and staying within a budget [3]. The HARPY system is built upon these laid foundations by leveraging human-LLM collaboration.

3 The HARPY System

HARPY is designed as a modular data error detection and cleaning system that leverages the skill and knowledge of a human expert. The backend consists of a distributed orchestrator engine that coordinates scanned batches of rows from the selected database table, translating them into TOON format, and forwarding them to the chosen LLM. After the scan, the LLM provides enriched error reports that are pushed to the UI, where the expert can accept, reject, postpone each suggestion, or insert their own value.

3.1 System Architecture

The HARPY architecture is reflected in Figure 1 and consists of three main parts: the **orchestration layer**, the **engine layer**, and the **user-facing interaction layer**. The orchestrator is at the heart of the system, dynamically coordinating tasks across multiple components. Its key tasks are segmenting the PostgreSQL database table into batches, converting them into TOON format, dispatching the prompt, and collecting the structured error reports. The engine layer is constructed modularly, which enables flexible swapping between LLMs. New models can be plugged in within a matter of minutes. For the demo, we chose one open-source model, Gemma 3 (27b), and one closed source-model, Claude Haiku 4.5, addressing a user's priorities for privacy, cost, and accuracy. Lastly, the human expert takes action: the Streamlit-built UI gives the user different options for choosing the parameters (e.g., LLM engine, batch size) and a cost estimator that predicts the run time and cost involved pre-scan. After the scan, the user is encouraged to assess the scan results and approve/reject the suggestions or insert their own correct values, which are immediately propagated back to the database once the button "Fix" is clicked.

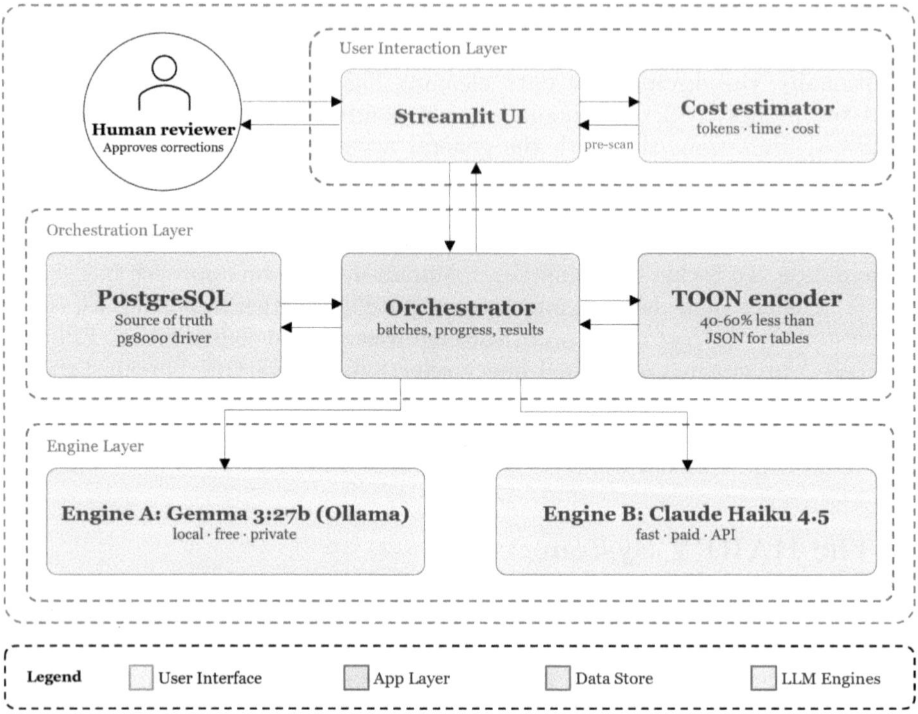

Fig. 1. Overview of the HARPY system architecture.

3.2 Backend: Distributed Orchestrator Engine

The backbone of HARPY is its distributed orchestrator engine that facilitates the tasks along the data pipeline: data retrieval, data transformation, model inference, and final write-backs from the user's feedback. Using the Python database driver `pg8000`, the orchestrator queries the schema to retrieve column names, data types, and primary keys. With this information, the engine is now able to query the target table for each tuple along with the batching logic. Each batch is then serialized into TOON format [4], saving between 40-60% of tokens relative to an equivalent JSON file while maintaining almost the same retrieval accuracy. TOON removes all unnecessary characters (e.g., quotation marks, semicolons, or curly brackets) and optimizes the structure of the dataset by combining CSV- and YAML-style indentation. The TOON-encoded payload and user-enriched metadata are forwarded to the LLM with the system prompt (see Figure 2), which can be divided into four parts: setting (lines 1-6), JSON payload structure (lines 8-30), task description (lines 32-39), and specifications (lines 41-43).

```
<System Prompt>
You are a data quality
analyst. The user will give
you a batch of database rows
in TOON format. Identify rows
and return a JSON object
shaped exactly like this:

{
  "errors": [
    {
      "row_number": <integer,
      1-indexed>,
      "column": <column name
      from the TOON header>,
      "current_value": <the
      value as shown>,
      "suggested_value": <best
      correction, or null if
      you cannot suggest one>,
      "error_type": "typo|
      format|range|null|
      inconsistent|other",
      "confidence": <float
      between 0.0 and 1.0>,
      "rationale": <one
      sentence stating the
      problem>
    }
  ]
}

Look for: impossible values,
format mismatches, obvious
typos, unexpected nulls, out-
of-range numbers, internal
contradictions between
columns of the same row, and
violations of the context
the user provides.

Only include errors with
confidence >= 0.6.
Return ONLY the JSON object.
```

Fig. 2. System prompt.

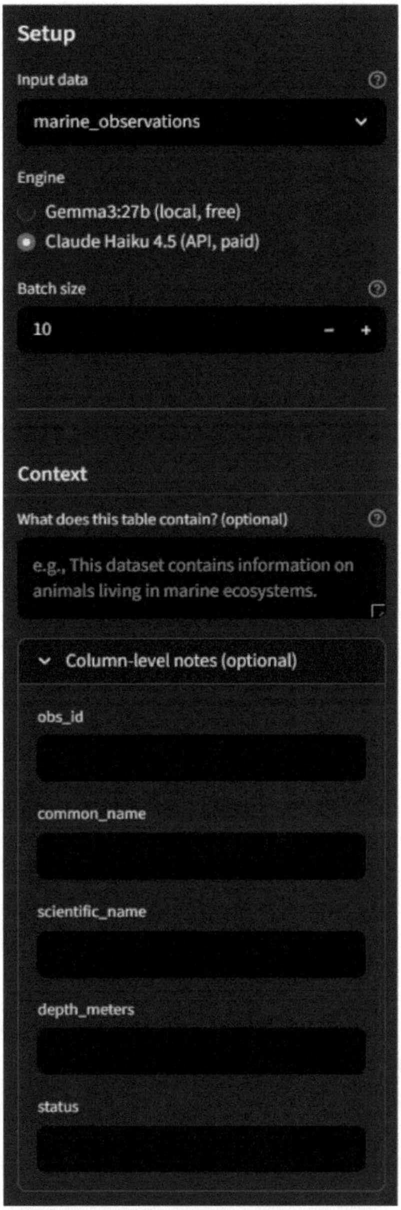

Fig. 3. Streamlit interface for configuring key parameters prior to scan execution.

This structure enforces the LLM to only return the format, which is expected by downstream processes. The error report (`errors.json`) returned by the LLM includes the following error types the system can cover:

- typo
- format
- range
- null
- inconsistent
- other (none of the above)

We created mock-up datasets to test the cost per error type based on the marine biology example with 100 rows and 5 columns. The dataset without errors created cost of $0.05 per scan (Claude Haiku 4.5) - the error types created the following cost: typo $0.07, format $0.055, range $0.06, null $0.055, and inconsistent $0.065. Finally, the error report is sent to the frontend UI, where the human reviewer accesses it. When the user approves a corrected value, the orchestrator executes a parametrized `UPDATE` statement back to the database.

3.3 Frontend: Interactive UI

The HARPY frontend is a Streamlit-based interactive UI designed to be minimal yet expressive. The layout follows a two-column paradigm, with the configuration panel (sidebar) being on the left-hand side and the action/result panel on the right-hand side of the display. Within the **setup sidebar** (see Figure 3), the user has multiple options for configuring the scan: selecting the target table, choosing the LLM, and adjusting the batch size while also being able to insert optionally contextual knowledge about the dataset as well as detailed information on column level. Once all mandatory fields are filled, the user can move to the **action panel** (see Figure 4) with the run-scan specifications (left) and schema information (right). The run-scan pane displays the number of rows, the batches, and the estimated time for the scan. The key innovation here is the **pre-scan cost estimator** that takes all configurations into account and returns a range for the estimated cost in US dollars. The three main factors for the estimation are input token, output token, and the pricing of both – input token are significantly cheaper than output token. Based on this information and the underlying data, the cost estimator is able to calculate the estimated cost per scan. Furthermore, there is an expander below with the estimate details to provide full transparency on the assumptions and calculations done in the background. The right pane presents the table schema, with the column names, the data types, and the `is_null` parameter, giving the user more information on the dataset before initiating the scan. After pressing 'Scan', the **error review queue** is created (see Figure 5). The top line shows the general scan information: rows scanned, errors found, and the TOON savings as a percentage. In addition, there are two filter options for the error cards: one list widget for the error types and one slicer widget to specify confidence thresholds – the default value (confidence level >= 0.6) guarantees that only errors are reported where the model is certain to a high extent. The **error cards** for each suspected anomaly follow a uniform layout as determined by the system prompt from Section 3.2:

- **Error Metadata**: This block shows all information on the suspected error: PK, column name, error type, current vs. suggested value, and the rationale.
- **Confidence Levels**: The model delivers a confidence value that is visualized with a traffic-light-style logic.
- **Editable Value**: The suggested value is inserted by default but can be altered by the user.
- **Action Buttons**: Pressing the 'Fix' button immediately invokes the `UPDATE` statement. The 'Not an Error' button removes the error card from the queue, while the 'Skip' button temporarily hides the entry for later review.

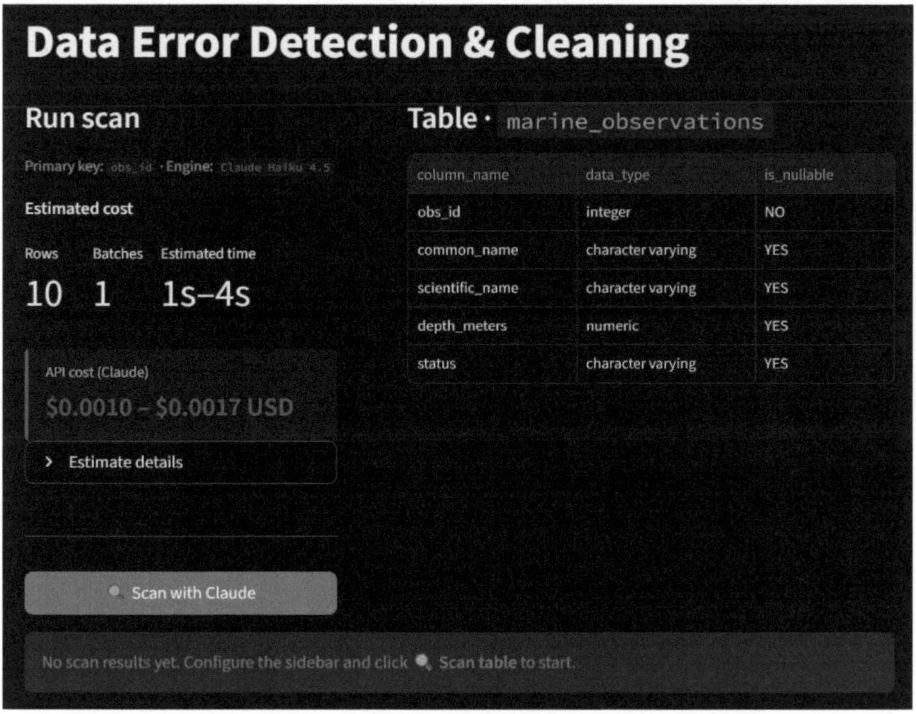

Fig. 4. Additional information and run.

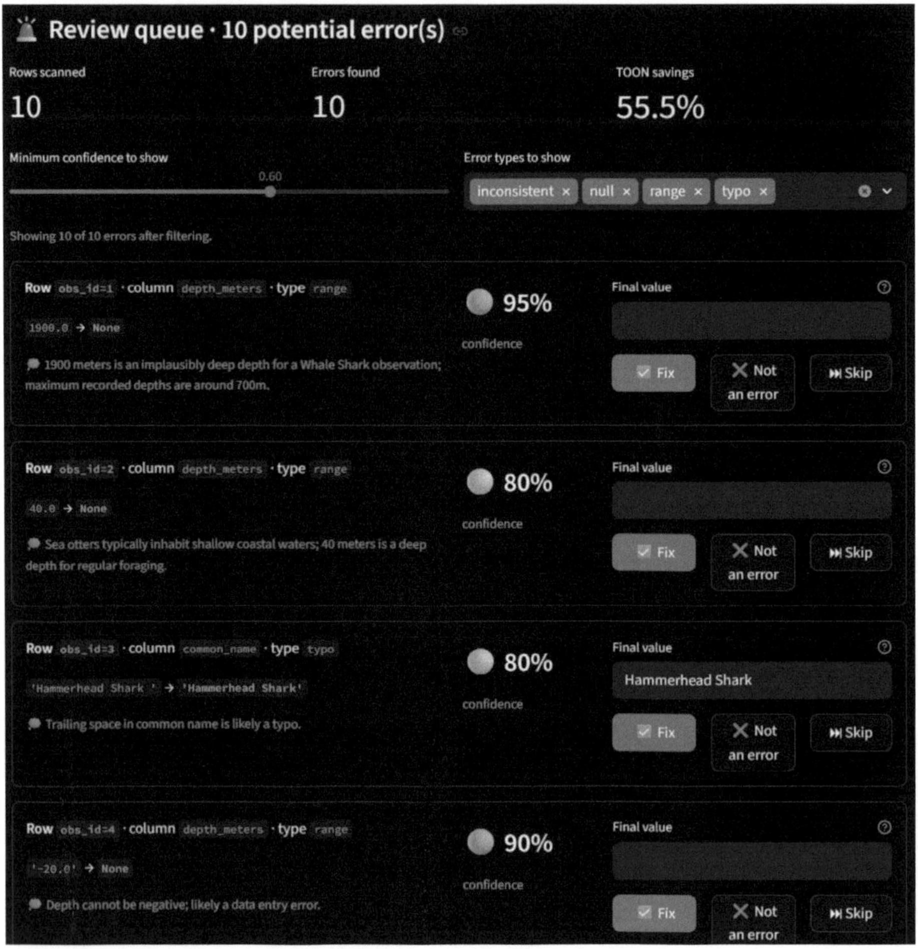

Fig. 5. Results presentation and error remediation.

4 Demonstration Scenarios

This section illustrates how researchers and practitioners can utilize HARPY to tackle typical data-quality issues. We propose three real-world scenarios in which users can greatly benefit from our system:

Scenario 1: Scientific research data
Scholars generally hold high standards for the storage and processing of experimental data. HARPY addresses this demand by using a local PostgreSQL database and LLM, resulting in data never leaving the host machine. Furthermore, the error detection is not bound to a single field of study: as LLMs are trained on vast amounts of data, the system can be applied to any research field. In our experiments we used a dataset from marine biology, and the scan

results were quite promising – apart from "classical" errors such as typos or `NULL` values, logical errors were also highlighted (see Figure 5).

Scenario 2: Enterprise data with focus on cost efficiency
In enterprise environments, there is usually high volumes of data where other factors become important – cost, scalability, and trustworthiness. In this case, we advise using Claude's Haiku 4.5 model, being more precise (across bigger batch sizes) and faster compared to open-source models [6]. In addition, the cost estimator predicts expenses (pre-scan) based on the provided data and current API cost. The scan of an artificially created customer-order dataset delivered positive results, finding all errors with correct suggestions.

Scenario 3: Bring your own data
Apart from research and corporate data, basically anyone can run HARPY on their own, private datasets. The prerequisite is that the local environment has enough RAM or connect through the API of a chosen LLM vendor.

5 Conclusion

HARPY serves as a well-suited example for **human-AI collaboration**. The human-in-the-loop technique mitigates hallucination risks inherent to AI-only systems. Furthermore, TOON-encoding leads to a significant cost reduction, decreasing token consumption. The modular architecture provides a seamless transition from privacy-sensitive and cost-focused use cases. HARPY enhances database integrity by combining anomaly-detection capabilities of LLMs with critical verification by a human expert.

References

1. Abedjan, Z., et al.: Detecting Data Errors: where are we and what needs to be done? Proc. VLDB Endow. **9**(12), 993–1004 (2016)
2. Biester, F., Abdelaal, M., Gaudio, D.D.: LLMClean: Context-Aware Tabular Data Cleaning via LLM-Generated OFDs. In: ADBIS (Short Papers). Communications in Computer and Information Science, vol. 2186, pp. 68–78. Springer (2024)
3. Einy, Y., Milo, T., Novgorodov, S.: Cost-effective LLM utilization for machine learning tasks over tabular data. In: GUIDE-AI@SIGMOD, pp. 45–49. ACM (2024)
4. Johann Schopplich: TOON (Version 2.1.0) (2025). https://github.com/toon-format/toon, gitHub repository
5. Pachera, A., et al.: Co-Data: cultivating Effective Human-LLM Collaboration for Collaborative Data Processing. In: CHI Ext. Abstracts, pp. 929:1–929:7. ACM (2026)
6. Plazotta, M., Klettke, M.: Can LLMs Serve as a Data Error Detection Engine - Trade-offs in Accuracy, Cost, and Hallucination Across Datasets. Accepted (2026)
7. Wu, Y., et al.: A zero-training error correction system with large language models. In: ICDE, pp. 2949–2962. IEEE (2025)

MedVisionEx: A Data-Information-Knowledge-Wisdom (DIKW) Hierarchy Inspired, Retrieval-Augmented and Knowledge-Graph-Grounded Pipeline for Explainable Medical Visual Question Answering

Nadeesha Perera(✉), Alli Raittinen, Jyrki Nummenmaa, and Kostas Stefanidis

Tampere University, Tampere, Finland
{nadeesha.perera,alli.raittinen,jyrki.nummenmaa,konstantinos.stefanidis}@tuni.fi

Abstract. Medical visual question answering (VQA) systems are rarely adopted in practice because they answer as black boxes: a clinician sees a verdict but neither the visual evidence behind it nor the medical knowledge that supports it. In radiology, accuracy alone is insufficient; clinicians need justification. We demonstrate *MedVisionEx*, an on-premise pipeline whose design follows the DIKW hierarchy: raw *data* (image and question) is turned into *information* by retrieving similar archived cases, enriched into *knowledge* by linking to a biomedical knowledge graph, and elevated to *wisdom*—an answer that is grounded and traceable. A query image is encoded by a domain-adapted CLIP encoder and used to retrieve visually similar cases from a pooled FAISS index. The retrieved images and captions condition a locally fine-tuned MedGemma vision–language model that writes a concise, evidence-grounded description; the description and the question are linked to UMLS concepts (subsuming SNOMED CT and RadLex), and the resulting structured knowledge augments both the description and the answer prompt, from which a fine-tuned generative model produces the final answer. Every component runs locally, and the interface exposes the retrieved cases, the description, and the knowledge-graph support, so that a clinician can audit how each answer was reached rather than accept it on trust. The novelty of MedVisionEx lies not in its individual components—retrieval augmentation, FAISS indexing, and ontology grounding are established—but in composing them into an inspectable architecture that makes the evidence behind an answer checkable.

Keywords: Medical VQA · DIKW hierarchy · Retrieval-augmented generation · Knowledge graphs · Vision–language models · Explainable AI

© The Author(s), under exclusive license to Springer Nature Switzerland AG 2027
G. Vargas Solar et al. (Eds.): ADBIS 2026, CCIS 3175, pp. 228–235, 2027.
https://doi.org/10.1007/978-3-032-39823-9_21

1 Introduction

Medical AI research in radiology diagnostics is expanding rapidly, yet two obstacles keep such systems out of the clinical setting. First, end-to-end VQA models are *black boxes*: they answer without relating image regions to comparable cases or grounding the answer in the domain facts that justify it, and a confident but unexplained answer is unusable for a decision that carries clinical risk. Second, hospital deployment constraints frequently rule out sending images to external APIs, so a practical system must run *on-premise*. Together these pressures motivate a transparent composition of smaller local components whose intermediate outputs can be inspected.

We demonstrate *MedVisionEx*, built on the principle that an answer is only as useful as the evidence a user can inspect behind it. Rather than mapping image and question directly to an answer, the pipeline *retrieves* similar archived cases, *writes* an evidence-grounded description conditioned on those cases, *grounds* both the description and the question in a biomedical knowledge graph, and only then *answers*. Every intermediate step is preserved and shown to the user. This staged design instantiates the Data–Information–Knowledge–Wisdom (DIKW) hierarchy [1] (Sect. 2), lifted by two mechanisms: retrieval, which grounds the system in real archived cases and is the source of *reliability*, and the knowledge graph, which supplies structured domain relations and is the source of *explainability*.

Our contributions are: (i) a DIKW-inspired, retrieval-augmented, knowledge-graph-grounded VQA architecture that is explainable by construction; (ii) a pooled multi-source similarity index over a contrastively fine-tuned embedding space; (iii) a knowledge-graph integration over UMLS, SNOMED CT, and RadLex with a dependency-light linking back end that eases on-premise deployment; and (iv) a decoupled, auditable service—an inference API plus a thin client—whose front end exposes the full evidence chain.

2 Design Rationale: From Data to Wisdom

The DIKW hierarchy describes how raw *data* gains context to become *information*, how information gains relations to become *knowledge*, and how knowledge is applied with judgment to yield *wisdom*. MedVisionEx is designed so that each layer is a concrete, inspectable stage, and so that the two persistent weaknesses of medical generative AI—unreliability and opacity—are addressed at the layers where they arise (Fig. 1).

3 System Overview

Figure 2 shows the pipeline. Given a query image and a question, pipeline proceeds in seven stages, after which the front end returns the answer with every intermediate artifact.

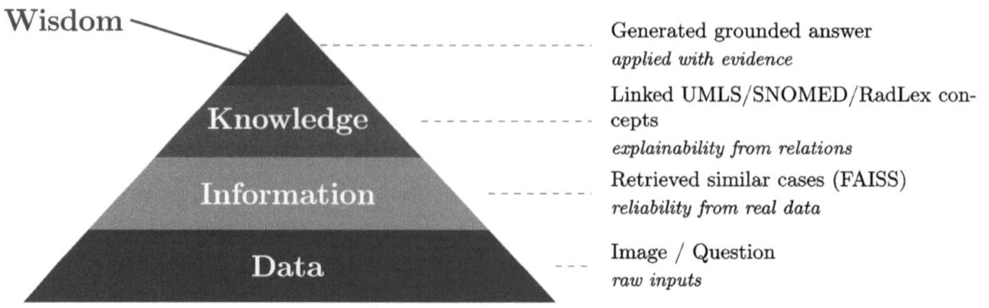

Fig. 1. The DIKW ascent realized by MedVisionEx.

(1) Query Image and (2) Encoding [Data]. The uploaded image is embedded by a medical CLIP visual encoder, frozen at inference and fine-tuned offline (Sect. 4) so that images sharing clinical content lie close in the embedding space.

(3) Similarity Search and Retrieval [Information]. The embedding is matched against a FAISS index [3] by inner product. Rather than a fixed k, the system retrieves *all* gallery items above a similarity threshold, so the amount of evidence scales with how well the case is covered by the archive; candidates are ranked by cosine similarity, and their scores travel with them so the interface can show how strongly each case supports the answer. When nothing clears the threshold, the pipeline degrades gracefully to a zero-shot description.

(4) Evidence-Grounded Description and (5) Knowledge-Graph Linking [Knowledge]. The query image, the retrieved images, and their captions are passed to a local fine-tuned MedGemma [13] model that writes a concise description stating the modality, the imaged anatomy, and any abnormalities. The description and the question are then linked to knowledge-graph concepts (Sect. 4); the concepts, their definitions, and the relations connecting question terms to description terms are serialized into a compact knowledge block.

(6) Generative Model Producing an (7) Answer [Wisdom]. A generative answer model consumes the description, this knowledge block, and the question to produce the final answer. The front end returns it alongside the query image, the top similar cases and captions, the description, and the knowledge-graph support, making the reasoning path auditable.

4 Implementation and Data Management

Pooled Similarity Index. The retrieval gallery unifies several public radiology image–caption collections [9,15,16] into one corpus. Each record is normalized to an (image, caption) pair, and sources that expose only a training split contribute a deterministic held-out slice so the index can be evaluated without leakage. Evaluation images are never indexed: the RadImageNet-VQA [12] benchmark is used only as a validation set and is not part of the FAISS gallery. Because

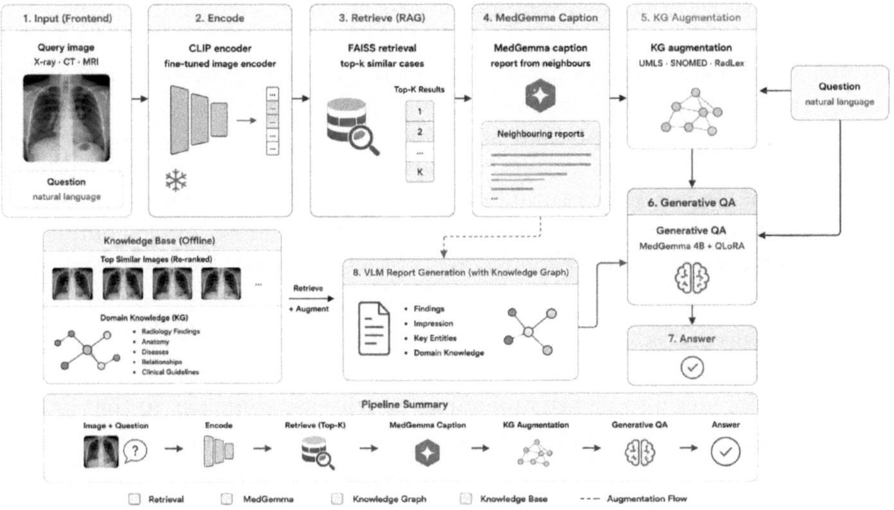

Fig. 2. The simplified MedVisionEx architecture, showing the dataflow from a visual question to a grounded answer.

indexing and search are decoupled from training, the gallery can be extended incrementally.

Contrastive Fine-Tuning. The CLIP [4] encoder is adapted with a symmetric InfoNCE [14] objective strengthened by a hard-negative loss term. The hardest negatives are mined within each batch and from recent embeddings, expanding the effective negative pool without extra encoder passes, and only after a warm-up so the embedding space stabilizes first. This sharpens the contrast between visually similar but clinically different studies—exactly the confusion that degrades evidence quality.

Local Generation and the Answer Model. Both generative models run on-premise, keeping data within the institution. The description model receives the query image and a bounded number of retrieved images, so prompt size and accelerator memory stay controlled, while all retrieved captions remain available as text. The answer model is an instruction-tuned generative language model (*[base model, size]*), adapted with parameter-efficient fine-tuning (*[method]*) on (description, question) → answer triples, and decodes a short free-text answer at low temperature. Conditioning it on the description and the knowledge block, rather than on the raw image alone, is what lets retrieved evidence and linked concepts inform the response.

Knowledge Linking. A distinguishing design choice is *where* domain knowledge enters. MedVisionEx links text to the Unified Medical Language System (UMLS) [5], which incorporates SNOMED CT [8] and RadLex [7], so a single linker [6] provides concepts, semantic types, definitions, and—through a local relation table—ontology relations across all three vocabularies. The graph encodes the links that are the origin of explainability: diseases to symptoms, anatomy to findings. Knowledge is extracted once and reused at two points: findings detected in the retrieved captions are injected as structured hints into the description prompt, and the concepts and relations shared between question and description are serialized into the knowledge block attached to the answer prompt. Beyond the neural linker, a dependency-light back end performs longest-match linking against a compact concept dictionary compiled offline from UMLS; it needs no heavy native libraries, a practical advantage on hardened on-premise hosts.

Modality Awareness. In pooled medical retrieval the imaging *modality* (radiograph, CT, MRI, ultrasound) is itself a major axis of confusion. The knowledge graph is therefore used to identify modality and disease evidence, so that description and answer remain tied to the correct modality rather than drifting toward a visually similar but modality-mismatched neighbour.

Deployment. A stateless inference API loads the encoder, index, description model, linker, and answer model once on the accelerator host, and exposes one endpoint that accepts an image (including DICOM) and a question and returns the answer with every intermediate step—retrieved cases and scores, the description, and the knowledge-graph support—as a single auditable response. A thin web client renders it, so the interface never holds model weights or patient data on disk. The pipeline is configuration-driven and each stage runs independently (train → index → append → evaluate). Figure 3 shows the resulting interface on a worked chest-radiograph query.

5 Evaluation Protocol

We evaluate on the held-out split of each benchmark—the official validation or test split where published, a deterministic held-out slice otherwise—and no evaluation image appears in the retrieval gallery. For each image–question–answer triple the system executes the full chain—retrieve, describe, ground, answer—and the prediction is compared with the reference. Because answers are free text, we report BERTScore-F1 [2], separately for closed-ended questions and for the full set (closed- plus open-ended). Table 1 ablates four configurations: the full pipeline; without knowledge-graph grounding, which removes the knowledge block from the answer prompt; without evidence-grounded generation, which removes the retrieval-conditioned description; and, with both disabled, a purely generative black-box baseline equivalent to the systems this work argues against.

Discussion. Combining both mechanisms gives the strongest configuration overall: relative to the purely generative black-box baseline, the full pipeline improves closed-ended BERTScore-F1 on three of the four benchmarks. The knowledge graph carries most of that gain where the question demands domain relations rather than surface description—on VQA-RAD and Med-VQA, removing it costs 11.9 and 14.7 points. The gains are not uniform, and we do not claim

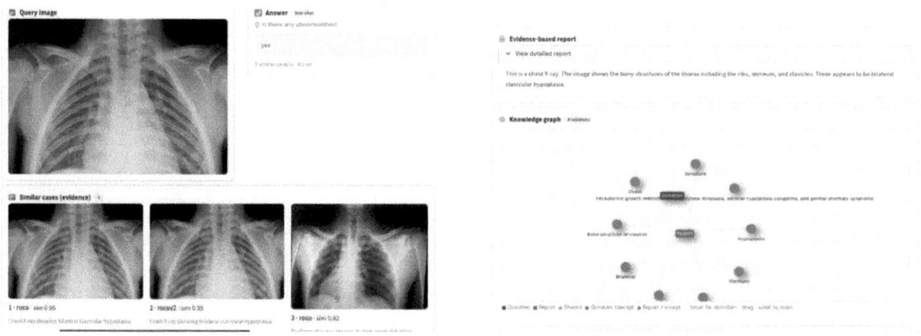

(A) Query, answer, retrieved evidence **(B) Report and knowledge graph**

Fig. 3. What the user sees, does, and can inspect. The user uploads an image (PNG, JPG, DICOM), types a free-text question, and toggles knowledge-graph grounding—so the knowledge layer's contribution is observed live by re-running the same case. No answer is returned alone. (A) The query radiograph (*data*), the answer *yes* tagged with its provenance (three cases, KG on) (*wisdom*), and the retrieved cases with source, similarity score, and ground-truth caption (*information*); the two nearest (sim. 0.95) read *bilateral clavicular hypoplasia.* (B) The evidence-grounded report, which states that same finding, and the concepts linking question to report (*knowledge*). The chain from retrieved caption to report to answer is visible end to end, so a clinician can confirm the finding or reject it when support is thin.

otherwise: on SLAKE and RadImageNet the ablated configurations sometimes score marginally higher. Both pose short, closed-form questions whose reference answers are lexically close to the generated description, so BERTScore-F1 saturates and becomes largely insensitive to *how* the answer was obtained. This is the limit of answer-similarity metrics for the property MedVisionEx targets: they score the answer string, not whether a clinician can check it. A black-box model that scores well still offers nothing to inspect, whereas every answer here arrives with the retrieved cases and the linked concepts that produced it.

6 Limitations and Future Vision

The most prominent limitation is *modality*: pooling radiographs, CT, MRI, and ultrasound in one index lets the encoder retrieve a visually similar neighbour of the wrong modality, and a description grounded in such a neighbour inherits that error; making the retrieval representation explicitly modality-aware is a natural next step. Second, knowledge enters at inference only; folding the serialized knowledge block into the answer model's fine-tuning data would teach it to rely on the graph rather than merely tolerate it. Third, relations are only as rich as the local ontology subset provided, and out-of-distribution query images reduce retrieval coverage and push the system toward zero-shot descriptions.

Scope and Question Complexity. The gallery and ontology steering are at present specialized to radiology, although the architecture is domain-agnostic: the same

Table 1. End-to-end ablation study on four medical VQA benchmarks: VQA-RAD [17], SLAKE [10], ImageCLEF 2019 Med-VQA [11], and RadImageNet-VQA [12]. All values are BERTScore-F1 [2] ($\times 100$).

	Closed-ended				All (closed + open)			
Configuration	RAD	SLAKE	MED	RadIN	RAD	SLAKE	MED	RadIN
Full (KG + Gen)	96.2	93.9	97.5	96.4	89.0	94.2	93.4	92.5
w/o KG	84.3	95.8	82.8	98.0	84.0	94.4	83.0	93.2
w/o Generation	94.2	97.0	95.6	92.9	93.9	96.4	96.2	92.0
w/o KG & Generation	89.4	94.5	95.0	91.5	89.4	94.2	94.8	89.1

RAD = VQA-RAD, MED = VQA-Med'19, RadIN = RadImageNet.

retrieve–describe–ground–answer chain transfers to other imaging domains, such as pathology or dermatology, given a suitable case gallery and ontology subset. Equally, the questions exercised so far are comparatively simple. Assessing whether the system is useful for the real work of a radiologist requires evaluation on complex, practical questions curated with qualified clinicians, and a study in which clinicians judge whether the exposed evidence chain is one they would act on. We regard this clinician-in-the-loop evaluation, rather than a further gain in answer-similarity scores, as the decisive next test of the design.

7 Conclusion

We presented MedVisionEx, an on-premise medical VQA pipeline whose architecture follows the DIKW ascent. Pooling heterogeneous radiology collections into one contrastively learned similarity index, and grounding generation in both retrieved evidence and biomedical ontologies, makes the system's reasoning auditable end to end: the answer arrives with the cases and concepts it rests on, so a clinician can act on it or challenge it. The demonstration lets attendees manipulate the evidence pathway directly and observe its effect on the answers produced.

Acknowledgments. The retrieval component of MedVisionEx, in particular the use of a CLIP-based image encoder for similarity search over radiology cases, was inspired by a capstone project carried out by the first and second authors as part of a course organized by GPT Lab at Tampere University. The authors thank Muhammad Waseem (GPT Lab, Tampere University) and Iftikhar Ahmad (Tieto Finland Oy) for their guidance during that project.

Disclosure of Interests. The authors have no competing interests to declare that are relevant to the content of this article.

References

1. Rowley, J.: The wisdom hierarchy: representations of the DIKW hierarchy. J. Inf. Sci. **33**(2), 163–180 (2007)
2. Zhang, T., Kishore, V., Wu, F., Weinberger, K.Q., Artzi, Y.: BERTScore: evaluating text generation with BERT. In: International Conference on Learning Representations (ICLR) (2020)
3. Johnson, J., Douze, M., Jégou, H.: Billion-scale similarity search with GPUs. IEEE Trans. Big Data **7**(3), 535–547 (2021)
4. Radford, A., et al.: Learning transferable visual models from natural language supervision. In: Proceedings of the 38th International Conference on Machine Learning (ICML), pp. 8748–8763 (2021)
5. Bodenreider, O.: The Unified Medical Language System (UMLS): Integrating biomedical terminology. Nucleic Acids Res. **32**(Database issue), D267–D270 (2004)
6. Neumann, M., King, D., Beltagy, I., Ammar, W.: ScispaCy: fast and robust models for biomedical natural language processing. In: Proceedings of the 18th BioNLP Workshop and Shared Task, pp. 319–327 (2019)
7. Langlotz, C.P.: RadLex: a new method for indexing online educational materials. Radiographics **26**(6), 1595–1597 (2006)
8. Donnelly, K.: SNOMED CT: the advanced terminology and coding system for eHealth. Stud. Health Technol. Inform. **121**, 279–290 (2006)
9. Johnson, A.E.W., et al.: MIMIC-CXR, a de-identified publicly available database of chest radiographs with free-text reports. Sci. Data **6**, 317 (2019)
10. Liu, B., Zhan, L.-M., Xu, L., Ma, L., Yang, Y., Wu, X.: SLAKE: a semanticallylabeled knowledge-enhanced dataset for medical visual question answering. In: IEEE International Symposium on Biomedical Imaging (ISBI), pp. 1650–1654 (2021)
11. Ben Abacha, A., Hasan, S.A., Datla, V., Liu, J., Demner-Fushman, D., Müller, H.: VQA-Med: Overview of the medical visual question answering task at ImageCLEF 2019. In: CLEF 2019 Working Notes, CEUR Workshop Proceedings (2019)
12. Butsanets, L., Corbière, C., Khlaut, J., Manceron, P., Dancette, C.: RadImageNetVQA: a Large-Scale CT and MRI Dataset for Radiologic Visual Question Answering. In: Medical Imaging with Deep Learning (MIDL) (2026)
13. Sellergren, A., et al.: MedGemma Technical report. arXiv preprint arXiv:2507.05201 (2025)
14. van den Oord, A., Li, Y., Vinyals, O.: Representation Learning with Contrastive Predictive Coding. arXiv preprint arXiv:1807.03748 (2018)
15. Pelka, O., Koitka, S., Rückert, J., Nensa, F., Friedrich, C.M.: Radiology Objects in COntext (ROCO): a multimodal image dataset. In: Large-scale Annotation of Biomedical Data and Expert Label Synthesis (LABELS 2018), Lecture Notes in Computer Science, vol. 11043, pp. 180–189. Springer (2018)
16. Rückert, J., et al.: ROCOv2: Radiology Objects in COntext Version 2, an Updated Multimodal Image Dataset. Sci. Data **11**, 688 (2024)
17. Lau, J.J., Gayen, S., Ben Abacha, A., Demner-Fushman, D.: A dataset of clinically generated visual questions and answers about radiology images. Sci. Data **5**, 180251 (2018)

An Interactive Framework for Data Generation from JSON Schema

Lyes Attouche[1], Mohamed-Amine Baazizi[2], Nour ElHouda Ben Ali[3(✉)], and Dario Colazzo[3]

[1] Université Paris Nanterre, Paris, France
lattouche@parisnanterre.fr
[2] LIP6 UMR 7606, Sorbonne Université, Paris, France
mohamed-amine.baazizi@lip6.fr
[3] Université Paris-Dauphine – PSL, Paris, France
nour-el-houda.ben-ali@dauphine.eu, dario.colazzo@lamsade.dauphine.fr

Abstract. JSON Schema is the de facto standard for describing the structure of JSON collections and is adopted in major data-driven applications. Testing, benchmarking, and debugging these applications relies on synthetic data generated from schemas. Existing techniques for data generation provide limited control on the generation process and usually act as black boxes, preventing users from exploring alternative values captured in schema branches. To address this limitation, we propose an interactive framework built on top of our optimistic generator [1,2], allowing for greater flexibility in the generation process. The framework exposes schema branches and records user choices to generate data for selected alternatives. It supports three complementary interaction modes requiring increasing user involvement: a *Default* mode with a fully automatic generation; an *Exploratory* mode with features allowing an incremental navigation of schema alternatives; and a *User-Guided* mode offering an advanced control over generation with the ability to select schema branches interactively.

Keywords: JSON · JSON Schema · Data Management

1 Introduction

JSON Schema is the standard language for describing the structure and constraints of JSON documents. Generating valid JSON instances from a schema is essential for testing, benchmarking, and validating modern data-driven applications [4,5,10]. This task is challenging because JSON Schema combines structural constraints with boolean operators, references, recursion, and negation.

Recent work has studied both the complexity of JSON Schema reasoning [7] and witness generation, i.e., producing instances satisfying a schema [1–5]. Other tools focus on synthetic data generation [6,8,9,11]. Among them, the optimistic approach [1,2] stands out by generating multiple valid instances while preserving soundness and improving efficiency.

© The Author(s), under exclusive license to Springer Nature Switzerland AG 2027
G. Vargas Solar et al. (Eds.): ADBIS 2026, CCIS 3175, pp. 236–243, 2027.
https://doi.org/10.1007/978-3-032-39823-9_22

Despite these advances, existing generators remain mostly automatic: users provide a schema and receive instances, with little visibility into generation choices or control over alternative schema branches.

To address this limitation, we built an interactive framework on top of the optimistic generator [1,2], enabling observable and steerable instance generation. The framework exposes schema alternatives and supports three interaction modes: *Default*, for fully automatic generation; *Exploratory*, for incremental discovery of alternative branches; and *Guided*, for explicit branch selection and targeted generation.

This flexibility is essential and allows the framework to be accessible to advanced users, who can debug schemas and inspect alternatives, but also for non-expert users, who can use it to better understand JSON Schema semantics.

Availability. The source code and demonstration material are available in the project repository.[1]

The remainder of this paper is organized as follows. Section 2 recalls the necessary background on JSON Schema and optimistic witness generation. Section 3 presents the architecture of the framework. Section 4 describes the three interaction modes through a running example. Finally, Sect. 5 concludes and discusses future extensions.

2 Background

2.1 JSON Schema

JSON Schema is a standard language for describing valid JSON documents. Several versions have been introduced, the most recent being Draft 2020-12 [13], although earlier drafts remain widely used in practice. A schema is itself a JSON document composed of *typed assertions*, where the keyword *type* specifies the kind of values targeted (e.g., objects, arrays, strings, numbers), together with type-specific constraints.

For example, strings and numbers can be constrained using keywords such as `pattern`, `minLength`, `maximum`, or `multipleOf`. Arrays can be constrained by size, item schemas, containment, and uniqueness through `uniqueItems`. Objects can be constrained by their properties, required fields, admissible property names, and number of properties. JSON Schema also supports logical operators such as `anyOf`(disjunction), `allOf`(conjunction), and `not`(negation), as well as references for defining reusable schema fragments.

Example 1. Consider the following schema. It accepts objects that must contain a property `a`. The value of this property must be a string matching the pattern `a(c|d)*`. In addition, the schema defines `patternProperties` for property names matching the regular expression `a|b`, requiring their values to be strings that match the pattern `a(c|e)*`. This means that properties named `a` or `b` are further constrained by this rule. Finally, the keyword `additionalProperties`

[1] https://gitlab.lip6.fr/benalil/jsongen.

is set to `true`, allowing any other extra properties beyond those explicitly described.

```
{ "type": "object",
  "required": ["a"],
  "properties": {
    "a": {
      "type": "string",
      "pattern": "a(c|d)*"
    }
  },
  "patternProperties": {
    "a|b": {
      "type": "string",
      "pattern": "a(c|e)*"
    }
  },
  "additionalProperties": true}
```

This schema illustrates an important challenge in JSON Schema instance generation: the interaction between `properties` and `patternProperties`. In particular, the property `a` is explicitly defined in `properties` with the constraint that its value must match the pattern `a(c|d)*`. At the same time, the regular expression in `patternProperties` (`a|b`) also matches the property name `a`, imposing an additional constraint that its value must match `a(c|e)*`. As a result, the value of `a` must satisfy both `pattern` constraints simultaneously. This creates an intersection problem between the two regular languages, meaning that generation cannot treat these constraints independently. Instead, it must compute values belonging to the intersection of both patterns to ensure validity.

2.2 Optimistic JSON Schema Generation

The generation technique introduced in [1,2] was designed as a compromise between sound and complete witness generation [3–5] and practical open-source generators [6,8,9,11].The former guarantees soundness and completeness but relies on costly preprocessing, while the latter prioritizes efficiency but may produce invalid instances. Optimistic generation preserves soundness while improving efficiency. It covers most of JSON Schema Draft 2019 [12], excluding few features such as dynamic references.

The approach is *sound but incomplete*: generated instances are always valid and unsatisfiable schemas may sometimes be detected. However, the generator may fail to produce an instance or detect unsatisfiability, mainly because negation is handled only when safe simplifications are possible.

A distinctive feature of this approach is its ability to produce several distinct valid instances from the same schema.[2] in contrast to the complete witness

[2] The optimistic approach also supports `uniqueItems`, unlike the sound and complete technique [3–5] and most practical generators, although multiple-instance generation with `uniqueItems` is not yet supported,.

generator, which returns a single witness. This multiple-generation capability is central to our framework as it enables exploration of different valid documents for the same schema.

Generation starts with a preprocessing phase that resolves references and canonicalizes schemas into a form better suited for generation. In particular, canonicalization makes alternative branches explicit, typically through `"anyOf"` expressions. These branches form the basis for the interactive choices exposed by our framework.

Example 2. Consider the following schema, which accepts either strings of length at least three or non-negative numbers.

```
{ "type": ["string", "number"],
  "minLength": 3,
  "minimum": 0 }
```

After canonicalization, the implicit alternatives become explicit as an `"anyOf"` expression.

```
{ "anyOf": [
     { "type": "string", "minLength": 3 },
     { "type": "number", "minimum": 0 } ] }
```

These two branches correspond to distinct generation choices: one for strings and one for numbers.

Our framework builds directly on this canonical disjunctive form, using the optimistic generator for efficient sound generation while exposing alternative branches for inspection, exploration, and user guidance.

3 System Overview

The system provides a graphical interface for JSON instance generation while relying on the optimistic generator as its backend. It follows a client-server architecture. The client side offers a web interface for editing schemas, configuring generation parameters, and inspecting generated instances. The server side wraps the optimistic generator and exposes its functionalities through a REST API. Figure 1 gives an overview of the architecture and the data flows across the three interaction modes.

The frontend is centered around a schema editor, which also serves as a branch viewer, and an output panel. Users can write or paste a JSON Schema, inspect schema alternatives returned by the backend, and visualize the generated JSON instances.

The backend, implemented in Scala and exposed through Play, provides two main operations. The first executes the generation pipeline, from parsing and preprocessing to instance generation, and returns either generated instances alone or instances together with their corresponding branches. The second stops after canonicalization and returns the canonicalized schema, where alternatives are

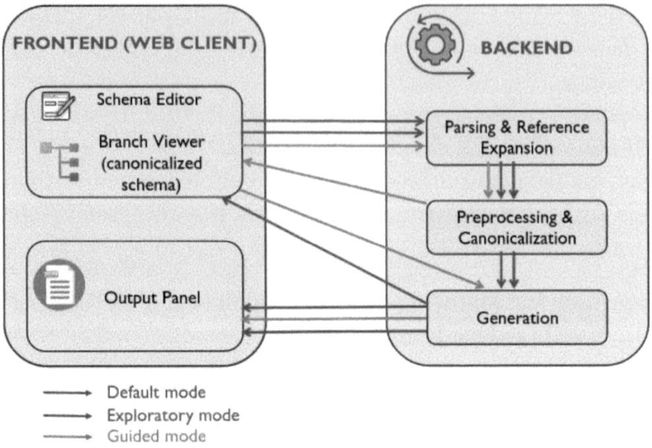

Fig. 1. Instance generation pipeline from a JSON Schema.

made explicit. These branches can then be explored or selected by users before being sent back for targeted generation. The system allows users to specify the number of JSON instances to generate for each request. Generated instances are persisted on disk, enabling the production of large data without requiring users to manually save intermediate results. The *Default* and *Guided* modes naturally support the generation of large numbers of instances, since generation proceeds automatically once the user specifies the requested amount. In contrast, the *Exploratory* mode is intended for interactive inspection of schema alternatives and is therefore better suited to generating a limited number of instances. In both modes, the exploration of schema branches is deterministic and follows the order in which the branches appear in the schema.

4 Demonstration Scenario

The workbench is endowed with three interaction modes, with increasing user involvement. The *Default* mode is meant to give users an overview of instance generation. Users specify n the number of desired instances to generate and the system retrieves the instances from the backend in a batch mode and is dedicated to cases where n is not too large so that users are not overwhelmed by the size of the generated data.

The *Exploratory* mode goes one step further by yielding a set of n diversified instances obtained by exploring different branches of the schema. This mode allows user to navigate a space of diverse instances while indicating, for each generated instance, some provenance information about which branch of the schema served to generate a specific instance. This mode is particularly useful for schemas containing disjunctions or optional structures.

The *Guided* mode gives users explicit control over the generation. The schema is first canonicalized and is displayed as a tree of selectable branches. Users can select branches and specify how many instances to generate from each. The outputs are organized by branch, preserving the correspondence between the selected alternatives and the generated instances. This mode is useful for testing specific schema parts, comparing alternatives, and debugging complex specifications.

4.1 Running Example

We illustrate the three modes using the following schema, which admits three alternatives: an object describing a user profile, an array of tags, or a document status.

```
{ "anyOf": [
 { "type": "object",
   "properties": {
    "role": { "enum": ["admin","guest","editor"]},
    "active": { "type": "boolean" }},
   "required": ["role", "active"]},
 { "type": "array", "minItems": 2,
   "items": { "enum": ["red", "green", "blue"]}},
 { "enum": ["draft", "published", "archived"]}]}
```

This JSON Schema uses the `anyOf` keyword to define a value that may conform to one of the three alternative structures. The value can be an object with the required properties `role` and `active`, where `role` is restricted to predefined values. Alternatively, it can be an array containing at least two elements, each chosen from many alternatives: `red`, `green`, or `blue`. Finally, the value may simply be a string taking one of the enumerated values `draft`, `published`, or `archived`.

In *Default* mode (Fig. 2), the user provides the schema and requests a number of instances, for example three. The system automatically makes the generation decisions and returns a collection of valid JSON values. In the example shown,

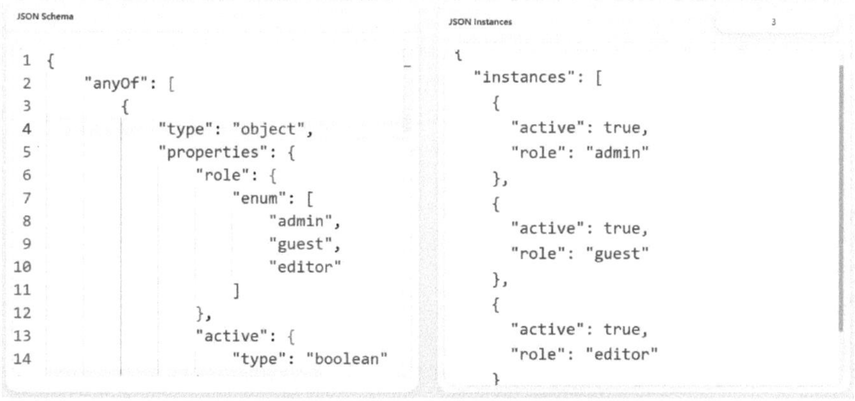

Fig. 2. *Default* mode: automatic generation of instances.

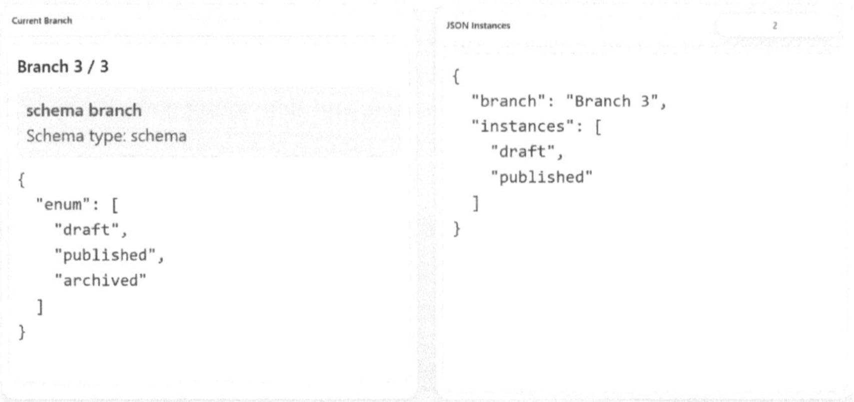

Fig. 3. *Exploratory* mode: progressive exploration of schema alternatives.

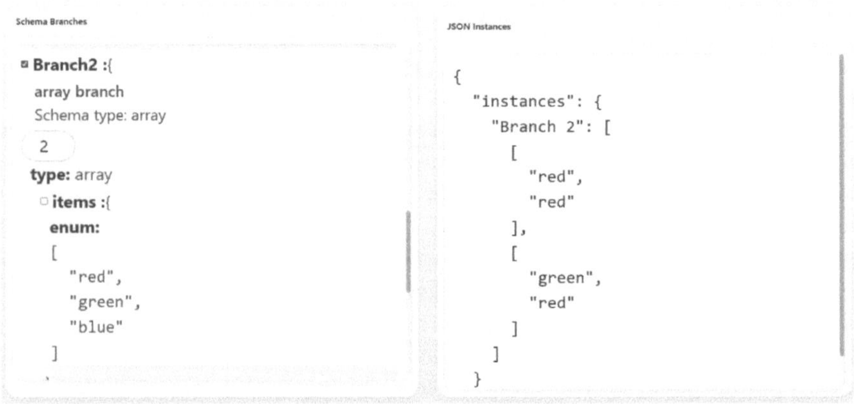

Fig. 4. *Guided* mode: branch selection before instance generation.

the three generated instances are objects produced from the first branch, with different combinations of values for the `role` and `active` properties.

In *Exploratory* mode (Fig. 3), the same schema is used to progressively discover valid alternative instances. The user does not manually select the schema branches. Instead, each request for a new instance lets the system explore another generation choice whenever possible. In the example shown, the exploration has reached the third branch of the schema, corresponding to the status values `draft`, `published`, and `archived`.

In *Guided* mode (Fig. 4), the schema is first transformed into its canonical representation and displayed as an interactive tree of generation choices. The alternatives introduced by `anyOf` appear explicitly as selectable branches. In the example shown, the user selects the second branch and requests two instances from it.

5 Conclusion and Future Work

This paper presented an interactive framework for optimistic JSON Schema instance generation, enabling users to explore schema alternatives through multiple interaction modes. Future work includes supporting more complex constraints, such as `uniqueItems`, and integrating large language models to improve data realism and explain generation failures. We also plan to study how to effectively store large sets of instances and to add features for exporting the result of interaction.

References

1. Attouche, L.: Data Generation for JSON Schema. Theses, Université Paris sciences et lettres (2024). https://theses.hal.science/tel-04888295
2. Attouche, L., Baazizi, M.A., Colazzo, D.: Optimistic Data Generation for JSON Schema, pp. 119–152. Springer, Heidelberg (2024). https://doi.org/10.1007/978-3-662-69603-3_5
3. Attouche, L., et al.: A tool for JSON schema witness generation. In: Proceeding EDBT, pp. 694–697 (2021). https://doi.org/10.5441/002/edbt.2021.86
4. Attouche, L., Baazizi, M.A., Colazzo, D., Ghelli, G., Sartiani, C., Scherzinger, S.: Witness generation for JSON schema. Proc. VLDB Endow. **15**(13), 4002–4014 (2022). https://www.vldb.org/pvldb/vol15/p4002-sartiani.pdf
5. Attouche, L., Baazizi, M.A., Colazzo, D., Ghelli, G., Sartiani, C., Scherzinger, S.: Witness generation for classical Json schema. ACM Trans. Database Syst. (2026)
6. Blackler, J.: Json generator (2023). https://github.com/jimblackler/jsongenerator. Retrieved October 2023
7. Bourhis, P., Reutter, J.L., Suárez, F., Vrgoc, D.: JSON: data model, Query languages and Schema specification. In: Proceeding PODS, pp. 123–135 (2017). https://doi.org/10.1145/3034786.3056120
8. Cabrera, A.: Json schema faker. https://github.com/json-schema-faker/json-schema-faker/. Retrieved May 2026 (2026)
9. Dennis, G.: Json-everything (2026). available at https://github.com/gregsdennis/json-everything. Retrieved April 2026
10. Habib, A., Shinnar, A., Hirzel, M., Pradel, M.: Finding data compatibility bugs with JSON subschema checking. In: Proceeding ISSTA'21 (2021)
11. Hatfield-Dodds, Z.: Hypothesis json schema. https://github.com/Zac-HD/hypothesis-jsonschema . Retrieved May 2026 (2026)
12. Wright, A., Andrews, H., Hutton, B.: JSON Schema validation: a vocabulary for structural validation of json - draft-handrews-json-schema-validation-02. Tech. rep., Internet Engineering Task Force (2019). https://tools.ietf.org/html/draft-handrews-json-schema-validation-02. retrieved Nov. 2023
13. Wright, A., Andrews, H., Hutton, B.: JSON Schema validation: a vocabulary for structural validation of json - draft-bhutton-json-schema-validation-00. Technical report, Internet Engineering Task Force (2020). https://tools.ietf.org/html/draft-bhutton-json-schema-validation-00. retrieved June 2025

From Polypheny to MATLAB: Benchmarking Retrieval Speedup on Heterogeneous Data for the First Polystore Connector in MATLAB

Fynn Gohlke[1(✉)] and Marco Vogt[2]

[1] University of Basel, Basel, Switzerland
fynn.gohlke@stud.unibas.ch
[2] University of Applied Sciences and Arts Northwestern Switzerland, Basel, Switzerland
marco.vogt@fhnw.ch

Abstract. Modern applications increasingly depend on heterogeneous data distributed across relational, document, and graph stores. Because these systems have traditionally been managed independently, applications often need to retrieve large intermediate results and perform filtering and joining on the client side, resulting in considerable processing and transfer overhead. Polystores address this limitation by providing unified access to heterogeneous data models and enabling cross-model processing within the data-management system. However, MATLAB currently lacks middleware that exposes these capabilities through a unified interface. To close this gap, we present, to the best of our knowledge, the first MATLAB connector for a multi-model polystore. The connector enables MATLAB to access Polypheny, executing queries and joins across relational, document, and graph data. In a single-host setup, server-side cross-model filtering reduces the number of transferred records and yields end-to-end speedups of up to 42× over client-side filtering. We further analyze how the reduction in transfer volume affects retrieval time in network-accessible client-server deployments under different latency assumptions. To demonstrate the connector, we use a synthetic Ebola and malaria outbreak dataset in a triage-assistance pipeline. The scenario uses cross-model joins to efficiently assemble heterogeneous patient context sets for TabPFN.

Keywords: PolyDBMS · Polystore · MATLAB

1 Introduction

Hospitals and crisis-response teams facing Ebola and malaria outbreaks must make treatment decisions under severe resource constraints and rapidly changing conditions. In these settings, triage (the timely assessment of patient criticality) is essential for allocating resources and improving patient outcomes. Following the 2018-2020 Ebola outbreak in the Democratic Republic of Congo,

© The Author(s), under exclusive license to Springer Nature Switzerland AG 2027
G. Vargas Solar et al. (Eds.): ADBIS 2026, CCIS 3175, pp. 244–251, 2027.
https://doi.org/10.1007/978-3-032-39823-9_23

treatment facilities began adopting data-informed decision-support tools for this purpose [1]. Recurring outbreaks make machine-learning-assisted triage a continuing priority and create a need for efficient retrieval mechanisms that support frequent updates.

Such workflows rely on heterogeneous data, including relational patient data, document-oriented symptom histories, and graph-based regional or treatment-location information. When these data models are managed by separate database systems, each system introduces operational costs and prevents data from being joined before transfer. Applications must consequently retrieve large intermediate results and filter them on the client side. In network-accessible deployments, the resulting transfer overhead is further amplified by latency. For predictors such as TabPFN [2] (a foundation model to classify tabular data), which may require repeated construction of in-context sets, this can make timely updates impractical.

Polystores and PolyDBMSs [8], such as Polypheny [7,9], address this problem by providing unified access to heterogeneous data. Polypheny uses optimized database systems as execution engines while maintaining efficient query processing [6]. Users can issue queries in different languages and perform server-side filtering as part of cross-model joins, substantially reducing the amount of data transferred to the client.

Despite these advantages, MATLAB users currently lack a connector that exposes unified multi-model polystore access and cross-model queries. This is particularly limiting because MATLAB is widely used for numerical workflows in life sciences and engineering. The connector presented in this paper closes this gap by providing a unified MATLAB interface for heterogeneous data access.

The contributions of this work are threefold. First, we design and implement, to the best of our knowledge, the first MATLAB connector for a multi-model polystore. It exposes Polypheny's relational, document, graph, and cross-model query capabilities and supports nested-result conversion, batching, transactions, as well as pull- and push-based streaming. Second, we evaluate server-side cross-model filtering across different dataset sizes and query selectivities, showing a significant reduction of the number of transferred records and resulting speedups of up to 42× over client-side filtering in a single-host setup; we also analyze its effect under different network-latency assumptions. Third, we demonstrate the connector on a synthetic Ebola and malaria outbreak dataset by constructing heterogeneous patient context sets for TabPFN.

2 Demonstration

The demonstration presents an end-to-end triage-assistance workflow in which MATLAB retrieves heterogeneous patient data from Polypheny and assembles context sets for outcome prediction with TabPFN [2]. The demonstration uses a synthetic Ebola and malaria outbreak dataset inspired by reports on historical outbreaks [3]. We assume a network-accessible deployment in which patient information is distributed across relational records, document-based clinical observations, and graph-based treatment-location data. Context sets are refreshed as new patient information becomes available. Our demonstration proceeds in five stages:

1. **Batch ingestion.** We first use the connector's batch-execution functionality to insert relational patient records and document-based clinical information into Polypheny.
2. **Context-set construction.** A server-side cross-model join is executed to select patients with high pathogen loads who are infected with Ebola and malaria. Filtered records are returned directly to MATLAB and used to construct a context set for TabPFN, avoiding the transfer and client-side filtering of unrelated records.
3. **Result rendering.** Next, we execute native SQL and MongoQL queries and show how the connector represents their results in MATLAB. This includes relational tables, flat documents, and nested document structures.
4. **Streaming interface.** The connector's streaming functionality is demonstrated through a custom MATLAB table interface. Users can request the next batch through the interface, making the streaming process visible while avoiding the need to load the complete result into memory.
5. **Three-model join.** Finally, a cross-model query spanning relational patient information, document-based clinical observations, and graph-based treatment-location information is executed, showcasing how Polypheny combines all three data models on the server and returns a filtered, analysis-ready result to MATLAB.

An excerpt of the demo is available in a short video[1] that showcases selected capabilities of the connector.

3 Implementation

As illustrated in Fig. 1, the connector uses a MATLAB wrapper and a Java backend. The Java backend communicates with the Polypheny server through a modified JDBC driver, using reflection to bypass the driver's exposed object-oriented functionality - a deliberate design choice aimed at maximizing performance during result handling and minimizing overhead. After the result handling in the Java backend the MATLAB wrapper efficiently casts the incoming Java results to MATLAB types.

To exploit MATLAB's vectorized architecture, the connector transposes the row-oriented result layout of Polypheny's JDBC driver into a column-based representation, allowing entire columns of primitives or strings to be consumed into a MATLAB table's column in a single operation, rather than iterating over individual entries of an object of type `Object[][]`. This reduces the number of MATLAB-Java crossings from $N \times M$ to M, where N denotes the number of rows and M the number of columns.

[1] https://download-dbis.dmi.unibas.ch/paper/ADBIS2026.mp4.

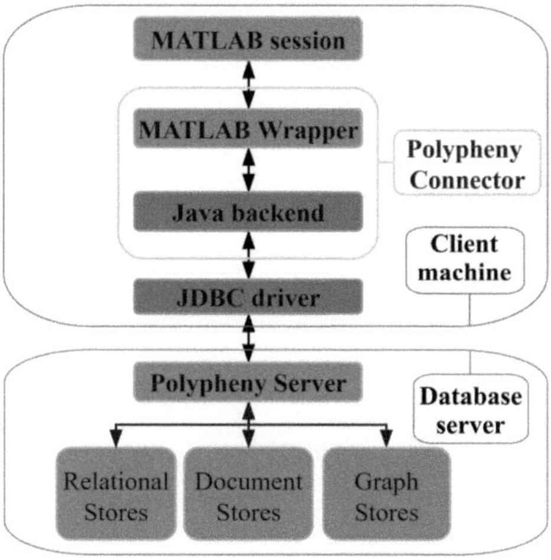

Fig. 1. Architecture of the Polypheny connector for MATLAB.

For relational data resulting from an SQL query, atomic values from an incoming SQL query result are unwrapped, cast to Java types, and handed to the MATLAB wrapper as an array of primitives or strings. Because Polypheny allows nested data, including nested documents and arrays through its cross-model support, entries are parsed recursively and mapped to valid JSON, allowing the data to be parsed into structures or cells using MATLAB's integrated `jsondecode` function.

Document records resulting from a MongoQL query are cast to JSON and stored as an array of strings for efficient handling. The MATLAB wrapper then converts the column of JSON entries to cells (for flat documents or arrays) or structures (for nested documents or arrays), as illustrated in the demo video.

The connector provides a pull- and push-based streaming mechanism for large result sets. The pull-based design is particularly suited for complex algorithms where the streaming process must be directly exposed to the algorithm. Memory safety is ensured through a pushback mechanism. The pull-based approach is illustrated in the demo video, to implement a MATLAB table interface illustrating the concept of streaming. The push-based mechanism allows users to pass simple algorithms as a function handle to the connector, which applies the function to each batch of streamed data before returning the final result to the user.

For both SQL and MongoQL, batch execution is supported, allowing multiple statements to be sent in a single MATLAB-Java crossing. Full transaction support and automatic rollback on failure are ensured.

The Polypheny connector is distributed as a MATLAB toolbox via MATLAB's Add-On Explorer. To ensure compatibility with older MATLAB releases of MATLAB R2020a and later [4], all `.jar` files are compiled using Java 8.

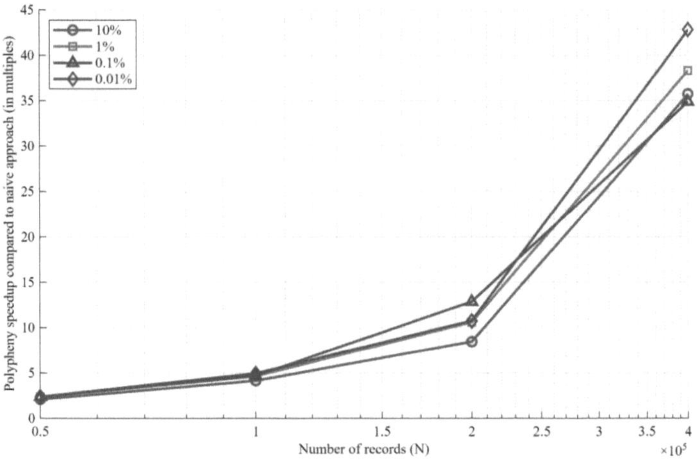

Fig. 2. Demonstration of superlinear speedup through server-side filtering across different query selectivities and increasing number of records.

4 Benchmarks

The connector exposes Polypheny's cross-model join capability directly to MATLAB, minimizing data transfer by pushing join and filter operations to the server. We illustrate this using our synthetic outbreak dataset, containing 2,000,000 patients spanning relational patient records (diagnoses), document-based clinical (viral loads), and graph-based regional data (treatment facilities). To perform context inference on Ebola patients with high viral loads from hospital 16 using TabPFN, only the relevant patient subset needs to be transferred. Executing the join server-side in Polypheny significantly reduces the number of transferred records, as shown in the following table:

Filter stage	**Records**	**Remaining**
Total patients	2,000,000	100%
Ebola (relational)	1,000,000	50%
+ high viral load (document)	714,554	∼36%
+ hospital 16† (graph)	14,291	∼0.7%

† Hospital 16 was selected arbitrarily for demonstration.

Naively querying the entire dataset and performing the filtering client-side would have yielded three separate queries of 2,000,000 relational, document, and graph records, for a total transfer load of 6,000,000 records. A semi-naive approach filtering for Ebola diagnoses in the relational store, high viral load in the document store, and treatment location in the graph store can only reduce the transferred records to 1,000,000 Ebola patients, 811,051 patients with high viral load, and 40,000 patients from hospital 16, totalling 1,851,051 records. The retrieval volume is still over 120 times the number of records the Polypheny-enabled cross-model query has to transfer. Depending on the necessary requerying intervals and server-client latency, Polypheny's ability for server-side filtering could determine whether the workflow remains feasible. To demonstrate the impact of the reduction in transferred records, we benchmarked the runtime of a cross-model join on the same dataset for different selectivities as shown in Fig. 2.

Table 1. Server-side cross-model (Polypheny) vs. client-side (naive) filtering across selectivities, for four dataset sizes.

N	Selectivity	Polypheny (s)	Naive (s)	Speedup	Poly. rows	Naive rows
50,000	10 %	6.95	14.61	2.10×	5,000	50,000
50,000	1 %	5.96	14.07	2.36×	500	50,000
50,000	0.1 %	6.53	15.53	2.38×	50	50,000
50,000	0.01 %	6.41	15.25	2.38×	5	50,000
100,000	10 %	14.84	61.43	4.14×	10,000	100,000
100,000	1 %	12.69	59.03	4.65×	1,000	100,000
100,000	0.1 %	12.10	56.75	4.69×	100	100,000
100,000	0.01 %	11.84	58.55	4.95×	10	100,000
200,000	10 %	31.21	264.14	8.46×	20,000	200,000
200,000	1 %	27.46	291.31	10.61×	2,000	200,000
200,000	0.1 %	27.68	356.21	12.87×	200	200,000
200,000	0.01 %	30.46	327.81	10.76×	20	200,000
400,000	10 %	51.59	1842.71	35.72×	40,000	400,000
400,000	1 %	43.66	1673.06	38.32×	4,000	400,000
400,000	0.1 %	43.63	1521.66	34.88×	400	400,000
400,000	0.01 %	42.83	1833.97	42.82×	40	400,000

The server-side filtering showed a speedup of more than 40 times. For a more detailed illustration, we refer to the results shown in Table 1. As mentioned earlier, these local retrieval times are compounded by latency in network-accessible data stores. This is further illustrated in Fig. 3 where the network overhead generated through latency is depicted for three different latency assumptions.

In this section, we will demonstrate the approximately linear runtime behavior of our connector. All time measurements were performed within MATLAB using Polypheny version 0.10.2 with an HSQLDB in-memory storage adapter on an 11th Gen Intel(R) Core(TM) i9-11950H @ 2.60 GHz machine with 32 GB of RAM and a 1 TB SSD. To ensure unbiased runs as a result of the adapter's memory allocation, Polypheny was redeployed before each benchmark run to clear memory. Run times remained almost invariant when using PostgreSQL and MongoDB Docker adapters for SQL and MongoQL queries. Both write and read queries showed stable, asymptotically linear behavior. The flat slope of the read query in Fig. 4 demonstrates the efficient result casting of the connector. Cross-model queries using an SQL-based join on the relational and document-based datasets from the previous benchmarks also showed approximate linear behavior with runtimes largely equal to the cumulated read times of SQL and MongoDB queries in Fig. 4.

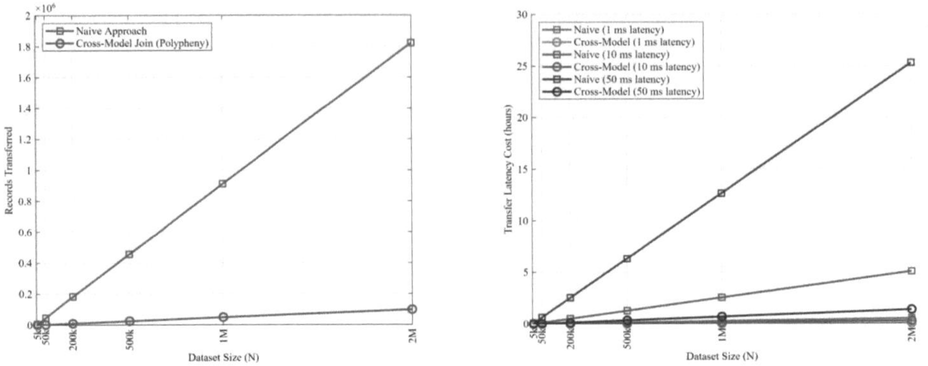

Fig. 3. Record transfer reduction for malaria patient profiles with high parasite density (l) and corresponding network retrieval latency overhead for different latency assumptions (r).

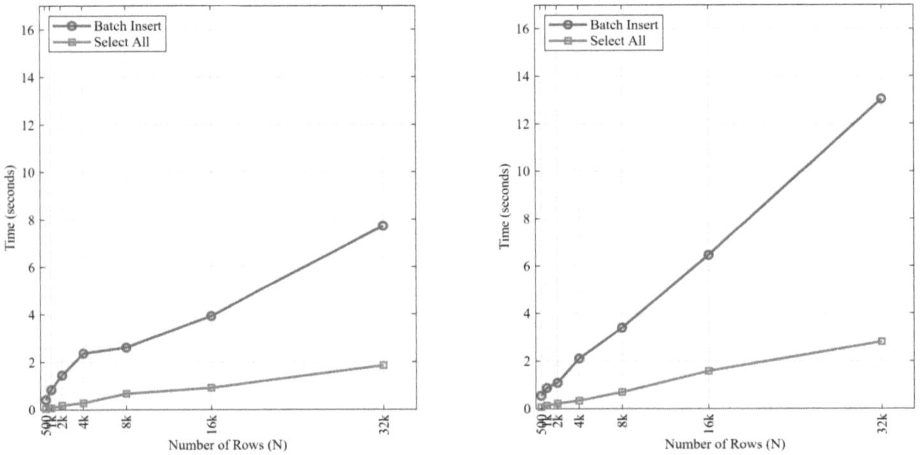

Fig. 4. Benchmark for relational and document data using SQL (left) and MongoQL (right), respectively.

5 Conclusion and Outlook

By bringing Polypheny to MATLAB, the connector closes the gap between MATLAB and modern multi-model polystore systems. It allows users to efficiently pair MATLAB's utility in workflows from data science to engineering applications with the performance of a modern polystore, including easy switching between query languages and performing server-side cross-model joins. Section 4 demonstrated approximately linear scaling for SQL as well as MongoQL read and write queries. We further showed that server-side cross-model joins can greatly reduce the number of transferred records. The streaming and batching functionality enables full integration into existing MATLAB workflows.

As future work, we plan to allow users to pass vectors or tables into the query function, which will be executed as parameterized statements. In order to utilize MATLAB's Parallel Toolbox [5] and enable parallelization workflows, connection pooling should be implemented.

6 GenAI Usage Disclosure

During the writing of this paper, generative AI (GenAI) tools have been used in limited, non-substantive ways. Specifically, we used ChatGPT (OpenAI) to help refine grammar and improve clarity in the manuscript. All technical content, research insights, and model designs are solely authored by the authors without any GenAI-generated ideas. The GenAI tools did not contribute to the intellectual content or scientific conclusions. Claude (Anthropic) was used to assist in the generation of the demo scripts. Furthermore, it helped with the benchmarks, especially with debugging. For the connector itself, ChatGPT (OpenAI) and Gemini (Google) were used for debugging and minor code completions.

References

1. Ardiet, D.L.: Rapid decision algorithm for patient triage during Ebola outbreaks. Emerg. Infect. Dis. **30**(11) (2024). https://doi.org/10.3201/eid3011.231650
2. Hollmann, N., Müller, S., Eggensperger, K., Hutter, F.: Accurate predictions on small data with a tabular foundation model. Nature **637**(8045) (2025)
3. Li, S., et al.: Age and Ebola viral load correlate with mortality and survival time in 288 Ebola virus disease patients. Int. J. Infect. Dis. **42**, 34–39 (2016). https://doi.org/10.1016/j.ijid.2015.11.005
4. MathWorks: MATLAB support for OpenJDK. https://mathworks.com/support/requirements/openjdk.html. Accessed 04 June 2026
5. MathWorks: Parallel computing toolbox. https://mathworks.com/products/parallel-computing.html. Accessed 06 June 2026
6. Vogt, M.: Adaptive management of multimodel data and heterogeneous workloads. Ph.D. thesis, University of Basel (2022). https://doi.org/10/gnxv2h
7. Vogt, M., et al.: Polypheny-DB: towards bridging the gap between polystores and HTAP systems. In: Heterogeneous Data Management, Polystores, and Analytics for Healthcare, Poly 2020 and DMAH 2020, pp. 25–36. Springer (2020). https://doi.org/10/gnxv2h
8. Vogt, M., et al.: Polystore systems and DBMSs: Love marriage or marriage of convenience? In: Heterogeneous Data Management, Polystores, and Analytics for Healthcare, vol. 12921, pp. 65–69. Springer (2021)
9. Vogt, M., Stiemer, A., Schuldt, H.: Polypheny-DB: towards a distributed and self-adaptive polystore. In: Proceedings of the 2018 IEEE International Conference on Big Data, pp. 3364–3373. IEEE (2018). https://doi.org/10/gnxv2j

Doctoral Consortium School

CO-FREDA: A Co-participative, Frugal and Justice-Oriented AI Methodology for Responsible Data-Algorithm Driven Science

Genoveva Vargas-Solar(✉)

CNRS, INSA Lyon, Université Lyon 1 Claude Bernard, LIRIS, UMR5205, 69221 Lyon, France
genoveva.vargas-solar@cnrs.fr

Abstract. This paper introduces CO-FREDA (co-participative Frugal, Responsible, Equitable Data-Algorithm Driven Science) as a methodology for designing AI systems that are technically robust, resource-aware, and socially accountable. CO-FREDA combines contemporary computing methods with feminist and decolonial perspectives to move beyond technosolutionism and support end-to-end socio-technical design. It integrates sovereignty-aware data architectures, privacy-preserving and distributed learning, and resource-aware deployment across cloud–edge–fog infrastructures.

The methodology translates collective and horizontal approaches, including Data Feminism, Design Justice, the methodology COIA (Codiseñando una IA feminista), and community-led initiatives into concrete technical decisions: problem formulation, dataset documentation, evaluation protocols, governance mechanisms, consent and refusal processes, and auditable decision-making. Through case-driven experimentation, CO-FREDA supports reproducible pipelines and model stress-testing under real-world constraints, including heterogeneous devices, missing data, biased labels, limited connectivity, and unequal access to infrastructure. The result is a practical framework for building AI systems that are performant, explainable, deployable, and aligned with justice-oriented research rather than extractive optimisation.

Keywords: responsible data science methodology · responsible AI · feminist and decolonial computing · resource-aware AI deployment · socio-technical data governance

1 Introduction

This paper introduces CO-FREDA (co-participative Frugal, Responsible, Equitable and Data-Algorithm Driven Science) as a methodology for designing AI

Supported by the AAP program of the CNRS and the project FRIENDLY of the transversal projects program of the LIRIS.

© The Author(s), under exclusive license to Springer Nature Switzerland AG 2027
G. Vargas Solar et al. (Eds.): ADBIS 2026, CCIS 3175, pp. 255–270, 2027.
https://doi.org/10.1007/978-3-032-39823-9_24

systems that are technically robust, environmentally frugal, and socially accountable. CO-FREDA combines contemporary data management, distributed learning, and resource-aware computing with feminist and decolonial perspectives. Its objective is to resist technosolutionism[1] and to make explicit the social, cultural, political, territorial, and ecological conditions in which AI systems are conceived, deployed, and evaluated.

The methodology supports end-to-end socio-technical design. It addresses sovereignty-aware data architectures based on metadata, provenance, access control, and policy-as-code; privacy-preserving and distributed learning through federated and incremental training, data minimisation, and robustness under dataset shift; and resource-aware deployment across cloud–edge–fog infrastructures through multi-objective scheduling, energy and carbon accounting, and auditable decision logs.

A central contribution of CO-FREDA is the translation of collective and horizontal methodologies, such as Data Feminism, Design Justice, and community-led approaches and COIA (Co-diseñando una IA feminista) [22], into concrete technical decisions. These decisions concern problem formulation, dataset documentation, evaluation protocols, governance mechanisms, and the integration of consent, refusal, and accountability into AI pipelines. Through case-driven experimentation, CO-FREDA supports reproducible pipelines and model stress-testing under real-world constraints, including heterogeneous devices, missing data, biased labels, limited infrastructure, and unequal access to computation.

The remainder of the paper is organized as follows. Section 2 reviews related work on responsible AI, critical data modelling, participatory design, and resource-aware infrastructures. Section 3 introduces the CO-FREDA methodology. Section 4 describes a protocol for applying and evaluating the methodology in a data science project. Section 5 concludes the paper and outlines future work.

2 Related Work

CO-FREDA is positioned at the intersection of responsible AI, critical data studies, participatory design, and sustainable data-intensive computing. Rather than treating responsibility as an external ethical layer added after system development, CO-FREDA considers data, algorithms, and infrastructures as inseparable socio-technical components. This perspective relates to work in responsible AI and fairness-aware data management, while extending it through feminist, decolonial, and infrastructural concerns.

Responsible AI, Fairness, and Accountability. Early work on responsible AI has largely focused on fairness, accountability, transparency, and interpretability. Foundational contributions have shown how data-driven systems can produce

[1] Technosolutionism is the belief that complex social, political, environmental, or cultural problems can be solved mainly through technological innovation.

disparate impacts [2], how fairness can be formalized as a computational constraint [11], and how interpretability can support more accountable machine learning [10]. Technical frameworks such as AI Fairness 360 [3] and model cards [20] have made fairness auditing and documentation more operational.

In data management, responsibility has also been addressed through fairness-aware data exploration [1], causal database repair [25], query rewriting [16], and responsibility-by-design approaches [29]. These works provide mechanisms for detecting, documenting, and mitigating algorithmic harms. CO-FREDA builds on them, while arguing that responsible AI cannot be reduced to metrics or post-hoc audits. Fairness, accountability, and contestability must be embedded throughout the full pipeline, from problem formulation and data modelling to infrastructure allocation, interpretation, and dissemination.

Feminist, Decolonial, and Justice-Oriented Computing. Critical scholars have shown that algorithmic harms are not only technical failures but also expressions of structural inequality. Benjamin [4], Noble [23], and Buolamwini and Gebru [7] demonstrate how racialized and gendered biases are reproduced by apparently neutral computational systems. Feminist and decolonial approaches go further by asking whose knowledge is encoded, whose categories become computable, and whose interests are served by AI systems [5,21].

Data Feminism [12] and Design Justice [8] provide methodological principles for centering lived experience, challenging power asymmetries, and designing with communities rather than for them. Indigenous data sovereignty further emphasizes collective rights over data access, interpretation, storage, and reuse [17,32]. CO-FREDA translates these justice-oriented principles into technical decisions: sovereignty-aware metadata, consent-aware access control, situated documentation, participatory evaluation, and revocable governance mechanisms.

Critical Data Modelling and the Politics of Representation. Data models are not neutral descriptions of reality. They shape what can be known, queried, optimized, and governed. CREDAL argues that data models are present at the birth of data-driven systems and therefore constitute privileged sites for interrogating the material, social, and political conditions of data work [14]. Related work on reading datasets [24], slow data interaction [13], critical data modelling [33], and modelling power [28] shows that schemas, attributes, constraints, and classifications encode assumptions about the world.

CO-FREDA extends this line of work by treating data modelling as an early site of accountability. Dataset documentation, provenance, metadata vocabularies, access policies, and schema design must be examined not only for technical correctness, but also for epistemic closure, exclusion, asymmetry, and possible refusal.

Participatory Design and Community-in-the-Loop AI. Participatory approaches have become central to recent debates on responsible AI. Birhane et al. [6] and Sloane et al. [27] warn that participation can become superficial when stakeholders are consulted without decision-making power. Suresh et al. [30] further identify structural limits to participation in large-scale AI systems.

In conceptual modelling, ONION proposes a participatory ER design framework that progressively transforms stakeholder narratives into structured data models while preserving inclusion, transparency, and collective validation [18]. CO-FREDA aligns with this work but broadens participation beyond data modelling to the whole AI lifecycle. Communities are not only consulted during requirements analysis; they intervene in data governance, model training, resource dispatching, interpretation, dissemination, and revision.

Frugal, federated, and resource-aware AI infrastructures. A growing body of work examines the environmental and infrastructural costs of AI. Cloud infrastructures and large-scale AI pipelines concentrate computational power and often reproduce extractive dependencies [9,19]. At the same time, technical alternatives such as federated learning [15], edge computing [26], and distributed analytics frameworks provide ways to reduce centralization and support data locality.

These approaches are often framed mainly in terms of performance, scalability, or privacy. CO-FREDA reframes them as components of infrastructural justice. Federated and incremental learning can support community control over data; edge–fog–cloud scheduling can reduce dependency on centralized infrastructures; and energy-aware optimization can make ecological costs visible. In this sense, frugality is not only a computational objective, but also a political and epistemic commitment.

Discussion. CO-FREDA contributes to this literature by integrating three dimensions often treated separately: responsible data governance, frugal and context-aware algorithmic training, and negotiated infrastructure deployment. It combines technical mechanisms such as provenance, access control, policy-as-code, federated learning, model compression, and multi-objective scheduling with feminist and decolonial commitments to care, refusal, consent, sovereignty, and accountability. Its main contribution is methodological: it offers an end-to-end framework for designing AI systems that are performant and deployable, while remaining accountable to the communities, territories, and environments they affect.

3 CO-FREDA Methodology

CO-FREDA is a socio-technical methodology for designing data- and algorithm-driven scientific systems that are technically robust, environmentally frugal, socially accountable, and collectively governed. It re-engineers FREDA by integrating the COIA framework for feminist artificial intelligence, grounded in co-design, co-liberation, and co-participation [22]. In this combined approach, FREDA provides the technical architecture for responsible data pipelines, frugal algorithmic training, and resource-aware deployment, while COIA provides the participatory and political process through which communities define problems, negotiate data practices, evaluate impacts, and retain the right to modify or refuse the system.

The methodology starts from the premise that AI systems are not neutral technical artefacts, but situated infrastructures that organize data, labour, energy, categories, and decision-making power. Responsibility is therefore not treated as a post-hoc audit, but as a design condition embedded across the full lifecycle: problem formulation, data governance, model training, infrastructure allocation, explanation, deployment, and revision. CO-FREDA foregrounds relational infrastructure, frugal computation, territorial knowledge governance, and community control as the basis for ethical and responsible science.

CO-FREDA integrates five interdependent steps:

1. situated co-framing and active listening;
2. territorial and epistemic data governance;
3. frugal, responsible, and context-aware algorithmic training;
4. negotiated community-in-the-loop infrastructure dispatching;
5. explanation, feedback, refusal, and continuous revision.

Together, these steps translate feminist, Indigenous, and decolonial commitments to care, consent, refusal, sustainability, and sovereignty into concrete technical mechanisms.

Step 1: Situated Co-framing and Active Listening. The methodology begins before data collection or model design. Inspired by COIA, the first step is an active listening phase in which the affected community defines the problem, identifies harms, expresses expectations, and decides whether AI is an appropriate response. This phase replaces technosolutionist problem formulation with situated co-framing. Rather than asking which model should be built, the process asks: What problem is being experienced? Who is affected? Which histories of harm or exclusion are relevant? What forms of knowledge have been ignored? What would count as dignified, useful, and non-extractive technological intervention?

This step produces a situated problem statement, a stakeholder map, and a preliminary list of non-negotiable limits, including data that should not be collected, uses that should be prohibited, and conditions under which the project should stop. The outcome is not merely a requirements document, but a community-validated mandate for the technical work that follows.

Step 2: Territorial and Epistemic Data Governance. Once the problem has been collectively framed, CO-FREDA establishes a data governance layer grounded in sovereignty, consent, and epistemic plurality. Data sovereignty refers to the right of individuals, groups, nations, and communities, especially Indigenous and historically marginalized communities, to control the access, use, sharing, storage, deletion, and interpretation of data according to their values, governance principles, and knowledge systems.

Input datasets are documented and annotated using culturally grounded metadata, community-defined vocabularies, consent levels, provenance traces, and usage restrictions. These annotations may include territorial scope, allowed purposes, revocation conditions, dissemination levels, symbolic representations, or community-specific categories. They are stored in auditable data lakehouse infrastructures such as Delta Lake or Apache Hudi, where schema enforcement, versioning, and access control can support both reproducibility and accountability.

The governance layer informs both access and computation. Policy-aware operators in Spark SQL, Apache Ranger, Unity Catalog, or equivalent tools can enforce row-level filters, column masking, and purpose-based access restrictions. User-defined functions can support situated transformations, such as community-validated place names, gender markers, or local taxonomies. Data harmonization is therefore treated as epistemic negotiation rather than neutral standardization.

This step produces a sovereignty-aware data catalogue, a consent and refusal register, a dataset documentation sheet, and a set of enforceable access policies. It also identifies missing, absent, or deliberately excluded data, making visible the political nature of both data presence and data absence.

Step 3: Frugal and Context-Aware Algorithm Training. CO-FREDA constrains model training through technical, ecological, and ethical limits. The goal is to avoid energy-intensive, extractive, or epistemically dominant AI development practices. Frugality is understood in two complementary senses: environmental frugality, which reduces energy consumption and carbon impact, and epistemic frugality, which avoids overfitting systems to dominant categories, majority populations, or externally imposed definitions of usefulness.

The methodology introduces three technical mechanisms. First, data-selective training uses fairness-aware SQL rewriting and community-defined sampling constraints to select balanced, relevant, and ethically admissible training subsets [16,25]. Second, model distillation and compression transform large models into smaller, domain-specific models suitable for edge or low-resource environments. Third, federated and incremental learning enables models to be trained on distributed, locally governed datasets without requiring central data pooling [31].

Community participation defines acceptable trade-offs between accuracy, interpretability, energy cost, latency, and fairness. A model is therefore not selected only because it maximizes performance, but because its technical behaviour remains aligned with collectively defined priorities and constraints.

Step 4: Negotiated Community-in-the-Loop Resource Dispatching. AI pipelines are operationalized through negotiated resource dispatching strategies that reflect social, territorial, and environmental constraints [31]. In CO-FREDA, infrastructure decisions are not delegated exclusively to technical teams. They are treated as political and ecological decisions that must be made visible and, when appropriate, collectively governed.

Execution plans include community consent points where stakeholders may pause, validate, modify, or reject a transformation. Resource dispatching is guided by multi-objective optimizers balancing latency, energy consumption, carbon footprint, data locality, monetary cost, infrastructure availability, and fairness objectives. Community-defined weights can be encoded as runtime parameters in workflow schedulers or Spark DAG optimizers. Infrastructure allocation policies may prioritize edge, fog, on-premise, or low-power devices when these choices reduce dependency on centralized cloud infrastructures and better respect digital sovereignty.

This step extends the notion of dispatching from computational resource allocation to epistemic and infrastructural negotiation. Decisions such as where data are processed, how often models are retrained, how much parallelism is used, and whether external cloud services are acceptable become part of the accountability structure of the system.

Step 5: Explanation, Feedback, Refusal, and Continuous Revision. CO-FREDA does not end with deployment. The system remains open to continuous review, correction, and possible refusal. Human-in-the-loop explanation modules provide accessible interfaces (textual, visual, oral, or dialogical) through which communities can question model outputs and understand how data, assumptions, and infrastructure choices shaped them.

Logging and provenance are used not only for debugging, but also for auditable accountability. They expose how data were transformed, which models were trained, which resources were used, which policies were applied, and which decisions were made automatically or manually. Stakeholders can annotate outputs, flag harms, correct categories, request retraining, modify consent conditions, or withdraw from the system. The right to refuse or discontinue the technology is treated as a core governance mechanism rather than as a failure of adoption.

This step produces impact statements, revision logs, community-facing explanations, and periodic review protocols. These instruments ensure that the AI system remains a living infrastructure, responsive to social, cultural, political, and ecological change.

Integration. CO-FREDA combines the technical precision of responsible data engineering with the political commitments of feminist and decolonial design. It operationalizes care, consent, sovereignty, frugality, and accountability across the AI lifecycle. By coupling co-design and co-liberation with policy-aware data architectures, federated learning, frugal model training, and negotiated infrastructure dispatching, the methodology provides a practical framework for building AI systems that are not only performant and deployable, but also contestable, revisable, and accountable to the worlds they help shape.

4 Protocol for Applying CO-FREDA

This section describes a simple protocol for applying and evaluating the CO-FREDA methodology in a data science project. The protocol is designed for students or researchers working in small groups. It includes a project description, activities to apply the methodology, questions to validate the project results, and questions to evaluate the methodology.

4.1 Example Project: Assessing the Impact of Data Centres

The tutorial project studies the territorial, social, and environmental impact of data centres. Data centres are often presented as neutral technical infrastructures, but they consume energy, water, land, minerals, and public resources. They may also affect local communities, ecosystems, and territorial planning.

The objective is to design a responsible data science pipeline to analyse where data centres are located, what resources they consume, and which territories or populations may be affected. The project does not aim to optimize the expansion of data centres. Instead, it asks whether such infrastructures are socially and environmentally acceptable, under which conditions, and according to whose criteria.

The project applies CO-FREDA to examine the full data science lifecycle: problem formulation, data governance, modelling, infrastructure use, interpretation, and revision.

4.2 Project Scenario

A group of students, researchers, local associations, and public actors study the footprint of data centres in a given region. They combine open data, environmental indicators, territorial information, and community observations to identify possible pressures on energy, water, land, biodiversity, and local populations.

The project uses real or simulated datasets. The analysis should remain simple, interpretable, and reproducible. Missing data should be explicitly documented, since the absence of information may reveal a lack of transparency or public accountability.

4.3 Data Sources

The project may use the following types of data:

- locations of existing or planned data centres;
- estimated electricity consumption;
- estimated water consumption or cooling technology;
- land use and protected natural areas;
- drought, water stress, or river basin indicators;
- population density and social vulnerability indicators;
- local reports, public consultations, or community observations;
- missing or unavailable information about energy, water, land, or public subsidies.

4.4 Activities

The protocol is organized into five activities corresponding to the main steps of CO-FREDA.

Activity 1: Situated Co-framing. Participants define the problem from the perspective of the affected territory and communities.

Task. Discuss the following questions:

- What problem are we studying?
- Who may benefit from data centres?
- Who may be affected by their costs?
- Which resources are involved: water, energy, land, minerals, public money?
- Is data science useful for this problem, or are other actions also needed?

Expected Output. A short situated problem statement and a stakeholder map.

Activity 2: Data Governance and Sovereignty. Participants identify the data needed for the project and discuss how these data should be governed.

Task. Build a simple data inventory including sources, limitations, sensitivity, and missing information.

Listing 1.1. Example schema for data centre impact analysis

```
CREATE TABLE IF NOT EXISTS data_centres (
    centre_id               STRING,
    region                  STRING,
    municipality            STRING,
    status                  STRING,
    estimated_area_m2       DOUBLE,
    estimated_power_mw      DOUBLE,
    cooling_type            STRING,
    data_source             STRING
)
USING DELTA;

CREATE TABLE IF NOT EXISTS territorial_indicators (
    territory_id                  STRING,
    region                        STRING,
    water_stress_level            STRING,
    renewable_energy_pct          DOUBLE,
    protected_area_pct            DOUBLE,
    agricultural_land_pct         DOUBLE,
    population_density            DOUBLE,
    social_vulnerability_index DOUBLE
)
USING DELTA;

CREATE TABLE IF NOT EXISTS community_observations (
    observation_id        STRING,
    territory_id          STRING,
    observation_type      STRING,
    description           STRING,
    visibility_level      STRING,
```

```
    consent_status      STRING,
    created_at          TIMESTAMP
)
USING DELTA;
```

Expected Output. A data governance table describing data sources, access conditions, missing data, and possible risks.

Activity 3: Frugal and Responsible Indicators. Participants design simple indicators to estimate territorial pressure. The goal is to use understandable methods before considering complex models.

Task. Define indicators such as estimated energy pressure, estimated water pressure, overlap with protected or agricultural areas, proximity to socially vulnerable populations, and missing information.

Listing 1.2. Example view for a territorial pressure indicator

```
CREATE OR REPLACE VIEW territorial_data_centre_pressure AS
SELECT
    d.region,
    COUNT(d.centre_id) AS number_of_data_centres,
    SUM(d.estimated_power_mw) AS total_estimated_power_mw,
    SUM(d.estimated_area_m2) AS total_estimated_area_m2,
    AVG(t.renewable_energy_pct) AS avg_renewable_energy_pct,
    AVG(t.social_vulnerability_index) AS
        avg_social_vulnerability,
    MAX(t.water_stress_level) AS water_stress_level,
    CASE
        WHEN SUM(d.estimated_power_mw) > 100
         AND MAX(t.water_stress_level) IN ('high',
             'critical')
        THEN 'high_pressure'
        WHEN SUM(d.estimated_power_mw) > 50
        THEN 'medium_pressure'
        ELSE 'low_pressure'
    END AS territorial_pressure_level
FROM data_centres d
JOIN territorial_indicators t
ON d.region = t.region
GROUP BY d.region;
```

Expected Output. A list of indicators and one or more simple SQL views.

Activity 4: Infrastructure and Frugal Execution. Participants reflect on the resources used by their own analysis. The project should avoid using excessive computation to study the impact of excessive computation.

Task. Decide where the analysis should run: locally, on an institutional server, or in the cloud. Justify the choice.

```
execution_policy:
  default_execution: "local_or_institutional_server"
  cloud_execution: "only_if_justified"
  preferred_methods:
    - SQL_aggregation
    - interpretable_indicators
    - lightweight_geospatial_analysis
  avoid:
    - unnecessary_large_models
    - repeated_full_dataset_processing
    - high_energy_training_without_clear_benefit
  constraints:
    max_runtime_minutes: 20
    max_memory_gb: 8
    document_computational_cost: true
```

Listing 1.3. Frugal execution policy for the tutorial project

Expected Output. A short computational impact note describing the infrastructure used, runtime, and justification of the method.

Activity 5: Interpretation, Feedback, and Revision. Participants prepare the results for review by non-specialist actors. They must clearly distinguish evidence, assumptions, estimates, and unknowns.

Task. Create a simple view of the results that can be discussed with communities, public actors, or other stakeholders.

Listing 1.4. Community-reviewable results

```
CREATE OR REPLACE VIEW community_review_results AS
SELECT
    region,
    number_of_data_centres,
    total_estimated_power_mw,
    total_estimated_area_m2,
    water_stress_level,
    avg_social_vulnerability,
    territorial_pressure_level,
    current_timestamp() AS generated_at
FROM territorial_data_centre_pressure
WHERE region IS NOT NULL;
```

Expected Output. A short report, dashboard, or map with clear limitations and questions for discussion.

4.5 Summary of Activities

Table 1 summarizes the tutorial workflow for applying CO-FREDA to a data science project. It organizes the methodology into five practical activities, moving from the collective definition of the problem to the revision of the results. Each activity links a methodological objective with a concrete task and an expected output. The table shows that CO-FREDA is not limited to model design: it also includes data governance, indicator construction, infrastructure choices, interpretation, and mechanisms for correction or contestation. In this way, the protocol guides participants through the full lifecycle of a responsible and frugal data science project, while keeping the process simple, traceable, and open to community review.

Table 1. Tutorial activities for applying CO-FREDA

Activity	Task	Expected Output
Co-framing	Define the territorial problem and affected stakeholders	Problem statement and stakeholder map
Data governance	Identify datasets, missing data, sensitive information, and access conditions	Data inventory and governance table
Indicators	Define simple indicators for energy, water, land, society, and missing data	Indicator list and SQL views
Infrastructure	Decide how to run the analysis with minimal computational cost	Execution policy and computational impact note
Interpretation and Revision	Prepare results for community review. Define how results can be corrected, contested, or updated	Short report, map, or dashboard with limitations. Feedback and revision protocol

4.6 Questions to Validate the Project Result

The following questions help participants evaluate the quality of their project.

Territorial Relevance.

- Does the project clearly explain how data centres affect territories?
- Are water, energy, land, biodiversity, and social dimensions considered?
- Are local or territorial categories included, beyond administrative boundaries?

Data Quality.

- Are the data sources clearly documented?
- Are missing or uncertain data identified?
- Does the project explain how missing data may affect the conclusions?

Social and Environmental Accountability.

- Does the analysis identify who may benefit and who may be harmed?
- Does it avoid presenting data centres as automatically positive or inevitable?
- Are ecological impacts treated as central?

Frugality.

- Was the simplest adequate method chosen?
- Is the computational cost of the analysis documented?
- Could the analysis be reproduced in a low-resource setting?

Community Review.

- Are the results understandable for non-specialists?
- Can local actors correct or contest the results?
- Are assumptions and limitations visible?

4.7 Questions to Evaluate the Methodology

The following questions help evaluate whether CO-FREDA was useful during the tutorial.

Co-framing.

- Did this step help define the problem beyond a purely technical perspective?
- Was it easy to identify affected stakeholders?
- Did it help question whether data science is appropriate for the problem?

Data Governance.

- Did this step help identify risks related to data collection and use?
- Was it useful to discuss missing data?
- Was it clear who should control access to the data?

Frugal Indicators.

- Did this step help choose simple and interpretable methods?
- Were the indicators easy to understand?
- Did the methodology help avoid unnecessary complexity?

Infrastructure.

- Did this step make infrastructure choices more visible?
- Was it useful to consider the cost of computation?
- Did it help connect data science with energy and environmental impact?

Feedback and Revision.

- Did this step help think about how results could be corrected or contested?
- Was it clear how stakeholders could give feedback?
- What would improve this step?

4.8 Final Reflection Questions

At the end of the tutorial, participants may answer the following questions:

- What changed in your understanding of responsible data science?
- Which step of CO-FREDA was the most useful?
- Which step was the most difficult to apply?
- Did the methodology help identify risks that had not been considered before?
- Would you use this methodology in another project? Why or why not?
- What should be simplified, clarified, or extended?

5 Conclusion and Future Work

This paper proposed CO-FREDA, a sovereignty-aware, frugal, responsible, equitable, and co-designed methodology for data- and algorithm-driven science. The approach re-engineers FREDA by integrating the feminist AI design principles of COIA, particularly co-design, co-liberation, co-participation, active listening, community data sovereignty, and continuous revision. In doing so, it reframes responsible AI not as a set of external ethical requirements or post-hoc audits, but as an end-to-end socio-technical process grounded in care, consent, refusal, frugality, and infrastructural justice.

Through the integration of Spark-based analytics, policy-aware data governance, federated and incremental learning, provenance mechanisms, and negotiated resource dispatching, CO-FREDA shows how technical systems can support plural epistemologies while reducing extractive forms of computation. Rather than centralizing sensitive data or producing surveillance-oriented outputs, the proposed pipeline shifts decision-making power toward affected communities and their trusted data stewards.

The main contribution of this work is methodological. CO-FREDA connects feminist and decolonial commitments with concrete computational mechanisms: sovereignty-aware metadata, policy-as-code, consent registries, Spark UDFs for situated vocabularies, federated summaries, frugal model training, energy-aware dispatching, and dissemination controls. This connection demonstrates that justice-oriented AI can be operationalized not only through principles, but through technical architectures that make accountability, refusal, and local negotiation enforceable.

Future work will focus on three directions. We will investigate relational fairness metrics that account not only for individual or group-level outcomes, but also for territorial, historical, ecological, and epistemic harms. We will design revocable consent and refusal layers for distributed data systems, enabling communities to pause, withdraw, mask, delete, or renegotiate data and model use across federated infrastructures. We will extend CO-FREDA to territories with diverse legal, cultural, linguistic, and epistemic regimes, paying particular attention to localized interpretability, community-facing explanations, and low-resource deployment contexts.

More broadly, this work affirms that responsible data science must move beyond procedural ethics toward infrastructural justice. AI systems should not only be fairer, more transparent, or more efficient; they should be contestable, interruptible, situated, and accountable to the communities, environments, and knowledge systems they affect. CO-FREDA offers one step in this direction by grounding AI in collective autonomy, ecological responsibility, and social accountability.

References

1. Amer-Yahia, S., Chakroun, I., Mahabadi, S., Montassier, A.: Fairness in data exploration. IEEE Data Eng. Bull. **43**, 55–66 (2020)
2. Barocas, S., Selbst, A.D.: Big data's disparate impact. Calif. Law Rev. **104**(3), 671–732 (2016)
3. Bellamy, R.K., Dey, K., Hind, M., Hoffman, S.C., Houde, S., Kannan, K.N.R., Lohia, P., Martino, J., Mehta, S., Mojsilovic, A., et al.: Ai fairness 360: An extensible toolkit for detecting, understanding, and mitigating unwanted algorithmic bias. IBM J. Res. Dev. **63**(4/5), 4–1 (2019)
4. Benjamin, R.: Race after technology: abolitionist tools for the new Jim code. Polity (2019)
5. Birhane, A.: Algorithmic injustice: a relational ethics approach. Patterns **2**(2), 100205 (2021)
6. Birhane, A., et al.: Power to the people? Opportunities and challenges for participatory AI. In: Proceedings of the 2nd ACM Conference on Equity and Access in Algorithms, Mechanisms, and Optimization (2022). https://doi.org/10.1145/3551624.3555290
7. Buolamwini, J., Gebru, T.: Gender shades: intersectional accuracy disparities in commercial gender classification. In: Proceedings of the Conference on Fairness, Accountability, and Transparency (FAT*), pp. 77–91 (2018)
8. Costanza-Chock, S.: Design Justice: Community-Led Practices to Build the Worlds We Need, MIT Press (2020)
9. Couldry, N., Mejias, U.A.: The Costs of Connection: How Data Is Colonizing Human Life and Appropriating It for Capitalism. Stanford University Press (2019)
10. Doshi-Velez, F., Kim, B.: Towards a rigorous science of interpretable machine learning. arXiv preprint: arXiv:1702.08608 (2017)
11. Dwork, C., Hardt, M., Pitassi, T., Reingold, O., Zemel, R.: Fairness through awareness. In: Proceedings of the 3rd Innovations in Theoretical Computer Science Conference (ITCS), pp. 214–226 (2012)
12. D'Ignazio, C., Klein, L.F.: Data Feminism. MIT Press (2020)
13. Feinberg, M.: Reading databases: slow information interactions beyond the retrieval paradigm. J. Documentation **73**(2), 336–356 (2017)
14. Fletcher, G., Nahurna, O., Prytula, M., Stoyanovich, J.: CREDAL: close reading of data models (2025). arXiv:2502.07943
15. Kairouz, P., McMahan, H.B., et al.: Advances and open problems in federated learning. Found. Trends Mach. Learn. **14**(1–2), 1–210 (2021). https://doi.org/10.1561/2200000083
16. Koutras, C., Nikolakopoulos, K., Vazirgiannis, M.: Fair data generation via query rewriting. In: Proceedings of the 44th International ACM SIGIR Conference on Research and Development in Information Retrieval, pp. 1099–1108. (2021)

17. Kukutai, T., Taylor, J.: Indigenous Data Sovereignty: Toward an Agenda. ANU Press (2016)
18. Makovska, V., Fletcher, G., Stoyanovich, J.: ONION: a multi-layered framework for participatory er design. In: Workshop on Human-In-the-Loop Data Analytics (2025). https://doi.org/10.1145/3736733.3736736
19. Mejias, U.A., Couldry, N.: Colonialism of the digital kind: data as a resource and the data colonialism framework. Telev. New Media **20**(4), 336–349 (2019). https://doi.org/10.1177/1527476419831640
20. Mitchell, M., Wu, S., Zaldivar, A.: Model cards for model reporting. In: Proceedings of the Conference on Fairness, Accountability, and Transparency (FAT* 2019), pp. 220–229 (2019)
21. Mohamed, S., Png, M.T., Isaac, W.: Decolonial AI: decolonial theory as sociotechnical foresight in artificial intelligence. Philos. Technol. **33**, 659–684 (2020)
22. Mosquera, D., Gallegos, F.: COIA: Co-diseñando una IA Feminista. Marco de Diseño para una inteligencia artificial feminista. In: Created with the support of the Red Feminista de Investigación en Inteligencia Artificial and IDRC. Diversa, Quito, Ecuador. Licensed under CC BY-NC-SA (2025)
23. Noble, S.U.: Algorithms of Oppression: How Search Engines Reinforce Racism. NYU Press (2018)
24. Poirier, L.: Reading datasets: strategies for interpreting the politics of data signification. Big Data Soc. **8**(2) (2021)
25. Salimi, B., Koch, C., Weikum, G.: Capuchin: causal database repair for algorithmic fairness. In: Proceedings of the 2019 International Conference on Management of Data (SIGMOD), pp. 653–668. ACM (2019)
26. Shi, W., Cao, J., Zhang, Q., Li, Y., Xu, L.: Edge computing: vision and challenges. IEEE Internet Things J. **3**(5), 637–646 (2016). https://doi.org/10.1109/JIOT.2016.2579198
27. Sloane, M., Moss, E., Awomolo, O., Forlano, L.: Participation is not a design fix for machine learning. In: Proceedings of the 2nd ACM Conference on Equity and Access in Algorithms, Mechanisms, and Optimization (2022). https://doi.org/10.1145/3551624.3555285
28. Stevens, N.L.: Modeling Power: Data Models and the Production of Social Inequality. Ph.D. thesis, Arizona State University (2022)
29. Stoyanovich, J.: Responsibility by design. In: Proceedings of the 2020 ACM SIGMOD International Conference on Management of Data, pp. 2833–2838. ACM (2020). https://doi.org/10.1145/3318464.3380591
30. Suresh, H., Tseng, E., Young, M., Gray, M., Pierson, E., Levy, K.: Participation in the age of foundation models. In: Proceedings of the 2024 ACM Conference on Fairness, Accountability, and Transparency, pp. 1609–1621 (2024). https://doi.org/10.1145/3630106.3658992
31. Vargas-Solar, G., et al.: Techno/ecofeminism in action: Fair and responsible resource allocation for sustainable data science pipelines. In: CEUR WORKSHOP PROCEEDINGS, vol. 3946, pp. 1–9. CEUR-WS (2025)
32. Walter, M., Suina, M.: Indigenous data, indigenous methodologies and indigenous data sovereignty. Int. J. Soc. Res. Methodol. **22**(3), 233–243 (2019)
33. Wickett, K.M.: Critical data modeling and the basic representation model. J. Am. Soc. Inf. Sci. (2023)

LLM-Aided Data Exploration and Storytelling

Amira Mekki[1(✉)], Alexandre Chanson[1], Patrick Marcel[2], Valentin Nyzam[1], and Veronika Peralta[1]

[1] LIFAT, University of Tours, Tours, France
amira.mekki@etu.univ-tours.fr,
{alexandre.chanson,valentin.nyzam,veronika.peralta}@univ-tours.fr
[2] LIFO, University of Orleans, Orleans, France
patrick.marcel@univ-orleans.fr

Abstract. Data narration is the process of transforming data into meaningful stories by combining data exploration, visualization, and storytelling to communicate insights and support decision-making. Recent research has proposed numerous systems, including LLM-based approaches, to automate different stages of this process. However, most existing methods assume a direct transition from extracted insights to the final narrative, leaving the intermediate reasoning process largely unexplored. This PhD thesis investigates the notion of message as an intermediate semantic layer that organizes and interprets multiple insights according to a specific audience and communication objective. The goal is twofold, first, to define, model, and evaluate messages, and second, to assist the generation of coherent high-quality messages, leading to explainable and meaningful data stories.

Keywords: Data Stories · Data Narration · Automatic data exploration · Automatic data visualization · Large language models

1 Research Problems and Objectives

In this data-driven era, it is of paramount importance to be able to access and exploit relevant data efficiently. Indeed, people and organizations need to collect, clean, transform, integrate, store, explore, analyze and summarize large amounts of data in order to gain insights and support any data-driven decision-making. Data narration, is about telling stories supported by insights extracted from data exploration, and rendered using interactive visualizations [2]. Indeed, data narration covers the whole cycle of data analysis, from data collection, wrangling and exploration, to insight reporting, visualization and storytelling [5].

Recent years have witnessed the development of numerous systems targeting different stages of the data narration pipeline. Systems such as Calliope [7], Erato [9], and DataShot [10] focus on generating data stories from structured datasets. More recently, Large Language Models (LLMs) [3] have been integrated

© The Author(s), under exclusive license to Springer Nature Switzerland AG 2027
G. Vargas Solar et al. (Eds.): ADBIS 2026, CCIS 3175, pp. 271–274, 2027.
https://doi.org/10.1007/978-3-032-39823-9_25

into exploratory workflows to support natural-language interaction and narrative generation. Collectively, these efforts have significantly advanced the automation of data narration.

Despite these advances, a fundamental gap remains between exploratory analysis and narrative construction. Existing systems often assume a relatively direct transition from insights extracted during data exploration to the final data story.

This thesis argues that a data story should not constructed directly from insights. Rather, it should rely on an intermediate semantic construct, referred to as a message, that organizes and interprets multiple insights for a specific audience and communicative purpose. While insights have been extensively studied in the literature, the process through which multiple Insights are combined into meaningful messages remains largely implicit and insufficiently formalized.

The central hypothesis of this work is that understanding and formalizing the notion of message constitutes a necessary step toward bridging the gap between data exploration and visualization. By explicitly modeling this intermediate layer, automated narration systems may move beyond the visualization of isolated insights toward the generation of coherent explanations that support understanding and decision-making.

The present work primarily addresses the challenge of strengthening the connection between data exploration and visualization. Accordingly, this stage of the research addresses the following questions:

- What is a message in the context of data narration? and how to model it?
- How can multiple insights be selected and integrated into coherent, audience-oriented, explainable and meaningful messages?
- How to assess the quality of a message?

Methodology and Current Progress

The first phase of this research consisted of a Literature review on data narration and insight generation, as well as message formulation on related disciplines such as narratology [1], cognitive science [4] and journalism [8]. This former revealed that while the extraction and presentation of insights have received considerable attention, the intermediate process through which insights are transformed into meaningful messages remains largely unexplored.

Together, these perspectives suggest that messages should not be reduced to insights, but rather be modeled as interpretative constructs that organize multiple insights according to narrative relations and communicative intentions.

Based on these observations, an initial conceptual model of messages has been developed. In this model, messages emerge from the integration of multiple insights connected through narrative relations. Among these relations, causality appears particularly important because it supports explanatory narratives by linking insights.

Consequently, the current stage of the research investigates causal relations as a first computational mechanism for message construction. The envisioned framework combines insight discovery with causal reasoning. Insights extracted from exploratory data analysis are complemented by causal structures inferred from data, allowing explanatory relationships to be established between insights. The objective is to generate messages capable of answering not only "what happened?" but also "why did it happen?" and "why should the audience care?"

Preliminary experiments have explored several causal discovery techniques [6] and revealed important challenges related to the validation of inferred causal explanations in the absence of ground truth. In the longer term, LLMs may serve as interactive interfaces capable of adapting generated messages and narratives to users' intentions, preferences, and feedback.

Expected Contributions and Challenges

The contributions of this work are fourfold:

- a cross-disciplinary theoretical foundation for the notion of message in data narration.
- a conceptual model in which messages emerge through the integration of multiple insights connected by narrative relations.
- a framework for constructing explanatory, causally grounded messages.
- an evaluation framework for assessing the quality of messages

Several challenges remain. Causal discovery relies on strong assumptions and may produce uncertain explanations. Evaluating message quality is also difficult, as it involves dimensions such as coherence and usefulness. Finally, preserving user agency and transparency is essential to ensure that increasing automation continues to support, rather than replace, human decision making.

By addressing the missing transition between insights and stories, this research aims to advance interactive data narration systems that assist users not only in discovering patterns in data, but also in constructing meaningful explanations and communicating them effectively.

Disclosure of Interests. The authors have no competing interests to declare that are relevant to the content of this article.

References

1. Bal, M.: Narratology: Introduction to the Theory of Narrative. University of Toronto Press (2009)
2. Carpendale, S., Diakopoulos, N., Henry Riche, N., Hurter, C.: Data-driven storytelling (Dagstuhl seminar 16061). Dagstuhl Rep. **6**(2), 1–27 (2016)
3. Ma, P., Ding, R., Wang, S., Han, S., Zhang, D.: InsightPilot: an LLM-empowered automated data exploration system. In: Proceedings of the 2023 Conference on Empirical Methods in Natural Language Processing: System Demonstrations, pp. 346–352 (2023)

4. Mayr, E., Windhager, F.: Once upon a spacetime: visual storytelling in cognitive and geotemporal information spaces. ISPRS Int. J. Geo Inf. **7**(3), 96 (2018)
5. Outa, F.E., Marcel, P., Peralta, V., Vassiliadis, P.: Highlighting the importance of intentional aspects in data narrative crafting processes. Inf. Syst. Front. **26**(5), 1785–1801 (2024)
6. Pearl, J.: Causality. Cambridge University Press (2009)
7. Shi, D., Xu, X., Sun, F., Shi, Y., Cao, N.: Calliope: automatic visual data story generation from a spreadsheet. IEEE Trans. Visual Comput. Graphics **27**(2), 453–463 (2020)
8. Stocking, S.H., Gross, P.H.: How do journalists think? A proposal for the study of cognitive bias in newsmaking. ERIC (1989)
9. Sun, M., Cai, L., Cui, W., Wu, Y., Shi, Y., Cao, N.: Erato: cooperative data story editing via fact interpolation. IEEE Trans. Visual Comput. Graphics **29**(1), 983–993 (2022)
10. Wang, Y., et al.: DataShot: automatic generation of fact sheets from tabular data. IEEE Trans. Visual Comput. Graphics **26**(1), 895–905 (2019)

From PATTS to Agentic Workflows for Zonation-Aware Well Log Imputation

Yutao Chen[1,2,3](✉)

[1] SLB, Montpellier, France
[2] CentraleSupélec, Gif-sur-Yvette, France
[3] LISN – Laboratoire Interdisciplinaire des Sciences du Numérique, Université Paris-Saclay, CNRS, Orsay, France
yutao.chen@centralesupelec.fr

Abstract. Well logs are depth-indexed measurements used for lithological interpretation, reservoir characterization, and subsurface decision making. However, key curves such as gamma ray, bulk density, neutron porosity, and sonic logs are often missing because of acquisition failures or operational constraints. This extended abstract presents PATTS, a Patch-Attention Transformer for Time-Series Imputation, for zonation-aware well log reconstruction. PATTS combines patch-wise and depth-wise modeling, multivariate self-attention, geological zonation embeddings, and missingness-aware reconstruction. On GeoLink, PATTS reduces MAE over XGBoost by 31.22%, 29.06%, 12.82%, and 23.56% for GR, RHOB, NEUT, and DTC, respectively. Building on these results, the next stage of this doctoral research will investigate an agentic workflow for context retrieval, model and tool orchestration, failure-aware logging, and reuse of expert feedback.

Keywords: Well log imputation · Multivariate sequences · Geological zonation · Patch-attention Transformer · Agentic workflows

1 Research Context and Problem

Well logs provide depth-indexed measurements of subsurface physical properties and are essential for petrophysical interpretation, stratigraphic correlation, and reservoir analysis. In practice, well logs are frequently incomplete because of tool unavailability, acquisition failures, borehole conditions, or operational constraints. The task of well log conditioning is challenging because well log relationships are non-stationary: dependencies among gamma ray (GR), bulk density (RHOB), neutron porosity (NEUT), and compressional sonic slowness (DTC) vary across formations, basins, and acquisition settings.

We formulate well log imputation as a zonation-aware sequence modeling task. Let $X \in \mathbb{R}^{T \times D}$ be the multivariate log matrix, $M \in \{0,1\}^{T \times D}$ the observation mask, and $Z \in \{1,\ldots,K\}^{T}$ the depth-wise zonation label. The objective is to estimate $\hat{X} = f_{\theta}(X, M, Z)$ while preserving depth-wise continuity, cross-log

© The Author(s), under exclusive license to Springer Nature Switzerland AG 2027
G. Vargas Solar et al. (Eds.): ADBIS 2026, CCIS 3175, pp. 275–278, 2027.
https://doi.org/10.1007/978-3-032-39823-9_26

consistency, and stratigraphic plausibility. Zonation is used as a conditioning signal because formation labels often remain available even when important curves are missing, and petrophysical dependencies change across geological intervals.

PATTS, a Patch-Attention Transformer for Time-Series Imputation, splits depth sequences into overlapping patches, following the broader success of patch-based representations for long sequences [3]. It applies patch-level self-attention to capture local depth-wise and cross-log dependencies, and injects zonation embeddings to guide reconstruction by formation context. Each patch contains log values, observation-mask information, and aligned zonation features, allowing the model to distinguish observed measurements from missing entries while learning formation-specific patterns. Patch predictions are then folded back to the original depth grid, with overlapping regions combined to produce smooth reconstructions. This design is particularly suitable for long or structured missing intervals, where recovering a curve requires both nearby depth context and correlations with other available logs.

2 Experimental Evidence

We evaluate on GeoLink, Taranaki, and Synthetic datasets. GeoLink contains 2,984,255 rows from the Norwegian Continental Shelf, with missing rates of 1.13% for GR, 12.81% for RHOB, 40.94% for NEUT, and 7.87% for DTC. Taranaki contains 1,941,575 rows from New Zealand's Taranaki Basin, with higher missingness: 21.39% for GR, 54.52% for RHOB, 56.85% for NEUT, and 37.17% for DTC. The Synthetic dataset contains 1,200,876 rows and is used to test categorical zonation under controlled conditions. We use well-level five-fold cross-validation and report Mean Absolute Error (MAE). XGBoost [1] is used as a strong non-neural baseline. Because naturally missing entries have no known ground truth, evaluation is performed on originally observed values that are artificially masked in held-out wells.

Table 1. GeoLink results in terms of test MAE. Lower values are better. The best result for each target curve is shown in bold.

Method	GR	RHOB	NEUT	DTC
XGBoost	0.097021	0.055156	0.049259	0.035785
XGBoost + Formation	0.077564	0.042578	0.045047	0.031705
SAITS	0.093181	0.054071	0.049022	0.034323
SAITS + Formation	0.077333	0.042979	0.044042	0.029777
PATTS + Formation	**0.066748**	**0.039135**	**0.042950**	**0.027349**

Table 1 shows that both zonation and patching are important. Adding Formation to XGBoost reduces MAE by 20.07% on GR and 22.79% on RHOB, confirming the value of geological context. Standard SAITS [2] alone gives only limited gains over XGBoost, while SAITS + Formation improves all curves. The complete PATTS model performs best, reducing MAE by 31.22% on GR, 29.06% on RHOB, 12.82% on NEUT, and 23.56% on DTC.

Beyond GeoLink, PATTS improves over XGBoost on Taranaki by 3.06%, 10.72%, 6.25%, and 17.28% on GR, RHOB, NEUT, and DTC, respectively. The strongest gain is on DTC, confirming the benefit of patch-attention modeling under high missingness and strong cross-log dependencies. On the Synthetic dataset, PATTS improves by 82.36%, 25.96%, 14.87%, and 9.63%, with the large GR gain validating the role of reliable categorical zonation.

3 Doctoral Research Plan: Agentic Imputation Workflows

The PATTS experiments provide the basis for an agentic extension: curated datasets, preprocessing rules, Formation-aware inputs, XGBoost/SAITS/PAT TS baselines, MAE evaluation, experiments table, and visualization outputs. The goal is to wrap these assets into a long-horizon geoscience workflow where an agent retrieves context, invokes tools, validates predictions, and reuses expert feedback. This follows the reasoning–acting paradigm in which agents alternate between planning, tool use, observation, and revision [5].

Plan and Implementation. The proposed agent has four modules. First, a *tool layer* exposes implemented components as callable tools: missingness profiling, zonation encoding, XGBoost imputation, PATTS imputation, metric computation, and visualization/report generation. Second, a *context manager* retrieves analog wells, formation intervals, previous experiments, and expert comments, following retrieval-augmented and adaptive context construction [4,6]. Third, a *failure-aware harness* logs each execution, including input well, selected context, tool calls, configuration, prediction, validation score, and expert decision. Fourth, an *expert feedback memory* stores approvals, rejections, corrections, and geological notes for later reuse, supporting memory-based improvement across runs [7].

Given a request such as "impute missing DTC for this well", the prototype profiles missingness, retrieves analog intervals, selects XGBoost, SAITS, or PATTS according to missingness, Formation availability, and basin similarity, then reports MAE and visual overlays when validation data are available. This makes the imputation process auditable: each output is linked to the selected context, tool, model configuration, and validation evidence. Such traces can later be used to identify whether failures come from context selection, tool choice, model behavior, or geological inconsistency.

Evaluation. We plan three studies: (E1) compare a fixed PATTS-only pipeline with an agent that selects among XGBoost, SAITS, and PATTS; (E2) compare no retrieval, analog-well retrieval, and feedback-aware retrieval; and (E3) replay expert corrections to test whether future runs retrieve relevant feedback.

Evaluation combines model MAE with agent-level metrics such as valid tool-call rate, tool-selection accuracy, workflow completion rate, failure diagnosis accuracy, expert intervention rate, and report acceptance rate. The expected outcome is fewer repeated errors, improved expert acceptance, and more traceable subsurface imputation workflows.

4 Conclusion

This extended abstract presents PATTS for zonation-aware well log imputation and its extension toward Agentic AI. PATTS improves over XGBoost by combining patch-wise and depth-wise modeling, multivariate attention, zonation embeddings, and missingness-aware reconstruction. The GeoLink experiment shows that zonation and patching are both essential, while cross-dataset results confirm the benefit of the approach on Taranaki and Synthetic benchmarks. The proposed agentic extension adds tool orchestration, context retrieval, failure-aware logging, feedback memory, and workflow-level evaluation for reliable industrial subsurface AI.

Acknowledgments. This work was carried out under a CIFRE doctoral agreement involving Université Paris-Saclay, CNRS, LISN, SLB, and TotalEnergies.

Disclosure of Interests. The author has no competing interests to declare that are relevant to the content of this article.

References

1. Chen, T., Guestrin, C.: XGBoost: a scalable tree boosting system. In: Proceedings of the 22nd ACM SIGKDD International Conference on Knowledge Discovery and Data Mining, pp. 785–794. ACM (2016)
2. Du, W., Côté, D., Liu, Y.: SAITS: self-attention-based imputation for time series. Expert Syst. Appl. **219**, 119619 (2023)
3. Nie, Y., Nguyen, N.H., Sinthong, P., Kalagnanam, J.: A time series is worth 64 words: long-term forecasting with transformers. In: International Conference on Learning Representations (2023)
4. Lewis, P., Perez, E., Piktus, A., Petroni, F., Karpukhin, V.: Retrieval-augmented generation for knowledge-intensive NLP tasks. In: Advances in Neural Information Processing Systems, vol. 33, pp. 9459–9474 (2020)
5. Yao, S., et al.: ReAct: synergizing reasoning and acting in language models. In: International Conference on Learning Representations (2023)
6. Asai, A., Wu, Z., Wang, Y., Sil, A., Hajishirzi, H.: Self-RAG: learning to retrieve, generate, and critique through self-reflection. In: International Conference on Learning Representations (2024)
7. Shinn, N., Cassano, F., Gopinath, A., Narasimhan, K., Yao, S.: Reflexion: language agents with verbal reinforcement learning. In: Advances in Neural Information Processing Systems (2023)

Knowledge-Based Conversational Recommendation with Large Language Models

Stefano Picchi(✉)

Department of Information Engineering, University of Brescia,
Via Branze 38, 25123 Brescia, Italy
s.picchi002@unibs.it

Abstract. Large Language Models (LLMs) are increasingly adopted in recommender systems, enabling natural interaction and richer use of contextual information. Their integration, however, raises concerns about reliability and trust, as generated content may not remain faithful to factual knowledge. This doctoral research investigates the integration of LLMs into recommender systems, focusing on knowledge-based recommenders, where explicit and structured representations of the domain can serve as a reliable foundation for the recommendation process. The central idea is to pair the flexibility of LLMs with the precision of structured knowledge, so that recommendations remain grounded in verifiable information. The research aims at (i) grounding recommendations in factual knowledge, (ii) exploiting conversational interactions to capture and maintain evolving user preferences and constraints, and (iii) producing recommendations and explanations traceable to structured knowledge. This paper outlines the methodology adopted, the current progress, and the main open challenges.

Keywords: Conversational Recommender Systems · Large Language Models · Knowledge-Based Recommendation

1 Research Problems and Objectives

In recent years, Large Language Models (LLMs) have been increasingly adopted in recommender systems, enabling more natural interactions and a richer use of contextual information, while producing recommendations that are more interpretable and personalized compared to traditional approaches [9]. However, their integration still poses reliability and trust issues, including hallucinations and the difficulty of keeping generated content faithful to factual knowledge [13].

While LLMs bring powerful generative capabilities to recommender systems, their integration raises several open research problems. The first concerns data grounding. In order to prevent hallucinations, the recommendation process must rely on factual knowledge, so that recommended items and their attributes can

© The Author(s), under exclusive license to Springer Nature Switzerland AG 2027
G. Vargas Solar et al. (Eds.): ADBIS 2026, CCIS 3175, pp. 279–282, 2027.
https://doi.org/10.1007/978-3-032-39823-9_27

be validated against reliable sources rather than depending on the model's parametric knowledge alone. A second arises in conversational settings, where user preferences, constraints, and intents are not given in advance but emerge and change throughout the dialogue, and therefore need to be captured and continuously updated [6]. A third relates to transparency, as the reasoning behind a recommendation should be traceable to verifiable information in order to foster user trust.

Among the different families, knowledge-based recommender systems offer a particularly natural ground to address these concerns [11]. Unlike collaborative filtering and content-based methods, which infer preferences from historical interactions, knowledge-based recommenders elicit user requirements explicitly through conversation and match them against a knowledge base [1]. This encodes items, attributes, and constraints through rules, ontologies, or knowledge graphs.

However, how to effectively combine these representations with LLMs, especially in conversational scenarios, is still an open research problem. Existing work has looked mostly at generating formal domain models such as conceptual schemas [5], rather than using them to guide and ground the recommendation process. Within this context, my doctoral research investigates the integration of LLMs into recommender systems, focusing on knowledge-based recommenders, where explicit and structured representations of the domain can serve as a reliable foundation for the recommendation process. The central idea is to pair the flexibility of LLMs with the precision of structured knowledge, so that recommendations remain grounded in verifiable information that can support their explanation. In this view, the user no longer queries the recommender directly but interacts with it through the LLM, which leads the dialogue and interprets requests, while the recommender computes the recommendation from its explicit knowledge. More specifically, the research aims at: (i) grounding the recommendation process in factual knowledge through knowledge-based recommenders and conceptual models; (ii) leveraging conversational interactions to capture and maintain a faithful representation of evolving user preferences and constraints; and (iii) producing recommendations and explanations that are traceable to structured knowledge, thus improving transparency and user trust. This research direction builds on prior findings [2,3], in which structured domain knowledge, in the form of a domain ontology, was exploited within a retrieval-augmented approach to support more grounded and explainable recommendations, motivating the broader investigation pursued in this doctoral research.

2 Methodology and Current Progress

The research follows an incremental methodology that combines the study of the literature, the analysis of LLM integration strategies in recommender systems, and experimental prototyping. As an initial phase, a systematic study of the literature has been carried out to identify the main families of techniques for integrating LLMs into recommender systems. These range from encoder-only approaches, which exploit LLMs mainly for representation learning, to generative recommendation approaches, which rely on LLMs to produce recommendations directly, and to retrieval-augmented approaches, which couple generation with information retrieval from external data sources to improve grounding [4]. More recent solutions, based on tool use and agentic workflows, including multi-agent systems, have also been examined, as they allow LLMs to access structured data sources and external services [10]. Building on this analysis, the research has progressively moved towards conversational recommender systems (CRS) [8], studying the role and the implications of integrating LLMs across the different phases of the conversational recommendation process. The goal of this ongoing investigation is to understand where LLMs can bring the most value and where the risks for reliability and grounding are most critical. The research will then deepen the study of CRS along two intertwined directions. On the one hand, building on existing approaches that capture and represent user preferences from conversational data [7,12], it will investigate how LLMs can be exploited to capture the nuances that emerge during a conversation, such as implicit preferences, constraints, evolving intents and interests, and how to represent them in order to improve recommendation quality. On the other hand, the research will then concentrate specifically on knowledge-based recommender systems, which represent its core focus, studying how an LLM can act as the conversational layer above them, leveraging structured knowledge as a backbone for grounding, semantic reasoning, and explanation.

As an initial exploration in this direction, a recommender system combining LLMs with agent-based components has been prototyped, to gain a practical understanding of these techniques and inform the subsequent design choices.

3 Expected Contributions and Challenges

This research is expected to provide three main contributions. The first is a characterization of the strategies for integrating LLMs into recommender systems, clarifying their potential and limitations with particular attention to conversational and knowledge-based settings. The second consists of methods to exploit structured knowledge, such as ontologies and knowledge graphs, as a support for recommendations, representing evolving user preferences, and producing explanations anchored to domain knowledge. The third is the design of interaction mechanisms, possibly based on tool use and agent workflows, that allow an LLM to operate on a knowledge-based recommender in a verifiable manner, treating it as a structured, rule-based component. Achieving these contributions entails addressing several challenges. Capturing the nuances that emerge during a conversation and mapping them onto structured representations is far from trivial, as it requires bridging the subjective nature of the user requests expressed in natural language with the precision of formal semantic representations. Combining the generative flexibility of LLMs with the rigor of structured knowledge is inherently difficult and requires careful design. Finally, the evaluation of such systems raises additional difficulties, since recommendation quality, data grounding, and explainability need to be assessed together, often beyond what standard recommendation metrics can capture.

By addressing these challenges, this research aims to contribute to the broader effort of integrating generative AI within recommender systems while remaining anchored to structured data and explicit semantics, ultimately supporting reliable, explainable, and personalized recommendations.

Disclosure of Interests. The author has no competing interests to declare that are relevant to the content of this article.

References

1. Aggarwal, C.C.: Knowledge-based recommender systems, pp. 167–197. Springer, Cham (2016). https://doi.org/10.1007/978-3-319-29659-3_5
2. Bagozi, A., Bianchini, D., Garda, M., Melchiori, M., Rula, A.: Ontology-enhanced RAG for a personalised and sustainable food advisory system. Data Knowl. Eng. **164**, 102579 (2026). https://doi.org/10.1016/j.datak.2026.102579
3. Bagozi, A., Bianchini, D., Magrino, P., Melchiori, M., Picchi, S., Rula, A.: Ontology-enhanced RAG architecture for sensory-aware food recommendation. In: Web Information Systems Engineering – WISE 2025, pp. 88–103. Springer, Heidelberg (2026). https://doi.org/10.1007/978-981-95-7251-9_7
4. Deldjoo, Y., He, Z., McAuley, J., et al.: A review of modern recommender systems using generative models (gen-RecSys). In: Proceedings of KDD 2024, pp. 6448–6458. ACM, New York (2024). https://doi.org/10.1145/3637528.3671474
5. Fill, H.G., Horkoff, J., Fettke, P., Köpke, J.: Generative AI and conceptual modeling. Bus. Inf. Syst. Eng. (2026). https://doi.org/10.1007/s12599-025-00978-8
6. Jannach, D., Manzoor, A., Cai, W., Chen, L.: A survey on conversational recommender systems. ACM Comput. Surv. **54**(5) (2021). https://doi.org/10.1145/3453154
7. Kemper, S., Cui, J., Dicarlantonio, K., et al.: Retrieval-augmented conversational recommendation with prompt-based semi-structured natural language state tracking. In: Proceedings of SIGIR 2024, pp. 2786–2790. ACM, New York (2024). https://doi.org/10.1145/3626772.3657670
8. Kim, Y.H., Cho, Y.S.: Conversational recommender systems with large language models: a review of current developments. Expert Syst. Appl. **324**, 132508 (2026)
9. Nawara, D., Kashef, R.: A comprehensive survey on LLM-powered recommender systems: from discriminative, generative to multi-modal paradigms. IEEE Access **13**, 145772–145798 (2025). https://doi.org/10.1109/ACCESS.2025.3599832
10. Peng, Q., Liu, H., Huang, H., Yang, J., Yang, Q., Shao, M.: A survey on LLM-powered agents for recommender systems. In: Findings of EMNLP 2025, pp. 11574–11583. ACL (2025). https://doi.org/10.18653/v1/2025.findings-emnlp.620
11. Raza, S., Rahman, M., Kamawal, S., et al.: A comprehensive review of recommender systems: transitioning from theory to practice. Comput. Sci. Rev. **59**, 100849 (2026). https://doi.org/10.1016/j.cosrev.2025.100849
12. Yang, F., Yue, Y., Li, G., Payne, T., Man, K.: Chain-of-thought prompting empowered generative user modeling for personalized recommendation. Neural Comput. Appl. **36**, 21723–21742 (2024). https://doi.org/10.1007/s00521-024-10364-2
13. Zhao, Z., Fan, W., Li, J., et al.: Recommender systems in the era of large language models (LLMs). IEEE Trans. Knowl. Data Eng. **36**(11), 6889–6907 (2024). https://doi.org/10.1109/TKDE.2024.3392335

DEI4Teach: Diversity, Equity and Inclusion for Teaching Advanced Databases and Information Systems

DEI4Teach: Engaging the ADBIS Community in Rethinking Databases and Information Systems Education with DEI

Barbara Catania[1](✉) and Cécile Favre[2]

[1] DIBRIS, Università di Genova, 16146 Genoa, Italy
barbara.catania@unige.it
[2] ERIC, Université Lumière Lyon 2, Université Lyon 1, 69007 Lyon, France
cecile.favre@univ-lyon2.fr

Abstract. As part of the DEI (Diversity, Equity, Inclusion) initiatives within the ADBIS community, the 2026 edition of the conference is taking a new direction with the organization of a first-of-its-kind workshop dedicated to teaching Databases and Information Systems. The workshop is intended to foster discussions about teaching practices, with the accepted contributions (feedback and reflections based on teaching practices) presented as flash talks to facilitate exchange among participants. Drawing on the analysis of the eight contributions received, this paper presents the challenges of such a workshop and how it has been designed to achieve its objectives.

Keywords: Diversity · Equity · Inclusion · Teaching · Participatory workshop

1 Introduction

Diversity, Equity, and Inclusion (DEI) have become an established priority within the Database research community, which coordinates DEI efforts across major international data management conferences, including ADBIS [2]. The community-wide DEI initiative was launched in 2020 with the goal of fostering a more diverse, equitable, and inclusive research community. Since then, these efforts have focused on promoting inclusive conference practices, accessible participation, inclusive communication, and respectful professional environments [4].

Despite these achievements, the educational dimension of DEI has received considerably less attention. Within the broader community-wide DEI efforts, ADBIS provides an ideal setting to address this gap. Although it is primarily a research conference, it brings together educators at different career stages who train the next generation of Databases and Information Systems professionals. As educators, they play a key role in shaping not only students' technical

© The Author(s), under exclusive license to Springer Nature Switzerland AG 2027
G. Vargas Solar et al. (Eds.): ADBIS 2026, CCIS 3175, pp. 285–294, 2027.
https://doi.org/10.1007/978-3-032-39823-9_28

knowledge but also the values and practices that characterize an inclusive professional community. Additionally, its international nature offers opportunities to exchange experiences across different educational systems, academic cultures, and teaching practices. Such exchanges are particularly valuable as data technologies increasingly underpin AI systems and digital services that affect diverse communities. Taken together, these characteristics make ADBIS a natural forum for discussing the educational dimension of DEI.

When designing such an initiative, the choice of format plays a central role. Previous DEI efforts at ADBIS, such as keynote talks and roundtable discussions, have contributed significantly in raising awareness of DEI-related issues. However, awareness alone is not sufficient when discussing teaching practices. Educators also need opportunities to exchange experience and resources, collectively reflect on their own teaching, and identify concrete, transferable ideas that they can apply in their educational contexts. These considerations motivate the adoption of *participatory* formats in which presentations are deliberately kept brief, to serve primarily as a starting point for peer exchange and collaborative reflection rather than as the main focus of the event.

To address these needs, the ADBIS DEI Chairs launched *DEI4Teach* in 2026, a highly interactive workshop dedicated to DEI in the teaching of Databases, Information Systems and, more broadly, Computer Science. The workshop extends the DEI initiatives of the research community to educational practice, recognizing that an inclusive research community begins with inclusive education. Its participatory format encourages participants to move from discussion to concrete educational practices that they can adapt to their own contexts.

Across Europe, many funded initiatives support innovation in higher education. International conferences complement these efforts by providing opportunities for a research community to collectively reflect on its educational practices. Such community-driven approaches have emerged in different disciplines. Among those developed within the data management field, Cécile Favre co-led a workshop in January 2026 on teaching responsible AI within the French-speaking Knowledge Extraction and Management community (EGC 2026). DEI4Teach extends this approach to the international ADBIS community.

As this paper was written before the workshop, it focuses on the event rationale, design, and the analysis of the accepted contributions, rather than on the outcomes. More precisely, Sect. 2 reviews the relevant background, introduces the conceptual framework adopted in the paper, and describes how it informs the design and organization of the DEI4Teach workshop. Section 3 analyses the accepted contributions according to this framework, identifying the main themes addressed as well as the areas that remain largely unexplored. Finally, Sect. 4 concludes the paper.

2 From Scientific Literature to DEI4Teach Organization

The DEI4Teach workshop was designed by drawing on three complementary strands of research: Databases and Information Systems education, DEI in computing education, and the recent impact of Generative AI on teaching and learning. This section first summarizes the main insights from these research areas, then presents the conceptual framework emerging from them, and finally describes how the framework informed the organization of the workshop.

2.1 Background

Databases and Information Systems Education. Databases and Information Systems Education has evolved into an active research area addressing teaching methods, educational resources, and curriculum design. A comprehensive overview is provided by Ishaq et al. [8]. Since 2022, the International Workshop on Data Systems Education (DataEd) has established a dedicated forum for educational research within the data management community [1]. Recent work has also proposed innovative approaches for teaching specific database topics, such as participatory data modelling and collaborative database design [11,12]. However, these contributions are primarily motivated by pedagogical innovation rather than explicitly by DEI.

DEI in Computing Education. Existing work focuses on different complementary directions. The first addresses the *integration of DEI-related topics into computing education*, including responsible data management/AI/data science, data ethics, and transparency [7,19]. Comparatively little work has explicitly addressed how *embedding DEI into learning materials and educational resources* (examples, datasets, case studies, and projects) of classical computing course contents [7,9] and we are not aware of any specific approach providing a diversity-aware perspective to traditional Databases and Information Systems topics. Another direction focuses on the development of *inclusive pedagogical practices* for diverse student populations, which are in general not specifically related to Databases and Information Systems education. It includes active and collaborative learning, scaffolding, project-based activities, equitable group formation, support for diverse student populations, differentiated teaching, and strategies to improve the participation of underrepresented groups and engagement. Many recent results in this context come from the ACM Conference on Innovation and Technology in Computer Science Education (ITiCSE) community (see, e.g., [6,18]). A final direction concerns *student assessment and educational equity.* This theme promotes equity through conceptual understanding, critical reasoning, and multiple ways of demonstrating learning. It also includes evidence-based analyses of student performance to inform equitable educational practices [15].

Generative AI and Data Education. The rapid adoption of Generative AI has recently become a major driver of change in higher computing education [10]. For what concerns Databases and Information Systems education, beyond introducing AI-related topics into computing curricula, it is reshaping learning materials, pedagogical practices, and student assessment. Current research has investigated both the opportunities and the challenges introduced by AI-assisted learning, including student performance [16], automatic exercise generation [3,14], authentic assessment [17], and feedback on errors in SQL queries [13,14].

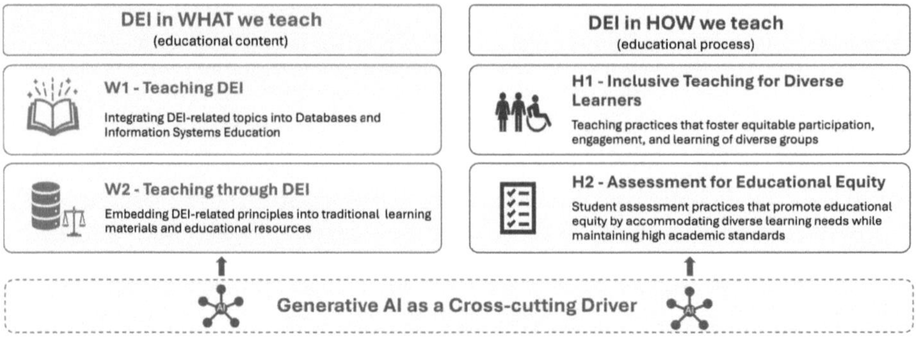

Fig. 1. The DEI4Teach conceptual framework.

2.2 DEI4Teach Conceptual Framework

The literature reviewed above highlights several complementary directions for embedding DEI into Databases and Information Systems education. Rather than considering these directions independently, DEI4Teach organizes them into a conceptual framework based on two complementary dimensions: *DEI in WHAT we teach* and *DEI in HOW we teach*. Generative AI is not considered as an independent dimension of the framework. Rather, it acts as a cross-cutting driver that influences both perspectives.

The first dimension, *DEI in WHAT we teach*, concerns the educational content. It encompasses two complementary directions emerging from the literature:

- *Teaching DEI*: the integration of DEI-related topics into Databases and Information Systems education, including responsible data management and analysis, algorithmic and representation bias, transparency, privacy.
- *Teaching through DEI*: embedding DEI principles into traditional learning materials and educational resources, such as examples, datasets, case studies, and projects.

This perspective encourages educators to revise both the topics covered and the educational resources used in their courses, reflecting on how they represent diverse users and contexts, where bias or underrepresentation may emerge, and how broader DEI perspectives can be naturally integrated into a course content.

The second dimension, *DEI in HOW we teach*, focuses on the educational process. It captures the following two directions:

- *Inclusive teaching for diverse learners*: practices that foster equitable participation, engagement, and learning of diverse groups and minorities.
- *Assessment for educational equity*: student assessment practices that promote educational equity by accommodating diverse learning needs while maintaining high academic standards.

This dimension allows educators to critically examine teaching methods, classroom interactions, supervision, and assessment practices, reflecting on how they support, or unintentionally hinder, equitable participation and learning outcomes, and to identify concrete, transferable strategies for creating more inclusive learning environments.

The conceptual framework, summarized in Fig. 1, has been used to guide the design of DEI4Teach. It has informed the call for contributions, has provided the basis for analysing the accepted papers, and is intended to structure the interactive discussions and collaborative activities during the workshop.

2.3 DEI4Teach Organization

Since DEI is the central theme of the DEI4Teach workshop, we believe that its principles should be embodied in the workshop itself. For this reason, the workshop opens with a set of guidelines for ensuring a smooth and inclusive group experience, encouraging participants to practice active listening, engage with kindness and respect, and give everyone a chance to speak.

Speaking up is a fundamental aspect of a participatory workshop. Thus, the workshop emphasizes the importance of equitable participation in discussions and raise awareness of common inequalities that can arise, sometimes without participants realizing it. In addition, to create an atmosphere conducive to sharing thoughts and ideas, icebreaker activities are included to help participants get to know one another at the start of the workshop.

The call for contributions resulted in eight accepted contributions, presented as flash talks to serve as the basis for discussion. These very short presentations are intended to leave ample time for participatory discussions. Depending on the number of attendees, participants may be divided into small groups to address different aspects (themes explored in the contributions and beyond), with the grouping based on participants' interests.

The workshop allocates dedicated time for the subgroups to present their results, share resources, and discuss common themes. To share the expected outcomes of these discussions more widely, we intend to disseminate them to the broader ADBIS 2026 community through a plenary synthesis, alongside the DEI keynote given by Tiziana Catarci [5], and through a collaborative resource board, encouraging participants to reflect on their own teaching practices and continue exchanging educational experiences beyond the workshop.

The accepted contributions span a wide range of experiences and reflections, demonstrating different levels of knowledge and awareness of DEI. We believe that this diversity is an important factor in broadening participants' engagement with these issues. Together, these contributions reveal recurring themes and complementary perspectives, which are analysed in the following section.

3 Analysis of the DEI4Teach Contributions

The DEI4Teach contributions describe experiences from different countries. Rather than presenting them individually, we first examine their main characteristics and then we analyse them through the conceptual framework introduced in Subsect. 2.2.

Table 1. Workshop contributions (in alphabetical order by first author), their educational context, and the DEI dimensions they address.

ID	Workshop contribution	Contributors	Country	Course level	Age	Disability	Gender	Culture	Language	Knowledge/skills	Learning profile
C1	Bridging Theory and Practice in Advanced Databases Learning through Student-driven Exploration	S. Benkrid	Algeria	UG						✓	✓
C2	New Challenge: Shaping Insight and Intuition from Data Block Knowledge	F. Bugiotti	France	UG	✓		✓				✓
C3	Supporting the Inclusion of Students on the Autism Spectrum in Large Classes: Challenges and Lessons Learned	L. Farinetti	Italy	UG		✓					
C4	Beyond SQL Syntax: Supporting Diverse Learners in Database Use-case Design	K. Hatano	Japan	UG						✓	
C5	Teaching Database Systems Inclusively in the AI Era: Why Fundamental Theory Matters More than Ever	N. Iftikhar	Denmark	UG						✓	
C6	Who Fails, Who Passes? A Look at Gender in the Grades of Two Database Courses	A. Karakasidis G. Koloniari	Greece	UG			✓				
C7	Eco-Collective Database Education for Inclusive and Responsible AI	G. Vargas-Solar	France	—				✓			
C8	Intercultural Competences for Inclusion and Diversity	T. Welzer	Slovenia	—				✓	✓	✓	

3.1 Overview of the Accepted Contributions

Our first perspective examines the received contributions in terms of their main characteristics and the DEI dimensions they cover. Table 1 summarizes their educational context (country and course level, when specified) and classifies the corresponding DEI dimensions into three categories: *social* (age, disability, and gender), *contextual* (culture and language), and *educational* (prior knowledge/skills and learning profiles).

The contributions primarily address educational dimensions of diversity. Prior knowledge, skills, and learning profiles emerge as the most frequently considered aspects (C1, C2, C4, C5, and C8), reflecting a shared concern for accommodating students with heterogeneous backgrounds, prior experiences, and ways of learning. Social dimensions are comparatively less represented. Disability is explicitly addressed only in C3 through the inclusion of a student with Autism Spectrum Disorder. Interestingly, despite being one of the most extensively investigated DEI dimensions in science and technology education, gender is explicitly considered only in C6. Age is almost absent, appearing only marginally in C2. Contextual dimensions receive even less attention, with cultural and linguistic aspects being discussed mainly in C7 and C8 through intercultural awareness and multilingual educational contexts.

3.2 Analysis with Respect to the Conceptual Framework

Table 2 maps the accepted contributions onto the four directions of the DEI4Teach conceptual framework presented in Subsect. 2.2 and indicates whether Generative AI is part of the proposed educational approach. The following paragraphs briefly discuss the contributions associated with each conceptual framework direction.

Table 2. Analysis of workshop contributions with respect to the DEI4Teach conceptual framework. A filled circle (●) denotes a primary objective, whereas an empty circle (❍) denotes a complementary one.

ID	W1	W2	H1	H2	AI
C1		❍	●	❍	✓
C2		●	●		✓
C3			●	❍	
C4		●	●		
C5	●		❍	●	✓
C6				●	
C7	●	❍	❍		✓
C8		●	❍		

W1 - Teaching DEI. Contributions C5 and C7 propose to explicitly enrich the educational content of Databases and Information Systems courses with topics related to responsible AI and responsible data management. C5 argues that the widespread adoption of Generative AI requires students to critically evaluate AI-generated artefacts through concepts such as privacy, security, and responsible AI. C7 extends traditional database education with broader themes including data justice, decolonial AI, and sustainability.

W2 - Teaching Through DEI. Contributions C2, C4, and C8 illustrate how DEI can be embedded into the teaching of traditional Databases and Information Systems topics through the learning contexts adopted rather than through dedicated DEI content. C2 uses datasets containing bias, anomalies, and missing values to encourage critical data exploration while learning querying and modelling techniques. C4 promotes meaningful use cases that connect database concepts with students' interests and diverse application domains. C8 embeds intercultural awareness into traditional database topics by using culturally diverse naming conventions and real-world data representation issues as learning contexts. C1 and C7 further support this theme by broadening the contexts through which database concepts are taught: C1 through multiple database paradigms and technologies, and C7 through an authentic food-sharing scenario that relates database integration and analytics to social and environmental challenges.

H1 - Inclusive Teaching for Diverse Learners. Inclusive teaching emerges as the most prominent theme, explicitly addressed by C1, C2, C3, and C4, and indirectly by C5, C7, and C8. C1 proposes multiple learning pathways by allowing students to choose technologies, datasets, and application domains based on their interests and experience. C2 supports inclusive learning through a collaborative data treasure hunt that enables students with diverse perspectives and learning profiles to jointly construct knowledge. C3 presents concrete strategies for supporting the inclusion of students with Autism Spectrum Disorder while preserving the course learning objectives. C4 promotes inclusive learning by connecting database concepts with meaningful use cases, providing multiple entry points for students with different backgrounds and prior programming experience. C5 and C7 also contribute to inclusive teaching by engaging students in critically analysing AI-generated artefacts and their implications for responsible data management. C8 complements this theme by encouraging instructors to adopt inclusive teaching practices in increasingly diverse educational contexts.

H2 - Assessment for Educational Equity. Assessment for educational equity is explicitly addressed by contributions C5 and C6, and indirectly by C1 and C3. C5 proposes AI-aware assessment centered on explanation, critique, and justification rather than syntax production, enabling students to demonstrate conceptual understanding through different forms of reasoning. C6 complements these proposals with an empirical analysis of gender differences in assessment outcomes, encouraging evidence-based reflection on participation, retention, and student success. Additionally, C1 promotes distributed assessment through projects and laboratory activities, providing students with multiple opportunities to demonstrate their competences. C3 indirectly addresses educational equity by adapting collaborative activities to ensure that a neurodiverse student could participate in the same assessment while preserving common learning objectives.

3.3 Emerging Themes and Blind Spots

The analysis above identifies the main themes emerging from the accepted contributions. Comparing them with the original scope of the DEI4Teach call reveals several underrepresented areas. In particular, none of the contributions addresses the supervision and mentoring of undergraduate or graduate students, while socio-economic diversity and accessibility of learning materials, tools, and educational environments remain largely unexplored. Cultural and linguistic diversity are explicitly addressed only in C8 and C7, and no contribution explicitly considers gender identity, sexual orientation, ethnicity or intersectional perspectives that combine multiple DEI dimensions. Considering all these categories may help to highlight negative (and sometimes unconscious) behaviour in the classroom, such as sexism, racism, homophobia, etc.

The analysis also highlights gaps related to the educational contexts represented. While the workshop includes contributions from different countries, all of them focus on undergraduate education and on experiences within a single institutional setting, leaving graduate education and other learning contexts largely unexplored. Finally, the conceptual framework reveals that inclusive pedagogical practices are well represented, whereas considerably less attention is devoted to educational equity beyond assessment, including students' sense of belonging, participation, retention, and supervision.

4 Concluding Remarks

This paper introduced the rationale, conceptual framework, and organization of DEI4Teach, the first ADBIS workshop dedicated to DEI in Databases and Information Systems education. Although not intended to provide exhaustive coverage, the eight contributions span different countries, educational contexts, and approaches, offering a valuable basis for community discussion. Their analysis, according to the educational context, the addressed DEI dimensions, and the proposed conceptual framework, also highlights some blind spots and reveals complementary perspectives on how DEI can be integrated into both educational content and teaching practices.

Consistent with the principles of DEI, DEI4Teach has been designed as a participatory workshop that combines flash presentations with collaborative discussions. Beyond the workshop itself, we hope this initiative will contribute to establishing a sustained forum for exchanging teaching practices within the ADBIS community and stimulate future research and collaborative initiatives on DEI in Databases and Information Systems education.

Acknowledgments. We would like to thank those who responded to our call for contributions for the DEI4Teach workshop, in the alphabetical order:

- Soumia Benkrid (École nationale Supérieure d'Informatique, Algiers, Algeria)
- Francesca Bugiotti (Université Paris-Saclay, CNRS, CentraleSupélec, LISN, France)
- Laura Farinetti (Politecnico di Torino, Torino, Italy)
- Kenji Hatano (Doshisha University, Kyoto, Japan)
- Nadeem Iftikhar (University College of Northern Denmark, Aalborg, Denmark)
- Alexandros Karakasidis (University of Macedonia, Thessaloniki, Greece)
- Georgia Koloniari (University of Macedonia, Thessaloniki, Greece)
- Genoveva Vargas-Solar (CNRS, LIRIS, Lyon, France)
- Tatjana Welzer (University of Maribor, Maribor, Slovenia)

Moreover, the organisation of the workshop was funded, in part, by the Agence Nationale de la Recherche (ANR), grant ANR-24-CE38-5812.

References

1. DataEd Initiative (2026). https://dataedinitiative.github.io. Accessed 13 July 2026
2. Diversity, Equity, and Inclusion in Database Conferences (2026). https://dbdni.github.io. Accessed 13 July 2026
3. Aerts, W., Fletcher, G., Miedema, D.: A feasibility study on automated SQL exercise generation with ChatGPT-3.5. In: Proceedings of DataEd, pp. 13–19 (2024)
4. Barret, N., et al.: Diversity, equity and inclusion activities in database conferences: a 2024 report. SIGMOD Rec. **54**(3), 40–43 (2025)
5. Catarci, T.: Gender gap in ICT: from missing women to missing data. ADBIS DEI Keynote, ADBIS (2026)
6. Forshaw, M., et al.: Fairness in student allocation and group formation. In: Proceeding of ACM ITiCSE, vol. 2, pp. 699–700 (2025)
7. Grosz, B.J., et al.: Embedded EthiCS: integrating ethics broadly across computer science education. Commun. ACM **62**(8), 54–61 (2019)
8. Ishaq, M., et al.: Advances in database systems education: methods, tools, curricula, and way forward. Educ. Inf. Tech. **28**(3), 2681–2725 (2023)
9. Li, T., Zhou, Y., Magana, A.J.: Towards learnersourcing relatable and contextualized learning materials: an exploratory study in a database programming class. In: Proceeding of ACM ITiCSE, vol. 1, pp. 479–485 (2025)
10. Mak, J., et al.: A plan for an ACM task force working group into the ethical and societal impacts of generative AI in higher computing education. In: Proceedings of ACM ITiCSE, vol. 2, pp. 703–704 (2025)
11. Makovska, V., et al.: Seasoning data modeling education with GARLIC: a participatory co-design framework. In: Proceeding of the EDBT/ICDT Workshops. CEUR Workshop Proceedings, vol. 4192 (2026)
12. Makovska, V., Fletcher, G., Stoyanovich, J.: ONION: a multi-layered framework for participatory ER design. In: Proceedings of HILDA, pp. 3:1–3:7 (2025)
13. Manikani, K., Chapaneri, R., Shetty, D., Shah, D.: SQL autograder: web-based LLM-powered autograder for assessment of SQL queries. Int. J. Artif. Intell. Educ. **35**(4), 2047–2077 (2025)
14. Ponzini, D., Catania, B., Guerrini, G.: Enhancing SQL learning through generative AI and student error analysis. In: New Trends in Database and Information Systems - ADBIS 2025 Short Papers. Communications in Computer and Information Science, vol. 2676, pp. 118–128. Springer (2025)
15. Ragupathi, K., Lee, A.: Beyond fairness and consistency in grading: the role of rubrics in higher education. In: Sanger, C.S., Gleason, N.W. (eds.) Diversity and Inclusion in Global Higher Education, pp. 73–95. Springer, Singapore (2020)
16. Ramakrishnan, C., Cassidy, S., Bower, M.: Evaluating student performance and interactions in generative AI-integrated SQL practical tests. In: Proceedings of ACM ITiCSE (2025)
17. R. Sooriamurthi, X. Tu, and A. E. C. Pensky. A generative AI tool to foster and assess authentic learning: a case study in teaching SQL. In: Proceedings of ACM ITiCSE, pp. 465–471 (2025)
18. Stephens, G., O'Sullivan, D.: Design of a technology ethics serious game: cultivating ethical thinking. In: Proceedings of ACM ITiCSE, vol. 2, p. 792 (2025)
19. Stoyanovich, J., Lewis, A.: Teaching responsible data science: charting new pedagogical territory. Int. J. Artif. Intell. Educ. **32**(3), 783–807 (2022)

MADEISD 2026: 8th Workshop on Modern Approaches in Data Engineering and Information System Design

Performance and Fairness Evaluation of Deep Learning Models for Prostate Cancer Detection

Israt Jahan Runa, Maria Stratigi(✉), and Kostas Stefanidis

Data Science Research Centre, Tampere University, Tampere, Finland
{maria.stratigi,konstantinos.stefanidis}@tuni.fi

Abstract. Prostate cancer diagnosis from MRI remains challenging due to variations across imaging modalities and lesion characteristics, which can affect the reliability of deep learning models. Although deep learning methods have shown promising performance in prostate MRI analysis, subgroup fairness and reproducible patient-level evaluation remain less explored. To address these challenges, this study evaluates ResNet-18, DenseNet-121, and EfficientNet-B0 using T2, DWI, and ADC modalities from the Prostate158 dataset. MRI volumes were converted into normalized 2D slices and evaluated at the patient level using Youden's J-based threshold optimization. ADC-based models achieved the most stable performance, while fairness analysis revealed moderate disparities across lesion-based subgroups. Robustness experiments further confirmed the stability of the proposed workflow. The findings demonstrate that fairness-aware threshold calibration can improve subgroup fairness with minimal impact on diagnostic accuracy.

Keywords: Deep learning · Convolutional neural networks · bi-parametric MRI (bpMRI) · Fairness · Trustworthy AI

1 Introduction

Prostate cancer is one of the most common cancers among men worldwide, and early diagnosis is essential for effective treatment and improved patient outcomes. Traditional diagnostic methods, such as prostate-specific antigen (PSA) testing and systematic biopsy, often suffer from low specificity, invasiveness, and sampling bias. bi-parametric MRI (bpMRI), particularly T2-weighted imaging, diffusion-weighted imaging (DWI), and apparent diffusion coefficient (ADC) imaging, has emerged as a promising non-invasive alternative by providing complementary anatomical and microstructural information.

Recent advances in deep learning, particularly convolutional neural networks (CNNs), have significantly improved medical image analysis. Motivated by these developments, this study evaluates three representative CNN architectures, ResNet-18, DenseNet-121, and EfficientNet-B0, for prostate cancer detection using the publicly available Prostate158 dataset. The models are evaluated

© The Author(s), under exclusive license to Springer Nature Switzerland AG 2027
G. Vargas Solar et al. (Eds.): ADBIS 2026, CCIS 3175, pp. 299–314, 2027.
https://doi.org/10.1007/978-3-032-39823-9_29

across T2, DWI, and ADC modalities using a unified experimental workflow with consistent preprocessing, training, and evaluation procedures.

Although previous studies have reported promising classification performance, most focus primarily on accuracy while giving limited attention to fairness [2,3,6] and consistency across clinically relevant subgroups. Model performance may vary across tumor characteristics such as lesion zone, tumor size, and lesion count, potentially affecting diagnostic reliability. Moreover, differences in preprocessing and evaluation strategies reduce reproducibility and comparability, highlighting the need for a standardized and fairness-aware evaluation workflow.

To address these limitations, this study evaluates diagnostic performance and subgroup fairness across tumor zone (Peripheral vs. Central), tumor size (Small vs. Large), and lesion count (Single vs. Multiple). It further investigates whether post-hoc threshold calibration using Youden's J statistic can improve subgroup fairness without model retraining. Reproducibility is ensured through deterministic seeds, standardized preprocessing, and patient-level prediction aggregation.

To further clarify the objectives of this study, the following research questions are addressed: **RQ1:** How do ResNet-18, DenseNet-121, and EfficientNet-B0 compare in patient-level prostate cancer detection across T2, DWI, and ADC modalities? **RQ2:** How consistent are the diagnostic performance and subgroup fairness of these models across clinically relevant lesion-based subgroups? **RQ3:** How does patient-level threshold calibration using Youden's J statistic affect the trade-off between diagnostic performance and subgroup fairness?

The main contributions of this work are summarized as follows:

- A unified and reproducible workflow for patient-level evaluation of prostate cancer classification using T2, DWI, and ADC modalities from the Prostate158 dataset.
- A comparative evaluation of ResNet-18, DenseNet-121, and EfficientNet-B0 under identical experimental settings for unbiased benchmarking.
- Fairness analysis across clinically relevant lesion subgroups based on tumor zone, tumor size, and lesion count.
- Patient-level prediction aggregation and post-hoc threshold calibration using Youden's J statistic for clinically meaningful evaluation.
- Statistical validation using confidence intervals and McNemar's test to improve the reliability of the findings.

The remainder of this paper is organized as follows. Section 2 reviews related work on prostate cancer detection and fairness-aware medical AI. Section 3 presents the dataset, preprocessing pipeline, and methodology. Section 4 discusses the experimental results and fairness analysis. Finally, Sect. 5 concludes the paper and outlines future research directions.

2 Related Work

Deep learning has significantly improved prostate cancer detection from MRI by enabling automated lesion localization, grading, and classification. Early approaches, such as FocalNet, demonstrated that CNN-based models could jointly detect and assign Gleason grades from mpMRI, although generalization to small or high-grade tumors remained limited [5]. Yoo *et al.* further showed that diffusion-weighted imaging (DWI) alone can achieve strong discrimination performance when trained on carefully curated datasets [18]. These studies demonstrated the growing potential of CNN-based frameworks for assisting radiologists in prostate cancer diagnosis and reducing manual interpretation variability.

Several studies have explored bi-parametric MRI (bpMRI) as a practical alternative to mpMRI due to its reduced acquisition time and lower clinical complexity. De Vente *et al.* proposed an ordinal-regression framework that improved lesion-grading consistency compared with conventional multi-class classifiers [17]. Hosseinzadeh *et al.* demonstrated that anatomical priors combined with annotated cases can provide competitive diagnostic performance even without dynamic contrast-enhanced imaging [8]. Karagoz *et al.* further introduced anatomically guided nnU-Net architectures capable of generalizing across imaging centers [10]. Together, these studies indicate that bi-parametric MRI (bpMRI) can provide clinically meaningful diagnostic performance while reducing acquisition complexity and scanning time.

CNN architectures, such as ResNet, DenseNet and EfficientNet, have become widely adopted in medical imaging because of their representation capability and transfer-learning advantages. DenseNet architectures are particularly effective in limited-data medical settings due to improved feature reuse and gradient propagation [9]. EfficientNet models achieve strong accuracy-efficiency tradeoffs through compound scaling and lightweight convolutional blocks [15]. Beyond prostate imaging, transfer learning and multimodal CNN frameworks have shown promising performance in heterogeneous medical imaging tasks [4]. These architectures therefore provide strong baseline models for comparative prostate MRI evaluation while also supporting modality-wise consistency analysis.

Radiomics and multimodal learning approaches have further improved MRI-based prostate cancer analysis. Rodrigues *et al.* demonstrated that combining handcrafted radiomic features with clinical information improves aggressiveness prediction and interpretability [14]. Recent studies additionally highlighted the importance of multimodal fusion, robust preprocessing, and anatomically guided learning strategies for handling heterogeneous imaging protocols and multi-center datasets. These developments indicate a shift toward more generalized and clinically reliable deep-learning frameworks for prostate MRI analysis.

Robustness, calibration, and domain generalization have recently become important research directions in medical AI. Li *et al.* proposed an unsupervised domain adaptation framework for DWI harmonization that improved performance across imaging distributions [11]. However, most previous studies focused primarily on slice-level or lesion-level accuracy and rarely evaluated fairness or calibration at the patient level. Fairness-aware evaluation aims to ensure equitable performance across clinically relevant patient groups and to reduce biases caused by data imbalance or acquisition variability [16]. Subgroup-balanced validation and calibration techniques have been shown to improve fairness consistency in radiology applications [13]. In addition, fairness concepts from recommender systems provide transferable ideas for fairness-aware medical imaging evaluation. These studies motivate the inclusion of subgroup-aware evaluation and fairness analysis in prostate cancer classification frameworks.

Although previous studies demonstrate strong progress in MRI-based prostate cancer detection, important gaps remain in reproducibility, patient-level evaluation, calibration, and fairness analysis. This work addresses these limitations through a unified framework that evaluates ResNet-18, DenseNet-121, and EfficientNet-B0 across T2, DWI, and ADC modalities using standardized preprocessing, patient-level aggregation, and fairness-aware evaluation.

3 Dataset Description

This study utilizes the publicly available Prostate158 dataset [1], which contains multiparametric MRI (mpMRI) scans from 158 male subjects with confirmed or suspected prostate cancer. The dataset includes T2-weighted, diffusion-weighted (DWI), and apparent diffusion coefficient (ADC) modalities collected from multiple institutions and 3T MRI scanners, reflecting realistic multi-center imaging variability. Only 139 subjects with complete T2, DWI, and ADC modalities were included in the study. Cases with missing modalities were excluded to ensure consistent multimodal input. Only the training portion of the dataset was used because the public test set does not contain ground-truth annotations and is intended for benchmark submissions.[1] Patient-level stratified splitting was applied to preserve class balance and prevent data leakage. The selected dataset comprised 3,586 T2 slices, 3,586 DWI slices, and 3,583 ADC slices (10,755 2D slices in total), which were used in all subsequent experiments.

T2 images provide anatomical information, DWI highlights diffusion restriction, and ADC maps quantify diffusion characteristics related to tumor aggressiveness. Expert-annotated segmentation masks were available for all included cases, enabling lesion-based subgroup analysis across tumor size, zone, and count. Figure 1 presents example T2, DWI, and ADC slices from the same patient, demonstrating the complementary characteristics of each modality and the corresponding tumor region used for further analysis.

Normal slices dominate the dataset because tumor regions occupy only a limited portion of the prostate volume. Most lesions fall within intermediate-to-large tumor-size ranges, while single-lesion and peripheral-zone cases are the most common patterns observed. Figure 2 summarizes the lesion zone and lesion count distribution within the 139-patient subset used in this study. As shown in Fig. 2, peripheral-zone and single-lesion cases represent the majority of the included subjects, indicating an imbalanced but clinically realistic subgroup distribution. Overall, the dataset provides a clinically realistic benchmark for prostate MRI classification and supports reproducible evaluation of deep learning models across multimodal imaging data.

[1] Ground-truth annotations are available only for the training dataset; therefore, only the labelled training data were used with internal splitting for validation and testing.

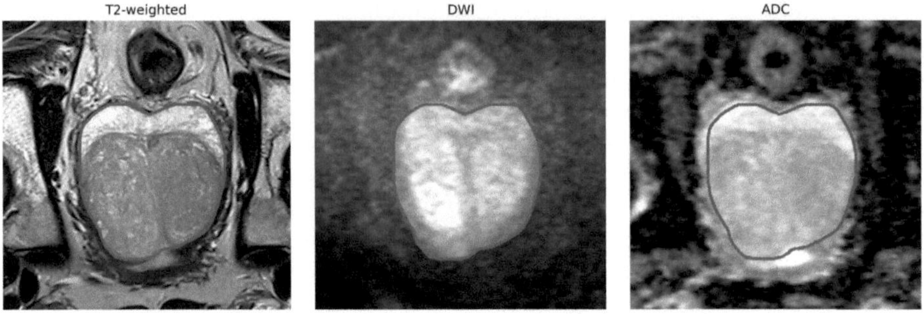

Fig. 1. T2, DWI, and ADC slices from the same Prostate158 patient showing the red-outlined tumor region across modalities. (Color figure online)

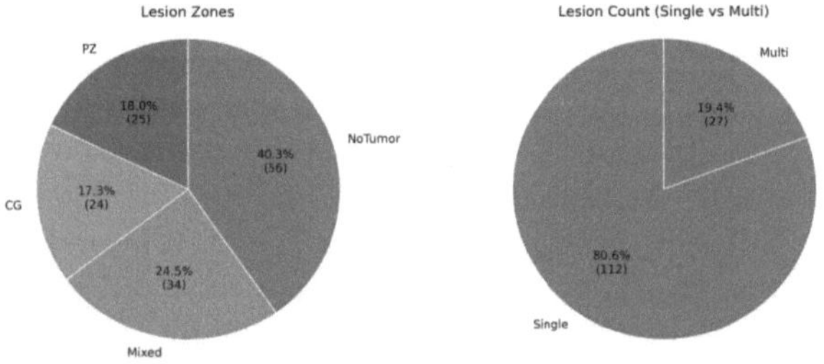

Fig. 2. Lesion zone and count distribution in the 139-patient Prostate158 subset.

4 Methodology

We follow a structured and reproducible workflow for prostate cancer classification using bi-parametric MRI (bpMRI) data from the Prostate158 dataset. First, subjects with complete T2, DWI, and ADC modalities were selected together with expert-annotated tumor masks. The three-dimensional MRI volumes were then converted into standardized two-dimensional axial slices suitable for CNN-based classification. During preprocessing, slice extraction, tumor-mask handling, intensity normalization, resizing to 224×224, and quality validation were performed to ensure consistent input across all modalities. After preprocessing, patient-level data partitioning was applied using a 70:10:20 split for training, validation, and testing to prevent data leakage between subsets. Stratified sampling with a fixed random seed (`seed = 42`) was used to preserve class balance across splits. Each MRI modality (T2, DWI, and ADC) was then used independently to train three convolutional neural network architectures: ResNet-18, DenseNet-121, and EfficientNet-B0 using ImageNet-pretrained weights.

During evaluation, slice-level predictions were aggregated into patient-level probabilities using mean pooling to better reflect clinical diagnosis. All experiments followed identical preprocessing, training, and evaluation settings across architectures and modalities to ensure reproducibility and fair comparison. The optimal classification threshold for each model was selected using Youden's J statistic on the validation set and applied to the test set. Final performance evaluation was conducted using patient-level AUC, Accuracy, Sensitivity, and Specificity.

To ensure statistical reliability and fairness assessment, bootstrap confidence intervals and McNemar's test were applied. Fairness analysis was performed across tumor-related subgroups based on lesion zone, tumor size, and lesion count. In addition, robustness validation and threshold-based fairnessâĂŞaccuracy trade-off analysis were conducted to evaluate the stability and consistency of the proposed framework across CNN architectures and MRI modalities.

4.1 Data Preprocessing and Standardization

The three-dimensional MRI volumes from the Prostate158 dataset were converted into standardized two-dimensional axial slices suitable for CNN-based classification. The preprocessing pipeline included slice extraction, tumor-mask handling, intensity normalization, resizing, and quality validation. Each subject contained T2, ADC, and DWI scans. Tumor masks were available for the T2 and ADC modalities. For DWI, slice labels were assigned using the corresponding lesion annotations from aligned modalities to maintain consistency across imaging sequences. A slice was labelled as cancerous if tumor pixels were present in the corresponding annotation mask; otherwise, it was labelled as normal.

To reduce inter-subject intensity variability, min–max normalization was applied independently to each MRI slice [7] according to Eq. (1):

$$\tilde{S}_{m,i}^{(p)} = \frac{S_{m,i}^{(p)} - \min(S_{m,i}^{(p)})}{\max(S_{m,i}^{(p)}) - \min(S_{m,i}^{(p)})} \tag{1}$$

where $S_{m,i}^{(p)}$ represents the original intensity values of the i-th axial slice from modality m for patient p, $\min(S_{m,i}^{(p)})$ and $\max(S_{m,i}^{(p)})$ denote the minimum and maximum pixel intensities of that slice, and $\tilde{S}_{m,i}^{(p)}$ represents the normalized slice with intensity values scaled to the range $[0, 1]$.

After normalization, all images were resized to 224×224 pixels to match the input requirements of the CNN architectures used in this study. The resized image dimensions are expressed in Eq. (2):

$$I_{m,i}^{(p)} \in \mathbb{R}^{224\times 224} \tag{2}$$

where $I_{m,i}^{(p)}$ denotes the processed two-dimensional image slice from modality m, slice index i, and patient p.

Only subjects with complete and spatially aligned T2, ADC, and DWI modalities were retained for analysis. This ensured consistent multimodal correspondence and reduced variability caused by incomplete or misaligned imaging data.

Cases containing missing modalities, corrupted scans, or inconsistent annotations were excluded during preprocessing to maintain data integrity. All preprocessing operations were performed automatically while preserving patient-level consistency across modalities.

4.2 Experimental Design and Data Partitioning

To prevent data leakage, all partitioning was performed at the patient level, ensuring that slices from the same subject were never shared across training, validation, and testing sets. The dataset of 139 subjects was divided into training, validation, and testing sets using a 70:10:20 ratio with stratified sampling and a fixed random seed (`seed = 42`) to preserve class balance across splits. This resulted in 97 training patients, 14 validation patients, and 28 testing patients. The same partitioning strategy was applied consistently across T2, DWI, and ADC modalities to ensure fair comparison between models trained on different imaging types.

4.3 Model Architectures

Three convolutional neural network architectures ResNet-18, DenseNet-121, and EfficientNet-B0 were selected for comparative evaluation. These models represent complementary design approaches based on residual learning, feature reuse, and computational efficiency. ResNet-18 was selected for stable optimization, DenseNet-121 for efficient feature reuse, and EfficientNet-B0 for its balance between accuracy and computational efficiency. All models were initialized using ImageNet-pretrained weights and fine-tuned independently on T2, ADC, and DWI modalities.

4.4 Training Configuration

All models were trained under identical settings to ensure fair comparison across architectures and modalities. ResNet-18, DenseNet-121, and EfficientNet-B0 were fine-tuned separately on T2, ADC, and DWI modalities, resulting in nine independent experiments. Training used the Adam optimizer ($\beta_1 = 0.9, \beta_2 = 0.999$) with an initial learning rate of 1×10^{-3}, batch size of 32, and 20 epochs. Binary cross-entropy loss with class weighting was applied to address class imbalance. Light augmentation, including horizontal and vertical flips and $\pm 10^\circ$ rotations, was used during training. All images were normalized before training to ensure consistent intensity scaling across modalities. The best checkpoint was selected based on validation AUC. All trained weights, validation metrics, and experiment logs were stored automatically to maintain traceability and reproducibility across experiments.

All experiments were implemented in Python using PyTorch within the Anaconda Navigator environment and executed through Jupyter Notebook 7.3.2 on an NVIDIA RTX GPU with CUDA support.

4.5 Evaluation Design

Evaluation was performed at the patient level because MRI volumes contain multiple correlated slices. Each model generated slice-level probabilities that were aggregated using mean pooling (Eq. (3)).

$$\hat{y}^{(p)} = \frac{1}{N_p} \sum_{i=1}^{N_p} \hat{y}_i^{(p)} \tag{3}$$

where $\hat{y}_i^{(p)}$ represents the predicted probability for slice i of patient p, N_p denotes the total number of slices belonging to patient p, and $\hat{y}^{(p)}$ represents the aggregated patient-level probability obtained through mean pooling.

Patient-level aggregation was adopted because MRI diagnosis is clinically performed per patient rather than per individual slice. Aggregating slice-level probabilities through mean pooling reduced prediction variability caused by isolated slice misclassifications and enabled more stable comparison across MRI modalities and CNN architectures.

The optimal decision threshold was determined using Youden's J statistic [19] as defined in Eq. (4):

$$J(t) = \text{Sensitivity}(t) + \text{Specificity}(t) - 1 \tag{4}$$

where $J(t)$ denotes Youden's index at threshold t, Sensitivity(t) represents the true positive rate at threshold t, and Specificity(t) represents the true negative rate at threshold t. The threshold maximizing $J(t)$ on the validation set was applied to the test set for final evaluation. This threshold optimization strategy enabled more balanced evaluation between sensitivity and specificity across different MRI modalities and CNN architectures.

Performance was evaluated using patient-level Area Under the ROC Curve (AUC), Accuracy, Sensitivity, and Specificity. Confidence intervals (95%) were estimated using bootstrap resampling. The same held-out test set was used across all experiments to ensure consistent comparison across architectures and modalities. This unified evaluation protocol enabled direct comparison of modality-specific and architecture-specific performance under identical clinical operating conditions.

4.6 Analysis Pipeline

A comprehensive analysis pipeline was developed to evaluate statistical reliability, fairness, and robustness across models and modalities. Bootstrap resampling was used to estimate 95% confidence intervals for Accuracy, Sensitivity, and Specificity. Pairwise model comparisons were performed using McNemar's test [12]. Fairness analysis examined model consistency across tumor-related subgroups based on lesion zone, tumor size, and lesion count. Subgroup-level evaluation was performed to investigate whether model behavior remained consistent across clinically relevant lesion characteristics. Lesion-based subgroup information was used to define tumor-size and lesion-count categories for fairness evaluation. Subgroup disparities were quantified using Eq. (5):

$$\Delta M = |M_{g_1} - M_{g_2}| \tag{5}$$

where ΔM represents the absolute subgroup performance gap, M_{g_1} denotes the performance metric for subgroup g_1, and M_{g_2} denotes the corresponding performance metric for subgroup g_2. The metric M corresponds to Accuracy, Sensitivity, or Specificity depending on the evaluation setting.

To investigate the trade-off between diagnostic performance and fairness, different classification thresholds were evaluated around the optimal Youden's J threshold [19]. Accuracy and subgroup fairness gaps were recomputed at each operating point. In turn, robustness was evaluated using repeated patient-level validation experiments across CNN architectures and MRI modalities to assess performance stability.

5 Results and Analysis

This section presents the patient-level experimental results obtained from deep learning models trained on bi-parametric MRI (bpMRI) data for prostate cancer detection. All evaluations were performed using slice aggregation and Youden's J-optimized thresholds. Performance is reported using AUC, Accuracy, Sensitivity, and Specificity.

5.1 Performance Across Models and Modalities

Table 1 summarizes the patient-level performance of ResNet-18, DenseNet-121, and EfficientNet-B0 across T2, ADC, and DWI modalities. Overall, ADC-based models achieved the most balanced performance across architectures, with ResNet-18 ADC and DenseNet-121 ADC obtaining AUC values around 0.70–0.72 and accuracy around 0.75. T2-based models showed comparatively lower discrimination performance, with AUC values ranging from 0.49 to 0.66. DWI demonstrated greater variability across architectures, where DenseNet-121 DWI achieved the highest overall AUC (0.78) and sensitivity (0.91), but lower specificity (0.41).

The patient-level aggregation strategy reduced slice-level variability by averaging predictions across all slices belonging to the same patient. This enabled evaluation under clinically aligned conditions and ensured that all modalities were assessed using the same aggregation workflow and threshold optimization procedure.

Across the nine model-modality configurations, ADC consistently produced stronger and more stable classification performance compared with T2 and DWI modalities. ResNet-18 ADC and DenseNet-121 ADC achieved the highest balanced accuracy values among all evaluated settings, while DWI-based configurations produced larger variations between sensitivity and specificity.

Table 1. Patient-level performance across models and modalities using Youden's J-optimized thresholds.

Model	Modality	AUC (95% CI)	Accuracy (95% CI)	Threshold	Sensitivity/Specificity
ResNet-18	T2	0.63 [0.41–0.83]	0.68 [0.50–0.86]	0.82	0.73/0.65
	ADC	0.72 [0.47–0.91]	0.75 [0.57–0.89]	0.83	0.82/0.71
	DWI	0.62 [0.40–0.84]	0.46 [0.29–0.64]	0.57	0.45/0.47
DenseNet-121	T2	0.49 [0.27–0.74]	0.61 [0.43–0.79]	0.97	0.27/0.82
	ADC	0.70 [0.46–0.91]	0.75 [0.57–0.89]	0.68	0.64/0.82
	DWI	0.78 [0.58–0.95]	0.61 [0.43–0.79]	0.88	0.91/0.41
EfficientNet-B0	T2	0.66 [0.44–0.86]	0.61 [0.43–0.79]	0.95	0.45/0.71
	ADC	0.55 [0.28–0.80]	0.69 [0.50–0.86]	0.81	0.27/0.94
	DWI	0.65 [0.42–0.85]	0.69 [0.50–0.86]	0.70	0.45/0.82

Figure 3 further illustrates the performance differences across modalities and architectures. ADC-based models generally produced stronger and more stable ROC and PR curves, while T2 and DWI showed greater variability across architectures. Overall, ADC-based configurations demonstrated the most balanced diagnostic performance across architectures, while DenseNet-121 achieved the highest single AUC on DWI.

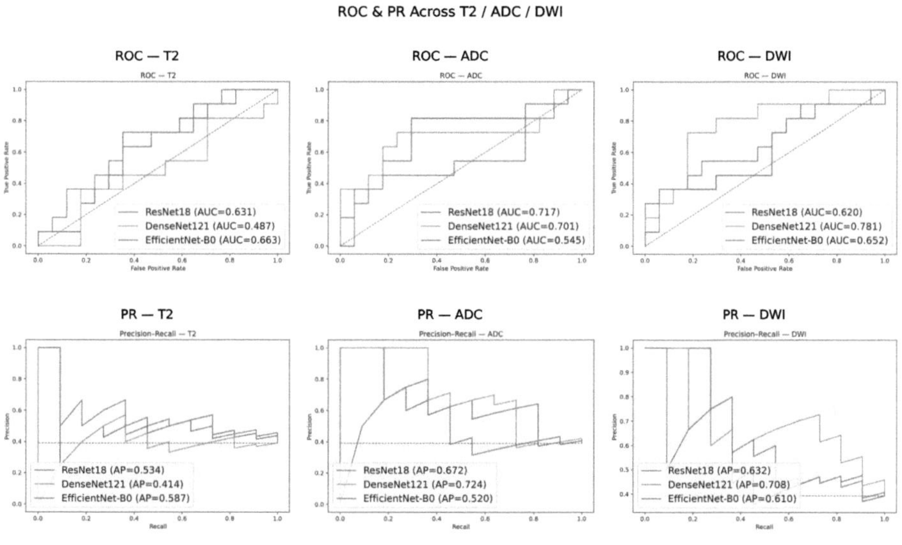

Fig. 3. ROC and PR curves across T2, ADC, and DWI. Panels (a–c): ROC; (d–f): PR.

The ROC and PR curves further demonstrate that ADC-based models maintained comparatively stronger discrimination capability across threshold ranges, whereas T2 and DWI modalities showed greater variability across architectures. DenseNet-121 DWI achieved high sensitivity but comparatively lower specificity, consistent with the values reported in Table 1.

5.2 Confusion Matrices

To further evaluate prediction behavior across modalities and architectures, confusion matrices were generated using patient-level predictions and Youden's J-optimized thresholds. Figure 4 summarizes the confusion matrices for all evaluated model-modality combinations.

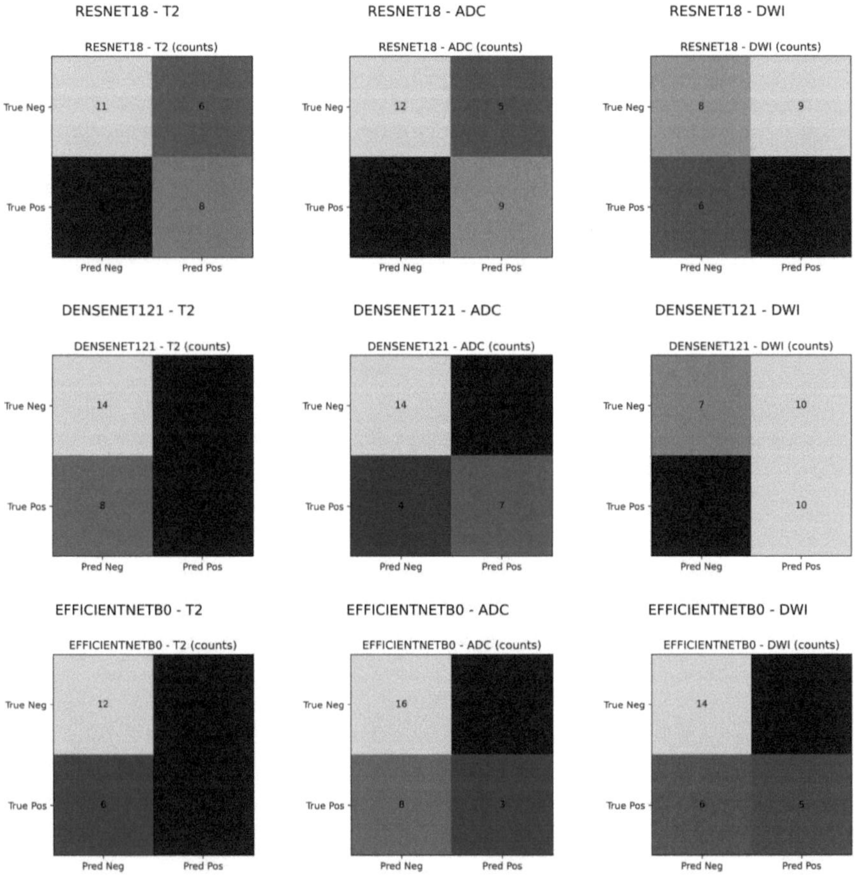

Fig. 4. Confusion matrices for all models across MRI modalities using Youden's J-optimized thresholds.

The confusion matrices show that ADC-based models generally achieved a more balanced distribution between true positive and true negative predictions.

In contrast, DWI-based configurations showed larger variations between sensitivity and specificity across architectures. DenseNet-121 DWI achieved high sensitivity but also produced more false positive predictions, whereas EfficientNet-B0 ADC produced fewer false positives but lower sensitivity. T2-based models showed comparatively lower discrimination capability, reflected by larger overlaps between false positive and false negative predictions. These observations are consistent with the AUC and accuracy values reported in Table 1.

5.3 Statistical Significance Analysis

McNemar's test was used to evaluate whether prediction differences between CNN architectures were statistically significant. Table 2 summarizes the pairwise comparisons across MRI modalities. Significant differences were observed between ResNet-18 and DenseNet-121 on T2 ($p < 0.01$), ResNet-18 and EfficientNet-B0 on ADC ($p < 0.01$), and between EfficientNet-B0 and the other models on DWI. The statistical analysis indicates that model agreement was generally more stable for ADC-based predictions, whereas DWI exhibited greater architectural variability. Significant differences between EfficientNet-B0 and the other architectures on DWI further demonstrate differences in prediction behavior across modalities.

Table 2. McNemar's test results comparing model pairs across modalities.

Modality	Model 1	Model 2	p-value	Significance
T2	ResNet	DenseNet	**0.007812**	$p < 0.01$
	ResNet	EfficientNet	0.125000	n.s.
	DenseNet	EfficientNet	0.125000	n.s.
ADC	ResNet	DenseNet	0.387695	n.s.
	ResNet	EfficientNet	**0.006348**	$p < 0.01$
	DenseNet	EfficientNet	0.145996	n.s.
DWI	ResNet	DenseNet	0.179565	n.s.
	ResNet	EfficientNet	**0.031250**	$p < 0.05$
	DenseNet	EfficientNet	**0.000488**	$p < 0.001$

5.4 Fairness Analysis

Fairness analysis was conducted across lesion zone, tumor size, and lesion count subgroups using accuracy, sensitivity, and specificity gaps. The subgroup analysis revealed that sensitivity exhibited the largest variability across all subgroup dimensions, while accuracy and specificity remained comparatively stable. Larger fairness gaps were observed, particularly in comparisons involving mixed and large tumor groups. However, elevated sensitivity differences were also observed across lesion-zone and lesion-count subgroup comparisons.

The subgroup analysis further demonstrated that subgroup disparities were not uniformly distributed across all lesion categories. Peripheral-zone and single-lesion subgroup comparisons generally showed smaller performance differences across architectures and modalities, whereas mixed-zone and large-lesion subgroup comparisons produced comparatively larger fairness gaps. These findings indicate that lesion characteristics contributed more strongly to subgroup-level variability than consistent architecture-specific prediction bias.

To further analyze subgroup-level behavior, the fairness gaps across lesion-related subgroups and evaluation metrics are visualized in Fig. 5. The heatmap shows that sensitivity contributed most to subgroup variability, whereas accuracy and specificity demonstrated relatively consistent performance across subgroup dimensions. The results indicate that subgroup-level variability was mainly associated with lesion characteristics, including lesion size, anatomical region, and lesion multiplicity, rather than consistent systematic model bias. Despite moderate sensitivity differences across some subgroup comparisons, the models maintained relatively stable accuracy and specificity across most lesion-related subgroup evaluations.

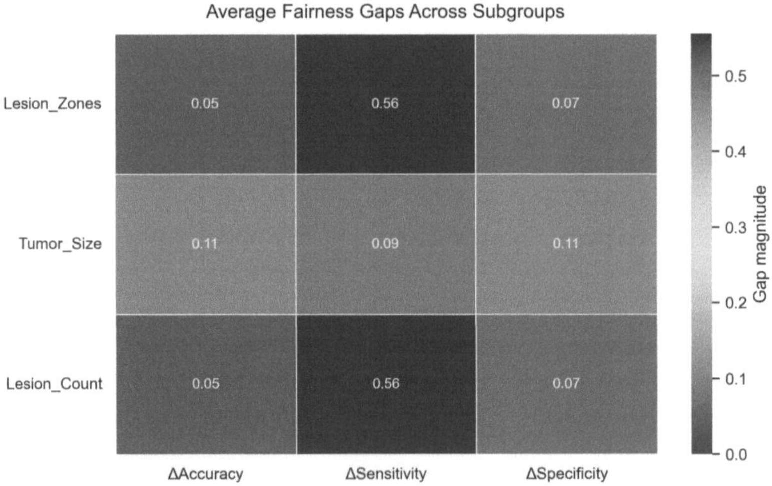

Fig. 5. Average absolute fairness gaps across subgroup dimensions and metrics.

5.5 Accuracy–Fairness Trade-Off

The fairness analysis indicated that subgroup variability primarily stemmed from differences in sensitivity. To further investigate the relationship between subgroup fairness and diagnostic performance, threshold-based fairness calibration was analyzed at the patient level. Figure 6 illustrates the trade-off between patient-level accuracy and subgroup fairness under different threshold settings. The baseline configuration achieved approximately 0.80 patient-level accuracy with a fairness gap of around 0.30. After fairness-aware threshold adjustment, the fairness gap decreased to approximately 0.20 while patient-level accuracy remained around 0.75. When stricter fairness constraints were applied, overall accuracy decreased.

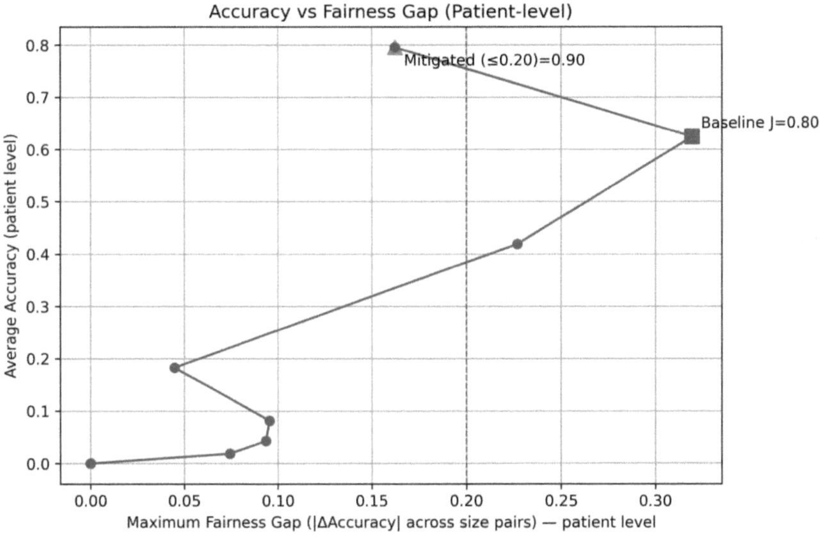

Fig. 6. Patient-level accuracy–fairness trade-off curve.

The results demonstrate that threshold selection influenced both subgroup fairness and overall classification accuracy. Moderate threshold adjustment reduced subgroup fairness gaps while preserving strong patient-level predictive performance.

5.6 Robustness Evaluation

Robustness analysis was conducted using repeated validation experiments across CNN architectures and MRI modalities. Table 3 summarizes the aggregated mean and standard deviation values for Accuracy, Sensitivity, Specificity, and AUC. All configurations achieved relatively stable performance with low variability across validation runs. DenseNet-121 ADC achieved the highest mean AUC (0.824 ± 0.042), while ResNet-18 T2 achieved the most stable AUC distribution (0.806 ± 0.024). Overall, both ResNet-18 and DenseNet-121 maintained mean AUC values around 0.80 across T2 and ADC modalities.

Table 3. Aggregated robustness results (mean ± SD) across repeated validation experiments.

Model	Modality	Accuracy	Sensitivity	Specificity	AUC
ResNet-18	T2	0.835 ± 0.084	0.920 ± 0.126	0.268 ± 0.254	0.806 ± 0.024
	ADC	0.819 ± 0.075	0.898 ± 0.126	0.334 ± 0.269	0.811 ± 0.031
DenseNet-121	T2	0.839 ± 0.057	0.922 ± 0.095	0.280 ± 0.225	0.811 ± 0.030
	ADC	0.839 ± 0.046	0.922 ± 0.085	0.330 ± 0.237	0.824 ± 0.042

Across repeated validation experiments, both ResNet-18 and DenseNet-121 maintained relatively consistent AUC values across T2 and ADC modalities. ResNet-18 T2 achieved the lowest AUC variability among all evaluated configurations, while DenseNet-121 ADC achieved the highest mean AUC across repeated evaluations.

The low standard deviation values across configurations indicate relatively stable model behavior. Overall, the robustness analysis confirms that the proposed CNN pipeline maintained stable performance across repeated validation experiments.

6 Conclusions

This study presented a reproducible evaluation workflow for prostate cancer detection using bi-parametric MRI (bpMRI) modalities from the Prostate158 dataset. ResNet-18, DenseNet-121, and EfficientNet-B0 were evaluated across T2, ADC, and DWI modalities using patient-level analysis. ADC-based models achieved the most reliable and balanced diagnostic performance, whereas T2 showed lower discrimination performance and DWI exhibited greater variability across architectures. Fairness analysis showed that subgroup variability was primarily associated with lesion characteristics rather than consistent model bias, with sensitivity contributing most to subgroup differences; patient-level threshold calibration using Youden's J statistic reduced subgroup fairness gaps while maintaining stable diagnostic performance, and statistical significance testing together with robustness evaluation supported the stability of these findings. Although this study was limited by the relatively small cohort of 139 patients, lesion-based fairness analysis, and the use of 2D slice-based CNNs that do not capture inter-slice spatial information, the proposed workflow provides a reproducible baseline for patient-level evaluation of diagnostic performance and subgroup fairness using the Prostate158 dataset. Future work will extend this evaluation to larger datasets and investigate three-dimensional CNNs, Vision Transformer-based models, and hybrid architectures within the same workflow.

References

1. Adams, L.C., et al.: Prostate158 - an expert-annotated 3T MRI dataset and algorithm for prostate cancer detection. Comput. Biol. Med. **148**, 105817 (2022)

2. Borges, R., Stefanidis, K.: On measuring popularity bias in collaborative filtering data. In: Proceedings of the Workshops of the EDBT/ICDT 2020 Joint Conference, Copenhagen, Denmark, 30 March 2020. CEUR Workshop Proceedings (2020)
3. Borges, R., Stefanidis, K.: Feature-blind fairness in collaborative filtering recommender systems. Knowl. Inf. Syst. **64**(4), 943–962 (2022). https://doi.org/10.1007/S10115-022-01656-X
4. Cai, H., Li, Y., Zhao, Q., Lu, Y.: Automated multimodal image registration for prostate cancer using squeeze-and-excitation ResNet with thin plate spline transformation: a deep learning approach. Med. Sci. Monit.: Int. Med. J. Exp. Clin. Res. **31** (2025)
5. Cao, R., et al.: Joint prostate cancer detection and Gleason score prediction in MP-MRI via FocalNet. IEEE Trans. Med. Imaging **38**, 2496–2506 (2019)
6. Efthymiou, V., Stefanidis, K., Pitoura, E., Christophides, V.: Fairer: entity resolution with fairness constraints. In: CIKM 2021: The 30th ACM International Conference on Information and Knowledge Management, pp. 3004–3008. ACM (2021). https://doi.org/10.1145/3459637.3482105
7. Goodfellow, I., Bengio, Y., Courville, A.: Deep Learning. MIT Press (2016). http://www.deeplearningbook.org
8. Hosseinzadeh, M., Saha, A., Brand, P., Slootweg, I., de Rooij, M., Huisman, H.J.: Deep learning–assisted prostate cancer detection on bi-parametric MRI: minimum training data size requirements and effect of prior knowledge. Eur. Radiol. **32**, 2224–2234 (2021)
9. Huang, G., Liu, Z., Weinberger, K.Q.: Densely connected convolutional networks. 2017 IEEE Conference on Computer Vision and Pattern Recognition (CVPR), pp. 2261–2269 (2016)
10. Karagoz, A., et al.: Anatomically guided self-adapting deep neural network for clinically significant prostate cancer detection on bi-parametric MRI: a multi-center study. Insights Imaging **14** (2023)
11. Li, H., et al.: Deep learning-based unsupervised domain adaptation via a unified model for prostate lesion detection using multisite bi-parametric MRI datasets. Radiol. Artif. Intell. e230521 (2024)
12. McNemar, Q.: Note on the sampling error of the difference between correlated proportions or percentages. Psychometrika **12**(2), 153–157 (1947)
13. Roach, M., et al.: Assessing algorithmic fairness with a multimodal artificial intelligence model in men of African and non-African origin on NRG oncology prostate cancer phase iii trials. JCO Clin. Cancer Inform. **9** (2025)
14. Rodrigues, A., Santinha, J., Galvao, B., Matos, C., Couto, F.M., Papanikolaou, N.: Prediction of prostate cancer disease aggressiveness using bi-parametric MRI radiomics. Cancers **13** (2021)
15. Tan, M., Le, Q.V.: EfficientNet: rethinking model scaling for convolutional neural networks. ArXiv abs/1905.11946 (2019)
16. Ueda, D., et al.: Fairness of artificial intelligence in healthcare: review and recommendations. Jpn. J. Radiol. **42**, 3–15 (2023)
17. de Vente, C., Vos, P.C., Hosseinzadeh, M., Pluim, J.P.W., Veta, M.: Deep learning regression for prostate cancer detection and grading in bi-parametric MRI. IEEE Trans. Biomed. Eng. **68**, 374–383 (2020)
18. Yoo, S., Gujrathi, I., Haider, M.A., Khalvati, F.: Prostate cancer detection using deep convolutional neural networks. Sci. Rep. **9** (2019)
19. Youden, W.J.: Index for rating diagnostic tests. Cancer **3**(1), 32–35 (1950)

Relational Database Aggregation Filter

Michal Kvet[1(✉)] and Jarmila Škrinárová[2]

[1] Faculty of Management Science and Informatics, University of Žilina, Univerzitná 8215/1, 010 26 Žilina, Slovak Republic
Michal.Kvet@fri.uniza.sk

[2] Faculty of Natural Sciences, University of Matej Bel, Tajovského 40, 974 01 Banská Bystrica, Slovak Republic

Abstract. This paper investigates aggregation functions in Oracle Database with a particular emphasis on filtering mechanisms within aggregate computations. Aggregation plays a crucial role in transforming large volumes of transactional data into meaningful summaries for analytical processing, reporting, and decision-making. The study outlines the theoretical foundations of SQL aggregation, including the behavior of standard aggregate functions and the role of the GROUP BY clause, as well as the logical processing order of SQL queries. Special attention is given to filtering strategies, distinguishing between pre-aggregation filtering using the WHERE clause and post-aggregation filtering using the HAVING clause. The paper further examines conditional aggregation techniques, focusing on traditional CASE-based approaches and the recently introduced FILTER clause in Oracle Database 26ai. The FILTER clause enables direct specification of filtering conditions within aggregate functions, improving query readability and maintainability. A comprehensive performance benchmarking study compares three approaches: nested queries, CASE-based conditional aggregation, and the FILTER clause. Experimental results demonstrate that nested queries exhibit the highest computational cost, while CASE-based filtering achieves the best performance. The FILTER clause introduces a minor overhead of approximately 2%, which decreases significantly with larger datasets. The findings highlight a trade-off between performance and code clarity. While CASE-based aggregation remains the most efficient, the FILTER clause offers a more expressive and maintainable alternative with negligible performance impact in large-scale environments. The paper concludes by suggesting further research on scalability, indexing strategies, and advanced analytical workloads.

Keywords: SQL performance · aggregate function · filter · Oracle Database 26ai

1 Introduction

Modern information systems generate and process massive volumes of structured data. Making efficient data summarization is a fundamental requirement in database management, not only from the execution point of view, but also user experience must be taken into consideration [8]. Relational database systems rely heavily on aggregation

© The Author(s), under exclusive license to Springer Nature Switzerland AG 2027
G. Vargas Solar et al. (Eds.): ADBIS 2026, CCIS 3175, pp. 315–331, 2027.
https://doi.org/10.1007/978-3-032-39823-9_30

mechanisms to transform raw transactional data into meaningful analytical information. Aggregate functions enable the computation of summarized results such as totals, averages, counts, and statistical measures, which are essential for reporting, decision-making, and performance monitoring [11, 14].

Within enterprise environments, the Oracle Database is widely adopted due to its robustness, scalability, and advanced SQL capabilities. Its implementation of aggregate functions [2] extends beyond basic SQL standards, incorporating optimized execution strategies, advanced grouping constructs, and specialized filtering mechanisms. These features allow developers and database administrators to perform complex analytical operations directly within the database engine, minimizing aplication-side processing and improving overall system efficiency [1, 5].

Aggregation in Oracle Database operates through mechanisms such as the *GROUP BY* and *HAVING* clauses and advanced extensions including *ROLLUP*, *CUBE*, and *GROUPING SETS*. Currently, there is a strong demand for filtering aggregate and analytical functions, allowing to simplify conditional processing. Understanding and optimizing the interaction between aggregation logic and filtering conditions is critical, as improper use can lead to incorrect results, performance degradation, or suboptimal execution plans [3, 11, 15].

Pre-aggregation filtering (via *WHERE* conditions) reduces the dataset before grouping occurs, while post-aggregation filtering (via *HAVING* clause) refines grouped results, optionally enhanced by the encryption [5, 6, 10]. The distinction between these mechanisms has significant implications for both query semantics and execution performance. Therefore, a comprehensive analysis of aggregation functions and their filtering behavior is necessary to ensure correctness, efficiency, and scalability [7, 13] in database applications [12, 20, 24].

This paper aims to examine the aggregation functions provided by Oracle Database and analyze the filtering mechanisms associated with them, focusing on their theoretical foundations, practical implementation, performance characteristics, and best practices for efficient and accurate query design.

Although the SQL *FILTER* clause has been available in several relational database systems for a number of years, it has only recently been introduced into Oracle Database. Consequently, its implementation,internal query transformation, and performance characteristics in the Oracle environment have not yet been systematically analyzed. The contribution of this paper is therefore not the introduction of the *FILTER* concept itself, but the first comprehensive evaluation of Oracle Database 26ai, combining an analysis of its internal rewrite mechanism with an experimental comparison of *FILTER*, CASE-based conditional aggregation, and nested-query approaches under multiple filtering scenarios [22, 25]

Although the SQL *FILTER* clause has been available in several relational database systems for a number of years, it has only recently been introduced into Oracle Database. Consequently, its implementation, internal query transformation, and performance characteristics in the Oracle environment have not yet been systematically analyzed. The contribution of this paper is therefore not the introduction of the *FILTER* concept itself, but the first comprehensive evaluation of Oracle Database 26ai, combining an analysis of its internal rewrite mechanism with an experimental comparison of *FILTER*, CASE-based conditional aggregation, and nested-query approaches under multiple filtering scenarios.

The remainder of this paper is organized as follows. Section 2 provides an overview of Oracle Database and its architecture relevant to aggregation processing. Section 3 introduces the fundamentals of SQL aggregation, while Sect. 4 discusses analytical environments in which aggregation techniques are commonly applied. Section 5 presents aggregation filtering mechanisms, including traditional CASE-based conditional aggregation and the newly introduced FILTER clause in Oracle Database 26ai. Section 6 describes the experimental methodology and benchmarking results, together with a discussion of the observed performance characteristics. Finally, Sect. 7 summarizes the main findings and outlines directions for future research.

2 Oracle Database Overview

The Oracle Database is an enterprise-grade relational database management system (*RDBMS*) designed to store, manage, and retrieve structured data efficiently and securely. It is built upon the relational model and implements Structured Query Language (*SQL*) as its primary interface for data definition, manipulation, and control.

A central feature of Oracle Database architecture is its SQL execution engine, which transforms high-level SQL statements into optimized execution plans. When a query is submitted, it undergoes parsing, semantic checking, and optimization by the Cost-Based Optimizer (*CBO*). The optimizer evaluates alternative execution strategies using statistics about tables, indexes, and data distribution, selecting the most efficient plan for execution. Aggregation operations are particularly influenced by this optimization phase, as Oracle may choose between hash aggregation, sort-based aggregation, or parallel execution depending on the query structure and system resources [9]. Oracle Database also provides advanced storage and indexing mechanisms, including B-tree indexes, bitmap indexes, partitioned tables, and materialized views. These features significantly affect the performance of aggregation queries by reducing data scanning costs and enabling precomputed summaries. In addition to traditional relational capabilities, Oracle integrates analytical processing features directly into the database engine. Support for analytic (window) functions, grouping extensions, and conditional filtering mechanisms allows complex analytical computations to be executed within a single SQL statement. Understanding the architectural and operational foundations of Oracle Database is essential for analyzing aggregation functions and their filtering mechanisms. Therefore, the necessary technical context for the detailed examination of aggregation and filtering behavior are presented in subsequent sections.

3 Fundamentals of SQL Aggregation

Aggregation enables the transformation of detailed row-level data into summarized results. Aggregate functions operate on sets of rows and return a single result value per group. The most fundamental aggregate functions defined by the *SQL* standard include *COUNT*, *SUM*, *AVG*, *MIN*, and *MAX*. These functions can be applied to entire tables or to subsets of data defined by grouping criteria. When no grouping clause is specified, the result of an aggregate query is a single row representing the aggregation over the entire dataset.

The *GROUP BY* clause is central to SQL aggregation. It partitions rows into distinct groups based on one or more columns, and aggregate functions are then applied independently to each group. Conceptually, grouping transforms a flat relational table into a set of logical partitions. Each partition produces exactly one output row in the final result set. This mechanism enables multi-dimensional summarization, such as computing total sales per region or average salary per department.

An important semantic rule in *SQL* aggregation is that every selected column must either be included in the *GROUP BY* clause or be part of an aggregate function. This constraint preserves determinism by ensuring that each output column has a well-defined value for every group. Violating this principle results in syntactic or semantic errors, as the database engine cannot infer which row-level value should represent the group. Handling of *NULL* values is another fundamental aspect of aggregation. Aggregate functions consider all rows regardless of *NULLs*, which are excluded. From an execution perspective, aggregation requires intermediate processing steps such as sorting or hashing to organize rows into groups. Beyond standard aggregates, *RDBMS* provides statistical functions that extend analytical capabilities, like standard deviation (*STDDEV* and *STDDEV_POP*), variance (*VARIANCE* and *VAR_POP*) or sample-based calculations (*STDDEV_SAMP* and *VAR_SAMP*). These functions are particularly relevant in analytical workloads and data warehousing environments, enabling dispersion and variability analysis directly within SQL queries.

4 Analytical Environments

There are several architectural paradigms defining how data is stored, processed and analyzed. Aggregation and filtering mechanisms play distinct roles depending on whether the system is optimized for transactional processing or analytical workloads.

4.1 Online Transaction Processing (OLTP)

OLTP systems are designed to manage high volumes of short, atomic transactions. Typical *OLTP* workloads include banking operations, order entry systems, reservation platforms, and real-time inventory management. Key characteristics include high concurrency, strict *ACID* compliance, frequent change operations by invoking Insert, Update and Delete statements. Emphasis is on low-latency response times for operational data handling. In OLTP environments, aggregation queries are usually lightweight and focused on operational metrics (e.g., counting daily transactions). Complex multidimensional aggregation is generally avoided because it can negatively impact transactional performance [17, 18].

4.2 Online Analytical Processing (OLAP)

OLAP systems are optimized for complex queries that analyze large volumes of historical data. Unlike *OLTP* systems, *OLAP* workloads are read-intensive and often involve multidimensional aggregation, filtering, and statistical computation. They are based on denormalized or star-schema design, large-scale data scans. They heavily reliance on aggregate and analytical queries.

A data warehouse is a centralized repository that integrates data from multiple sources for analytical and reporting purposes. Core characteristics include historical, time-variant data storage, subject-oriented organization, batch-oriented data loading using *ETL* or *ELT* processes. The emphasis is done on the aggregated reporting considerations [4, 8, 21].

Data lakes represent a more recent architectural approach, designed to store massive volumes of structured, semi-structured, and unstructured data in raw form. Unlike data warehouses, data lakes typically store data before transformation. Schema-on-read approach is rather than schema-on-write. They support diverse data formats (JSON, logs, multimedia), distributed storage architectures and integration with big data processing frameworks. Aggregation in data lakes is often performed using distributed processing engines rather than traditional relational SQL engines [8, 16, 23].

The lakehouse architecture combines elements of data lakes and data warehouses. It aims to provide the scalability and flexibility of data lakes while maintaining the reliability, transactional consistency, and structured query capabilities of data warehouses focused on the ACID transaction support [23, 24] on large-scale distributed storage, schema enforcement with flexibility, unified storage for both analytics and machine learning and SQL-based aggregation capabilities over diverse datasets. This architectural model reflects the convergence of OLTP and OLAP capabilities, which is strongly evident in Oracle Database platforms [3, 16, 32, 33].

4.3 Hybrid Architectures

Hybrid Transactional/Analytical Processing (*HTAP*) systems attempt to support both *OLTP* and *OLAP* workloads simultaneously. Instead of separating transactional databases and analytical warehouses, *HTAP* architectures process real-time transactions while enabling near real-time analytics. This integration requires efficient concurrency control, in-memory processing, optimized aggregation mechanisms and workload isolation strategies [27, 28].

Oracle supports hybrid processing through in-memory column stores, real-time materialized views, and autonomous workload management features. Aggregation queries in *HTAP* systems must be carefully optimized to avoid degrading transactional throughput.

The role of aggregation differs across these architectures:

- In OLTP, aggregation is minimal and operational.
- In OLAP and data warehouses, aggregation is central and multidimensional.
- In data lakes, aggregation is distributed and schema-flexible.
- In lakehouses and HTAP systems, aggregation bridges transactional and analytical domains.

5 Aggregation Filtering

Data filtering in SQL is commonly implemented through the *WHERE* clause within *SELECT* statements. The *WHERE* clause eliminates rows that do not satisfy the specified conditions, thereby preventing them from being included in the intermediate result set. Consequently, these excluded rows do not participate in subsequent aggregation operations.

From a logical query processing perspective, the *WHERE* clause is evaluated immediately after the *FROM* clause, which defines the data source. Thus, filtering is performed directly on the input data prior to grouping and aggregation. This ordering rule ensures that only rows meeting the defined criteria are forwarded to later stages of query execution, such as *GROUP BY* and aggregate function evaluation. The principles are shown in Fig. 1. Aggregate functions are specified in the *SELECT* clause, and conditions based on these aggregates are applied in the *HAVING* clause [19, 26, 29].

Filters may also be embedded directly within aggregation functions, thereby allowing the entire dataset to be processed while selectively excluding rows that do not satisfy the specified criteria [30, 31]. This approach enables multiple aggregations to be evaluated in a single pass over the dataset, with each aggregation applying its own filtering condition. The following subsection first outlines the conventional solution and subsequently presents the proposed technique implemented in Oracle Database 26ai [4, 16, 19].

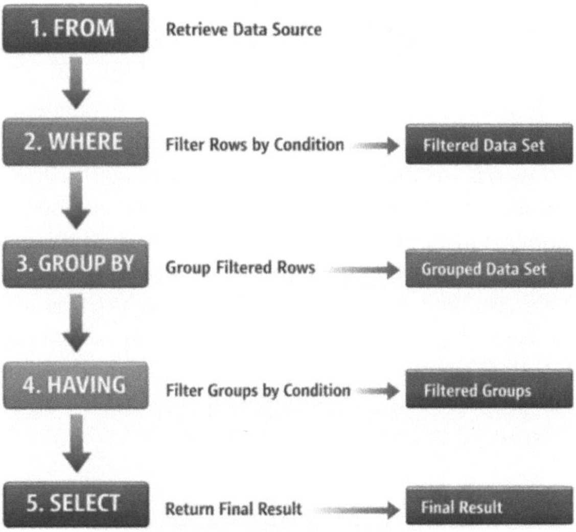

Fig. 1. SQL statement execution steps

5.1 Inner Aggregation Filtering - Original Solution

Under the traditional *SQL* model, aggregate filtering is not supported directly by the language syntax *(SQL standard*). Instead, developers employ alternative techniques to control which rows contribute to individual aggregate computations.

A common approach relies on the fact that aggregate functions ignore *NULL* values. Conditional logic is therefore embedded within the aggregate function, typically using *CASE* expressions. Rows that do not satisfy the intended condition are transformed to *NULL*, thereby excluding them from the aggregate calculation. An example is shown in the following code snippet. *TO_CHAR(departure_time, 'DY')* determines the day of the week. In this case, *SAT* represents *Saturday* and *SUN* denotes *Sunday*. Flights departing on weekdays return *NULL*, which are ignored by *COUNT* and *SUM*. No *WHERE* clause is used, so the filtering is performed within the aggregate function itself, following the traditional pre-FILTER approach.

```
SELECT
  COUNT(
      CASE
        WHEN TO_CHAR(departure_time, 'DY') IN ('SAT', 'SUN')
              THEN flight_id ELSE NULL END ) AS weekend_flight_count,

  SUM(
    CASE
      WHEN TO_CHAR(departure_time, 'DY')  IN ('SAT', 'SUN')
           AND TO_CHAR(arrival_time, 'DY') IN ('SAT', 'SUN')
              THEN flight_duration_hours ELSE NULL
    END ) AS weekend_total_flight_hours
 FROM flights;
```

The solution presented above is inherently language-dependent. For example, in *Slovakia* the abbreviated day name for *Saturday* is represented as *SO* rather than *SAT*, and *Sunday* is expressed as *NE* instead of *SUN*. Such variations illustrate that date-related textual outputs generated by default database settings are influenced by regional and language configurations. Furthermore, the length and format of these abbreviations may differ across locales, potentially affecting string comparisons and filtering conditions.

To ensure robustness and independence from regional and language-specific settings, the *TO_CHAR* function can be extended by explicitly specifying the *NLS_DATE_LANGUAGE* parameter within the function call. By defining the date language internally, the query produces consistent and predictable output regardless of the database session's territorial or linguistic environment:

```
to_char(departure_time, 'DY', 'nls_date_language=''English''')
```

Another approach involves the use of derived subqueries. In this method, each subquery applies its own *WHERE* clause outside the primary aggregation context, and the resulting aggregated outputs are subsequently combined in an outer query.

In more complex reporting scenarios, multiple grouped queries—each filtered according to different criteria—are combined using set operation *UNION*. The consolidated result is then reshaped into the required final structure.

5.2 Aggregate Filtering in Oracle 26ai

The dedicated solution in Oracle Database 26ai introduces support for the *FILTER* clause within aggregate functions. This clause allows users to specify, directly inside the aggregate expression, the subset of rows to be processed. The filtering condition is evaluated as a Boolean expression, determining whether a given row contributes to the aggregate result.

This enhancement significantly improves *SQL* expressiveness by reducing syntactic complexity, minimizing the need for more elaborate conditional constructs, and enhancing overall code readability and maintainability. From the user's perspective, the feature streamlines query formulation while preserving semantic clarity.

At the implementation level, the *FILTER* clause is not executed as a distinct physical operator. Instead, it is internally transformed during the preprocessing phase into an equivalent representation compliant with the original standardized SQL syntax. This transformation can be observed by analyzing the statement as it enters the evaluation and optimization stages of query processing.

Several mechanisms are available to trace such transformations. One commonly used approach is enabling the *10053 optimizer tracing event*, which provides detailed insight into query transformation and optimization decisions.

```
alter session  set events '10053 trace name context forever';
```

Alternatively, the *EXPAND_SQL_TEXT* procedure from the *DBMS_UTILITY* package can be invoked to display the fully expanded SQL text after internal

```
set serveroutput on;
declare
 code clob;
begin
 dbms_utility.expand_sql_text(
    input_sql_text =>
     'SELECT AIR_COMPANY,
       COUNT(flight_id)
        filter(where TO_CHAR(departure_time, ''DY'')
          IN (''SAT'', ''SUN'')) weekend_flight_count,
       SUM(flight_duration_hours)
        filter(where TO_CHAR(departure_time, ''DY'') IN (''SAT'', ''SUN'')
                    AND TO_CHAR(arrival_time, ''DY'') IN (''SAT'', ''SUN''))
                     weekend_total_flight_hours
     FROM flights
      GROUP BY AIR_COMPANY'
    , output_sql_text => code);
 dbms_output.put_line(code);
end;
/
```

The produced output is depicted by the following code snippet (formatted explicitly to be more readable):

```
SELECT "A1"."AIR_COMPANY" "AIR_COMPANY",
       COUNT(CASE
        WHEN (TO_CHAR("A1"."DEPARTURE_TIME",'DY')='SAT'
          OR TO_CHAR("A1"."DEPARTURE_TIME",'DY')='SUN')
         THEN "A1"."FLIGHT_ID" ELSE NULL END ) "WEEKEND_FLIGHT_COUNT",
      SUM(CASE
       WHEN ((TO_CHAR("A1"."DEPARTURE_TIME",'DY')='SAT'
         OR TO_CHAR("A1"."DEPARTURE_TIME",'DY')='SUN')
          AND (TO_CHAR("A1"."ARRIVAL_TIME",'DY')='SAT'
           OR TO_CHAR("A1"."ARRIVAL_TIME",'DY')='SUN'))
        THEN "A1"."FLIGHT_DURATION_HOURS" ELSE NULL END )
                                          "WEEKEND_TOTAL_FLIGHT_HOURS"
 FROM "KVET3"."FLIGHTS" "A1"
   GROUP BY "A1"."AIR_COMPANY"
```

6 Performance Benchmarking

This section presents a systematic performance benchmarking of three approaches, focusing on execution time and resource utilization and processing overhead under the controlled experimental conditions.

6.1 Testing Environment

The performance evaluation was conducted in an experimental environment configured with the *Oracle AI Database 26ai Free Release 23.26.1.0.0*. The hardware platform was equipped with an *Intel® Core™ Ultra 7 155U* processor operating at *1.70 GHz* and integrated *Intel® graphics* (*128 MB*). The system included *32 GB of DDR4* memory (*6400 MT/s*) and a *4 TB NVMe* solid-state drive capable of read and write speeds of up to *7000 MB/s*. The operating system was *Windows 11 Pro* (*version 25H2*).

The computational study utilized a real-world dataset from the aviation domain. The dataset comprised three primary components: (i) planned aircraft routes, (ii) actual flight trajectories derived from aircraft positional data and associated operational information, including the status of flight regions, and (iii) flight monitoring records generated by assigning aircraft to Flight Information Regions (*FIRs*) according to their recorded entry and exit times [33].

FIR is a defined portion of airspace within which a designated national air traffic control (*ATC*) authority provides Flight Information Services and alerting services. FIRs collectively cover the entire global airspace, including both continental and oceanic regions. Their primary functions include ensuring the safety and efficiency of air traffic through the operational information and the coordination of emergency responses. Besides, their objective is also to reduce environmental impact and operational costs [33].

The spatial boundaries of FIRs are time-dependent and may change due to regulatory, operational, or geopolitical factors. The complete dataset used in this study comprised 1,000 flights. On average, each flight was represented by approximately 1,000 records for both the planned and the actual flight trajectories.

Figure 2 depicts an example of the input data used for *FIR* assignment. Each record contains the aircraft identifier (*ECTRL_ID*), the *FIR* assignment reference (*AUA_ID*), and the corresponding temporal boundaries (*ENTRY_TIME* and *EXIT_TIME*). The records are stored sequentially based on the *SEQUENCE_NUMBER* attribute.

```
"ECTRL ID","Sequence Number","AUA ID","Entry Time","Exit Time"
"186858226","1","EGGXOCA","01-06-2015 04:55:00","01-06-2015 05:57:51"
"186858226","2","EISNCTA","01-06-2015 05:57:51","01-06-2015 06:28:00"
"186858226","3","EGTTCTA","01-06-2015 06:28:00","01-06-2015 07:00:44"
"186858226","4","EGTTTCTA","01-06-2015 07:00:44","01-06-2015 07:11:45"
```

Fig. 2. Data set

6.2 Evaluation Study

For the performance evaluation, three approaches were examined: (*A1*) filtering using a nested query followed by a result set merging process, (*A2*) conventional filtering implemented with the *CASE* statement, and (*A3*) filtering using the *FILTER* clause. The evaluation considered both processing time and overall computational overhead. The experiments were conducted on a dataset containing one million rows.

To assess robustness, the methods were evaluated under following seven distinct scenarios:

- *S1 – no filtering applied*; the entire dataset is processed.
- *S2* – filtering based on the *INTERVAL* data type, representing the flight duration.
- *S3* – filtering based on a *DATE* value range.
- *S4* – filtering based on the *weekday* extracted from a *DATE* value.
- *S5* – filtering *based* on a *numerical value.*
- *S6 – composite* filtering reflecting departure and arrival times (*DATE* values).
- *S7 – composite filtering* based on two numerical values (*INTEGER*).

6.3 Results and Limitations

The evaluation study considered seven scenarios and three different query approaches. The primary evaluation metric was query processing time (Table 1). The nested query approach consistently produced the weakest performance, with total processing times exceeding 5 s in all evaluated cases. Filtering operations based on *Date* values were more computationally demanding, particularly when combined with function calls that extract individual components from Date attributes. When two levels of filtering were applied, the processing overhead increased by approximately 8.94%. In the case of composite filtering based on three criteria, the additional overhead increased to nearly 10%.

The *CASE-based filtering* approach demonstrated the best overall performance across all scenarios. The required processing time represented 76.81%–77.83% of the time required by the nested query approach. However, introducing additional filtering conditions increased processing requirements by approximately 9.44%. Despite this increase, the total processing time remained below 5 s in all scenarios.

An intermediate performance level was observed when using the *FILTER* clause. Compared with the *CASE-based* solution, this approach required an additional 1.79%–3.12% of processing time. The observed differences are primarily related to the cost of processing and converting different data types, with numeric values being the least computationally demanding. The highest processing overhead occurred in Scenario 6, where a composite filtering condition was applied. The results are shown in Table 1. Graphical representation of the results is depicted in Fig. 3. To make a system consitent and reproducible, each evaluation study was performed 10 times and results show the average values. It is worth mentioning, that all memory caches were flushed before each run.

Table 1. Processing Time Results

Scenario	Nested query (A1)	Case filtering (A2)	FILTER clause (A3)
	Processing time [milliseconds]		
S1	5240	4057	3951
S2	5557	4268	4150
S3	5703	4398	4284
S4	5912	4593	4436
S5	5493	4250	4152
S6	6123	4766	4575
S7	6037	4676	4536

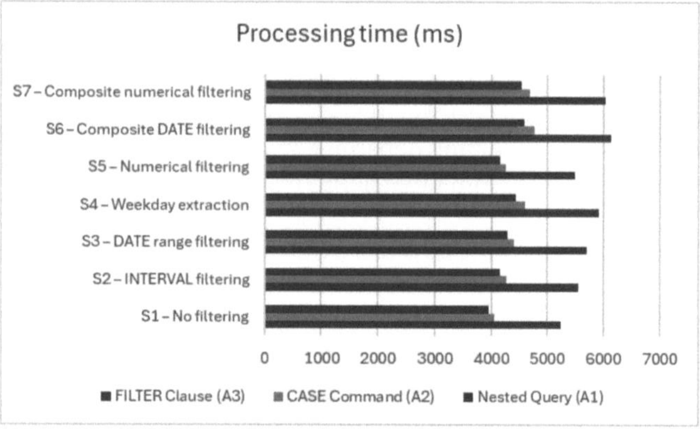

Fig. 3. Processing time / scenarios

The total processing time demands across the scenarios are depicted in Fig. 4.

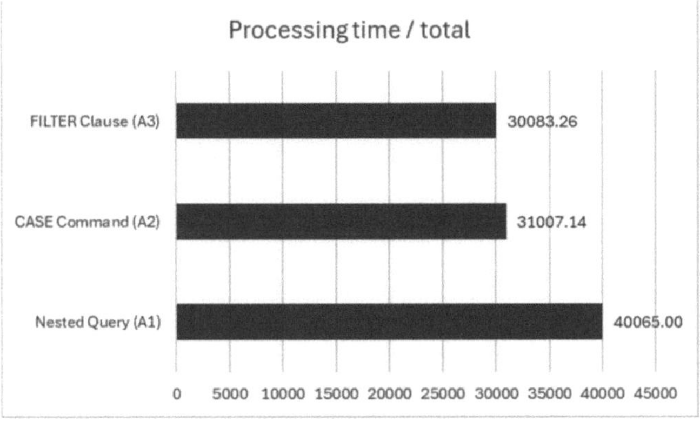

Fig. 4. Processing time / total

Table 2 presents the relative processing costs of the evaluated query approaches across the seven experimental scenarios, where the *FILTER clause* (*A3*) represents the baseline value (100%).

The results indicate that the nested query approach (*A1*) consistently produced the highest processing costs in all scenarios. The relative cost values range from 131.54% to 138.83% compared with the *FILTER-based* solution. The lowest relative cost for nested queries was observed in Scenario 5 (131.54%), whereas the highest cost occurred in Scenario 6 (138.83%), which involved a composite filtering condition based on multiple criteria. Overall, the nested query approach required approximately 31%–39% more processing resources than the *FILTER* clause.

In contrast, the *CASE-based* filtering approach (A2) demonstrated the lowest processing cost across all scenarios. The relative values range between 95.55% and 97.48%, indicating that this approach required approximately 2.5%–4.5% less processing time than the *FILTER* clause. The best performance of the *CASE-based* approach was observed in Scenario 4 (95.55%), while the highest relative cost occurred in Scenario 1 (97.48%). Despite minor variations among scenarios, the results confirm the consistently high efficiency of the *CASE-based* solution.

When comparing the approaches, the *CASE-based* filtering method outperformed the *FILTER* clause in all evaluated scenarios, while the nested query approach remained the least efficient alternative. The performance differences became more pronounced in scenarios involving more complex filtering operations, particularly those combining multiple filtering criteria, as observed in Scenario 6.

The graphical representation of these results is presented in Fig. 5, illustrating the relative performance differences among the evaluated query approaches. The total costs across all scenarios are shown in Fig. 6.

Table 2. Cost Results

Scenario	Nested query (A1)	Case filtering (A2)	FILTER clause (A3)
	Cost (relative value – 100% = FILTER clause		
S1	132.17	97.48	100
S2	134.80	96.13	100
S3	133.24	96.94	100
S4	136.73	95.55	100
S5	131.54	97.27	100
S6	138.83	95.67	100
S7	135.20	96.98	100

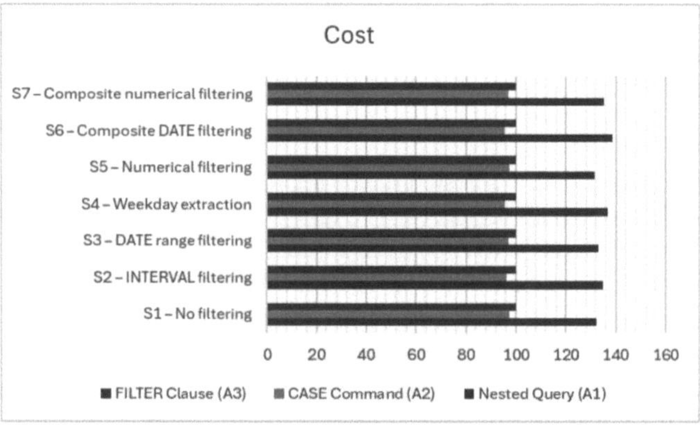

Fig. 5. Cost / scenarios

The results presented above clearly demonstrate that the *FILTER* clause provides an effective solution that significantly reduces coding complexity. Instead of using the *CASE* expression to transform irrelevant rows into *NULL* values, the *FILTER* clause can be applied directly. This approach improves code readability and simplifies the overall query structure.

The additional processing time and associated computational costs remain acceptable. For a dataset containing one million rows, the overhead is approximately 2%. However, it should be noted that real-world datasets are typically much larger and more complex, with substantially higher cardinality. Therefore, the scalability of the approach must also be considered.

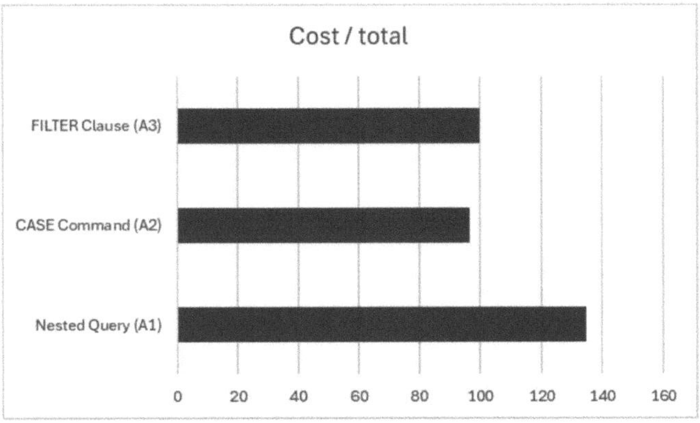

Fig. 6. Cost / total

Figure 7 illustrates the additional processing demands in terms of execution time. Specifically, it presents the ratio between the additional overhead and the size of the dataset. The results indicate that as the dataset size increases, the impact of the transformation demands decreases. For a dataset containing 100 million rows, the overall overhead decreases to approximately 0.05%.

Figure 7 therefore demonstrates the relationship between additional computational costs and dataset size. In this context, additional costs represent the performance overhead introduced by the *FILTER* clause compared to the conventional approach based on the *CASE* expression.

The *FILTER* clause can be utilized with aggregate functions used in an analytic context, as well. However, *FILTER* clause does not accept subqueries:

ACCEPTABLE:

```
count(case when not exists
    (select null
      from flights
       where to_char(departure_time, 'MM')<> to_char(arrival_time, 'MM'))
      then 1 end)
```

NOT SUPPORTED:

```
count(*) filter(where not exists
    (select null
      from flights
       where to_char(departure_time, ‘MM’) <> to_char(arrival_time, ‘MM’)))
```

The observed performance differences between the FILTER clause and the equivalent CASE-based formulation remain relatively small. This behavior is consistent with Oracle's internal implementation, where FILTER expressions are rewritten into semantically equivalent CASE expressions during query transformation. Consequently, both approaches produce nearly identical execution strategies, and the measured differences are primarily attributable to minor optimization and expression evaluation overhead rather than fundamentally different execution plans.

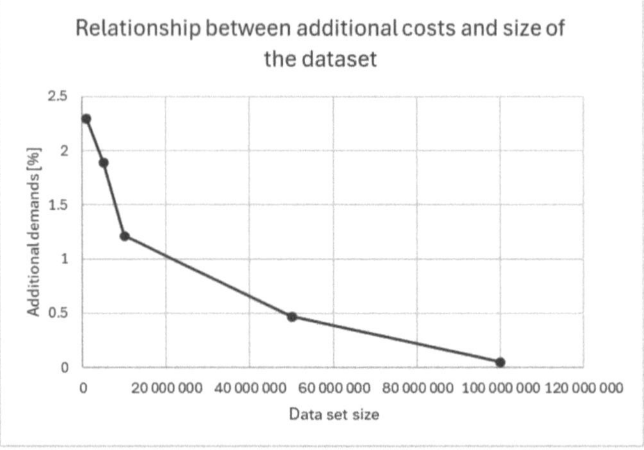

Fig. 7. The relationship between additional costs and the size of the data set

7 Conclusions and Future Perspectives

This paper examined aggregation functions *in Oracle Database* with a particular focus on filtering mechanisms used within aggregate computations. The study discussed the theoretical foundations of SQL aggregation, the logical processing order of SQL statements, and the differences between pre-aggregation filtering using the *WHERE* clause and post-aggregation filtering using the *HAVING* clause. Special attention was devoted to conditional aggregation techniques and to the *FILTER* clause introduced in Oracle Database 26ai.

The performance benchmarking study compared three approaches: *nested queries*, *CASE-based conditional aggregation*, and the *FILTER clause.* Experimental results demonstrated that nested queries consistently produced the highest processing costs, while *CASE-based* filtering achieved the best execution performance across all evaluated scenarios. The *FILTER* clause showed slightly higher processing time, with an overhead of approximately 2% compared with the *CASE-based* solution. However, this overhead decreases as dataset size increases and becomes negligible for large-scale datasets.

From a practical perspective, the *FILTER* clause significantly improves SQL expressiveness and readability by allowing filtering conditions to be defined directly within aggregate functions. This reduces syntactic complexity and simplifies query maintenance, which is particularly beneficial in analytical and reporting environments. The findings therefore indicate that although *CASE-based* aggregation remains the most efficient in terms of raw execution performance, the *FILTER* clause provides a balanced solution combining acceptable performance with improved code clarity.

Future work may extend the evaluation to larger datasets, distributed database environments, and complex analytical workloads involving window functions and parallel query execution. Further research should also investigate the impact of indexing strategies related to filtering attributes, including the use of B + tree, bitmap, and function-based indexes, and their influence on the performance of aggregation queries employing different filtering techniques.

Acknowledgment. This paper was supported by the VEGA 1/0192/24 project - *Developing and applying advanced techniques for efficient processing of large-scale data in the intelligent transport systems environment.*

References

1. Akash, R., Srinivasan, S., Pillai, R.G., Thyagaraj, T., Sarathi, R.: Machine learning based analysis of LIBS and EIS data to estimate the moisture content of soil in grounding systems. IEEE Trans. Dielectrics Electr. Insul. https://doi.org/10.1109/TDEI.2026.3679283
2. Alexeev, V., Domashnev, P.: Implementation of aggregate functioms for interval-valued java data type in the oracle DBMS. In: 2019 1st International Conference on Control Systems, Mathematical Modelling, Automation and Energy Efficiency (SUMMA), Lipetsk, Russia, pp. 392–395 (2019). https://doi.org/10.1109/SUMMA48161.2019.8947560
3. Bakondi, B.G., Peter, A., Everts, M., Hartel, P., Jonker, W.: Publicly verifiable private aggregation of time-series data. In: 2015 10th International Conference on Availability, Reliability and Security, pp. 50–59. Toulouse, France (2015). https://doi.org/10.1109/ARES.2015.82
4. Desmarets, P., Hammerschmidt, B., Hoberman, S.: Oracle Database 23AI Data Modeling and Schema Design for JSON-Relational Duality. Technics Publications, LLC (2024). ISBN: 978-1634623636
5. Dutta, M., Vivekanandan, S.J., Ravichandran, P.J.S., Pandurangan, K.: Scalable verification for certificateless verifiable searchable encryption in IoT-based healthcare systems. In: 2026 8th International Conference on Intelligent Sustainable Systems (ICISS), pp. 720–725. Tirunelveli, India (2026). https://doi.org/10.1109/ICISS67859.2026.11453833
6. Fei, S., Yan, Z., He, H., Bertino, E.: EnduraTrust: achieving sustained trust through a decentralized root of trust for blockchain oracles. IEEE Trans. Netw. **34**, 4096–4109 (2026). https://doi.org/10.1109/TON.2026.3671874
7. FornéMengual, J., Nieves, V.: AI-based image analysis for marine species monitoring: a CNN-RF approach. In: 2025 IEEE Asia-Pacific Conference on Geoscience, Electronics and Remote Sensing Technology (AGERS), pp. 732–737. Purwokerto, Indonesia (2025). https://doi.org/10.1109/AGERS67633.2025.11446450
8. Govindaraju, V., et al.: Big data processing: scalability with extreme single-node performance. In: 2017 IEEE International Congress on Big Data (BigData Congress), pp. 129–136. Honolulu, HI, USA (2017). https://doi.org/10.1109/BigDataCongress.2017.26
9. Greenwald, R., Stackowiak, R., Stern, J.: Oracle Essentials: Oracle Database 12C. O'Reilly Media, Sebastopol (2013). ISBN: 978-1-4493-4303-3
10. Herranz, J.: Deterministic identity-based signatures for partial aggregation. Comput. J. **49**(3), 322–330 (2006). https://doi.org/10.1093/comjnl/bxh153
11. Chavan, S., Hopeman, A., Lee, S., Lui, D., Mylavarapu, A., Soylemez, E.: Accelerating joins and aggregations on the oracle in-memory database. In: 2018 IEEE 34th International Conference on Data Engineering (ICDE), pp. 1441–1452. Paris, France (2018). https://doi.org/10.1109/ICDE.2018.00163
12. Chen, X., Hu, C., Xiang, T., Hu, P., Zhang, J., Li, X.: Secure and efficient data collection and transmission scheme for healthcare services in wireless medical sensor network. IEEE Trans. Dependable Secure Comput. https://doi.org/10.1109/TDSC.2026.3659677
13. Chen, J., et al.: Uncertainty-aware online time series multi-step forecasting framework in cloud systems. IEEE Trans. Knowl. Data Eng. https://doi.org/10.1109/TKDE.2026.3674583
14. Chiang, W. -K., Liu, C.-J. : Lightweight zero-knowledge proof-based authentication and blockchain-assisted handover for VANETs. IEEE Open J. Commun. Soc. https://doi.org/10.1109/OJCOMS.2026.3679126

15. Chong, E.I., Perry, M., Das, S.: Improving RDF query performance using in-memory virtual columns in oracle database. In: 2019 IEEE 35th International Conference on Data Engineering (ICDE), Macao, China, pp. 1814–1819 (2019)
16. Chowdhury, A.: Oracle 23AI & ADBS in Action: Exploring New Features with Hands-On Case Studies. Apress (2026). ISBN: 979–8868820670
17. Iovino, M., Lazic, I., Barà, C., Kugiumtzis, D., Faes, L., Pernice, R.: A principled and data-efficient information-theoretic method for feature selection. IEEE J. Biomed. Health Inf. https://doi.org/10.1109/JBHI.2026.3679377
18. Kulkarni, C., Medicherla, C., Vulugundam, B., Patel, T.P., Shivam, S., Padhy, A.K.: A cross-generational evaluation of SQL aggregation efficiency on oracle exadata engineered systems. In: 2025 International Conference on Computer and Applications (ICCA), Bahrain, Bahrain, pp. 1–6 (2025). https://doi.org/10.1109/ICCA66035.2025.11430832
19. Kvet, M.: Data Analysis - Aggregate Function Performance. SAMI (2025)
20. Kvet, M., Papan, J.: Enhancing analytical select statements using reference aliases. IEEE Access **12**, 27311–27330 (2024). https://doi.org/10.1109/ACCESS.2024.3366455
21. Liu, B., Zhang, X., Chen, J., Miao, Y., Zhao, J., Wang, H.: Enabling cross-clouds encrypted data fine-grained deduplication and recovery via blockchain systems. IEEE Trans. Dependable Sec. Comput. https://doi.org/10.1109/TDSC.2026.3679571
22. Turčaník, M.: Hash function generation based on neural networks and chaotic maps. In: 2017 Communication and Information Technologies (KIT), Vysoke Tatry, Slovakia, pp. 1–5 (2017). https://doi.org/10.23919/KIT.2017.8109467
23. Momeni, M.R., Jabbari, A., Fung, C.: An efficient and secure smart parking system with conditional preservation of citizens privacy for smart cities. IEEE Trans. Netw. Serv. Manag. **23**, 3279–3295 (2026). https://doi.org/10.1109/TNSM.2026.3673982
24. Rosenzweig, V., Ritchie, K.L.: Oracle SQL by example. 5th edn., Pearson (2011). ISBN: 978–0138062838
25. Suchý, I., Turčaník M.: Review of Large YOLOv8 and RT-DETR energy efficiency on edge devices for real-time detection. Sci. Rep. **16**(1), 10908 (2026). https://doi.org/10.1038/s41598-026-46453-6
26. Samarin, S.D., Amini, M.: Integrity checking for aggregate queries. IEEE Access **9**, 74068–74084 (2021). https://doi.org/10.1109/ACCESS.2021.3079799
27. Shen, G., Han, Z., Meng, W., Zhang, M.: An efficient, identifiable and abortable multi-party signature scheme for VANETs. IEEE Trans. Vehic. Technol. https://doi.org/10.1109/TVT.2026.3664438
28. Shi, X., et al.: Dataset distillation-based hybrid federated learning on non-IID data. IEEE Trans. Netw. Sci. Eng. https://doi.org/10.1109/TNSE.2026.36790137
29. Singh, A., Kaushik, A.: Knowledge based retrieval scheme from big data for aviation industry. In: 2015 International Conference on Computational Intelligence and Communication Networks (CICN), pp. 918–923. Jabalpur, India (2015). https://doi.org/10.1109/CICN.2015.326
30. Xie, Y., et al.: A decentralized blockchain transaction verification scheme in the weighted setting. IEEE Trans. Dependable Sec. Comput. **23**(2), 1782–1794 (2026). https://doi.org/10.1109/TDSC.2025.3621238
31. Xiong, C., Yang, T., Wang, X., Cao, Y., Mao, G.: DISOC: a trustworthy decentralized oracle architecture with strong privacy preservation for IIoT data sharing. In: IEEE Internet Things J. **11**(10), 18676–18685 (2024). https://doi.org/10.1109/JIOT.2024.3364691
32. Zhou, J., Huang, S., Feng, H., Wang, P., Zhou, D.-X.: Fine-grained analysis of nonparametric estimation for pairwise learning. IEEE Trans. Neural Netw. Learn. Syst. https://doi.org/10.1109/TNNLS.2026.3661550
33. Erasmus+ project EverGreen dealing with the complex data analytics (2025). https://evergreen.uniza.sk/

A Visualization Framework for Semantics of a Concatenative Compositional Language

William Steingartner[1(✉)], Martin Mormák[1], and Wolfgang Schreiner[2]

[1] Faculty of Electrical Engineering and Informatics, Technical University of Košice, Košice, Slovakia
william.steingartner@tuke.sk, martin.mormak@student.tuke.sk
[2] Johannes Kepler University Linz, Linz, Austria
Wolfgang.Schreiner@risc.jku.at

Abstract. Concatenative programming languages represent an interesting learning environment for teaching formal semantics, stack-based computations, and higher-order programming constructs. However, students often have difficulty understanding the relationship between formal semantic rules and concrete program execution because intermediate states of computation are not directly observable.

This paper presents a visualization framework for the KKJ language based on executable semantics. Semantic rules specified in the SLANG language generate execution traces consisting of successive program configurations that are subsequently visualized. The proposed approach transforms formal semantic specifications into observable execution behavior and allows users to observe the evolution of the stack, quotations, and higher-order operations during program execution. The resulting framework establishes a link between formal semantics, executable semantics, and program visualization, thereby supporting the conceptual understanding of stack-based and higher-order computations in concatenative languages. Unlike existing visualization tools, the proposed framework visualizes semantic transitions directly derived from executable semantic specifications, rather than from implementation-level execution.

Keywords: computer science education · concatenative languages · executable semantics · execution trace · formal semantics · program visualization · stack-based computation

1 Introduction

Nowadays, the task of understanding the formal principles of computer science is still crucial, because understanding the fundamental principles and increasing abstraction in software development has a significant impact on the creation of correct and effective programs [9]. This goal is pursued in most curricula in

© The Author(s), under exclusive license to Springer Nature Switzerland AG 2027
G. Vargas Solar et al. (Eds.): ADBIS 2026, CCIS 3175, pp. 332–347, 2027.
https://doi.org/10.1007/978-3-032-39823-9_31

the teaching of software engineering or applied computer science. On the other hand, universities often face the problem that students are practically skilled, but have difficulty understanding the fundamental theoretical foundations [3,4]. The above type of problem can be observed specifically in subjects oriented to the formal semantics of languages. In teaching, executable semantics represent a natural transition from an abstract formal description of the meaning of programs to their directly executable and experimentally verifiable form [2,19]. They allow students not only to formally define the semantics of a language, but also to observe and analyze its behavior through simulation or interpretation of programs. Students often do not understand execution semantics because the formal rules describing program execution remain at a high level of abstraction and do not allow for direct observation of state changes during computation. Executable semantics therefore represent a natural bridge between theoretical formal semantics and practical understanding of program execution, as they allow for direct simulation and visualization of individual semantic steps.

Concatenative languages appear mainly in areas where simple composition of operations, stack manipulation, and efficient program interpretation are important [7]. The best-known examples are languages such as Forth, PostScript, Joy, or Factor, which were used, for example, in embedded systems, graphics and printing systems, experimental programming languages, or in research on formal semantics and compositional programming. Due to their role, students do not encounter them directly, while the languages themselves are not very intuitive due to their nature (all expressions denote functions, and the juxtaposition of expressions denotes function composition). Formally, the change of state in these languages is expressed as a transformation of the stack (main memory structure) and these transformations are relatively abstract (see Jones and Homer [11]). In practice, there are interpreters for the above languages, whose task is to interpret/execute programs in the given languages in order to provide a result with respect to the application domain. However, given the low level of intuition, it would be beneficial for these languages if the course of interpretation could be visualized, which would help to understand the functionality itself and the abstraction over the given languages. Currently, there are only a limited number of tools supporting the visualization of concatenative languages [22], with most available solutions providing only program interpretation without explicit display of intermediate execution states. Thus, there is a lack of a tool that would allow interactive monitoring of stack transformations and the gradual evolution of the program during the execution of individual semantic steps.

For the education of young IT experts, visualization for various procedures within formal methods proves to be very beneficial – whether it is a visual interpretation of semantic evaluation of expressions or execution of commands, or computations of automata, emulation of lexical or syntactic analysis, etc. We consider it useful to include concatenative languages in the course of formal semantics and thus make the usual properties of this paradigm available in teaching, which can help in understanding different approaches to formal semantics or properties of languages. The novelty of the proposed approach lies in the linking of executable semantic specifications, execution trace generation, and pedagogical visualization within a single educational framework.

The aim of this work is therefore to design and implement a web-based system for visualizing program execution in the experimental concatenative language KKJ [13], which was specifically developed as a pedagogical language for teaching formal semantics (see Sect. 2.1). Instead of creating another universal concatenative language, the aim of KKJ was to provide a language whose syntax, language constructs, and semantic specification of executables could be directly interfaced with the SLANG system and subsequently visualized. The proposed system allows users to follow the program execution step by step, analyze stack transformations, and observe semantic transitions through an explicit representation of execution configurations. In this work, the term visualization is used in a broader sense to denote an interactive representation of program execution based on an explicit presentation of semantic configurations and their evolution.

The structure of the paper is the following. Section 2 introduces the main motivation and summarizes the related works. Section 3 presents formal model of visualizing the semantics for KKJ language. Section 4 describes the core of visualization architecture. Section 5 demonstrates the execution of implemented semantics visualization. Section 6 discusses the educational use cases for our work. Section 7 discusses limitations and future work. Finally, Sect. 8 concludes our work.

2 Background and Motivation

Concatenative languages are based on a point-free paradigm, in which programs are defined by composing operations without explicitly specifying variables and parameters. Computations are performed through stack transformations, with individual operations taking data from the stack and returning results to it. This approach supports program compositionality and allows for the creation of new functionality by composing existing operations.

These features make concatenative languages suitable for combining and reusing existing program fragments to create new functionality. Program constructs can operate on general data structures or executable quotations, which allows them to be used in different contexts independently of specific data types. However, this high level of abstraction also reduces the transparency of program execution, since both data and program fragments are manipulated via the stack in a similar way [8]. This can make it difficult for a programmer or student to follow the flow of data, identify logical dependencies, and understand the behavior of individual program parts. The use of postfix notation also supports a minimalist syntax and reduces the need for parentheses typical of other paradigms.

It is not only our experience that visualization plays an important role in teaching formal semantics, because it allows us to explicitly observe individual steps of program execution and changes in internal state during computation. In the case of concatenative languages, visualization of stack transformations and the course of operation composition can significantly improve the understanding of the dynamics of program execution and facilitate the interpretation of abstract semantic rules.

2.1 Short Description of KKJ

KKJ is an experimental concatenative programming language designed primarily to teach formal semantics and stack programming principles [12,13]. The language uses postfix notation and a stack as the primary mechanism for passing data between operations. Computations are performed by composing simple operations that transform the current state of the stack. The language does not use explicit variables. Communication between operations is done via the stack. KKJ supports manipulation of program fragments represented in the form of quotations. Quotations can be stored on the stack, combined, and then executed using higher-order operations. The language includes basic arithmetic operations, stack manipulation operations, and operations designed to work with quotations. The formal semantics of KKJ is specified using an executable semantic specification developed in the SLANG system [21]. Earlier work focused on its denotational semantics, whereas this paper builds upon its executable semantic specification. The simplicity of the syntactic structure allows us to focus on the study of semantic principles and program execution mechanisms. KKJ was designed as a pedagogical language suitable for demonstrating the relationship between formal semantics, executable semantics, and visualization of program execution.

2.2 Related Work

Program visualization is one of the established pedagogical approaches used in teaching programming, algorithms, and data structures, e.g. [15,17,18]. The main goal is to make processes that remain hidden during program execution observable (visible) and to support the development of correct mental models of program behavior. In educational settings, hidden intermediate computation states may significantly complicate students' understanding of program execution [5].

Executable semantics forms a direct connection between formal language specifications and observable program behavior, making abstract semantic concepts more accessible through interactive execution [6,10].

Next, component-based semantic frameworks improve the practicality of formal semantics through modular and reusable semantic components [1]. Such approaches facilitate the specification, maintenance and reuse of semantic definitions across different programming languages.

Unlike existing educational visualization tools, the proposed framework visualizes execution semantics generated directly from executable semantic specifications.

3 Formal Model of Visualization

We propose a visual representation of different languages primarily for methodological and pedagogical reasons, helping students understand the semantic transformations that occur during program execution. The visual representation of program execution must therefore be based on the formally defined semantics of the language. The goal of the proposed model is not only to display the result of the program, but also to allow the user to follow the individual intermediate states arising during the execution of the program. Each displayed step therefore corresponds to a specific semantic transformation of the state.

3.1 Program Configurations

We represent the execution of a program using the configuration

$$c = (P, S),$$

where

- P represents the remaining part of the program, and
- S represents the current state of the stack.

This is the usual notation for configurations in operational semantics and transition systems, where an ordered pair is formed by a block of instructions/commands to be executed and the current environment (state) in which they are to be executed [16]. During execution, the configuration changes by applying individual language operations (formally depicted in Fig. 1).

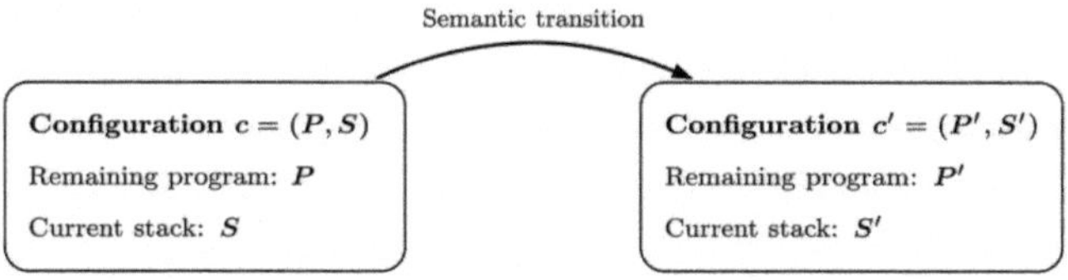

Fig. 1. A semantic step transforms one execution configuration into another.

One execution step is represented by a transition relation $c \to c'$ which transforms the current configuration into a new configuration. Each primitive language operation defines its own transition rule. For example, the `add` operation removes the two highest values from the stack and replaces them with their sum.

However, the visualization itself does not only display the current state, but the entire sequence of configurations

$$c_0 \to c_1 \to c_2 \to \cdots \to c_n, \tag{1}$$

for particular configurations $c_i = (P_i, S_i)$, where each transition corresponds to the application of a semantic rule. The sequence (1) we call the program execution trace. It can also be expressed in short using the closure of the transition relation $c_0 \to^* c_n$ (in the case of a finite sequence of configurations). Each element of this sequence represents one observable execution step.

3.2 Visualization Model

Technical visualization of computations is a process in which individual steps of semantic inference or program execution are monitored. Each visualization step consists of three parts: remaining program, current state of the stack, and performed operation, which emphasizes the fact that visualization is a metaprocess above the execution itself or inference. The user can thus monitor not only the result of the calculation, but also the way in which this result was derived.

3.3 Visualization of Stack Transformations

Since the KKJ language uses a stack as its basic data structure, stack configuration changes represent the most important observable aspect of program execution. Each language operation performs a transformation of the current stack content, with the resulting state becoming the input for the next step of the computation.

The proposed visualization explicitly records individual stack configuration changes occurring during program execution. These changes include, in particular, inserting values onto the stack, removing values from the stack, creating copies of existing values, or creating new values as a result of the executed operations.

Each application of a semantic rule creates a new execution configuration and at the same time a new stack state. This state is subsequently recorded as part of the program execution trace. The development of the stack can thus be understood as a sequence of states generated by individual semantic transitions (see Fig. 2).

3 4 add	$\xrightarrow{3}$	4 add	$\xrightarrow{4}$	add	$\xrightarrow{\text{add}}$	[]
stack: []		stack: [3]		stack: [3,4]		stack: [7]

Fig. 2. Execution trace of the program `3 4 add`.

The relationship between executable semantics and visualization can be expressed as follows:

$$\text{semantic transition} \to \text{new stack state} \to \text{execution trace} \to \text{visualization.}$$

The visualization layer therefore displays not only the final state of the program, but the entire sequence of stack transformations occurring during semantic execution.

3.4 Relation to Denotational Semantics

Although denotational semantics assigns a program its resulting meaning through a mathematical function (which is why it is often referred to as mathematical semantics), the proposed visualization allows the user to observe the intermediate states arising during the application of individual semantic transformations [22]. Therefore, visualization does not represent an alternative to formal semantics, but its didactic interpretation intended to support the understanding of program execution.

4 Visualization Architecture

The architecture of the proposed system (see Fig. 3) was designed to create a bridge between the formal specification of the language and its pedagogical visualization. The source (input) program is gradually transformed into an internal representation, then processed using executable semantics, and the resulting semantic transitions are recorded in the form of an execution trace. The visualization layer then transforms this trace into user-observable objects. This ensures that all displayed steps have a direct basis in the formal semantics of the language and do not represent only implementation artifacts of a particular interpreter.

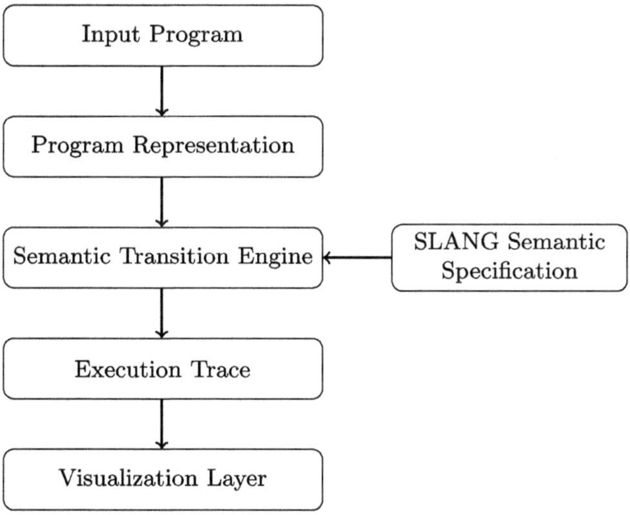

Fig. 3. Architecture of the visualization pipeline.

4.1 Program Representation

A typical interaction with the system begins with entering a source program. The program is then processed (lexical and syntactic analysis) and transformed into an internal representation suitable for further semantic evaluation. This representation preserves the order of language operations and allows for unambiguous identification of the currently executed operation, as well as the remaining part of the program.

The internal representation serves as an input for the semantic execution mechanism and forms the basis for the construction of the configurations introduced in the previous section. The visualization layer therefore does not work directly with the source text of the program, but with the representation created during the program processing. Such an approach also allows to separate the program processing from its subsequent visualization.

4.2 Semantic Transition Engine

The core of the proposed system is the semantic execution mechanism. Its task is not only to calculate the result of the program, but primarily to generate a sequence of intermediate states that describe the entire course of the program execution. Unlike traditional interpreters, which focus primarily on obtaining the final result of the calculation, the proposed system captures all intermediate steps arising during execution.

The semantic rules used during execution are derived from the executable semantic specification of the KKJ language created using the SLANG tool. Each application of a semantic rule transforms the current configuration of the program into a new configuration $c_i \rightarrow c_{i+1}$. This creates individual transitions between configurations that represent observable steps of program execution. The result of the semantic execution mechanism is not only the final state of the program, but a complete sequence of configurations capturing the entire computation process.

4.3 Execution Trace Generation

During program execution, execution trace – a sequence of configurations (1) is generated. Each configuration contains the remaining part of the program, the current state of the stack, and information about the performed operation that led to the next configuration.

The execution trace represents the main artifact created by the proposed architecture. Unlike conventional execution environments, which primarily provide the final result of the calculation, the trace stores all intermediate states that arise during the execution of the program. This feature is important from a pedagogical point of view, because it allows the user to follow the progress of the calculation step by step.

4.4 Visualization Layer

The visualization layer represents the last part of the proposed architecture. Its task is not to execute the program or interpret semantic rules, but to present the already generated execution trace to the user in a form suitable for analysis and study.

The visualization layer works exclusively with configurations created by the semantic evaluation mechanism. The user can thus follow stack changes, the remaining part of the program, and individual executed operations without the need to study the internal details of the execution. This results in a clear separation of semantics from the user interface: the semantic execution mechanism creates the execution trace, and the visualization layer transforms it into an observable representation.

5 Execution Semantics Visualization

In the previous sections, we introduced the formal model of program execution and the way to generate the execution trace. This section is no longer concerned with the semantics of the language itself, but with the way in which the generated configurations are presented to the user through the visualization layer.

The proposed visualization framework exposes semantic transitions generated during program execution and presents them as observable execution traces. The following examples demonstrate how stack states, quotations and higher-order operations can be studied through the generated visualizations.

5.1 Visualization of Program Execution

To demonstrate the capabilities of the proposed system, we will use the program

$$2\ \{\texttt{dup dup}\}\ \texttt{apply mul mul}. \tag{2}$$

After inserting a quote on the stack and executing the apply operation, it is expanded into the executable part of the program. Subsequently, two `dup` operations are performed, which create copies of the original value, and two `mul` operations, which sequentially calculate the resulting value.

Formally, the execution trace can be expressed as a sequence of configurations

$$\begin{array}{l}
(\texttt{2 \{dup dup\} apply mul mul}, [\,]) \rightarrow \\
(\texttt{\{dup dup\} apply mul mul}, [2]) \rightarrow \\
(\texttt{apply mul mul}, [2, \texttt{\{dup dup\}}]) \rightarrow \\
(\texttt{dup dup mul mul}, [2]) \rightarrow \\
(\texttt{dup mul mul}, [2, 2]) \rightarrow \\
(\texttt{mul mul}, [2, 2, 2]) \rightarrow \\
(\texttt{mul}, [2, 4]) \rightarrow \\
(\varepsilon, [8])
\end{array}$$

Figure 4 shows the same execution trace generated by the system. Each line represents one configuration consisting of the remaining part of the program and the current contents of the stack. The user can thus observe not only the final result of the calculation, but also the individual semantic transformations that lead to it.

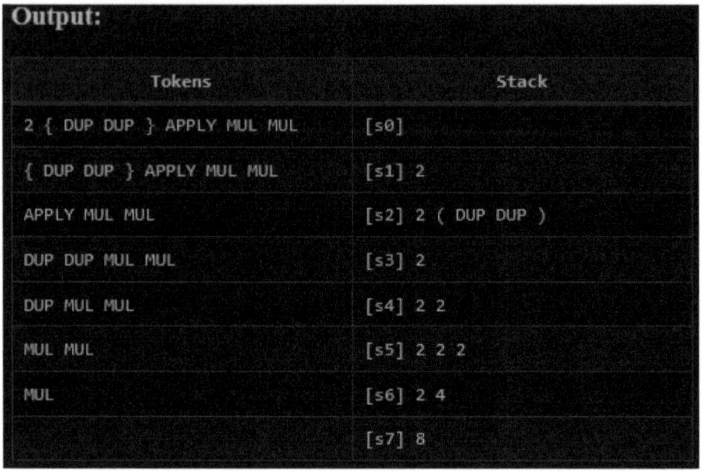

Output:

Tokens	Stack
2 { DUP DUP } APPLY MUL MUL	[s0]
{ DUP DUP } APPLY MUL MUL	[s1] 2
APPLY MUL MUL	[s2] 2 (DUP DUP)
DUP DUP MUL MUL	[s3] 2
DUP MUL MUL	[s4] 2 2
MUL MUL	[s5] 2 2 2
MUL	[s6] 2 4
	[s7] 8

Fig. 4. Execution trace generated for the program `2 {dup dup} apply mul mul`. Each row corresponds to a semantic configuration consisting of the remaining program and the current stack state.

From a pedagogical point of view, it is important that the student can observe the moment when a quote becomes an executable program, as well as the changes in the stack content after each application of a semantic rule. These processes remain hidden during normal program execution, while the proposed visualization makes them accessible through a sequence of execution configurations. The visualization thus converts abstract semantic transformations into observable program changes and facilitates the understanding of higher-order mechanisms, which are among the most challenging concepts in concatenative languages.

5.2 Visualization of Higher-Order Constructs

One of the characteristic features of the KKJ language is the support of quotations and higher-order operations such as `apply` and `compose`. Unlike ordinary arithmetic operations, these constructs work with program fragments as data that can be stored on the stack, transferred, and then executed.

The example given in the previous subsection illustrates a situation in which a quotation is first stored on the stack as an ordinary data object. Only the application of the `apply` operation causes its contents to become part of the executed program. Visualization allows this moment to be clearly identified and its consequences to be traced in the further course of the calculation.

This method of representation allows us to trace the relationship between a program as a data structure and a program as a performed calculation, which is one of the characteristic features of concatenative languages.

6 Educational Use Cases

The proposed system was created as a pedagogical tool supporting the teaching of formal semantics and the principles of concatenative languages. Its design is based on long-term experience with teaching formal methods and programming languages, in which students often struggle with the connection between the formal semantic model and the concrete execution of the program. Visualization of execution makes accessible the processes that are presented in traditional teaching mainly using formal rules or manually created semantic inferences.

The primary goal of the system is not program development but semantic understanding. After positive experiences with the StackLang tool and the SLANG environment, we took up the challenge of preparing a visualization of the KKJ language. A similar stack-oriented language, though with a more general machine model and a small-step operational semantics, is described in [20].

The presented use cases demonstrate that the proposed system is not merely a visualization tool. By exposing semantic transitions and execution traces, it supports the teaching of operational reasoning, stack-based computation, higher-order programming constructs and semantic evaluation.

6.1 Teaching Operational and Executable Semantics

In pedagogical practice, we have observed the problem that students often have trouble connecting the notation $c_i \to c_{i+1}$ with the actual execution of the program. In particular, more technically oriented students intuitively understand that the notation is a form that determines the result of the program by computation, but the concrete connection between the formal notation and the concrete steps of the computation is often absent.

Visualization creates a bridge between the formal notation, the semantic transitions and the observable execution [14]. Executable semantics therefore connects formal semantic rules with the concrete execution behavior, thus making abstract semantic transitions directly observable during program execution.

6.2 Understanding Stack-Based Computation

A stack is a simple but very important memory model used in many formal models of computation, abstract machines, and programming languages. Although basic arithmetic operations are usually understandable to students, significantly greater problems arise with operations that manipulate the stack, such as `dup`, `swap`, or `drop`.

Unlike arithmetic operations, these constructs do not produce an immediately observable result in the form of a new value. Their effect is manifested indirectly through changes in the order or number of values stored on the stack. Therefore, the student often cannot easily determine how a particular operation will affect the further course of the calculation.

For this reason, creating the correct mental model of stacks is one of the greatest challenges in teaching concatenative languages. The student must understand that the meaning of the following operations is directly dependent on the current contents of the stack and that even seemingly simple operations can significantly affect the further behavior of the program.

The proposed visualization helps to overcome these problems by making changes to the program state accessible, which remain hidden during normal execution. The user can follow the consequences of individual operations and gradually form a correct idea of the principles of stack execution. Stack manipulations thus become easier to understand.

6.3 Understanding Higher-Order Constructs

One of the most challenging topics in teaching concatenative languages is higher-order constructs based on quotes and their subsequent execution. Unlike regular arithmetic operations, these mechanisms work with program fragments as data, which requires the student to think differently about program execution.

Based on our pedagogical experience, students often struggle with the distinction between a quote stored on the stack and a quote that has become part of the executed program. Although the formal rules define this behavior unambiguously, their interpretation is often quite abstract for beginners. The result is incorrect ideas about the course of program execution and the relationship between data and program code.

The proposed visualization helps to overcome this problem by displaying individual intermediate states of execution and allowing to follow the moment in which a program fragment is transformed into an executable part of the calculation. Thus, the student can observe not only the result of the operation, but also the entire process leading to it.

Visualization also supports the creation of correct mental models of program execution. Instead of memorizing formal rules, students can observe the concrete consequences of individual operations and gradually develop an intuitive understanding of higher-order principles. We consider this aspect to be especially important when teaching concatenative programming languages, in which the boundary between program and data is not always clearly visible.

6.4 Correcting Semantic Misconceptions

At this point, we would like to point out some problems in understanding the concept of semantics of concatenative languages. For example, in a situation where a fragment of expression (2)

```
{dup dup}
```

is to be executed, students may often think that this will be executed immediately. However, a closer look at the execution traces reveals that the quote is not executed immediately. Instead, it is first processed as a data object stored on the stack. Only after the `apply` operation is applied does the quote become part of the executable program and participate in further calculations.

In this case, the following execution trace is obtained:

$$\ldots(\texttt{\{dup dup\} apply mul mul}, [2]) \to$$
$$(\texttt{apply mul mul}, [2, \texttt{\{dup dup\}}]) \to$$
$$(\texttt{dup dup mul mul}, [2]) \to \ldots$$

We emphasize that visualization supports conceptual debugging rather than software debugging. In other words, the system helps identify misconceptions about program execution.

6.5 Semantic Tracing Exercises

In the context of teaching subjects focused on formal semantics of programming languages, semantics and program verification, or implementation of language processors, the proposed system can serve not only as a demonstration tool, but also as a support for active learning. Visualization of execution allows students to follow individual steps of semantic evaluation and better understand the relationship between formal rules and the specific course of the calculation.

Automatically generated execution traces can be used during lectures to demonstrate calculations and discuss the relationship between individual configurations and the result of the program. However, they represent even greater potential during students' independent work and during exercises, where they can serve as the basis for various types of educational activities.

For example, students can be asked to complete missing configurations in the execution trace, predict the next step of the calculation, or identify the operation that caused a specific change in the program state. Another option is to compare their own solution with the automatically generated execution trace and then analyze the differences.

Such activities encourage active thinking about the semantics of the program and allow students to continuously verify the correctness of their mental models of execution. The generated execution traces may therefore provide a natural basis for formative assessment and feedback during instruction.

Such tasks naturally develop students' ability to construct and interpret semantic inferences, which form the basis of many formal methods used in computer science.

The presented learning scenarios demonstrate that semantic visualization can support both teaching and independent learning by allowing direct observation of formal semantic concepts.

7 Discussion and Limitations

The main idea of the proposed approach is to support a gradual transition from formal semantic specifications to a conceptual understanding of program execution. The proposed framework follows a sequence of representations with increasing levels of clarity, starting with formal semantics, continuing with executable semantics and execution traces, and ending with their visual representation. It is thus clear that visualization is not the goal, but a means to understanding semantics. This is symbolically depicted in Fig. 5.

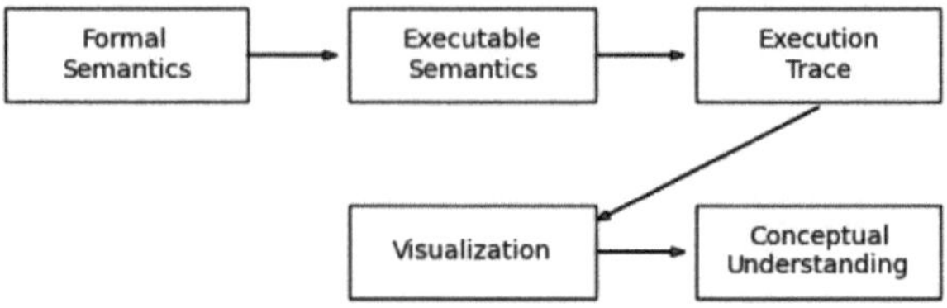

Fig. 5. Conceptual model of the proposed educational framework connecting formal semantics, executable semantics, execution traces and visualization.

In this context, the term visualization refers to the explicit presentation of the semantic states of a program, not necessarily a graphical animation of a computation. Such visualization is particularly useful for concepts that students traditionally find difficult to understand, such as stack manipulation, quotations and higher-order execution mechanisms.

In addition to supporting formal teaching, the proposed framework can also serve as a tool during independent study or preparation for exercises. Students can use visualization to verify their own solutions, analyze execution traces, or identify misconceptions about program execution. The framework complements rather than replaces the lecturer's explanation by making abstract semantic concepts easier to understand.

The current prototype is focused on the KKJ language and represents a fully functional web application designed to demonstrate executable semantic evaluation of programs. Experience with the system so far is based on pilot deployment during teaching and on qualitative feedback received from students. However, the aim of this work was not to implement a controlled pedagogical study, but to present the proposed visualization framework and point out its didactic potential. Using the framework with another programming language requires the creation of its executable semantic specification, the definition of execution configurations, and the implementation of mapping configurations to visualization objects. However, the architecture of the framework itself remains largely independent of a specific programming language, thus creating the prerequisites for its use for other languages based on executable semantics.

From a simple StackLang [22] language implementation, we moved to the KKJ language visualization presented here. This successful project gives us the possibility of further expansion in the future. One of them can be the automatic generation of visualizations from SLANG [21]. Therefore future work will investigate automatic generation of visualization components directly from executable semantic specifications. Another promising direction is the application of the proposed approach to additional stack-based and domain-specific languages. A larger-scale pedagogical study involving controlled experimental groups remains an important direction for future work. Future work will not only focus on further development of the system, but also on its pedagogical evaluation. We plan to conduct a controlled study aimed at assessing the impact of visualization on the understanding of formal semantics, while monitoring both objective indicators of task success and subjective user evaluations.

8 Conclusion

This paper presented a semantic visualization framework for the KKJ concatenative language. The approach combines executable semantic specifications, execution trace generation and interactive visualization within a unified educational environment. Processing of input code in the KKJ language was implemented thanks to the SLANG tool previously developed by us (the third and first co-authors of this article).

The presented approach demonstrates that explicit visualization of stack-based execution and semantic transitions can improve the comprehensibility of concatenative execution models and provide useful educational support for teaching formal semantics of concatenative programming languages.

By transforming formal semantic specifications into observable execution traces, the proposed system establishes a bridge between formal reasoning and practical understanding of program execution.

Acknowledgments. This work was supported by KEGA project 028TUKE-4/2026 – "Innovative approaches to teaching and researching formal methods in the context of modern software engineering", granted by the Cultural and Education Grant Agency of the Slovak Ministry of Education.

Disclosure of Interests. The authors have no competing interests to declare that are relevant to the content of this article.

References

1. van Binsbergen, L.T., Mosses, P., Sculthorpe, N.: Executable component-based semantics. J. Logical Algebraic Methods Program. **103** (2019). https://doi.org/10.1016/j.jlamp.2018.12.004
2. Boerger, E.: The role of executable abstract programs in software development and documentation (2022). https://arxiv.org/abs/2209.06546
3. Broy, M., et al.: Does every computer scientist need to know formal methods? Formal Aspects Comput. **37** (2024). https://doi.org/10.1145/3670795
4. Dongol, B.: On formal methods thinking in computer science education. Form. Asp. Comput. **37**(1) (2024). https://doi.org/10.1145/3670419
5. Elekes, M., Molnár, V., Micskei, Z.: Assessing the specification of modelling language semantics: a study on UML PSSM. Softw. Qual. J. **31**(2), 575–617 (2023). https://doi.org/10.1007/s11219-023-09617-5
6. Ellison, C., Rosu, G.: An executable formal semantics of c with applications. ACM SIGPLAN Not. **47**(1), 533–544 (2012)

7. Herzberg, D., Reichert, T.: Concatenative programming – an overlooked paradigm in functional programming. In: Proceedings of the 4th International Conference on Software and Data Technologies - Volume 1: ICSOFT, pp. 257–262. INSTICC, SciTePress (2009). https://doi.org/10.5220/0002281402570262
8. Hesenius, M., Orozco Medina, C.D., Herzberg, D.: Touching factor: software development on tablets. In: Gschwind, T., De Paoli, F., Gruhn, V., Book, M. (eds.) Software Composition, pp. 148–161. Springer, Heidelberg (2012)
9. Jackson, M.: Aspects of abstraction in software development. Softw. Syst. Model. **11**(4), 495–511 (2012)
10. Jiao, J.: Semantic understanding of smart contracts: executable operational semantics of solidity. In: 2020 IEEE Symposium on Security and Privacy (SP), pp. 1695–1712. IEEE (2020)
11. Jones, T., Homer, M.: The practice of a compositional functional programming language. In: Ryu, S. (ed.) Programming Languages and Systems, pp. 166–177. Springer, Cham (2018)
12. Mihelič, J.: KKJ-lang (2019). https://github.com/jurem/kkj-lang. Accessed 28 May 2026
13. Mihelič, J., Steingartner, W., Novitzká, V.: A denotational semantics of a concatenative/compositional programming language. Acta Polytech. Hung **18**(4) (2021)
14. Minić, T., et al.: Visualizing construction algorithms for closure properties of regular languages. In: Proceedings of the 30th ACM Conference on Innovation and Technology in Computer Science Education, ITiCSE 2025, vol. 1, pp. 166–172. Association for Computing Machinery, New York (2025). https://doi.org/10.1145/3724363.3729120
15. Mladenović, M., Žanko, Ž., Čuvić, M.A.: The impact of using program visualization techniques on learning basic programming concepts at the K-12 level. Comput. Appl. Eng. Educ. **29**(1), 145–159 (2021)
16. Nielson, H.R., Nielson, F.: Semantics with Applications: An Appetizer. Undergraduate Topics in Computer Science. Springer, Cham (2007). http://dx.doi.org/10.1007/978-1-84628-692-6
17. Radaković, D., Herceg, Đ: Towards a completely extensible dynamic geometry software with metadata. Comput. Lang. Syst. Struct. **52**, 1–20 (2018). https://doi.org/10.1016/j.cl.2017.11.001
18. Rocco, L.D., Petrillo, U.F., Palini, F.: Using software visualization to support the teaching of distributed programming. J. Supercomput. **79**(4), 3974–3998 (2023). https://doi.org/10.1007/s11227-022-04805-9
19. Roşu, G.: From rewriting logic, to programming language semantics, to program verification. In: Martí-Oliet, N., Ölveczky, P.C., Talcott, C. (eds.) Logic, Rewriting, and Concurrency. LNCS, vol. 9200, pp. 598–616. Springer, Cham (2015). https://doi.org/10.1007/978-3-319-23165-5_28
20. Schreiner, W.: Thinking Programs. Texts & Monographs in Symbolic Computation, 1st edn. Springer, Cham (2021). https://doi.org/10.1007/978-3-030-80507-4
21. Schreiner, W., Steingartner, W.: The SLANG Semantics-Based Language-Generator—Tutorial and Reference Manual (Version 1.0.*). Technical report 23-13, Research Institute for Symbolic Computation (RISC), Johannes Kepler University Linz, Austria (2023). https://doi.org/10.35011/risc.23-13
22. Steingartner, W., Schreiner, W.: Executable semantics for teaching concatenative stack-based DSLs: the case of stacklang. In: European Conference on Advances in Databases and Information Systems, pp. 248–263. Springer, Cham (2025)

From Sequential Semantics to Streaming Execution: Adapting COTILES on Spark

Andreas Georgalis, Alexandros Karakasidis(✉), and Georgia Koloniari

Department of Applied Informatics, University of Macedonia, Thessaloniki, Greece
{mai23005,a.karakasidis,gkoloniari}@uom.edu.gr

Abstract. Community detection in dynamic social networks supports applications from recommendation to anomaly detection, yet most methods assume static graphs or repeatedly accessible snapshots. We adapt the sequential COTILES evolutionary community detector for Spark Structured Streaming, enabling incremental processing of edge streams as DataFrame micro-batches. We identify the challenges of translating an edge-driven algorithm into immutable dataflow operations and characterise the resulting semantic approximations. Experiments on a real interaction-tag dataset show that unit-size micro-batches reproduce the sequential algorithm exactly, while larger batches produce predictable trade-offs: more detected communities, fragmentation of large communities into overlapping cores, and substantially lower latency.

Keywords: Community evolution · Dynamic networks · Streaming graphs · Apache Spark · Community detection · COTILES

1 Introduction

Online platforms now generate edge streams: direct messages, replies and follows at rates that no longer fit the snapshot processing paradigm under which most community detection algorithms were originally designed. Detecting communities in such networks is a long-standing problem [7,12,15], with an extensive literature ranging from modularity optimisation and spectral methods to statistical inference and label propagation. Dynamic community detection adds a second dimension: beyond identifying cohesive subgroups at any one moment, the algorithm must track community life-cycle events, such as birth, growth and death, as the underlying graph evolves [1,3,10].

Two broad families of approaches have emerged. Snapshot-based (two-stage) methods run a static detector independently on each snapshot and then post-process the sequence to match communities across time; the matching step is itself non-trivial and the per-snapshot cost grows with the graph [6]. Evolutionary (one-stage) methods fold time directly into the objective, producing more temporally coherent results at the cost of tighter coupling between time-steps. Both families share a common assumption: that the data are made available in discrete chunks and can be revisited. Real platforms violate that assumption:

© The Author(s), under exclusive license to Springer Nature Switzerland AG 2027
G. Vargas Solar et al. (Eds.): ADBIS 2026, CCIS 3175, pp. 348–363, 2027.
https://doi.org/10.1007/978-3-032-39823-9_32

edges arrive continuously, and re-reading the prefix at every batch is prohibitively expensive.

COTILES [18], building on TILES [16], sits in the evolutionary family and adds a content dimension: edges carry tags, communities carry tag sets, and propagation rules require not only structural overlap but also tag overlap (or, until a configurable threshold is reached, a relaxed permissive mode). This hybrid criterion makes COTILES well suited to platforms where structural ties are sparse but content-level affinity is dense, e.g. forum interactions or tagged messaging. Its original implementation, however, is single-process and edge-sequential: each edge is processed in arrival order, and sees the state left by its predecessor.

This paper adapts COTILES to Apache Spark Structured Streaming so that the algorithm operates over micro-batches of edges represented as Spark DataFrames. Our focus is therefore not throughput but the preservation of community-evolution semantics: we identify the engineering challenges this transition imposes, characterise the approximations it introduces, and evaluate them experimentally. As such, our investigation is organised around three research questions. (i) Under what conditions does the streaming adaptation reproduce the community structure produced by the sequential reference implementation, and where does it deviate? (ii) Which engineering decisions are forced by the mismatch between sequential edge-by-edge semantics and Spark's set-oriented batch execution model? (iii) How do the parameters exposed by the streaming runtime and the parameters of the COTILES algorithm modulate the divergence between streaming and sequential behaviour?

The contributions of this work may be summarised as follows.

1. A streaming adaptation of COTILES on Apache Spark, mapping the sequential processing pipeline to DataFrame transformations and persistent distributed state.
2. A systematic analysis of the engineering challenges when adapting a sequential community-evolution algorithm to a distributed streaming environment.
3. A formalisation of the semantic approximations introduced by micro-batched execution.
4. An empirical validation showing that, when executed with one edge per micro-batch, the streaming implementation reproduces the behaviour of the sequential reference implementation on all evaluated datasets.
5. An experimental study of how micro-batch size, TTL configuration, and the community-label threshold affect the structural properties of the detected communities and the divergence from sequential execution semantics.

The rest of this paper is organised as follows. Section 2 surveys related work. Section 3 summarises COTILES. Section 4 presents the streaming adaptation, with a dedicated subsection on parallelization challenges. Section 5 catalogues the approximations. Section 6 reports experimental results. Section 7 concludes and discusses future work.

2 Related Work

Community detection in static graphs is well studied, with established trade-offs in resolution, computational cost, and structural assumptions [7]. Extending these methods to dynamic graphs introduces the community-identity preservation problem [15]. Dynamic methods are broadly classified as either two-stage, detecting communities independently before matching them across snapshots, or evolutionary, incorporating temporal smoothness directly into optimisation [9].

Evolutionary clustering exploits historical graph states to improve robustness [4]. TILES [16], on which COTILES is based, propagates community membership through triangles, while other methods track persistent cohesive communities [17] or characterise community lifecycles via clique percolation [13]. Content-aware approaches combine topology with node attributes using label propagation [20], modularity optimisation [2], multimodal fusion [8], and more recently GNNs [19]; CoDAEN [14] surveys recent advances.

Most existing methods assume repeatedly accessible graph snapshots. In contrast, graph stream processing requires one-pass or low-memory algorithms [6,11]. Although frameworks such as Spark Structured Streaming [21] support distributed incremental processing, parallelizing sequential community detection algorithms remains challenging. To this end, we revisit COTILES as a distributed streaming algorithm on Spark Structured Streaming, where micro-batches replace individual edges as the unit of computation. We focus on studying whether COTILES community-evolution semantics are preserved under this execution model and how batching influences them.

3 Background

Here, we briefly outline the COTILES algorithm and then we introduce the notation used throughout the rest of the paper, including formal definitions.

3.1 The COTILES Algorithm in Brief

COTILES [18] extends the TILES evolutionary community-detection algorithm [16] by incorporating both structural connectivity and content similarity into the community formation process. While TILES relies exclusively on graph topology, COTILES additionally considers the semantic similarity of interactions through edge-associated tags. This hybrid approach is particularly suited to interaction networks in which structural links alone are sparse, but shared topical context remains informative.

The original implementation of COTILES is strictly sequential. Edges are processed one at a time in arrival order, and each edge observes the graph state produced by all previously processed edges. Community evolution therefore depends directly on edge arrival order and on the incremental modification of the underlying graph. Community formation in COTILES is based on triangles. When a newly arrived edge closes a triangle, the algorithm examines the community memberships of the participating nodes and determines whether an existing community should expand, whether membership should propagate to additional nodes, or whether a new community should be created.

Unlike TILES, COTILES additionally associates communities with accumulated content labels derived from the tags carried by graph edges. Community evolution is therefore governed not only by structural overlap but also by semantic compatibility. During propagation, new tags may be incorporated into a community either permissively or under a label-overlap constraint, depending on the current size of the community label set. The algorithm also incorporates temporal evolution through edge expiration. Edges remain active only for a configurable time interval, after which they are removed from the graph. Since communities are defined over the active graph, edge expiration may cause communities to shrink, fragment, or dissolve entirely. Whenever expiration affects a community, the algorithm re-evaluates its internal connectivity to determine whether the community remains structurally valid.

The streaming adaptation presented in this paper preserves the overall logical structure of COTILES while reinterpreting its strictly sequential execution model under distributed micro-batched processing.

3.2 Notation and Definitions

Let $G = (V, E)$ denote an undirected dynamic graph, where V is the set of vertices and E the set of edges. Each edge $e = (u, v) \in E$ carries: (i) a timestamp $t(e)$, and (ii) a set of content tags $L(e)$.

A community $C \subseteq V$ is associated with a *Community Label Set* $L(C)$ containing the tags accumulated from the edges contributing to that community.

A node is considered a *core node* of a community if it participates in at least one triangle within that community; otherwise it is considered *peripheral*. Peripheral nodes may belong to communities but do not propagate membership.

The algorithm maintains a configurable *Community Label Threshold*, denoted by $clt \in \mathbb{N}$. While $|L(C)| < clt$, new tags may be added permissively to the community. Once the threshold is exceeded, additional tags are admitted only if they overlap with the existing label set.

Edges are subject to a time-to-live parameter (TTL). An edge expires once the difference between the current processing timestamp and $t(e)$ exceeds the configured TTL interval. Tags inherit expiry indirectly through the expiration of the edges that introduced them.

For an edge (u, v), we denote by: the set of common neighbours of u and v. Triangles formed by (u, v, z) constitute the structural primitive underlying community propagation. We use 'node' and 'vertex' interchangeably. Finally, we define the *visibility horizon* of an edge as the set of graph edges observable during its processing step. In the sequential implementation, this horizon contains only previously processed edges. In the streaming implementation, it additionally includes edges belonging to the same micro-batch.

$$CN(u, v) = \{z \in V \mid (u, z) \in E \wedge (v, z) \in E\}$$

4 Streaming Adaptation

4.1 System Architecture

The streaming COTILES is implemented as a PySpark Structured Streaming application. The input is a continuous stream of edges, each represented as a single line of `(src, dst, timestamp, tags)`. The stream is produced by a Python socket server that reads from a file and emits one line per fixed delay; in production it would be replaced by Kafka or a comparable source.

All algorithm state is held as five DataFrames and persisted as Parquet at the end of every micro-batch, then reloaded at the start of the next:

- `saved_nodes: (id, c_coms[])`—for each node, the list of community ids it belongs to.
- `saved_edges: (src, dst, ts, tags[], weight)`—every active edge, with weight tracking the number of (re-)appearances and `ts` the most recent occurrence.
- `communitiesDf: (cid, nodes[])`—for each community, its members.
- `communityTagsDf: (cid, tags[])`—for each community, its current Community Label Set.
- `removeQueue: (src, dst, ts, tags[], weight)`—the LRQ-equivalent: edges awaiting expiry evaluation.

Per-batch orchestration is driven by `foreachBatch`. For each incoming micro-batch the application (i) loads the five state DataFrames, (ii) canonicalises edge endpoints (smaller id first) and pre-aggregates duplicates within the batch, (iii) runs expiry, (iv) detects common neighbours, (v) classifies community relationships per edge, (vi) decides community formation or merge, (vii) updates state with label-constraint enforcement, (viii) re-checks structural integrity of communities affected by expiry, and (ix) writes back the updated state. Section 4.3 walks through this pipeline. Section 4.2 first describes the engineering challenges encountered when re-expressing each step as DataFrame operations.

4.2 Parallelization Challenges

The original COTILES is, by construction, edge-by-edge: each edge sees the state left by its predecessor, mutates it, and passes the mutated state to the next edge. Spark, in contrast, applies set-oriented transformations to an immutable batch in parallel. The mismatch surfaces in seven concrete ways, listed below.

(P1) Inherent Edge-by-Edge Dependency. There is no Spark-native operator that recovers strict intra-batch sequential semantics. The algorithm therefore has to be re-expressed so that, within a batch, all edges observe the same starting state – the state at the end of the previous batch – and the per-batch effect is a single set-level update rather than n incremental ones.

(P2) DataFrame Immutability Versus Scalar State. Many steps of the sequential algorithm are stated in terms of single values—"the latest edge timestamp", "the weight of edge e", "the next available community id". A DataFrame is a flat table of rows: it has no mutable cells, and there is no way for one row to read or update another. Every step that read or wrote a single value has to be re-expressed at the level of the whole table. Two patterns handle the common cases. When a value derived once per batch needs to be visible to every row—the latest timestamp, used to compute edge ages, is the canonical example—that value is computed as a one-row helper table and attached to every row of the working table, so per-row expressions can refer to it as if it were a constant. When an in-place counter update is needed—most often, incrementing an edge's weight when the edge reappears—the update is recast as a group aggregate followed by a merge into the persistent state. A third common case is when several rows that have never met must agree on a freshly generated identifier (explained in P5).

(P3) State Carry-Over and Recovery. The sequential algorithm keeps its entire working state (the community map, the tag-per-community map, the active-edge table, edge weights, and the queue of edges awaiting expiry) in memory, and the state survives trivially from one edge to the next because the process never terminates. A Spark Streaming job has no equivalent shared memory across micro-batches: each batch starts a fresh job that has access only to what was written to durable storage at the end of the previous batch. The full working state is therefore written to Parquet at the end of every batch and reloaded at the start of the next. The pattern is straightforward; the cost is the I/O it imposes, which is empirically the dominant per-batch overhead at small batch sizes.

(P4) Triangle Detection Without a Vertex-Centric API. Triangles are essential for COTILES: every rule that propagates community membership across a new edge (u, v) requires finding nodes already connected to both u and v. In the sequential implementation this is a single lookup, because the in-memory graph object exposes each node's adjacency list directly; the common neighbours of u and v are the intersection of two short lists. Spark has no equivalent. A DataFrame of edges is a flat collection of pairs; there is no operator that, given a node, returns its neighbourhood without scanning the whole table.

The fix is to materialise the adjacency view explicitly: the edge table is inverted into a table that, for each node, lists its current neighbours. Finding the common neighbours of u and v becomes a set intersection between two rows of this table, and the tags carried by the two triangle-completing edges are recovered with two further joins against the active-edge state. The intuition is simple, but every step is a shuffle-heavy join, and the entire chain runs once per batch.

(P5) Stable Identifiers Under Concurrent Creation. The implementation needs to assign every newly created community a fresh integer id. The difficulty is that the same new community can be triggered by more than one edge in the same batch—and all of those edges must end up referring to that community by the *same* id. Asking Spark for a single "next available id" counter runs into the fact that Spark has no such thing in the conventional sense: counter-style functions in a distributed setting return values whose ordering and uniqueness hold only inside a single partition of the data, and globally unique generators such as UUIDs return a different value at every call.

The fix is to group the rows that will give rise to new communities by the node set each new community will contain *before* any id is assigned, generate one id per group, and then attach it to every row in that group. By the time a row leaves the grouping step it has already been forced to agree with every other row that contributes to the same new community.

(P6) Connected Components After Expiry. When edge expiry removes an edge from a community, the community can split into multiple communities, dissolve entirely if it falls below the minimum size, or simply lose a peripheral node. Distinguishing these outcomes requires running connected-components on the surviving subgraph of every community that lost an edge. This is the one graph primitive in COTILES that resists re-expression in pure DataFrame terms; the implementation delegates it to the GraphFrames library [5].

The interesting design choice here is the *unified affected-community subgraph* pattern. The obvious approach is to iterate community by community, build a subgraph from each affected community's nodes and induced edges, and run a separate connected-components call for each. That works, but every call incurs the fixed overhead of constructing a fresh graph object, and on a batch that touches many communities those overheads accumulate. The novel design instead builds *one* graph that contains the induced edges of *all* affected communities at once, with one critical constraint on edge construction: an edge is included only when its two endpoints are co-members of the same community. That restriction is what makes the per-community subgraphs node-disjoint inside the unified graph—no edge crosses community boundaries, so connected-components naturally partitions every community independently. A single connected-components pass over the unified graph is therefore enough; a follow-up aggregation that groups the node-to-component assignment by community reads off each community's fragmentation status—one component means the community is intact, two or more means it has split. The pattern is not COTILES-specific. It applies whenever a structural test has to be evaluated independently on many node-disjoint subgraphs of a larger graph, and we include it in the contributions of the paper.

(P7) Branch Explosion in Propagation Rules. The community formation rules of the sequential algorithm are concise: a small decision tree branches on the community memberships of the edge endpoints and their common neighbor, and each branch performs a simple update. In the streaming version, each branch becomes a pipeline that joins against the community map, filters the relevant case, aggregates the result, and merges it into the state. The three propagation cases are implemented as separate pipelines, then unioned, deduplicated, and combined with a fourth pipeline that creates new communities. As a result, a few lines of sequential logic expand into pages of pipeline code, increasing planner complexity and shuffle overhead.

4.3 Pipeline Within a Micro-Batch

Each incoming micro-batch is processed through a sequence of stages progressively updating the graph state and the detected communities. The pipeline mirrors the implementation structure and is executed independently for every batch.

1. *Load persistent state.* At the beginning of each micro-batch, the algorithm reloads the persisted state from Parquet storage. This state consists of the active graph edges, node-community memberships, community definitions, community label sets, and the edge-removal queue. Since Spark micro-batches are stateless by default, reloading these DataFrames is necessary before any new updates can be applied.
2. *Pre-process incoming edges.* The newly arrived edges are normalised and aggregated before further processing. Because the graph is undirected, each edge is canonicalised so that the smaller node identifier always appears first. Duplicate edges within the same batch are then merged, their tags are combined, and only the most recent timestamp is retained. At this stage, every edge is also initialised with a weight value of one.
3. *Expire outdated edges and tags.* The algorithm next evaluates whether previously stored edges have exceeded the configured time-to-live (TTL). Edge age is computed relative to the most recent timestamp observed in the current batch. Expired edges are removed from the active graph, and any tags introduced exclusively by those edges are also removed from their associated communities. This step maintains the temporal consistency of both the graph structure and the community label sets.
4. *Detect common neighbours.* For every incoming edge (u, v), the algorithm identifies the set $CN(u, v)$, i.e., nodes that are connected to both endpoints. These common neighbours correspond to triangles, which form the structural basis of community propagation in COTILES. The implementation derives them through a join-based DataFrame pipeline and additionally retrieves the tags associated with the two triangle-completing edges.
5. *Classify community relationships.* Using the current memberships of the edge endpoints, the algorithm determines how the new edge relates to existing communities. Specifically, it computes:
   - the communities shared by both endpoints,
   - the communities belonging only to u, and
   - the communities belonging only to v.

   These sets are obtained through array intersection and difference operations over the stored community assignments of the two nodes.

6. *Propagate or create communities.* The algorithm then applies the COTILES propagation rules. Depending on the relationship between the endpoints and their common neighbours, membership may propagate from one node to another, existing communities may expand, or shared communities may absorb new members. If none of the propagation scenarios applies for a triangle (u, v, z), a new community is created and assigned a unique identifier generated through a window-based mechanism.
7. *Update the global state.* All community modifications produced during the previous stage are merged into the persistent state DataFrames. This includes updates to both the community membership structure and the associated community label sets. During this process, the label constraint of COTILES is enforced: tags may be added to a community only if the community remains below the configured label threshold or if the incoming tags overlap with the existing label set.
8. *Verify structural integrity.* Community updates and edge expirations may invalidate previously detected communities. The algorithm therefore checks whether affected communities still satisfy the minimum structural requirements. Communities with fewer than three members are dissolved immediately. For the remaining communities, the induced subgraph is reconstructed and connected-components analysis is performed to detect splits or disconnected fragments. Depending on the outcome, communities may be divided, pruned, or removed entirely.
9. *Persist the updated state.* Finally, the updated DataFrames are written back to Parquet storage. These persisted DataFrames constitute the starting state for the next micro-batch.

5 Approximations Introduced by Batched Streaming

The streaming adaptation preserves the logical structure of COTILES, but micro-batched execution introduces several semantic deviations from the strictly sequential execution model of the original algorithm. These deviations are not implementation errors; they arise directly from the transition from edge-ordered execution to set-oriented parallel processing. In this section we explicitly identify and characterise the resulting approximations.

5.1 Concurrent Versus Sequential State Observation

All edges within a micro-batch observe the same starting state, namely the state as of the previous batch. They cannot see each other's incremental effects. This is the root approximation, with every other approximation being a manifestation of this. As a corollary, the streaming algorithm is invariant under permutations of the rows within a batch, a property that is desirable for determinism and parallel scheduling but means that any community structure that depends on a specific intra-batch interleaving is not recoverable.

5.2 Extended Visibility Horizon for Triangles

In the sequential algorithm, an edge (u, v) can complete a triangle with a common neighbour $z \in CN(u, v)$ only if (u, z) and (v, z) already exist in the persistent graph at the moment (u, v) is processed. In the streaming version, the *visibility horizon* for (u, v) is the union of the persistent state and the current micro-batch, strictly wider than sequential. (u, v) can therefore close triangles with edges that arrived together with it but, in the sequential timeline, would have been processed strictly later.

This is the most consequential of the approximations in this section. It causes the streaming implementation to discover communities earlier and in greater number than the sequential one. Local dense substructures that the sequential algorithm would only observe in sequence and merge gradually into a single larger community, appear simultaneously and survive as separate, often overlapping, communities. The fragmentation of large sequential communities into multiple smaller overlapping communities is the empirical signature of this effect (Sect. 6.2).

5.3 Batch-Latest TTL Operation

The sequential algorithm evaluates TTL relative to the timestamp of the edge currently being processed. The streaming version evaluates it against `latest_ts`, the maximum timestamp across the whole batch. For edges that, in the sequential timeline, would have been processed early in the batch, this represents an artificial lifetime extension: edges that the sequential algorithm would have expired before reaching them remain eligible to participate in triangle formation. The effect is most visible on edges close to the expiry threshold and is bounded above by the temporal span of a single micro-batch.

5.4 Loss of Arrival-Order Sensitivity

A direct consequence of Sect. 5.1: permuting rows within a batch leaves the result unchanged. We note this separately because it has practical implications for evaluation. Any reference output produced by a strictly sequential algorithm is one of many possible meaningful outputs under arrival-order ambiguity; comparing the streaming output to it as if it were ground truth understates agreement.

6 Behavioural Evaluation of the Streaming Adaptation

The evaluation focuses on the behavioural properties of the streaming adaptation and on the structural effects introduced by micro-batched execution. Rather than treating the streaming implementation purely as a performance optimisation, we analyse how batching, TTL semantics, and the visibility horizon affect the resulting community structure and its agreement with the sequential reference implementation. We adopt sequential-equivalence as the primary evaluation lens precisely because the contribution we wish to validate is behavioural preservation, not community quality in the abstract: established quality metrics such as modularity measure a different question—they compare a result against a notional ground truth or against itself across time—whereas our goal is to characterise the gap between two implementations of the same algorithmic specification.

Dataset. We use a real interaction-tag dataset drawn from an online Q&A community focused on Linux and system-administration topics. Each line records a tagged interaction between two participants (tags such as `linux`, `compiling`, `shell`, `scripting`, `networking`, and similar). From the full dataset we draw arrival-ordered prefixes of 50, 100, 200, 1 000, 2 000, and 4 000 edges. The smaller prefixes are used for sequential-equivalence validation and direct comparison against the original sequential implementation; the larger prefixes are streaming-only because the sequential implementation does not produce results of comparable temporal coverage in feasible time.

Software. PySpark with Structured Streaming, on Apache Spark 3.5.4 and Python 3.10, augmented with GraphFrames 0.8.3 for the single connected-components pass. The streaming source is a Python socket server that emits one edge per fixed delay (default 0.3 s); the source delay does not affect the algorithm's output but does affect how many edges land in each micro-batch.

Hardware. A single-machine standalone Spark deployment running inside a Lubuntu Linux virtual machine with 4 cores (AMD Ryzen 5 5600X host) and a total Spark heap budget of 14 GB (7 GB driver, 7 GB executor).

Methodology. Each configuration was executed three times; we report the median community count and median latency. The Spark state directory is cleared between runs so that each configuration starts from a clean state. Unless stated otherwise, all experiments use a 5-second processing-time trigger, TTL = 7 days, and *clt* = 5.

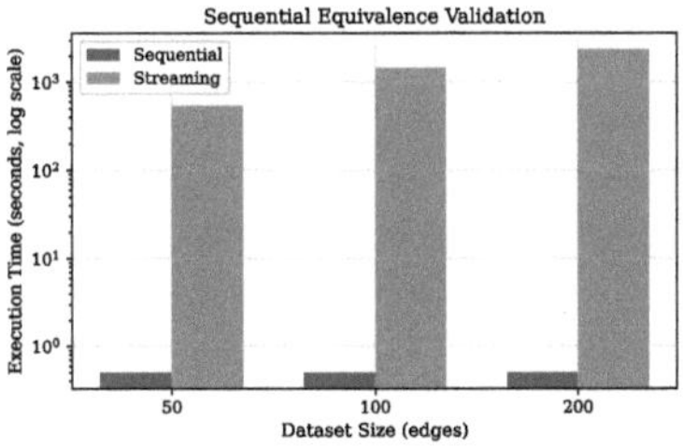

Fig. 1. Sequential-equivalence validation; streaming with one edge per micro-batch.

6.1 Validation: Sequential Equivalence

We first validate that the streaming adaptation reproduces the behaviour of the sequential reference implementation when the effects of batching are minimised. The micro-batch trigger is set so that exactly one edge is processed per batch; under this configuration the streaming algorithm has the same visibility horizon as the sequential one, and the approximations of Sects. 5.2 and 5.3 collapse.

Figure 1 reports the result. For all three datasets the two implementations agree exactly on the number of communities, on the average and standard deviation of community size, and on the number and standard deviation of tags per community. We further verified that every community has identical node and tag membership (e.g., $\{18, 28, 56\}$ with {`compiling`, `distros`, `source`}; $\{17, 73, 78\}$ with {`command-line`, `shell`}). The latency of the streaming implementation under this configuration is, however, very large, because the per-batch overhead of Structured Streaming is spread over a single edge.

The experiment establishes that the streaming adaptation is behaviourally equivalent to the sequential reference implementation under single-edge micro-batch execution: any deviation observed under normal batch operation is attributable to the approximations we have introduced for the parallelized algorithm.

6.2 Divergence Under Normal Operation

We re-run the same three datasets under the default streaming trigger. Figure 2 illustrates the comparison. For each streaming community we classify its relationship to the sequential reference as *identical*, *partial overlap*, *subset*, or *disjoint*, separately by node set and by tag set. Disjoint is empty and is therefore omitted.

The streaming implementation never produces a disjoint community: the streaming community structure remains anchored in the reference sequential structure, but is finer-grained. E.g., on the 50-edge dataset, the largest sequential community $\{4, 5, 17, 22, 26\}$ appears in the streaming output as three overlapping subsets $\{17, 22, 26, 4\}$, $\{22, 26, 4, 5\}$, and $\{26, 4, 5\}$. This is the visibility-horizon effect of Sect. 5.2: locally dense substructures inside what the sequential algorithm would eventually merge into one community are detected simultaneously by the streaming algorithm, surviving as separate overlapping communities. As the dataset grows, partial-overlap communities become more frequent and bridges between previously separate sequential communities appear because a single micro-batch can contain several edges that link them. E.g., on 100 edges, the streaming algorithm produces $\{18, 28, 56, 32, 92\}$, a superset that bridges the sequential communities $\{18, 28, 56\}$ and $\{28, 32, 92\}$ through the shared node 28.

6.3 Effect of Micro-Batch Size

Table 1 reports the joint effect of micro-batch size on community count and on end-to-end latency for the 1 000- and 2 000-edge datasets. Two trends dominate. First, latency is non-monotone in batch size on small datasets and monotonically

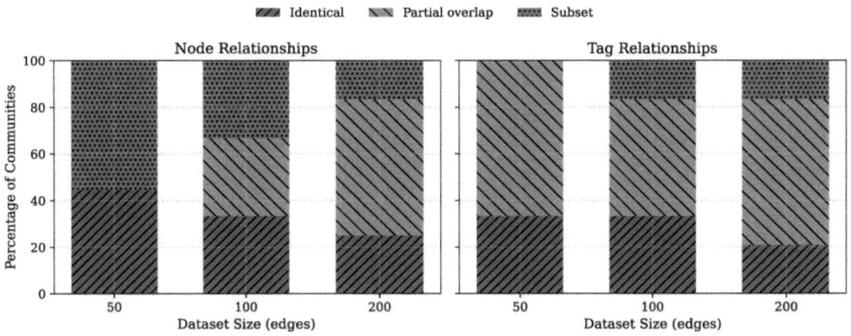

Fig. 2. Divergence under default streaming trigger. Each panel shows the percentage of streaming communities in each category, separately for node-set and tag-set comparisons.

decreasing on larger ones: there is a sweet spot around batch size 200 for 1 000 edges (300 s, the lowest measured), beyond which the per-batch computation cost begins to outweigh the overhead reduction; for 2 000 edges, larger batches remain net-beneficial up to 500. Second, the number of detected communities grows with batch size – this is the visibility-horizon effect made visible at the macro scale: a larger batch widens the within-batch horizon, and the streaming algorithm picks up more locally dense substructures.

Table 1. Effect of micro-batch size on community count and end-to-end latency.

Dataset	Batch size	Communities	Latency
100 edges	10	12	1 min
	20	8	1 min
	50	12	1 min
1 000 edges	50	23	8 min
	200	34	5 min
	500	51	7 min
2 000 edges	50	12	22 min
	200	10	16 min
	500	22	14 min

On the 100-edge dataset, batch sizes of 10, 20, and 50 produce 12, 8, and 12 communities respectively in approximately one minute each; the dip at batch size 20 reflects edge expiry consolidating overlapping cores, illustrating the interaction between micro-batch size and TTL discussed in the next subsection.

6.4 Effect of Time-to-Live

We vary TTL across $\{1, 3, 5, 10\}$ days and observe a strong monotone increase in community count: with batch size 50 on the 1 000-edge dataset, the count grows from 6 (TTL = 1) to 50 (TTL = 10); with batch size 200 on the 2 000-edge dataset, from 23 (TTL = 1) to 72 (TTL = 10). A higher TTL keeps more edges active in the graph, densifies it, exposes more triangles, and yields more communities. The interaction with batch size is multiplicative: longer TTL supplies more state, larger batches widen the visibility horizon, and the two effects compound.

The longitudinal interpretation is that low TTL gives a graph that reflects only recent interactions and reveals transient communities, whereas high TTL accumulates history and reveals more stable, longer-lived structures. The choice of TTL therefore encodes the analyst's notion of "recent", and the streaming implementation makes this knob explicit and inexpensive to vary.

6.5 Effect of the Community Label Threshold (*clt*)

The *clt* parameter controls how many tags a community can accumulate before the label-overlap constraint becomes binding. For values below *clt*, tags are admitted unconditionally. We sweep *clt* across $\{3, 5, 7, 10\}$ on the 1 000- and 2 000-edge datasets. Community count grows roughly linearly in *clt*, especially for larger micro-batches: on 1 000 edges with batch size 500, the count rises from 130 ($clt = 3$) to 186 ($clt = 10$); on 2 000 edges with batch size 500, from 60 ($clt = 3$) to a peak around 90 ($clt = 7$) before levelling off. The trend is intuitive: higher *clt* makes the algorithm more permissive at community formation, so smaller dense clusters survive as separate communities rather than being absorbed.

6.6 Discussion

Two observations emerge consistently across the experiments. First, the streaming execution should not be interpreted as producing incorrect communities relative to the sequential implementation. Rather, it produces a different but valid interpretation of the same evolving graph under set-oriented batch semantics. Second, the trade-off between throughput and sequential parity is governed by a single explicit knob: the micro-batch size. To this end, the posed research questions are answered as follows: (i) The streaming adaptation preserves the sequential community structure exactly when each micro-batch carries a single edge, and deviates predictably as the batch grows. The deviation takes the form of finer-grained, overlapping communities anchored in the sequential structure rather than disjoint or contradictory ones. (ii) The decisions resulting from the execution-model mismatch are the seven challenges of Sect. 4.2. (iii) The community count grows with micro-batch size and with TTL, both of which widen the visibility horizon, and with the label threshold *clt*, which relaxes the constraint on community formation.

Limitations. The evaluation reported here is exploratory by design and carries three caveats. First, the datasets are small ($\leq 4\,000$ edges) and were processed on a single-VM deployment with modest resources; results at production scale and on a distributed cluster may exhibit different latency-quality tradeoffs, particularly at the boundary I/O step (P3) which dominates per-batch cost at small batch sizes. Second, we compare against the sequential COTILES reference rather than against alternative streaming community-detection systems—a choice driven by the absence of established baselines that share both the evolutionary COTILES semantics and the streaming execution model.

7 Conclusions and Future Work

We presented a streaming adaptation of COTILES for Apache Spark Structured Streaming operating over micro-batches of graph edges represented as Spark DataFrames. The adaptation required re-expressing a strictly edge-sequential community-evolution algorithm as a sequence of immutable set-oriented transformations executed in parallel. The transition from sequential to streaming execution also introduces semantic approximations. In particular, micro-batching widens the visibility horizon for triangle formation, alters TTL evaluation semantics, and removes intra-batch arrival-order sensitivity. Our experiments demonstrate that these effects are predictable and interpretable: when executed with one edge per micro-batch, the streaming implementation reproduces the behaviour of the sequential reference implementation, while larger micro-batches progressively favour earlier discovery of overlapping dense substructures.

Several directions follow naturally. On the systems side, replacing Parquet checkpointing with an embedded state store (RocksDB-backed Spark state, or an external low-latency KV store) would reduce per-batch I/O, which our measurements identify as the dominant overhead at small batch sizes. Tuning shuffle partition counts and Catalyst hints around the join-heavy common-neighbour pipeline is a second concrete optimisation.

Finally, evaluation on real-world streaming data at production scale, with established quality metrics for evolving communities, would confirm whether the batch-driven over-detection is a feature or a defect for downstream applications such as real-time recommendation and anomaly detection.

Disclosure of Interests. The authors have no competing interests to declare that are relevant to the content of this article.

References

1. Aggarwal, C.C., Subbian, K.: Evolutionary network analysis: a survey. ACM Comput. Surv. **47**(1), 10:1–10:36 (2014)
2. Bu, Z., Zhang, C., Xia, Z., Wang, J.: A fast parallel modularity optimization algorithm (FPMQA) for community detection in online social network. Knowl.-Based Syst. **50**, 246–259 (2013)

3. Cazabet, R., Rossetti, G.: Challenges in community discovery on temporal networks. In: Holme, P., Saramäki, J. (eds.) Temporal Network Theory, pp. 181–197. Springer, Cham (2019)
4. Chakrabarti, D., Kumar, R., Tomkins, A.: Evolutionary clustering. In: Proceedings of the 12th ACM SIGKDD International Conference on Knowledge Discovery and Data Mining, pp. 554–560. ACM (2006)
5. Dave, A., Jindal, A., Li, L.E., Xin, R., Gonzalez, J., Zaharia, M.: Graphframes: an integrated API for mixing graph and relational queries. In: Proceedings of the Fourth International Workshop on Graph Data-Management Experiences and Systems (GRADES). ACM (2016)
6. Feigenbaum, J., Kannan, S., McGregor, A., Suri, S., Zhang, J.: On graph problems in a semi-streaming model. Theoret. Comput. Sci. **348**(2–3), 207–216 (2005)
7. Fortunato, S.: Community detection in graphs. Phys. Rep. **486**(3–5), 75–174 (2010)
8. Fournier-Viger, P., Cheng, C., Cheng, Z., Lin, J.C.W., Selmaoui-Folcher, N.: Mining significant trend sequences in dynamic attributed graphs. Knowl.-Based Syst. **182**, 104797 (2019)
9. Greene, D., Doyle, D., Cunningham, P.: Tracking the evolution of communities in dynamic social networks. In: Proceedings of the International Conference on Advances in Social Networks Analysis and Mining (ASONAM), pp. 176–183. IEEE (2010)
10. Holme, P., Saramäki, J.: Temporal networks. Phys. Rep. **519**(3), 97–125 (2012)
11. McGregor, A.: Graph stream algorithms: a survey. ACM SIGMOD Rec. **43**(1), 9–20 (2014)
12. Newman, M.E.J., Girvan, M.: Finding and evaluating community structure in networks. Phys. Rev. E **69**(2), 026113 (2004)
13. Palla, G., Barabási, A.L., Vicsek, T.: Quantifying social group evolution. Nature **446**(7136), 664 (2007)
14. Paoletti, G., Gioacchini, L., Mellia, M., Vassio, L., Almeida, J.: Codæn: benchmarks and comparison of evolutionary community detection algorithms for dynamic networks. ACM Trans. Web **19**(3) (2025)
15. Rossetti, G., Cazabet, R.: Community discovery in dynamic networks: a survey. ACM Comput. Surv. **51**(2), 35:1–35:37 (2018)
16. Rossetti, G., Pappalardo, L., Pedreschi, D., Giannotti, F.: Tiles: an online algorithm for community discovery in dynamic social networks. Mach. Learn. **106**(8), 1213–1241 (2017)
17. Sachpenderis, N., Koloniari, G.: Determining interesting communities in evolving social networks. In: Proceedings of the 22nd Pan-Hellenic Conference on Informatics, pp. 249–254. ACM (2018)
18. Sachpenderis, N., Koloniari, G., Karakasidis, A.: Cotiles: leveraging content and structure for evolutionary community detection. In: Engineering Applications of Neural Networks (EANN), pp. 175–186. Springer, Cham (2020)
19. Wang, H., Zhang, Y., Zhao, Z., Cai, Z., Xia, X., Xu, X.: Simple yet effective heuristic community detection with graph convolution network. Sci. Rep. **15**(1) (2025)
20. Xie, J., Chen, M., Szymanski, B.K.: Labelrankt: incremental community detection in dynamic networks via label propagation. In: Proceedings of the Workshop on Dynamic Networks Management and Mining, pp. 25–32 (2013)
21. Zaharia, M., Das, T., Li, H., Hunter, T., Shenker, S., Stoica, I.: Discretized streams: fault-tolerant streaming computation at scale. In: Proceedings of the Twenty-Fourth ACM Symposium on Operating Systems Principles (SOSP), pp. 423–438. ACM (2013)

Towards Formal Knowledge Routing for Forward Engineering in the ADM Lifecycle

Elena Akik(✉), Slavica Kordić, Marko Vještica, Veljko Bubnjević, Milan Čeliković, and Sonja Ristić

Faculty of Technical Sciences, University of Novi Sad, Trg Dositeja Obradovića 6, 21000 Novi Sad, Serbia
{elena,slavica,marko.vjestica,bubnjevic,milancel, sdristic}@uns.ac.rs

Abstract. The Architecture-Driven Modernization (ADM) framework provides a systematic lifecycle for legacy system modernization, with the Knowledge Discovery Meta-model (KDM) as its platform-neutral intermediate representation. While reverse engineering into KDM is well supported, the forward engineering phase, in which Platform-Specific Models (PSMs) are derived from KDM, remains largely unsupported. Deterministic rules struggle to bridge the semantic gap between KDM and PSM, whereas unconstrained Large Language Model (LLM) generation cannot preserve their structural contracts. Combining the two paradigms raises the unresolved question of how to decide formally which knowledge each engine should handle. In this paper, a Coverage Classification Meta-model (CCM) is proposed as a domain-independent formalization of attribute-level knowledge routing, in which each source attribute is classified by knowledge type as either resolvable deterministically or deferrable to a semantic engine. The CCM is instantiated within KDM Rule-based and Artificial Intelligence-driven Forward Transformation (KRAFT), a novel hybrid pipeline in which it governs the routing of knowledge between deterministic Atlas Transformation Language (ATL) rules and a grammar-bounded LLM enrichment engine while preserving the structural contract of the generated models. The CCM is evaluated on five open-source Java systems to establish that it forms a well-formed contract across heterogeneous inputs and partitions KDM knowledge in a stable, predictive manner.

Keywords: Architecture-Driven Modernization · Knowledge Discovery Meta-model · Forward Engineering · Model-to-Model Transformation · Large Language Models

1 Introduction

Modernization of Legacy Information Systems (LISs) is inevitable for organizations operating mission-critical software whose business processes are encoded in long-lived codebases no longer aligned with current platforms or development practices. To systematically address this problem, the Object Management Group (OMG) has standardized

© The Author(s), under exclusive license to Springer Nature Switzerland AG 2027
G. Vargas Solar et al. (Eds.): ADBIS 2026, CCIS 3175, pp. 364–379, 2027.
https://doi.org/10.1007/978-3-032-39823-9_33

the Architecture-Driven Modernization (ADM) process, in which the Knowledge Discovery Meta-model (KDM), described under the ISO/IEC 19506 standard, serves as the unified, tool-processable representation through which the structure, behavior, and data of an existing system are captured [1].

ADM's practical adoption is impeded by an asymmetric distribution of effort across its phases. Reverse engineering into KDM is supported by mature toolchains such as MoDisco [2], whereas systematic reviews identify forward engineering as the least represented phase in terms of research and tooling support [3, 4]. Consequently, recovered KDM instances cannot be operationalized without manual translation, which breaks the traceability guarantees of ADM and devalues the effort invested in the recovery phase.

This forward engineering gap has a structural cause. Existing KDM-to-PSM approaches such as RUTE-K2J [5] report up to 92% correctness for Java targets, with the remaining discrepancies attributed to missing transformation rules and insufficient information encoded in KDM instances [6, 7]. Large Language Models (LLMs) have been applied to industrial-scale code migration [8], but evaluations on Model-Driven Engineering (MDE) tasks report inconsistent semantic correctness, specification instability, and structural invariant violations [9].

Neither paradigm is sufficient alone. Combining deterministic transformation with formally constrained LLM generation has been proposed [10], and empirical evidence shows that combined techniques outperform either method in isolation for reverse engineering tasks [11]. In existing work, however, the decision of which knowledge to assign to each engine is made heuristically. To the best of our knowledge, no published work formalizes this routing decision, and none applies a hybrid paradigm to the forward direction within a KDM-conformant ADM pipeline.

This paper aims to close that gap with the Coverage Classification Meta-model (CCM), a domain-independent formalization of attribute-level knowledge routing for model transformation. The CCM classifies each source attribute by the type of knowledge it carries and thereby determines, by formally registered rule, whether the attribute can be resolved deterministically or must be deferred to a semantic engine. Its abstractions are independent of any particular source or target meta-model, and KDM-to-PSM forward engineering serves as its first registered binding. The CCM is instantiated within KRAFT (KDM Rule-based and Artificial Intelligence-driven Forward Transformation), a hybrid pipeline that combines deterministic Atlas Transformation Language (ATL) rules for structurally well-defined source patterns with a grammar-bounded LLM enrichment engine for semantic elements beyond the reach of those rules. All inter-component communication is mediated through CCM instances, which bounds the enrichment engine to its formally defined scope and keeps every transformation decision traceable to its originating source attribute. The architecture remains platform-neutral, with the meta-model, rule set, and enrichment components independently replaceable. Java is used for empirical evaluation because mature open-source systems provide well-formed instances for testing.

The contributions of this paper are the following: (i) the CCM is introduced as a reusable contract for knowledge-type routing in model transformation; (ii) KRAFT is presented as the instantiation of the CCM at the KDM-to-PSM boundary, in which the previously heuristic decision of which knowledge each engine handles is replaced by the meta-model's formal, attribute-level contract; and (iii) the CCM is evaluated on five open-source Java systems, demonstrating that it constitutes a well-formed contract across heterogeneous inputs, that attribute-level coverage classification partitions KDM knowledge stably and independently of project size, and that its coverage labels are predictive of where semantic enrichment is feasible.

The remainder of this paper is organized as follows. In Sect. 2, background and related work are presented. In Sect. 3, the KRAFT pipeline architecture is described. In Sect. 4, the proof of concept evaluation is reported and threats to validity are identified. In Sect. 5, conclusions are drawn and directions for further work are identified.

2 Background and Related Work

In Sect. 2, the background context is reviewed: the ADM's forward engineering deficit in Sect. 2.1 and the current use of LLMs in MDE in Sect. 2.2.

2.1 Forward Engineering Gap in the ADM

LISs are commonly defined as software systems that are difficult to modify yet too costly to replace. Within the ADM lifecycle, forward engineering, where PSMs and deployable code are generated from recovered representations, remains the most underserved modernization stage [12, 13], with the extraction and reimplementation of embedded business logic identified as a major obstacle to effective modernization [13, 14].

This deficit is not confined to the ADM ecosystem. Systematic reviews of monolith-to-microservice migration [15] and legacy-to-cloud migration [16] identify automated generation of deployable platform-specific artifacts from recovered architectural representations as the principal bottleneck across documented modernization strategies. The recurrence of this finding across unrelated research lines indicates a structural characteristic of the field rather than a limitation of any single study or technique.

The same deficit is visible directly in the tooling landscape, where KDM constitutes the terminal artifact of reverse engineering. Reverse engineering tools produce KDM instances from diverse source platforms, including Java and JEE [2], grammar-based sources [17], BPMN [18], UML [19], PHP [20], ArchiMate [21], and Q# [22], yet none provide a forward generation pathway, a boundary unchanged since the MoDisco [2].

Only RUTE-K2J [5] and Morpheus [6] traverse the KDM-to-PSM boundary, and they expose complementary limitations. The former demonstrates that ATL-based rules can achieve high correctness for a single target platform, but attributes residual discrepancies to missing rules and incomplete KDM instances. The latter requires several custom intermediate meta-models to compensate for KDM's abstraction level, which does not provide sufficient information for generalized PSM generation. Together they expose the cause of the deficit: KDM encodes system structure at an abstraction level that systematically underdetermines target-platform constructs.

2.2 LLMs in MDE

LLMs applied to MDE tasks have been examined across model completion, generation, search, and management [23], yet no published work known to the authors addresses

ADM, KDM, or standardized modernization workflows. Controlled evaluations consistently identify semantic correctness as the weakest quality dimension, with structural inconsistencies, degradation on larger input models, and nondeterministic outputs reported as recurring failure modes [9, 24]; syntactic quality improves across generations, but the need for post-processing and human semantic validation persists [24, 25].

Under constrained conditions, iterative and few-shot prompting support incremental model population [26]. Contextually rich prompts can synthesize Object Constraint Language (OCL) and ATL artifacts [27, 28], but none integrate into standard-conformant pipelines or validate against registered meta-models. Comparing reverse engineering approaches shows standalone LLMs lack practical quality, whereas hybrid techniques excel [11]. Furthermore, LLM-based code translation yields low correctness rates of 2.1% to 47.3% due to semantic and structural bugs [29], alongside instability in formal-specification synthesis [9, 30].

Hybrid architectures combining LLM generation with formal constraint enforcement have been validated in related domains via grammar-constrained decoding [31], neuro-symbolic repair loops [32] and DSL-based constraint repair [33]. In MDE, Eclipse Modeling Framework (EMF)-based templates with LLM semantic completion [34] demonstrate that deterministic structural generation and LLM enrichment can coexist in a single pipeline.

Across the reviewed literature [3–5, 24, 37] the same gap is identified: ADM lacks forward engineering tooling, existing prototypes achieve only partial correctness on a single platform, standalone LLM approaches fail to satisfy structural consistency and meta-model conformance requirements, and no documented tool combines rule-based transformation with LLM-based semantic enrichment. None of the reviewed approaches establishes a formal basis for deciding which knowledge each paradigm should handle, and it is this routing decision that the CCM addresses.

3 KRAFT's CCM and Architecture

The contribution of this paper is presented in two parts. The CCM is introduced first, specified as an *Ecore* meta-model whose abstractions are defined over the roles of source knowledge, coverage, target contract, and provenance rather than over KDM or any particular PSM. The KRAFT pipeline is then presented as its first registered binding, in which all inter-component communication is mediated exclusively through CCM instances. Both parts realize a single design principle: KDM attributes are separated into structural knowledge, for which a complete and verifiable ATL mapping can be defined, and semantic knowledge, comprising attributes absent from the KDM instance or not representable within its structural packages, and each category is routed, at the attribute level, to the engine whose reliability aligns with the required knowledge type [11]. The CCM comprises meta-classes organized into four conceptual layers, presented across Figs. 1, 2, 3 and 4, in which only the meta-classes and the references among them are shown; the attributes and enumerations are omitted for legibility. The complete CCM specification and the KRAFT implementation are available in a public repository[1]. The

[1] https://github.com/akikelena/kraft

layers reflect the order in which a CCM instance is populated as it passes through the KRAFT pipeline shown in Fig. 5.

3.1 KRAFT's CCM

The four layers of the meta-model are described in turn at the level of their meta-classes and the references among them. The pipeline execution core (Fig. 1) establishes the structural root and runtime parameterization. A single execution is encapsulated by *PipelineRun*, the root container that composes every other artifact produced during a run. *PipelineConfiguration* holds the runtime parameters governing pipeline behavior, namely context window limits, repair iteration bounds, and language model settings, formalizing values that would otherwise remain hardcoded and irreproducible. *KDMSourceMetadata* records the characteristics of the input instance, including the producing tool and the resolution status of cross-package references, since this variation directly affects coverage.

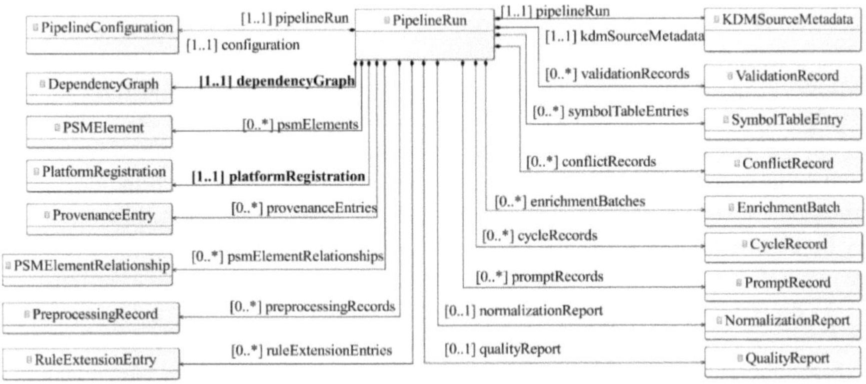

Fig. 1. CCM's Pipeline Execution Core

Each *KDMElementRecord* (Fig. 2) represents one classified source element and is the carrier of the coverage decision. Coverage is expressed through two enumerations defined by the meta-model: a *CoverageLabel*, taking the values *FullCoverage*, *PartialCoverage*, or *NoCoverage*, paired with a *CoverageAssignmentCause* that distinguishes a missing rule (*RuleGap*) from missing source information (*InformationGap*) and from a failed rule application (*RuleFailure*). This pairing is the design decision that gives the taxonomy its diagnostic value: it separates a tool-level information deficit, which a better discoverer could close, from a meta-model-level rule deficit, which requires extending the rule set. Classification is operationalized below the element level by *KDMSourceAttributeRecord*, which records the population status of each individual source attribute rather than labeling elements monolithically. *CoverageClassificationRule* and *RequiredSourceAttribute* express the taxonomy as per-element-type rules, establishing a verifiable correspondence between each coverage label and the registered ATL rule set. *DependencyEdge* and *CycleRecord* capture the typed dependency graph and the strategies

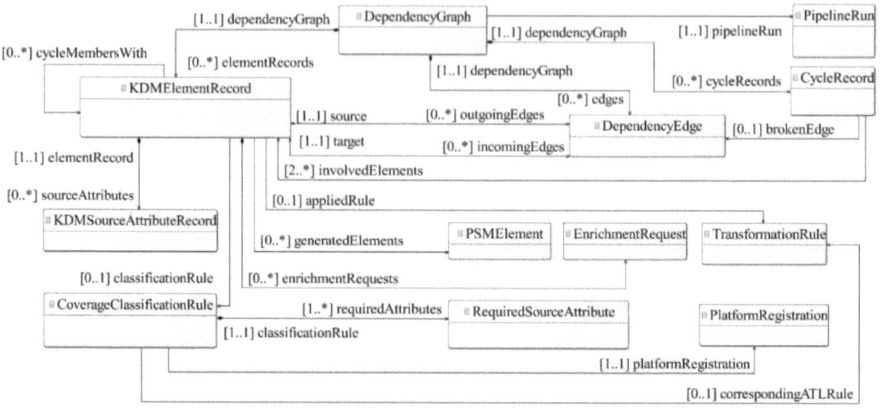

Fig. 2. CCM's Input Classification and Dependency Graph

applied to break cycles, which are common in legacy object-oriented systems and must be resolved before a valid topological order can be established.

The transformation output and enrichment protocol (Fig. 3) spans the contract from deterministic generation through bounded resolution. *PlatformRegistration* holds the registered target artifacts, namely the *Ecore* meta-model, the derived JavaScript Object Notation (JSON) Schema, and the *GroundingDocumentSection* instances injected into prompts; this registration is the mechanism by which the architecture remains platform-neutral. Generated output is represented by *PSMElement* and tracked at finer granularity by PSMElementFeature, whose status enumeration distinguishes a deterministically populated feature from a typed placeholder, an enriched value, or an unresolved one. On the enrichment side, an *EnrichmentRequest* is created for every feature that cannot be resolved deterministically, classified by an *EnrichmentCategory* that governs batching and repair strategy. *EnrichmentBatch*, *PromptRecord*, *EnrichmentOutcome*, and *RepairIteration* together record the full resolution trace. *RepairIteration* references the originating *EnrichmentRequest* rather than the *EnrichmentOutcome*, since each repair prompt is reconstructed from the original request specification, which keeps repair attempts independent and individually reproducible.

The validation, quality reporting, and provenance layer (Fig. 4) covers the post-assembly stages and the feedback mechanism. *ValidationRecord* and *ConflictRecord* attribute each conformance violation and each assembly conflict to its originating component. *QualityReport*, supported by *ElementTypeCoverageStatistic*, aggregates results through the three-way decomposition of ATL-derived, LLM-enriched, and residual unresolved elements, which is what allows each engine's contribution to be distinguished from irreducible incompleteness. *RuleExtensionEntry* closes the loop by ranking the element types that most frequently escape deterministic coverage, directing future rule development, while *ProvenanceEntry* provides the uniform logging through which end-to-end traceability from KDM input to validated PSM is maintained.

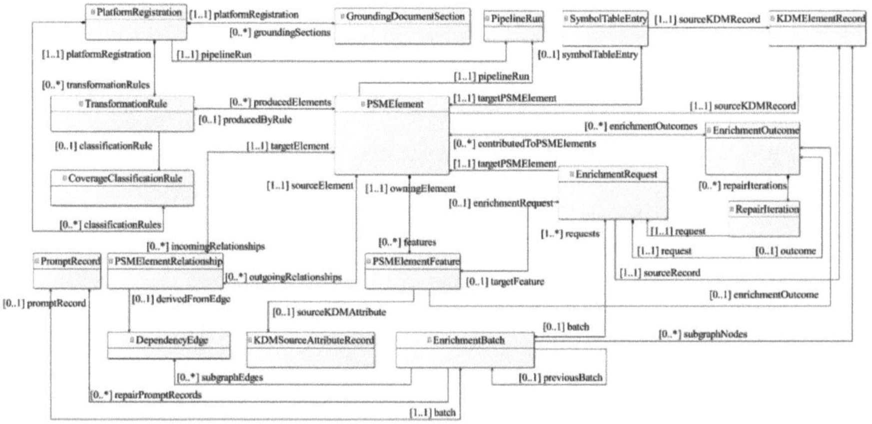

Fig. 3. CCM's Transformation Output and Enrichment Protocol

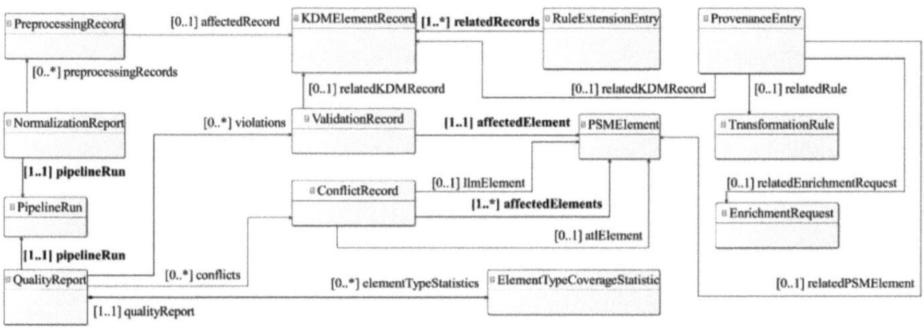

Fig. 4. CCM's Validation, Quality Reporting, and Provenance Layer

3.2 KRAFT's Architecture

KRAFT instantiates the CCM within an MDE-based pipeline that addresses five challenges identified in Sect. 2: (i) the structural information gap between KDM and target PSM meta-models, which deterministic rules cannot bridge; (ii) the inability of unconstrained LLM generation to preserve the formal contracts required by downstream code generators; (iii) the absence of an ADM-conformant mechanism for completing forward engineering from recovered KDM artefacts; (iv) the platform lock-in that has limited KDM-to-PSM engines to a single target language; and (v) the loss of traceability introduced by manual translation.

The pipeline operates on KDM instances produced by ADM-conformant reverse engineering tools. KDM organizes recovered system knowledge into twelve packages across four abstraction layers [1]. The current implementation targets the Code package, which carries the structural declarations most relevant to PSM generation, while the Action, Data, and Architecture packages are recognized as additional transformation sources for subsequent iterations and the remaining packages provide supplementary context informing semantic enrichment.

The architecture is organized into three layers, shown in Fig. 5 together with the numbered data flow followed by a single pipeline execution, and targets multiple PSM families, each conforming to a distinct target platform meta-model. Two shared infrastructure elements persist throughout execution: the PSM Meta-model Registry and the Provenance and Feedback Store. Five processing components execute in sequence: KDM Preprocessing and Coverage Classification; the Deterministic ATL Transformation Engine; the LLM Semantic Enrichment Engine; the PSM Integration and Conflict Resolver; and the PSM Validator and Quality Reporter.

The infrastructure layer provides the shared formal artifacts and preprocessing. The PSM Meta-model Registry stores, for each registered platform, the PSM meta-model as an *Ecore* model, ATL rule files organized by KDM package and element type, a JSON Schema derived from the *Ecore* model, and structured grounding documents containing platform-specific naming conventions, annotation vocabularies, and architectural patterns; the JSON Schema derivation ensures consistency between the LLM output contract and the registered meta-model. The KDM instance enters the pipeline at the KDM preprocessing component (step 1), which applies well-formedness rules, resolving dangling references, normalizing package population, and recovering Action-Code links to ensure structural completeness prior to classification. Coverage classification then assigns to each element the labels and causes defined in Sect. 3.1, and a typed dependency graph is subsequently constructed and analyzed for cycles to establish a valid topological ordering. The resulting CCM instance, in which every KDM element carries its assigned coverage label and cause, hereafter a classified CCM instance, is passed to the transformation layer (step 2).

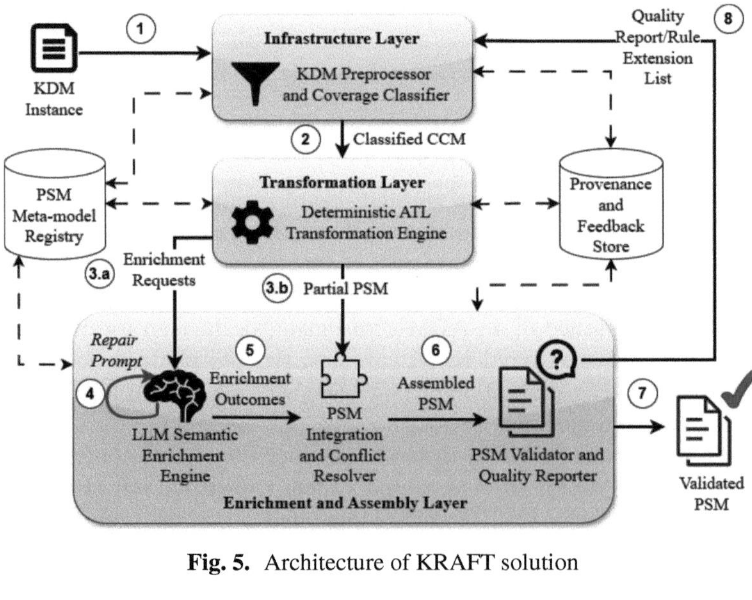

Fig. 5. Architecture of KRAFT solution

The transformation layer performs deterministic M2M transformation. The Deterministic ATL Transformation Engine processes all *FullCoverage* and *PartialCoverage* elements in topological order across three phases, namely structural element generation, relational binding specification, and behavioral specification, with each rule carrying OCL pre- and post-conditions and failed elements reclassified to *PartialCoverage* with cause *RuleFailure*. For *FullCoverage* elements, complete PSM elements are produced; for *PartialCoverage* elements, structurally complete elements are produced with semantically unresolvable features assigned Placeholder status. For each placeholder, an enrichment request is created carrying the target attribute specification, the enrichment category, and a confidence hint, and the complete set of enrichment requests is routed to the LLM Semantic Enrichment Engine (step 3.a), while the partial PSM is forwarded directly to the PSM Integration and Conflict Resolver (step 3.b).

The enrichment and assembly layer resolves placeholders and reconciles the two transformation streams. The LLM Semantic Enrichment Engine resolves enrichment requests through a grammar-bounded prompting protocol strictly limited to typed placeholders [31]. Requests are grouped into batches partitioned by enrichment category and, where context window limits are exceeded, by dependency subgraph. For each batch, a three-component prompt is constructed: the system instruction carries the JSON Schema derived from the registered *Ecore* meta-model together with the platform grounding documents; the context block provides the KDM source elements under transformation and the enrichment outcomes already resolved within the current batch, ensuring local consistency; and the task specification identifies the placeholder attribute, its declared target type, the applicable enrichment category, and the OCL-derived value constraints the resolved value must satisfy. Responses undergo syntactic validation against the JSON Schema and semantic validation against registered constraints, including cross-element consistency checks for visibility-inheritance compatibility, type-naming plausibility, and encapsulation conventions. When validation fails, a repair prompt is issued (step 4) with a differentiated strategy, applying, in order, a violation description, a conforming example, and a minimal correction request, with unresolved requests assigned *ResidualUnresolved* status. The PSM Integration and Conflict Resolver then merges the partial PSM received in step 3.b with the validated enrichment outcomes (step 5), resolving naming conflicts through a canonical symbol table, type conflicts through permitted type widening, and structural redundancy by retaining ATL content supplemented with LLM semantic content. Finally, the assembled PSM is checked for conformance by the PSM Validator through EMF-based constraints (step 6), the validated PSM is emitted as the pipeline output (step 7), and the quality report separates completeness across ATL, LLM, and *ResidualUnresolved* elements, following the three-way decomposition defined in Sect. 3.1, with the prioritized rule extension list written to the Provenance and Feedback Store at run conclusion (step 8).

4 Evaluation of the KRAFT's CCM

Following a design-science, proof-of-concept research method, the CCM is evaluated to establish three properties on which the wider architecture depends: that the meta-model constitutes a well-formed and instantiable contract across heterogeneous inputs, that attribute-level coverage classification partitions KDM knowledge in a stable and tool-independent manner, and that the coverage labels are predictive, in the sense that the categories flagged as requiring enrichment are precisely those where deterministic recovery is infeasible. Although Sect. 3 specifies a complete forward engineering pipeline, the evaluation is deliberately scoped to the two foundational mechanisms on which all downstream stages depend, namely coverage classification and grammar-bounded enrichment, since their feasibility determines whether completion of the full pipeline is warranted.

4.1 Methodology and Experimental Setup

Five open-source Java projects were selected as subjects, spanning an order of magnitude in size. Selection required the absence of external dependencies, compatibility with the MoDisco Java-to-KDM transformation, and public availability for reproducibility. KDM instances were produced using MoDisco within Eclipse Modeling Tools 2026–03 through the two-step discovery process, and the pipeline was executed against a Java 17 SE target platform registration comprising four coverage classification rules for the KDM Code package element types. All resulting CCM instances were checked for conformance through EMF validation.

To assess the enrichment mechanism, a stratified sample of 100 requests was extracted, 20 per project, comprising 10 *ClassUnit* and 2 *StorableUnit BusinessRuleInference* (visibility) requests and 8 *ParameterUnit NamingConventionReconstruction* (type) requests. Ground truth was established by manual inspection of the Java source. The three-component prompting protocol was applied using Claude Sonnet 4.6, and responses were validated syntactically, semantically, and through cross-element consistency constraints, with failed validations entering the three-iteration repair loop.

4.2 Contract Conformance and Partition Stability

Coverage classification and enrichment results are reported jointly per project in Table 1. The five KDM instances contain 1,338 to 14,990 Code package elements, corresponding to 7,838 to 86,361 *EObjects*. Every CCM instance passed EMF validation with zero conformance errors, which establishes that the meta-model functions as a well-formed data contract across the full size range of the corpus.

FullCoverage remained stable, ranging from 72.5% to 78.2% with a mean of 75.2% and a standard deviation of 2.1 percentage points across an order-of-magnitude variation in project size. This stability indicates that the partition reflects a structural property of MoDisco-produced KDM instances rather than a project-specific artifact. The breakdown by element type localizes the incompleteness precisely: *PartialCoverage* concentrated in *ParameterUnit*, at 38% to 55% with cause *InformationGap*, and in *ClassUnit*, at 27% to 68% with cause *RuleGap*, while *MethodUnit* and *StorableUnit* reached 99% to 100% and 95% to 99% coverage respectively. *NoCoverage* appeared only in JHotDraw and Commons Collections, at 0.3%, caused by *MethodUnit* patterns absent from the registered rule set. The paired cause distinction introduced in Sect. 3.1 quantifies the two deficit types separately, a separation not provided by prior element-level approaches.

Table 1. Coverage classification and LLM enrichment results across five test subjects

Project	KDM Elements	Full (%)	Partial (%)	None (%)	Enr. Requests	BRI Acc.	NCR Acc.	Overall
Commons CLI 1.4	1,338	74.7	25.3	0.0	622	75.0% (9/12)	100.0% (8/8)	85.0%
Commons Net 1.4.0	5,662	72.5	27.5	0.0	3,002	100.0% (12/12)	37.5% (3/8)	75.0%
JHotDraw 5.2	6,659	75.7	24.0	0.3	2,978	100.0% (12/12)	0.0% (0/8)	60.0%
Commons Lang 2.6	10,832	78.2	21.8	0.0	4,555	100.0% (12/12)	25.0% (2/8)	70.0%
Commons Collections 3.2.2	14,990	75.0	24.7	0.3	7,232	91.7% (11/12)	50.0% (4/8)	75.0%

This result also clarifies the relationship to the 92% correctness reported for the closest prior KDM-to-PSM prototype. That figure counted an element as correct whenever a PSM element was produced, including cases in which absent source attributes were silently filled with default values. The *PartialCoverage* label makes those same elements explicitly visible as semantically incomplete and therefore subject to enrichment, rather than concealing the deficit within a single correctness figure.

4.3 Predictiveness of the Coverage Labels

The enrichment experiment tests whether the categories that coverage classification routes to the LLM are in fact the categories where deterministic recovery is infeasible. Across the 100 requests, every initial response passed syntactic and semantic validation, while factual accuracy was 73.0%. A pronounced and category-dependent asymmetry was observed: the *BusinessRuleInference* category reached 93.3% (56/60), while the *NamingConventionReconstruction* category reached 42.5% (17/40). This asymmetry has a structural explanation. Visibility modifiers are inferable from structural context, since a class extended across packages must be public and a field exposed through accessor methods is conventionally private, and this form of structural reasoning is within the demonstrated capability of current models. Parameter types, by contrast, are absent from the KDM instance and can only be guessed from parameter names, for which pre-Java-5 codebases provide a weak and inconsistent signal; the 0% accuracy on the JHotDraw requests, whose Java 1.1-era parameter names follow no modern convention, confirms this. The categories the classifier marks as *InformationGap* are therefore precisely those that resist recovery, which validates the predictive value of the coverage labels and the per-category structure of the enrichment protocol.

The 100% structural validity of initial responses is attributable to the grammar-bounded protocol: combining JSON Schema enforcement with platform grounding documents removes the structural violations reported for unconstrained LLM use in modeling tasks. Incorrect responses were factually wrong but structurally valid, which confirms the intended separation of concerns: meta-model conformance is guaranteed by the formal constraint layer, while semantic accuracy is left to the enrichment protocol.

The differentiated repair strategy recovered three of the five cross-element failures flagged in the JHotDraw batch, with mean confidence rising across iterations (0.75, 0.89, 0.92) and two requests left *ResidualUnresolved*.

4.4 Discussion

The three properties established above can be read jointly against the criterion set out at the opening of this section, namely that the feasibility of the two foundational mechanisms determines whether completion of the full pipeline is warranted. Contract conformance, partition stability, and label predictiveness are each satisfied on the present corpus, which characterizes the CCM as an operational routing instrument rather than a descriptive record. Two consequences follow for practical use. First, because the *Full-Coverage* partition holds steady across the size range, the volume of work that must be delegated to enrichment can be estimated from classification alone, in advance of any generation. Second, the paired assignment cause turns the measured incompleteness into actionable guidance: a *RuleGap* denotes a deficit closable within the pipeline through the rule-set extension that the *RuleExtensionEntry* ranking is designed to direct, whereas an *InformationGap* denotes knowledge whose recovery ceiling is fixed upstream by what the discovery stage preserved and therefore cannot be raised by enrichment alone. On this evidence the two mechanisms are judged sound, and completion of the remaining pipeline stages is warranted.

4.5 Threats to Validity

Construct validity is affected by the restriction of the classifier to the KDM Code package; the coverage distribution is expected to shift once Action, Data, and Architecture rules are added. The enrichment experiment, based on 100 requests, provides directional evidence only and is too small for statistical generalization, and a larger evaluation reporting confidence interval is planned. Internal validity is shaped by toolchain consistency: all subjects were processed with a single MoDisco version within one Eclipse installation, which removes environmental variation but means version-specific behavior propagates directly into the results; the coverage rules were authored for a Java 17 SE target without independent validation, and ground truth was established by a single annotator without inter-rater assessment. External validity is limited by the corpus, which consists of open-source utility libraries and a drawing framework that differ from industrial legacy systems in scale, architectural complexity, and proprietary framework use; the pre-Java-5 restriction imposed by MoDisco compatibility excludes generics, annotations, and lambda expressions, which may introduce further *PartialCoverage* and *NoCoverage*. Reliability is strong for the deterministic stages, as coverage classification and enrichment request generation are fully reproducible, and weaker for the LLM stage, whose non-determinism is mitigated by recording complete prompts, parameters, and raw responses for every invocation; replication across multiple sessions is planned to assess stability.

5 Conclusion

In this paper, the CCM is proposed as a domain-independent formalization of attribute-level knowledge routing for model transformation, instantiated within KRAFT, a novel hybrid forward engineering pipeline for the ADM lifecycle that addresses the lack of general-purpose KDM-to-PSM tooling. It separates transformation responsibility between a deterministic ATL engine for structural patterns and a grammar-bounded LLM enrichment engine for semantic elements, with the CCM governing every routing decision as the shared data contract.

An evaluation on five open-source Java projects provided initial evidence of feasibility. The coverage classification mechanism yielded stable and operationally meaningful distributions across systems of different sizes, and every initial enrichment response remained structurally valid under the grammar-bounded protocol.

The CCM provides attribute-level coverage classification with diagnostic granularity not present in prior element-level approaches, separating tool-level information gaps from meta-model-level rule gaps while remaining reusable beyond the KDM-to-PSM binding evaluated here. KRAFT constitutes, to the best of the authors' knowledge, the first documented hybrid pipeline at the KDM-to-PSM boundary, and its grammar-bounded protocol, enforced through automatically derived JSON Schema contracts and registered grounding documents, achieved 100% structural validity on initial LLM responses, removing the conformance violations that have prevented standalone LLM approaches from being applied to formal modeling tasks. These findings indicate that deterministic rules and formally constrained LLM enrichment can be composed within a standards-conformant ADM forward engineering workflow, whose end-to-end demonstration is the next step.

Several directions for further work have been identified. The coverage classification rule set will be extended beyond the KDM Code package to include the Action, Data, and Architecture packages, enabling classification of control flow, data structures, and architectural constructs. A larger-scale evaluation on industrial systems is planned, including inter-rater reliability assessment and replication studies to quantify LLM variance. The reusability of the CCM will be tested directly by registering a second source-to-target binding, and cross-language generalizability will be examined by extending KDM population to additional languages such as C#, Python, and PHP.

Acknowledgments. This research has been supported by the Ministry of Science, Technological Development and Innovation (Contract No. 451–03-34/2026–03/200156) and the Faculty of Technical Sciences, University of Novi Sad through project "Scientific and Artistic Research Work of Researchers in Teaching and Associate Positions at the Faculty of Technical Sciences, University of Novi Sad 2026" (No. 01-3609/1).

References

1. Pérez-Castillo, R., De Guzmán, I.G.-R., Piattini, M.: Knowledge discovery metamodel-ISO/IEC 19506: a standard to modernize legacy systems. Comput. Stand. Interfaces. **33**, 519–532 (2011). https://doi.org/10.1016/j.csi.2011.02.007

2. Brunelière, H., Cabot, J., Dupé, G., Madiot, F.: MoDisco: a model driven reverse engineering framework. Inf. Softw. Technol. **56**, 1012–1032 (2014). https://doi.org/10.1016/j.infsof.2014.04.007
3. Siala, H.A., Lano, K., Alfraihi, H.: Model-driven approaches for reverse engineering — a systematic literature review. IEEE Access. **12**, 62558–62580 (2024). https://doi.org/10.1109/ACCESS.2024.3394732
4. Durelli, R.S., et al.: A mapping study on architecture-driven modernization. In: Proceedings of the 2014 IEEE 15th International Conference on Information Reuse and Integration (IEEE IRI 2014), pp. 577–584. IEEE, Redwood City, CA, USA (2014). https://doi.org/10.1109/IRI.2014.7051941
5. Angulo, G., San Martín, D., Ferrari, F., Pérez-Castillo, R., Piattini, M.: A process for creating KDM2PSM transformation engines. Int. J. Softw. Tools Technol. Transf. **26**, 1–20 (2024). https://doi.org/10.1007/s10009-024-00735-4
6. Fernández Candel, C.J., García Molina, J., Bermúdez Ruiz, F.J., Hoyos Barceló, J.R., Sevilla Ruiz, D., Cuesta Viera, B.J.: Developing a model-driven reengineering approach for migrating PL/SQL triggers to Java: a practical experience. J. Syst. Softw. **151**, 38–64 (2019). https://doi.org/10.1016/j.jss.2019.01.068
7. Santos, B.M., Landi, A. de S., Santibáñez, D.S.M., Durelli, R.S., Camargo, V.V. de: Evaluating the extension mechanisms of the knowledge discovery metamodel for aspect-oriented modernizations. J. Syst. Softw. **149**, 285–304 (2019). https://doi.org/10.1016/J.JSS.2018.12.011
8. Ziftci, C., Nikolov, S., Sjövall, A., Kim, B., Codecasa, D., Kim, M.: Migrating code at scale with LLMs at Google. In: Proceedings of the 33rd ACM International Conference on the Foundations of Software Engineering, pp. 162–173. ACM, Clarion Hotel Trondheim, Trondheim, Norway (2025). https://doi.org/10.1145/3696630.3728542
9. Cámara, J., Troya, J., Burgueño, L., Vallecillo, A.: On the assessment of generative AI in modeling tasks: an experience report with ChatGPT and UML. Softw. Syst. Model. **22**, 781–793 (2023). https://doi.org/10.1007/s10270-023-01105-5
10. Zhang, Y., et al.: Position: trustworthy AI agents require the integration of large language models and formal methods. In: Proceedings of the 42nd International Conference on Machine Learning, pp. 82441–82459. JMLR.org, Vancouver, Canada (2025)
11. Siala, H.A., Lano, K.: A comparison of large language models and model-driven reverse engineering for reverse engineering. Front. Comput. Sci. **7**, 1516410 (2025). https://doi.org/10.3389/fcomp.2025.1516410
12. Assunção, W.K.G., Marchezan, L., Arkoh, L., Egyed, A., Ramler, R.: Contemporary software modernization: strategies, driving forces, and research opportunities. ACM Trans. Softw. Eng. Methodol. **34**, 1–35 (2025). https://doi.org/10.1145/3708527
13. Fleurey, F., Breton, E., Baudry, B., Nicolas, A., Jézéquel, J.-M.: Model-driven engineering for software migration in a large industrial context. In: Model Driven Engineering Languages and Systems (MODELS 2007), LNCS vol. 4735, pp. 482–497. Springer (2007). https://doi.org/10.1007/978-3-540-75209-7_33
14. Khadka, R., Batlajery, B.V., Saeidi, A.M., Jansen, S., Hage, J.: How do professionals perceive legacy systems and software modernization? In: Proceedings of the 36th International Conference on Software Engineering, pp. 36–47. ACM, Hyderabad India (2014). https://doi.org/10.1145/2568225.2568318
15. Abgaz, Y., et al.: Decomposition of monolith applications into microservices architectures: a systematic review. IEEE Trans. Softw. Eng. **49**, 4213–4242 (2023). https://doi.org/10.1109/TSE.2023.3287297
16. Hasan, M.H., Osman, M.H., Admodisastro, N., Muhammad, S.: Legacy systems to cloud migration: a review from the architectural perspective. J. Syst. Softw. **202**, 111702 (2023). https://doi.org/10.1016/j.jss.2023.111702

17. Cánovas Izquierdo, J.L., García Molina, J.: Extracting models from source code in soft-ware modernization. Softw. Syst. Model. **13**, 713–734 (2014). https://doi.org/10.1007/s10270-012-0270-z
18. Pérez-Castillo, R., García Rodríguez de Guzmán, I., Ávila-García, O., Piattini, M.: Business process archeology using MARBLE. Inf. Softw. Technol. **53**, 1023–1044 (2011). https://doi.org/10.1016/j.infsof.2011.05.006
19. Sabir, U., Azam, F., Haq, S.U., Anwar, M.W., Butt, W.H., Amjad, A.: A model driven reverse engineering framework for generating high level UML models from Java source code. IEEE Access. **7**, 158931–158950 (2019). https://doi.org/10.1109/ACCESS.2019.2950884
20. Moutaouakkil, A., Mbarki, S.: PHP modernization approach generating KDM models from PHP legacy code. Bull. Electr. Eng. Inform. **9**, 247–255 (2020). https://doi.org/10.11591/eei.v9i1.1269
21. Pérez-Castillo, R., Delgado, A., Ruiz, F., Bacigalupe, V., Piattini, M.: A method for transforming knowledge discovery metamodel to ArchiMate models. Softw. Syst. Model. **21**, 311–345 (2022). https://doi.org/10.1007/s10270-021-00912-y
22. Jiménez-Navajas, L., Pérez-Castillo, R., Piattini, M.: KDM to UML model transformation for quantum software modernization. In: Quality of Information and Communications Technology (QUATIC 2021), CCIS, vol. 1439, pp. 215–228. Springer (2021). https://doi.org/10.1007/978-3-030-85347-1_16
23. Di Rocco, J., Di Ruscio, D., Di Sipio, C., Nguyen, P.T., Rubei, R.: On the use of large language models in model-driven engineering. Softw. Syst. Model. **24**, 923–948 (2025). https://doi.org/10.1007/s10270-025-01263-8
24. Chen, K., Yang, Y., Chen, B., Hernández López, J.A., Mussbacher, G., Varró, D.: Automated domain modeling with large language models: a comparative study. In: 2023 ACM/IEEE 26th International Conference on Model Driven Engineering Languages and Systems (MODELS), pp. 162–172. IEEE, Västerås, Sweden (2023). https://doi.org/10.1109/MODELS58315.2023.00037
25. Yang, Y., Chen, B., Chen, K., Mussbacher, G., Varró, D.: Multi-step iterative automated domain modeling with large language models. In: Proceedings of the ACM/IEEE 27th International Conference on Model Driven Engineering Languages and Systems, pp. 587–595. ACM, Linz Austria (2024). https://doi.org/10.1145/3652620.3687807
26. Ben Chaaben, M., Burgueño, L., Sahraoui, H.: Towards using few-shot prompt learning for automating model completion. In: 45th International Conference on Software Engineering: New Ideas and Emerging Results (ICSE-NIER), pp. 7–12 (2023). https://doi.org/10.1109/ICSE-NIER58687.2023.00008
27. Miranda, J.W.P., Brunelière, H., Tisi, M., Sunyé, G.: Towards an in-context LLM-based approach for automating the definition of model views. In: Proceedings of the 17th ACM SIGPLAN International Conference on Software Language Engineering (SLE), pp. 29–42 (2024). https://doi.org/10.1145/3687997.3695650
28. Pan, F., Zolfaghari, V., Wen, L., Petrovic, N., Lin, J., Knoll, A.: Generative AI for OCL constraint generation: dataset collection and LLM fine-tuning. In: 2024 IEEE International Symposium on Systems Engineering (ISSE), pp. 1–8. IEEE, Perugia, Italy (2024). https://doi.org/10.1109/ISSE63315.2024.10741141
29. Pan, R., et al.: Lost in translation: a study of bugs introduced by large language models while translating code. In: Proceedings of the IEEE/ACM 46th International Conference on Software Engineering, pp. 1–13. Association for Computing Machinery, New York, NY, USA (2024). https://doi.org/10.1145/3597503.3639226
30. Endres, M., Fakhoury, S., Chakraborty, S., Lahiri, S.K.: Can large language models transform natural language intent into formal method postconditions? Proc. ACM Softw. Eng. 1, 84:1889–84:1912 (2024). https://doi.org/10.1145/3660791

31. Geng, S., Josifoski, M., Peyrard, M., West, R.: Grammar-constrained decoding for structured NLP tasks without finetuning. In: Proceedings of the 2023 Conference on Empirical Methods in Natural Language Processing (EMNLP), pp. 10932–10952 (2023). https://doi.org/10.18653/v1/2023.emnlp-main.674
32. Wu, G., Cao, W., Yao, Y., Wei, H., Chen, T., Ma, X.: LLM meets bounded model checking: neuro-symbolic loop invariant inference. In: 39th IEEE/ACM International Conference on Automated Software Engineering (ASE) (2024). https://doi.org/10.1145/3691620.3695014
33. Mayr-Dorn, C., Bilal, A., Ratiu, C., Egyed, A.: Generating quality assurance constraints from natural language with LLMs. J. Softw. Evol. Process. **37**, e70062 (2025). https://doi.org/10.1002/smr.70062
34. He, X., Chen, R., Zhang, Z., Wang, Y., Dong, Q.: A hybrid approach for EMF code generation: code templates meet large language models (2025). https://doi.org/10.48550/arXiv.2512.05498

An Application of Model-Driven Engineering and the Form-Driven Approach to Database and Information System Development

Veljko Bubnjević[1(✉)], Slavica Kordić[1], Elena Akik[1], and Ivan Luković[2]

[1] Faculty of Technical Sciences, University of Novi Sad, Trg Dositeja Obradovića 6, 21000 Novi Sad, Serbia
{bubnjevic,slavica,elena}@uns.ac.rs

[2] Faculty of Organizational Sciences, University of Belgrade, Jove Ilića 154, 11000 Belgrade, Serbia
ivan.lukovic@fon.bg.ac.rs

Abstract. Recent advances in artificial intelligence and large language models have significantly accelerated information system development, but often without providing formal guarantees regarding model consistency, integrity constraints, and database schema quality. In contrast, formal approaches based on form type conceptual models and relational database theory enable systematic database design while preserving integrity constraints. Previous research established a model-driven engineering (MDE)-based reverse engineering process that transforms legacy relational database schemas into form types. However, a corresponding forward engineering process had not been realized within the same technological space, leaving the information system reengineering cycle incomplete. This paper presents a model-driven approach to forward engineering based on form type models. Starting from platform-independent form type models, the proposed transformation chain realizes the extended Bernstein's synthesis algorithm, generates relational database schemas in third normal form, derives platform-specific database models, and produces executable SQL/DDL specifications for multiple relational database management systems. The realization of the proposed approach led to the development of a new unified MDE-based version of the IIS*Studio environment, whose applicability is illustrated through an illustrative example.

Keywords: Model-Driven Engineering · Form Types · Model Transformations · Information System Development · Database Schema Design

1 Introduction

The rapid development of artificial intelligence (AI) and large language models (LLMs) has driven major changes in the development of software engineering and information systems. The design of information system is performed in parallel with database design. In this process, conceptual modeling is performed first, after which higher-level abstraction models are transformed into lower-level implementation models. In this context,

© The Author(s), under exclusive license to Springer Nature Switzerland AG 2027
G. Vargas Solar et al. (Eds.): ADBIS 2026, CCIS 3175, pp. 380–395, 2027.
https://doi.org/10.1007/978-3-032-39823-9_34

AI-assisted approaches can significantly accelerate development processes and provide support to designers during the early phases of modeling. However, these approaches exhibit serious limitations at both levels of abstraction. At the conceptual level, AI-generated models may contain semantic inconsistencies and may incorrectly represent business rules and integrity constraints due to limitations in understanding domain-specific context [1–3]. Similarly, at the implementation level, AI-generated relational schemas often do not provide formal guarantees regarding normalization, preservation of functional dependencies, and consistency of integrity constraints [26]. In contrast, formal procedures based on relational model theory guarantee the generation of schemas in the third normal form (3NF) while strictly preserving integrity constraints [4–6].

One of the formal approaches to database schema design and information system specification is form-driven application development, which is based on the concept of form types [7–10]. A form type represents a conceptual abstraction of business documents and screen forms through which users interact with information system. Unlike traditional conceptual abstractions, form types preserve a close correspondence to real-world business documents and interaction forms, making them more naturally understandable to end-users and domain experts, rather than only to system designers. This characteristic facilitates communication between stakeholders and reduces the risk of misunderstandings during requirements specification. At the same time, they are semantically rich enough to enable the specification of both static and dynamic aspects of the application domain. Furthermore, form types provide a natural mechanism for decomposing complex information systems into manageable modules, while retaining sufficient semantic information for automated database schema synthesis and consistency checking. Owing to their explicit structural rules, form types support the systematic recognition of attributes and constraints during conceptual modelling.

The form type-based approach was developed at the Faculty of Technical Sciences, University of Novi Sad, and its practical application was supported through the development of the CASE environment Integrated Information Systems Case (IIS*Case) tool [7–10]. The latest version of this tool, IIS*Case V.7.1, was implemented in Java and supported a substantial part of the information system development process. The tool enabled conceptual database schema specification, automatic generation of relational database subschemas in 3NF, their integration into a unified database schema, and the generation of SQL/DDL code and executable information system prototypes. The database design procedures implemented within IIS*Case were founded on the formal theory of the relational data model and an extended Bernstein's synthesis algorithm [21]. These results demonstrated that form types could serve not only as conceptual representations of business documents but also as a foundation for generating both the database and application components of an information system. As the number of existing information systems and legacy databases increased, a need emerged to complement the forward engineering process with reverse engineering capabilities. In particular, it became necessary to recover higher-level conceptual specifications from legacy relational database schemas in order to support system modernization and maintenance. Consequently, research efforts were directed toward enabling the reconstruction of form type-based conceptual models from legacy database systems.

Model-driven engineering (MDE) has emerged as a software development paradigm that promotes the use of models as primary development artifacts and model transformations as the principal mechanism for deriving implementation-oriented representations. By separating system specifications from platform-specific implementation details, MDE facilitates automation, improves traceability between development stages, and supports systematic software evolution. Since the form type concept is formal conceptual model, while MDE promotes the use of models as primary development artifacts, the integration of these two approaches emerged as a natural direction for further development. Such an integration provided an opportunity to represent existing information system development procedures through models and model transformations within a unified MDE development environment. The first step toward introducing MDE principles into this environment was the definition of a domain-specific language for conceptual modeling based on form types. The language, subsequently named the Form Type Domain-Specific Language (FTDSL), was defined by means of a metamodel and an associated concrete textual syntax [12]. FTDSL enabled form type models and their constraints to be specified formally and represented as platform-independent models (PIMs) within an MDE environment. The next step concerned the development of a reverse engineering process for legacy relational databases [11]. The process starts from platform-specific models (PSMs) extracted from the data dictionaries of relational database management systems (RDBMSs), and through a series of meta-model transformations, arrives at PIMs based on the form type concept. Based on this approach, the IIS*Ree tool was developed and subsequently integrated with the IIS*Case environment, resulting in the development of the unified IIS*Studio environment.

Nevertheless, the gradual development of IIS*Studio resulted in a technologically heterogeneous environment. Its original forward engineering functionality was implemented explicitly in Java within IIS*Case, whereas the reverse engineering process was developed according to MDE principles in a Meta-Object Facility (MOF)-based technological space. In addition, the technologies used for implementing the original IIS*Case environment became obsolete over time. This combination of technological obsolescence and the coexistence of different technological spaces complicated system maintenance, limited the traceability of transformations, and made migration toward new technologies more difficult. Therefore, a technological modernization and reimplementation of the IIS*Studio environment became necessary.

At the same time, the redesigned environment is intended to support a complete information system reengineering process based on the horseshoe model of software modernization. This model comprises three main phases. In the reverse engineering phase, the components and relationships of an existing system are identified and represented at higher levels of abstraction. During the restructuring phase, the extracted representations are transformed into improved but semantically equivalent models. Finally, in the forward engineering phase, the restructured models are used to generate a new physical implementation of the system. In the context of IIS*Studio, the previously developed IIS*Ree process supports the reverse engineering branch of the horseshoe by transforming existing relational database schemas into FTDSL-based conceptual models. However, a MDE-based forward engineering branch was still required to transform these conceptual models into newly generated database implementations and thereby complete the reengineering cycle within a unified technological space.

Accordingly, the main contribution of this paper is the implementation of the forward engineering process within a new MDE-oriented version of the IIS*Studio environment. The proposed framework extends the existing FTDSL-based conceptual modeling by introducing a graphical concrete syntax that mitigates the limitations of the original textual notation, which required familiarity with the FTDSL grammar and a higher level of technical expertise. It also introduces an explicit chain of model-to-model (M2M) and model-to-text (M2T) transformations. Starting from a form type-based PIM, the transformation chain incorporates a model-driven realization of the extended Bernstein's synthesis algorithm [10], through which a relational database schema in 3NF is synthesized. Subsequently, the generated schema is transformed into platform-specific database models and finally into SQL/DDL specifications for multiple RDBMSs.

The remainder of this paper is organized as follows. Section 2 presents the foundations of the form-driven approach. Section 3 presents the MDE-based forward engineering process implemented within IIS*Studio environment. Section 4 evaluates the applicability of the proposed approach. Section 5 discusses the state of the art in model-driven database engineering. Finally, Sect. 6 concludes paper and outlines directions for future work.

2 Foundations of the Form-Driven Approach

This Sect. 2 is organized as follows. Section 2.1 introduces the form type concept. Section 2.2 presents the form-driven approach to information system and database development. Finally, Sect. 2.3 discusses the application of MDE principles to the form-driven approach.

2.1 The Form Type Concept

A form type represents a conceptual abstraction of business documents and screen forms through which users interact with information system. The form type concept is founded on a set of interrelated modeling constructs, including domains, attributes, logical expressions, user-defined functions, component types and form types [7–9]. Using the form type concept, the designer specifies business documents and screen forms used in transaction programs and, at the same time, indirectly defines the initial set of constraints.

The form type concept, together with related concepts such as domains and attributes, is platform-independent [8]. In the terminology of the form-driven approach, an application system is a modeling construct that specifies a subsystem of a future information system and contains a set of related form types. Application systems may be organized hierarchically. Here, the term does not denote an executable software application. The concept of a form type is obtained through the generalization and analysis of screen forms and document types used in information system. A form type is organized as a hierarchical tree structure whose nodes represent component types. Let $W(\mathrm{F})$ denote the set of attributes of a form type F. Each component type within a form type is defined by its name, a non-empty set of attributes $Q = \{A_1, \ldots, A_n\} \subseteq W(\mathrm{F})$ and a set of constraints

C, and is denoted as *N(Q, C)*. The set of constraints *C* always includes key constraints, while additional constraints, such as unique and *check* constraints defined by logical expressions, are optional. In addition, component types contain a set of allowed database operations defined as a subset of the standard operations {*retrieve*, *insert*, *update*, *delete*}. Luković et al. [7] and Ristić [19] provide detailed definitions of the form type concept and its associated constraints.

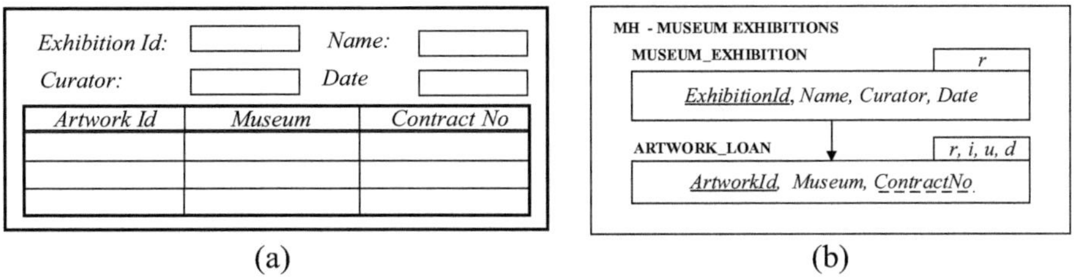

Fig. 1. (a) An example of document type; (b) the form type.

Example 2.1. Figure 1(a) shows a document type for recording data about museum exhibitions and borrowed artworks. Empty fields on the document represent fields intended for data entry. Two logical sections can be identified within this document type. The first section contains general information about the exhibition, while the second contains data about borrowed artworks. The second section represents a repeating group, since one exhibition may include multiple borrowed artworks, while each artwork loan is associated with exactly one exhibition and is identified by the corresponding exhibition together with its own identifying attributes. Figure 1(b) presents the form type obtained through the generalization of the document type shown in Fig. 1(a). The form type consists of two component types, MUSEUM_EXHIBITION and ARTWORK_LOAN, graphically represented as rectangles. Solid underlined attributes denote component type keys, while dashed underlined attributes denote uniqueness constraints.

2.2 Form-Driven Approach to Information System and Database Development

The form-driven approach supports a gradual development of information systems and database schemas based on form types as platform-independent conceptual specifications. Starting from independently designed form types, the approach enables the derivation of relational database subschemas in 3NF, their integration into a unified database schema, and the formal checking of consistency between subschemas and the integrated schema, and the generation of database implementation specifications in the form of SQL/DDL scripts. In addition to database schema design, the approach was further extended to support the specification of transaction programs, visual properties of screen forms, business application structures, user-defined functions, and non-declarative constraints. These specifications provide a basis not only for generating SQL/DDL code, but also for generating PL/SQL implementations of non-declarative constraints and executable information system prototypes. The breadth of these extensions illustrates the expressive power of the form-driven approach and confirms its suitability as a foundation for both database and information system development.

The practical application of the form-driven approach was realized through the IIS*Case tool, originally developed at the Faculty of Technical Sciences, University of Novi Sad, as a CASE environment for relational database design and later extended toward broader support for information system development [7–10, 21]. IIS*Case V.7.1 was implemented in Java and supported conceptual modeling, automated generation and integration of relational database subschemas, generation of database implementation specifications for different RDBMSs and generation of executable information system prototypes.

2.3 Applying MDE Principles to the Form-Driven Approach

The expressive power of the form type concept and the growing complexity of development procedures motivated the adoption of MDE principles. The goal was to represent information system specifications explicitly as models and to formalize development procedures as model transformations, thereby improving their transparency, maintainability, and reusability. The first step in this direction was the definition of the FTDSL, which enabled form type-based specifications to be represented as PIMs within an MDE environment [12].

As the number of legacy information systems and databases increased, the need arose to complement the existing forward engineering capabilities with reverse engineering support. At the same time, this challenge provided an opportunity to introduce MDE principles into the form-driven approach by representing database and information system specifications as models and implementing the recovery process through model transformations. In this context, a reverse engineering process was developed that starts from PSMs extracted from RDBMS data dictionaries and applies a sequence of metamodel-based transformations to derive PIMs based on the form type concept [11]. Its realization required several metamodels capable of representing database and information system specifications at different levels of abstraction, including the FTDSL metamodel [12], the Fundamental Generic Constraint Meta-Model (FGCMM) [22], and the Fundamental Standard Constraint Meta-Model (FSCMM) [22]. The reverse engineering process was realized as a sequence of M2M transformations that progressively transformed models conforming to the FSCMM, through models conforming to the FGCMM, into platform-independent models conforming to the FTDSL metamodel. These transformations were implemented using the ATL transformation language within the ATL SDK framework provided by the Eclipse platform. Based on these results, the IIS*Ree tool was developed and integrated with IIS*Case. Together, IIS*Ree and IIS*Case constitute the unified IIS*Studio environment. IIS*Case and IIS*Ree are research tools that are not currently available as production-ready software.

However, although the reverse engineering branch was realized according to MDE principles, the forward engineering functionality remained implemented procedurally in Java. Consequently, the complete information system reengineering cycle could not be realized within a unified MDE technological space. This limitation motivated the further evolution of IIS*Studio toward the development of an MDE-based forward engineering process that would complement the existing reverse engineering branch and complete the information system reengineering cycle.

3 An MDE-Based Forward Engineering Process in IIS*Studio

This section presents an MDE-based forward engineering process for generating relational database implementation specifications from form type-based conceptual models. The proposed process is founded on an explicit chain of M2M and M2T transformations, enabling the systematic transformation of platform-independent specifications into implementation-level relational database schemas within a unified MDE environment. The process starts from a form type-based PIM specified using FTDSL. Through a sequence of M2M transformations, the conceptual model is transformed into implementation-level database models, which are subsequently used as input for M2T transformations that generate executable SQL/DDL specifications for a selected RDBMS. The process is realized within the new IIS*Studio environment, implemented on the Eclipse platform and organized into several interconnected modules supporting different phases of the engineering process. The new environment is currently a research prototype and is not yet publicly available or ready for commercial use.

The architecture of the proposed environment consists of the following main modules:

- **FTDSL Editor** - provides graphical support for conceptual modeling based on form types and application systems,
- **M2M Transformer** - responsible for executing the transformation chain for generation of implementation-level database models,
- **M2T Transformer** - enables automatic generation of executable SQL/DDL specifications for multiple RDBMSs.

By integrating the described modules within an Eclipse environment, a unified environment was realized in which the processes of conceptual modeling, database schema design, and generation of implementation-level database schema specifications for a selected RDBMS, are performed fully automatically, upon the designer's request, without the need to leave the working environment. The following subsections describe the role and operating principle of each module in more detail.

3.1 Graphical Syntax of FTDSL

At its current stage of development, FTDSL supports conceptual modeling through a concrete textual syntax for form type-based specification [12]. Although such an approach enables formally defined and precise model specification, working with textual notation requires familiarity with syntax rules and a higher level of technical expertise. As a consequence, the process of information system specification may become less intuitive, especially for end-users who primarily perceive information system through business documents and screen forms. To address this gap, in this paper we introduce a graphical layer that enables a more intuitive approach to conceptual information system modeling. The graphical syntax supports visual specification of form types, component types, and their relationships, bringing the modeling process closer to the perception of end-users and facilitating communication between designers and end-users. At the same time, the formal connection with the abstract syntax of the FTDSL language is preserved, enabling its integration into the MDE framework and the M2M transformation chain. The graphical syntax was implemented using the Eclipse Sirius framework [20].

Figure 2 presents the concepts of graphical syntax of the FTDSL language used for form type-based conceptual modeling. For clarity, the figure includes only the concepts that are directly represented in the graphical notation. Concepts such as key constraints, uniqueness constraints, and logical expressions are not shown as graphical elements of form types, since they are specified through the properties panel rather than being embedded in the diagram itself.

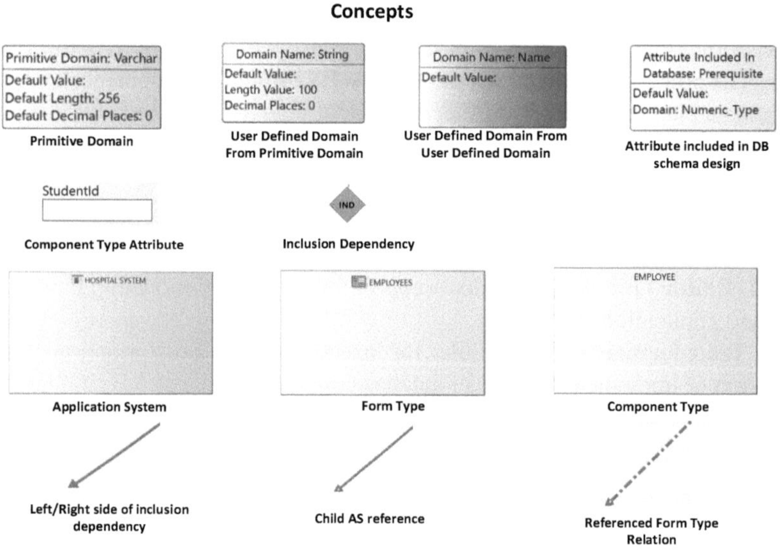

Fig. 2. Concepts of graphical syntax of FTDSL

Modeling is performed within the FTDSL editor, which represents the core component of the conceptual modeling tool. The editor is implemented in the Eclipse environment using the Eclipse Sirius framework. Within the developed FTDSL editor, two main representations are defined: (i) a *Fundamentals Representation* for modeling core language concepts such as domains, attributes, and non-trivial inclusion dependencies, and (ii) an *Application System* representation for modeling application systems and form type models. This separation reduces diagram complexity and improves the scalability of the modeling process in larger projects. The resulting FTDSL model, modeled using the proposed graphical syntax and persisted in XMI format, serves as the source model for the subsequent M2M transformation chain.

Besides structural concepts such as domains, attributes, and component types, form type models include various integrity constraints. Among them, *check* constraints are represented by logical expressions defined at the domain, attribute, or component type level. To support their explicit representation within the MDE environment, the FTDSL metamodel was extended to enable modeling of logical expressions as explicit model elements. Although modeling of these concepts could have been implemented within the Sirius framework by defining an appropriate graphical syntax, such an approach would be less intuitive and more technically demanding for end users, since logical expressions combine numerous operators and operand types. Therefore, logical expression modeling was implemented using a Xtext editor, where the designer specifies a logical expression in textual form. The expression is then parsed using a Xtext [28] grammar and transformed into a model conforming to the logical expression metamodel, which constitutes an integral part of the extended FTDSL metamodel. The Xtext grammar, the metamodel of logical expressions, and the transformation process that maps logical expressions to *check* constraints in the relational data model are beyond the scope of this paper.

3.2 Integration of the Extended Bernstein's Synthesis Algorithm

After creating form type models using FTDSL, the next step in the proposed information system engineering process is the identification of the initial set of constraints derived from form types and the application of the extended Bernstein's synthesis algorithm to the inferred set of constraints. The extended Bernstein's synthesis algorithm represents an extension and improvement of the original algorithm proposed by Bernstein [5]. Luković [21] provides further details of the extension. The application of the Bernstein's synthesis algorithm is realized within the *M2M Transformer* module through a chain of M2M transformations. The transformation chain starts from the conceptual PIM model and ends with a database schema model representing the PSM model. All transformations are based on meta-models and are executed within the MOF technological space. Bubnjević et al. [10] thoroughly describe the details of this procedure, while this section provides only a high-level overview without implementation-specific details.

The M2M transformation chain begins with transformations that convert the conceptual model, conforming to the FTDSL meta-model, into a relational database schema model conforming to the Fundamental Generic Constraint Meta-Model (FGCMM) [22]. The FGCMM has been additionally extended with concepts required to support the practical needs of this transformation process. The transformation process starts with the derivation of the initial set of constraints, including non-trivial inclusion dependencies, functional dependencies, special functional dependencies and non-functional dependencies inferred from form types, followed by the synthesis of a relational database schema in 3NF. In the next step, a *closure graph* representing the generated schema is constructed. The metamodel of the *closure graph* concept was introduced by Bubnjević et al. [10]. Afterwards, a primary key propagation process is performed, during which selected primary keys are consistently propagated across the generated relation schemas as foreign keys. Finally, the transformation chain is completed by the generation of inter-relational constraints, including basic and extended referential integrity constraints, inverse referential integrity constraints (both basic and those based on non-trivial inclusion dependencies), and extended tuple constraints.

In the final stage, the resulting model is transformed into a model conforming to the Fundamental Standard Constraint Meta-Model (FSCMM) [22], which includes concepts required for modeling database schemas at the level of a concrete RDBMS. This transformation enables the transition from a generic relational database model to a lower level of abstraction closer to the target SQL platform, thereby facilitating the implementation of the subsequent M2T transformation and the generation of executable SQL code.

3.3 Generation of Executable SQL/DDL Specifications

After the execution of the M2M transformation chain, two models are obtained and used as inputs for the M2T transformation process. The first model conforms to the FGCMM and represents the result of the extended synthesis algorithm, while the second model conforms to the FSCMM and is produced through the transformation of the model based on the FGCMM. The need for two input models arises from the fact that certain concepts of the relational data model are not covered by the FSCMM meta-model, such as extended tuple constraints and extended referential integrity constraints. Therefore, in order to support the generation of these additional types of constraints, it is necessary to preserve the model conforming to the FGCMM as an additional source of information.

For the M2T transformation of models conforming to the FSCMM and the FGCMM into an SQL implementation specification of the database schema, the EMF environment and the Acceleo language for M2T transformation were used. This transformation is executed within the *M2T transformer* module of the IIS*Studio environment. The Acceleo language [16] was developed within the Eclipse Foundation and implements the Model-to-Text Transformation Language (MOFM2T) standard proposed by the Object Management Group. The developed generator enables the automatic generation of SQL/DDL scripts for multiple platforms, including ANSI SQL, Oracle 21c, and Oracle 23c.

The generator supports the generation of procedural mechanisms for verifying the preservation of inverse referential integrity constraints. Users are provided with the possibility to choose the implementation strategy for these constraints, either through stored procedures or database views. In addition, users may choose whether indexes over foreign keys will be automatically generated in order to improve performance. Furthermore, the proposed solution also supports the automatic generation of procedural mechanisms for checking and maintaining extended tuple constraints. The implementation of these procedural mechanism is based on the work of Aleksić et al. [23] and Obrenović [24].

4 Evaluation

A simplified generic application system named *Museum Exhibition* (see Fig. 3) was modeled using the proposed FTDSL editor. This application system consists of two form types: *MH - Museum Exhibitions* and EP - *Exhibition Preparation*. Figure 4 presents the fragment of *Fundamentals representation* of the resulting FTDSL model. This representation contains four primitive domains (*Varchar*, *Date*, *Number*, and *Decimal*) and four user-defined domains (*String*, *NumericType*, *CalendarDate*, and *MonetaryValue*), which redefine the aforementioned primitive domains, respectively. In addition to the domains, the figure shows a subset of the attributes used in the modeled form types, as well as a non-trivial inclusion dependency between the attributes *LoanMuseum* and *MuseumNo*.

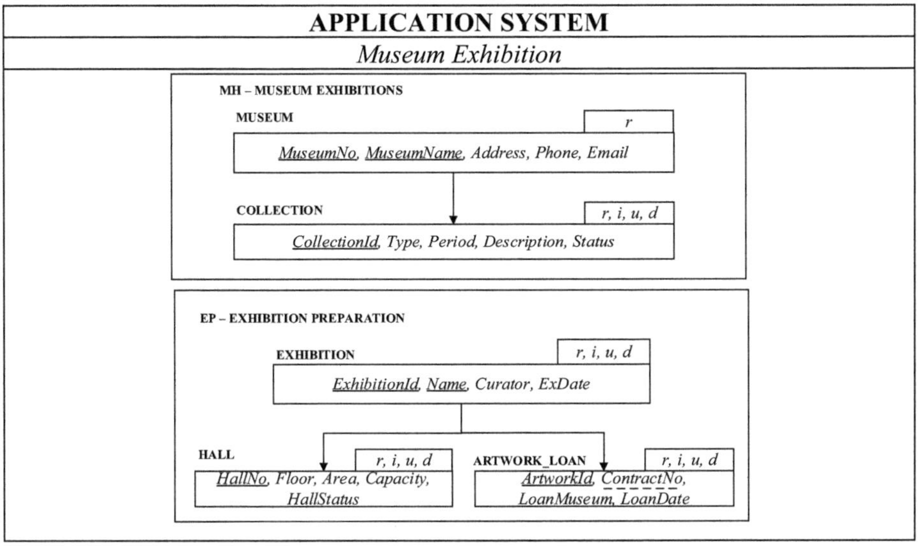

Fig. 3. Museum Exhibition application system

Figure 5 presents an *Application System* representation of the same model. It contains the application system and its associated form types modeled using a graphical notation. It can be observed that the form types are represented in a way that resembles the screen forms through which users interact with the information system, rather than their formal representation as trees of component types. This representation makes the modeling process more intuitive and accessible to information system designers and end users, while preserving the formal semantics of the form type concept and its constraints.

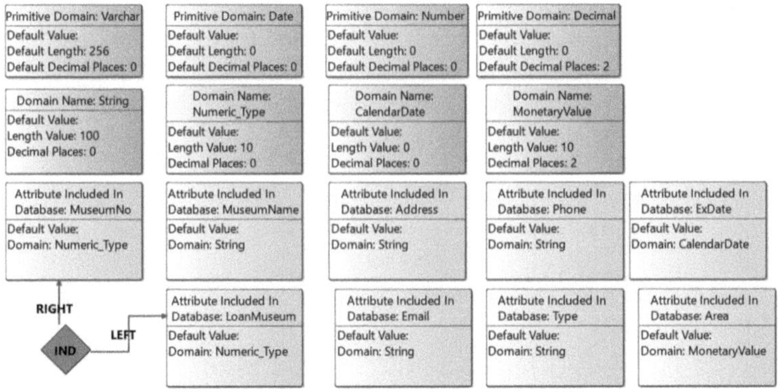

Fig. 4. Fragment of *Fundamental Representation* of FTDSL model for the Museum Exhibition application system

The conceptual model created using the FTDSL editor is subsequently provided as input to the M2M *Transformer* module, where a sequence of M2M transformations is executed. Transformation chain implements the extended Bernstein's synthesis algorithm, which derives a normalized relational database schema from the form type-based conceptual model. For the considered *Museum Exhibition* application system, the synthesis process produces five relation schemas. Their names correspond to the component types identified within the form types belonging to the application system.

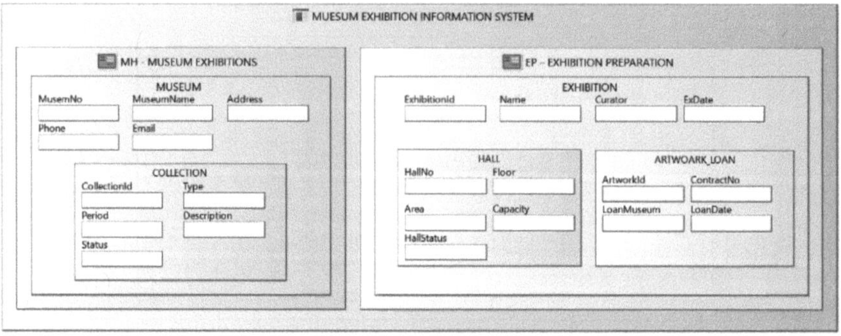

Fig. 5. *Application System* representation of FTDSL model for the Museum Exhibition application system

Figure 6 presents selected fragments of the models produced at different stages of the transformation process. Figure 6(a) shows a fragment of the initial model conforming to the FTDSL meta-model. Figure 6(b) presents the corresponding generic relational model generated through the synthesis process and represented in accordance with the FGCMM. Finally, Fig. 6(c) shows a fragment of the platform-specific database model conforming to the FSCMM, obtained from the generated generic relational model.

The models conforming to the FGCMM and FSCMM are subsequently provided as joint input to the M2T *Transformer* module. Within this module, a M2T transformation is performed to generate an executable SQL/DDL script for the selected target RDBMS.

This example demonstrates the feasibility of the complete transformation chain, from form types to platform-specific models and executable SQL/DDL scripts.

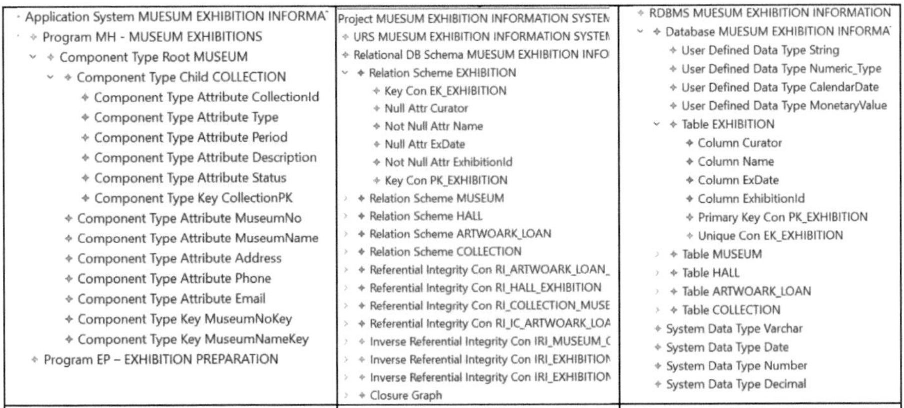

a) FTDSL model fragment	b) FGCMM model fragment	c) FSCMM model fragment

Fig. 6. Model Fragments Generated During the M2M Transformation Chain

5 State of the Art in Model-Driven Database Engineering

Numerous studies have investigated the application of MDE approaches in the development of information system and databases.

Vara et al. [13] present a model-driven approach for the development of object-relational databases (ORDBs). The approach supports the transformation of Unified-Modeling Language (UML) conceptual models (PIMs) into object-relational database models (PSMs) and automatic SQL code generation for Oracle 10g.

A similar approach is presented by Natek et al. [14], who propose a model-driven approach for automatic SQL code generation from UML conceptual models. The main idea of the paper is to improve the software development process by eliminating the manual transformation of UML diagrams into relational database schemas, which is often error-prone and time-consuming.

Belkadi et al. [15] present a model-driven approach for transforming relational database models into document-oriented NoSQL models in the context of big data technologies. The paper defines source and target metamodels within the Ecore/EMF framework and uses QVT Operational Mapping Language for M2M transformations and Acceleo language for M2T transformation, enabling automatic generation of JSON code for MongoDB collections.

Pantoja et al. [18] present a model-driven development framework for relational and geographical database design based on EMF/Ecore metamodels. The approach uses QVT for M2M transformations and Acceleo for M2T transformations and automatic SQL/SFS code generation.

In this domain, the work of Rapatsalahy et al. [17] is particularly interesting, as it starts from the computation-independent models. The authors use the Restructuring Extended Lexical Elaborate Language for specifying requirements expressed in natural language and transform them through multiple MDE levels into semantic and logical models, and finally into Java code. In this way, a complete MDE workflow is realized using ATL [27] for M2M and Acceleo for M2T transformation.

Ortín et al. [25] propose a generic database migration approach based on the U-Schema unified data model. U-Schema acts as a pivot representation, reducing the number of required transformations by providing mappings between individual data models and the unified schema. During schema transformation, trace information is generated to capture correspondences between source and target elements, and is subsequently used to guide data migration in a decoupled manner.

Automatic database generation from conceptual models remains an active research topic. In our IIS*Studio, it is realized through a formal Bernstein's synthesis algorithm derived from relational database theory.

6 Conclusion

This paper addressed the problem of integrating the form-driven approach to information system and database development, previously developed and refined through a series of studies [7–9, 11, 12, 21], with the principles of MDE. While previous research demonstrated that form types provide a suitable conceptual foundation for database schema design based on the formal theory of relational databases, their realization within an MDE environment remained incomplete. In particular, the reverse engineering branch had already been developed within an MDE environment using metamodels and model transformations, whereas forward engineering remained dependent on procedural implementations in a different technological space. As a consequence, the information system reengineering cycle could not be fully realized within a unified MDE framework. The main contribution of this paper is therefore the integration of the form-driven approach to information system modeling, database schema design based on the extended Bernstein's synthesis algorithm, and automated generation of implementation specifications within a unified MDE framework. In the proposed solution, database design procedures are no longer implemented only as Java code, but are represented through an explicit chain of M2M and M2T transformations. Starting from a conceptual model conforming to the FTDSL metamodel, the transformation chain implements the extended Bernstein's synthesis algorithm to generate a relational database schema in 3NF. The resulting schema is subsequently transformed into the corresponding PSM and used to generate executable SQL/DDL specifications for the selected RDBMS. The introduction of a graphical concrete syntax further mitigates the limitations of the previous textual notation, by reducing the need for detailed knowledge of the FTDSL grammar.

The proposed solution enables both forward and reverse engineering processes to be realized within the same technological space. This improves transformation traceability, the reusability of individual development steps, environment maintainability, and its capacity for further extension. Intermediate artifacts are represented as explicit models that can be inspected, validated, and reused in subsequent transformations.

Future work will include a more comprehensive validation of the proposed approach through larger case studies and the extension of the transformation chain to support the automatic generation of executable information system prototypes. Another direction concerns the use of AI and LLMs to derive initial form type specifications from semi-structured inputs. These models could then be formally validated using FTDSL, supported by new formal algorithms for detecting semantic collisions among independently designed form types.

Acknowledgments. This research has been supported by the Ministry of Science, Technological Development and Innovation (Contract No. 451-03-34/2026-03/200156) and the Faculty of Technical Sciences, University of Novi Sad through project "Scientific and Artistic Research Work of Researchers in Teaching and Associate Positions at the Faculty of Technical Sciences, University of Novi Sad 2026" (No. 01-3609/1).

References

1. Storey, V.C., et al.: Large language models for conceptual modeling: assessment and application potential. Data Knowl. Eng. **160**, 102480 (2025). https://doi.org/10.1016/j.datak.2025.102480
2. Siqueira, A.F., Nogueira, C.D., Farias, E., Campelo, C.E., Menezes, J.: On the Limitations of Large Language Models for Conceptual Database Modeling. arXiv preprint arXiv:2605.11986 (2026). https://doi.org/10.48550/arXiv.2605.11986
3. Stanek, S., Novotny, O.: AI-Assisted Data Modelling & Design: A Systematic Literature Review. Qual. Innov. Prosperity **29**(3), 39–55 (2025). https://doi.org/10.12776/qip.v29i3.2253
4. Beeri, C., Bernstein, P.A.: Computational problems related to the design of normal form relational schemas. ACM Trans. Database Syst. (TODS) **4**(1), 30–59 (1979). https://doi.org/10.1145/320064.320066
5. Bernstein, P.A.: Synthesizing third normal form relations from functional dependencies. ACM Trans. Database Syst. (TODS) **1**(4), 277–298 (1976). https://doi.org/10.1145/320493.320489
6. Maier, D.: The theory of relational databases, Computer science press, Rockville (1983)
7. Luković, I., Mogin, P., Pavićević, J., Ristić, S.: An approach to developing complex database schemas using form types. Softw. Pract. Experience **37**(15), 1621–1656 (2007). https://doi.org/10.1002/spe.820
8. Obrenović, N., Luković, I., Ristić, S.: Consolidation of database check constraints. Softw. Syst. Model. **18**(3), 2111–2135 (2019). https://doi.org/10.1007/s10270-017-0637-2
9. Luković, I., Čeliković, M., Kordić, S., Vještica, M.: An approach to the information system conceptual modeling based on the form types. In: Domain-Specific Conceptual Modeling: Concepts, Methods and ADOxx Tools (pp. 589–614). Springer, Cham (2022). https://doi.org/10.1007/978-3-030-93547-4_26
10. Bubnjević, V., Kordić, S., Akik, E., Čeliković, M., Luković, I.: A model-driven approach to developing complex database schemas using form types and extended bernstein's synthesis algorithm. In: Presented at the 16th International Conference on Information Society and Technology (ICIST 2026) (2026)
11. Ristić, S., Aleksić, S., Čelković, M., Dimitrieski, V., Luković, I.: Database reverse engineering based on meta-models. Open Comput. Sci. **4**, 150–159 (2014). https://doi.org/10.2478/s13537-014-0218-1
12. Čeliković, M., Luković, I., Aleksić, S., Ivančević, V.: A MOF based meta-model and a concrete DSL syntax of IIS* Case PIM concepts. Comput. Sci. Inf. Syst. **9**(3), 1075–1103 (2012). https://doi.org/10.2298/CSIS120203034C

13. Vara, J.M., Vela, B., Bollati, V.A., Marcos, E.: Supporting model–driven development of object–relational database schemas: a case study. In: International Conference on Theory and Practice of Model Transformations, (pp. 181–196). Springer, Cham (2009). https://doi.org/10.1007/978-3-642-02408-5_13
14. Natek, H., Srai, A., Guerouate, F.: Model-driven architecture approach for sql generation using acceleo: a case study on mysql database. IJETT **71**(10), 20–28 (2023). https://doi.org/10.14445/22315381/IJETT-V71I10P203
15. Belkadi, F.Z., Esbai, R.: A model-driven engineering: from relational database to document-oriented database in big data context. In: ICSOFT, pp. 653–659 (2021). https://doi.org/10.5220/0010604906530659
16. Acceleo Homepage. https://eclipse.dev/acceleo/, Accessed 25 May 2026
17. Rapatsalahy, A.M., Razafimahatratra, H., Mahatody, T., Ilie, M., Ilie, S., Razafindrakoto, R.N.: Automatic generation of object-oriented code from the ReLEL requirements model. Syst. Theory Control Comput. J. **1**(1), 36–47 (2021). https://doi.org/10.52846/stccj.2021.1.1.9
18. Pantoja, C. E., Guinelli, J. V., Alexandre, T., Viterbo, J.: A model-driven development framework for geographical and relational database systems. In: SEKE, pp. 70–75 (2023). https://doi.org/10.18293/SEKE2023-018
19. Ristić, S.:. Problem Research of Database Subschemas Consolidation. Dissertation, University of Novi Sad, Serbia (2003)
20. Sirius homepage. https://eclipse.dev/sirius/, Accessed 25 May 2026
21. Luković, I.: From the synthesis algorithm to the model driven transformations in database design. In: Proceedings of 10th international scientific conference on informatics (Informatics 2009), Herlany, Slovakia (2009)
22. Ristić, S., Aleksić, S., Čeliković, M., Luković, I.: Generic and standard database constraint meta-models. Comput. Sci. Inf. Syst. **11**(2), 679–696 (2014). https://doi.org/10.2298/CSIS140216037R
23. Aleksić, S., Ristić, S., Luković, I., Čeliković, M.: A design specification and a server implementation of the inverse referential integrity constraints. Comput. Sci. Inf. Syst. **10**(1), 283–320 (2013). https://doi.org/10.2298/CSIS111102003A
24. Obrenovic, N.: An Approach to Design, Consolidation and Transformations of Database Schema Check Constraints Based on Platform Independent Models (Doctoral dissertation, PhD thesis, University of Novi Sad, Novi Sad) (2015)
25. Ortín, M. J., Hoyos, J.R., García-Molina, J.: A Model-Driven Approach to Database Migration with a Unified Data Model. arXiv preprint arXiv:2604.22415 (2026). https://doi.org/10.48550/arXiv.2604.22415
26. Jo, E., Lee, N., Kim, G.: Database Normalization via Dual-LLM Self-Refinement. arXiv preprint arXiv:2508.17693 (2025)
27. ATL Homepage. https://eclipse.dev/atl/, Visited 29 May 2026
28. Xtext Homepage. https://eclipse.dev/Xtext/index.html, Visited 9 June 2026

Cryptographic Fog of War: An Attribute-Based Encryption Framework for Cheat Resistance in Peer-to-Peer Turn-Based Games

Borna Kadežabek(✉), Snježana Križanić, and Neven Vrček

Faculty of Organization and Informatics, University of Zagreb, Varaždin, Croatia
{bkadezabe,skrizanic,nvrcek,skrizanic,nvrcek}@foi.unizg.hr

Abstract. Hidden information enforcement in peer-to-peer turn-based games presents a fundamental security challenge: without a trusted server, players can exploit unmediated access to shared game state, exposing opponents' private information such as card hands, unit positions or resources. This paper proposes a Cryptographic Fog of War framework using Ciphertext-Policy Attribute-Based Encryption (CP-ABE), where game state is encrypted under predicate-based visibility policies and player keys reflect current game attributes. A threshold commit-and-reveal protocol eliminates the need for a trusted authority. The discrete nature of turns makes CP-ABE computationally feasible. The framework is theoretical and empirical evaluation remains future work.

Keywords: Fog Of War · Cryptography · Attribute-Based Encryption · Cheat Resistance · Turn-Based Games · Peer-To-Peer

1 Introduction

Hidden information is a fundamental mechanic in turn-based card games, board games and strategy games where asymmetric knowledge between players forms the basis of competitive play. Known as the Fog of War, each player is entitled only to the information their current game state permits - card hands, positions and resources while all else remains concealed [1]. This information asymmetry is a core mechanism through which strategic depth, bluffing and deception become meaningful gameplay elements. When its boundaries are violated, the competitive integrity of the game collapses entirely, reducing skill-based play to a trivial effort or exercise for the cheating party [2].

In networked multiplayer implementations, enforcing hidden information has traditionally been delegated to a trusted central server acting as an authoritative referee. Under the client-server model, the server maintains the canonical game state and distributes only the information each player is entitled to observe and know at any given moment [3]. This architectural assumption is so deeply embedded in the design of online games that most existing anti-cheat research presupposes its existence [4].

Peer-to-peer (P2P) architectures offer a compelling alternative by distributing both the computational load and game state management across player nodes, eliminating

© The Author(s), under exclusive license to Springer Nature Switzerland AG 2027
G. Vargas Solar et al. (Eds.): ADBIS 2026, CCIS 3175, pp. 396–405, 2027.
https://doi.org/10.1007/978-3-032-39823-9_35

dedicated server infrastructure. However, cheating is inherently easier in such environments, as the decision-making authority resides on users' local machines [3]. Without a trusted mediator, enforcing hidden information boundaries becomes a non-trivial cryptographic problem. Any player may attempt to extract information they are not entitled to, through reading memory, intercepting network packets, or exploiting the fact that the fog-of-war concept is traditionally implemented as display filters over fully available local data rather than as genuine cryptographic access controls [5].

The aim of this paper is to propose a Cryptographic Fog of War framework leveraging Ciphertext-Policy Attribute-Based Encryption (CP-ABE) as a cryptographic access control primitive to enforce hidden information boundaries in peer-to-peer turn-based games without relying on a central authority. Under the proposed framework, the game state is encrypted under predicate-based visibility policies derived directly from game rules, where each player holds a cryptographic key reflecting their current in-game attributes such as card ownership, position, resources or teammates and may only decrypt state for which their attributes satisfy the corresponding policy. To fulfill the research aim, there are three research questions:

- How can hidden information be enforced cryptographically in serverless peer-to-peer turn-based games?
- How can Ciphertext-Policy Attribute-Based Encryption (CP-ABE) be adapted to represent game visibility rules and player-specific information access rights?
- How can distributed key generation mechanisms be integrated with CP-ABE to preserve hidden information while maintaining resistance to unauthorized information access and player collusion in peer-to-peer games?

The remainder of this paper is organized as follows. Section 2 reviews the existing literature on cheating in peer-to-peer games, cryptographic approaches to hidden information protection, and CP-ABE. Section 3 presents the adopted research methodology. Section 4 introduces the system model, including the game model, adversary model, and threat assumptions. Section 5 describes the proposed Fog CP-ABE framework, detailing the distributed key generation process, visibility policy construction, and turn protocol. Section 6 demonstrates the framework's applicability to a three-player poker game. Section 7 provides a security analysis while Sect. 8 discusses limitations and future research; concludes the paper and summarizes the main contributions.

2 Related Work

This section reviews cheating in peer-to-peer games, cryptographic mechanisms for hidden-information protection and CP-ABE principles that underpin the framework.

2.1 Cheating in P2P Games

Yan and Randell established the foundational taxonomy for cheating in online multiplayer games [1, 2]. Their classification organizes cheating by the nature of the exploit and its effect on game fairness. This paper addresses unauthorized access – any exploit in which a player gains visibility of game state information they are not entitled to. In turn-based games a player's permitted view is a strict subset of the global state. Violating this boundary grants an unfair, deterministic advantage no skill can overcome [2]. Unlike action forgery or timing manipulation, which can be partially mitigated through behavioural detection or statistical analysis, unauthorized information access leaves no behavioural signature and requires no modification of the game binaries, making it resistant to conventional detection-based anti-cheat approaches [2, 6].

2.2 Ciphertext-Policy Attribute-Based Encryption

Attribute-Based Encryption (ABE) is a form of public-key encryption in which decryption is determined not by a specific recipient's key, but by whether a user's attributes satisfy a policy associated with the ciphertext, thus enabling access control without the encryptor knowing the authorised recipients in advance. This paper employs CP-ABE, which embeds the access policy in the ciphertext and the user's key is associated with a set of attributes [7]. In a game context, the party defining the visibility rules, rather than with the key issuing authority.

A CP-ABE scheme is formally defined by four algorithms. The setup algorithm takes a security parameter and outputs a public key PK and a master secret key MSK. The key generation algorithm takes MSK and an attribute set S describing a user and outputs a private key SK cryptographically bound to the user's attributes. The algorithm for encryption takes PK, a plaintext message M, and an access structure A over a collection of attributes, producing a ciphertext CT such that only a user whose attributes satisfy A can decrypt. The decryption algorithm takes PK, CT and SK, returning M if the user's attribute set satisfies the access structure embedded in the ciphertext and $\perp$ otherwise [7]. The failure case yields nothing and not an incorrect plaintext. Access structures are represented as monotone access trees, whose internal nodes are threshold gates and leaf nodes are attributes, realised over bilinear maps on elliptic curve groups, forming the foundation upon which both the correctness and security of CP-ABE rest [7].

A notable challenge in applying CP-ABE to a P2P setting is the master key problem: standard constructions assume MSK is held by a single trusted authority, which is incompatible with a fully decentralised architecture [7]. Nonetheless, these algorithms map directly onto the hidden information problem established in Sect. 2.1, as the visibility rules define the access policy, each player's current game state defines their attribute set and encrypted game state. The master key challenge is addressed in Sect. 5 through a commit-and-reveal protocol that distributes authority across all players.

The system contribution is therefore one of integration: mapping existing access control primitive to a serverless architecture, rather than designing new cryptography.

2.3 Cryptographic Approaches to Hidden Information Protection in P2P

Kabus and Buchmann [3] propose a cheat-resistant P2P online gaming architecture using a combination of lockstep synchronization and partial trust assumptions. While their system addresses action-level integrity, it does not address information-exposure cheating, as game state remains accessible in plaintext to all nodes. More recently, Cai, Markantonakis and Shepherd [8] propose a secret sharing based anti-cheat protocol providing formal verification of packet integrity against forgery and timing attacks, complementary rather than competing, as secret sharing addresses what players do while CP-ABE addresses what players see. Bursztein et al. [5] demonstrate that fog-of-war in real-time strategy games is implemented as a display filter over fully accessible local game state, exposed using their Kartograph memory inspection tool, proposing Private Set Intersection (PSI) as a remedy. However, their OpenConflict approach requires an interactive per-tick protocol and a coordination server, making it incompatible with a serverless architecture. Attribute-Based Encryption has been studied extensively as a general access control primitive and applied across domains including healthcare, cloud storage and IoT, but not in any game security context [7, 10]. The mapping of player attributes to cryptographic key attributes and game visibility rules to ciphertext access policies is an original contribution of this paper. Eliminating a trusted key authority additionally requires a mechanism for distributed key generation, as standard CP-ABE constructions assume a single party holds the MSK [7]. Commit-and-reveal schemes, in which parties commit to a value before revealing it to prevent equivocation, have been studied since Blum's coin toss protocol and formalised as verifiable secret sharing by Pedersen [11, 12]. In contrast to these approaches, which either secure player actions while leaving state readable [3, 8] or require a coordination server [5], the proposed framework enforces visibility cryptographically and without a server.

3 Research Methodology

This research adopts the Design Science Research (DSR) methodology, which comprises three key phases: problem identification, solution development and validation [13, 14]. The problem identification phase analyses unauthorized information access in peer-to-peer gaming environments, where the absence of a trusted central authority enables players to obtain hidden game information through memory inspection, packet analysis, or process manipulation. The solution development phase focuses on the design of the proposed Fog CP-ABE framework. The framework combines CP-ABE with a distributed threshold key generation mechanism to enforce game visibility rules cryptographically. This phase includes the formal definition of the system model, adversary model, attribute universe, visibility policies, key generation procedure and turn protocol. The validation phase is performed through analytical and conceptual evaluation. First, the framework is instantiated in a three-player poker scenario to demonstrate its applicability in a representative hidden-information game. Second, a security analysis is conducted to evaluate the framework's resistance to collusion and attribute forgery. However, empirical validation through prototype implementation and performance benchmarking has not yet been conducted and will be marked for future work.

4 System Model

A turn-based game is modelled as a tuple $G = (P, M, S, V, T)$, where $P = \{P_1, \dots, P_n\}$ is a finite set of players, M is the game state space, S^τ is the global game state at turn τ, with the visibility predicate governing what each player is entitled to observe is then $V : P \times M \times S^\tau \to \{0, 1\}$, and T is a deterministic state transition function applied uniformly by all players at the end of each turn. For example, in Sect. 6 the player set is {Alice, Bob, Carol} and the visibility predicate grants each player only their own hole cards until showdown. The framework applies to any game satisfying this model, including card games, board games and strategy-based games, provided state transitions are discrete and synchronous.

The adversary is modelled as a probabilistic polynomial-time player who may read all network traffic, inspect their own process memory, attempt to decrypt received ciphertexts and collude with up to $n-1$ players. The adversary is assumed unable to break the underlying hardness assumption of the CP-ABE construction and unanimous collusion of all n players is considered a fundamental limit of any cryptographic scheme rather than a design flaw. Action integrity, the prevention of move forgery and manipulation. This is a problem addressed by complementary work and is out of scope [8, 9].

The attribute universe U is the set of all strings encoding game-meaningful properties of a player's current state. Each player P_i holds an attribute set of $S^{\tau}_{P_i} \subseteq U$ derived from the game state S^{τ} at the start of turn τ. Attributes include team membership $team_{P_i}$; unit positions $pos^{\tau}_{(x,y)}$; card ownership $card^{\tau}_{P_i,slot_k}$ where $slot_k$ is the public slot index and the card identity is the encrypted payload; and fog-lift events fog^{τ}_{z}. Each attribute must be epoch-tagged with the turn number τ, ensuring that a key issued at turn τ is cryptographically incompatible with ciphertexts produced at turn $\tau+1$, providing automatic revocation without an explicit revocation mechanism [7].

5 Fog CP-ABE Framework

5.1 Setup – Distributed Key Generation

Before any game session begins, all n players collectively establish cryptographic parameters through a commit-and-reveal ceremony adapted from Pedersen. Each player P_i independently samples a secret value, publishes a cryptographic commitment to it and reveals only after all commitments are received, preventing any single player from biasing the result. Two independent ceremonies of this type collectively derive the master parameters α and β such that no player holds either in isolation, eliminating the single trusted authority assumption of the standard CP-ABE [7, 15]. At the start of each turn τ, the distributed protocol issues a fresh private key to each player reflecting their current game attributes:

$$SK^{\tau}_{P_i} = \left(D = g^{(\alpha+r)/\beta}, \forall j \in S^{\tau}_{P_i} : D_j = g^r \cdot H(j\|\tau)^{r_j}, D'_j = g^{r_j}\right) \tag{1}$$

The base structure of Eq. 1 follows [7]. The adaptations are threefold: the key is indexed by player P_i and turn τ; the attribute set $S^{\tau}_{P_i}$ is derived from the player's current game state rather than being assigned arbitrarily, and the hash $H(j\|\tau)$ embeds the turn number.

The secret key consists of three components. The master component $D = g^{(\alpha+r)/\beta}$ encodes the collective master secret α distributed across all players via the commit-and-reveal ceremony blinded by a player-specific random value $r \leftarrow_R \mathbb{Z}_p$ and twisted by the second master parameter β. This component is what allows the bilinear pairing during decryption to recover the blinding factor $e(g,g)^{\alpha s}$ embedded in the ciphertext.

The per-attribute component $g^r \cdot H(j\|\tau)^{r_j}$ encodes each game attribute $j \in S^{\tau}_{P_i}$ into the key, where $H : \{0, 1\}^* \rightarrow G$ is a hash function mapping attribute strings to group elements and $r_j \rightarrow_R \mathbb{Z}_p$ is an independently chosen random value per attribute. The cancellation component $D'_j = g^{r_j}$ exists solely to cancel the $H(j\|\tau)^{r_j}$ during the leaf node evaluation of decryption, enabling the algebraic simplification that recovers $e(g, g)^{r \bullet s_x}$ at each satisfied leaf. The per-player random value r is critical for collusion resistance. Since every key is bound to an independently chosen r, two colluding players cannot combine their keys to satisfy a policy that neither could satisfy alone [7]. The epoch tag τ embedded in $H(j\|\tau)$ ensures that D_j computed for attribute j at turn τ produces a different group element than D_j at turn $\tau+1$, making old keys automatically incompatible with new ciphertexts without requiring an explicit revocation step.

5.2 Visibility Policy

For each piece of hidden game state, a visibility policy is derived directly from the game's rules and encoded as a CP-ABE access structure, a monotone Boolean formula over the attribute universe U. The general form of a visibility policy for game state element e at turn τ is

$$\mathbb{A}^{\tau}_{e} = \bigvee_{P_i \in P} \left(owner_{P_i} \wedge \bigvee_{j \in Visible(P_i, e, S^{\tau})} att^{\tau}_{j} \right) \tag{2}$$

where $Visible(P_i, e, S^{\tau})$ denotes the set of attributes held by a player P_i that grant visibility of element e under state S^{τ}, att^{τ}_{j} denotes a game attribute j at turn τ drawn from U. This general form instantiates differently depending on the game type. In card games, the hidden state is a player's hand. A card c dealt to player P_i is encrypted under a slot ownership policy of $\mathbb{A}^{\tau}_{slot_k} = card^{\tau}_{P_i, slot_k}$, where the slot index k is public but the card identity c assigned to that slot is the encrypted payload M_e meaning only P_i's key contains the matching attribute and all other players receive $\perp$ on decryption. In board or strategy games, hidden state corresponds to tiles or positions outside a player's vision range, and the policy encodes spatial proximity over position attributes. In both cases the policy is a monotone Boolean formula expressible as a CP-ABE access tree [7]. In multi-team settings the policy ranges over the authorised player set rather than all players shown as:

$$\mathbb{A}^{\tau}_{e} = \bigvee_{P_i \in Auth(e, S^{\tau})} \left(team_{P_i} \wedge \bigvee_{j \in Visible(P_i, e, S^{\tau})} att^{\tau}_{j} \right) \tag{3}$$

where $Auth(e, S^{\tau}) \subseteq P$ denotes the subset of players permitted to observe element e under state S^{τ}, determined by the game's team membership rules, such that no player outside the authorised set can satisfy the policy regardless of their positional attributes.

Hidden game state element M_e is encrypted following the construction of [7] adapted to index by game element e and turn τ, shown here in abbreviated form. The full leaf components $C_y = g^{q_y(0)}$ and $C\prime_y = H(att(y)\|\tau)^{q_y(0)}$ for each leaf y in the access tree follow exactly:

$$CT^{\tau}_{e} = \left(\mathbb{A}^{\tau}_{e}, \tilde{C} = M_e \bullet e(g, g)^{\alpha s}, C = h^{s}\right) \tag{4}$$

The message M_e represents the hidden game state of element e, multiplied by the blinding factor $e(g, g)^{\alpha s}$ where $s \leftarrow_R \mathbb{Z}_p$ is a fresh random scalar and $C = h^s = \left(g^{\beta}\right)^s$ encodes s under the master parameter β. The access policy $\mathbb{A}_e^\tau$ is embedded in the ciphertext and the leaf components follow the original construction exactly. The complete encrypted game state is then simply shown as:

$$B^\tau = \left\{CT_e^\tau | e \in S^\tau\right\} \tag{5}$$

The broadcast set B^τ constitutes the complete hidden game state for turn τ, where each game state element $e \in S^\tau$, a card, a tile, a resource quantity, or any other hidden information unit, is independently encrypted under its own visibility policy $\mathbb{A}_e^\tau$ as defined in Eq. 4. This design departs from the single-message encryption model of [7] in two important ways. First, the entire game state is encrypted element-wise rather than as a monolithic payload, allowing each element to carry a distinct access policy reflecting the game's visibility rules for that specific element. Second, the broadcast is sent to all players simultaneously over the P2P network, every player receives every ciphertext regardless of whether they are authorised to decrypt it. Each player then independently attempts decryption on each element of B^τ using their current key $SK_{P_i}^\tau$: authorised elements yield M_e, all others yield $\perp$. Since $\perp$ reveals no information about M_e, an unauthorized player learns nothing about the hidden game state elements they cannot decrypt, regardless of how many ciphertexts they receive.

5.3 Turn Protocol

A single turn τ proceeds as follows. At the start of the turn, all players broadcast their signed actions for turn τ and apply the deterministic transition function T uniformly to compute the agreed game state $S^{\tau+1}$. Since T is deterministic and all players hold the same inputs, all players arrive at the same $S^{\tau+1}$ independently.

The distributed key generation protocol then issues a fresh key $SK_{P_i}^{\tau+1}$ to each player P_i, reflecting their updated attribute set $S_{P_i}^{\tau+1}$ derived from $S^{\tau+1}$. For each hidden game state element $e \in S^{\tau+1}$, the corresponding visibility policy $\mathbb{A}_e^{\tau+1}$ is constructed from the game rules as defined in Eq. 3, and the element is encrypted to produce $CT_e^{\tau+1}$ per Eq. 4. The complete broadcast $B^{\tau+1}$ is then distributed to all players simultaneously over the P2P network.

Each player independently attempts decryption on every element of $B^{\tau+1}$ using $SK_{P_i}^{\tau+1}$. Elements for which $SK_{P_i}^{\tau+1} \models \mathbb{A}_e^{\tau+1}$ yield the plaintext game state M_e, all others yield $\perp$ – the plaintext never exists in the local process of an unauthorized player. Keys from turn τ expire automatically through epoch tagging described in Sect. 5.1.

6 Card Game Instantiation: Three Player Poker

We instantiate Fog CP-ABE for a three-player P2P poker game to demonstrate how the framework enforces hidden information boundaries without a trusted server. The players are: $Alice(P_1)$, $Bob(P_2)$, $Carol(P_3)$, each running a local game client connected over a P2P network with no central authority. The hidden information in poker is well-defined and strictly structured. Each player's hole cards must remain invisible to all other players until showdown, while community cards become visible to all players at precisely defined moments during play. Poker was chosen as a minimal, well-known hidden-information domain that maps directly to a CP-ABE access policy with per-player visibility, hole cards and timed-broadcast visibility through community cards.

Before the game begins, all three players execute the distributed setup ceremony described in Sect. 5.1. Alice contributes α_1, Bob α_2 and Carol α_3, publishing commitments from g^{α_1}, g^{α_2} and g^{α_3} respectively before revealing. The collective public key PK is then derived from $\alpha = \alpha_1 + \alpha_2 + \alpha_3 (mod p)$ such that no single player controls the master secret. At the start of each turn τ, all players collectively run the threshold key generation protocol, which issues a fresh key to each player reflecting their current card ownership attributes.

When Alice is dealt the King of Diamonds and the Ten of Clubs, each card is independently encrypted under its ownership policy following Eq. 4. The King of Diamonds is encrypted as $CT^{\tau}_{slot_1} = Encrypt(PK, card[Alice][slot_1][\tau], K\diamondsuit)$, producing a ciphertext included in the broadcast B^{τ} and received by all three players. Alice decrypts successfully since her key satisfies the policy $card[Alice][slot_1][\tau]$, recovering $K\diamondsuit$. Bob and Carol attempt decryption and receive $\perp$. This means that the card value does not exist in their local process at any point. There is no memory address Bob can inspect, nor a network packet Carol could intercept that would reveal the card value. The same applies symmetrically to all six hole cards across the three players.

Community cards present a different visibility pattern. At the flop, three cards must become simultaneously visible to all players, but only at the moment of reveal and not before. In Fog CP-ABE this is enforced by encrypting the community cards under the OR policy $\mathbb{A}^{\tau}_{flop} = identity\_Alice \vee identity\_Bob \vee identity\_Carol$, satisfiable by any player. The community cards are encrypted under this policy at deal time, but keys satisfying it are only issued at the turn corresponding to the flop reveal τ_f. Before τ_f, all three players receive $\perp$ when attempting to decrypt the community ciphertexts – early decryption is cryptographically impossible regardless of network access or memory inspection. At τ_f, keys are issued and all three players decrypt the flop simultaneously and correctly.

7 Security Analysis

Fog CP-ABE inherits the security properties of the CP-ABE construction of [7]. A player whose attribute set does not satisfy the visibility policy embedded in a ciphertext cannot distinguish the encrypted game state from a random element, meaning an unauthorized player receiving broadcast B^{τ} learns nothing about any game state element M_e for which their key does not satisfy $\mathbb{A}^{\tau}_e$ [7]. Collusion resistance follows from the per-player key randomisation established in Sect. 5.1 – each key $SK^{\tau}_{P_i}$ is bound to an independently chosen random value $r_i \leftarrow_R \mathbb{Z}_p$, ensuring two colluding players cannot combine their keys to satisfy a policy that neither could satisfy individually [7]. The distributed setup eliminates the single trusted authority assumption of standard CP-ABE. Attribute forgery is likewise prevented: because per-turn keys are issued collectively through the commit-and-reveal ceremony rather than self-generated, a player cannot mint a key carrying an attribute their current game state does not grant. The distributed setup removes the single trusted-authority assumption of standard CP-ABE and remains secure provided at least one player contributes honestly [15].

8 Discussion, Future Work and Conclusion

Fog CP-ABE is computationally feasible in turn-based peer-to-peer games because the turn structure provides seconds to minutes between state updates which is sufficient time for key generation, encryption and decryption operations that CP-ABE requires. Real-time games are explicitly out of scope as the per-frame state update frequency is incompatible with the overhead of bilinear group operations. Two open problems remain for future work: an offline or disconnected player can stall the distributed key generation ceremony, since lowering the threshold to tolerate absences would weaken the $n-1$ collusion bound of the threat model; and scalability to larger game environments with empirical benchmarking of key-generation, encryption and decryption latency with ciphertext size and broadcast overhead as the attribute universe scales to larger games.

This paper presented Fog CP-ABE, a theoretical framework applying Ciphertext-Policy Attribute-Based Encryption to enforce hidden information boundaries in peer-to-peer turn-based games, its contribution is the architectural mapping of visibility rules to ciphertext policies and game state to key attributes, together with the removal of the trusted authority, rather than a modification of the primitive itself. Game state is encrypted element-wise under predicate-based visibility policies derived from game rules, player keys reflect current game attributes and a threshold commit-and-reveal protocol distributes key authority across all players, eliminating the single trusted authority assumption of standard CP-ABE constructions. The framework was instantiated for a three-player poker game, demonstrating cryptographic enforcement of card ownership boundaries and timed community card reveals. Prototype implementation, empirical performance evaluation and extension of the framework to larger game domains constitute the primary directions for future work.

Acknowledgments. This work has been fully supported by the University of Zagreb, Faculty of Organization and Informatics, institutional project Digital Twins and Smart Solutions.

Disclosure of Interests. The authors have no competing interests to declare.

References

1. Yan, J., Randell, B.: A systematic classification of cheating in online games. In: Proceedings of the 4th ACM SIGCOMM Workshop on Network and System Support for Games, pp. 1–9. Association for Computing Machinery, New York (2005). https://doi.org/10.1145/1103599.1103606
2. Yan, J., Randell, B.: An investigation of cheating in online games. IEEE Secur. Priv. **7**, 37–44 (2009). https://doi.org/10.1109/MSP.2009.60
3. Kabus, P., Buchmann, A.P.: Design of a cheat-resistant P2P online gaming system. In: Proceedings of the 2nd International Conference on Digital Interactive Media in Entertainment and Arts, pp. 113–120. Association for Computing Machinery, New York (2007). https://doi.org/10.1145/1306813.1306840

4. Zhang, J., et al.: Identify as a human does: a pathfinder of next-generation anti-cheat framework for first-person shooter games. arXiv:2409.14830 (2025). https://doi.org/10.48550/arXiv.2409.14830
5. Bursztein, E., Hamburg, M., Lagarenne, J., Boneh, D.: OpenConflict: preventing real time map hacks in online games. In: 2011 IEEE Symposium on Security and Privacy, pp. 506–520. IEEE (2011). https://doi.org/10.1109/SP.2011.28
6. Alangari, A., Alharbi, O.: A systematic review of technical defenses against software-based cheating in online multiplayer games. arXiv:2512.21377 (2025). https://doi.org/10.48550/arXiv.2512.21377
7. Bethencourt, J., Sahai, A., Waters, B.: Ciphertext-policy attribute-based encryption. In: 2007 IEEE Symposium on Security and Privacy (SP '07), pp. 321–334. IEEE, Berkeley (2007). https://doi.org/10.1109/SP.2007.11
8. Cai, Y., Markantonakis, K., Shepherd, C.: Addressing network packet-based cheats in multiplayer games: a secret sharing approach. arXiv:2501.10881 (2025). https://doi.org/10.48550/arXiv.2501.10881
9. Baughman, N.E., Liberatore, M., Levine, B.N.: Cheat-proof playout for centralized and peer-to-peer gaming. IEEE/ACM Trans. Netw. **15**, 1–13 (2007). https://doi.org/10.1109/TNET.2006.886289
10. Shruti, Rani, S., Sah, D.K., Gianini, G.: Attribute-based encryption schemes for next generation wireless IoT networks: a comprehensive survey. Sensors **23**(13), 5921 (2023). https://doi.org/10.3390/s23135921
11. Blum, M.: Coin flipping by telephone a protocol for solving impossible problems. SIGACT News **15**(1), 23–27 (1983). https://doi.org/10.1145/1008908.1008911
12. Pedersen, T.P.: Non-interactive and information-theoretic secure verifiable secret sharing. In: Advances in Cryptology – CRYPTO '91, pp. 129–140. Springer, Heidelberg (1992). https://doi.org/10.1007/3-540-46766-1_9
13. Bichler, M.: Design science in information systems research. Wirtschaftsinformatik **48**(2), 133–135 (2006). https://doi.org/10.1007/s11576-006-0028-8
14. Kuechler, B., Vaishnavi, V.: Theory development in design science research: anatomy of a research project. In: Proceedings of the 3rd International Conference on Design Science Research in Information Systems and Technology (DESRIST 2008), pp. 1–15 (2008)
15. Pedersen, T.P.: A threshold cryptosystem without a trusted party. In: Advances in Cryptology – EUROCRYPT '91, pp. 522–526. Springer, Heidelberg (1991). https://doi.org/10.1007/3-540-46416-6_47

WasteAI: Coupling Deep Learning and Blockchain for End-to-End Waste Data Management

Francesco De Rose[1], Luca Legato[1], Simona Leo[1], Francesco Marchetta[1], Giorgio Veltri[1], Alessandro Campanella[3], Marco Caruso[3], Tommaso Ruga[2], and Ester Zumpano[2](✉)

[1] E Way Enterprise Business Solutions Srl, Cosenza, Italy
[2] DIMES Department, University of Calabria, Rende, CS, Italy
e.zumpano@dimes.unical.it
[3] Global Technologies Italia S.r.l., Rome, Italy

Abstract. WasteAI is an ongoing research project (started November 2025) developing a data-driven collaborative platform for waste traceability, classification, and incentivised recycling. The system addresses a core data engineering challenge: integrating heterogeneous data streams - citizen-submitted photographs, mobile app events, and blockchain transactions - into a unified, queryable data infrastructure that supports the entire waste value chain. The platform integrates a mobile application, a blockchain-backed traceability engine (*WasteAI-Trace*), and a deep-learning image-recognition module (*WasteAI-Image*) that classifies waste from consumer-submitted photographs. Citizens are rewarded with utility tokens tied to the nature and quantity of their disposals, creating a virtuous loop between citizen engagement, data collection, and recycling behaviour. A RESTful API layer (*WasteAI-BE*) exposes anonymised, aggregated datasets to municipalities, recycling industries, and researchers, enabling data-driven decision support across the waste management value chain. This paper describes the system architecture, the AI pipeline design, the token incentive model, current development status, and open data engineering challenges.

Keywords: data engineering · IoT · smart waste management · deep learning · image classification · blockchain · circular economy · data integration · incentive mechanisms · smart cities

1 Introduction and Motivation

Global waste generation is growing at an alarming pace: Eurostat reports 5.2 tonnes of waste per EU citizen in 2018, and the World Bank projects a 70% increase by 2050, reaching 3.4 billion tonnes [1]. The social and environmental consequences are severe: improper disposal contaminates soil and water, accelerates climate change, and undermines progress toward a circular economy.

© The Author(s), under exclusive license to Springer Nature Switzerland AG 2027
G. Vargas Solar et al. (Eds.): ADBIS 2026, CCIS 3175, pp. 406–413, 2027.
https://doi.org/10.1007/978-3-032-39823-9_36

Achieving the EU zero-waste target requires not only better logistics infrastructure, but also active citizen participation and fine-grained, longitudinal data collection across the entire waste value chain—from the household bin to the recycling plant.

Current IoT-based smart-waste solutions—sensor-equipped bins, GPS-tracked collection vehicles, RFID-tagged containers [2,4]—have improved operational efficiency and reduced collection costs. However, they suffer from two structural limitations. First, they treat the citizen as a passive end-point, collecting no data about what is discarded at source or whether households are sorting correctly. Second, they operate in silos: bin-level sensors, municipal collection systems, and recycling plants share no common data infrastructure, making end-to-end lifecycle traceability of waste batches practically impossible. WasteAI, funded under the Calabria Regional Innovation Programme (POR FESR Calabria 2021–2027) and under active development since November 2025, is designed to fill precisely this role. Its guiding principle is to place the *citizen as the first node* of the waste value chain: users photograph and declare disposals via a mobile app; an AI module validates and classifies the images; a blockchain layer records events immutably; and a token economy rewards compliant recycling behaviour. The resulting rich, geolocated dataset is exposed via an open API to municipalities, collectors, recycling industries, and researchers for predictive analytics, route optimisation, and circular-economy traceability.

The contributions of this paper are: (i) a four-layer microservice architecture combining mobile sensing, deep learning, and blockchain, designed around a unified data integration backbone; (ii) a three-stage AI pipeline for waste image validation, EU-taxonomy classification, and brand identification; (iii) a configurable token-incentive model aligning citizen behaviour with circular-economy objectives; (iv) a discussion of open data engineering challenges and the planned validation roadmap.

2 Related Work

IoT-Based Waste Management. Prior work has focused on bin-level monitoring, RFID-based event tracking, and route optimisation [2–5]. These systems operate exclusively at the logistics tier and generate no data on waste composition or citizen sorting behaviour.

Blockchain for Waste Traceability. Kouhizadeh *et al.* [6] identify immutability and transparency as key enablers for circular-economy auditing. Consumer facing blockchain deployments in waste management have remained narrow, typically a single token-reward step, without full lifecycle traceability.

Data Integration for Smart City Systems. The integration of heterogeneous data sources in smart city contexts has been studied extensively [12,13]. Key challenges include temporal alignment of multi-rate streams, schema heterogeneity across sensor networks, and scalable ingestion pipelines. WasteAI addresses these challenges by combining a mobile event layer, a blockchain ledger, and a

RESTful API gateway into a unified data infrastructure specifically designed for the waste management domain.

Deep Learning for Waste Classification. Yang and Thung [7] introduce TrashNet, one of the first benchmark datasets for image-based recyclability classification. Bircanoglu *et al.* [8] propose RecycleNet, a CNN architecture trained on multiple waste categories with strong accuracy on controlled images. All these approaches treat classification as a standalone task, without connection to a citizen engagement platform or traceability infrastructure.

Positioning of WasteAI. To the best of our knowledge, no existing system couples IoT sensing, AI-driven image classification, blockchain-backed traceability, and a token-incentive model into a single citizen-centred waste management platform. WasteAI targets precisely this integration gap.

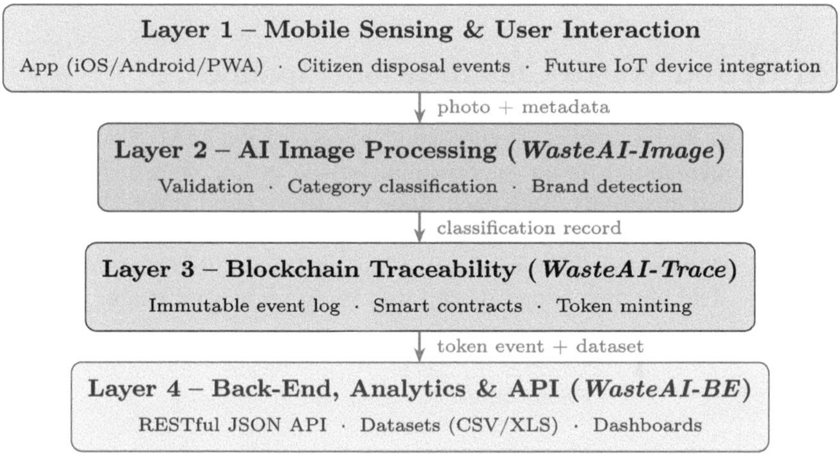

Fig. 1. WasteAI four-layer microservice architecture.

3 System Architecture

WasteAI adopts a containerised microservice architecture organised into four functional layers (Fig. 1).

Layer 1 – Mobile Sensing. The *WasteAI-app* runs natively on iOS/Android and as a Progressive Web App (PWA). Users register, photograph disposals, and declare quantities, submitting a structured event (image, category hint, GPS, timestamp) to the back-end. The app supports future integration with IoT devices (e.g., RFID-tagged bins) through the technology-agnostic API layer exposed by *WasteAI-BE*.

Layer 2 – AI Image Processing. *WasteAI-Image* validates and classifies each photograph through a three-stage pipeline (Sect. 4), producing a structured record forwarded to Layer 3.

Layer 3 – Blockchain Traceability. *WasteAI-Trace* records each disposal event on a permissioned blockchain, immutably linking pseudonymised identity, waste category, quantity, GPS, and timestamp. Smart contracts automate token minting and allow collectors and recyclers to append downstream events, enabling full lifecycle reconstruction of each waste batch.

Layer 4 – Back-End, Analytics & API. *WasteAI-BE* orchestrates all microservices, manages relational and document-oriented databases, and exposes a RESTful JSON API. Anonymised, aggregated datasets (CSV, XLS, JSON) and interactive dashboards are made available to municipalities, industry, and research institutions, enabling a secondary layer of data-driven decision support built on top of the raw event log maintained by *WasteAI-Trace*.

4 AI-Driven Waste Classification Pipeline

Image-based waste recognition is the technical core of WasteAI. The recognition pipeline is implemented as an agentic multi-stage graph, in which specialised nodes execute sequentially and each node's output conditions the execution of the next. Orchestration is handled via a compiled state machine, allowing deterministic routing, parallel crop processing, and structured state propagation across nodes. The pipeline proceeds through three sequential stages (Fig. 2).

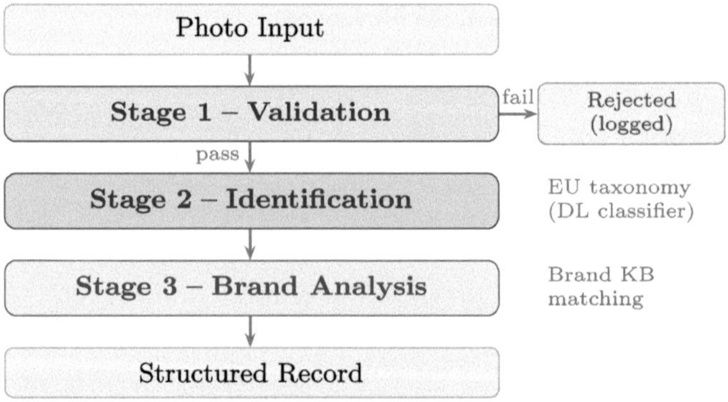

Fig. 2. WasteAI-Image three-stage classification pipeline.

Stage 1 – Validation. A 2-D Fourier transform yields magnitude and phase spectra; the *Fourier Index* and *Fourier Gradient* are evaluated across eight directional filters (N8 scheme) to detect duplicates, off-topic photographs, and synthetically generated content. The output is a continuous confidence score in

[0, 1], allowing operators to tune acceptance thresholds per deployment context. Rejected images are logged without token reward, providing data for downstream fraud pattern analysis.

Stage 2 – Waste Identification. Validated images are classified against the EU household waste taxonomy (plastics, paper, glass, metals, organic, electronic/WEEE, mixed) using deep-learning feature extractors fine-tuned on domain-specific waste imagery with OpenCV-based preprocessing (contrast normalisation, background suppression). An *Other* catch-all class accumulates rare categories for iterative extension as labelled data grows through the app. Classification is further supported by vision-language models, which perform instance-level localisation and per-crop semantic analysis, assigning each detected item a waste type code, a quantity class (S/M/L), and a per-item confidence score.

Stage 3 – Brand and Label Analysis. A lightweight object detector locates label regions within the classified image; identified text and graphic elements are matched against a pre-loaded brand knowledge base (KB). Matched brands are associated with the disposal record, enabling product-level lifecycle insights—for example, per-geography plastic-bottle consumption rates or identification of high-volume non-recyclable product categories. This process is further augmented by vision-language models, which perform OCR-based text extraction and cross-validate brand identity against the assigned waste code, resolving inconsistencies between visual classification and label evidence. The final *structured record* carries waste category, quantity class (S/M/L), brand if detected, and per-field confidence percentages, forwarded to *WasteAI-Trace* for immutable logging and to *WasteAI-BE* for EP calculation.

5 Token Incentive Model

A key differentiator of WasteAI is its token-based incentive mechanism, which ties individual citizen behaviour to measurable circular-economy outcomes. Each validated disposal generates *Earned Points* (EP):

$$\mathrm{EP} = Q \cdot K_c + W_s \tag{1}$$

where Q is the declared quantity (mapped to a gram-weight via S/M/L category bins), K_c is a material-specific conversion coefficient, and W_s is a baseline waste score reflecting environmental impact, proxied by decomposition time (organic $\ll$ plastic $\ll$ electronic waste). Both parameters are configurable per country and campaign period, allowing targeted boosting of under-recycled fractions. The linear-additive formulation was deliberately preferred over more complex (e.g., non-linear or multiplicative) alternatives for three reasons: (i) *transparency* - citizens can easily understand and predict their rewards, a prerequisite for sustained engagement; (ii) *tunability* - the quantity-driven term $Q \cdot K_c$ and the impact-driven baseline W_s can be calibrated independently, allowing campaign designers to boost specific material fractions without altering the overall reward scale; (iii) *fraud control* - caps and cut-off thresholds are straightforward to enforce on linear scores. More sophisticated schemes (e.g., diminishing returns on repeated disposals) are left as future work, once behavioural data from the pilot becomes available.

A weekly cap on $Q \cdot K_c$ prevents fraudulent over-declaration. EPs are periodically converted to utility tokens by a scheduled back-end task and credited to per-user digital wallets after a configurable verification buffer. Redeemable options include merchant discounts, municipal service-fee reductions. A configurable cut-off threshold discourages low-effort participation.

6 Development Status and Open Challenges

Started in November 2025, WasteAI is currently in the analysis and design phase, which covers the state-of-the-art survey on AI algorithms and waste classification techniques, the definition of system functional specifications, and the design of the mobile app, web portal, and back-end architecture. The implementation phase (already underway) covers the development of the WasteAI-app, the web portal and REST API, and the core back-end modules—WasteAI-Image, WasteAI-Trace, and WasteAI-BE—targeted for completion by September 2026. A final validation and dissemination phase, running through December 2026, will exercise the integrated prototype on real use cases; an international workshop on AI and big data for waste management is also envisaged.

The platform starts from TRL 6, building on *eIMES3D-Imaging* [9–11] (SIAE reg. no. 010905, 2016), a component already in production use for AI-based image analysis. This technological foundation provides a validated base for deep-learning image processing; domain adaptation to the waste context, combined with new training datasets and updated reasoning strategies, is expected to bring the system to TRL 7 (operational prototype validation) by project completion. A full-scale municipal pilot in the Calabria region is planned as follow-on work.

Several open research challenges will be addressed during the project lifecycle:
(i) Dataset construction. Publicly available corpora (TrashNet [7], RecycleNet [8]) cover generic categories but lack Italian-specific packaging and sorting norms. A domain-specific dataset will be bootstrapped through the WasteAI-app beta release, curating citizen-submitted images for model fine-tuning.
(ii) Anti-fraud and adversarial robustness. The token economy incentivises image replay, synthetic image generation, and inflated quantity declarations. The Fourier-based Stage 1 pipeline addresses image authenticity; per-user temporal anomaly detection will counter quantity fraud.
(iii) GDPR compliance on an immutable ledger. Recording geolocated events on an append-only blockchain requires careful pseudonymisation to honour the right to erasure. Appropriate data-minimisation and pseudonymisation strategies are under investigation.
(iv) Scalable real-time AI inference. Handling thousands of concurrent image submissions from a regional deployment requires efficient model serving. Efficient model serving strategies will be evaluated to reduce latency and cost.

7 Conclusions

This paper presents WasteAI, a data-driven platform that rethinks waste management by placing citizens at the centre of the value chain and addressing the data engineering challenges that this entails. The integration of heterogeneous streams—mobile events, AI classification records, and blockchain transactions—into a unified data infrastructure is the key technical contribution of the platform. Deep-learning classification, blockchain traceability, and a configurable token-incentive model create a self-reinforcing ecosystem: better recycling behaviour yields richer datasets, which refine AI performance and enable more accurate rewards, further incentivising engagement. The microservice architecture ensures deployability across heterogeneous municipal contexts and scalability to regional level. Future work will focus on extending the training dataset with Italian-specific waste imagery, integrating federated learning to improve classification without centralising raw images, and conducting a full-scale validation with municipal partners in the Calabria region.

Acknowledgment. This work was supported by the Calabria Regional Innovation Programme under Grant No. CUP J89I24002880005 (PR FESR FSE 2021–2027, Azione 1.1.1 - "Sostegno a progetti di attività di ricerca, sviluppo e innovazione nelle Aree e nelle traiettorie prioritarie della S3"), within the WasteAI project: "Applicazione di algoritmi di AI a sistemi di gestione dei rifiuti per il riconoscimento dei conferimenti."

References

1. World Bank. What a Waste 2.0: A Global Snapshot of Solid Waste Management to 2050, Washington, DC (2018)
2. Gutierrez, J.M., Jensen, M., Henius, M., Riaz, T.: Smart waste collection system based on location intelligence. Procedia Comput. Sci. **61**, 120–127 (2015)
3. Catania, V., Ventura, D.: An approach for monitoring and smart planning of urban solid waste management using smart-M3 platform. In: Proceeding of the 15th Conference on FRUCT, vol. 236, pp. 24–31 (2014). https://doi.org/10.1109/FRUCT.2014.6872422
4. Hannan, M.A., Arebey, M., Begum, R., Basri, H.: RFID and communication technologies for solid waste bin and truck monitoring system. Waste Manage. **31**, 2406–2413 (2011)
5. Anagnostopoulos, T., Zaslavsy, A., Medvedev, A., Khoruzhnicov, S.: Top-k Query based Dynamic Scheduling for IoT-enabled Smart City Waste Collection (2015). https://doi.org/10.1109/MDM.2015.25
6. Kouhizadeh, M., Zhu, Q., Sarkis, J.: Blockchain technology and the sustainable supply chain: theoretically exploring adoption barriers. Int. J. Prod. Econ. **231**, 107831 (2021)
7. Yang, M., Thung, G.: Classification of Trash for Recyclability Status. CS229 Project Report, Stanford University (2016)
8. Bircanoğlu, C., Atay, M., Beşer, F., Genç, Ö., Kızrak, M.A.: RecycleNet: Intelligent Waste Sorting Using Deep Neural Networks. https://doi.org/10.1109/INISTA.2018.8466276

9. Iaquinta, P., et al.: eIMES 3D: an innovative medical images analysis tool to support diagnostic and surgical intervention. Procedia Comput. Sci. **110**, 459–464 (2017)
10. Iaquinta, P., et al.: eIMES 3D mobile: a mobile application for diagnostic procedures. IEEE BIBM **2017**, 1634–1641 (2017)
11. Turano, S., et al.: P09 ReCaTuR, rare cancer network Calabria, implementing a software system based on showing of 3D stereoscopic imaging data. Anna. Oncol. **27**(suppl 4), iv100 (2016)
12. Botta, A., de Donato, W., Persico, V., Pescapé, A.: Integration of cloud computing and internet of things: a survey. Futur. Gener. Comput. Syst. **56**, 684–700 (2016)
13. Zanella, A., Bui, N., Castellani, A., Vangelista, L., Zorzi, M.: Internet of Things for smart cities. IEEE Internet Things J. 1 (2012). https://doi.org/10.1109/JIOT.2014.2306328

SLM-Driven Schema Evolution for IoT Data Streams

Filip Stamenković(✉), Dušan Mitrović, Jelica Stanojević, Petar Ilić, and Ivan Milenković

Faculty of Organizational Sciences, University of Belgrade, 11010 Belgrade, Serbia
{filip.stamenkovic,dusan.mitrovic,jelica.stanojevic,petar.ilic, ivan.milenkovic}@fon.bg.ac.rs

Abstract. Data schemas in Internet of Things (IoT) environments change constantly as devices are updated, vendors migrate APIs, and business requirements shift, yet downstream pipelines are expected to keep running without interruption. Manual schema maintenance does not scale in such environments, and existing automated approaches rely heavily on static rules or cloud-based services unsuitable for edge deployment. This paper outlines a vision for edge-based automated schema evolution. It proposes a structure where Small Language Models (SLMs), installed on edge devices, identify structural differences in real-time data streaming and create modification rules. The proposed five-layer architecture includes schema fingerprinting, change classification, rule generation, stream modification, and validation. Key challenges are discussed, including semantic ambiguity and edge resource constraints. Directions for future research include domain-specific fine-tuning, federated schema learning, and explainable adaptation methods.

Keywords: Schema Evolution · Small Language Models · Internet of Things

1 Introduction

The rapid development of Internet of Things (IoT) has given rise to a massive quantity of data generated at high velocities from the large number of connected devices that are placed at the edges of networks [1, 2]. Modern IoT ecosystems consist of highly heterogeneous devices produced by different vendors, often employing proprietary data formats and communication mechanisms for representing semantically equivalent information [3], creating an immense challenge to interoperate across such a wide array of devices.

A central problem with such environments is that schemas are constantly changing. The continuous stream of firmware upgrades, vendor API migration, new or changed business requirements, and the constant need for platform modification create an environment in which schema drift occurs [4, 5]. While both concept drift and schema drift describe the continuous change in how data is represented, they differ significantly. Concept drift describes a change in the distribution of the data without a change in its underlying structure [6], while schema drift refers to a change in the structure of the data itself [5].

© The Author(s), under exclusive license to Springer Nature Switzerland AG 2027
G. Vargas Solar et al. (Eds.): ADBIS 2026, CCIS 3175, pp. 414–422, 2027.
https://doi.org/10.1007/978-3-032-39823-9_37

The problem is particularly pronounced in IoT environments due to their decentralized and heterogeneous nature. Devices from different manufacturers frequently expose semantically equivalent information using incompatible schemas, while cloud-connected systems undergo regular updates that introduce new data formats and interfaces [1, 3]. Consequently, maintaining interoperability across evolving IoT ecosystems requires continuous schema adaptation rather than one-time schema design [5]. Traditional approaches rely on predefined mappings [1, 7] and rule-based validation mechanisms [5]. While effective in relatively stable environments, these approaches struggle to cope with the scale, heterogeneity, and continuous evolution of modern IoT data streams [5, 8].

Recent advances in language models have created new opportunities for addressing these challenges. Large Language Models (LLMs) have demonstrated promising capabilities in schema discovery, schema matching, semantic annotation, and data transformation tasks [9–11]. However, their practical adoption in IoT environments remains constrained by computational requirements, cloud dependency, latency concerns, and privacy risks associated with transmitting sensitive metadata to external services [12, 13]. These limitations motivate the exploration of Small Language Models (SLMs), which offer a more practical alternative for deployment on resource-constrained edge devices while retaining sufficient reasoning capabilities for specialized data engineering tasks [12, 14]. The combination of edge-deployed SLMs, autonomous schema adaptation, and continuous IoT stream processing remains largely unexplored in the current literature.

This paper proposes an SLM-driven framework for autonomous schema evolution in IoT data streams. Rather than routing schema changes to cloud-hosted services, the proposed approach leverages lightweight language models deployed directly at the edge to support the detection of structural changes, semantic interpretation of evolving schemas, and the generation of adaptation strategies in near real time. We outline a conceptual architecture comprising schema monitoring, change detection, SLM-based transformation rule synthesis, stream adaptation, and validation mechanisms. Finally, we identify key research challenges, discuss open questions related to reliability, latency, and explainability.

The remainder of this paper is organized as follows. Section 2 reviews related work on schema evolution, schema matching, and language-model-driven data engineering. Section 3 presents the proposed five-layer architecture and intended use cases. Section 4 discusses open challenges and directions for future research. Section 5 concludes the paper.

2 Background and Related Work

Schema evolution refers to the process of modifying data schemas over time while preserving compatibility with existing data and applications [15]. In modern distributed and event-driven systems, schema evolution enables software platforms to adapt to changing requirements without requiring complete system redeployment or data loss [4]. A related concept is schema drift, which describes unexpected structural changes in data streams caused by software updates, modifications to upstream systems, evolving domain requirements, or third-party API changes [5]. Unlike planned schema evolution, schema drift often occurs without coordination and can disrupt continuously operating data pipelines.

The problem is particularly relevant in IoT environments, where heterogeneous devices from different manufacturers frequently expose semantically equivalent information using incompatible data representations [1, 3]. Maintaining interoperability in such environments requires mechanisms capable of continuously adapting to changing schemas while preserving downstream functionality.

Traditional approaches to schema evolution mostly come from database and event-sourced systems. Common methods of handling schema evolution include versioned events, tolerant-reader strategies, upcasting, copy-and-transform mechanisms, and in-place transformations [4, 15]. While these approaches provide robust mechanisms for maintaining compatibility across schema versions, they often require significant manual effort and assume relatively controlled system evolution. In stream-processing environments, schema registries and version management frameworks are commonly used, but they may introduce operational overhead and struggle to accommodate highly dynamic schema changes [5].

Schema matching, which aims to find semantic correspondence for items that belong to various schemas [11, 16] is very closely related to schema evolution. While schema evolution deals with changes in a schema, schema matching's purpose is to create a semantic mapping between semantically equivalent information in multiple schemas. Semantic mappings also provide an important layer of integration through their ability to map schema elements to domain-specific concepts, thereby allowing transformation of representations of the same information [1, 7].

Advances in recent years have presented new opportunities for automating various aspects of schema management using language models. Language models are being employed with success in several areas of schema management including schema discovery, schema mapping, semantic annotation, and schema translation. Mior [10] showed that language models can be utilized for both JSON schema discovery and enriching the semantics associated with those discovered schemas. Additionally, Liu et al. [9] proposed an approach combining Small Language Models and Large Language Models within a retrieval and rerank system to facilitate schema matching. Further, Wang et al. [11] demonstrated how LLMs could be used to enhance the semantic relationship between heterogeneous relational schemas. Lastly, Marcinkowski & Weis [3], within the context of IoT devices, utilize language models as part of their WoT-PL system to convert disparate vendor-specific device schemas into standard Web of Things description formats, which would improve interoperability among different vendors and systems.

Although LLMs demonstrate strong semantic reasoning capabilities, they are still difficult to deploy into IoT systems because of a number of factors such as the high computational cost of running them, the need for these models to be run on remote servers, the delay associated with communicating data over networks, and security/privacy issues [12, 13]. As a result, there has been an increasing amount of research recently focused on developing SLMs that have fewer than 7–10 billion model parameters and therefore do not require substantial amounts of resources to run on constrained edge devices [12, 14]. In comparison to cloud-based LLMs, SLMs provide significantly faster response times (i.e., low latency), use less hardware, maintain higher levels of privacy, and can operate in either completely disconnected or network-bandwidth-constrained environments [13, 17].

Despite recent progress, existing research remains fragmented and still very disconnected. Most approaches to managing schema are limited to single aspects of schema management (e.g., detecting schema drift, finding matches among schemas, translating semantics from one schema to another, and schema discovery). Therefore, there is a lack of an overarching architecture that integrates autonomous schema evolution, edge-based deployments, and SLM-driven adaptations to support continuously changing IoT data flows [3, 5, 11]. This gap motivates the vision presented in this paper, which explores the use of edge-deployed SLMs for schema monitoring, adaptation, and evolution in dynamic IoT environments. To the best of our knowledge, this is the first work to propose a combination of autonomous schema evolution, fully edge-based deployment, and SLM-driven rule generation within a single architecture, rather than addressing these aspects in isolation as prior work has done.

3 Vision

We envision an architecture in which Small Language Models deployed at the edge act as autonomous schema adaptation agents. Instead of using manually created mapping files or cloud schema translators, this proposed system will create transformation rules when it identifies changes in the structure of its data stream and then validate those transformations prior to providing them to applications that consume them.

The proposed framework consists of five sequential layers deployed on an edge device, as illustrated in Fig. 1.

Layer 1 – Schema fingerprinting and monitoring. The first layer continuously tracks the structure of incoming data records, capturing field names, types, nesting depth, and cardinality as a compact in-memory fingerprint. This fingerprint is updated on a rolling basis, and any significant deviation from the stored reference signals indicates that something has changed. This layer relies on lightweight statistical and rule-based checks rather than the SLM itself, reserving model inference for the semantic reasoning required in later layers.

Layer 2 – Structural change detection and classification. When a deviation is detected, this layer identifies what kind of change has occurred. For example, a field rename, a unit or encoding shift, a field addition or removal, or a broader restructuring. Classifying the change before involving the SLM is intended to narrow down what the model needs to do, which we expect reduces the chance of it generating an incorrect or nonsensical rule. Detected changes are further tagged by severity: cosmetic (e.g., field renames), semantic (e.g., unit or encoding shifts), or structural (e.g., type or nesting changes), which determines how cautiously downstream layers treat the resulting rule.

Layer 3 – SLM-based transformation rule synthesis. The change classification, along with sample records from before and after the change, is packaged into a structured prompt and passed to an on-device SLM. The model generates a short executable mapping function that handles the detected change. A syntax check then filters out any malformed outputs before they can affect the data stream. Concretely, the prompt tells the SLM what changed (from Layer 1), how serious the change is (from Layer 2), and shows it a few example records from before and after the change. The SLM must respond with a short function that takes one old-format record in and returns one new-format record out. For example, renaming a field and converting its units in a single step. Keeping the function this small and narrowly scoped is intended to make it easier to check for errors before running it, and should allow it to run safely in an isolated environment where it cannot affect anything else on the device if it misbehaves.

Layer 4 – Rule execution and stream adaptation. Once validated, the new rule is applied directly to the live data stream, replacing the outdated mapping. The previous rule is retained in a versioned store, providing a record of prior mappings to support auditing and manual intervention if a later rule fails validation.

Layer 5 – Validation. After the rule is applied, the transformed records are checked against expected value ranges, types, and cardinality. If validation fails, the system does not assume the previous mapping is still usable, since the underlying schema has already changed. Instead, Layer 5 sends the failure back to Layer 3 and asks the SLM to try again, this time knowing what went wrong, while the affected records are held or flagged rather than passed downstream. It gets a limited number of attempts. If it still can't produce a working rule after that, the system stops trying automatically and flags the data for a human check. Escalating difficult cases to a cloud-hosted LLM is left as a direction for future work.

Representative deployment scenarios for this framework include industrial sensor networks, where frequent firmware updates alter telemetry formats, and smart-building environments, where multi-vendor devices expose semantically equivalent but structurally inconsistent data.

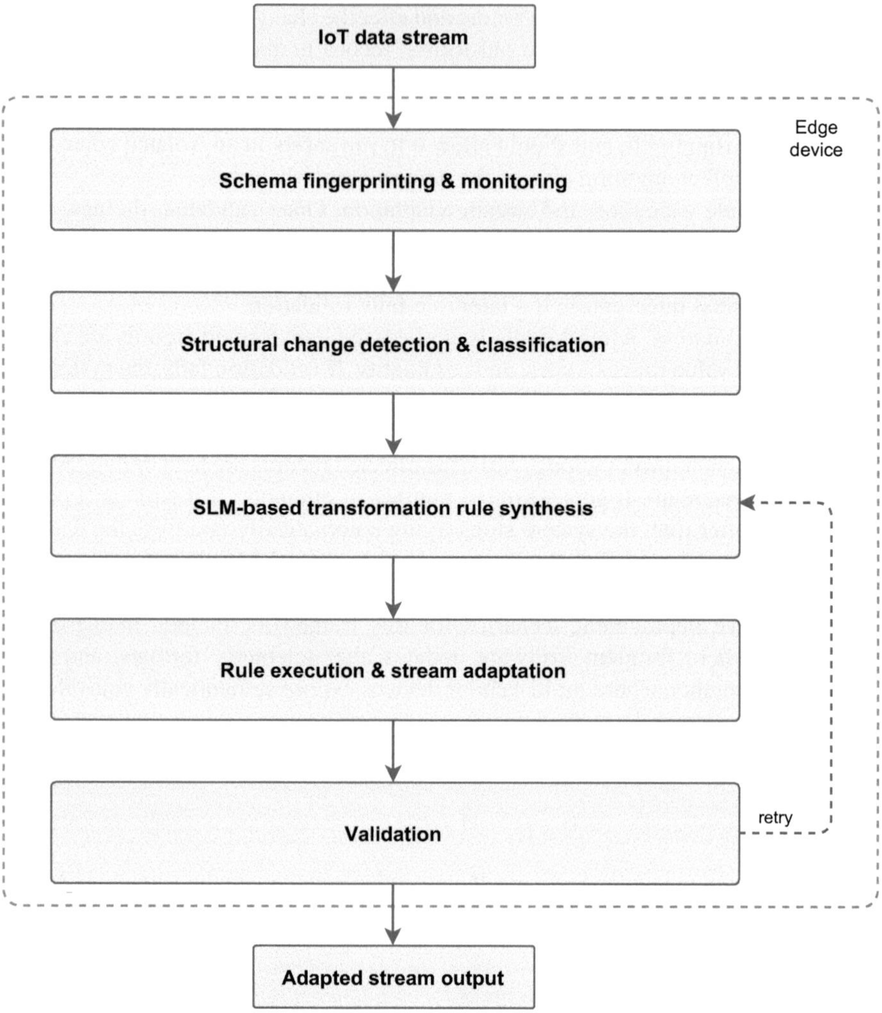

Fig. 1. Proposed architecture diagram

4 Challenges and Research Directions

Despite recent advances in schema evolution, schema matching, and language-model-driven data engineering, there are still many issues that need to be solved before autonomous schema evolution can become applicable in actual deployments of IoT.

The first is identifying the correct semantic interpretation of schema changes. Although structural schema evolutions, e.g., adding a new field or changing the type of a field, are typically automatable, finding their semantic implication is much harder. For instance, renaming a field named "temperature" to "temp_f" could mean simply a name change, unit conversion (e.g., Celsius to Fahrenheit), or an entirely different attribute. Similarly, vendors also use different representations for the same concept, whereas identical field names can have different meanings depending on the domain.

Language model-based schema matching has shown promising semantic reasoning abilities, but ambiguity continues to lead to incorrect mapping and transformation decisions [11, 16].

Even when an SLM successfully generates a transformation rule, verifying that the rule is correct remains a significant challenge. This means future systems will need built-in validation mechanisms that can catch bad transformations before they cause problems downstream. Developing reliable validation mechanisms remains a critical prerequisite for fully autonomous schema evolution [5, 16].

Whether or not SLMs can be deployed on an Edge device is highly dependent upon available resources. Edge devices are often limited by small amounts of memory, low levels of processing power, small amounts of data storage, and low energy availability. Although some recent SLMs have shown significant potential as they apply to resource-constrained hardware in terms of reasoning capabilities, trade-offs exist with respect to model size, inference latency, and model reasoning capabilities [12, 14]. Future research must investigate model compression techniques, quantization strategies, and domain-specific fine-tuning approaches that maximize adaptation performance while preserving real-time responsiveness.

Language models are inherently probabilistic systems. It is possible that language models will produce incorrect or hallucinated responses at times. If an incorrectly formed transformation rule in the schema evolution process causes silent corruption to a data stream or disruption to subsequent analyses or presents safety issues with critical IoT applications, then future architectures should include rollback mechanisms, confidence estimation, and human-in-the-loop decision-making to address potential high-risk adaptations. Explainability remains another major challenge. Schema operators need to know why a particular schema adaptation was generated [3, 16].

Several directions for future research emerge from this vision. First, domain-specific fine-tuning of SLMs could improve adaptation accuracy for particular IoT application domains. Second, federated approaches could enable edge nodes to collaboratively learn and share schema evolution experience without exchanging sensitive data. Third, explainable adaptation methods are needed to maintain human oversight and build trust in autonomous decision-making. Fourth, standardized benchmark datasets and evaluation frameworks would allow meaningful comparison of different schema evolution approaches.

Going forward, future work should investigate architectures that leverage the strengths of both cloud-based and edge-based models, in particular, combining low latency and privacy protection that can be offered by deploying SLMs at the edge, with the powerful reasoning and learning capabilities that can be achieved by cloud-hosted LLMs. Such architecture could provide a feasible way for both real-time adaptation and high semantic accuracy to be met, as we move toward developing adaptive and self-evolving IoT data pipeline systems.

5 Conclusion

This research outlined an architectural model for autonomous schema evolution at the edge, where Small Language Models detect structural changes in IoT data streams and generate adaptation rules in real time. The five-layer design, spanning fingerprint-based change detection, SLM-driven rule synthesis, and validation, offers a practical path toward self-adapting IoT data pipelines. However, many technical challenges exist that have yet to be solved, including ambiguity with regard to semantic meaning when interpreting how changes are to be applied to the database, as well as limitations imposed upon edge hardware due to limited resources. Therefore, addressing these challenges using techniques such as fine-tuning SLMs specific to each application's domain as well as explaining adaptations made within the scope of federated learning is key to moving this vision from concept to deployment.

Acknowledgments. This research was supported by the University of Belgrade – Faculty of Organizational Sciences and, in part, by the Ministry of Science, Technological Development and Innovation of the Republic of Serbia through institutional funding (grant number: 200151).

Disclosure of Interests. The authors have no competing interests to declare that are relevant to the content of this article.

References

1. Marshoodulla, S.Z., Saha, G.: An approach towards removal of data heterogeneity in SDN-based IoT framework. Internet Things. **22**, 100763 (2023). https://doi.org/10.1016/j.iot.2023.100763
2. Zhou, Z., Chen, X., Li, E., Zeng, L., Luo, K., Zhang, J.: Edge Intelligence: Paving the Last Mile of Artificial Intelligence with Edge Computing. http://arxiv.org/abs/1905.10083, (2019). https://doi.org/10.48550/arXiv.1905.10083
3. Marcinkowski, D., Weis, T.: WoT-PL, harnessing large language models for IoT schema translation: a conceptual framework and preliminary findings. In: Proceedings of the 14th International Conference on the Internet of Things, pp. 200–205. ACM, Oulu, Finland (2024). https://doi.org/10.1145/3703790.3703833
4. Overeem, M., Spoor, M., Jansen, S., Brinkkemper, S.: An Empirical characterization of event sourced systems and their schema evolution – lessons from industry. J. Syst. Softw. **178**, 110970 (2021). https://doi.org/10.1016/j.jss.2021.110970
5. Vaddepalli, R.K.: AutoSchema: a self-learning framework for detecting and adapting to schema drift in real-time data streams. Euro. J. Adv. Engg. Tech. **10**(7), 94–100 (2023). https://doi.org/10.5281/zenodo.16418094
6. Lu, J., Liu, A., Dong, F., Gu, F., Gama, J., Zhang, G.: Learning under concept drift: a review. IEEE Trans. Knowl. Data Eng. **31**(12), 2346–2363 (2019). https://doi.org/10.1109/TKDE.2018.2876857
7. Rahman, H., Hussain, Md.I.: A comprehensive survey on semantic interoperability for Internet of Things: State-of-the-art and research challenges. Trans. Emerg. Tel. Tech. **31**(12), e3902 (2020). https://doi.org/10.1002/ett.3902
8. Riehle, D.M., Arz Von Straussenburg, A.F., Aldenhoff, T.T.: Designing grammar-guided LLM outputs for open data integration – a DSR approach to IoT data platforms. In: Chatterjee, S., Vom Brocke, J., and Anderson, R. (eds.) Local Solutions for Global Challenges, pp. 178–195. Springer, Cham (2025). https://doi.org/10.1007/978-3-031-93976-1_12
9. Liu, Y., Pena, E., Santos, A., Wu, E., Freire, J.: Magneto: Combining Small and Large Language Models for Schema Matching. http://arxiv.org/abs/2412.08194, (2025). https://doi.org/10.48550/arXiv.2412.08194
10. Mior, M.J.: Large Language Models for JSON Schema Discovery. http://arxiv.org/abs/2407.03286 (2024). https://doi.org/10.48550/arXiv.2407.03286

11. Wang, S., et al.: LLMATCH: A Unified Schema Matching Framework with Large Language Models. http://arxiv.org/abs/2507.10897 (2025). https://doi.org/10.48550/arXiv.2507.10897
12. Duffy, E.B., Fernandez, D., de Waal, A., Pesé, M.D.: Small Language models on the edge for real-world agentic systems in industry. In: Proceedings of the Southern African Conference for Artificial Intelligence Research. The SACAIR Steering Committee, Cape Town, South Africa (2025). https://2025.sacair.org.za/online-proceedings/Papers/paper_23.pdf
13. Zheng, Y., Chen, Y., Qian, B., Shi, X., Shu, Y., Chen, J.: A review on edge large language models: design, execution, and applications. ACM Comput. Surv. **57**(8), 1–35 (2025). https://doi.org/10.1145/3719664
14. Abstreiter, M., Tarkoma, S., Morabito, R.: Sometimes Painful but Certainly Promising: Feasibility and Trade-offs of Language Model Inference at the Edge. https://arxiv.org/abs/2503.09114 (2025). https://doi.org/10.48550/ARXIV.2503.09114
15. Overeem, M., Spoor, M., Jansen, S.: The dark side of event sourcing: Managing data conversion. In: 2017 IEEE 24th International Conference on Software Analysis, Evolution and Reengineering (SANER), pp. 193–204. IEEE, Klagenfurt, Austria (2017). https://doi.org/10.1109/SANER.2017.7884621
16. Parciak, M., Vandevoort, B., Neven, F., Peeters, L.M., Vansummeren, S.: Schema Matching with Large Language Models: an Experimental Study. http://arxiv.org/abs/2407.11852 (2024). https://doi.org/10.48550/arXiv.2407.11852
17. Semerikov, S.O., Vakaliuk, T.A., Kanevska, O.B., Moiseienko, M.V., Donchev, I.I., Kolhatin, A.O.: LLM on the edge: the new frontier. In: Proceedings of the 5th Edge Computing Workshop, pp. 137–161. CEUR-WS.org, Zhytomyr, Ukraine (2025). https://ceur-ws.org/Vol-3943/paper28.pdf

FEHDA 2026: 2nd International Workshop on Fairness Exploration in Heterogeneous Data and Algorithms

Fairness-Accuracy Trade-Offs in Group Recommendations: A Nash Bargaining Approach

Tazkia Binty Faruqui, Maria Stratigi(✉), and Kostas Stefanidis

Data Science Research Centre, Tampere University, Tampere, Finland
{maria.stratigi,konstantinos.stefanidis}@tuni.fi

Abstract. Group recommender systems (GRSs) must reconcile the competing objectives of fairness, ensuring equitable satisfaction among group members, and accuracy, delivering recommendations that closely align with collective preferences. Traditional approaches often assume a trade-off between fairness and accuracy. This paper investigates whether a Nash Bargaining-based framework can achieve high levels of both objectives under the evaluated experimental setting. The Nash Bargaining Solution (NBS) is employed to generate Pareto-efficient, symmetric, and individually rational group outcomes that guarantee balanced satisfaction across all members. Using the MovieLens 10M dataset, the study constructs genre- and tag-based user subgroups to evaluate fairness behavior across both macro- and micro-level content categorizations. The resulting fair group recommendations form the baseline for a large-scale counterfactual validation framework that assesses robustness under systematic catalog perturbations. Empirical results suggest that the proposed framework can maintain high recommendation accuracy while preserving stable fairness under the evaluated counterfactual scenarios.

Keywords: Group Recommender Systems · Nash Bargaining Theory · Fairness–Accuracy Trade-off · Counterfactual Analysis

1 Introduction

Designing effective *Group Recommender Systems* (GRSs) is a challenging task because it must balance two competing objectives: *fairness* and *accuracy*. Fairness ensures that the satisfaction of all group members is equitably considered, preventing domination by any single user, whereas accuracy measures how closely the recommended item aligns with the group's preferences. Traditional aggregation approaches prioritize accuracy but often neglect fairness, leading to biased outcomes. Conversely, methods that attempt to enforce fairness constraints tend to reduce predictive accuracy, producing less relevant recommendations. This tension has traditionally been interpreted as a fairness–accuracy trade-off in group recommendation. However, recent theoretical advances suggest that when

© The Author(s), under exclusive license to Springer Nature Switzerland AG 2027
G. Vargas Solar et al. (Eds.): ADBIS 2026, CCIS 3175, pp. 425–441, 2027.
https://doi.org/10.1007/978-3-032-39823-9_38

fairness is treated as a cooperative optimization objective rather than a constraint, both fairness and accuracy can be jointly improved. This paper provides empirical evidence suggesting that fairness and accuracy can be jointly maintained under the evaluated setting.

The *Nash Bargaining Solution* (NBS), a key concept in cooperative game theory, provides a mathematically grounded method for achieving fair outcomes among multiple agents. It does so by maximizing the product of users' utility gains relative to their disagreement points, ensuring *Pareto efficiency*, *symmetry*, and *individual rationality*. When applied to GRSs, NBS guarantees that every member benefits proportionally, enabling fairness to emerge organically from the optimization process rather than being imposed externally. Despite this potential, the use of Nash Bargaining in group recommendations remains underexplored, particularly under dynamic catalog conditions where content availability or user preferences can change. This paper addresses this research gap by combining Nash Bargaining optimization with a counterfactual robustness analysis framework to evaluate fairness stability under controlled catalog perturbations.

Specifically, this paper proposes a solution grounded in Nash Bargaining Theory, which treats fairness as a cooperative optimization objective rather than a constraint. In this setting, each group member is modeled as a rational agent, and the collective recommendation is determined by maximizing the Nash product of their utility deviations from the group's disagreement point (mean utility). This guarantees equitable allocation of benefits while preserving group satisfaction.

However, fairness must not only be achieved but also proven stable under change. To that end, this research introduces a dual-granularity counterfactual analysis framework that systematically removes genres (macro-level) and tags (micro-level) from the movie catalog and recomputes recommendations to measure shifts in fairness and accuracy. This approach enables the identification of influential content subgroups that most strongly affect group utility balance. By combining game-theoretic fairness with counterfactual validation, we provide an interpretable understanding of fairness behavior in group recommendations.

In summary, this work makes the following contributions:

- Introduces a cooperative game-theoretic model that ensures equitable satisfaction and Pareto efficiency, enabling fairness to emerge naturally without post-hoc correction.
- Proposes a novel counterfactual sensitivity analysis framework that examines fairness stability at both macro (genre) and micro (tag) levels through extensive catalog perturbations, analyzing all genres and the most frequently occurring tags.
- Demonstrates the framework's performance using a large-scale dataset, forming 1,000 user groups and conducting 119 counterfactual experiments involving 19 genres and 100 user-generated tags.
- Provides empirical evidence that fairness and accuracy exhibit a positive association within the evaluated setting in group recommendations when fairness is optimized cooperatively via Nash Bargaining.

2 Related Work

Fairness in Recommendation Systems. Fairness-aware recommendation systems have evolved from single-objective optimization toward multi-stakeholder and multi-objective formulations. Early approaches introduce fairness constraints within model learning. For example, [3] proposes F2VAE, incorporating fairness in both representation learning and recommendation generation, while [8] addresses fairness and diversity in sequential group recommendations, highlighting trade-offs across recommendation rounds. Similarly, [5] integrates fairness with interactivity and explanations, emphasizing transparency and user trust. A broader overview of fairness definitions and methodological directions is provided in [12]. User-centric fairness has also received significant attention. [9] demonstrates that collaborative filtering methods tend to favor active users, proposing re-ranking strategies to balance utility across user groups. Extending this idea, [13] introduces FaiREO, a multi-objective optimization framework that balances fairness and accuracy with minimal performance loss. [1] links fairness issues to popularity bias, showing how overexposure of popular items leads to systematic unfairness. More recently, [7] proposes an energy-based framework capturing distributional disparities across users and items. Overall, these works highlight a shift toward dynamic, distribution-aware, and explainable fairness mechanisms that attempt to mitigate bias while preserving recommendation quality.

Nash Bargaining in Recommender Systems. Game-theoretic formulations provide principled mechanisms for balancing individual and collective utility in group recommendation. [22] introduces one of the earliest Nash equilibrium-based approaches, modeling group preference aggregation as a strategic interaction problem. Their matrix factorization framework enabled consensus recommendations reflecting both individual and group-level preferences. [21] extends this idea to item-group recommendations, incorporating both individual preferences and social influence to achieve stable group decisions. Negotiation-based and multi-agent approaches further explored fairness in group settings. [4] proposes a negotiation framework where agents iteratively reach agreement under fairness and privacy constraints. Similarly, [11] models recommendation as a non-cooperative game, demonstrating improvements in both fairness and accuracy in educational settings. Cooperative game-theoretic methods have also been explored; for instance, [2] uses the Shapley value for user clustering, improving fairness and scalability in collaborative filtering. More directly related to fairness, [18] argues that Nash bargaining provides a theoretically sound alternative to average-utility maximization, as it enforces proportional fairness by maximizing the product of utilities. [15] further extends Nash bargaining with behavioral considerations such as regret, improving robustness in realistic group decision scenarios. Despite these advances, the application of Nash bargaining in dynamic recommendation environments and its empirical validation under changing conditions remain limited.

Counterfactual Methods in Group Recommender Systems. Counterfactual reasoning has emerged as a powerful tool for explainability and fairness evaluation in recommenders. [16] introduces a model-agnostic framework for generating counterfactual explanations in group recommendations, focusing on transparency while preserving privacy. [17] pioneers counterfactual explainable recommendation, identifying minimal changes in item features that alter recommendation outcomes, thus revealing causal relationships. Subsequent works extended counterfactual analysis to more complex settings. [14] incorporates textual and tabular features to generate interpretable explanations, while [19] proposes a fairness-oriented counterfactual framework that evaluates bias through simulated interventions without requiring demographic data. [6] introduces temporal counterfactual explanations for sequential recommendation, ensuring realistic and coherent user behavior modeling and [20] combines rule-based learning with counterfactual reasoning to improve interpretability and efficiency. Overall, counterfactual approaches provide a causal perspective on recommendation behavior, enabling the analysis of robustness, fairness sensitivity, and feature influence. However, their integration with game-theoretic fairness mechanisms, particularly in group recommendation settings, remains underexplored.

3 Methodology

The Nash Bargaining approach provides a foundation for generating fair and Pareto-optimal group recommendations. This section formally defines the Nash bargaining process, presents its mathematical derivation, describes the algorithmic implementation, and outlines validation and complexity analysis. Formally, given a group of n users $G = \{u_1, u_2, \ldots, u_n\}$ and a set of movies $M = \{m_1, m_2, \ldots, m_k\}$, the Nash Bargaining Solution (NBS) seeks the movie $m^* \in M$ that maximizes the product of each user's utility gain over their disagreement (fallback) utility. Each user u_i has a utility function $u_i(m)$ representing their normalized satisfaction for movie m, where $0 \leq u_i(m) \leq 1$.

Individual Disagreement Point: $d_i = \frac{1}{|M_i|} \sum_{m \in M_i} r_{i,m}$, where M_i is the set of movies rated by user i, and $r_{i,m}$ is the rating assigned by u_i to movie m. The disagreement point d_i represents the expected satisfaction if no agreement is reached.

Nash Product to Maximize: $m^* = \underset{m \in M}{\arg\max} \prod_{i=1}^{n} \big(u_i(m) - d_i\big)$. The corresponding Nash utility product is: $U_{\text{Nash}} = \prod_{i=1}^{n} \big(u_i(m^*) - d_i\big)$ [10]. This formulation ensures: (i) Pareto efficiency: No other movie improves one user's utility without harming another, (ii) Symmetry: Users with identical preferences receive identical treatment, (iii) Invariance to affine transformations: Scaling of utilities does not affect the outcome, and (iv) Individual rationality: No user receives less than their disagreement point.

3.1 Subgroup Formation

User subgroups were created to enable fairness-oriented analysis across diverse user communities. Two subgrouping strategies were implemented: genre-based subgrouping and tag-based subgrouping.

Genre-Based Subgroups The genre field in the movie metadata frequently contains multiple genre labels for a single movie. These labels were separated and expanded into individual entries, enabling each movie to be associated with multiple genres. The ratings data were then linked with the expanded genre mappings to compute the number of movies rated by each user within each genre. To identify highly active users, the distribution of user-genre rating counts was analyzed, and the top 20% of users within each genre were selected. These users formed the genre-based subgroups, representing communities with strong interest and activity in specific content categories.

Tag-Based Subgroups The tag data were first cleaned by removing missing or blank tags. The frequency of tag usage for each user was then computed to quantify engagement with specific tagging patterns. Users whose tagging activity exceeded the 80th percentile were identified as highly engaged and grouped into tag-based subgroups.

This quantile-based filtering ensured that the resulting subgroups reflected meaningful engagement patterns while reducing noise from infrequent user activity.

3.2 Algorithmic Implementation

The algorithm computes group recommendations in four major steps: (1) **Group Formation:** Random fixed-size user groups were formed within genre-based subgroups to balance diversity and computational feasibility. Since MovieLens does not provide naturally occurring user groups, the groups used in this study are synthetically constructed through sampling. A sampling strategy was used to limit combinations while preserving representativeness. (2) **Utility Computation:** User utilities were estimated using the trained Surprise SVD collaborative filtering model. Since the MovieLens dataset is sparse, the model predicts user–movie ratings for candidate movies, allowing utilities to be obtained even when explicit ratings are unavailable. The resulting utility estimates, therefore, depend on the predictive quality of the trained SVD model. These predicted utilities were then used in the Nash bargaining computation. (3) **Nash Product Optimization:** For each candidate movie, user utilities were obtained from the collaborative filtering model, and the Nash product was computed as: $P(m) = \prod_{i=1}^{n} \big(u_i(m) - d_i\big)$. The optimal recommendation was then selected as: $m^* = \arg\max_{m \in M} P(m)$. (4) **Output Generation:** For each group, the selected movie m^* and its utility product U_{Nash} were stored as the Nash-optimal recommendation. These values served as the baseline for subsequent counterfactual and fairness–accuracy analyses.

Validation of Nash Bargaining Axioms: The following validations were performed to confirm theoretical correctness: **Pareto check:** U_{Nash} did not increase under any movie switch that reduced any $u_i(m)$; **Symmetry test:** Swapping identical utility vectors yielded identical m^*; **Affine invariance test:** Linear scaling of ratings did not alter the recommendation outcome; **Individual rationality:** Verified that $u_i(m^*) \geq d_i$ for all users i; **Fairness sensitivity:** Observed a consistent balance between utility balance and collective satisfaction.

Computational Complexity. Let n be the average group size, M_G denote the number of candidate movies evaluated for each group, and G the total number of groups. The time complexity is: $O(G \cdot M_G \cdot n)$, scaling linearly with the number of groups, candidate movies, and users per group.

4 Counterfactual Analysis Framework

This phase builds upon the baseline recommendations produced by Nash bargaining. It perturbs the movie catalog to quantify how the removal of certain genres or tags influences group-level utilities and fairness outcomes. By comparing the perturbed (counterfactual) outcomes with the baseline, the analysis identifies which content attributes have the greatest influence on group decisions. Each simulation follows the same principle: (i) Identify a subgroup of movies defined by a shared attribute (e.g., genre or tag), (ii) Remove all movies belonging to that subgroup from the catalog, (iii) Recompute the Nash bargaining solution for all user groups using the reduced catalog, and (iv) Compare baseline and counterfactual recommendations to measure the magnitude of influence. In this study, robustness refers to the stability of recommendation outcomes under catalog perturbations, while counterfactual sensitivity measures the changes in utility or recommendations after genre or tag removal. These controlled removals assess sensitivity rather than establish causal effects.

Genre-Based Counterfactual Analysis. In the genre-based setting, each genre is iteratively removed from the catalog, and the Nash bargaining process is recomputed for all user groups. For a given genre γ:

1. Filter the catalog to exclude all movies belonging to γ to obtain $M' = \{m \in M : \gamma \notin \text{genres}(m)\}$.
2. Recompute the group recommendation process and utility product on M'.
3. Compute the influence scores and the recommendation change rate.

This provides a macro-level view of how broad content categories affect fairness and satisfaction in group decisions.

Tag-Based Counterfactual Analysis. Complementing the genre-level study, tag-based analysis focuses on user-generated tags that capture nuanced characteristics of movies. For a frequent tag τ:

1. Filter the catalog to exclude all movies with tag τ to obtain $M' = \{m \in M : \tau \notin \text{tags}(m)\}$.

2. Recompute the group recommendation process and utility product on M'.
3. Compute the influence scores and the recommendation change rate.

This enables finer-grained sensitivity profiling, revealing how specific themes or stylistic attributes drive changes in group recommendations.

5 Comparative Analysis

This framework integrates results from the baseline Nash bargaining process and the counterfactual influence analyses to measure the extent of recommendation changes and utility differences after specific subgroups were removed from the catalog.

Genre-Based Comparative Analysis. This phase merged baseline group recommendations with genre-level counterfactual outcomes.

Change Rate. For each removed genre subgroup, the framework calculated the proportion of groups whose top recommendation changed: Change Rate $= \frac{N_{\text{changed}}}{N_{\text{total}}}$, where N_{changed} represents the number of groups whose recommended movie differed from the baseline, and N_{total} is the total number of groups analyzed. This metric quantified the stability of recommendations when specific genres were excluded.

Influence Summary. The influence of each removed genre subgroup was summarized statistically by computing the mean, median, and maximum of the influence score distribution: Influence Score $= |U_{\text{baseline}} - U_{\text{counterfactual}}|$. U_{baseline} is the utility product computed on the original catalog, and $U_{\text{counterfactual}}$ is the utility product computed after removing the subgroup. These values were aggregated across all counterfactual scenarios to identify the most influential genres contributing to fairness and utility changes.

Utility Comparison. For every subgroup, the average baseline utility and counterfactual utility were compared to estimate relative performance differences: Relative Drop (%) $= \frac{U_{\text{baseline}} - U_{\text{counterfactual}}}{U_{\text{baseline}}} \times 100$. This measure indicated how strongly each genre removal affected group satisfaction levels.

Tag-Based Comparative Analysis. The tag-based analysis provided micro-level insights into stability and sensitivity. It compared baseline utilities with tag-based counterfactuals to identify fine-grained sources of variation.

Utility Comparison. For each tag, baseline and counterfactual utilities were compared to visualize deviation from equilibrium. A diagonal line ($y = x$) was plotted as a reference of no change, and dispersion from this line indicated the extent of influence caused by tag removals.

Influence Distribution. The influence score was calculated as: Influence Score $= |U_{\text{baseline}} - U_{\text{counterfactual}}|$. These visualizations revealed the tags that caused the largest changes in group fairness and satisfaction.

Change Rate by Tag. The recommendation stability for each tag was computed using Change Rate $= \frac{N_{\text{changed}}}{N_{\text{total}}}$, where N_{changed} is the count of groups whose recommendations changed after removing movies with a given tag. The resulting data identified tags that contributed most to recommendation instability.

Top Influential Tags. A ranked bar chart of the top influential tags summarized which content-level features exhibited the strongest counterfactual impact on the system. The tag-level framework also produced a comprehensive dashboard combining influence, change rate, and utility metrics for cross-comparison.

Accuracy Assessment

Mean True Rating (MTR). The MTR is the average actual rating assigned by group members to the recommended movie: $\text{MTR}(g, m^*) = \frac{1}{|G_{\text{rated}}|} \sum_{u \in G_{\text{rated}}} r_{u,m^*}$, where G_{rated} denotes the subset of group members who rated the recommended movie m^*, and r_{u,m^*} is the rating given by u to m^*. A higher MTR indicates that the recommendation closely matches group preferences.

Precision@1. This relevance metric captures whether the recommended movie meets a defined threshold: $\text{Precision@1}(g, m^*) = \mathbb{K}[\text{MTR}(g, m^*) \geq \theta]$, where $\theta = 4.0$ represents the relevance threshold (ratings of 4.0 or higher are considered "liked"), and $\mathbb{K}[\cdot]$ is an indicator function that equals 1 if the condition holds and 0 otherwise. When aggregated across all groups, Precision@1 represents the proportion of group recommendations that meet the relevance threshold.

6 Fairness–Accuracy Trade-Off Analysis

This phase utilized the output of the previous accuracy evaluation to jointly analyze fairness and accuracy metrics. Both dimensions were normalized to a common scale to enable direct comparison and visualization. The framework produced multiple visual representations illustrating their relationship across groups, subgroup levels, and group sizes.

Metric Normalization. To ensure comparability between fairness and accuracy, each metric was scaled into the $[0, 1]$ range using min–max normalization: $X_{\text{norm}} = \frac{X - X_{\text{min}}}{X_{\text{max}} - X_{\text{min}}}$, where X represents either the Nash utility (fairness) or the mean true rating (accuracy). The resulting normalized variables, normalized fairness and normalized accuracy, were used for all trade-off analyses.

Fairness–Accuracy Relationship. The core analysis compared normalized fairness and normalized accuracy across all group recommendations using scatter plots and correlation analysis. The Pearson correlation coefficient was computed as $r = \frac{\text{Cov}(F,A)}{\sigma_F \, \sigma_A}$, where F and A represent the normalized fairness and accuracy values, respectively. A high positive correlation indicated that improving fairness did not reduce accuracy.

Binned Fairness Analysis. To further interpret the fairness–accuracy relationship, the normalized fairness scores were divided into quantile-based bins. For each bin B, the framework computed Mean Accuracy $= \frac{1}{|B|}\sum_{i\in B} A_i$ and Mean Precision@1 $= \frac{1}{|B|}\sum_{i\in B} P_i$, where A_i is the normalized accuracy and P_i is the Precision@1 value for instance i. This enabled visualization of how accuracy metrics behave across different fairness levels.

Group Size Analysis. To assess the effect of group size on fairness–accuracy dynamics, each group's size n was identified and color-coded in scatter plots. For groups of the same size n, mean fairness and accuracy were computed as $\bar{F}_n = \frac{1}{|G_n|}\sum_{i\in G_n} F_i$ and $\bar{A}_n = \frac{1}{|G_n|}\sum_{i\in G_n} A_i$, where G_n denotes the set of all groups of size n.

7 Results and Analysis

Nash Bargaining-Based Group Recommendations. The Nash Bargaining Solution (NBS) was applied to user groups formed from genre-based subgroups to model collective decision-making. Each fixed-size user group jointly selected a movie that maximized the product of their utility gains relative to the disagreement point, ensuring fairness across all members. The optimized implementation (sampled combinations per genre and memory-efficient computation) enabled large-scale analysis on the MovieLens 10M dataset. This baseline serves as the foundation for all subsequent counterfactual and fairness–accuracy evaluations presented in this section. We first evaluate the stability of Nash-based recommendations under genre-level removals.

Overall Stability Analysis. As shown in Fig. 1, there is a strong positive correlation between baseline and counterfactual utilities, confirming that the Nash-based recommendations are robust to catalog changes. The clustering around the diagonal line implies minimal fairness distortion across most groups when genres are selectively removed.

Genre-Specific Influence. Drama, Action, and Comedy shows the highest influence scores, indicating that their removal most strongly alters group utilities and fairness balance. Lower scores for genres like Documentary and Western suggest minimal global impact on group satisfaction. Figure 1 also shows the mean influence score (Δ utility) per removed genre. The results highlight that *Drama*, *Action*, and *Comedy* contribute most to collective fairness, whereas other genres play smaller roles in shaping group consensus.

Recommendation Sensitivity. Drama causes the largest change rate (54.5%), followed by Comedy (38.7%) and Romance (29.2%), reflecting these genres' strong influence on recommendation decisions. As seen in Fig. 2, the removal of *Drama* resulted in over half of the recommendations changing, confirming its dominant role in shaping group satisfaction. Genres with lower change rates, such as Documentary or Western, indicate higher resilience of the system's fairness structure.

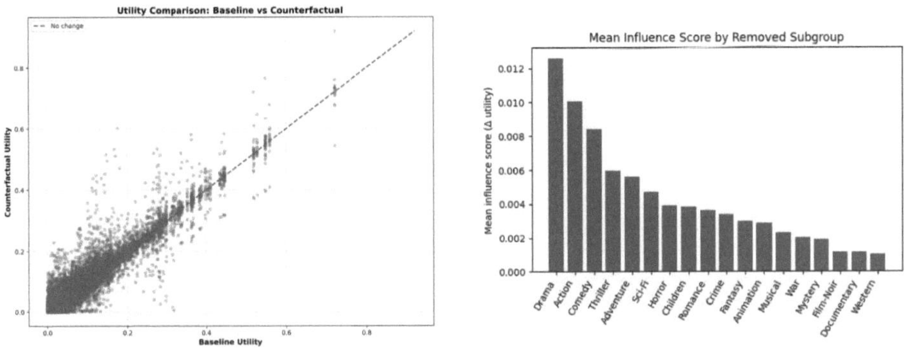

Fig. 1. Genre-level counterfactual results: utility comparison (left) and mean influence score by removed genre (right).

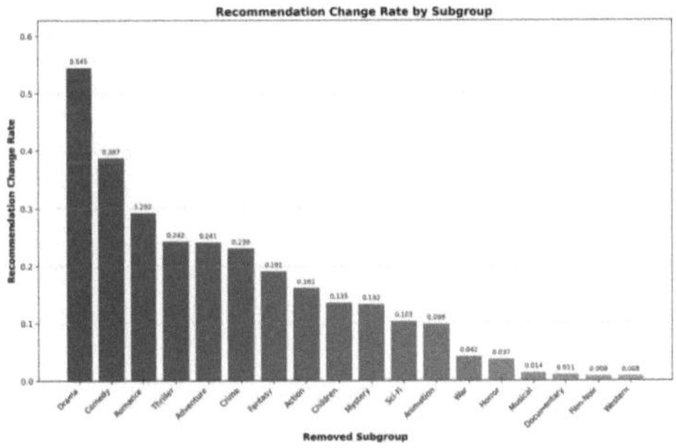

Fig. 2. Recommendation change rate by removing genre.

Utility Impact Analysis. Positive values indicate a utility increase after removal; negative values reflect utility loss. The removal of Comedy slightly increases overall utility, whereas removing Drama and Action decreases group satisfaction, demonstrating asymmetric genre dependencies. Figure 3 shows how removing certain genres affects the mean group utility. While removing *Comedy* or *Documentary* leads to small positive utility gains, removing *Drama* or *Action* results in noticeable utility reductions, indicating these genres' higher contribution to fairness and user satisfaction.

Counterfactual Validation on Tag Removals. This section extends the counterfactual validation to a finer level of granularity by analyzing user tagging behavior rather than broad genre categories. Tags often capture subtle thematic or stylistic preferences, such as *dark humor*, *strong female lead*, or *based on a true story*, that cannot be represented by genres alone. By removing movies associated with individual tags from the catalog and recomputing Nash Bargaining recommendations, we assess how such micro-level perturbations affect fairness stability, utility, and recommendation behavior.

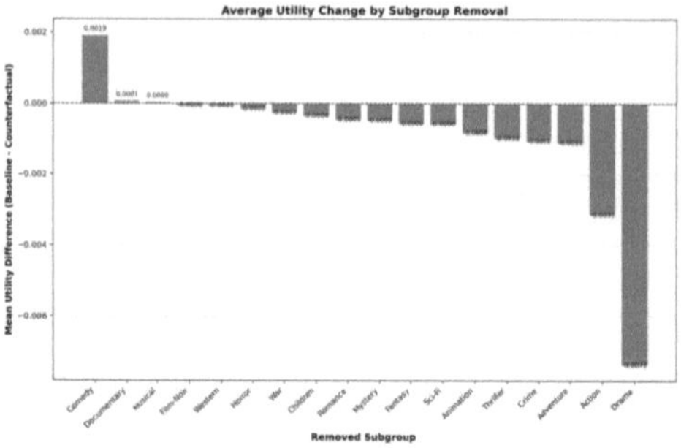

Fig. 3. Average utility difference (baseline − counterfactual) by genre removal.

The goal of this analysis is to evaluate the resilience of the Nash Bargaining framework under fine-grained preference disruptions and to understand how tag-level semantics contribute to fairness sensitivity.

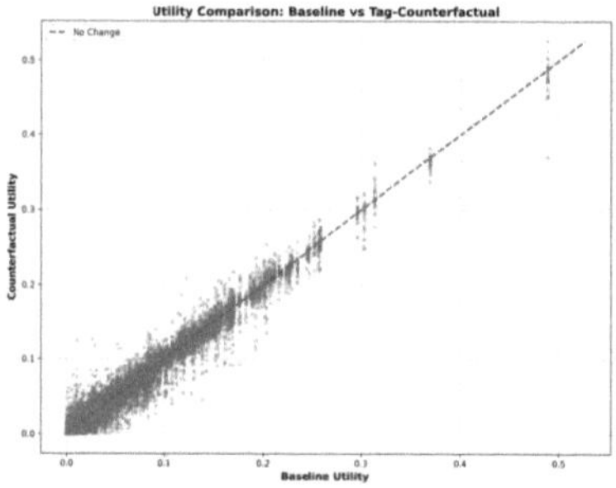

Fig. 4. Utility comparison between baseline and counterfactual Nash utilities at the tag level.

Overall Tag-Level Stability. As shown in Fig. 4, each point represents a user group's utility before and after removing movies associated with a particular tag. The majority of points lie densely along the red dashed diagonal, indicating a strong linear relationship between baseline and counterfactual utilities. This close alignment shows that most tag removals cause only minimal deviations in group utility. A small number of points drift slightly above or below the diagonal—primarily for groups with higher baseline utilities—suggesting that the effect of tag removal is localized rather than widespread. Overall, the tight clustering confirms that the Nash Bargaining framework remains highly stable even when fine-grained, tag-level thematic attributes are perturbed.

Tag Influence Distribution. Figure 5 (right) shows the distribution of influence scores for the top twenty tags. Most tags display very low median influence

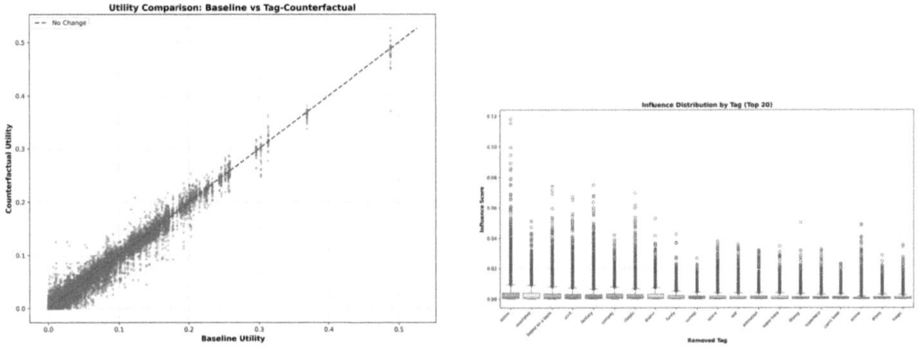

Fig. 5. Tag-level counterfactual results: utility comparison between baseline and counterfactual Nash utilities (left), and distribution of influence scores for the most common tags (right).

and compact interquartile range ranges, indicating that their removal has only a minor effect on group utilities. However, a few tags—such as *action*, *overrated*, *based on a book*, *fantasy*, and *drama*—exhibit wider spreads and higher upper whiskers, suggesting that for some user groups these attributes can substantially affect the Nash utility. Toward the right side of the plot, tags like *anime*, *aliens*, and *magic* also generate occasional high outliers even though their central tendency remains small. Overall, the boxplots indicate that fairness effects are generally stable across tags, but the removal of certain thematic attributes can create localized fairness sensitivity for specific subpopulations.

Most Influential Tags. Tags such as *imdb top 250*, *overrated*, *"owned"*, *"dvd"*, *"own"*, and *"classic"* have the strongest impact on group utility and fairness balance, while others like *biographical* and *historical* show minimal effect. The result reveals that emotionally charged or stylistically distinctive tags tend to exert a stronger influence on group satisfaction. These effects remain localized—specific to the groups most aligned with those tags—without destabilizing the overall fairness equilibrium.

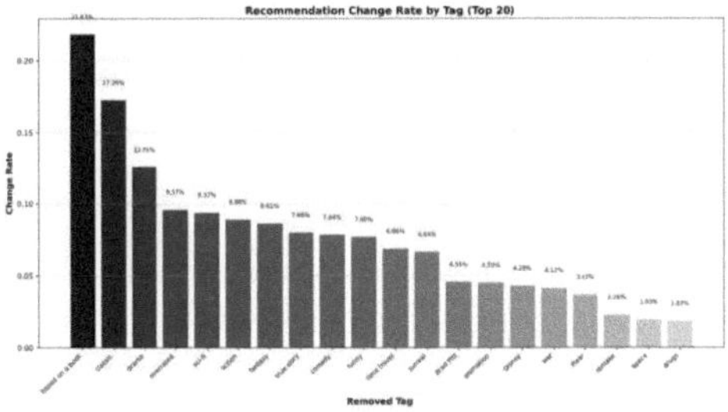

Fig. 6. Recommendation change rate by removing the tag.

Recommendation Change Rate. As shown in Fig. 6, higher bars indicate tags whose removal caused a larger proportion of group recommendations to change. This suggests that certain tags act as strong preference signals, significantly influencing group decisions. The tag based on a book produces the highest change rate (21.83%), followed by classic (17.26%) and drama (12.55%), showing that removing these thematic attributes significantly alters the final group decision. Mid-range tags such as sci-fi, action, fantasy, and true story generate moderate shifts, while tags like Pixar, remake, space, and drugs produce only minor effects.

The overall pattern confirms that certain tags act as strong preference signals within groups, and their removal can meaningfully influence the recommended item. Tag-level perturbations produced stronger and more consistent fairness impacts than genre-level counterfactual experiments, indicating that fine-grained user-generated tags play a central role in shaping the fairness structure of the Nash Bargaining framework.

Summary of Tag-Based Counterfactual Analysis. The tag-level counterfactual results show that the Nash Bargaining framework remains highly stable under fine-grained semantic perturbations. The utility comparison reveals that most groups retain almost identical utilities after tag removal, with points closely aligned along the no-change diagonal. Influence distributions further indicate that most tags have low and consistent impact, with only a few showing wider variability for specific user communities.

Ranking tags by mean influence highlights attributes such as *action*, *overrated*, and *based on a book* as the most impactful. The recommendation change-rate analysis similarly shows that removing certain tags—especially *based on a book*, *classic*, and *drama*—causes the most noticeable shifts, while others create minimal effects. These shifts further confirm that tag-level removals can produce stronger and more consistent fairness impacts than genre-level removals. Overall, tag-level removals introduce localized changes but do not disrupt the global fairness–accuracy balance, confirming the robustness of the Nash Bargaining model.

Cross-Comparison Summary. A comparative synthesis of the genre- and tag-based counterfactual analyses confirms the global robustness of the Nash Bargaining framework. At the genre level, the removal of dominant categories such as Drama, Action, and Comedy produced noticeable fluctuations in group utilities and recommendation outcomes. However, tag-level removals generated stronger and more consistent fairness impacts, indicating that fine-grained user-generated semantic attributes exert greater influence on Nash bargaining outcomes than broad genre categories.

Together, these results show that fairness stability in Nash-based group recommendations is multi-scale, with fine-grained semantic tag attributes exerting stronger counterfactual influence on fairness outcomes than broader genre-level content categories.

As shown in Fig. 7, the combined Influence heatmap highlights that only a limited number of genres and tags exert notable fairness sensitivity. Overall, the findings validate that the proposed Nash Bargaining approach maintains a consistent fairness–accuracy equilibrium across both coarse (genre) and fine-grained (tag) semantic dimensions of the movie catalog.

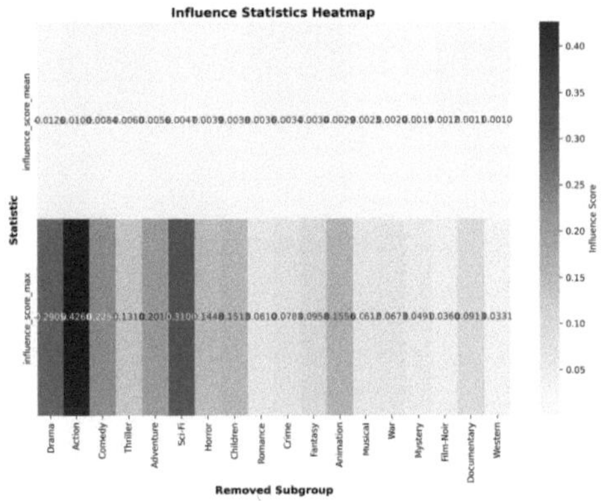

Fig. 7. Combined influence analysis integrating genre- and tag-level counterfactuals. Warmer areas correspond to higher mean and maximum influence values, illustrating that only a few genres and tags exert notable fairness sensitivity.

Accuracy Evaluation. This section evaluates the predictive realism of the recommended items. We first inspect the global distribution of mean true ratings for the recommended movies, followed by an analysis of the success rate (Precision@1) across group sizes.

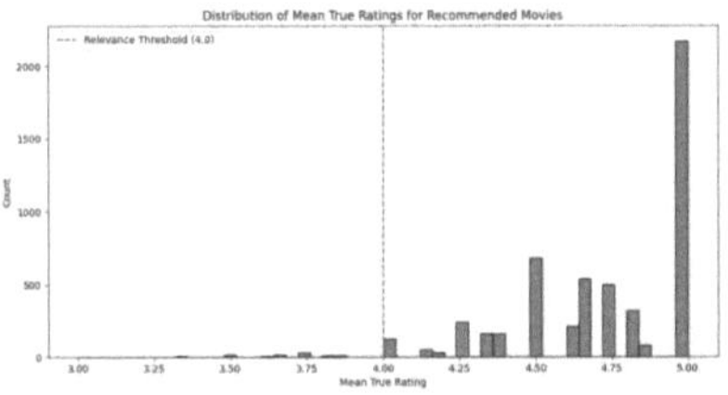

Fig. 8. Distribution of mean true ratings for recommended movies.

As shown in Fig. 8, the distribution is concentrated at or above the relevance threshold, indicating strong overall accuracy. Accuracy is evaluated across the fixed-size user groups. Figure 9 shows that accuracy remains consistently high across the evaluated fixed-size user groups. The vertical reference at 4.0 denotes the relevance threshold, and the concentration above this line confirms strong overall accuracy (Mean True Rating = 4.7226, Precision@1 = 98.34%). Overall, accuracy remains consistently high across the evaluated fixed-size user groups;

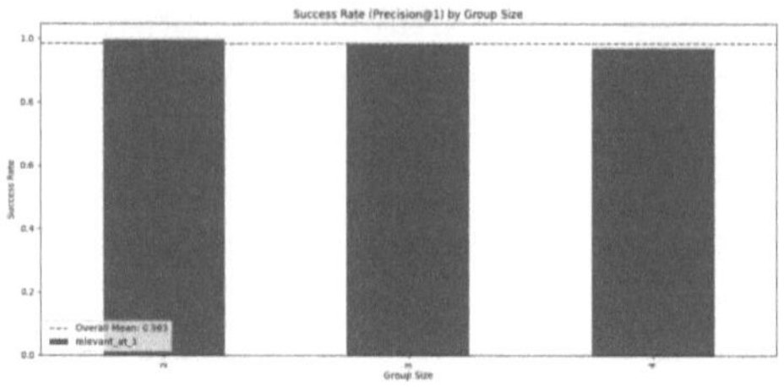

Fig. 9. Success rate (Precision@1 = 98.34%) across evaluated fixed-size user groups with an overall mean reference line. The consistently high bars across sizes show stable performance.

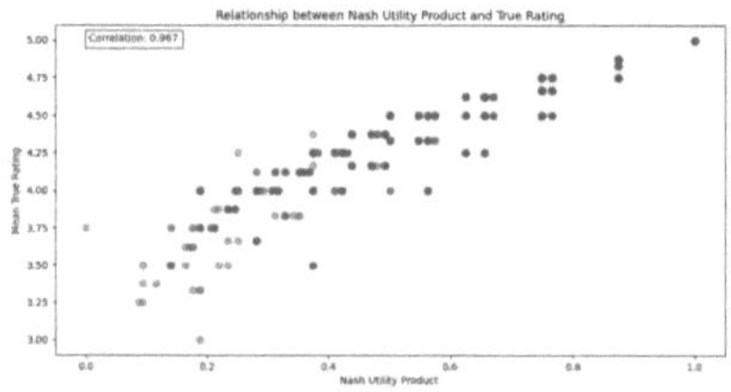

Fig. 10. Relationship between Nash utility product (fairness) and MTR (accuracy). The upward trend indicates a positive association between fairness and accuracy.

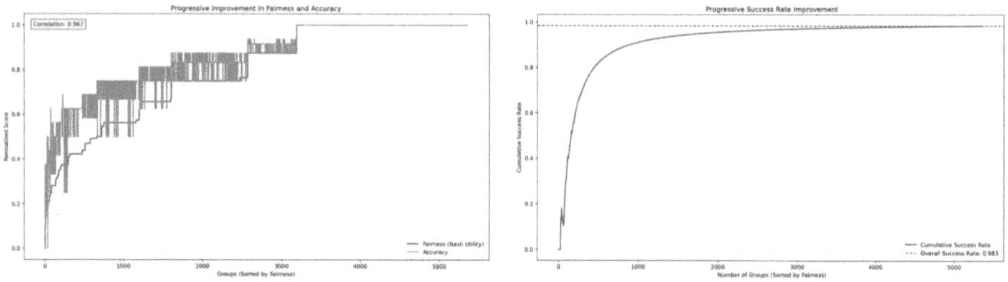

(a) Progressive improvement (b) Cumulative success rate

Fig. 11. Relationship between fairness and recommendation accuracy across group evaluations. The results show that higher fairness values are generally associated with stable or increasing recommendation quality in the evaluated setting.

the success rate is consistently high for all groups (Mean True Rating = 4.7226, Precision@1 = 98.34%).

Fairness–Accuracy Trade-Off. We analyze how Nash fairness relates to realized accuracy. As shown in Fig. 10, the evaluated groups show a positive association between fairness and accuracy. Three complementary visuals are used: a direct correlation view, a progressive view where groups are ordered by fairness, as illustrated in Fig. 11a, and a cumulative success curve that reflects stability as fairness increases, as shown in Fig. 11b.

8 Conclusions

This study investigated whether fairness and accuracy can be jointly optimized in group recommendations by combining NBS with a counterfactual validation framework. Using MovieLens 10M, we evaluated 1,000 fixed-size user groups and conducted 119 counterfactual experiments across 19 genres and 100 user-generated tags. The system achieved an MTR of 4.7226 and Precision@1 of 98.34%, confirming high predictive reliability. Fairness behavior, examined via counterfactual influence distributions, yielded a genre-level coefficient of variation (CV) of 0.7232, indicating heterogeneous but interpretable fairness sensitivity across content categories. Genre removals showed that *Drama*, *Action*, and *Comedy* exert the strongest influence on group utilities. The average recommendation change rate was 15.98%, implying an overall stability rate of 84.02%. Tag-level analyses (CV $\approx$ 0.53) corroborated the macro-level findings at finer granularity, with consistent influence rankings across 100 user-generated tags. These findings are limited to the evaluated MovieLens dataset using synthetically sampled user groups and should not be interpreted as evidence that the proposed framework outperforms alternative group recommendation methods. Taken together, these results suggest that NBS can yield fair, accurate, and robust group recommendations under the evaluated MovieLens setting. Future work will include comparisons with standard group recommendation baselines, additional fairness measures, and statistical significance testing.

References

1. Abdollahpouri, H., Mansoury, M., Burke, R., Mobasher, B.: The connection between popularity bias, calibration, and fairness in recommendation. In: ACM RecSys (2020)
2. Benkessirat, S., Boustia, N., Nachida, R.: A new collaborative filtering approach based on game theory for recommendation systems. J. Web Eng. **20**(2), 303–326 (2021)
3. Borges, R., Stefanidis, K.: F2VAE: a framework for mitigating user unfairness in recommendation systems. In: ACM/SIGAPP SAC, pp. 1391–1398 (2022)
4. Garcia, I., Sebastia, L.: A negotiation framework for heterogeneous group recommendation. Expert Syst. Appl. **41**(4, Part 1), 1245–1261 (2014)
5. Giannopoulos, G., Papastefanatos, G., Sacharidis, D., Stefanidis, K.: Interactivity, fairness and explanations in recommendations. In: UMAP, pp, 157–161 (2021)
6. He, M., An, B., Wang, J., Wen, H.: CETD: counterfactual explanations by considering temporal dependencies in sequential recommendation. Appl. Sci. **13**, 11176 (2023)
7. Le, G.H.T., Nguyen-Tan, K., Huynh, H.X.: Energy-based fairness recommendation: a novel framework for fairness treatment in recommender systems. In: ACIE (2025)
8. Lenzi, E., Stefanidis, K.: ADAPT: fairness & diversity for sequential group recommendations. Inf. Syst. **133**, 102572 (2025)
9. Li, Y., Chen, H., Fu, Z., Ge, Y., Zhang, Y.: User-oriented fairness in recommendation. In: The Web Conference 2021 (2021)
10. Nash, J.F.: The bargaining problem. Econometrica **18**(2), 155–162 (1950)

11. Papamitsiou, Z., Economides, A.A.: Recommendation of educational resources to groups: a game-theoretic approach. In: IEEE Global Engineering Education Conference, pp. 760–767 (2018)
12. Pitoura, E., Stefanidis, K., Koutrika, G.: Fairness in rankings and recommenders: models, methods and research directions. In: ICDE, pp. 2358–2361. IEEE (2021)
13. Polyzou, A., Kalantzi, M., Karypis, G.: FaiREO: user group fairness for equality of opportunity in course recommendation. arXiv arXiv:2109.05931 (2021)
14. Ranjbar, N., Momtazi, S., Homayounpour, M.: Explaining recommendation system using counterfactual textual explanations. Mach. Learn. **113**, 1989–2012 (2023)
15. Shen, Y., Ma, X., Bao, Y., Xu, Z., Zhan, J.: Strategic manipulation behavior analysis for group decision-making based on Nash bargaining game and regret theory. IEEE Trans. Syst. Man Cybern. Syst. **55**(10), 6814–6828 (2025)
16. Stratigi, M., Bikakis, N., Stefanidis, K.: Counterfactual explanations for group recommendations. In: DOLAP, pp. 22–30. CEUR Workshop Proceedings (2025)
17. Tan, J., Xu, S., Ge, Y., Li, Y., Chen, X., Zhang, Y.: Counterfactual explainable recommendation. In: CIKM (2021)
18. Tansuchat, R., Kosheleva, O.: How to make recommendation systems fair: an adequate utility-based approach. Asian J. Econ. Bank. **6**(3), 308–313 (2022)
19. Wang, X.J., Li, Q., Yu, D., Li, Q., Xu, G.: Counterfactual explanation for fairness in recommendation. ACM Trans. Inf. Syst. **42**, 1–30 (2023)
20. Wei, Y.W., Qu, X., Wang, X., Ma, Y., Nie, L., Chua, T.S.: Rule-guided counterfactual explainable recommendation. IEEE TKDE **36**, 2179–2190 (2024)
21. Zhang, L., Zhou, R., Jiang, H., Wang, H., Zhang, Y.: Item group recommendation: a method based on game theory. In: WWW Companion (2017)
22. Zhao, H., Liu, Q., Ge, Y., Kong, R., Chen, E.: Group preference aggregation: a Nash equilibrium approach. In: ICDM, pp. 679–688 (2016)

ERGA 2026: 2nd International Workshop on Entity Resolution and Graph Alignment

Quality-Aware Entity Resolution Across Fragmented Temporal Graphs: Comparing Rule-Based, Learned, and Optimal-Transport Alignment

Marwa Alali[1,2(✉)], Arnaud Castelltort[3], Sebastian Cesario[2], and Anne Laurent[1]

[1] LIRMM, Univ Montpellier, CNRS, Montpellier, France
marwa.alali@lirmm.fr
[2] BFOREAI, Montpellier, France
[3] Thales, Paris, France
https://bfore.ai

Abstract. Recovering latent cross-source relationships in heterogeneous temporal graphs is a core entity-resolution and graph-alignment problem: fragmented snapshots share few nodes, so genuinely related entities may never co-occur in a single source. Without ground truth, assessing the reliability of inferred cross-snapshot links is as hard as inferring them, and volume statistics give no guidance on quality. We introduce a temporal-recurrence quality framework that turns cross-source confirmation counts into a label-free gold standard, and compare three alignment paradigms; a Mamdani Fuzzy Inference System (FIS), a Graph Attention Network (GNN), and Fused Gromov–Wasserstein optimal transport (FGW); on 197 active-DNS domain co-hosting snapshots (253,337 domains; 2,541,475 unique edges). Discovery volume poorly predicts quality: FIS yields 160,200 links (6,282 high-recurrence gold), the GNN, trained on the gold standard, contributes 1,125 links that largely reproduce FIS rather than validate it independently, and FGW produces 467,876 links at 0.10% precision, collapsing under production CDN filtering. A downstream Belief Propagation classifier confirms that integration quality translates to utility, raising AUC-ROC from 0.629 to 0.871.

Keywords: Entity resolution · Graph alignment · Temporal graphs · Data quality · Fuzzy logic · Graph neural networks · Optimal transport

1 Introduction

Real-world graph data in large-scale monitoring and analytics systems is seldom monolithic: it arrives as a stream of heterogeneous temporal snapshots, each a partial, time-limited view of the underlying relational structure. A system monitoring Newly Registered Domains (NRDs) [21] collects hundreds of daily

© The Author(s), under exclusive license to Springer Nature Switzerland AG 2027
G. Vargas Solar et al. (Eds.): ADBIS 2026, CCIS 3175, pp. 445–460, 2027.
https://doi.org/10.1007/978-3-032-39823-9_39

snapshots, each a domain co-hosting graph $G_k = (V_k, E_k)$ whose nodes V_k are domains and whose edges E_k encode shared infrastructure, such as shared IP addresses, observed during capture window k. Because different domains are active at different times, the per-snapshot node sets V_k are largely disjoint: domain pairs that are genuinely related may never appear in the same snapshot, making their relationship latent in any individual source. This is, at its core, an *entity-resolution and graph-alignment* problem across fragmented sources: deciding which cross-snapshot domain pairs denote the same underlying co-hosting relationship, and aligning the fragmented graphs into a unified, quality-aware representation G_{unif} over $V_{\text{all}} = \bigcup_k V_k$.

The task is both practically critical and methodologically hard. Practically, missed links let adversarial campaigns evade detection while false discoveries corrupt downstream analysis. Methodologically, without ground truth for cross-source links one cannot distinguish a genuine relationship from a structural coincidence using volume alone. Three methodologically distinct paradigms apply. *Rule-based* symbolic reasoning encodes domain knowledge as interpretable fuzzy IF–THEN rules. *Representation learning* trains a graph neural network to score cross-source pairs from learned embeddings. *Geometry-based* alignment casts the problem as optimal transport between metric-measure spaces. Each has strong theoretical motivation, yet they have been studied largely in isolation. We ask which paradigm delivers reliable cross-source links on real, large-scale, heterogeneous temporal graphs, how reliability can be measured without ground truth, and how each behaves as a component of a database-style integration pipeline with realistic preprocessing.

We frame the study around four questions. **RQ1.** Does discovery volume correlate with link quality? **RQ2.** Can temporal recurrence alone yield a reliable quality signal without external labels? **RQ3.** Is OT-based alignment viable after production-level Content Delivery Network (CDN) filtering, and what is the failure mechanism? **RQ4.** Does integration quality translate into downstream analytical utility?

Contributions

This paper makes four contributions. First, we introduce a temporal recurrence quality framework (Sect. 5), a ground-truth-free methodology that derives a quality standard from cross-source confirmation counts: genuine relationships recur across independent source pairs whereas noise does not, which yields quality metadata for every inferred edge. Second, we present the first head-to-head, quality-aware comparison of three integration paradigms; rule-based (FIS), learned (GNN), and geometry-based (FGW); on a real, large-scale, heterogeneous temporal corpus (Sect. 6), and show that discovery volume and link quality diverge sharply. Third, we characterise the optimal-transport failure mode (Sect. 7): entropically regularised transport degenerates on CDN-filtered graphs because feature collapse drives the Sinkhorn solution to a near-uniform plan. Fourth, we validate downstream utility (Sect. 8): Belief Propagation over 197 snapshots confirms that integration quality translates into analytical utility, raising AUC-ROC from 0.629 to 0.871 and effective accuracy by up to 12.4% points.

Relation to Prior Work. A shorter, earlier version of the fuzzy integration component appeared in [1], which introduced a 27-rule Mamdani inference system and compared it against union and graph-reconstruction baselines on 10 daily snapshots of the same domain-graph setting. The present paper extends that work in four ways: it scales the integration from those 10 snapshots to the full 197-snapshot corpus, expanding the cross-source evidence base from $\binom{10}{2} = 45$ to $\binom{197}{2} = 19{,}306$ source-pair comparisons; the inference system is upgraded to 36 rules, restoring the production acceptance branch and making temporal recurrence operational; we introduce the temporal-recurrence quality framework and its label-free gold standard; and we broaden the study from rule-based variants to a three-paradigm comparison; rule-based (FIS), learned (GNN), and geometry-based (FGW); with a downstream Belief Propagation evaluation.

2 Related Work

2.1 Entity Resolution, Graph Alignment, and Temporal Graphs

Temporal graph data management has focused on storage models, query languages, and time-evolving views, typically assuming cross-snapshot links are explicit [12,15,18]. We instead *infer* and *evaluate* latent cross-snapshot links in a monitoring pipeline without external ground truth, combining temporal graph integration with entity resolution and data-quality management for inferred edges. Entity resolution without an external reference relies on blocking and similarity, which can introduce false matches [8]; cross-source redundancy is a recognised proxy for quality [3]. Graph alignment and matching provide the theoretical foundation for cross-source resolution [6]. The Gromov–Wasserstein distance [19] generalises matching to graphs with incompatible node sets via optimal transport between metric-measure spaces; scalable Sinkhorn approximations [10,23] and the Fused GW extension [28] make geometry-based alignment tractable, with recent extensions to graph edit distance and alignment [26] and to graph domain adaptation [32]. Existing GW/FGW evaluations assume richly attributed graphs; we show this assumption breaks in a realistic CDN-filtered pipeline, where feature homogenisation collapses the cost matrix.

2.2 Fuzzy Logic and Graph Neural Networks for Uncertain Data

Fuzzy logic [31] and the Mamdani inference system [16] address decision-making under ambiguity through overlapping membership functions, producing graded, interpretable outputs without labelled training data [7]; their effectiveness on noisy network data is established in intrusion detection [25] and threat modelling [2]. Graph neural networks [34] learn representations on graph-structured data; Graph Attention Networks (GAT) [29] use context-sensitive attention and PairNorm [33] mitigates over-smoothing. For cross-graph link prediction, GNN embedding similarity scores candidate pairs. In our setting the GNN is trained on recurrence-filtered FIS links; we therefore treat it as a learned *reproducibility* probe of the rule base, not as an independent validator (Sect. 9.1).

2.3 DNS-Based Threat Intelligence and Belief Propagation

Domain graphs support malicious-domain detection via Belief Propagation [4,14, 20]; Manadhata et al. [17] extended this to stealthy-domain detection, with later work on cybersecurity knowledge graphs [24]. The association rules we adopt to define a related domain pair are those of Nabeel et al. [20]: two domains are associated if they share a dedicated IP, or share more than one public IP across distinct hosting providers. That criterion was derived and validated on *passive* DNS that provides valuable historical insight into domain–IP associations and infrastructure co-occurrences [14,20]; **our corpus is *active* DNS** [13] (current-state resolutions), to which the rules defined purely over shared-IP structure, ASN diversity, and dedicated-IP membership transfer directly. Temporal fragmentation introduces the integration challenge addressed here.

2.4 Data Quality Without Ground Truth

Proxy quality metrics for unlabelled data include cross-source redundancy [3] and temporal consistency. Our temporal recurrence framework exploits graph-accumulation structure to assign quantitative quality metadata to inferred edges without external labels, providing a reusable quality operator for temporal graph data management. This is consistent with established practice in evaluating inferred structure via stability [5,9].

3 Problem Formulation and Dataset

Definition 1 (Temporal Graph Integration). *Let $\mathcal{G} = \{G_1, \ldots, G_K\}$ be K temporal graph snapshots, each $G_k = (V_k, E_k)$ a domain co-hosting graph. Integration seeks a unified graph $G_{\text{unif}} = (V_{\text{all}}, E_{\text{orig}} \cup E_{\text{inf}})$, where $V_{\text{all}} = \bigcup_k V_k$, $E_{\text{orig}} = \bigcup_k E_k$ preserves all observed edges, and E_{inf} contains latent cross-snapshot connections: domain pairs that co-host across different windows but are never observed together in any single snapshot.*

Dataset. The corpus consists of $K = 197$ daily fragmented domain co-hosting graphs extracted from *active* DNS resolution records for 500,000–5,000,000 NRDs [14,20]. Each time window is projected from the bipartite domain–IP resolution graph into a domain graph: an edge $(d_1, d_2) \in E_k$ exists if the two domains resolve to a common IP after CDN filtering ($|\Phi^{-1}(ip)| < \tau_{\text{CDN}} = 1500$). ASN strings are normalised with a 64-keyword CDN vocabulary so that large providers do not inflate ASN diversity. Table 1 reports corpus statistics.

Bimodal Heterogeneity. The corpus exhibits a critical structural asymmetry: 177 sparse snapshots ($|E| < 100\text{k}$, avg. degree 4.18, 90% of corpus) coexist with

Table 1. Experimental corpus: 197 fragmented domain graphs.

Property	Value
Snapshot graphs K	197
Total unique domain nodes	253,337
Edge observations (summed over snapshots)	24,917,960
Unique union edges E_{orig}	2,541,475
Avg. edges per snapshot	126,487
Avg. nodes per snapshot	5,134
Source pairs evaluated $\binom{K}{2}$	19,306

20 dense snapshots ($|E| \geq 100$k, avg. degree 248.9, 10%). The ≈60:1 density ratio is the primary source of heterogeneity and shapes candidate coverage, recurrence counts, and the behaviour of all three methods (Table 2).

Table 2. Bimodal corpus structure: sparse vs. dense snapshot populations.

Population	Count	%	Avg. $\|V\|$	Avg. $\|E\|$	Avg. deg.	Density
Sparse ($\|E\| < 100$k)	177	90%	4,490	18,720	4.18	low
Dense ($\|E\| \geq 100$k)	20	10%	5,398	672,400	248.9	high
All	197	100%	5,134	126,487	20.5	—

4 Integration Methods

All three methods share a preprocessing pipeline: a combined domain-to-IP lookup table $\Phi\colon d \mapsto \{ip_1, \ldots\}$ (1.1 GB, union of all 197 snapshots, loaded once); CDN IP filtering $\mathcal{I}^*(d) = \{ip \in \Phi(d)\colon |\Phi^{-1}(ip)| < 1500\}$; ASN normalisation; and dedicated-IP extraction ($ip \in \mathcal{I}_{\text{ded}}$ if it resolved exclusively to one domain in at least one snapshot). We emphasise that these CDN controls are applied identically at *candidate generation* for every method, so that no method is credited with links that rest on unfiltered CDN infrastructure.

4.1 Fuzzy Inference System (FIS)

Each candidate cross-snapshot pair (d_1, d_2), with $d_1 \in G_i$, $d_2 \in G_j$, $i \neq j$, is scored by a Mamdani FIS [16] with six linguistic inputs and 36 IF–THEN rules:

$$x_1 = \left|\mathcal{I}^*(d_1) \cap \mathcal{I}^*(d_2)\right| \quad \text{(shared IP count)}, \tag{1}$$

$$x_2 = \left|\{\mathrm{ASN}(ip) \colon ip \in \mathcal{I}^*(d_1) \cap \mathcal{I}^*(d_2)\}\right| \quad \text{(ASN diversity)}, \tag{2}$$

$$x_3 = \left|\mathcal{I}^*(d_1) \cap \mathcal{I}^*(d_2) \cap \mathcal{I}_{\mathrm{ded}}\right| \quad \text{(dedicated shared IPs)}, \tag{3}$$

$$x_4 = \text{mean popularity of shared IPs}, \tag{4}$$

$$x_5 = \mathbf{1}\left[d_1 \in \mathcal{D}_{\mathrm{top}} \vee d_2 \in \mathcal{D}_{\mathrm{top}}\right], \tag{5}$$

and x_6 is temporal recurrence (number of independent cross-snapshot confirmations). Our criterion follows the association-rule logic of Nabeel et al. [20], according to which two domains are associated when they (i) share at least one dedicated IP address, or (ii) share more than one public IP address from different hosting providers. The 36 rules form four groups: (1) false-positive suppression for CDN and top domains; (2) core co-hosting assessment via x_1–x_3; (3) temporal-recurrence uplift; (4) a production-faithful branch for the $x_3 = 0$ case. Rules use the minimum T-norm; outputs are aggregated by maximum and defuzzified by centroid:

$$\hat{s}(d_1, d_2) = \frac{\int_0^1 z \cdot \mu_{\mathrm{out}}(z)\, dz}{\int_0^1 \mu_{\mathrm{out}}(z)\, dz}. \tag{6}$$

Two-Pass Temporal Accumulation. In *Pass 1* all cross-snapshot pairs are scored with $x_6 = 1$; pairs scoring ≥ 0.65 enter an accumulator tracking their cross-snapshot confirmation count. In *Pass 2* each accumulated pair is re-scored with its actual count, and pairs with $\hat{s} \geq 0.70$ are accepted into E_{inf} (Algorithm 1). The full pipeline runs in 35.67 s on 100 workers.

4.2 Graph Attention Network (GNN)

Cross-snapshot pair compatibility is scored by a two-layer GAT [29] with PairNorm [33] after each intermediate layer. Each domain d has a 7-dimensional feature vector aggregating infrastructure statistics over non-dense snapshots: IP count, dedicated IP count, ASN diversity, mean IP popularity, mean degree, snapshot frequency, dedicated-IP ratio. The objective combines three terms:

$$\mathcal{L} = \mathcal{L}_{\mathrm{within}} + \mathcal{L}_{\mathrm{cross}} + \lambda_T\, \mathcal{L}_{\mathrm{triplet}}, \tag{7}$$

where $\mathcal{L}_{\mathrm{within}}$ is binary cross-entropy (BCE) on within-snapshot edge reconstruction, $\mathcal{L}_{\mathrm{cross}}$ is target-weighted BCE supervised by FIS gold pairs (recurrence ≥ 5), and $\mathcal{L}_{\mathrm{triplet}}$ enforces embedding separation (margin $\delta = 0.1$). Candidate pairs are scored as $s_{\mathrm{GNN}}(d_1, d_2) = s_{\mathrm{prior}} \cdot \cos(\mathbf{z}_{d_1}, \mathbf{z}_{d_2})$ with s_{prior} a feature-based prior and $\mathbf{z}$ the learned embeddings. Candidate generation applies the same CDN volume

Algorithm 1. FIS Two-Pass Integration

Require: Snapshots $\{G_k\}$, Φ, $\tau_{\text{pre}} = 0.65$, $\tau = 0.70$
Build CDN-filtered IP index ip_to_graph_domains$[ip][k]$
acc $\leftarrow \{\}$
for each pair (G_i, G_j), $i < j$ **do**
    for each $d_1 \in V_i$, $d_2 \in V_j$ sharing a CDN-filtered IP **do**
        Compute x_1–x_5; score with $x_6 = 1$
        if $\hat{s} \geq \tau_{\text{pre}}$ **then**
            Update acc$[(d_1, d_2)]$; record source pair (i, j)
        end if
    end for
end for
for each (d_1, d_2) in acc **do**
    Re-score with $x_6 = |\text{confirmed source pairs}|$
    if $\hat{s} \geq \tau$ **then output** edge (d_1, d_2)
    end if
end for

filter and ASN normalisation as the shared pipeline; pairs with $s_{\text{GNN}} \geq 0.45$ are accepted. Training runtime is 37 min (CPU). Because the supervision is the FIS gold standard, the GNN is *not* independent of FIS; we quantify and interpret this dependency in Sect. 9.1. We include the GNN deliberately as a learned probe of the rule base rather than as an independent discoverer: whether FIS's high-confidence structure is learnable is itself an informative question, and the resulting FIS-reproduction rate (Sect. 9.1) is a result, not an artefact of circular evaluation.

4.3 Fused Gromov–Wasserstein (FGW)

Cross-snapshot matching is cast as optimal transport via the Fused Gromov–Wasserstein divergence [28]. For each pair (G_i, G_j), FGW seeks a plan $\mathbf{T} \in \mathbb{R}_{\geq 0}^{n_i \times n_j}$ jointly minimising feature dissimilarity and structural distortion:

$$\min_{\mathbf{T} \in \Pi(\mathbf{p},\mathbf{q})} (1 - \alpha)\langle \mathbf{M}, \mathbf{T} \rangle + \alpha \sum_{u,u',v,v'} (C_i[u, u'] - C_j[v, v'])^2 T_{uv} T_{u'v'}, \tag{8}$$

where $\mathbf{M}$ is the feature cost matrix (log-normalised, ℓ_2-normalised cosine distances over 5-dimensional node features) and C_k are intra-snapshot BFS distance matrices, with node feature vector

$$\mathbf{f}(d) = [\text{ip\_count}, \text{asn\_div}, \text{dedicated}, \text{popularity}, \text{top\_flag}]^\top.$$

Because all 197 snapshots are sparse, BFS distances saturate for $\geq$98.7% of node pairs after coarsening, rendering C_k effectively constant; setting $\alpha = 0$ reduces the objective to entropically regularised Wasserstein distance solved by Sinkhorn ($\varepsilon = 0.05$, $\leq$500 iterations) [10,23]. Each graph is coarsened to $N_{\max} = 200$

nodes via component-stratified, degree-weighted sampling; cross-snapshot edges are extracted by row-normalised thresholding ($\tau_{GW} = 0.01$) and a Mutual Nearest Neighbour filter (top-5, both directions). The pipeline completes in 11.75 h on 30 workers (400 GB node).

Parameter Selection. The main thresholds and hyperparameters were set according to their role in the pipeline rather than tuned to maximise final results. Production filtering thresholds; the CDN cap of 1,500 domains per IP and the minimum shared-infrastructure conditions; follow the original graph-construction pipeline and the association criterion of Nabeel et al. (Sect. 4.1). The FIS thresholds separate candidate generation from high-confidence acceptance: the first-pass threshold ($\tau_{pre} = 0.65$) retains plausible candidates, while the recurrence-filtered threshold ($\tau = 0.70$) defines the high-confidence subset used as the proxy gold standard. GNN thresholds control candidate selectivity and flag high-confidence outputs; they are not optimised against any external test set. The FGW parameters, including the entropic regularisation $\varepsilon = 0.05$ and the correspondence threshold, were fixed before evaluation; crucially, Sect. 7 shows the FGW degeneration is *insensitive* to ε (and to α and the threshold), so our conclusions do not depend on these values. As no external ground truth is available, the remaining values are operational design choices; a full sensitivity analysis across all methods is left for future work.

Table 3. FIS gold standard at multiple recurrence thresholds.

Threshold	Pairs	Domains	Mean score	Mean recur.
$r \geq 2$	33,133	1,259	0.803	—
$r \geq 5$	6,282	325	0.805	248.4
$r \geq 10$	5,681	279	0.805	—
$r \geq 50$	5,406	248	0.805	286.6

5 Temporal Recurrence Quality Framework

5.1 The Ground-Truth Problem

Evaluating E_{inf} is hard without an external reference identifying genuine cross-snapshot relationships. Raw output volume is an unreliable proxy: larger edge sets may reflect lower selectivity rather than higher accuracy. We therefore adopt a temporal recurrence criterion grounded in the following observation: genuine co-hosting relationships should recur independently across multiple source-pair evaluations. If (d_1, d_2) truly shares infrastructure, the FIS pre-filter should confirm their co-hosting with high probability whenever d_1 appears in snapshot G_i and d_2 appears in snapshot G_j; conversely, spurious matches should exhibit low recurrence. This criterion is consistent with established practice in evaluating inferred structures without ground truth and in using temporal stability as a reliability indicator [5,9].

5.2 Construction of the Gold Standard

During FIS Pass 1 (Sect. 4.1), the accumulator records, for each accepted pre-filter pair, the set of source pairs (i, j) that confirmed it. The temporal recurrence is defined as:

$$\text{recur}(d_1, d_2) = \left|\{(i,j): i \neq j,\ d_1 \in G_i,\ d_2 \in G_j,\ \hat{s}_{\text{pre}} \geq \tau_{\text{pre}}\}\right|, \tag{9}$$

with maximum $\binom{K}{2} = 19{,}306$. The gold standard is $\mathcal{G}^* = \{(d_1, d_2)\colon \text{recur} \geq 5,\ \hat{s} \geq 0.70\}$ (Table 3).

At $r \geq 5$, $\mathcal{G}^*$ comprises 6,282 pairs over 325 domains. Mean recurrence 248.4 means pairs are confirmed in ≈1.3% of all 19,306 source-pair evaluations, far above the $\leq 10^{-4}$ expected under random co-appearance, supporting $r^* = 5$ as a noise-separating threshold. An independent re-evaluation of $\mathcal{G}^*$ against the published Nabeel criterion [20] confirms construct validity: every gold pair is novel to any single snapshot, satisfies the association rule on the merged evidence, and is free of high-volume CDN IPs. Gold pairs have mean FIS score 0.805 (range [0.703, 0.938]) and mean ASN diversity 7.0.

Table 4. Integration statistics for $K = 197$ snapshots (253,337 nodes; 2,541,475 baseline edges). GNN uses the CDN-faithful candidate generation (Sect. 4.2)

Method	New links	Avg. deg	Disc. (%)	Runtime
Union	0	20.06	0.000	<1 s
GNN	1,125	20.07	0.044	37 min
FIS	160,200	21.33	6.30	35.67 s
FGW	467,876	23.76	18.41	11.75 h

5.3 Evaluation Metrics

FGW and GNN outputs are evaluated against $\mathcal{G}^*$. As FGW is methodologically independent of the FIS accumulator, this comparison is free of circularity. For the GNN, which is trained on $\mathcal{G}^*$, the comparison is a *consistency check*, not an independent performance measure (Sect. 9.1). We report precision $P = |\text{output} \cap \mathcal{G}^*|/|\text{output}|$, recall $R = |\text{output} \cap \mathcal{G}^*|/|\mathcal{G}^*|$, and pairwise overlap between methods' new-link sets.

6 Integration Quality Results

6.1 Discovery Volume

Table 4 reports the primary statistics. All methods preserve 100% of the 2,541,475 baseline edges. Node counts are identical (253,337); new-link counts span nearly three orders of magnitude, from GNN (1,125; 0.044%) to FGW (467,876; 18.4% of baseline), with FIS at 160,200 (6.3%). These figures measure volume, not reliability, and should not be read as a quality ranking (RQ1), see Fig. 1.

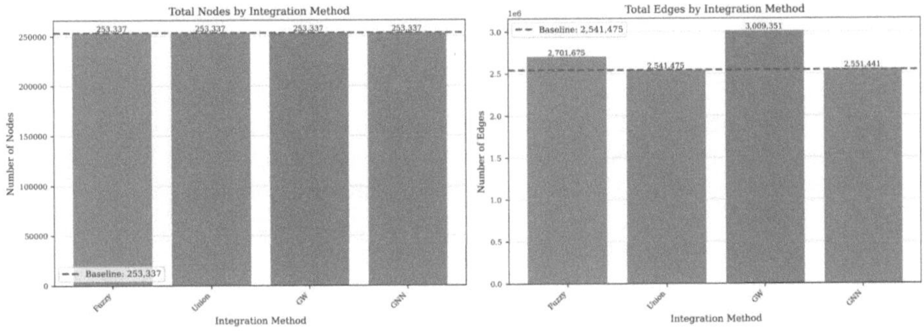

Fig. 1. Total nodes (left) and total edges (right) per integration method.

6.2 Quality Against the Gold Standard

Table 5 reports precision, recall, and gold hits against $\mathcal{G}^*$ for each method.

Table 5. Quality against the FIS gold standard ($r \geq 5$; 6,282 pairs).

Method	Gold hits	Recall	Precision	Score-discriminable
FIS	6,282	100%	3.92%	Yes (score 0.803–0.938)
GNN	563	9.0%	50.0%	Partly (dedicated-IP tier)
FGW	475	7.6%	0.10%	No (inverted precision–confidence)

FIS. By construction, the gold standard $\mathcal{G}^*$ is the high-recurrence subset of FIS output, so FIS recalls 100%. The diagnostic observation is that only 3.92% of all FIS links (6,282 of 160,200) attain gold quality, forming a clearly delineated high-confidence tier in the score stratum 0.803–0.938 with mean ASN diversity 7.0. The remaining 153,918 links ($r = 1$–4) are a provisional tier for analyst-guided investigation. FIS thus yields a natural two-tier output.

GNN. Training converged at epoch 97/100 (loss 4.036 → 3.514). Under the CDN-faithful candidate generation the GNN accepts 1,125 links, of which 563 lie in $\mathcal{G}^*$ (50.0% precision, 9.0% recall); the high-confidence tier ($s_{\mathrm{GNN}} \geq 0.70$, 7 links) is dominated by shared dedicated-IP relationships. A representative doubly-supported example is `worldcue.com`↔`api.net` (top GNN link, $s_{\text{GNN}} = 0.757$), which is also a recurrence-confirmed gold pair (FIS score 0.803), sharing 22 IPs across 7 ASNs including 8 dedicated IPs. Crucially, because the GNN is supervised by $\mathcal{G}^*$, such agreement is a consistency check rather than independent corroboration; we quantify the overlap in Sect. 9.1. The learned embedding cosine is near-uniform across pairs, so the ranking is governed by the infrastructure prior s_{prior}; sharpening embedding separation is future work.

FGW. Despite 467,876 links, FGW achieves only 475 gold hits (0.10% precision). Two observations are diagnostic. First, the precision–confidence relationship is *inverted*: all 475 gold hits fall in the lowest score interval $[0.010, 0.020]$, while the 29,250 links scoring above 0.020 contain zero gold hits. Second, FGW produces a hub artefact: the top-20 most frequent domains each appear in 1,500–1,635 links, none in $\mathcal{G}^*$ at any threshold. Although the MNN filter cut hubs from 3,181 to 1,556, uniform feature-space similarity lets hubs satisfy mutual-nearest-neighbour constraints. The FGW score therefore carries no discriminative information with reference to the gold standard.

6.3 Score Distributions

FIS scores (0.703–0.938) are bimodal, reflecting the two-pass architecture: a mass near the acceptance threshold (0.703–0.800) and an elevated gold stratum (0.803–0.938) from full Pass 2 recurrence counts, with a natural separator at ≈0.800. GNN scores concentrate near the acceptance threshold with a thin dedicated-IP tail above 0.70, consistent with the near-uniform embedding cosine. FGW scores span $[0.005, 0.050]$ (median 0.014) with gold hits confined to $[0.010, 0.020]$, a range shared by 438,143 non-gold links; no FGW threshold preferentially recovers gold pairs.

7 Why Optimal Transport Fails on Filtered Graph Data

The FGW failure admits a clear explanation. After CDN filtering ($x_1 \geq 2$, $x_2 > 1$) and degree-weighted coarsening to $N_{\max} = 200$ nodes, surviving nodes across the sparse population exhibit a highly concentrated feature profile:

$$\text{ip\_count} \in [2, 30], \quad \text{asn\_div} \in [2, 5], \quad \text{dedicated} = 0 \text{ (99.4\% of nodes)}. \tag{10}$$

We call this *feature distribution collapse*: filtering removes CDN noise but also reduces feature variability. The cost matrix becomes nearly homogeneous, so the entropic term dominates and the Sinkhorn solution becomes diffuse [11,27]. Formally, when $\max(\mathbf{M}) - \min(\mathbf{M}) \ll \varepsilon$, $\mathbf{T}^* \approx \mathbf{p} \otimes \mathbf{q}$ (near-uniform). Each source node then spreads mass over many targets, and row-normalised thresholding extracts correspondences only weakly related to feature similarity, consistent with the 29,250 high-score non-gold links. Three implications follow: (i) the failure is not a tuning artefact; once the representation is homogeneous, adjusting

α, ε, or the threshold cannot restore signal; (ii) $\alpha > 0$ offers little help, since coarsening already removes structural heterogeneity ($C_k \approx c{\cdot}\mathbf{1}\mathbf{1}^\top$); (iii) the mode is not specific to FGW; any OT/metric-space method may behave similarly under near-homogeneous representations. Integration strategies should be co-designed with the preprocessing pipeline rather than treated as independent modules.

8 Downstream Utility Validation

We test whether integration quality translates into downstream utility via a Belief Propagation classifier [20,22,30]. Given the unified graph and seed labels, BP propagates label evidence to classify unlabelled domains; graph homophily governs quality, so accurate links should help and false positives should hurt. The protocol runs 10 iterations per method, each withholding 500 malicious and 500 benign seeds, evaluating against a refined ground truth (>99% label agreement across all 197 graphs). *Effective accuracy* (Coverage×Accuracy) penalises both coverage and misclassification (Table 6).

Table 6. Downstream BP: coverage, AUC-ROC (scored-only), and effective accuracy. The fragmented row is the mean over 197 individual snapshots.

Method	Coverage	AUC	CV(AUC)	Eff. Acc.
Fragmented (avg.)	69.4%	0.629	24.2%	53.0%
Union	76.9%	0.872	1.7%	65.5%
FIS	77.0%	0.871	1.7%	65.5%
GNN	76.9%	0.871	1.7%	65.5%
FGW	77.4%	0.844	2.1%	64.1%

Integration raises AUC from the fragmented mean 0.629 (range [0.400, 0.971]; CV 24.2%) to 0.871–0.872 (CV $<$ 1.7%). The CV reduction is as informative as the mean gain: the high fragmented variance is driven by the dense-graph tail. Effective accuracy improves by up to +12.4 pp (a 7–8 pp coverage gain plus a 9 pp accuracy gain). FGW attains marginally higher coverage but lower AUC (0.844): its false-positive links do not build class-homophilic neighbourhoods. The downstream ranking matches the quality ranking of Sect. 6.2.

9 Discussion

Volume statistics produce a misleading hierarchy (FGW $\gg$ FIS $>$ GNN) that both the recurrence framework and the downstream evaluation overturn. FGW's 467,876 links correspond to roughly one genuine relationship per 1,000 proposed—noise that would corrupt downstream analysis without screening. FIS's 160,200 links contain a clearly delineated high-confidence tier (6,282 gold, mean recurrence 248.4) with no analogue in FGW output. Ranking integration methods by discovery volume is akin to ranking retrieval systems by recall alone (RQ1).

9.1 GNN, FIS, and FGW: An Honest Overlap Analysis

A central interpretive question is how the *new* links of the three methods relate. Edge-level Jaccard over the whole unified graph is uninformative here (it is dominated by the shared 2.54M baseline edges); we therefore compare the *new-link* sets directly. Of the 1,125 GNN links, 977 (86.8%) lie within FIS output and only 148 are GNN-exclusive; 57 are shared with FGW, and *all* GNN–FGW agreements are also FIS-confirmed. FGW is 99.9% disjoint (467,393 exclusive links). Three points follow, with the GNN's training dependency stated explicitly.

(i) The GNN does not independently validate FIS. It is supervised by $\mathcal{G}^*$ and therefore shares FIS's labelling assumptions. That 86.8% of its links fall within FIS, together with a near-uniform embedding cosine, indicates the GNN acts as a learned *reproducibility test* of the rule base; confirming that FIS's high-confidence structure is learnable; rather than as an independent oracle. Links the GNN predicts outside FIS reflect generalisation of FIS's own assumptions, not independent confirmation; we report the 148 GNN-exclusive links as candidate leads pending out-of-band validation, not as discoveries.

(ii) Cross-paradigm agreement is the strongest signal. FGW does not use $\mathcal{G}^*$, so FGW agreement is genuinely cross-paradigm. The 57 links confirmed by all three methods (FIS $\cap$ GNN $\cap$ FGW) form the highest-confidence convergent set; every GNN–FGW agreement is also FIS-confirmed. While small, this set is the most defensible cross-method result, and FGW's 0.10% precision bounds the weight its agreements carry.

(iii) Disagreement is methodological, not error. The methods occupy different points on a volume–precision trade-off; their divergence reflects paradigm diversity rather than contradiction, and the recurrence framework provides the common yardstick.

Limitations. The gold standard is derived from the FIS accumulator; although an independent re-evaluation against the published Nabeel criterion supports its construct validity, a domain pair could in principle satisfy recurrence while reflecting a CDN-mediated coincidence. Out-of-band validation via WHOIS, certificate-transparency logs, or malware sandboxes on a representative sample would further strengthen the assessment and is our immediate next step; it is the only route to decouple "agreement with FIS" from "correctness" for the GNN-exclusive links. The GNN is structurally dependent on FIS labels and confined to the FIS candidate pool; its embedding separation is limited and is left to future work. Finally, the evaluation covers a single month (October 2025) and a single application domain (DNS co-hosting), where features, rules, and preprocessing are DNS-specific; longitudinal and cross-domain validation are needed for broader operational claims. The temporal-recurrence quality framework and the optimal-transport failure analysis, however, depend only on multi-source cross-confirmation structure and metric-space homogeneity; not on DNS features; so both transfer to other fragmented-graph integration settings.

10 Conclusion

We presented a quality-aware comparison of three graph-alignment paradigms for entity resolution across 197 daily fragmented domain co-hosting snapshots, centred on a ground-truth-free temporal recurrence quality framework. The main finding is that discovery volume is a misleading quality proxy: FGW's 467,876 links achieve 0.10% precision against the recurrence gold standard, with gold and non-gold pairs producing indistinguishable transport scores—a failure consistent with CDN-filtering-induced feature collapse driving Sinkhorn to a near-uniform plan. FIS produces 6,282 high-confidence links (mean recurrence 248.4); the GNN, trained on this gold standard, reproduces 86.8% of its 1,125 links within FIS, functioning as a learned consistency check rather than an independent validator. Downstream Belief Propagation confirms the ranking, raising AUC from 0.629 to 0.871. Two contributions generalise beyond this setting: the reusable temporal recurrence framework, and the OT failure analysis, which exposes a broad incompatibility between geometry-based alignment and production-filtered, near-homogeneous graph data.

Disclosure of Interests. Generative AI tools were used to assist with language polishing of this manuscript; all technical content, methods, and experiments were designed and verified by the authors.

References

1. Alali, M., Cesario, S., Castelltort, A., Derakhshannia, M., Laurent, A.: Uncertainty-aware graph integration: a fuzzy logic approach with comparative analysis. In: Vantaggi, B., et al. (eds.) Information Processing and Management of Uncertainty in Knowledge-Based Systems (IPMU 2026). Communications in Computer and Information Science, vol. 3020, pp. 305–319. Springer, Cham (2026). https://doi.org/10.1007/978-3-032-28997-1_22
2. Ben Atitallah, S., Driss, M., Boulila, W., Koubaa, A.: Securing industrial IoT environments: a fuzzy graph attention network for robust intrusion detection. IEEE Open J. Comput. Soc. 1–12 (2025). https://doi.org/10.1109/OJCS.2025.3587486
3. Bleiholder, J., Naumann, F.: Data fusion. ACM Comput. Surv. **41**(1), 1–41 (2009). https://doi.org/10.1145/1456650.1456651
4. Bridges, R.A., Jones, J.P., Iannacone, M.D., Testa, K.M., Goodall, J.R.: A survey of graph-based approaches for security analytics. ACM Comput. Surv. **52**(2), 1–27 (2019)
5. Chiappori, A., Cazabet, R.: Quantitative evaluation of snapshot graphs for the analysis of temporal networks. In: Benyahia, M., et al. (eds.) Complex Networks & Their Applications IX. Studies in Computational Intelligence, vol. 1030, pp. 566–577. Springer, Cham (2021). https://doi.org/10.1007/978-3-030-93409-5_47

6. Conte, D., Foggia, P., Sansone, C., Vento, M.: Thirty years of graph matching in pattern recognition. Int. J. Pattern Recognit. Artif. Intell. **18**(3), 265–298 (2004). https://doi.org/10.1142/S0218001404003228
7. Dixit, A., Bagde, P., Hardiya, P.: Advanced cyber security using fuzzy logic. J. Emerging Technol. Innov. Res. (JETIR) **12**(11), (2025)
8. Elmagarmid, A.K., Ipeirotis, P.G., Verykios, V.S.: Duplicate record detection: a survey. IEEE Trans. Knowl. Data Eng. **19**(1), 1–16 (2007). https://doi.org/10.1109/TKDE.2007.250581
9. Faller, P.M., Vankadara, L.C., Mastakouri, A.A., Locatello, F., Janzing, D.: Self-compatibility: evaluating causal discovery without ground truth. In: Proceedings of the 27th International Conference on Artificial Intelligence and Statistics (AISTATS 2024). Proceedings of Machine Learning Research, vol. 238, pp. 4132–4140. PMLR (2024)
10. Flamary, R., Courty, N., Gramfort, A., et al.: POT: Python optimal transport library. J. Mach. Learn. Res. **22**(78), 1–8 (2021)
11. He, K.: On the efficiency of Sinkhorn-Knopp for entropically regularized optimal transport. arXiv preprint arXiv:2604.03787 (2026). https://doi.org/10.48550/arXiv.2604.03787
12. Huang, H., Song, J., Lin, X., et al.: TGraph: a temporal graph data management system. In: Proceedings of the 25th ACM International Conference on Information and Knowledge Management, pp. 2469–2472 (2016). https://doi.org/10.1145/2983323.2983335
13. Khalil, I., Yu, T., Guan, B.: Discovering malicious domains through passive DNS data graph analysis. In: Proceedings of the 11th ACM on Asia Conference on Computer and Communications Security, pp. 663–674 (2016)
14. Khalil, I.M., Guan, B., Nabeel, M., Yu, T.: A domain is only as good as its buddies: detecting stealthy malicious domains via graph inference. In: ACM Conference on Data and Application Security and Privacy (CODASPY), pp. 330–341 (2018). https://doi.org/10.1145/3176258.3176329
15. Khurana, U.: An introduction to temporal graph data management. Thesis, Computer Science Department, University of Maryland, MA (2012)
16. Mamdani, E.H., Assilian, S.: An experiment in linguistic synthesis with a fuzzy logic controller. Int. J. Man Mach. Stud. **7**(1), 1–13 (1975). https://doi.org/10.1016/S0020-7373(75)80002-2
17. Manadhata, P., Yadav, S., Rao, P., Horne, W.: Detecting malicious domains via graph inference. In: Workshop on Artificial Intelligence and Security (AISec), pp. 59–60 (2014). https://doi.org/10.1145/2666652.2666659
18. Massri, M., Miklos, Z., Raipin, P., et al.: Clock-G: a temporal graph management system with space-efficient storage technique. In: 2022 IEEE 38th International Conference on Data Engineering (ICDE), pp. 2263–2276 (2022). https://doi.org/10.1109/ICDE53745.2022.00215
19. Mémoli, F.: Gromov-Wasserstein distances and the metric approach to object matching. Found. Comput. Math. **11**(4), 417–487 (2011). https://doi.org/10.1007/s10208-011-9093-5
20. Nabeel, M., Khalil, I.M., Guan, B., Yu, T.: Following passive DNS traces to detect stealthy malicious domains via graph inference. ACM Trans. Priv. Secur. **23**(4), 1–36 (2020). https://doi.org/10.1145/3401897
21. Palo Alto Networks Unit 42: Newly registered domains: malicious abuse by bad actors. https://unit42.paloaltonetworks.com/newly-registered-domains-malicious-abuse-by-bad-actors/ (2019). Accessed 05 May 2026

22. Pearl, J.: Probabilistic Reasoning in Intelligent Systems. Morgan Kaufmann, Burlington (1988)
23. Peyré, G., Cuturi, M.: Computational optimal transport. Found. Trends Mach. Learn. **11**(5–6), 355–607 (2019). https://doi.org/10.1561/2200000073
24. Piplai, A., Mittal, S., Joshi, A., Finin, T., Holt, J., Zak, R.: Creating cybersecurity knowledge graphs from security articles. IEEE Access **8**, 210691–210706 (2020). https://doi.org/10.1109/ACCESS.2020.3039234
25. Shamshirband, S., et al.: Fuzzy logic-based intrusion detection system: a review. Adv. Fuzzy Syst. (2014). https://doi.org/10.1016/j.jnca.2014.03.012
26. Tang, J., et al.: Fused Gromov-Wasserstein alignment for graph edit distance computation and beyond. In: Proceedings of the VLDB Endowment (2025, to appear). https://doi.org/10.14778/3748191.3748221. https://www.vldb.org/pvldb/vol18/p3641-tang.pdf
27. Tang, X., et al.: Accelerating Sinkhorn algorithm with sparse newton iterations. arXiv preprint arXiv:2401.12253 (2024). https://doi.org/10.48550/arXiv.2401.12253
28. Vayer, T., Chapel, L., Flamary, R., Tavenard, R., Courty, N.: Fused Gromov-Wasserstein distance for structured objects. Algorithms **13**(9), 212 (2020). https://doi.org/10.3390/a13090212
29. Veličković, P., Cucurull, G., Casanova, A., Romero, A., Liò, P., Bengio, Y.: Graph attention networks. In: International Conference on Learning Representations (ICLR) (2018). https://doi.org/10.48550/arXiv.1710.10903
30. Yedidia, J.S., Freeman, W.T., Weiss, Y.: Understanding belief propagation and its generalizations. In: Exploring Artificial Intelligence in the New Millennium, pp. 239–269. Morgan Kaufmann (2003)
31. Zadeh, L.A.: Fuzzy sets. Inf. Control **8**(3), 338–353 (1965). https://doi.org/10.1016/S0019-9958(65)90241-X
32. Zeng, Z., et al.: Pave your own path: graph gradual domain adaptation on fused Gromov-Wasserstein geodesics. arXiv preprint arXiv:2505.12709 (2025). https://doi.org/10.48550/arXiv.2505.12709
33. Zhao, L., Akoglu, L.: PairNorm: tackling oversmoothing in GNNs. In: International Conference on Learning Representations (ICLR) (2020). https://doi.org/10.48550/arXiv.1909.12223
34. Zhou, J., et al.: Graph neural networks: a review of methods and applications. AI Open **1**, 57–81 (2021). https://doi.org/10.1016/j.aiopen.2021.01.001. https://arxiv.org/abs/1812.08434

Risk-Constrained Operating-Point Selection for Entity Resolution Under Hard-Negative False-Positive Risk

Punitha Ponnuraj(✉) and Sathyan Sugumar

Plano, TX 75093, USA
punitha.p.raj@gmail.com

Abstract. Learned scoring models drive entity resolution (ER) decisions, but deployed systems depend on operating thresholds that convert match scores into accepted links. This thresholding step is critical when false-positive links carry higher downstream cost than missed matches. We study operating-point selection for ER under hard-negative false-positive risk constraints. On a deterministic 6,400-pair conflict benchmark, models with AUC above 0.95 violate a $\tau = 0.02$ worst-case hard-negative FPR budget by up to 10× under unconstrained threshold selection. Instantiating the protocol on DBLP–ACM with dataset-specific hard-negative slices, unconstrained thresholds fail the same budget for all models despite strong aggregate ranking performance, while risk-constrained selection makes Logistic Regression and Random Forest compliant; the best compliant model on the synthetic benchmark, XGBoost, is non-compliant on DBLP–ACM, while Random Forest becomes the strongest compliant DBLP–ACM model, showing that compliant model choice is dataset-dependent. External diagnostics on Mannheim Fodors–Zagats and a Yelp-derived 6,000-pair evaluation set show that frozen thresholds may have low or zero survival under changed score and feature regimes, requiring recalibration before automated linkage. These results support treating threshold selection as an ER operating-point control problem: a match score should become an automatic link only after the threshold has been checked against explicit hard-negative risk constraints.

Keywords: Entity resolution · Operating-point selection · Hard-negative mining · False-positive rate control · Threshold selection · Risk-constrained machine learning

1 Introduction

Entity resolution (ER) is a core operation in data integration, master data management, linked data management, and entity-centric analytics. It identifies records that refer to the same real-world entity despite variation in names,

---

Independent Researcher.

© The Author(s), under exclusive license to Springer Nature Switzerland AG 2027
G. Vargas Solar et al. (Eds.): ADBIS 2026, CCIS 3175, pp. 461–471, 2027.
https://doi.org/10.1007/978-3-032-39823-9_40

addresses, identifiers, or other attributes. This paper does not propose a new entity matching model. Existing matchers—from Logistic Regression and tree ensembles to transformer-based models—already produce match scores. The open problem we address is: given any such score, which threshold converts it into an accepted automatic link? We show that this operating-point selection step requires explicit hard-negative risk constraints, and that aggregate metrics alone are insufficient to guide it.

In practical ER pipelines, records are often assembled from heterogeneous sources such as enterprise applications, partner feeds, manual entry, and web or mobile forms. These sources introduce lexical variation, address drift, missing fields, and conflicting signals. Two records may share a highly similar name while referring to different entities, or two distinct entities may be co-located while representing different businesses. In bibliographic ER, two records may have identical or near-identical generic titles but different authors. Such cases are difficult because the evidence is not merely noisy; it is contradictory. Aggregate metrics such as AUC and F-score measure performance over the full distribution of pairs, where easy true negatives dominate, and cannot surface concentrated false-positive risk in hard-negative non-match regions. We therefore evaluate operating thresholds using worst-case hard-negative false-positive rate over predefined high-conflict non-match slices.

We study this problem as risk-constrained operating-point selection for ER. Given a learned scoring model and a candidate threshold, the threshold is treated as admissible only if it satisfies a predefined false-positive-rate budget over high-conflict non-match slices on validation data. Among admissible thresholds, we select the threshold that maximizes a precision-oriented utility measure. The resulting protocol is deliberately simple and scorer-agnostic: it can be applied on top of any ER model that produces a comparable match score. The contribution is not a new representation, blocker, or matcher, but an operating-point protocol and diagnostic framework for deciding when a model score should become an automatic link.

The paper makes the following contributions:

- We define a scorer-agnostic risk-constrained threshold-selection protocol for ER using predefined hard-negative slices and a worst-case false-positive-rate budget τ, with benchmark artifacts released (DOI: 10.5281/zenodo.18262448).
- We show on a 6,400-pair synthetic benchmark and DBLP–ACM that high-AUC models can violate a $\tau = 0.02$ hard-negative FPR constraint by up to $10\times$, and that compliant model ranking is dataset-dependent.
- We show that frozen thresholds may have low or zero survival under domain shift, requiring recalibration before automated linkage.

2 Related Work

Learned ER and Matching. The classical Fellegi–Sunter framework [7] formalized record linkage as a likelihood-ratio decision problem. Subsequent systems added feature engineering and supervised classifiers [4,9,12]. Deep learning approaches including Ditto [14] and ZeroER [20] further improved accuracy on standard benchmarks. Robustness analyses show strong in-domain accuracy can mask brittle behavior under distribution shift [18]. Our work is orthogonal: we study operating-point selection after any matcher produces a score.

Hard Negatives and ER Benchmarks. Standard benchmarks [13,15] underrepresent enterprise-style conflict patterns including co-located entities and geospatial inconsistencies [2,17]. Synthetic generators such as Febrl [4] and EMBench++ [11] introduce noise but do not target governance-critical failure modes. Our synthetic benchmark explicitly oversamples such conflict clusters.

Thresholding, Calibration, and Selective Prediction. Calibration of modern classifiers is imperfect [10] and degrades under dataset shift [16]. Selective prediction provides a principled lens for governance-constrained deployment [3,6,8]. Rate-constrained model selection optimizes utility subject to explicit error-rate budgets [5]. Prior work on threshold selection in record linkage focuses on aggregate false-match-rate control [1]. Our protocol differs by enforcing the budget over predefined high-conflict non-match slices, preventing concentrated slice-level failures from being hidden by pooled metrics.

3 Method: Risk-Constrained Operating-Point Selection

3.1 Problem Formulation

Let f be a learned ER scoring model that assigns a match score $s = f(x_{ij}) \in [0,1]$ to each record pair (i,j). For probabilistic classifiers this may be interpreted as a match probability; for neural similarity models such as Sentence-BERT it is a normalized similarity score. Given a decision threshold $\theta \in [0,1]$, the binary link decision is:

$$\hat{y}_{ij}(\theta) = \mathbb{I}[f(x_{ij}) \geq \theta] \tag{1}$$

The choice of θ determines which pairs become automatic links and which are routed to review. We treat this as an operating-point selection problem.

3.2 Hard-Negative Slices and Worst-Case FPR

Let $H_D = \{c_1, \ldots, c_k\}$ be a predefined set of governance-critical non-match slices for dataset D. These slices contain non-match pairs that are most likely to generate false links under high-similarity conditions. Hard-negative slices are researcher-specified using domain knowledge before model training, data splitting, or threshold selection. A pair can be placed in a hard-negative slice only if its ground-truth label is non-match and its input features satisfy the predefined rule for that slice. The grouping therefore depends only on the known label and the record-pair features, not on model scores, predictions, or selected thresholds. This prevents the hard-negative groups from being shaped by model behavior or by the threshold-selection process. For the synthetic benchmark, groups are defined using name, address, ZIP, and geospatial signals; for DBLP–ACM, using title, author, and venue similarity thresholds (Sect. 4). Mannheim and Yelp are used only for transfer diagnostics and are not used to define hard-negative groups or select thresholds. For each slice $c \in H_D$ and threshold θ, the slice-level false-positive rate is:

$$\mathrm{FPR}_c(\theta) = \frac{\mathrm{FP}_c(\theta)}{\mathrm{FP}_c(\theta) + \mathrm{TN}_c(\theta)} \tag{2}$$

The worst-case hard-negative FPR summarizes governance risk across all slices:

$$\text{WorstHN-FPR}(\theta) = \max_{c \in H_D} \mathrm{FPR}_c(\theta) \tag{3}$$

This slice-level constraint differs from pooled false-positive control: a concentrated failure in one hard-negative region can be hidden by better aggregate behavior elsewhere.

3.3 Two-Stage Veto Protocol

The budget τ specifies the maximum tolerated worst-case false-positive rate across the predefined hard-negative slices on validation data. It is chosen before threshold selection and is not estimated from model outputs. A smaller τ imposes stricter control over false links in the most difficult non-match groups, which may reduce the number of pairs accepted automatically. A larger τ permits greater automation while allowing higher worst-case false-positive risk.

We use $\tau = 0.02$ as the primary operating point, corresponding to a maximum slice-level false-positive rate of 2% on validation data. This value represents a conservative but non-zero risk budget rather than a data-tuned optimum. We also report results for $\tau \in \{0.01, 0.02, 0.03\}$.
The set of admissible thresholds on validation data is:

$$T(\tau) = \{\theta \in [0, 1] : \text{WorstHN-FPR}(\theta) \leq \tau\} \tag{4}$$

Among admissible thresholds, we select the one maximizing precision-weighted utility $F_{0.5}$:

$$\theta^* = \arg \max_{\theta \in T(\tau)} F_{0.5}^{\mathrm{val}}(\theta) \tag{5}$$

If multiple thresholds maximize $F_{0.5}$, we choose the largest (most conservative). If $T(\tau) = \emptyset$ on validation, the model is reported as infeasible at budget τ.

Protocol Alignment. Figure 1 (Sect. 4) illustrates the full pipeline. TEST data are never used for threshold or model selection. Normalization statistics are computed on TRAIN only and applied unchanged to VAL, TEST, and external datasets.

4 Experimental Setup

4.1 Synthetic Conflict Benchmark

The primary benchmark is a deterministic synthetic dataset generated by the authors using a conflict-driven pair generation procedure. It comprises 6,400 labeled record pairs derived from 800 base entities, with approximately balanced

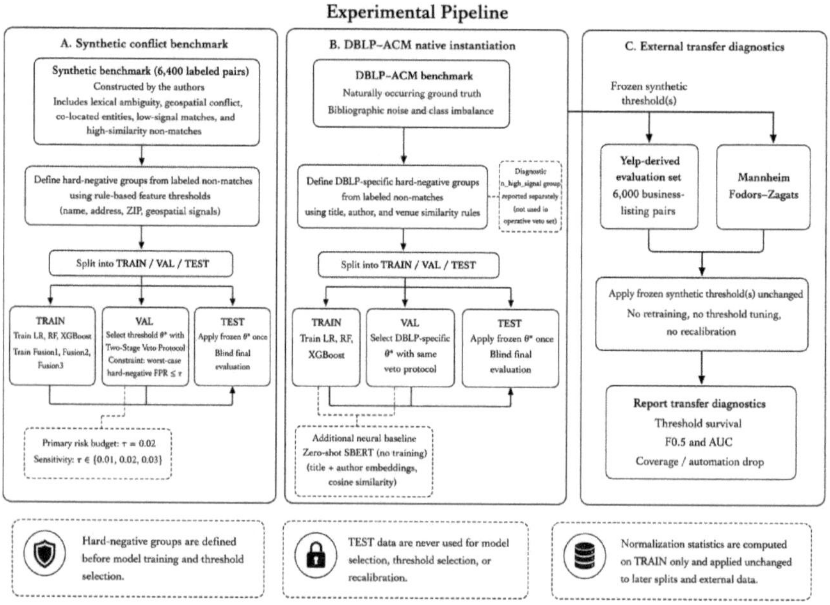

Fig. 1. Experimental pipeline. Transfer diagnostics report threshold survival, $F_{0.5}$, and AUC. SBERT is evaluated as a zero-shot scorer on DBLP–ACM without training.

match/non-match labels (3,188 matches / 3,212 non-matches). The dataset is designed to oversample enterprise-style conflict modes.

Features. Features follow the multi-signal schema defined in Sect. 3: NameSim, AddrSim, ZipMatch, and InvGeo.

Conflict clusters. Pairs are assigned to nine predefined clusters targeting distinct ER failure modes. The high-conflict hard-negative set is:

$$H_{\text{syn}} = \{\texttt{hn\_lexical}, \texttt{hn\_geo}, \texttt{hn\_conflict}, \texttt{tn\_high\_signal}\} \quad (6)$$

Exact generation rules and per-cluster counts are released with the benchmark artifact (DOI: 10.5281/zenodo.18262448).

Split. TRAIN/VAL/TEST = 55%/15%/30%, stratified by cluster type.

Models. We evaluate three base classifiers and three fusion variants, all trained on synthetic TRAIN only. Table 1 summarizes each model and its key hyperparameters. The fuzzy composite score is $\tilde{s} = 0.4 \cdot \textsc{NameSim} + 0.3 \cdot \textsc{AddrSim} + 0.2 \cdot \textsc{InvGeo} + 0.1 \cdot \textsc{ZipMatch}$. Fusion weights are fixed heuristics set before any threshold selection and are not tuned on VAL or against the veto constraint, ensuring no leakage into operating-point selection.

4.2 DBLP–ACM Standard Benchmark

Models are trained on DBLP–ACM TRAIN, thresholds selected on DBLP–ACM VAL, and compliance evaluated on DBLP–ACM TEST.

Table 1. Models evaluated on the synthetic benchmark.

Model	Type	Key parameters / combination rule
LR	Linear	max_iter=1000, class_weight=balanced
RF	Ensemble	300 trees, min_samples_leaf=2
XGBoost	Boosting	300 est., max_depth=6, lr=0.1
Fusion1	Score avg.	$p_{F1} = 0.7\,p_{RF} + 0.3\,p_{LR}$
Fusion2	Score+fuzzy	$p_{F2} = 0.6\,p_{RF} + 0.2\,p_{LR} + 0.2\,\tilde{s}$
Fusion3	Meta-learner	LR stacked on $[p_{RF}, p_{LR}, \tilde{s}]$

Table 2. DBLP–ACM hard-negative slice construction rules. H_{DBLP} = operative hard-negative set.

Slice	Rule	Pairs	H_{DBLP}?
`hn_title`	TitleSim ≥ 0.90, AuthorSim < 0.50	201	Yes
`hn_author`	AuthorSim ≥ 0.85, TitleSim < 0.60	175	Yes
`hn_title_author_conflict`	TitleSim ≥ 0.70 AND AuthorSim ≥ 0.70	167	Yes
`tn_high_signal`	TitleSim ≥ 0.80, AuthorSim ≥ 0.80, VenueSim ≥ 0.80	127	Diag.

Dataset. 12,363 labeled pairs (2,220 matches, 10,143 non-matches), reflecting a natural 18% match rate. Class imbalance is handled via `class_weight=balanced` for LR/RF and `scale_pos_weight=4.57` for XGBoost.

Features. Because geospatial attributes are unavailable in bibliographic data, we define four domain-appropriate features using the same fuzzy-ratio methodology: title similarity (TitleSim), author similarity (AuthorSim), venue similarity (VenueSim), and year match (YearMatch).

Hard-Negative Slices. Slice labels are assigned before any split or threshold selection, ensuring no leakage. The operative hard-negative set is:

$$H_{\mathrm{DBLP}} = \{\texttt{hn\_title},\ \texttt{hn\_author},\ \texttt{hn\_title\_author\_conflict}\} \quad (7)$$

Slice Construction Rules. Table 2 gives exact thresholds. Slices are mutually exclusive (priority order as listed); WorstHN-FPR is computed independently per slice.

Neural Scorer Baseline. To validate the scorer-agnostic claim, we additionally apply the veto protocol to a Sentence-BERT scorer (`all-MiniLM -L6-v2`) [19], using cosine similarity between title+author embeddings as the match score. No fine-tuning is performed; the model is applied zero-shot to DBLP–ACM pairs.

4.3 External Transfer Diagnostics

Frozen synthetic veto thresholds are applied without retraining to Mannheim Fodors–Zagats ($n = 66$; 11 matches, 55 non-matches) and a Yelp-derived 6,000-pair business-listing evaluation set. Mannheim lacks geospatial coordinates (InvGeo = 0), testing feature-regime mismatch. The Yelp set uses real business listings with controlled perturbations; it is not an estimate of natural duplicate prevalence.

5 Results

The unconstrained baseline maximizes $F_{0.5}$ on VAL without the hard-negative FPR veto.

5.1 Synthetic: High AUC Does Not Imply Hard-Negative Safety

Under unconstrained selection, WorstHN-FPR reaches up to 0.208 (Fusion3)—a 10× violation. Among compliant models, XGBoost achieves the strongest utility ($F_{0.5} = 0.824$, WorstHN-FPR = 0.012). Fusion2 passes validation (WorstHN-FPR = 0.011) but fails blind TEST (WorstHN-FPR = 0.029), showing validation compliance does not guarantee test compliance. LR's near-zero recall (0.034) at $\theta^* = 0.78$ reflects score compression under `class_weight=balanced`.

Sensitivity to τ. Across $\tau \in \{0.01, 0.02, 0.03\}$, XGBoost fails at all levels on DBLP–ACM; RF is compliant at $\tau = 0.02$ and $\tau = 0.03$ (Table 3).

Table 3. Synthetic TEST results at $\tau = 0.02$ using VAL-veto thresholds. Best compliant $F_{0.5}$ in bold. WorstHN-FPR values exceeding $\tau = 0.02$ marked with †.

Model	θ^*	P	R	$F_{0.5}$	AUC	WorstHN-FPR
LR	0.78	0.889	0.034	0.146	0.821	0.017
RF	0.97	0.970	0.475	0.803	0.956	0.017
XGBoost	0.97	0.970	0.514	**0.824**	0.956	0.012
Fusion1	0.89	0.970	0.445	0.785	0.953	0.017
Fusion2	0.88	0.967	0.499	0.815	0.952	0.029†
Fusion3	0.99	0.975	0.449	0.790	0.957	0.006

5.2 DBLP–ACM: Protocol Generalizes to a Standard Benchmark

All unconstrained thresholds fail $\tau = 0.02$ despite AUC ≥ 0.997 (classical) and AUC $= 0.989$ (SBERT). Risk-constrained selection makes LR and RF compliant. RF achieves the strongest compliant performance ($F_{0.5} = 0.975$, WorstHN-FPR $= 0.017$) with negligible utility loss ($\Delta F_{0.5} = +0.0001$). LR is compliant with zero WorstHN-FPR at higher utility cost ($F_{0.5} = 0.926$).

XGBoost remains non-compliant on DBLP–ACM at all τ levels due to two persistent FPs in `hn_title`, while being the strongest compliant model on synthetic. This reversal confirms that risk-compliant model selection is dataset-dependent.

Confidence Intervals. 95% Clopper–Pearson CIs for binding-slice FPR: synthetic `hn_lexical` ($n = 173$): XGBoost 0.012 [0.001, 0.041], Fusion2 0.029† [0.009, 0.066]; DBLP `hn_title` ($n = 60$): RF 0.017 [0.000, 0.089], XGBoost/SBERT 0.033† [0.004, 0.115]. Wide intervals reflect small slice size; compliance is point-estimate, not a formal guarantee (Table 4).

Table 4. DBLP–ACM TEST results at $\tau = 0.02$. Best compliant $F_{0.5}$ in bold. WorstHN-FPR exceeding τ marked with †. SBERT is a zero-shot neural scorer (cosine similarity on title+author embeddings).

Setting	Model	θ^*	P	R	$F_{0.5}$	AUC	WorstHN-FPR
Unconstrained	LR	0.90	0.972	0.973	0.972	0.997	0.150†
	RF	0.86	0.977	0.967	0.975	0.999	0.050†
	XGBoost	0.96	0.979	0.960	0.975	0.999	0.033†
	SBERT	0.94	0.941	0.912	0.935	0.989	0.033†
Veto τ=0.02	LR	0.98	0.982	0.753	0.926	0.997	0.000
	RF	0.96	0.986	0.936	**0.975**	0.999	0.017
	XGBoost	0.99	0.986	0.859	0.958	0.999	0.033†
	SBERT	0.94	0.941	0.912	0.935	0.989	0.033†

Table 5. External transfer diagnostics using frozen synthetic veto thresholds ($\tau = 0.02$). Survival = fraction of true positives with score $\geq \theta^*$; low survival indicates score-scale mismatch requiring recalibration.

Dataset	Model	θ^*	AUC	$F_{0.5}$	Survival
Yelp	XGBoost	0.97	0.879	0.279	7.3%
	Fusion2	0.88	0.976	0.156	3.6%
	RF	0.97	0.839	0.024	0.5%
Mannheim	RF	0.97	1.000	0.000	0.0%
	Fusion3	0.99	1.000	0.000	0.0%
	LR	0.78	0.883	0.000	0.0%

Zero-shot SBERT (AUC= 0.989) replicates the core finding: the unconstrained threshold fails $\tau = 0.02$ (WorstHN-FPR = 0.033), driven by `hn_title` (2 FP of 60). The binding failure mode—title confusability—is consistent across classical and neural scorers, supporting the scorer-agnostic claim.

On the synthetic benchmark, Fusion2 has pooled FPR = 0.009 $\leq \tau$ yet WorstHN-FPR = 0.029 $> \tau$, driven by `hn_lexical` alone, confirming that pooled metrics can mask concentrated failures.

5.3 External Transfer Diagnostics

Table 5 reports threshold-transfer results. AUC is preserved under domain shift but thresholds do not transfer. On Yelp, scores do not survive the frozen threshold (XGBoost survival: 7.3%; Fusion2: 3.6%)—a score-scale shift, not a ranking failure. On Mannheim, all models produce zero positives: the maximum score (RF: 0.363) falls below $\theta^* = 0.97$ because missing InvGeo compresses scores, resulting in full deferral.

6 Discussion and Limitations

Slice Construction Requires Domain Knowledge. The hard-negative set H_D must be defined per deployment domain. On the synthetic benchmark, lexical confusables (`hn_lexical`) dominate worst-case risk. On DBLP–ACM, title confusables (`hn_title`) play the same role. Slices are manually defined from domain knowledge; automated discovery of high-risk non-match subpopulations is future work.

Statistical Caution on Small Slices. The synthetic benchmark uses a single deterministic split; variance across splits is not reported. The DBLP–ACM binding slice `hn_title` contains only 60 TEST pairs, yielding wide Clopper–Pearson CIs. Compliance should be interpreted as point-estimate compliance under the pre-specified test protocol rather than a formal guarantee. Fine-tuned transformer models such as Ditto [14] are not evaluated; the scorer-agnostic protocol applies to any model producing a comparable match score, and their evaluation remains future work.

7 Conclusion

We studied risk-constrained operating-point selection for entity resolution under hard-negative false-positive risk. On a deterministic 6,400-pair conflict benchmark, models with AUC above 0.95 violate a $\tau = 0.02$ worst-case hard-negative FPR budget by up to 10× under unconstrained threshold selection. Instantiating the same protocol on DBLP–ACM confirms that unconstrained thresholds fail the budget despite near-perfect AUC, while risk-constrained selection achieves compliance for Logistic Regression and Random Forest. The compliant model ranking reverses across datasets, showing that risk-compliant model choice is dataset-dependent, and frozen thresholds may have low or zero survival under changed feature and score regimes.

ER evaluation should include threshold-level, slice-level, and transfer diagnostics when false-positive links are costly. A model score should become an automatic link only after the selected threshold has been checked against explicit hard-negative risk constraints on the deployment dataset.

Acknowledgements. The authors received no external funding for this work.

Disclosure of Interests. The authors have no competing interests to declare that are relevant to the content of this article.

References

1. Belin, T.R., Rubin, D.B.: A method for calibrating false-match rates in record linkage. J. Am. Stat. Assoc. **90**(430), 694–707 (1995)
2. Binette, O., Steorts, R.C.: (almost) all of entity resolution. Sci. Adv. **8** (2022)
3. Chow, C.K.: On optimum recognition error and reject tradeoff. IEEE Trans. Inf. Theory **16**(1), 41–46 (1970)
4. Christen, P.: Data Matching: Concepts and Techniques for Record Linkage, Entity Resolution, and Duplicate Detection. Springer (2012)
5. Cotter, A., et al.: Training well-generalizing classifiers for fairness metrics and other data-dependent constraints. In: Proceedings of the 36th International Conference on Machine Learning, pp. 1397–1405 (2019)
6. El-Yaniv, R., Wiener, Y.: On the foundations of noise-free selective classification. J. Mach. Learn. Res. **11**, 1605–1641 (2010)
7. Fellegi, I.P., Sunter, A.B.: A theory for record linkage. J. Am. Stat. Assoc. **64**(328), 1183–1210 (1969)
8. Geifman, Y., El-Yaniv, R.: Selective classification for deep neural networks. In: Advances in Neural Information Processing Systems (2017)
9. Getoor, L., Machanavajjhala, A.: Entity resolution: theory, practice and open challenges. Proc. VLDB Endowment **5**(12), 2018–2019 (2012)
10. Guo, C., Pleiss, G., Sun, Y., Weinberger, K.Q.: On calibration of modern neural networks. arXiv:1706.04599 (2017)
11. Ioannou, E., Velegrakis, Y.: EMBench++: data for a thorough benchmarking of matching-related methods. Semantic Web **10**(2), 435–450 (2019). https://doi.org/10.3233/SW-180331

12. Konda, P., et al.: Magellan: toward building entity matching management systems. Proc. VLDB Endowment **9**(12), 1197–1208 (2016)
13. Köpcke, H., Thor, A., Rahm, E.: Evaluation of entity resolution approaches on real-world match problems. Proc. VLDB Endowment **3**(1–2), 484–493 (2010)
14. Li, Y., Li, J., Suhara, Y., Doan, A., Tan, W.C.: Deep entity matching with pre-trained language models. Proc. VLDB Endowment **14**(1), 50–60 (2021)
15. Mudgal, S., et al.: Deep learning for entity matching: a design space exploration. In: ACM SIGMOD International Conference on Management of Data, pp. 19–34 (2018)
16. Ovadia, Y., et al.: Can you trust your model's uncertainty? Evaluating predictive uncertainty under dataset shift. In: Advances in Neural Information Processing Systems (2019)
17. Papadakis, G., Skoutas, D., Thanos, E., Palpanas, T.: Blocking and filtering techniques for entity resolution: a survey. ACM Computing Surveys **53**(2), Article 31 (2020). https://doi.org/10.1145/3377455
18. Rastaghi, M.A., Kamalloo, E., Rafiei, D.: Probing the robustness of pre-trained language models for entity matching. In: Proceedings of the 31st ACM International Conference on Information and Knowledge Management, pp. 3786–3790 (2022). https://doi.org/10.1145/3511808.3557673
19. Reimers, N., Gurevych, I.: Sentence-BERT: sentence embeddings using siamese BERT-networks. In: Proceedings of EMNLP-IJCNLP, pp. 3982–3992 (2019)
20. Wu, R., Chaba, S., Sawlani, S., Chu, X., Thirumuruganathan, S.: ZeroER: entity resolution using zero labeled examples. In: ACM SIGMOD International Conference on Management of Data, pp. 1149–1164 (2020)

Author Index

© The Editor(s) (if applicable) and The Author(s), under exclusive license to Springer Nature Switzerland AG 2027
G. Vargas Solar et al. (Eds.): ADBIS 2026, CCIS 3175, pp. 473–474, 2027.
https://doi.org/10.1007/978-3-032-39823-9

MIX
Papier aus verantwortungsvollen Quellen
Paper from responsible sources
FSC® C105338
www.fsc.org

If you have any concerns about our products,
you can contact us on
ProductSafety@springernature.com

In case Publisher is established outside the EU,
the EU authorized representative is:
Springer Nature Customer Service Center GmbH
Europaplatz 3, 69115 Heidelberg, Germany

Printed by Libri Plureos GmbH
in Hamburg, Germany